SEVEN PILLARS OF WISDOM
A Triumph

The Complete 1922 Text

Wilder Publications, Inc.
PO Box 10641
Blacksburg, VA 24060

ISBN 10: 1-61720-183-9
ISBN 13: 978-1-61720-183-7
First Edition

10 9 8 7 6 5 4 3 2 1

SEVEN PILLARS OF WISDOM
A Triumph

T. E. Lawrence

CONTENTS

Introduction.. 8
Chapter 1: How and Why I Wrote. 8
Chapter 2: The Spirit of the Revolt. 11
Chapter 3: Arabia. 13
Chapter 4: The Nomadic Phase. 15
Chapter 5: Monotheism. 17
Chapter 6: The Autonomy Movement. 21
Chapter 7: Prelude of the Sherif.. 25
Chapter 8: The British Protagonists.. 29
Chapter 9: Jealousies of First Success. 33

Book I
Chapter 10: Storrs and Abdulla. 36
Chapter 11: Jidda. 42
Chapter 12: Ali, Zeid and Rabegh. 45
Chapter 13: Tehama and Shera. 50
Chapter 14: Feisal. 54
Chapter 15: The First Campaign. 56
Chapter 16: Morale. 61
Chapter 17: the Troops. 64
Chapter 18: Return to Egypt. 69

Book II
Chapter 19: Yenbo. 74
Chapter 20: Nakhl Mubarak — Bad News.. 76
Chapter 21: Cavil Routine. 79
Chapter 22: Defeat in Wadi Yenbo. 82
Chapter 23: Recovery. 86
Chapter 24: Read Justment — New Plans. 90
Chapter 25: Evacuating Yenbo. 94
Chapter 26: The Order of March. 99
Chapter 27: Marching. 105
Chapter 28: In Billi Country. 109
Chapter 29: Wejh. 113

Book III
Chapter 30: Rewards and Squabbles. 115
Chapter 31: Reorganisation. 119
Chapter 32: Conversion.. 121
Chapter 33: A Railway Offensive. 125
Chapter 34: To Abdulla.. 129
Chapter 35: Strategy and Tactics. 132

Chapter 36: Attacking Aba El Naam. 139
Chapter 37: Mining for Trains. 144
Chapter 38: Abdulla and Friends. 150
Chapter 39: Returning to Wejh. 154
Chapter 40: Auda and Akaba. 158

Book IV
Chapter 41: Geography of Akaba. 162
Chapter 42: From Wejh to El Kurr. 165
Chapter 43: In Abu Raga. 169
Chapter 44: Harrat El Aweirid. 174
Chapter 45: The Railway and El Haul. 178
Chapter 46: Wadi Fejr. 182
Chapter 47: The Biseita. 185
Chapter 48: Wadi Siriian. 189
Chapter 49: Howeitat Feasting. 193
Chapter 50: With the Tribes. 197
Chapter 51: Excursions. 201
Chapter 52: Bair. 205
Chapter 53: A Raiding Party. 209
Chapter 54: A Blank. 212
Chapter 55: Blood. 214
Chapter 56: Away to Take Akaba. 216
Chapter 57: A Fight. 220
Chapter 58: Akaba Taken. 225

Book V
Chapter 59: A Cross Sinai. 231
Chapter 60: Allenby. 235
Chapter 61: Rearrangement. 238
Chapter 62: On the Threshold of Syria. 243
Chapter 63: Syrian Towns. 247
Chapter 64: Syrian Politics. 248
Chapter 65: Irregular War. 251
Chapter 66: Distractions. 255
Chapter 67: Attitudes. 259
Chapter 68: Rum. 264
Chapter 69: Repairs. 267
Chapter 70: A Fresh Start. 270
Chapter 71: An Ambush. 273
Chapter 72: Loot. 276
Chapter 73: Escape. 280
Chapter 74: Raiding. 284
Chapter 75: Harvest. 289

Book VI
Chapter 76: Potentialities. 291
Chapter 77: A Foray. 294

Chapter 78: Forward. 297
Chapter 79: Night Marching. 301
Chapter 80: The Beni Sakhr. 306
Chapter 81: The Serahin. 310
Chapter 82: Azrak and Anyadh. 316
Chapter 83: The Bridge Dash. 320
Chapter 84: Waiting for Trains. 324
Chapter 85: A Rout. 328
Chapter 86: Teaching. 331
Chapter 87: Being Taught. 336
Chapter 88: Jerusalem. 341

Book VII
Chapter 89: A Local Offensive. 346
Chapter 90: Armoured Car Work. 350
Chapter 91: My Bodyguard. 353
Chapter 92: Direct Action. 358
Chapter 93: Tafileh. 361
Chapter 94: The Turks Attack. 364
Chapter 95: The Arabs Reply. 367
Chapter 96: The Weather Sums Up. 371
Chapter 97: Slow Progress. 376
Chapter 98: Winter Sports. 379
Chapter 99: Resignation. 383
Chapter 100: A New Engagement. 387

Book VIII
Chapter 101: A Big Scheme. 392
Chapter 102: Amman Fails. 399
Chapter 103: Withdrawal. 402
Chapter 104: Maan Fails. 406
Chapter 105: D Awnay Succeeds. 410
Chapter 106: A Gift of Camels. 414
Chapter 107: Covering Raids. 418
Chapter 108: Nasir Does Well. 421
Chapter 109: A Changed Plan. 424
Chapter 110: King Hussein Refuses. 427

Book IX
Chapter 111: Allenby Revives. 430
Chapter 112: Resentment in Akaba. 434
Chapter 113: Buxton Begins Work. 439
Chapter 114: The Rualla. 442
Chapter 115: Peace Negotiations. 448
Chapter 116: By Car to Azrak. 452
Chapter 117: Meeting at Bair. 456
Chapter 118: A Birthday. 458
Chapter 119: The Icc. 463

Chapter 120: Self Denial. 466
Chapter 121: King Hussein Again. 471

Book X
Chapter 122: Pleasure of Empty Azrak. 476
Chapter 123: Our Slow Collection. 480
Chapter 124: The First Railway. 483
Chapter 125: The Second Railway. 487
Chapter 126: The Third Railway. 492
Chapter 127: Check. 494
Chapter 128: The Nisib Bridge. 498
Chapter 129: An Aeroplane Adventure. 502
Chapter 130: Over to Allenby. 505
Chapter 131: Back to the Desert. 510
Chapter 132: A Surprise Move. 514
Chapter 133: In Hiding. 519
Chapter 134: A Night of Storm. 523
Chapter 135: With Tile British. 527
Chapter 136: Damascus. 533
Chapter 137: Making a State. 538
Chapter 138: Sanitary Men. 541
Chapter 139: Allenby Triumph. 545
Epilogue. 547

Introduction

Some Englishmen, of whom Kitchmer was chief believed that a rebellion of Arabs against Turks would enable England, while fighting Germany, simultaneously to defeat Turkey.

Their knowledge of the nature and power and country of the Arabic-speaking people made them think that the issue of such a rebellion would be happy: and indicated to them its probable character and method.

So they allowed it to begin, having obtained for it formal assurances of help from the British Government. Yet none the less the rebellion of the Sherif of Mecca came to most as a surprise and found the Allies unready. It aroused mixed feelings and made strong friends and strong enemies, amid whose clashing jealousies its affairs began to miscarry.

Chapter 1: How and Why I Wrote

The story which follows was first written out in Paris during the Peace Conference, from notes (mainly of impressions) jotted daily on the march, strengthened by some reports sent to my chiefs in Cairo. Afterwards, in the autumn of 1919, this first draft and some of the notes were lost. It seemed to me historically needful to reproduce the tale, as perhaps no one but myself in Feisal's army had thought of writing down at the time what we felt, what we hoped, what we tried. So it was built again with great repugnance in London in the winter of 1919-20, from memory and my surviving notes. The record of events was not dull in me, and perhaps few actual mistakes crept in — except in details of dates or numbers — but the outlines and significance of things had lost edge in the haze of new interests, and consequently the story lacked force. However, this was inevitable, and, as hardly anyone but myself saw the original edition, it would be silly to grow sorry for its loss.

Probably something should be said of the particularities of this draft. For the style of telling is owed a special apology. As a great reader of books, my own language has been made up by choosing from the black heap of words those which much-loved men have stooped to, and charged with rich meaning, and made our living possession. Everywhere there are such borrowed phrases and ideas, not picked out by footnotes and untidy quotation marks, since great lords of thought must be happy to see us tradesmen setting up our booths under their castle-walls, and dealing in their struck coinage. At least, I should be happy if anyone found a phrase of mine worth lifting.

The dates and places are correct, so far as my notes preserved them: but the personal names are not in the same case. Since we ended the adventure, some of those who worked with me have buried themselves in the shallow grave of public duty. Free use has been made of their names. Others still possess themselves, and here they keep their secrecy. Sometimes one man carries various names. This may hide individuality, and make the book a scatter of featureless puppets rather than a group of living people; but once good is told of a man, and again evil, and some would not thank me for either. It is often easier to bear undeserved blame than earned praise, and hard in writing an intimate story not to bring many facets of a man to the light.

Then there is the question of my British colleagues. This isolated picture throwing the main light upon myself is unfair to them. Especially I am most sorry that I have not told what the noncommissioned with us did. They were inarticulate, but wonderful, although without the motive, the imaginative vision of the End, which sustained their officers. Unfortunately my concern was limited to this End, and the book just a designed procession of Arab freedom from Mecca to Damascus. It was intended to rationalize the campaign, that everyone might see how natural the success was, and how inevitable, how little dependent on direction or brain, how much less on the outside assistance of the few British. It was an Arab war, waged and led by Arabs, for an Arab aim, in Arabia.

My proper share was a minor one, but because of a fluent pen, a free speech and a certain adroitness of brain, I took upon myself, as I describe it, a mock primacy. By the accidental judgment of a publicist who visited us in the field this mock primacy was published abroad as truth. In reality I held a subordinate official place. I never held any office among the Arabs, was never in charge of the British mission with them. Wilson, Joyce, Newcombe, Dawnay, and Davenport were all over my head. I flattered myself that I was too young, not that they had more heart or mind in the work. I did my best. Wilson, Joyce, Newcombe, Dawnay, Davenport, Buxton, Marshall, Stirling, Young, Maynard, Ross, Scott, Winterton, Lloyd, Wordie, Siddons, Goslett, Stent, Henderson, Williams,

Gilman, Garland, Brodie, Hornby, Peake, Scott-Higgins, Ramsay, Wood, Clayton, Bright, Macindoe, Greenhii, Grisenthwaite, Wade, Dowsett, Pascoe and the others also did their best. It would be impertinence in me to praise them. When I wish to say ill of anyone outside our number I do it: though there is less of this than was in my diary, by my own choice, for the passage of time seems to have bleached out men's stains. When I wish to praise outsiders, I do it: but our family affairs are our own. We did what we set out to do, and have the satisfaction of that knowledge. The others have liberty some day to put on record their story, one parallel to mine but not mentioning more of me than I of them, for each of us did his own job by himself and as he pleased, hardly seeing his friends.

In these pages is not the history of the Arab movement, but just of what happened to me in it. It is the narrative of what I tried to do in Arabia, and of some of what I saw there. It is a chronicle in the spirit of the old men who marched with Bohemond or Coeur de Lion. It treats of daily life, mean happenings, little people. Here are no lessons for the world, no events to shake peoples. It is filled with trivial things, partly that no one mistake it for history (it is the bones from which some day a man may make history), and partly for the pleasure it gave me to recall the fellowship of the revolt. We were fond together, and there are here memories of the sweep of the open places, the taste of wide winds, the sunlight, and the hopes in which we worked. It felt like morning, and the freshness of the world-to-be intoxicated us. We were wrought up with ideas inexpressible and vaporous, but to be fought for. We lived many lives in those whirling campaigns, never sparing ourselves any good or evil: yet when we achieved and the new world dawned, the old men came out again and took from us our victory, and remade it in the likeness of the former world they knew. Youth could win but had not learned to keep, and was pitiably weak against age. We stammered that we had worked for a new heaven and a new earth, and they thanked us kindly and made their peace. When we are their age no doubt we shall serve our children so.

This therefore is a faded dream of the time when I went down into the dust and noise of the Eastern market-places, and with my brain and muscles, with sweat and constant thinking, made others see my visions coming true. Those who dream by night in the dusty recesses of their minds wake in the day to find that all was vanity: but the dreamers of the day are dangerous men, for they may act their dream with open eyes, and make it possible. This I did. I meant to make a new nation, to restore to the world a lost influence, to give twenty millions of Semites the foundation on which to build an inspired dream-palace of their national thoughts. So high an aim called out the inherent nobility of their minds, and made them play a generous part in events: but when we won, it was charged against me that the British petrol royalties in Mesopotamia were become dubious, and French colonial policy mined in the Levant.

I am afraid that I hope so. We pay for these things too much in honor, and in innocent lives. I went up the Tigris with one hundred Devon Territorial: young, clean, delightful fellows, full of the power of happiness, and of making women and children glad. By them one saw vividly how great it was to be their kin, and English. And we were casting them by thousands into the fire, to the worst of deaths, not to win the war, but that the corn and rice and oil of Mesopotamia might be ours. The only need was to defeat our enemies (Turkey among them) and this was at last done in the wisdom of Allenby with less than four hundred killed, by turning to our uses the hands of the oppressed in Turkey. I am proudest of my thirty fights in that I did not have any of our own bloodshed. All the subject provinces of the Empire to me were not worth one dead English boy. If I have restored to the East some self-respect, a goal, ideals: if I have made the standard of rule of white over red more exigent, I have fitted those peoples in a degree for the new commonwealth in which the dominant races will forget their brute achievements, and white and red and yellow and brown and black will stand up together without side-glances in the service of the world.

We were three years over this effort, and I have had to hold back many things which may not yet be said. Even so, parts of this book will be new to nearly all who see it, and many will look for familiar things and not find them. At first I reported fully to my chiefs, but then learned that they were rewarding me on my own evidence. This was not as it should be. Honors may be necessary in a professional army, as so many emphatic mentions in dispatches, and by enlisting we had put ourselves, willingly or not, in the position of regular soldiers. I had, however, determined to accept nothing for my work on the Arab front. The Cabinet raised the Arabs to fight for us by definite promises of self-government afterwards. Arabs believed in persons, not in institutions. They saw in me a free agent of the British Government, and demanded from me an endorsement of our written promises. So I had to join the conspiracy, and, for what my word was worth, assured my men of their reward. In our two years' partnership under fire they grew accustomed to believing me, and to think my Government, like myself, well-meaning towards them. In this hope they performed some fine things; but of course instead of being proud of what we did together, I was continually and bitterly ashamed.

It was evident from the beginning that if we won the war these promises would be dead paper, and had I been an honest adviser of the Arabs I would have told them to go home, and not risk their lives fighting for such stuff: but I salved myself with the hope that by leading these Arabs madly in the final victory I would establish them, with arms in their hands, in a position so assured (if not dominant) that expediency would counsel to the Great Powers a fair settlement of their claims. It is not yet clear if I succeeded: but it is clear that I had no shadow of leave to engage them unknowing in such hazard. I risked being made a fraud, on my conviction that Arab help was necessary to our cheap and speedy victory in the East, and that better we win and break our word than lose. The dismissal of Sir Henry McMahon confirmed my belief in our essential insincerity, but I could not so explain myself to General Wingate, while the war lasted, since I was nominally under his orders, and he did not seem sensible of how false his own standing was. The only thing to do was to refuse rewards for being a successful trickster; and to prevent this unpleasantness arising again

I began in my reports to conceal the true stories of things, and to persuade the few Arabs who knew to an equal reticence. In this book also for the last time I mean to be my own judge of what to say.

Chapter 2: The Spirit of the Revolt

This phrase-book, this selection of some of all the goods found in my mind's store-house when the shouting was over and I had leisure to unlock memory and think contains a relative truth of what we did and said. Yet the hook of battle is a large one, and each of us sees only his little page. I am fully conscious that as in my heat I sometimes did ill, and saw imperfectly, so also I must have thought wrong.

The evil in the tale may be understood, if not excused, by our circumstances. We lived for years anyhow with one another in the naked desert, under the indifferent heaven. By day the hot sun fermented us, and we were dazed by the beating wind. At night we were stained by dew, and shamed into pettiness by the innumerable silences of stars. We were a very self centered army, without parade or gesture, devoted to freedom, the second of man's creeds, a purpose so ravenous that it devoured all our strength, a hope so transcendent that our earlier ambitions faded in its glare.

As time went by, the need to fight for the ideal increased in us to an unquestioning possession, riding with spur and rein over our doubts. Willy-nilly it became our faith. We had sold ourselves into its slavery, manacled ourselves together in its chain-gang, and bowed ourselves to serve its holiness with all our good and ill content. The mentality of ordinary human slaves is terrible — they have lost the world — and we had surrendered not our bodies only, but our souls to the overmastering greed of victory. By our own act we were drained of morality, of volition, of responsibility like dead leaves in the wind.

The everlasting battle stripped from us care of our own lives or of others'. We had ropes about our necks, and on our heads prices which showed that the enemy intended hideous tortures for us if we were caught. Each day some of us passed, and the living knew themselves just sentient puppets on God's stage: and indeed our task-master was merciless, merciless so long as our bruised feet could stagger forward on the road. The weak envied those tired enough to die, for success looked so remote, and failure a near and certain, if sharp, release from toil. We lived always in the stretch or sag of nerves, either on the crest or in the trough of waves of feeling. This impotency was bitter to us, and made us live only for the seen horizon, reckless what spite we inflicted or endured, since physical sensation showed itself mean and transient. Gusts of cruelty, perversions, lusts ran lightly over the surface without troubling us, for the moral laws which had seemed to hedge about these silly accidents must be yet fainter words. We had learned that there were pangs too sharp, grieves too deep and ecstasies too high for our finite selves to register. When emotion reached this pitch the mind choked, and memory went white till the circumstances were humdrum once more.

Such exaltation of thought, while it let adrift the spirit and gave it license in strange airs, lost it the old patient rule over the body. The body was too coarse to feel the utmost of our sorrows and of our joys. Therefore we abandoned it as rubbish; we left it below us, and it marched forward, a breathing simulacrum, on its own unaided level, subject to influences from which in normal times our instincts would have shrunk. The men were young and sturdy, and hot flesh and blood unconsciously claimed their right in them, and tormented their bellies with strange longings. The privations and dangers fanned this virile heat, in a climate as racking as can be conceived. We had no shut places to be alone in, no thick clothes to hide our nature. Man in all things lived candidly with man.

The Arab was by nature continent, and the use of universal marriage had nearly abolished irregular courses in the tribes. The public women of the rare settlements we entered in our months of wandering would have been nothing to our numbers, even had their raddled meat been palatable to a man of healthy parts. In horror of such sordid commerce our youths began indifferently to slake one another's needs in their own clean bodies — a cold convenience that by comparison seemed sexless and even pure. Later, some began to justify this sterile process, and swore that friends quivering together in the yielding sand, with intimate hot limbs in supreme embrace, found there hidden in the darkness a sensual coefficient of the mental passion which was welding our souls and spirits in one flaming effort. Some few, thirsting to punish the appetites they could not wholly prevent, took a savage pride in degrading the body, and offered themselves fiercely in any habit which promised physical pain or filth.

I was sent to these Arabs as a stranger, unable to think their thoughts or subscribe their beliefs, but charged by duty to lead them forward, and to develop to the highest any movement of theirs profitable to England in her war. If I could not assume their character I could at least conceal my own, and pass among them without evident friction, neither a discord nor a critic, but an unnoticed influence. Since I was their fellow, I will not be their apologist or advocate. Today in my old garments I could play the bystander, obedient to the sensibilities of our theater ... but it is more honest to record that these ideas and actions then passed naturally. What now looks wanton or sadist seemed in the field inevitable, or just unimportant routine.

Blood was always on our hands: we were licensed to it. Wounding and killing are ephemeral pains, and lie was very brief and sore with us. The sorrow of living was so great that the sorrow of punishment had him pitiless. We lived for the day, and died for it also. When we needed to punish we wrote our lesson with gun or whip immediately in the sullen flesh of the sufferer, and the case was beyond appeal. The desert did not afford the refined slow penalties of courts and galosh.

Of course our rewards and pleasures were as suddenly sweeping as our troubles, but to me in particular they bulked less large. Bedouin ways were hard even for those brought up to them, and for strangers terrible, a death in life.

When the march or labor ended I had no energy to record sensation, and while it lasted no leisure to see the spiritual loveliness that sometimes came upon us by the way. In my notes the cruel rather than the beautiful found place. We no doubt enjoyed more the rare moments of peace and forgetfulness, but I remember more the agony, the terrors, and the mistakes. Our life is not summed up in what I have written (there are things I will not repeat in cold blood for very shame of you, my friends), but what I have written was in and of our life. Pray God that men reading my story will not in the glamor of strangeness go out and prostitute themselves and their talents in the service of another race.

A man who gives himself to the possession of aliens leads a Yahoo lie, selling his soul to a brute. He is not of them. He may stand against them, persuade himself of a mission, batter and twist them into something which they of their own accord would not have been. Then he is exploiting his old environment to press them out of theirs. Or, after my model, he may imitate them so well that they imitate him back again. Then he is giving away his own environment: pretending to theirs; and pretenses are hollow worthless things. In neither case is he doing a thing of himself. The cleanest is to be himself without thought of conversion and to let them take what action or reaction they please from the example.

In my case the effort for these years to live in the dress of Arabs, and to imitate their mental foundation, quitted me of my English self; and let me look at the West and its conventions with new eyes, and destroyed it all for me. At the same time I could not sincerely take on the Arab skin: it was an affectation only. Easily was a man made an infidel: but hardly might he be converted to another faith.

I had dropped one form and not taken on the other, and was become like our legend of Mohammed's coffin, with a resultant feeling of intense loneliness in life, and a contempt, not for other men, but for all they do. Such detachment came to a man exhausted by prolonged physical effort and isolation. His body plodded on, mechanically, while his reasonable mind left hi, and from without looked down critically on him, and wondered what that futile lumber did, and why. Sometimes these selves would converse in the void, and then madness was very near, as I believe it would be near the man who could see things through the veils at once of two customs, two educations, two environments.

Chapter 3: Arabia

A first difficulty of the Arab movement was to say what the Arabs were. Being a manufactured people, their name had been changing its sense slowly year by year. Once it meant an Arabian: then it meant a Bedouin: now it was not a race, but a society growing together firmly. There was a country called Arabia, but this was nothing to the point. There was a language called Arabic, and there lay the test. It was the current tongue of Syria and Palestine, of all Mesopotamia, and of the great peninsula called Arabia on the map. Before the Muslim conquest these areas were inhabited by diverse peoples, speaking languages of the Arabic family. We called them Semitic, but (like most scientific terms) incorrectly. However, Arabic, Assyrian, Babylonian, Phoenician, Hebrew, Aramaic and Syrian were related tongues. The words Christ spoke on the Cross would be understood in the Hejaz today, and indications of common influences in the past, or even of a common origin, were strengthened by our knowledge that the manners and customs and appearances of the present Arabic-speaking peoples of Asia, while as varied as a field of poppies, had an equal and essential likeness. We might call them all cousins with perfect propriety, cousins fully if sadly aware of their own relationship.

The Arabic-speaking areas of Asia, in this sense, were a rough parallelogram. The north side ran from Alexandretta on the Mediterranean across Mesopotamia eastward to the Tigris. The south side was the coast of the Indian Ocean from Aden to Muscat. On the west it was bounded by the Mediterranean, by the Suez Canal, and by the Red Sea to Aden. On the east it was bounded by the Tigris valley, and then by the shore of the Persian Gulf to Muscat. This square of land, as large as India, formed the homeland of our 'Semites', the area in which no foreign race had kept a permanent footing, though Egyptians, Hittites, Philistines, Persians, Greeks, Romans, Turks and Franks had variously tried. All had in the end been broken, and their last scattered elements drowned in the strong characteristics of the Semitic race. Semites had sometimes pushed outside this area, and been drowned themselves in the outer world. Egypt, Algiers, Morocco, Malta Sicily, Spain, Cilicia and France absorbed and obliterated Semitic colonies. Only in Tripoli of Africa and in the everlasting miracle of Jewry, had distant Semites kept some of their identity and force.

The origin of these peoples was an academic question, but for the understanding of their revolt their present social and political differences were important, and could only be grasped by looking at their geography. This continent of theirs fell into certain great regions, which imposed varying habits on their inhabitants. On the west the parallelogram was framed, from Alexandretta to Aden, in a mountain belt called, in the north, Syria and thence southward first Palestine, then Midian, then Hejaz, and lastly Yemen. It had an average height of perhaps three thousand feet, with peaks of ten to twelve thousand feet. As it faced west it was well watered with rain and cloud from the sea, and in general was holly peopled. The south edge of the parallelogram was another range of inhabited hills, facing the Indian Ocean. The eastern frontier was all a plain, at first alluvial, and called Mesopotamia, but south of Basra a level littoral, called Kuwait, and Hasa and Gattar. Much of this plain was inhabited. These strips of inhabited hills and plains framed a great gulf of thirsty desert, in whose heart again was an archipelago of watered and populous oases called Kasim and Aridh. In this group of oases lay the true center of Arabia, the preserve of its native spirit, and its most conscious individuality. The desert lapped it round and kept it pure of contact.

The desert around the oases, which performed this great function and so made the character of Arabia, varied greatly in nature. South of the oases it appeared to be a pathless sea of sand, stretching nearly to the escarpment of the Indian Ocean shore. To the west of the oases, between them and the Hejaz hills, it was called Nejd, and was an area of gravel and lava with little sand in it. To the east of the oases, between them and Kuwait, it was a similar waste of gravel, but with some great stretches of soft sand making the road difficult. To the north of the oases the desert was at first a belt of sand and then an immense gravel and lava plain filling up everything between the eastern edge of Syria and the banks of the Euphrates where Mesopotamia began. The practicability of this northern desert for men and motor cars enabled the Arab Revolt to win its ready success.

These gross physical diversities molded the social history of Arabia. As a first point they cut off the Indian Ocean coast from the rest of the peninsula by an impassable barrier of sand, and so prevented it entering the history of the main body, or influencing in any way its moral or its conduct. Hadhramaut, as they called it, formed part of the history of the Dutch Indies, and it's thought swayed Java rather than Arabia.

The hills of the west and the plains of the east were the parts of Arabia which had always been most populous and most active. In particular on the west, the mountaineers of Syria and Palestine, of Hejaz and Yemen, had entered time and again into the current of our European life. Ethically they were in Europe, not in Asia, just as the Arabs looked always to the Mediterranean, not to the Indian Ocean. Their fertile and healthy hills were able to support a considerable population. They presented always a steep sharp face to the western sea, but on the east they were a long slope falling away slowly to the Persian Gulf: Most of their rainfall ran down short torrents into the beach: the rest drained away eastward, till it was swallowed up in the unprofitable desert. The exceptional rivers of the eastern face that broke through the hills westward and reached the sea (chief of them the Orontes and Litani, the Hamdh and Fatma) were all of them main distributors of the population: but they did not afford through-roads, and as the hills were usually impassable, trade or migration northward and southward had been compelled either to struggle up the narrow pathway of the beach, or to sweep along the great open plains of the eastern desert beyond the crests of the hills.

Chapter 4: The Nomadic Phase

The migration problem was the greatest and most complex force in Arabia, and varied in the different Arabic districts. In the north, in Syria, the birth-rate was low in the cities and the death-rate high, because of the unsanitary conditions and the hectic life led by the majority. In consequence the surplus of the peasantry found openings for themselves in the towns, and was swallowed up by them. In the Lebanon sanitation had been improved, and so each year a greater exodus of youth took place to America, threatening, for the first time since Greek days, to change the outlook of an entire district.

In Yemen the solution was different. There were no industries and no foreign trade to accumulate population in unhealthy places. The towns that existed were market towns, as clean and simple as ordinary villages. Therefore the population slowly increased, the scale of living had been brought down very low, and a congestion of numbers was generally felt. They could not emigrate overseas, for the Sudan was even worse country than Arabia, and the few poor tribes that did once venture across were compelled profoundly to modify their manner of life and their Semitic culture, in order to exist. They could not move north along the hills, for they were barred by the holy town of Mecca and its port Jidda, an alien belt, continually reinforced by strangers from India and Java and Bokhara and Mica, very strong in vitality, violently hostile to the Semitic consciousness, maintained in spite of economics and geography and climate by the artificial factor of a world religion.

The constipation of Yemen therefore became extreme, and found its only relief in the east, by forcing the weaker aggregations of its border down and down the slopes of the hills out along the Widian, the half-waste district of the great water-bearing valleys of Bisha, Dawasir, Ranya, and Taraba, which ran down from the complex of hills east and north towards the deserts of Nejd. These weaker clans had continually to exchange good springs and fertile palms for poorer springs and scantier palms, till at last they reached an area where a proper agricultural life became impossible. They then began to eke out their precarious husbandry by breeding sheep and camels, and in time came to depend more and more on these herds for their living. Finally some day there arrived a last impulse from the straining population behind them, and the border people, now almost wholly pastoral, were flung out of the furthest crazy oasis into the untraced wilderness as nomads.

This process, which could be watched today with individual families and tribes to whose stages an exact name and date could be put, must have been going on since the first day of full settlement of Yemen. The Widian below Mecca and Taif were crowded with the memories and place names of half a hundred tribes, which had gone from there and might be found today in Nejd, in Jebel Shammar, in the Hamad, or even in the frontiers of Syria and Mesopotamia.

There was the source of migration, the factory of nomads, the springing of the gulf-stream of desert wandering.

For the people of the desert were as little static as the people of the hills. The economic life of the desert was based on the supply of camels, which were to be best bred on the upland pastures, where strong nutritious thorns were produced by the rigor of the climate. By this industry the Bedouin lived, and it in turn molded their life, apportioned the tribal areas, and kept the clans revolving season by season through their rote of spring, summer and winter pasturages, as their herds cropped the scanty growths of each in turn. The camel markets in Syria, Mesopotamia and Egypt determined the population which the deserts could support, and regulated strictly their standard of living. So the desert also over peopled itself upon occasion, and everywhere there were heaving and thrusting of the crowded tribes, as they elbowed themselves by natural courses towards the light. They might not go south, for there was only inhospitable sand or sea. They could not turn westward, for there the hills of Hejaz were thickly lined by mountain peoples, taking full advantage of their defensiveness. Sometimes they went towards the central oases of Aridh and Kasim and, if the tribes looking for new homes were very strong and vigorous, might succeed in occupying parts of them.

If, however, the desert had not this strength, its peoples were pushed gradually north, up between Media of the Hejaz, and Kasim of Nejd, till they found themselves at the fork of two roads. They could strike eastward by Wadi Rumh or Jebel Shammar, to follow eventually the Batn into Shamiya, where they would at last become riverside Arabs of the lower Euphrates: or they could climb by slow degrees the ladder of western oases, Henakiyeh, Kheiber, Teima, Jauf, and the Sirhan, till fate saw them approaching Jebel Druse in Syria, or watering their herds in Tadmor of the northern desert on their way to Aleppo or to Assyria.

Not even then did the pressure cease: the inexorable trend northward continued. The tribes with their herds found themselves driven to the very edge of cultivation in Syria or Mesopotamia. Opportunity and their bellies persuaded them of the advantages of possessing goats, and then of possessing sheep: lastly they began to sow, if only a little barley for their animals. They were now no longer Bedouin, and they began to suffer like the villagers before them from the ravages of the nomads behind. Insensibly they made common cause with the peasants already on the soil, and found out that they too were peasantry. So we saw clans born in the highlands of Yemen, thrust unwillingly by stronger clans into the desert, where unwillingly they became nomad to keep themselves alive: and then we saw them wandering, every year of their thousand years moving a little further north or a little further east, as chance had sent them down one or other of the great well-roads of their wilderness: until finally this same pressure drove them from the desert again into the sown, by the like need of life, and with the like unwillingness of their first delicate experiment in nomad life. This was the circulation in the Semitic body, the life in its veins through all the ages. There were few, if indeed there was a single northern Semite, whose ancestors had not, at some dark age, passed through the desert. The mark of nomads, the most deep and biting of all social disciplines, was on every one of them in his degree.

Chapter 5: Monotheism

If tribesman and townsman in Arabic-speaking Asia were no different races, but just men in different social and economic stages, a family resemblance might be expected in the working of their minds, and so it is only reasonable that common elements appear in the product of all these Eastern peoples. In the very outset, at the first meeting with them, we found a universal clearness or hardness of belief, almost mathematical in its limitation, and which repelled us by its unsympathetic form. Semites had no half-tones in their register of vision. They were a people of primary colors, especially of black and white, who saw the world always in line. They were a certain people, despising doubt, that modem crown of thorns which some western thinkers wore with such a grace. They did not understand our metaphysical difficulties, our introspective questionings. They knew only truth and untruth, belief and unbelief; without our hesitating retinue of finer shades.

These people were black and white not only in its vision, but in its inmost furnishing, and black and white not merely in clarity, but in opposition. Their thoughts reclined most easily among extremes. They inhabited superlatives by choice. Sometimes the great inconsistencies seemed to possess them in joint sway; they excluded compromise, and pursued the logic of their opinions to its absurd ends, without perceiving any incongruity in their opposed conclusions. They oscillated with cool head and tranquil judgment from asymptote to asymptote, so imperturbably that they would seem hardly conscious of their giddy flight.

They were a limited narrow-minded people, whose inert intellects lay fallow in incurious resignation. Their imaginations were keen, but not creative. There was so little Arab art in Asia that they could almost be said to have had no art, though their classes were liberal patrons, and had encouraged whatever talents in architecture, or ceramic, or in handicraft their neighbors and helots displayed. Nor did they handle great industries; they had no organizations of mind or body anywhere. They invented no systems of philosophy, no complex mythologies. They steered their course between the idols of the tribe and cave: those of the theater and market-place were not within their sight. They were the least morbid of peoples, and accepted the gifts of life unquestioningly, as axiomatic. To them it was a thing inevitable, entailed on man, a usufruct, beyond control. Suicide was an impossible thing, and death no grief.

They were a people of spasms, of upheavals, of ideas, the race of the individual genius. Their movements were the more shocking by contrast with the quietude of every day, their great men greater by contrast with the humanity of their mob. Their convictions were by instinct, their activities intuitional. Their largest manufacture was of creeds: they were monopolists of revealed religions. Three of these efforts had endured among them: two of the three had also borne export (in modified forms) to non Semitic peoples. Christianity, translated into the diverse spirits of Greek and Latin and Teutonic tongues, had conquered Europe and America. Islam in various transformations was subjecting Africa and Asia. These were Semitic successes. Their failures they kept to themselves. The fringes of their deserts were strewn with the broken pieces of faiths which had suffered shipwreck.

It was significant that this wrack of fallen religions lay about the meeting of the desert and the sown. It pointed to the generation of all these creeds. They were assertions, not arguments, and so required a prophet to set them forth. The Arabs said there had been forty thousand prophets: we had records of at least some hundreds. None of them had been themselves of the wilderness, but their lives followed a pattern. Their birth set them in crowded places. An unintelligible, passionate yearning drove them out into the desert. There they lived a greater or lesser time in meditation and physical abandonment: and then they returned with their imagined message articulated, and preached it to their elderly, and now doubting associates. The founders of the three great creeds fulfilled this cycle: their possible coincidence was proved a law by the parallel life histories of the myriad others, the unfortunate who failed, whom we might judge of no less true profession, but for whom time and a disillusioned world had not heaped up dry souls ready to be set on fire. To the thinkers of the town the impulse into Nitria had ever been irresistible, not because of the probability of finding God dwelling there, but that in its solitude they heard more certainly the living word they had brought with them.

The base of all these Semitic creeds, the winners and the losers, was common in the one great idea of world-worthlessness. Their profound reaction against matter led them to preach bareness, renunciation, poverty: and the atmosphere of this invention stifled the minds of the desert pitilessly. A first knowledge of their sense of the purity of rarefaction was given me in early years, when we had ridden out over the rolling plains of North Syria to a far ruin of the Roman period which the Arabs believed was made by a prince of the border as a desert palace for his queen. The clay of its building was said to have been kneaded not with water but, for greater richness, with the precious essential oils of flowers.

My guides, sniffing the air like dogs, led me from one crumbling room to another, saying, 'This is Jessamine, this ambergris, this rose.' But at last Dahoum drew me: 'Come and smell the very sweetest scent of all': and we went into the main lodging, to the gaping window sockets of its eastern face, and there drank with open mouths of the effortless, empty, endless wind of the desert, throbbing past. That slow breath had been born somewhere beyond the distant Euphrates and had dragged its way across many days and nights of dead grass, to this first obstacle, the man-made walls of our broken palace. About them it seemed to fret and linger, murmuring some uncaught secret in baby-speech. This,' they told me, 'is the best: it has no taste.' My Arabs were turning their backs on perfumes and luxuries, and looking out towards the wilderness, choosing the things in which mankind had had no share or part.

The Bedouin of the desert had been born and had grown up in it, and had embraced this nakedness too harsh for volunteers with all his soul, for the reason, felt but inarticulate, that there he found himself indubitably free. He lost all material ties, all comforts, all superfluities or complications to achieve the personal liberty which haunted starvation and death. He saw no virtue in poverty herself: he enjoyed the little vices and luxuries — coffee, fresh water, women — which he could still preserve. In his life he had air and winds, sun and light, open spaces and great emptiness. There was no human effort, no fecundity in nature: just the heaven above and the unspotted earth beneath. There unconsciously he came near to God.

God was to him not anthropomorphic, not tangible, not moral or ethical, not concerned with the world or with him, not natural: but the being *axpuparoc, auxqparzuroc, avapnc* thus qualified not by divestiture, but by investiture, a comprehending being, the egg of all activity, with nature and matter just a glass reflecting Him. The Bedouin could not look for God within him: he was too sure that he was within God. He could not conceive anything which was or was not God. He alone was great, and yet there was a homey an everydayness of this climatic Arab God, who was their eating and their fighting and their lusting, the commonest of their thoughts, their commonest resource and companion, in a way impossible to those whose God was so wistfully veiled from them by despair of their unworthiness of him and the decorum of formal worship. They felt no incongruity in bringing God into their weaknesses and appetites, and invoked his name in the least creditable causes. He was the commonest of their words: and indeed we lost much eloquence by making him the shortest and ugliest of our monosyllables.

This creed of the desert seemed inexpressible in words and indeed in thought. It was easily felt as an influence and all those who went into the desert long enough to forget its open spaces and its emptiness were inevitably thrust upon God as their only refuge and rhythm of being. The Bedawi might be a nominal Sunni, or a nominal Wahabi, or anything else in the Semitic compass, and he would take it all very lightly, a little in the manner of the watchmen at Zion's gate who drank beer and laughed in Zion, because they were Zionists. Each individual nomad had his revealed religion, not oral or traditional or expressed but instinctive in himself, and so we get all the Semitic creeds with, in their character and essence, a stress on the emptiness of the world and the fullness of God, but according to the power and opportunity of the believer was the expression of them.

The desert-dweller could not take virtue for his belief. He had never been either evangelist or proselyte. He arrived at this intense condensation of himself in God by shutting his eyes to the world, and to all the complex possibilities latent in him which only contact with wealth and temptations could bring forth. He attained a sure trust and a powerful trust, but of narrow field! His sterile experience robbed him of compassion and perverted his human kindness to the image of the waste in which he hid. Accordingly he hurt himself, not merely to be free, but to please himself. There followed a delight in pain, a cruelty which was more to him than goods. The desert Arab found no joy like the joy of voluntarily holding back. He found luxury in abnegation, renunciation and self-restraint. He made nakedness of the mind as sensuous as nakedness of the body. He saved his own soul, perhaps, and without danger, but in a hard selfishness. His desert was made a spiritual ice-house, in which was preserved intact but unimproved for all ages a vision of the unity of God. To it sometimes the seekers from the outer world could escape for a season and look thence in detachment at the nature of the generation they would convert.

This faith of the desert was impossible in the villages or towns. It was at once too strange, too simple and too impalpable for export and common use. The idea, the ground-belief of all the Semite creeds was waiting there, but it had to be diluted to be made comprehensible to us. The scream of a bat was too shrill for many years: the desert spirit escaped through our coarser texture. The prophets returned to us from the desert with their glimpse of God, and through their stained medium (as through a dark glass) showed something of the majesty and brilliance whose 111 vision would blind us, deafen us, and silence us, as it had served the Bedouin, setting him, uncouth, a man apart. Their disciples, in the endeavor to strip themselves and their neighbors of all things according to the master's word, stumbled over human weaknesses and failed. To live, the villager or townsman must fill himself each day with all the pleasures of acquisition and accumulation, and by rebound off circumstance he became the grossest and most material of men. The shining contempt of life which led others into the barest asceticism drove him to despair. He squandered himself heedlessly, as a spendthrift ran through his inheritance of flesh in hasty longing for the end. The Jew in the Metropolis at Brighton, the miser, the worshiper of Adokoy, and the lecher in the stews of Damascus were all signs of the Semitic capacity of physical joy, and the expression of the same nerve which gave us at the other pole the self-denial of the Essenes the early Christians, or the first Khaliias, finding the way to heaven fairest for the poor in spirit. The Semite hovered between lust and self-denial.

When you had Arabs and an idea you could sway them as on a cord, and easily to yourself for the unfledged allegiance of their empty minds made them your obedient servants. None of them escaped, and the bond endured till you succeeded, and with successes came responsibility, and duty and engagements. Then your idea was gone, and your work ended, all in ruins. Without a creed you could take them to the four corners of the world (but not to heaven) by showing them the riches of earth and the pleasures of it — but if on your road, leading them in this fashion, you met the prophet of an idea, who had nowhere to lay his head, and who depended for his food on charity or birds — then they would all leave your wealth for his inspiration. They were incorrigibly children of the idea, feckless and color-blind, for whom body and spirit were forever and inevitably opposed.

The Semitic mind was strange and dark full of depressions and exaltations, lacking in rule, but with more of ardor and more fertile in belief than any other in the world. They were a people of starts, for whom the abstract was the strongest motive, the process of infinite courage and variety, and the end nothing. They were as unstable as water, and like water would perhaps finally prevail.

Since the dawn of life in successive waves they had been dashing themselves against the coasts of the flesh. Each wave was broken but, like the sea, wore away ever so little of the granite on which it failed, and some day, ages yet, might roll unchecked over the place where the material world had been, and God would move upon the face of those waters. One such wave (and not the least) I raised and rolled before the breath of an idea, till it reached its crest, and toppled over and fell at Damascus. The wash of that wave, thrown back by the resistance of vested things, will provide the matter of the following wave, when in fullness of time it shall be raised once more.

Chapter 6: The Autonomy Movement

The first great rush around the Mediterranean showed the world the power of an excited Arab for a short spell of intense physical activity: but when the effort burned out, the lack of endurance and routine in the Semitic mind became as evident. They neglected the provinces they had over-run, out of sheer distaste of system, and sought the help of their conquered subjects or of more vigorous foreigners to administer their ill-knit and inchoate empires. So, early in the middle ages, the Turks found a footing in the Arab states, first as servants, then as helpers, and then as a parasite growth which choked the life out of the old body politic. The last phase was of enmity, when the Hulagus or Tiurs sated on them their blood lust, burning and destroying everything that irked them with a pretension of superiority.

Arab civilization had been of a parasite nature, moral and intellectual rather than applied, and their lack of public spirit made their excellent private qualities a waste: but they were fortunate in their epoch. Europe had fallen barbarous, and the memory of Greek and Latin learning was slowly fading from men's minds. By this easy standard their imitative exercises had seemed like culture, their mental activity progressive, their state prosperous: and they had performed real service in preserving something of a classical past for a medieval future.

With the coming of the Turks this happiness became a dream. By stages the Semites of Asia passed under the yoke, and found it a slow death. Their material goods were stripped from them, and their spirits gradually shriveled by the numbing breath of a military government. Turkish rule was gendarme rule, and Turkish political theory was as crude as their practice. They taught the Arabs that the interests of religion were higher than those of nationality, that the petty concerns of the province were more than patriotism. They led them by subtle dissensions to distrust one another. The Arabic language was banished from courts and offices, from the Government service, and from superior schools. Arabs might only serve the state by the sacrifice of their racial characteristics.

These measures were not accepted quietly. Semitic tenacity showed itself in the many rebellions of Syria, Mesopotamia and Arabia against the grosser forms of Turkish penetration; and resistance was also made to the more insidious attempts at absorption. The Arabs would not give up their rich and flexible tongue for crude Turkish: instead they filled Turkish with Arabic words. Nor could they lightly forget the literary treasures of their language. They lost their geographical sense, and their racial and political and historical memories: but they clung the more tightly to their language, and erected it almost into a fatherland of its own. The first duty of every Muslim was to study the Koran, the sacred book of Islam, and incidentally the greatest Arab literary monument. The knowledge that this religion was his own, and that only he was perfectly qualified to understand and practice it, gave every Arab who thought abstractly a standard by which to judge the banal achievements of the Turks.

The superiority of the Turks over the Arabs in material possessions and in modem knowledge did not humiliate as much as it imitated by impressing a sense of inferior opportunity. Foreigners came to the Arabic countries, with knowledge far greater than anything the Turks could show and, unlike the Turks, eager to impart this knowledge. A great American college, splendidly equipped, was set up at Beirut and gave the people an example of sympathy and wisdom, in glaring contrast with the attitude of their Government. The Turks sowed jealousy and bitterness and ignorance.

The American schools taught by the method of enquiry, encouraged a scientific detachment and free exchange of views. Quite without intention they taught revolution, since it was impossible to be modem in Turkey, and at the same time loyal, if one belonged to any of the subject races — Greeks, Arabs, Kurds, Armenians or Albanians — over whom the Turks were so long helped to keep dominion.

Then came the Turkish Revolution, the fall of Abdul Hamid, and the supremacy of the Young Turks. The horizon momentarily broadened for the Arabs. The Young Turk movement was a revolt against the hierarchic conception of Islam and the pan-Islamic theories of the old Sultan, who had aspired, by making himself spiritual director of the Muslim world, to be also, beyond appeal, its director in temporal affairs. These young politicians rebelled against him and threw him into prison, under the impulse of constitutional theories of a sovereign state. So at a time when Western Europe was just beginning to climb out of nationality into internationality and to rumble with wars far removed from problems of race, Western Asia began to climb out of religious movements into politics, and to dream of wars for self-government and national freedom, instead of for faith or dogma. This tendency had broken out first and strongest in the Near East, in the little Balkan states, and nationality had sustained them through an almost unparalleled martyrdom to their goal of separation from Turkey. Afterwards there had been nationalist movements in Egypt, in India and in Persia, and for their final expression in Constantinople they were pointed and fortified by the new American ideas in education; which, when released in an old high-oriental atmosphere, made an explosive mixture.

The Young Turks in their confidence of first success were carried away by the logic of their principles, and in self-defense against pan-Islam preached Ottoman brotherhood. The gullible subject races, far more numerous than the Turks themselves, believed that they were called upon to co-operate in building a new East. They rushed to the task, full of Herbert Spencer and Alexander Hamilton, laid down sweeping platforms of ideas, and hailed the Turks as partners. The Turks were terrified at the forces that they had let loose, and closed them down as suddenly as they had called them out. The Turkification of Turkey, Neo-Turan, became the cry. It was another general theory, and sought to make everything and everybody in the empire Turkish, for the better, as the original virtues and families of the best Turks were from their Mongol stock Later on, this policy would turn them towards the rescue of their irredenta, the Turkish populations subject to Russia in central Asia: but first of all they must purge their empire of these irritating subject races who resisted the ruling stamp. The Arabs, as the largest alien component of Turkey, must first be dealt with. Accordingly the Arab deputies were scattered, the Arab societies forbidden, the Arab notables proscribed. The Arabic language and Arabic manifestations were suppressed by Enver Pasha more sternly than of old by Abdul Hamid.

However, the Arabs had tasted freedom: they could not change their ideas as quickly as their conduct, and the stiffer spirits among them were not easily put down. They read the Turkish papers within their reach, putting 'Arab' for 'Turk' in all the patriotic exhortations, and their suppression charged them with unhealthy violence. Deprived of constitutional outlets they became revolutionary. The Arab societies went underground, and changed from liberal clubs into conspiracies. The Akhua, the Arab mother society, was publicly dissolved. It was replaced in Mesopotamia by the dangerous Ahad, a very secret brotherhood, limited almost entirely to Arab officers in the Turkish army, who swore to acquire the military knowledge of their masters and to hold it against them, at the disposal of the Arab people, when the moment of rebellion came.

It was a large society, with a sure base in the wild part of southern Irak, where Sayid Taleb, the young John Wilkes of the Arab Movement, held the power in his unprincipled fingers. To it belonged seven out of every ten Mesopotamian-born officers, and their counsel was so well kept that members of it held high commands in Turkey to the last. When the crash came and Allenby rode across Armageddon and Turkey fell, one vice-president of the society was commanding the broken fragments of all the Palestine armies on the retreat, and another was directing the Turkish army across Jordan in the Amman area. Yet later, after the Armistice, great places in the Turkish service were still held by men ready to turn their knowledge to its destruction when the word was given them by their Arab leaders. To most of them the word was never given, for these societies were pro-Arab only, willing to fight for nothing but Arab independence, and they could see no advantage in supporting the Allies rather than the Turks, as they would not accept our assurances that we would leave them free. Indeed many of them preferred an Arabia united in miserable subjection to Turkey, to an Arabia divided up and slothful under the easier domination of several European powers in spheres of influence.

Greater than the Ahad was the Fetah, the society of freedom in Syria. The landowners, the writers, the doctors, the great public servants linked themselves in this society with a common oath, passwords, signs, a press, and a central treasury, to ruin the Turkish empire. With the noisy facility of the Syrian, an ape-like people with much of the Japanese quickness, but shallow, they speedily built up a formidable organization. They looked outside for help, and expected freedom to come by diplomacy, not by sacrifice. They corresponded with Egypt, with the Ahad (whose members, with true Mesopotamian dourness, rather despised them), with the Sherif of Mecca, and with Great Britain, everywhere seeking the ally who would serve their turn. They also were deadly secret, and the Turkish Government, though it suspected their existence, could never find evidence of their leaders or membership. It had to hold its hand and wait the opportunity to strike blindly.

The outbreak of war in 1914 seemed to the rulers of Turkey just this opportunity. The English and French withdrew their representatives, who had been public opinion in Turkey, and so they were nearly free of interference. The mobilization put the striking power of the country into the hands of the three men in Turkey, Enver, Talaat and Jemal, who were at once the most ruthless, the most logical and the most ambitious of the Young Turks. They set themselves to stamp out all non-Turkish elements in the State, especially Arab and Armenian nationalism. For the first step they found a specious and convenient weapon, in the secret papers of a French consul in Syria, who left behind him in his consulate correspondence about Arab freedom which had passed between him and an Arab club, not connected with the Fetah, but made up of the more talkative and less formidable intelligentsia of the Syrian coast. The Turks of course were delighted, for French 'colonial' aggression in North Africa had given them a black reputation in the Arabic-speaking Muslim world, and it served Jemal well to show their co-religionists how these Arab nationalists were infidel enough to prefer France to Turkey.

In Syria, of course, his disclosures had little novelty: but the members of the society were well-known and respected, if somewhat academic, members of the community, and their arrest and condemnation, and the crop of deportations, exiles and executions to which their trial led, moved the country to its depths, and taught the Arabs of the Fetah that if they did not profit by their lesson the fate of the Armenians would be upon them. The Armenians had been armed and organized, but their leaders had failed them, and so they had been disarmed, and destroyed piecemeal, the men by massacre, the women and children by being driven and over-driven naked and hungry along the wintry roads into the desert, common property of any passer-by, until death took them. The Young Turks had killed the Armenians not because they were Christians, but because they were Armenians, and for the same reason they herded Arab Muslims and Arab Christians into the same prisons, and hanged them together on the same scaffolds. Jemal Pasha united all classes, conditions and creeds in Syria, under pressure of a common misery and peril, and so made a concerted revolt possible.

The Turks suspected the Arab officers and soldiers in the army, and hoped to use against them the weapon which had served in the Armenian case. At first transport difficulties stood in their way, and there came a dangerous concentration of Arab divisions (nearly one third of the original Turkish m y was Arab) in North Syria early in 1915. They broke these up as soon as possible, marching them off to Europe, to the Dardanelles, to the Caucasus, on to the Canal — anywhere so long as they were put quickly into the firing line, or withdrawn far from the sight and help of their compatriots. The Holy War was proclaimed, to rally the old clerical elements to the Government banner, and to give it an odor of sanctity, and the Sherif of Mecca was invited, or rather ordered, to associate himself with the cry.

Chapter 7: Prelude of the Sherif

The position of the Sherif of Mecca had long been anomalous. The title 'Sherif' assumed descent from the prophet Mohammed through his daughter Fatima and Hassan her elder son. Authentic Sheds were inscribed on the family tree, an immense roll preserved at Mecca in custody of the Emir of Mecca, the elected Sherif of Sheds, supposed to be the senior and noblest of them all. The prophet's family had held temporal rule in Mecca for the last nine hundred years, and now counted some two thousand persons.

The Ottoman Government regarded this clan of manticratic peers with its usual mixture of reverence and distrust. They were too strong to destroy, so the Sultans salved their dignity by solemnly confirming them in their place. This empty approval acquired dignity by lapse of time, until the local choice for the succession began to feel that it added the final seal to his dignity. After a while the Turks found that they needed the Hejaz under their unquestioned sway, as part of the stage-furniture for their new pan-Islamic notion. The opportune Suez Canal enabled them to send a considerable garrison to the Holy Cities. Later they projected the Hejaz Railway, and increased Turkish influence among the tribes by money and intrigue and armed expeditions.

As the Sultan grew stronger, he ventured to assert himself more and more alongside the Sherif, even in Mecca itself, and upon occasion ventured to depose a Sherif too magnificent for his views and to appoint a successor from a rival family of the clan, in hopes of winning the usual advantages from dissension. Finally Abdul Hamid took away some of the family to Constantinople into honorable captivity. Amongst these was Hussein ibn Ali, the present ruler, who was held there for nearly eighteen years. He took the opportunity to provide his sons, Ali, Abdulla, Feisal and Zeid, with the modern education and experience which afterwards enabled them to lead the Arab armies to success.

When Abdul Hamid felt the less wise Young Turks reversed his policy, and sent back Sherif Hussein to Mecca as Emu, he at once set to work unobtrusively to restore the power of the Emirate, and strengthened himself on the old basis, keeping the while in close and friendly touch with Constantinople by the intermediary of his sons Abdulla, Vice-Chairman of the Turkish House, and Feisal, member for Jidda. They kept him properly informed of political opinion in the capital, until war broke out, and then they returned in haste to Mecca.

The outbreak of war put the Hejaz in great difficulty. The pilgrimage ceased, and with it all the revenues and business of the Holy Cities. There was reason to fear that the Indian food-ships would cease to come (since the Sherif became technically an enemy subject) and as the province produced almost no food of its own it would be precariously dependent on the goodwill of the Turks, who might starve it by closing the Hejaz Railway. Hussein had never been entirely at the Turks' mercy before, and at this unhappy moment they particularly needed his help in their 'Jihad', the Holy War of all Muslims against Christianity.

To become popularly effective this must be endorsed by Mecca, and if endorsed it might plunge the whole East in blood. Hussein was honorable, shrewd, obstinate and deeply pious. He felt that the Holy War was doctrinally incompatible with an aggressive war, and absurd with a Christian ally, Germany. So he refused the Turkish demand, and made at the same time a dignified appeal to the Allies, not to starve his province for what was not his people's fault. The Turks at once instituted a partial blockade of the Hejaz, by controlling the traffic on the pilgrim railway. The British left his coast open to regulated vessels.

The Turkish demand was, however, not the only one which the Sherif received. The oppressed peoples of Mesopotamia and Syria, the committees of the Ahad and the Fetah, were calling out to him, as the Father of the Arabs, the Muslim of Muslims, their greatest prince, their oldest notable, to save them from the sinister designs of Talaat and Jemal. They began in January 1915, when Yasin, head of the Mesopotamian officers, Ali Riza, head of the Damascus officers, and Abd el Ghani el Areisi representing the Syrian civilians, sent down to him a concrete proposal for a military mutiny in Syria against the Turks.

Hussein as politician, as prince, as Muslim, as modernist, and as nationalist was forced to listen to their appeal. He sent down Feisal, his third son, to Damascus, to discuss their projects as his representative and to make a report. He sent Ali, his eldest son, to Medina with orders to raise quietly, on any excuse he pleased, troops from the villagers and tribesmen of the Hejaz, and to hold them ready for action if Feisal called. Abdulla, his politic second son, was to apply to the British, and to sound them about help for the principle of an Arab revolt.

Feisal reported in January 1915 that the local conditions were good, but that the general war was not going well for their hopes. In Damascus were the Twenty-fifth Division, the Thirty-fifth, and the Thirty-sixth Division, all Arab troops ready for rebellion. In Aleppo Yasin had two other divisions riddled with Arab nationalism, which were certain to join in if the others began. There was only one Turkish division this side of the Taurus, so that it was certain that they would get possession of all Syria at the first effort. On the other hand public opinion was less ready, and the military class was quite sure that Germany would win the war, and win it soon. If, however, the Allies landed their Australian expedition, preparing in Egypt, at Alexandretta, and so covered the Syrian flank then it would be wise and safe to risk a German victory and the need to make a separate peace with the Turks.

A delay followed, as the Allies went to the Dardanelles, and not to Alexandretta. Feisal went there after them to get first-hand knowledge of the Gallipoli conditions, since a break-down of Turkey would be the Arab signal, and there followed a very long delay of all the months through which the Dardanelles campaign dragged itself out. In that slaughter-house the remaining Turkish first-line army was destroyed. The disaster to Turkey of their accumulated losses was so great that Feisal came back to Syria, judging it a possible moment in which to strike, but found that meanwhile the local situation had become unfavorable.

His Syrian supporters were under arrest or in hiding, and their friends being hanged in scores on political charges. He found the well-disposed Arab divisions either exiled to distant fronts, or broken up in drafts and distributed among Turkish units. The Arab peasantry was in the grip of Turkish military service, and Syria prostrate before the merciless Jemal Pasha. All his assets had disappeared. He wrote to his father that further delay was necessary, till England had been properly approached and Turkey reduced to extremities. Unfortunately England, their last possible resource, was in a deplorable condition. Her fleets and armies were falling back shattered, from the Dardanelles. The slow-drawn agony of Kut was in its last stage; and the Senussi rising, coincident with the entry of Bulgaria, threatened her on new flanks.

Feisal's correspondence with his father was an adventure in itself. They communicated by means of old retainers of the family, men above suspicion, who went up and down the Hejaz Railway, carrying their notes in sword-hilts, in cakes, sewn between the soles of their sandals, or in invisible writing on the wrappers of harmless packages. In all of them Feisal reported unfavorable things, and begged his father to wait for a wiser time.

His own position was hazardous in the extreme. He was at the mercy of all the members of the secret society, whose president he had been before the war. He had to live in Damascus, as the guest of Jemal Pasha, rubbing up hi military knowledge; for his brother Ali was raising the troops in the Hejaz on the pretext that he and Feisal would lead them against the Suez Canal to help the Turks.

So Feisal, as a good Ottoman and a general in the Turkish service, had to live at headquarters and endure acquiescently the insults and indignities heaped upon his race by Jemal in his cups.

Jemal would send for Feisal and take him with him to the hanging of his Syrian bends. These victims of justice could not show that they knew Feisal's real hopes (any more than he could show his mind by word or look), since they would have condemned his family, and perhaps the race, to the same fate.

Only once did he burst out, in the cry that these executions would cost Jemal all that he was trying to avoid — and it took the intercessions of his Constantinople friends, the chief men in Turkey, to save him from the price of those rash words.

Hussein, the father, was not a whit cast down by Feisal's discouragements. The Young Turks were to him godless transgressors of their creed and their human duty, traitors to the spirit of their time, and to the higher interests of Islam. He was cheerfully determined, though an old man of sixty-five, to wage war against them, relying upon justice to cover the cost. Hi eldest son collected the tribal levies gradually, and moved them into Medina. Hussein trusted so much in God that he let his military sense lie fallow, and thought Hejaz able to fight it out with Turkey on a fair field. So he sent Abd el Kader el Abdu to Feisal with a letter that the troops were now ready for inspection by him in Media before they started for the front. Feisal informed Jemal, and asked leave to go down and see them: but to his dismay Jemal replied that Enver Pasha the generalissimo was on his way to the province, and that they would all go together to Media to the inspection. Feisal had planned to raise his father's crimson banner as soon as he arrived in Medina and to take the Turks unawares, and here he was saddled with two uninvited guests to whom, by the Arab law of hospitality, he could do no harm, and who would probably delay his action so long that the whole secrecy of the revolt would be in jeopardy.

In the end matters passed off well, though the irony of the review was terrible. They watched the troops wheeling and turning in the dusty plain outside the city gate, rushing up and down in mimic camel-battle, or spurring their horses in the javelin game after immemorial Arab fashion. 'And are all these volunteers for the Holy War? Asked Enver at last, turning to Feisal. Yes', said Feisal. 'And will they fight to the death against the enemies of the faithful? 'Yes', said Feisal again, and then the Arab chiefs came up to be presented, and Ali ibn el Hussein of Modhig drew him aside whispering, 'My Lord, shall we kill them now? and Feisal said, 'No, they are our guests.' The Sheikhs protested, for they believed that there they could finish off the war in two blows. They were determined to force Feisal's hand, and he had to go among them, just out of earshot but in full view of the Turks, and beg for the lives of Enver and Jemal, who had murdered his best friends on the scaffold. In the end he was compelled to make excuses to the Turks, and take them back quickly to Medina, and picket the banqueting hall with his own slaves, and escort the dictators back to Damascus to save them born death on the way.

He explained this labored courtesy by the plea that it was the Arab manner to devote everything to guests, but both Enver and Jemal were deeply suspicious of what they had seen, imposed a strict blockade of the Hejaz and ordered large Turkish reinforcements thither. They wanted to detain Feisal in Damascus, but urgent telegrams came from Media demanding his immediate return to prevent disorder, and reluctantly Jemal let him go, on condition that his suite remained behind as hostages. Feisal found Medina full of Turkish troops, and the headquarters of the Twelfth Corps under Fakhri Pasha, the courageous old butcher who had 'purified' Zeitun and Urfa of Armenians.

However, it was now too late for prudence. Four days later his suite in Damascus took horse and rode out east into the desert to Nuri Shaalan to take refuge against the Turks, and the same day

Feisal showed his hand. When he raised the Arab flag, the pan-Islamic supra-national state for which Abdul Hamid had massacred and worked and died, and the German hope of the co-operation of Islam in the world-plans of the Kaiser, passed into the realms of dreams. By the mere fact of his rebellion the Sherif had closed these two fantastic chapters in history.

Rebellion was the gravest step which political man could take, and the success or failure of the Arab revolt was a gamble too hazardous for prophecy. Yet for once fortune favored the bold player, and the Arab epic tossed up its stormy road from birth through weakness, pain and doubt to red victory. It was the just end to an adventure which dared so much: but after the victory there came a slow time of disillusion, and then a night in which they found that all their hopes had failed them. Now at last may there be to them the white peace of the end, in the knowledge that they achieved a deathless thing, a lasting inspiration to the children of their race.

Chapter 8: the British Protagonists

I had been many years going up and down the Semitic East before the war, learning the manners of the villagers and tribesmen and citizens of Syria and Mesopotamia. My poverty had constrained me to mix with the humbler classes, those seldom encountered by European travelers, and thus my experiences gave me an unusual angle of view, one which enabled me to understand and think for the ignorant majority, as well as for the more enlightened, whose opinions mattered not so much for the day as for the morrow. In addition I had seen something of the broad political forces working in the minds of the Middle East, and especially had noted everywhere sure signs of the internal decay of Turkey.

Turkey was dying of over strain, of the attempt with diminished resources to hold, on the traditional terms, all the Empire bequeathed to it. It was as though the Turks had settled that they would be the one stable element in a changing world. The world at once left them out of its progress, and shortly it was evident that, even in their own homes, they were losing grip. Life was growing too complicated for this child-like people, whose strength had lain in simplicity and patience, and in their capacity for sacrifice. They were the slowest of the races of Western Asia, the least fitted to adapt themselves to new sciences of government and life, still less to invent new arts for themselves. Their administration since Mahmud had become perforce an affair of files and telegrams, of high finance, eugenics, calculations. Inevitably the old governors, who had governed by force of hand or force of character — illiterate, direct, personal — had to pass away. The rule was transferred to new men, with agility and suppleness to stoop to such machinery. The shallow and half-polished committee of the Young Turks was descendants of Greeks, Albanians, Circassians, Bulgars, Armenians, Jews — anything but Seljuks or Ottomans. The commons ceased to feel in tune with their governors, whose culture was Levantine, and whose political theory was French. Turkey was decaying from the head.

The old Turk remained a beast of burden in his village and an uncomplaining soldier abroad, loving the old ways steadily; while the subject races of the Empire, who formed nearly seventy per cent of its total population, grew daily in strength and knowledge; for their lack of tradition and responsibility, as well as their lighter and quicker minds, disposed them to accept new ideas. The former natural awe and supremacy of the Turkish name began to fade in the face of wider comparison. The changing relations and balance of Turkey and the subject provinces involved stronger garrisons, if the old ground was to be retained. Tripoli, Albania, Thrace, Yemen, Hejaz, Syria, Mesopotamia, Kurdistan, Armenia were all outgoing accounts, burdens on the peasants of Anatolia, and yearly devoured a larger draft of them. The burden fell most heavily on the poor villages, and each year it made these poor villages yet poorer. They took their fate unquestioning, resignedly, after the custom of Turkish peasantry. The unfortunate recruits were like sheep, neutrals without vice or virtue. Left alone, they did nothing, or perhaps sat down dully on the ground. Ordered to be kind, and without haste they were as good friends and as generous enemies as might be found. Ordered to outrage their fathers or disembowel their mothers, and they did it as calmly as they did nothing, or did well. There was about them a hopeless, fever-wasted lack of initiative, which made them the most biddable, the most enduring, and the least spirited soldiers in the world.

Such men were natural victims of their showy and vicious Levantine officers, to be driven to death or thrown away by neglect without reckoning. Indeed we found them just kept chopping blocks of their commanders' viler passions. So cheap did they rate them, that in connection with them they used none of the ordinary sanitary precautions. Medical examination of some batches of Turkish prisoners found nearly the half of them afflicted by unnatural diseases. Pox and it's like were not understood in the country, and the infection ran from one to another through the battalion, where the conscripts served for six or seven years, till at the end of their period the survivors, if they came from decent homes, were ashamed to return, and drifted either into the gendarme service, or as broken men into casual labor about the towns: and so the birth-rate fell. The Turkish race in Anatolia was dying of military service.

We could see that a new factor was needed in the East, some power or race which would outweigh the Turks in numbers, in output, and in mental activity. History gave no encouragement to think that these qualities could be supplied ready-made from Europe. The efforts of European powers to maintain a footing in the Asiatic Levant had been uniformly disastrous, and we disliked no Western people so much that we would inveigle them into a new adventure. Our successor and solution must be local, and fortunately the standard of efficiency required was local also. Their competition would be with Turkey, and Turkey was rotten. The sword had been the virtue of the children of Othman and swords had passed out of fashion nowadays, in favor of deadlier and more scientific weapons.

Some of us decided that there was latent power enough and to spare in the Arabic peoples, the greatest component of the old Turkish Empire, that prolific Semitic agglomeration, great in religious thought, reasonably industrious, mercantile, politic, yet solvent rather than dominant in character. They had served a term of five hundred years under the Turkish harrow, and had begun to dream of liberty: and so when at last by good fortune England fell out with Turkey, and war was let loose in the East and West at once, we who believed we held an indication of the future set out to bend England's efforts towards fostering a new Arabic world in hither Asia.

We were not so many, and we nearly all rallied round Clayton, the Chief of Intelligence, civil and military, in Egypt. Clayton made the perfect leader for such a hand of wild men as we were. He was calm, detached, clear-sighted, of unconscious courage in assuming responsibility, and gave an open run to his subordinates. His own views were general, like his knowledge, and he worked by influence rather than by direction. It was not easy just to descry this influence. He was like water, or permeating oil, soaking silently and insistently through everything. It was not possible to say where Clayton was or wasn't, and how much really belonged to him. He never led, but his ideas were abreast of those who did, while yet he impressed men by his sobriety, and by a certain quiet and stately moderation of hope. In practical matters he was loose, irregular, untidy, a man with whom wild men could bear.

The first of us was Ronald Storrs, Oriental Secretary of the Residency, the most brilliant Englishman in the Near East, and the deepest, though his eyelids were heavy with laziness, and his eyes dulled by care of self and his mouth made unbeautiful by hampering desires. None the less Storrs sowed what we reaped, and was always the first and greatest of us. His shadow would have covered our work and British policy in the East like a cloak, had he been able to deny himself to leave the world, and prepare his mind and body with the sternness of an athlete for a great fight.

George Lloyd entered our number. He gave us confidence, and lent us knowledge of money, and a sure guide in the subways of trade and politics, and the future arteries of the Middle East. We would not have done so much so soon without his partnership, but unfortunately he was born a restless soul, avid rather to taste than to create. To him many things were needful, and so he would not stay very long with us.

Then there was Mark Sykes, the imaginative prophet of unconvincing world-movements, and also a bundle of prejudices, intuitions and half-sciences. His ideas were of the outside, and he lacked patience to test his materials before deciding on his style of building.

He would take an aspect of the truth, detach it from its circumstances, inflate it, twist and model it, until its old likeness and its new unlikeness together made one laugh. His instincts lay in parody; by choice he was a caricaturist rather than an artist, even in his statesmanship. He saw the odd in everything, and missed the even.

He would sketch out in a few dashes of words a new world, all out of scale but so vivid a vision of some sides of the thing we hoped. His help did us great good and great harm. For this his last week in Paris atoned. He had returned from Syria, after his awful realization of the true shape of his dreams, to say gallantly, 'I was wrong; here is the truth.' His former friends would not see this new earnestness, and thought him fickle and in error: and before time proved him right he died. It was a tragedy of tragedies, for the Arab sake.

Not a wild man, but *Mentor* to all of us was Hogarth, our father confessor and adviser, who brought us the parallels and lessons of history, and moderation, and courage. To the outsider he was peacemaker (I was all claws and teeth, and had a devil) and made us lied and listened to, for his weight and judgment. He had a delicate sense of value, and would present clearly to us the forces hidden behind the lousy rags and festering skins that we knew as Arabs. Hogarth was our referee, and our untiring historian, who gave us his great knowledge and careful wisdom even in the smallest things, because he believed in what we were making. Behind him stood Cornwallis, a man rude to look upon, but apparently forged from one of those incredible metals whose melting point was thousands of degrees. So he could remain for months hotter than other men's white-heat, and yet look cold and hard. Behind him again were others, Newcombe, Parker, Graves, all of the creed, and laboring stoutly after their fashion.

We called ourselves 'Intrusive' as a band, for we meant to break into the accepted halls of English foreign policy, and build a new people in the East despite the rails laid down for us by our ancestors.

Therefore from our hybrid intelligence office in Cairo we began to work upon all our chiefs, far and near. McMahon was our first effort, and with his shrewd insight and tired, experienced mind he understood our design from the first showing and judged it good. Others, like Wemyss, Neil Malcolm, Wingate, supported us in their pleasure at seeing the purpose of the war turned constructive. Their combined advocacy confirmed Lord Kitchener in the opinion Storrs had given him years before when Sherif Abdulla had appealed to him in Egypt, and with his support McMahon at last achieved our foundation stone, the understanding with the Sherif of Mecca.

But before this we had had hopes of Mesopotamia. The Arab beginning of the Arab Independence Movement had been there, under the vigorous but unscrupulous impulse of Sayid Taleb, and later of Yasin el Hashimi and the military league. Aziz el Masri, Enver's rival, who was living, much indebted to us, in Egypt, was an idol of the Arab officers, and he was approached by Lord Kitchener in the first days of the war, in the hope of winning the Turkish Mesopotamian forces to our side. Unfortunately at that time Britain was bursting with confidence in an early and easy victory, and the smashing of Turkey was called a promenade. So the Indian Government was adverse to any pledges to the Arab nationalists which might limit their ambitions to make the intended Mesopotamian colony play the self-sacrificing role of a Burma for the general good. They broke off negotiations, rejected Aziz, and deported Sayid Taleb.

Then they marched into Basra by brute force. The enemy troops in Irak were nearly all Arabs who found themselves in the unenviable predicament of having to fight on behalf of their secular oppressors against the people whom they had long wanted as liberators, but who obstinately refused to play the part. As may be imagined they fought very badly, and our own forces won victory after victory till we became deluded with the idea that an Indian army was better than a Turkish army. There followed our rash advance to Ctesiphon, where we met native Turkish troops whose heart was in the game, and were abruptly checked. We fell back and the long misery of Kut began.

Meanwhile our Government repented and, for reasons not unconnected with the fall of Erzeroum, sent me out to Mesopotamia to see what could be done by indirect means to relieve the beleaguered garrison. The local British had the strongest objection to my coming, and two generals of them were good enough to explain that my mission (which they did not know) was dishonorable to a soldier (which I was not). As a matter of fact, it was too late for action, with Kut just dying, and in consequence I made no effort to do anything of what it had been in my mind and power to do.

The conditions were ideal for an Arab movement. The people of Nejef and Kerbela, far in the rear of Halil Pasha's army, were in actual revolt against him. The surviving Arabs in Halil's army were, on his own confession, openly disloyal to Turkey. The tribes of the Hai and Euphrates would have turned our way had they seen signs of grace from the British. If we had published the promises we had made to the Sherif; or even the proclamation we afterwards posted in Bagdad when we captured it, enough local fighting men would have joined us to cut the Turkish line of communication between Bagdad and Kut. A few weeks of that and the enemy would either have been forced to raise the siege and retire, or have suffered investment, outside Kut, nearly as stringent as the investment of Townsend within it. Time to develop such a scheme could have easily been gained. Had the British headquarters in Mesopotamia obtained from the War Office six more airplanes to increase the carriage of food by air to the garrison of Kuf Townsend's resistance might have been indefinitely prolonged. His defense was Turkishly impregnable, and only our blunders forced surrender upon him.

However, this was not the way of the directing parties there, and so I returned at once to Egypt, and till the end of the war the British in Mesopotamia remained substantially an alien force invading enemy territory. Allenby entered Syria as a friend, with the local people actively on his side. The British in Mesopotamia had the local people passively neutral or sullenly against them, and in consequence they had not the freedom of movement and elasticity of Allenby. The factors of number, climate and communications favored us in Mesopotamia more than in Syria, and our higher command there was, after the beginning, no less efficient and experienced, but their casualty lists compared with Allenby's, their wood-chopping tactics compared with his rapier-play, showed how formidably an adverse political situation cramped an operation.

Chapter 9: Jealousies of First Success

This check in Mesopotamia was a disappointment to us, but McMahon continued his negotiations with Mecca, and finally brought them to a successful conclusion in June 1916, despite the evacuation of Gallipoli and the surrender of Kut, and the generally unfortunate aspect of the war at the moment. Few people, even of those who knew all the course of the negotiations, had really believed that the Sherif would come out in arms on our side, and so his eventual rebellion and his opening his coast to our ships and help took us mainly by surprise. We found our difficulties then only beginning. The credit of the new factor was to McMahon and Clayton, and jealousies immediately raised their heads. Sir Archibald Murray, the General in Egypt, wanted, naturally enough, no competitor and no competing campaigns in his area. He disliked the civil power, which had so long kept the peace between himself and General Maxwell, and which might yet be a sprung on his rolling wheel. He could not be entrusted with the Arabian affair, for neither he nor his staff had the necessary competence to deal with such a curious a problem. On the other hand he could make the spectacle of the High Commission running a private war sufficiently ridiculous.

He was a very nervous mind, fanciful and even ungenerous. When he found the opportunity he bent his considerable powers to crab what he called the rival show.

He found help in his Chief of Staff, a man too good for so intolerable a post, General Lynden Bell, a red soldier with an instinctive shuddering away from politicians and a false heartiness.

His militarist conception of the necessary loyalties of his office involved him, chameleon-like, in the attempt to imitate the faults as well as the virtues of his chief. Two of the General Stag officers followed their leaders full cry: and so the unfortunate McMahon found himself deprived of Army help and reduced to waging his war in Arabia with the assistance of hi Foreign Office Attach&. Even these proved not quite honest. Sir Ronald Graham, whose six years' inconclusiveness in Egypt wrecked the Ministry of the Interior, and prepared the disorders of 1919, made up his mind for the first time, and when sent down to Suez to report on the situation to Lord Hardinge, was only able to beg him to remove McMahon. It was less diplomatic of him to boast of this exploit across Cairo, in the evening of the very day he had solemnly assured Sir Henry McMahon of the profoundly favorable impression his expose had made upon the Viceroy. Wingate, whose rather facile mind had believed itself the home of political insight in the Arab East, foresaw credit and great profit for the country in the new development: but as criticism slowly beat up against McMahon he disassociated himself from him, and at the same time came hints of how much better use might be made, by an experienced hand, of so subtle and involved a skein.

However it was, things in the Hejaz went from bad to worse. No proper British liaison staff was provided with the Arab forces in the field, no information was given the Sherifs, no tactical advice or strategy was suggested, no attempt made to find out the local conditions, and to see how existing allied resources in material could be adapted to suit their needs. The French Military Mission which Clayton's prudence had suggested should be sent down there to soothe our very suspicious allies, by allowing them to act counterpart to our own influence, was permitted to carry on an elaborate intrigue against Sherif Hussein in his towns of Jidda and Mecca, and to propose to him and to the British authorities measures insidiously calculated to ruin his cause in the eyes of all Muslims Wingate, now in military control of our co-operation with the Sherif, was deceived by them and supported the French suggestion of the landing of foreign troops at Rabegh, halfway between Medina and Mecca, to defend Mecca, and to block the further advance of the reinvigorated Turks from Medina. McMahon, in the multitude of counselors, became confused, and gave a handle to Murray to cry out against his vacillations and inconsistencies. The Arab Revolt became discredited, and Staff Officers in Egypt gleefully prophesied to us the near failure of the movement and the stretching of Sherif Hussein's neck on a Turkish scaffold.

My own private position was not easy meanwhile. I was a Staff Captain in Sir Archibald Murray's intelligence section, under Clayton, and my proper duties were the distribution of the Turkish Army and the preparation of maps. By natural inclination I had added to them the invention of the *Arab Bulletin* the secret weekly record of Middle-Eastern politics, and of necessity Clayton came more and more to need me in the military wing of the Arab Bureau, as the tiny Intelligence and war staff for foreign affairs, which he was now organizing for McMahon, was called. Colonel Holdich, Murray's Intelligence officer at Ismailia, eventually succeeded in driving Clayton out of the General Staff, and took his place in command of us. His first intention was to retain my services, not that he needed me, but to keep me away from the Arab affair. I learned of this from a friendly source, and decided that I must escape at once if ever.

A straight request was refused, so I took to stratagems. I became, on the telephone (G.H.Q. were at Ismailia, and I at Cairo), quite intolerable to the Staff on the Canal. I took every opportunity to rub into them their comparative ignorance and inefficiency (not difficult!) and irritated them yet further by literary airs, correcting split infinitives and tautologies in their reports.

In a few days they were bubbling over on my account, and at last determined at no price to endure me longer as a colleague. I took this strategic moment to ask for ten days' leave, saying that Storrs was going down to Jidda on business with the Grand Sherif, and that I would like a holiday and joy-ride in the Red Sea with him. They hated Storrs, and were glad to get rid of me for the moment. So they agreed at once, and began to prepare against my return some rare place to which I could be banished to rust out in idleness hereafter. Needless to say I had no intention of giving them such a chance: for while I would be very ready to hire my body out on any service, I could not treat my mind with such contempt. So I went to Clayton and told him my affairs, and he arranged for the Residency to make telegraphic application to the Foreign Office for my transfer to the Arab Bureau. The Foreign Office would treat directly with the War Office, and the Egypt command would be unable to block the business.

Then Storrs and I marched off to Suez together, very happily. It was a crooked way to get free, rather in the spirit of that principle of Eastern conduct which swears that by three sides is the best way across a square; but we were dealing with queer company, who could only be combated in their own manner, and I was confident in the final success of the Arab Revolt if it was properly advised.

I had been a mover in its beginning, and my hopes lay in it, and I was not strong enough to watch it being wrecked by the jealousies of little-spirited intriguers in Egypt, for their own satisfaction.

BOOK I

The Discovery of Feisal

I believed these misfortunes of the Revolt to be due mainly to faulty leaders, or rather to lack of leadership, Arab and English.

So I went down to Arabh to see and consider its great men. The first the Sherif Of Mecca, we knew to be aged Abdulla I found too clever, Ali too clean, Zeid too cool.

Then I made up-country to Feisal and found in him the leader with the necessary fire, and yet with reason enough to give effect to our science. His tribesmen seemed sufficient instruments, and his hills to provide a natural advantage.

So I returned pleased and confident to Egypt, and told my chiefs how Mecca was defended not by the obstacle of Rabegh, but by the fink-threat of Feisal in Jebel Subh.

Chapter 10: Storrs and Abdulla

In Suez was the Lama, a small converted liner, waiting, and in her we left immediately. These short voyages on warships were delightful interludes for us, the passengers, since naval officers had a good habit of talking an interesting shop among themselves, and by just sitting still and overhearing them one gained a better idea of their lives and ships than by days of solitary thinking. In an army mess the conversation, being non-technical, was dull. On this occasion, however, I felt some embarrassment. We were a mixed party on board, and disturbed the ship's company in their own element. Some of the juniors had turned out of their berths to give us sleeping space, and by day we filled up their living rooms with irregular talk Storrs was an intolerant brain, and seldom stooped to his company. On this occasion he was more abrupt even than usual. He turned twice round the deck, sniffed, 'No one worth talking to', and at once sat down in one of the two comfortable armchairs and began a deep discussion of Debussy with Aziz el Masri in the other. Aziz, the Arab-Circassian, ex-colonel in the Turkish army, now general in the Sherifian army, was on his way to Jidda to discuss with the Emir of Mecca some questions of the equipment and standing of the Arab regular army which he was forming at Rabegh. A few minutes later they had left Debussy, and were appreciating Wagner, Aziz in fluent German, and Storrs in alternate German, French and Arabic.

The ship's officers found it an unnecessary conversation, but could not interrupt it. Captain Scott, a hydrograph, led me off to cooler places, and we found common interests in revolver shooting and marine survey, and a common antipathy in coral reefs. The eastern coast of the Red Sea was fringed with reefs, mostly uncharted, and on them the patrol vessels were constantly going ashore. It did no harm; indeed, it did good, for the clean, gritty coral-fringes used to scrape from the ships' bottoms the accumulated weed of the past few months; but seamen were prejudiced against going aground, and these Red Sea captains could not overcome their training. Scott had been a famous victim on one occasion. He had spent weeks down near Kamaran charting a dangerous area, blank on the map, and was on his way home, triumphantly navigating on his new-drawn sheet, when he piled up the ship on a reef omitted from his work, because it, and it only, was adequately entered on the old chart. However, no one could throw stones at him, for every ship in the fleet had been ashore, except the *Hardinge,* which claimed a clean slate, but had to admit two broken rudders!

We had the usual pleasant run to Jidda, in the delightful sea climate of the Red Sea, never too hot while the ship was moving. By day we sat about in the shadow of the boat deck and for great part of the glorious nights we would tramp up and down the wet decks under the stars in the steaming breath of the southern wind: but when at last we anchored in the outer harbor off the white town hung between the blazing sky and its reflection in the mirage that swept and rolled over the wide lagoon, then the heat of Arabia came out like a drawn sword and smote us speechless. It was midday, and the noon sun in the east, like moonlight, put to sleep all the colors. There were only lights and shadows, the white houses and the black gaps of streets dividing them; in front, the shimmering whiteness of the haze on the inner harbor; behind, the dazzle of league upon league of featureless sand, running up to an edge of low hills, dimly suggested in the distant mist of heat. Just north of Jidda was a second group of black-white buildings, moving up and down like pistons in the mirage as the ship rolled to her anchor and the intermittent puffs of wind shifted the heat waves in the air. It looked horrible, and felt horrible, and we began to regret that so great a price had to be paid for the inaccessibility which made this part of the Empire safe from the armies of the Turk.

However, Colonel Wilson, the British representative with the new Arab state, had sent his launch out to meet us, and we had to go ashore, to learn the reality of the men living in that gummy mirage. Half an hour later Ruhi, his oriental assistant, was grinning a delighted welcome to his old patron Storrs (Ruhi looked more like a mandrake than a man) while the newly-appointed Syrian police and harbor officers were lining the customs' wharf to do honor to Azii el Masri. Sherif Abdulla, the second son of the old man of Mecca, was reported just arriving in the town. It was he we had hoped to meet, so our coming was auspicious, and we walked past the white masonry of the yet-building water gate, and through the oppressive alley of the food market on our way to the Consulate.

In the air, from the men to the dates and back to the meat, squadrons of flies danced up and down like particles of dust in the sun-shafts which stabbed to the darkest places of the booths through torn places in the wood and sackcloth awning overhead. The atmosphere was like a bath. The scarlet leathers of the armchair on the Lama's deck had dyed Storrs' white tunic and trousers as bright as themselves in their damp contact of the last four days, and now he began to shine like varnish through the stain, with the sweat running in his clothes. I was so fascinated watching him that I never noticed the deepened brown of my khaki drill, wherever it touched my body. He was wondering if the walk to the Consulate was long enough to wet me a decent harmonious color all over and I was wondering if everything he ever sat on would grow scarlet like him.

However, we reached the Consulate too soon for either hope, and there was Wilson in a shaded room with a lattice wall behind him, prepared to welcome the sea-breeze, which had lagged these last few days. He received us stiffly, for he was of the sober honest downright Englishmen, to whom Storrs was suspect, if only for his artistic sense: and his contact with me in Cairo had been short and sharp, a difference of opinion as to whether native clothes were an indignity for a British officer. I had called them uncomfortable merely: to him they were wrong. However, Wilson in spite of his personal feelings was all for the game. He had made the possible preparations for the forthcoming interview with Abdulla and was ready to afford every help he could. Besides, we were his guests, and he had the splendid hospitality of the East in his spirit.

Abdulla came to us softly, mounted on a white mare with a bevy of richly-armed slaves on foot about him, through the silent and respectful salutes of the townsmen. He was flushed with his success at Taif and inclined to be happy in his outlook upon lie. This cheerfulness made a favorable impression on me. I was seeing Abdulla for the first time, while Storrs was an old friend, and on the best of terms: yet before long, as they spoke together I began to suspect a constant cheerfulness in him. His eyes had a confirmed twinkle, and though only thirty-five, he was already beginning to put on flesh. This might be due to too much laughter. Life seemed very merry for Abdulla. He was short, strong, fair-skinned, with a carefully trimmed brown beard, a round smooth face, and full short lips. They called him the Albanian behind his back, because of his fair color. In manner he was very open, or affected to be, and charming on acquaintance. He stood not at all on ceremony, but jested with all comers in most easy fashion: yet when we fell into serious talk the veil of humor seemed to fade away. He then chose his words carefully, and argued shrewdly. Of course he was in discussion with Storrs, who demanded a high standard from his opponent.

The Arabs thought Abdulla a far-seeing statesman, and an astute Politician Astute he certainly was, but I suspected some insincerity throughout our talk His ambition was patent. Rumor made him the brain of his father, and of the Arab Revolt: but he seemed too easy for that. His object was of course the winning of Arab independence and the budding up of Arab nations, but in these states Abdulla meant to secure the pre-eminence at least of his family, quite possibly of himself. He was watching us and playing subtly for effect all the time.

On our part I was doing the same. The Sherifs rebellion had been going ill for the last few months, standing still, which with an irregular war was the prelude of disaster, and my conviction was that all it lacked was leadership; not intellect, nor cool judgment, nor political wisdom, but the fiery enthusiasm, the heedless burning torch which would set fire to everyone upon the path. My visit was really to see for myself who was the yet unknown master-spirit of the affair, and if he was capable of carrying the revolt to the distance and greatness I had conceived for it: and as our conversation proceeded I became more and more sure that Abdulla was too balanced, too cool, too humorous to be a prophet, especially the armed prophet whom history assured me was the successful type in such circumstances. His value would come perhaps in the peace after the movement had succeeded, as it had been before the outbreak, in laying the political groundwork of the Sherifs societies. During the physical struggle when singleness of eye, and magnetism, self-sacrifice and devotion were needed, Abdulla would be an inefficient instrument, a tool too complex for a simple purpose.

We talked to him first about the state of Jidda, to put him at ease by discussing in this first of our interviews the unnecessary subject of the Sherifs administration. He replied that the war was yet too much with them to let them think about civil government. They had inherited the Turkish system in the towns, and were continuing it on a more modest scale. They had appointed governors, and were assisting them by their own direct agents, in whose hands lay the real power, but who had to use it warily, to avoid rousing the jealousy of some local great one, who if angry might make an understanding with the Turks. The Turkish Government was often not unkind to strong men, who obtained considerable license on terms. Consequently some of the leading men in Hejaz regretted the coming of a native ruler who understood things better, and was harder to influence. Particularly in Mecca and Jidda public opinion was against an Arab state. The mass of citizens were foreigners,

Egyptians, Indians, Javanese, Africans and others, quite unable to sympathies with Arab aspirations, especially as voiced by the Bedouin with whom they had been for ever at war: for the Bedouin lived on what he could exact from the stranger who used his roads to journey over, or his valleys to live in, and he and the townsman bore one another a perpetual grudge.

Yet the Sherif was forced to depend much upon the tribes since they were his soldiers. His policy towards them was patriarchal. He dealt with the sheikhs as his officials, increasing their responsibility, and rewarding their services, largely. If they were unsatisfactory he put pressure on their followers to replace them by another member of the qualified family. This policy was not without danger; in theory the sheikh was an autocrat: in practice he was so bound by precedent and irrefragable public opinion that he was little more than a mouthpiece. By leaning too much on him it was possible to break him, and with him would go the last hope of combining the clans. The Bedouin were the only fighting men the Sherif had got and on their help the Revolt depended. He was arming them freely (did not a new prince in a new principality, according to book, always distribute arms?), paying many of them for their service in his forces, feeding their families while they were from home, and hiring from them their transport camels to maintain his armies in the field. Accordingly the country was prosperous, while the towns went short, yet the townsmen did not altogether wish to share the fortune of the tribes, since they had a terror of military service. The Turks had exempted the Holy Places from conscription, but the citizens now entertained a not unreasonable fear lest the Sherifs necessities destroy their most precious privilege.

Another grievance in the towns was in the matter of law. The Turkish civil code had been abolished, and a return made to the old religious law, the undiluted Koranic procedure of the Arab Kadi. Abdulla explained to us, smiling, that when there was time they would discover in the Koran such opinions and judgments as were required to make it suitable for modem commercial operations, like banking and exchange. Meanwhile of course the antique severity irked the easy citizens, who found their former pleasures of drink and gaming sternly put down. Months later two Arab officers who had gone to Mecca for a month's leave between two strenuous campaigns, when discovered in the Holy City with whiskey in their baggage, learned that war services and a western education availed nothing to save their persons from humiliating punishment at the hands of the Emir's justices. Many novelties came under the ban, amongst them gramophones, not on aesthetic grounds but because they were thought uncanny, improper, inexplicable, things unknown in the Prophet's days.

What the townsmen lost by the abolition of the civil law, the Bedouin gained. Sherif Hussein was a deep student of tribal polity and custom, and his wisdom silently sanctioned the restoration of the old order wherever it had retained its vitality. The higher government in Arabia had been something of an excrescence, a nuisance when it interfered with the family system which sufficiently restrained its members in normal times. Bedouin at odds with one another pleaded their own cases before their tribal lawman, an office hereditary in one most-respected family, and recognized by the payment of a goat per household as yearly due. Judgment was based on custom, formed by quoting from a great body of remembered precedent. It was delivered publicly without fee. In cases between men of different tribes the lawman of one was selected by mutual consent, or recourse was made to the lawman of a third tribe. If the case were contentious and difficult, the judge was supported by a jury of four, two nominated by plaintiff from the ranks of defendant's family, and two by defendant from plaintiffs family. Decisions were always unanimous.

We contemplated this vision which Abdulla drew for us, with sad thoughts of the Garden of Eden and all that Eve, now lying in her tomb just outside the city wall, had lost for average humanity: and then Storrs brought me into the discussion, by asking Abdulla to give his views on the military situation for my benefit, and for me to communicate to Headquarters in Egypt. Abdulla at once grew serious, and said that he wanted to urge upon the British their immediate and very personal concern in the matter. By our neglect to cut the Hejaz Railway the Turks had been able to collect transport and all kinds of supplies and to reinforce Medina heavily.

The Arabs had been driven back from the town, and the enemy were preparing a mobile column of all arms, for an advance on Rabegh. Feisal now in the hills across their road was by our neglect too weak in supplies, machine-guns and mountain guns to hold up their march. Ali and Zeid, his eldest and youngest brothers, were in Rabegh, but they were hampered in action because Hussein Mabeirig, the chief of the local Masruh Harb, had gone over to the Turks. His tribe now veiled their hostility to the Sherif: but if the Turks came forward they and all the Harb would join them. It would only remain for his father to put himself at the head of his own people of Mecca and die fighting before the Holy City.

At this moment the telephone rang; the Grand Sherif wanted to speak to Abdulla. He was told of the point which our conversation had reached, and at once confirmed that he would so act in the emergency. The Turks would enter Mecca over his dead body. To prevent such a disaster Abdulla asked that a British brigade, if possible of Muslim troops, be kept at Suez, with transport to rush it to Rabegh as soon as the Turks approached. What did we think of the proposal?

I replied, first, that Sherif Hussein had asked us not to cut the Hejaz line, since he would need it for his victorious advance into Syria. Secondly, that the dynamite we sent down had been returned with a note to say that it was too dangerous for the Arabs to use. Thirdly, that we had no specific demands for equipment from Feisal. With regard to the brigade for Rabegh, it was a large question.

Shipping was precious, and we could not hold empty transports indefinitely at Suez. A British brigade was a complicated affair, and would take long to embark and disembark. We had no Muslim units in our army. The Rabegh position was extended. A brigade would hardly hold it, and would be quite unable to also detach a force to prevent a Turkish column slipping past it inland. The most it could do would be to defend the beach, under our ships' guns, and that the ships would do as well, without troops.

Abdulla replied that ships were insufficient morally, as the Dardanelles fighting had destroyed the old legend of the British fleet and its omnipotence. No Turks could slip past Rabegh, for it was the only water-supply in the district, and they must water at its wells.

The earmarking of a brigade and transports need be only temporary, for he was taking his victorious Taif troops up the eastern road from Mecca to Medina, to encircle the Turks on the east. As soon as he was in position he would give orders to Ali and Feisal, who would close in from south and west, and their combined forces would deliver a grand attack in which Media would, please God, be taken. Meanwhile Aziz el Masri was molding the volunteers from Mesopotamia and Syria into a force at Rabegh. When we had brought the other Arab prisoners of war from India and Egypt to join them, there would be enough to take over the duties temporarily allotted to the British brigade. I said that I would represent his views to Egypt, but that the British were reluctant to spare troops from the vital defense of Egypt (though he was not to imagine that the Canal was in any danger from the Turks), and still more to send Christians to defend the people of the Holy City against their enemies, as some Muslims in India, who considered the Turks had an imprescriptibly right to the Caliphate and the Hararnein, would misrepresent our motives and actions. I thought that I would be able to urge his opinions more powerfully if I was able to report on the Rabegh question in the light of my own knowledge of the position and local opinion. I would also like to see Feisal, and talk over with him his needs, and the prospects of a prolonged defense of his hills by the tribesmen, if we strengthened him with materials. I would like to ride from Rabegh up the Sultani road towards Medina, as far as Feisal's camp.

Storrs then came in and supported me with all his might, urging the vital importance of full and early information, from a trained observer, for the British Commander-in-Chief in Egypt, and showing that his sending down me, his best qualified and most indispensable staff officer, proved the serious consideration being given to Arabian affairs by Sir Archibald Murray. Abdulla went to the telephone and tried to get his father's consent for me to go up the country. The Sherif viewed the proposal with grave distrust. Abdulla argued the point, made some advantage and transferred the mouthpiece to Storrs, who tried all his diplomacy on the old man. Storrs in full blast was a delight to listen to, in the mere matter of Arabic speech, and also a lesson to every Englishman alive on how to deal with suspicious or unwilling Orientals. It was nearly impossible to resist him for more than a few minutes, and in this case also he had his way. The Sherif asked again for Abdulla, and authorized him to write to Ali, and suggest that if he thought fit, and if conditions were normal, I might be allowed to proceed to Feisal's headquarters in Jebel Subh: — and Abdulla, under Storrs' influence, transformed this very guarded message into direct written instructions to Ali to mount me as well and as quickly as possible and to convey me, by sure hand, to Feisal's camp to confer with him. This was all I wanted, and half what Storrs wanted, and we adjourned for lunch.

Chapter 11: Jidda

We had been struck with the character of Jidda, on our way to the Consulate: so after lunch when it was a little cooler, or at least when the sun was not so bright, we wandered out to see the sights under guidance of Young, Wilson's assistant, a man who found good in many old things, but little good in things now being made. It was indeed a most remarkable town. The streets were narrow alleys, wood-roofed in the main bazaar but elsewhere open to the sky for the little gap between the tops of the lofty white-walled houses. They were built, four or five stories high, of coral rag, tied with wooden beams, and decorated with great bow-windows running from ground to roof in grey wooden panels. There was no glass in Jidda, but a profusion of good lattices, and some very delicate shallow chiseling on the panels of the window casings. The doors were heavy two-leaved slabs of teak-wood, deeply carved, often with wickets in them, and they had good hinges and ring-knockers of hammered iron. There was much fine molded or cut plastering, and on the older houses rich stone heads and jambs to the windows looking on the inner courts. The style of architecture was like crazy Elizabethan half-timber work, in the elaborate Cheshire fashion, but gone gimcrack to an incredible degree. House-fronts were fretted and pierced and pargetted till they looked as though cut out of cardboard for a romantic stage-setting. Every story jutted every window leaned one way or other; often the very walls sloped back or forward.

It was like a dead city, so clean underfoot, and so quiet. Its winding even streets were floored with damp sand, beaten hard by time and as silent to the tread as any carpet. The lattices and wall-returns deadened all reverberation of voices. There were no carts (and no streets wide enough for carts), no shod animals, no bustle anywhere. Everything was hushed, strained, and even furtive. The doors of houses shut softly as we passed. There were no loud dogs, no crying children: indeed except in the bazaar, still half asleep, there were few wayfarers of any kind, and the rare people we did meet, all thin, and as it were wasted by disease, with scarred hairless faces and screwed-up eyes, slipped past us quickly and cautiously, not looking at us. Their skimp white robes, shaved polls, with little skull-caps, the red cotton shawls round their shoulders, and their bare feet were so same as to be almost a uniform.

The atmosphere was oppressive, deadly. There seemed no life in it. It was not burning hot, but there was a moistness and sense of great age and exhaustion in the air, such as seemed to belong to no other place: not a passion of smells like Smyrna, Naples or Marseilles, but a feeling of long use, of the exhalations of many people, of continual bath-heat and sweat. One would say that for years Jidda had not been swept through by a firm breeze: that its streets kept their air from year's end to year's end, born the day they were built for so long as the houses should endure. There was nothing in the bazaars to buy.

In the evening the telephone rang, and the Sherif called Storrs to the instrument. He asked if we would not like to listen to his band. Storrs in astonishment asked what band, and congratulated his holiness on having advanced so far towards urbanity. The Sherif explained that the headquarters of the Hejaz Command under the Turks had had a brass band, which played each night to the

Governor General: and when the Governor General was captured by Abdulla at Taif his band was captured with him. The other prisoners were sent to Egypt to be interned, but the band was excepted. It was held in Mecca to give music to the victors. Sherif Hussein laid his receiver on the table of his reception hall, and we, called solemnly one by one to the telephone, heard the band as it played in the courtyard of the Palace at Mecca, forty-five miles away. Storrs expressed the general gratification, and the Sherif increasing his favor replied that the band should be sent down at once in our honor by forced march to Jidda, to play in our courtyard also. 'And,' he said, 'you may then do me the pleasure of ringing me up from your end that I may share your satisfaction.'

Next day Storrs visited Abdulla in his tent out by Eve's tomb, and together they inspected the hospital, the barrack, the town offices, and partook of the hospitality of the Mayor and the Governor. In the intervals of duty they talked about money, and the Sherifs title, and his relations with the other princes of Arabia and the general course of the war — all the commonplaces that should pass between envoys of two governments. It was tedious, and for the most part I held myself excused, since after a conversation in the morning I had firmly decided that Abdulla was not the leader I was looking for. We had asked him for a sketch of the genesis of the Arab Movement: and his reply illuminated his character. He had begun by a long description of Talaat, the first Turk to speak to him in terms of concern about the restlessness of the Hejaz. He wanted it properly subdued, and military service established, as elsewhere in the Empire. Mahmud Shefket supported him, since he was perturbed at the growing influence of Sherif Hussein amongst the Arab tribes. They conspired to send Vehib Pasha down as Turkish Commander in Chief and Governor General. He arrived with instructions which threw the province into a turmoil. Hussein appealed to the Turkish Ministry against the illegalities and encroachments of Vehib. He sent Feisal to represent his case in Constantinople, and by adroit lobbying secured Vehib's recall. Talaat became yet more nervous, and began to ascribe responsibility for the trouble to Abdulla. He offered him the Ministry of Wakf, to distract him, and when he refused it, the Vilayet of Yemen. Abdulla despised Talaat's intelligence, for showing his hand too openly.

He therefore made a plan of action to get independence for the Hejaz without going to war with Turkey, and after sounding Lord Kitchener without profit, dated it provisionally for 1915. He meant to call out the tribes and lay sudden hands on all the pilgrims, during the feast. They would have included many of the chief men of Turkey, and leading Muslims of Egypt, India, Java, Eritrea and Algiers. With these thousands of hostages in his hands he expected to attract the notice of the Great Powers concerned, and reckoned on their bringing pressure on the Porte to secure the release of their nationals. The Porte would have been powerless to deal with him militarily, and would have either made concessions to the Hejaz, or confessed its powerlessness to the foreign states. In the latter event, Abdulla would have approached them direct, ready to meet their demands, in return for a guarantee of immunity from Turkey. I did not like his scheme and was glad when he said with almost a sneer that Feisal had been afraid, and had begged his father not to follow Abdulla's advice. It sounded good for Feisal, toward whom my hopes of a great leader were now slowly turning.

In the evening Abdulla came to dine with Colonel Wilson. We received him in the courtyard on the house steps. Behind him were his brilliant household servants and slaves, and behind them a pale crew of bearded emaciated men with woebegone faces, wearing tatters of military uniform, and carrying tarnished brass instruments of music. Abdulla waved his hand towards them with a giggle and said, 'My Band.' We made them sit down on the benches in the forecourt, and Wilson sent them cigarettes, while we went up to the dining room whose great shuttered balcony overlooking the court was now opened right out, hungrily, for a sea breeze. As we sat down to meat, the band, under the guns and swords of Abdulla's retainers, began to play heartbroken Turkish airs in a leaderless fashion. Our ears ached with the noise: but Abdulla beamed with delight on us.

We were a curious party. Abdulla himself, Vice-President (in *Partibus*) of the Turkish Chamber and now Foreign Minister of the rebel Arab State: Wilson, Governor of the Red Sea Province of the Sudan, and His Majesty's Minister with the Sherif of Mecca: Storrs, Oriental Secretary successively to Gorst, Kitchener and McMahon in Cairo: Young, Cochrane and myself; hangers-on of the Staff Sayed Ali, a general in the Egyptian Army, and the commander of the detachment sent over by the Sirdar to help the first efforts of the Arabs; Azii el Masri, now Chief of Staff of the Arab regular army, but in old days Enver's rival, the leader of the Turkish and Senussi forces against the Italians, the chief conspirator of the Arab officers in the Turkish Army against the Committee of Union and Progress, a man condemned to death by the Turks for obeying the Treaty of Lausanne, and saved by *The Times* and Lord Kitchener.

We got tired of Turkish music, and asked for German. Aziz stepped out on the balcony and called down to the bandsmen in Turkish to play us something foreign. They struck shakily into 'Deutschland uber Alles' just as the Sherif came to his telephone in Mecca to listen to the music of our feast. There was a satisfying irony in that tune played in Jidda to the leaders of the new revolt in Islam by the captured band of the Turkish Governor of the Holy Places. We asked for more German music, and they played 'Ein' Feste Burg'. Then in the midst they died away into flabby discords of drums. The parchment had stretched in the damp air of Jidda. Men cried for fire, and Wilson's servants and Abdulla's bodyguard brought them piles of straw and packing cases. They warmed the drums, turning them round and round before the blaze, and then broke into what they said was the 'Hymn of Hate', though no one could recognize a European chord or discord in it all. Sayed Ali turned to Abdulla and said, 'It is a death march.' Abdulla's eyes widened: but Storrs spoke in quickly to the rescue and turned it to laughter, and we sent out rewards and the leavings of the feast to the sorrowful musicians, who could take no pleasure in our praises, but begged to be sent home. Next morning I left for Rabegh.

Chapter 12: Ali, Zeid and Rabegh

In the harbor at Rabegh lay the Northbook, *an Indian Marine ship commanded by Captain* Turton, who had shown decision at Kunfida a few months before. The Idrisi should have captured the town but showed himself lacking in spirit. So Turton went off and took it himself without loss, and hoisted the Idrisi flag, and sent word south to him that unless he hurried, his flag might suffer dishonor. Of course there followed great confusion and a dispute between the Sherif and the Idrisi as to whose was the miserable place. The Turks ended the dispute abruptly by coming back, and gave Turton a satisfactory chance of a second action. On board the *Northbook* was Colonel Parker, our liaison officer with Sherif Ali in command on shore, and through him was forwarded my letter from Abdulla, giving Ali his father's 'orders' to send me at once up to Feisal.

Ali was staggered by such instructions, but could not help himself; for his only telegraph to Mecca was by the ship's wireless, and he was ashamed to send personal remonstrances through us. So he made the best of it, and prepared for me his own splendid riding-camel, and saddled her with his own saddle, hung with luxurious housings and cushions of Nejd leather-work all pieced and inlaid in various colors, with plaited fringes and nets, embroidered with metal tissues. As a reliable man he chose out Obeid el Raashid, a Hawazim Harb tribesman, with his son, to guide me up country through the hills to Feisal's camp.

He did all this with the better grace for the countenance of Nuri Said, the Bagdadi Staff officer whom I had befriended once in Cairo when he was ill. Nuri was now acting as second-in-command of the regular force which Aziz el Masri was raising and training here. Another friend at court was Faiz el Ghusein, Ali's secretary. He was a Sulut sheikh from the Hauran, and a former official of the Turkish Government, who had escaped across Armenia during the war, and had eventually, reached Miss Gertrude Bell in Basra she had sent him on to me with a warm recommendation.

To Ali himself I took a great fancy. He was of middle height, thin. And looking already more than his seven years. He stooped a little. His skin was sallow, his eyes large and deep and brown, his nose thin and rather hooked his mouth sad and drooping. He had a spare black beard and very delicate hands. His manner was dignified and courteous, but simple, and he struck me as a conscientious careful pleasant gentleman, without great force of character, nervous and rather tired. Hi physical weakness (he was consumptive) made him subject to quick fits of shaking passion, preceded and followed by long moods of infirm obstinacy. He was bookish, learned in law and religion, and pious almost to the fanatical degree. He was too conscious of his high heritage to be ambitious, and his nature was too clean to see or suspect interested motives in those about him. Consequently he was much the prey of any constant companion, and a little too sensitive to advice for a great leader, though his purity of intention and conduct would gain him the affectionate regard of those who came into direct contact with him.

If Feisal turned out not to be a prophet, the revolt would make shift well enough with Ali for its head. I thought him more definitely Arab than Abdulla, or than Zeid, his young half-brother who was helping him at Rabegh, and who came down with Ali and Nun and Azii to the palm-groves to see me start. Zeid was a shy white beardless lad of perhaps nineteen, cold and flippant, no enthusiast for the Revolt. Indeed his mother was a Turk, and he had been brought up in the house all his life, so that he could hardly feel great sympathy with an Arab revival: but he did his best to be pleasant, and surpassed Ali, perhaps because his feelings were not much outraged at the departure of a Christian for the interior of the holy province under the auspices of the Emir of Mecca. Zeid of course was less qualified even than Abdulla to fulfill my quest for the born leader: though I liked him, and could see that he would be a decided man when he found himself.

Ali would not let me start till after sunset, that no one of his followers might see me leave the camp. He kept my journey a profound secret even from his slaves, and gave me an Arab cloak and head cloth to wrap round myself and my uniform, that I might present a proper silhouette in the dark upon my camel. I had no food with me, so he instructed Obeid to get something to eat at Bir el Sheikh, the first settlement, some sixty miles out, and ordered him most stringently to keep me from questioning and curiosity on the way, and to avoid all camps and encounters. The Masruh Harb, who inhabited Rabegh and district, only paid lip-service to the Sherif. Their real allegiance was to Hussein Mabeirig, the ambitious sheikh of the clan, who was jealous of the Emir of Mecca and had fallen out with him. He was now a fugitive from Ali's camp, living in the hills to the east, and was known to be in touch with the Turks. His people were not pro-Turkish, but owed him obedience. If he had heard of my departure he might have tried to intercept me on the way.

Obeid was a Hazimi, of the Beni Salem branch of Harb, and so not on good terms with the Masruh. This inclined him towards me: and when he had once accepted the charge of escorting me to Feisal we might rest in full confidence that his sincerity was engaged. The fidelity of road-companions was most dear to Arab tribesmen. The guide had to answer to a sentimental public with his lie for that of his fellow. One Harbi, who promised to take Huber to Medina, and broke his word and killed him on the road near Rabegh when he found out that he was a Christian, was ostracized by public opinion, and in spite of the religious prejudices in his favor had ever since lived miserably alone in the hills, cut off from friendly intercourse, and refused permission to marry any daughter of the tribe. So we could depend upon the good will of Obeid and his son, Abdulla, and Ali endeavored by detailed instructions to ensure that their performance should be as good as their intention.

We marched through the palm-groves which lay like a girdle about the scattered houses of Rabegh village, and then out under the stars along the Tehama, the sandy and featureless strip of desert along the western coast of Arabia between sea-beach and littoral hills, for hundreds of monotonous miles. In day-time this low plain was insufferably hot, and its waterless character made it a forbidding road: though also the inevitable road the more-fruitful hills in land were too rugged to afford passage north and south. The cold of the night was pleasant after the day of checks and discussions which had so dragged at Rabegh. Obeid led on without speaking, and the camels went silently over the soft flat sand. My thoughts as we went were how this was the Pilgrim Road, down which for uncounted generations the people of the north had come to visit the Holy City, bearing with them gifts of faith for the shrine: and it seemed that the Arab Revolt might be in a sense a return pilgrimage, to take back to the north, to Syria, an ideal for an ideal, a belief in liberty for their belief in a revelation.

We continued for some hours, without distinguishing any change except at times when the camels plunged and strained a little, and the saddles creaked. It meant that there the soft plain had merged into beds of drift-sand, dotted with tiny scrub, and therefore uneven going, for the plants collected little mounds about their roots, and the eddies of the sea-winds scooped hollows in the intervening spaces. Camels were not very sure-footed in the dark and, the star lighted sand carried little shadow, so that hummocks and holes were difficult to see. Before midnight we halted, and I rolled myself tighter in my cloak, and chose a hollow of my own size and shape, and slept well in it till nearly dawn.

As soon as he felt the air growing chill with the coming change Obeid got up, and two minutes later we were swinging forward again. An hour after and it grew bright, as we climbed up a low neck of lava, drowned nearly to the top with blown sand. This joined a small flow near the shore to the great common lava-field of all the central Hejaz, whose western edge ran up upon our right hand, and caused the coast road to lie where it did. The neck was stony, but only a few yards wide: on each side the blue lava humped itself into low shoulders, from which, so Obeid said, it was possible to see ships sailing on the sea Pilgrims had built cairns here beside the road. Sometimes they were individual works, of just three stones set up one above the other: sometimes they were common heaps, to which any disposed passer-by might add his stone not reasonably or with any known motive, but because others did, and perhaps they knew.

Beyond the ridge the path descended into a broad open place, the Masturah, or plain by which Wadi Fura flowed out. Seaming its surface with innumerable interwoven channels of loose stone, a few inches deep, were the beds of the flood water, on those rare occasions when there was rain in the Tareif, and Wadi Fura became a raging stream into the sea. The delta was about six miles wide, and down some part of it water flowed for an hour or two, or even for a day or two, every so many years. Underground there was plenty of moisture, protected by the overlying sand from the sun-heat, and thorn trees and loose scrub profited by it and flourished here. Some of the trunks were a foot through, and their height might be twenty feet. The trees and bushes stood somewhat apart, in clusters, and the hungry camels had cropped their lower branches. So they looked cared for, and had a premeditated air, which felt strange in the desert, more especially as the Tehama hitherto had been a sober bareness.

Two hours upstream from us, so Obeid said, was the throat where Wadi Fura issued from the last granite hills, and where had been built a little village, Khoreiba, of running water channels, and wells and palm-groves, inhabited by a small population of freedmen engaged in date-husbandry. This was important. We had not understood that the bed of Wadi Fura served as a direct road from near Medina to the neighborhood of Rabegh. It laid so far south and east of Feisal's supposed position in the hills that he could hardly be said to cover it. Abdulla also had not warned us of the existence of Khoreiba, and yet it materially affected the Rabegh question, by affording the enemy a possible watering place, safe from our interference, and from the guns of our warships. At Khoreiba the Turks could concentrate a large force to attack our supposed brigade in Rabegh.

In reply to further questions Obeid disclosed that at Hajar, east of Rabegh in the hills, was yet another supply of water, in the hands of the Masruh, and now the headquarters of Hussein Mabeirig, their Turcophil chief. The Turks could make that their next stage from Khoreiba towards Mecca, leaving Rabegh unmolested and harmless on their flank. It meant that the British brigade which Colonel Bremond and Abdulla had asked for would be quite useless to save Mecca from the Turks. For that purpose would be required a force with a front or a radius of action of some twenty miles, in order to deny all these three water-supplies to the enemy. Meanwhile in the early sunlight we lied our camels to a steady trot across the good going of these shingle-beds among the trees, making for Masturah well, the first stage out from Rabegh on the Pilgrim Road. There we would water, and halt a little. My camel was a delight to me, for I had not been on such an animal before. There were no good camels in Egypt, and those of the Sinai desert, while hardy and strong, were not taught to pace like these rich mounts of the Arabian princes.

Yet her refinements were in large part wasted on me, since they were afforded only to riders who had the knack and asked for them, and in my former journeys I had been content to be carried, rather than to ride my beast. It was very easy to sit on a camel's back, and stay there without falling off: but very difficult to understand and get the best out of the animal, so as to do long journeys without fatiguing either myself or her. Obeid gave me hints as we went: indeed it was one of the few subjects on which he would speak. Ali's strict injunctions to preserve me from all contact with the world seemed to have made him close his own mouth also.

We found the well quite near the north bank of the Masturah; beside it were some decayed stone walls which had been a hut, and opposite it some little shelters of branches and palm-leaves; under them some Bedouin were sitting. They were probably families out from their tents watching their camels but we did not greet them. Instead Obeid turned aside to the ruinous walls, and we dismounted by them, and I sat in their shade while he and Abdulla watered the animals, and drew a drink for themselves and for me. The well was old and broad, with good stone seining, and a strong coping round the top. It was about twenty feet deep and for the convenience of travelers without ropes, like us, a square chimney had been contrived in the masonry on one side, with foot and hand holds in the comers, in order that a man might descend to the water level and fill his goat-skin.

Idle passers-by had flung stones down the shaft, so that half the bottom of the well was choked with them, and the water not abundant: but yet there was some at all seasons, and if they had cleaned it, the supply would have been greater than they needed. Abdulla tied his flowing sleeves about his shoulders, tucked his gown under his cartridge belt and clambered nimbly down and up, bringing us each time four or five gallons in his water skin and pouring it for our camels into a stone trough beside the well. They drank about five gallons each, for they had been watered at Rabegh yesterday. After they had finished we let them moon about a little, while we sat in peace, breathing the light wind coming off the sea. Abdulla smoked a cigarette after his exertions.

Some Harb came up, driving a large herd of brood camels, and began to water them, having sent one man down the well to fill their large leather bucket, which the others drew up hand over hand with a loud staccato chant. We watched them, without intercourse, for these were Masruh, and we were Beni Salem, and while the two clans were now at peace, and might pass through each other's districts, it was only a temporary accommodation to further the Sherifs' war against the Turks, and had little depth of gladness in it. As we were watching the two riders, trotting light and fast on thoroughbred camels, drew towards us from the north. Both were young. One was richly dressed in cashmere robes, and a red silk embroidered head cloth. The other was plainer, in white cotton, with a red cotton head-dress.

They halted at the well, and the more splendid one slipped gracefully to the ground, without kneeling his camel, and threw his halter to his companion, saying carelessly, 'Water them while I go over there and rest.' Then he strolled over to us and sat down under our wall, after glancing at us with an air of affected unconcern. He offered me a cigarette, saying, Your presence is from Syria!' I parried politely, suggesting that he was from Mecca, to which he likewise made no direct reply. We spoke a little of the war and of the leanness of the Masruh she-camels in front of us.

Meanwhile the other rider was standing by rather vacantly, holding the two halters, waiting perhaps for the Harb to finish watering their herd before taking his turn. The young lord next me cried out sharply, 'What is it, Mustafa? Water them at once.' The servant came up and said dismally, they will not let me ....' 'God's mercy!' shouted his master, furiously, and he scrambled to his feet and hit the unfortunate Mustafa three or four sharp blows on the head and shoulders with his riding stick: 'Go and ask them.' Mustafa looked hurt, astonished, and angry as though he would hit back but thought better of it and hurried down to the well.

The Harb were shocked, and in pity made a place for him, and let his two camels drink from their trough. They whispered, 'Who is he? And Mustafa said, 'Our lord's cousin from Mecca.' At once they ran and untied a bundle from one of their saddles, and spread from it fodder of the green leaves and buds of the thorn-trees before the two riding camels. They gathered this by striking the low bushes with a heavy staff, till the broken tips of the branches rained down on a cloth stretched over the ground beneath.

The young Sherif watched them contentedly and when his camel had fed, climbed slowly and without apparent effort up its neck into saddle, where he settled himself leisurely, and took an unctuous farewell of us, asking God to requite the Arabs richly. They wished him a good journey, and he started southward, while Abdulla brought our camels, and we went off northward. Ten minutes later I heard a chuckle from old Obeid, and saw him smiling with delight between his grizzled beard and mustache

'What is upon you, Obeid? I said.

'My Lord, you saw those two riders at the well the Sherif and his servant?

'Yes, but they were Sherif Ali ibn el Hussein of Modhig, and his cousin Sherif Mohsin, lords of the Harith, who are blood enemies of the Masruh. They feared they would be delayed or driven off the water if the Arabs knew them. So they pretended to be master and servant from Mecca Did you see how Mohsin raged when Ali beat him? Ali is a devil. When he was eleven years old he escaped from his father's house to his uncle, who was a robber of pilgrims by trade, and with him he lived by his hands for many months, till his father caught him. He was with our lord Feisal from the first day's battle in Medina, and led the Ateiba in the fighting about the town, and in the plains round Aar and Bir Denvish. It was all camel-fighting, and Ali would have no man with him who could not do as he did, run beside his camel and leap with one hand into the saddle, carrying his rifle. The children of Harith are children of battle.' It was the first time Obeid had been full of words.

I drew him out gently, and gained long stories of these robber Shenfs of Modbig, the little village in the defile of Wadi Shamiya, the upper reaches of Fatima, where it broke from Nejd through the eastern divide of the Hejaz hills north of Mecca, on its course towards the sea. The place was rich, but small, and the most of it would fall to Ali some day: but others of the clan were poor, unable to live on their properties. In the days before Sherif Hussein they used to get their living on the roads, by holding up caravans of pilgrims or merchants (and indeed it was usually the same thing) on their way from Medina to Mecca or from Nejd, and taking toll of them. Hussein objected to this practice, and imprisoned most of them, till they promised amendment. In return he promised them honorable employment, and had since used them constantly in his wars, and in his mounted levies, as officers. So their fidelity, resource and courage found good scope. This boy, Ali, was too well off to need work: but his father to improve his mind sent him to Mecca, where he was brought up with the sons of the chief Abadla Sheds, to become learned in books as well as in games.

Chapter 13: Tehama and Shera

While he spoke we scoured along the dazzling plain, now nearly bare of trees, and turning slowly softer underfoot. At first it had been grey shingle, packed like gravel. Then the sand increased and the stones grew rarer, till we could distinguish the colors of the separate flakes, porphyry, green schist, basalt. At last it was nearly pure white sand, under which lay a harder stratum, good for the camels' pace. The particles of sand were clean and polished, and caught the blaze of sun like little diamonds in a reflection of the sun so fierce that after a little I could not endure to lower my glance to it. I puckered my lids together, and pulled the head cloth forward in a peak over my eyes, and beneath them too, like a beaver, to try to shut out the heat rising in glassy waves from the ground, beating up against my face. In front of us, eighty miles away, the huge peak of Jebel Rudhwa behind Yenbo was looming and fading in the dazzle of vapor which hid its foot. Quite near in the plain rose the little shapeless hills of Hesna, which seemed to block our way. To our right was the steep ridge of Beni Ayub, toothed and narrow like a saw-blade, the first edge of the sheaf of mountains between the Tehama and the high scarp of the table-land about Medina. These Tareif Beni Ayub fell away on their north into a blue series of smaller hills, soft in character, behind which lofty range after range in a jagged stairway, red now the sun grew low, climbed up to the towering central mass of Jebel Subh with its fantastic granite spires.

It was a fine sight but a rough one, and I wondered to Obeid how our road found way into the middle fastnesses. He explained briefly that a valley ran down from Bir el Sheikh, this side of the Hesna hills, and we would work up it into Wadi Mild a gorge by which the rainfall of the broad tableland towards Media reached the sea. Our road crossed its depths under Subh by Bir ibn Hassani tonight — or towards dawn, he added. A little later he turned to the right, off the Pilgrim Road, and took a short cut across gradually rising ground of flat basalt ridges, buried in sand till only their top most piles showed above the surface. It held moisture enough to be well grown over with hard, wiry grass and shrubs up and down the slopes, on which a few sheep and goats were pasturing. There he showed me a stone, which was the limit of the district of the Masruh, and told me with grim pleasure that he was now at home, in his friends' tribal property.

We often looked upon the desert as barren land, the free holding of whoever chose, but in fact each hill and valley in it had a man who was its acknowledged owner, and quick to assert the right of his family or clan to it, if there was aggression. Even the wells and trees had their masters, who allowed men to make firewood of the one and drink of the other freely, as much as was required for their need, but who would instantly check anyone trying to turn the property to account and to exploit it or its products among others for private benefit. The desert property was held in a crazed communism by which nature and the elements were for the free use of every known friendly person for his own purposes and no more. A logical outcome was the reduction of this license to privilege by the men of the desert, through their hardness to strangers among them without introduction or guarantee, since the common security lay in the common responsibility of kinsmen. Obeid was now in his own country, and so might relax his watch.

The valleys were becoming sharply marked, with clean beds of sand and shingle, and an occasional large boulder brought down by some flood. There were many broom bushes, restfully grey and green to the eye, and good &el, though useless as pasture. We ascended steadily till we rejoined the main track of the Pilgrim Road along which we held our way till sunset, when we were in sight of the hamlet of Bir el Sheikh. In the first dark, as the supper fires were lighted, we rode down its wide open street and halted. Obeid went into one of the twenty miserable huts, and in a few whispered words and long silences bought flour, of which with water he kneaded a dough cake two inches thick and six inches across, and then he buried it in the ashes of a brush wood fire, provided for him by a Subh woman whom he seemed to know. When the cake was warmed he drew it out of the fire, and clapped it to shake off the dust, then we shared it together, while Abdulla went away to buy himself tobacco.

They told me the place had two stone-lined wells at the bottom of the southward slope but I felt disinclined to go and look at them, for the long ride that day had tired my unaccustomed muscles, and the heat of the plain had been My skin was blistered by it, and my eyes ached with the glare of the light striking up off the ground, from the silver sand, and from the shining pebbles. My last two years had been spent in Cairo, writing all day and thinking hard in a little overcrowded room full of distracting noises, and a hundred rushing things to do, and without any bodily exertion except the need to come and go each day between the office and the hotel. In consequence the novelty of the change was a little severe, since time had not been given me to accustom myself to the pestilent beating of the Arabian sun, and the long monotony of camel pacing. There was to be another stage tonight, and a long day tomorrow before Feisal's camp would be reached.

So I was grateful for Obeid's cooking, and marketing, which spent one hour, and for the second hour of rest after it which we took by common consent, and was sorry when it ended and we remounted, and rode in pitch darkness up valleys and down valleys, passing in and out of bands of air, which were hot in the confined hollows, but fresh and breathing in the open places. The ground underfoot must have been sandy, because the silence of our passage hurt my straining ears; and smooth, for I was always falling asleep in the saddle, to wake a few seconds later suddenly and sickeningly, as I clutched by instinct at the saddle-post to recover my balance which had been thrown out by some irregular stride of the animal. It was too dark and the forms of the country too neutral, for my peering heavy-lashed eyes to see anything. At last we stopped for good, long after midnight, and I was rolled up in my cloak and asleep in a most comfortable little sand-grave, before Obeid had done knee-haltering my camel.

Three hours later we were on the move again, helped now by the last shining of the moon. We marched down Wadi Mared, the night of it dead, hot, silent, and on each side sharp-pointed hills stood up black and white in the colorless air. There were many trees. Dawn at last came to us as we passed out of the narrows into a broad place, over whose flat floor an uneasy wind was spinning circles in the dust, capriciously. The day strengthened always and now showed that our plain was a big valley running down from the east, into which fell smaller valleys from south and north. This was Wadi Milii in whose bed the Sultani Pilgrim Road passes through Jebel Subh on its way from Bir Abbas to Rabegh. Bir ibn Hassani was just to our right. The trim little settlement of absurd houses, brown and white, holding together for security's sake, looked doll-like and lonelier than the desert, in the shadow of the immense dark bulk of Subh behind. Subh is a wonderful hill for its abruptness and steepness. As we watched, the sun was fast coming up, and the fretted cliff thousands of feet above our heads became outlined in hard refracted shafts of white light against a sky still sallow with the tropic dawn.

We rode on to cross the great valley, past the houses whose chief resident was Sherif Ahmed el Mansur, brother of Mohsin of Jidda, and the Sherifs Emir of all the Harb, though more politician than soldier. A few minutes later a single camel rider, a garrulous old man, naming himself Khallaf; came out from among the houses and jogged over to join us. His salutation came after a pause in a long series of observations, and when it was returned he tried to force us into conversation. However, Obeid grudged his company, and gave him short answers. Khallaf persisted, and finally, to improve his footing, bent down and burrowed in his saddle pouch till he found and drew out a small covered pot of enameled iron, containing a liberal portion of the staple of travel in the Hejaz. It was made of the unleavened dough cake of yesterday, crumbled while still warm between the fingers, and moistened with liquid butter till its particles would only fall apart reluctantly. It was then sweetened with ground sugar and scooped up to be eaten like damp sawdust in pressed pellets with the fingers.

I ate a little, on this my first attempt, while Obeid and Abdulla played at it vigorously, so that for his bounty Khallaf went half hungry that morning and deservedly for it was thought effeminate by the Arabs to carry a provision of food for a little journey of one hundred miles. We were now friends, and the chat began again while Khallaf told us about the last fighting, and a reverse Feisal had had the day before. It seemed he had been beaten out of Kheif in the head of Wadi Safra and was now at Hamra, only a little way in front of us: or at least Khallaf thought he was there: we might learn for sure in Wasta, the next village on our road. The fighting had not been severe but the few casualties were all among the tribesmen of Obeid and Khallaf, and the names and hurts of each were told in order.

Meanwhile I looked about, interested to find myself in a new zone of country. The sand and detritus of last night and of Bu el Sheikh had vanished, and we were riding up a valley, the northern tributary of Milif, varying from two hundred to five hundred yards in width, of shingle and light soil, quite firm, with occasional small crags of hard shattered green stone cropping out of its midst. There were many well-grown thorn trees, some of them woody acacias thirty feet and more in height, beautifully green with enough of tamarisk and soft scrub to give the whole a charming well-kept park-like air, now in the long soft shadows of the early morning. The ground was so flat and clean, the pebbles so swept and variegated, their colors so joyfully blended that they gave a sense of design to the landscape, and this feeling was strengthened by the straight lines and sharpness of the hills. They raised each hand regularly, precipices perhaps two thousand feet in height, of granite-brown and dark porphyry-colored rock, with pink stains in them: and by a strange fortune these glowing hills rested on hundred-foot bases of the green cross-grained stone, whose pale unaccustomed color looked like a surface growth of moss.

We rode along this beautiful place for about seven miles, to a low watershed, crossed by a wall of broken granite slivers, now little more than a shapeless heap, but once no doubt a barrier of a sort. It ran from cliff to cliff, and even far up the hillsides, wherever their slopes were not too steep to climb. In the center, where the road passed, had been two small enclosures like pounds. I asked Khallaf what the purpose of the wall might be. He replied that he had been in Cairo and Constantinople and Damascus, and had many friends among the great men of Egypt. He asked me if I knew any of the English there, and was curious about my intentions and my history. He tried to trip me in Egyptian phrases. I answered in the Arabic of Aleppo, and then he spoke of prominent Syrians of this acquaintance. I knew them too, and he changed off into local politics, and asked leading questions, delicately and indirectly, about the Sherif and his sons, and what I thought Feisal was going to do. I understood less of this than he, and parried inconsequentially. Obeid came to my rescue and changed the subject. We afterwards knew that Khallaf was in Turkish pay, and used to send them 6equent news of what came past Bir ibn Hassani for the Arab forces.

Across the wall we were in an fluent of Wadi Sask, a more wasted and stony valley bounded by less brilliant hills. It ran into another, far down which to the west we could see a cluster of dark palm-trees, which the Arabs said was Jedida, one of the slave villages in Wadi Safra. We turned up another valley to the right, and across another saddle, and then downhill for a few miles to a comer shut in by tall cliffs. We rounded this and found ourselves suddenly in Wadi Sda, the valley of our seeking, and in the very midst of Wasta, the largest village of its upper reaches. Wasta seemed to be a number of little nests of houses, clinging to the hillsides each side the torrent-bed on banks of alluvial soil, or standing on detritus islands between the various deep-swept channels which made up the parent valley.

We rode across between two or three of these built-up islands, making for the far bank of the valley. On our way we came to the main bed of the winter floods, a sweep of white shingle and boulders, quite flat. Down its middle, from palm-grove on the one side to palm-grove on the other, was a reach of clear water, perhaps two hundred yards long and twelve feet wide, sand-bottomed, and bordered on each brink by a ten-foot lawn of thick green grass and flowers. When we stepped on it to wade over the water, halting a moment to let our camels put their heads down and drink their fill, the relief to our eyes after the day-long hard glitter of the pebbles was so sudden that involuntarily I glanced up to see if a cloud had not come over the face of the sun.

We rode up the far side of the stream to the garden from which it issued, sparkling in a stone-lined channel: and then we turned along the mud wall of the garden in the shadow of the palms, till we reached another of the detached hamlets. Obeid led the way up its little street (the houses were so low that from our saddles we looked down upon their mud roofs), and near one of the larger houses stopped, and beat upon the door of an uncovered court. A slave opened to us, and we dismounted in privacy. Obeid haltered the camels, loosed their saddle girths, and strewed down before them green fodder from a fragrant pile beside the gate. Then he led me into the guest room of the house, a dark, clean little mud-brick place, roofed with split palm-logs under hammered earth. We sat down on the palm-leaf mat along the dais for a little rest. The day was now very hot, and gradually we lay back side by side and then the hum of the bees in the gardens without, and of the flies passing back and forth over our veiled faces within, sent us all to sleep.

Chapter 14: Feisal

When we awoke we found a meal of bread and dates prepared for us by the people of the house. The dates were new, meltingly sweet and good, like none I had ever tasted. They told us that the locusts had made of them a small crop this year. The owner of the property, a Harbi, was away like his neighbors serving with Feisal, and his women and children were out in the hills in his goat-hair tents, pasturing his camels. At the most the tribal Arabs of Wadi Safia lived in their village houses four months in the year. For the other seasons the gardens were entrusted to their slaves, negroes like the grown lads who brought in the tray to us, and whose thick limbs and plump shining bodies looked curiously out of place among the bird-like Arabs. Khallaf told me the blacks were all originally 60m the Sudan, brought over as children by their nominal Takruri fathers, and sold in Mecca during the pilgrimage. When grown strong they were worth from fifty to eighty pounds apiece, and were looked after carefully as befitted their price. Some were kept as house or body servants with their masters, but the majority were sent out to the palm villages of the feverish valleys with running water, whose climate was too bad for an Arab to labor in, but where they flourished, and built themselves houses, and mated with women slaves, and did all the manual work of the holding.

They were very numerous — for instance there were thirteen villages of them in forty miles of this Wadi Safia — so they formed a society of their own, and had power to live much at their pleasure. Their work was hard, but the supervision loose, and escape easy. Their legal status was bad, for they had no appeal to tribal justice, or even to the Sherifs courts, but public opinion and self interest deprecated any cruelty towards them, and the tenet of the faith that to enlarge a slave was a good deed meant in practice that nearly all gained their freedom in the end. They made pocket money of their own during their service, if they were ingenious. Those I saw were in possession of property, and declared themselves contented. Wadi Safra had become their country, and they had no thought of leaving it. They grew melons, marrows, cucumbers, tobacco and grapes, for their own account, in addition to the dates they owed their masters. These masters were all Beni Salem, and their life must have been well lived, with the garden produce added to the ordinary subsistence of camel-breeding. Surplus dates were sent across to the Sudan by sailing dhow, and there exchanged for corn and luxuries.

After the midday heat was passed we mounted again, and rode up the clear slow rivulet until it passed into the shelter of the palm gardens, which were bounded with low walls of sun-dried clay. In and out between the tree roots were dug little canals a foot or two deep, so contrived that the stream might be let into them from the stone channel, and each tree watered in its turn. The main head of water was owned by the community, and shared out among the landowners for their plots of garden ground, for so many minutes or hours daily or weekly according to the traditional use. The water was a little brackish, as was needed for the best palms: but for drinking it was better to use one of the wells of private water in the groves. These wells were very frequent, and reached water three or four feet below the surface. They were used to supplement the easy watering from the spring, by bucket lift, and during the summer and autumn this was the main labor of the slaves.

Our way took us through the central village, and its market street. There was little in the shops, and all the places were decayed. A generation ago Wasta was populous, they said of a thousand houses, but there came a great wall of water down Wadi Safra, the embankments of many palm gardens were breached, and the palm-trees swept away. Some of the islands on which houses had stood for centuries were submerged, and the mud houses melted back again into mud, killing or drowning the unfortunate slaves within. The men could have been replaced, and the trees replanted, had the soil remained: but the gardens had been built up of earth carefully won from the normal freshets in years of labor, and this wave of water, eight feet deep and running in a race for three days, had reduced the plots in its track to the primordial banks of stones. Many of the surviving slaves fled the place, and the labor of the remainder had done little yet to restore the old prosperity, as there was the dread of a second disaster in their minds. Wadi Saka ran in flood every winter, often more than once, but the whole bed seldom filled: usually just a section came down in a thick muddy stream a foot or two deep, an annual benefaction to whose renewal of the tired soil was due its continued fertility. In the year of death there was a cloudburst somewhere in the hills. Wadi Safra had so large a drainage system that its catchments covered thousands of square miles, and from these polished granite hills every drop of fallen rain ran down as it would from glass.

A little way beyond Wasta was Kharma, a tiny settlement with rich palm-groves, where a tributary ran in from the north. Beyond Kharma the valley widened somewhat, to an average of perhaps four hundred yards, with a bed of fine shingle and sand, laid very smooth by the winter rains. The walls were of bare red and black rock, whose edges and ridges were sharp as knife-blades, and reflected the sun like metal. They made to seem very luxurious the freshness of the trees and grass. We now began to meet parties of Feisal's soldiers, and grazing herds of their riding camels. Before we reached Hamra every nook in the rocks or clump of trees was a bivouac. They cried cheery greetings to Obeid, who came to lie again, waved back and called to them, while he pressed on quickly to get his duty over. Hamra lay on our left. It seemed to be a village of about one hundred houses, buried in fertile gardens among gentle mounds of earth some twenty feet in height.

We forded a little stream, and went up a walled path between trees to the top of one of those mounds, and there made our camels kneel by the gate of the courtyard of a long low house. Obeid said something to a slave who stood there with a silver-Kited sword in his hand. He led me through a second gate into an inner cow, and across it I saw standing framed between the posts of a black doorway, a white figure waiting tensely for me. This was Feisal, and I felt at the glance that now I had found the man whom I had come to Arabia to seek, the leader alone needed to make the Arab Revolt win through to a success. He looked very tall and pillar-like, very slender, dressed in long white silk robes and a brown head cloth bound with a brilliant scarlet and gold cord. His eyelids were dropped, and his close black beard and colorless face were like a mask against the strange still watchfulness of his body. His hands were loosely crossed in front of him on his dagger.

I greeted him, and he made way for me into the room, and sat down on his carpet near the door. As my eyes grew accustomed to the shade I saw that the little room held many silent figures, all looking at me and at Feisal steadily. He remained staring down at his hands which were twisting slowly about his dagger. At last softly he inquired how I had found the journey. I spoke of the heat, and he asked how long from Rabegh, commenting that I had ridden fast for the season. 'And do you like our place here in Wadi Safra? 'Well; but it is far from Damascus.' There was a quiver, and everybody present stiffened where he sat, and held his breath for a silent minute. Some perhaps were dreaming of how far off success seemed to be, others thought my word a reflection on their late defeat. It had fallen like a sword into their midst, but Feisal at length lifted his eyes and smiled at me and said, 'Praise be to God, there are Turks nearer us than that.' We all smiled with him, and then I got up and excused myself for the moment.

Chapter 15: The First Campaign

I went away to a lush meadow under long arcades of tall palms with ribbed and groined branches where I found, pitched in the side-bays between the trees, a trim camp of Egyptian Army soldiers, under Zeki Bey, the Egyptian major sent over from the Sudan by Sir Reginald Wingate, the Sirdar, to help the Arab rebellion. They comprised a mountain battery, and some machine-guns, and looked smarter than they felt. Zeki himself was an amiable fellow, kind and hospitable to me in spite of his weak health and of his resentment at having been sent so far away into the desert to serve under such wild conditions. The Egyptians were home-loving persons, and comfortable. Strangeness was always a misery to them.

In this particular instance their hardships had a philanthropic end, which made it much harder to bear. They were fighting the Turks, for whom they had a sentimental regard, on behalf of the Arabs, an alien people speaking a kindred language to their own, but appearing therefore all the more unlike in character, and in the crudeness of their lie. The Arabs seemed hostile to, rather than appreciative of the material blessings of civilization. They often met with a ribald hoot well-meaning attempts to furnish their bareness. Englishmen were sure of their general excellence, and would persist in executing services so recognized, without grumbling too much: but the Egyptians lost faith.

They had neither that collective sense of duty towards their state, nor that feeling of individual obligation to help struggling humanity up its road. The vicarious policeman attitude, which was the strongest emotion of Englishmen when they saw another man's muddle, in their case was replaced by the instinct to pass by as far away as possible on the other side. So though all was well with these soldiers, and they had abundant rations, and good health and no casualties, yet they found fault with the handling of the universe, and hoped that I had come to set it right.

A little later Feisal came to see me, with Maulud Mukhlus, the Arab zealot of Tekrit, who had been twice degraded in the Turkish army for rampant nationalism, and had spent an exile of two years in Nejd with ibn Rashid as a secretary. He had commanded the Turkish cavalry reconnaissance before Shaiba, and had been captured by us there. As soon as he heard of the rebellion of the Sherif he had volunteered for him, and had been the first regular officer to join Feisal. He was now nominally his A.D.C. and took the first part in the conversation.

He said bitterly that their forces were in every way ill equipped: this was the main cause of their present plight. They received three thousand pounds a month from the Sherif, but little flour and rice, little barley, few rifles, insufficient ammunition, no machine-guns, and no mountain guns. I stopped right there, and said that my coming was expressly to learn what they lacked, and to report it: but that I could only work with them if they would explain to me their general situation. Feisal agreed that this was just, and began to sketch to me the history of their Revolt.

The first rush on Medina had been a desperate measure. The Arabs were ill-armed and short of ammunition, the Turks in great force since Fakhri's detachment had just arrived, and the troops to escort von Stotzingen to Yemen were still in the town. In the height of the crisis the Beni Ali broke: and the Arabs were thrust out beyond the walls. The Turks then opened fire on them with their artillery, and the Arabs, unused to this new arm, became terrified. The Ageyl and Ateiba got into safety, and refused to move out again. Feisal and Ali ibn el Hussein vainly rode about in front of their men in the open, to show them that the bursting shells were not as fatal as they sounded.

Meanwhile some of the Beni Ali approached the Turkish command with an offer to surrender, if their villages were spared. Fakhri played with the idea, and during this lull in hostilities surrounded the Awali suburb with his troops: then suddenly he ordered them to carry it by assault, and to massacre everything living within its walls. Hundreds of the inhabitants were raped and butchered, the houses fired, and living and dead alike thrown back into the flames. Fakhri and his men had served together and gained experience against the Armenians in the Urfa province.

This example of the Turkish mode of war sent a shock across Arabia, for the first rule of Arab war was that women were inviolable: the second was that the lives and honor of children too young to fight with men were to be spared: and a third, that property impossible to carry off should be left in place undamaged. The Arabs with Feisal perceived that they were opposed to new customs, and fell back out of touch to gain time to readjust themselves. There could no longer be any question of submission: the sack of Awali put upon them the duty of fighting to the last: but they were seeing that it would be a long affair and that with muzzle loading guns and hand arms they could hardly expect to win.

So they fell back from the level plains about Medina into the hills across the Sultani road about Aar and Raha and Bir Abbas, where they rested a little, while Ali and Feisal sent messenger after messenger down to Rabegh, their sea-base, to learn when fresh stores and money and arms were to be expected. The revolt had begun haphazard, on their father's orders, and no arrangements had been worked out for prolonging it: so the reply was only a little food. Later some Japanese rifles, mostly broken, were received. The barrels were so foul that the too-eager Arabs found them burst on the first trial. No money was sent up at all: and to take its place Feisal filled a decent chest with stones, had it locked and corded carefully, guarded on the march by his own slaves, and introduced meticulously into his tent each evening.

At last Ali went down to Rabegh to inquire what was wrong with their organization. He found that Hussein Mabeirig, its overlord, the great sheikh of the Masruh, and one of the chief men of all the Harb, had made up his mind that the Turks would be victorious (he had tried conclusions with them twice himself and had found them the stronger) and that therefore theirs was the best cause to follow. As the stores for the Shed were landed by the British he was appropriating them, and putting them into his own houses. Ali made a demonstration. Hi half-brother Zeid joined him from

Jidda with reinforcements and Sheikh Hussein in fear recanted of his evil-doing. Next night he slipped off to the hills, an outlaw, and the Arab leaders took possession of his villages. In them they found great stores of arms, and food for their armies for a month. They settled down to live in Rabegh.

This left Feisal alone up country, and he soon found himself isolated, in a hollow situation, driven to depend on his own resources. He bore it for a time, but in August took advantage of the visit to the newly-conquered Yenbo of Colonel Wilson to come down to the coast and meet him, and give in a full explanation of his urgent needs. Wilson was impressed with him and his story, and at once promised him a battery of mountain guns and some Maxims, to be handled by men and officers of the Egyptian

Army garrison in the Sudan. This explained the presence of Zeki Bey and his units. The Arabs rejoiced when they came, and believed that they were now the equals of the Turk: but the four guns were twenty-year-old Krupps, with a range of only three thousand yards, and their personnel were not eager enough in brain and spirit for irregular fighting.

However, they went forward with the mob, and drove in the Turkish outposts, and then their supports, until Fakhri became seriously alarmed and came down himself, inspected the front, and reinforced the threatened detachment at Bir Abbas, till it was some three thousand strong. The Turks had field guns and howitzers with them, and the advantage of high ground for observation. They began to wow the Arabs by indirect fire, and nearly dropped a shell on Feisal's tent while all the head men were conferring within. The Egyptian gunners were asked to return the fire, and smother the enemy guns. They had to plead that their weapons were useless, since they could not carry the nine thousand yards. They were derided, and the Arabs ran back again into the defiles.

Feisal was deeply discouraged, and sent word to his father that he might hold up the Turks for fifteen days or even twenty till reinforcements came or till the bulk of the enemy were drawn off by diversions made against Media from the southern or eastern roads. His father promised both, but since then he had been sitting up there in the hills fronting the Turks, by himself; while Abdulla had delayed at Mecca, and Ali and Zeid at Rabegh.

His men were tired. He had lost many of them. His only effective tactics against the enemy had been to chase in suddenly upon their rear by fast mounted charges, and many camels had been wounded, and many were worn out by these expensive measures. He felt unable any longer to carry all the war upon his own neck. Finally he had withdrawn the bulk of his forces here to Wadi Safia, leaving the Rahala and Radada tribes by Bir Abhas to keep up a constant pressure on the Turkish supply columns and communications. He had no fear that the enemy would come forward against him suddenly.

It became clear to me as he talked how very lightly he treated the Turks with whom he had been in contact, and how he seemed to despise them, while yet he could make no impression on them. His latest retirement to Hamra was not forced on him: it had happened because he had lost heart, because he was bored by his obvious impotence, and was determined for a little while to have rest and peace. The two sides were yet untried. The Turkish armament made them so superior at long range that the Arabs had never got to grips. For this reason most of the fighting had taken place at night, when the guns were blinded. To my ears they sounded oddly primitive battles, with torrents of words on both sides in a preliminary match of wits. After using up all the foulest terms of the languages they knew there would come the climax, when the Turks in frenzy called the Arabs 'English', and the Arabs screamed back 'German' at them. There were of course no Germans in the Hejaz, and I was the first Englishman up here: but each party loved cursing, and any charge would do.

I asked Feisal what his plans were now. He said that till Medina fell they were inevitably tied down there in the Hejaz dancing to Fakhri's tune. In his opinion the Turks were aiming at the recapture of Mecca; indeed they were already a long way on the road to it. The bulk of their strength was now at Bir Denvish, in a mobile column, which they could move either by the Sultani, by the Fura, or by the Gaha roads, for Rabegh.

There was no technical difficulty about the movement, and the choice of routes open to them kept the Arab forces in constant alarm. He personally was most afraid of the Fura road. Wadi Fura ran down in a long twisting defile, with half a dozen good oases of palms and running springs, to Khoreiba, the village near Masturah. It was the most direct and best watered road from Medina to Rabegh, and at this season the Turks could support themselves along it by means of the ripe dates in its palm-gardens.

His passive defense in the Subh hills had been shown impotent to stop them. When they next moved he must change ground, and pass to the offensive. He meant to retire further yet, out of Wadi Safra to Bir Said where he would be on the Wadi Yenbo border of the great Juheina tribe. He hoped to raise fresh levies from them, and to march eastwards towards Buwat and Bir Nasif, stations on the Hejaz Railway behind Medina. He intended to do this at the moment when Abdulla was advancing through the Mteir lava-desert to attack Medina from the east.

He hoped that Ali would go up simultaneously from Rabegh to attack Media from the south, while Zeid or Shakir moved into Wadi Safra, to engage the big Turkish force at Bir Abbas, and keep it out of the main battle. By this plan Fakhri would be threatened or attacked on all sides at once, and so he hoped the Arabs would take Medina, as they would have done had they only had two guns on the first occasion. At any rate, whatever was the success of the attack the concentration from three sides would at least break up the Turkish push outwards on the fourth, and would give Rabegh and the southern Hejaz a breathing space.

Maulud, who had sat fidgeting through our long slow talk, could no longer restrain himself and cried out to me, 'Don't write a history of us. What we need to do is fight and fight, and kill them. Give me a battery of Schneider quick-firing mountain guns, and some machine-guns, and I will finish this off for you. We talk and talk and do nothing.' I replied as warmly, and Maulud, a magnificent fighter, a man who regarded a battle won as a battle wasted, if he had not carried away some wound to prove his part in it, took me up. We wrangled while Feisal sat by and grinned delightedly at us.

This talk had been for him a holiday, and I think too he was encouraged at my coming, for he was a man of moods, flickering between glory and despair, and just now he was dead-tired. He looked years older than thirty-one, and his dark appealing eyes, set a little sloping in his face, were bloodshot, and his hollow cheeks deeply lined and puckered with reflection. His nature grudged thinking, for it crippled his speed in action: when he thought, his face shriveled into swift lines of pain. His hair and beard were dark, his nose high, his chin very short. In appearance he was tall, graceful and vigorous, with the most beautiful gait, and a royal dignity of head and shoulders. He obviously knew it, for a great part of his speaking was just sign and gesture.

His movements were impetuous; he showed himself hot-tempered and proud, sometimes unreasonable, and ran off soon tangents. He communicated a sense of abounding desire, untamed except by physical weakness, waiting always to leap out and strike. His personal charm, his imprudence, the pathetic hint of weakness in reserve made him the idol of his followers. One never asked if he were scrupulous: but he showed later that he could return trust for trust, and suspicion for suspicion. He was fuller of wit than of humor.

His training in Abdul Hamid's entourage had made him past master in diplomacy. His military service with the Turks had given him a working knowledge of tactics. His life in Constantinople, and in the Turkish parliament, had made him familiar with European questions and manners. He was a careful judge of men. If he had the strength to realize his dreams he would go very far, for he was all wrapped up in his work, and lived for nothing else: but I felt that either he would wear himself out by trying to seem to aim always a little higher than the truth, or that he would die of too much action. His men told me that after a long spell of hand-to-hand fighting, in which he had to guard himself, and lead the charges, and control and encourage his men, he had collapsed physically and was carried away from his victory, unconscious, with the foam flecking his lips.

Meanwhile here was offered to our hand, if we were big enough to take it, the finest instrument which God ever made for the Orient, the prophet who if veiled would give cogent form to the idea working behind the activity of the Arab Revolt. It was all and more than we had ever hoped for, much more than we had deserved in our halting course.

My duty was now to get back by the shortest road to Egypt, to tell the others what I knew: and this knowledge that evening in the palm wood grew and blossomed in my mind into a thousand branches, laden with fruit and shady leaves, beneath which I sat and half-listened, and saw visions, till the twilight deepened, and the night, and a line of slaves with lamps came down the winding paths between the tree trunks, and with Feisal and Maulud we walked back through the gardens, and up to the little house with its courts still full of waiting people, and to the hot inner room in which the familiars were assembled, and where we sat down together to the smoking bowl of rice and meat set for us for our supper, by the slaves.

Chapter 16: Morale

We were a mixed company, Sherifs, Meccans, sheikhs of the Juheina and Ateiba, Mesopotamians, Ageyl, and among them I threw apples of discord, inflammatory subjects of talk, to feel their mettle and beliefs without delay. Feisal, smoking innumerable cigarettes, kept command of the conversation whatever I did, and it was fine to see him do it. He showed himself a master of tact, with a real power of disposing men's feelings to his wish. Storrs was as efficient, but Storrs paraded his strength, exhibiting all his cleverness and machinery, the movements of his hands which made the creatures dance. Feisal seemed to govern his men unconsciously, hardly to know how he stamped his mind on them, hardly to care whether they obeyed or not. It was as great art as Storrs' and in addition it concealed itself for Feisal was born to this office.

The Arabs loved him openly: indeed these chance meetings made clear how to the tribes the Sherif and his sons were heroic. Sherif Hussein (Sayidna as they called him) was outwardly so clean and gentle-mannered as to seem almost weak, but this appearance hid a crafty policy, deep ambition, and an un-Arabian foresight, strength of character, and obstinacy. There was never need of an

Arab secret society in Mecca, for he had been always an Arab Government. In the towns he played Arabs' advocate with the Turkish Government, but in the country districts his influence was strong enough to be administrative and there his power lay, with his tastes and sympathies. His interest in natural history reinforced his sporting instincts and made him, when he pleased, a fair copy of a Bedouin prince while his Circassia mother had endowed him with qualities foreign to both Turk and Arab, and he displayed considerable astuteness in turning now one, now another of his assets to advantage.

An instance of his worldly wisdom was his upbringing of his sons. The Sultan had made them live in Constantinople, and receive a Turkish education. Sherif Hussein saw to it that the education was as good as Constantinople could afford. Then they came back to the Hejaz, young Levantine effendis, in European clothes, with Turkish manners. The father at once changed them into Arab dress and, to rub up their Arabic, gave them Meccan companions and sent them out into the wilds in command of small bodies of Ageyl Camel Corps, to patrol the pilgrim roads against robbers.

The young men thought it might be an amusing trip, but were rather dashed when their father forbade them special food, bedding, and soft-padded saddles. He would not let them back to Mecca even for the feast, but kept them out for months in all seasons guarding the roads day and night, learning to handle all manner of men, and their methods of riding and fighting. Soon they hardened, and became self-reliant and self-content. By now they were thorough Bedouin in experience, and their former education had given them the knowledge and experience of Turkish officials, and their descent that blend of native intelligence and vigor which so often comes in a crossed stock

It made them a formidable family group, at once admired and efficient, but left them curiously isolated in their world. They were natives of no country, lovers of no private plot of ground. They had no real confidants or advisers or ministers, and no one of them seemed really open to another, or to the father, of whom they all stood in awe.

Meanwhile, the wrangle after supper was in full career. As a supposed Syrian I made a sympathetic reference to the Arab leaders who had been executed in Damascus by Jemal Pasha. They took me up sharply; the published papers had disclosed that these men were in touch with foreign governments, and ready to accept French or British suzerainty as the price of help. Such was a crime against Arab nationality, and Jemal had only executed the implied sentence. Feisal smiled, almost winked, at me. 'You see,' he explained, 'we are now of necessity allies of the British. We are delighted to be their friends, most grateful for their help, most expectant of our future profit: but we are not British subjects. We would be more at ease if they were not so disproportionate an ally.

'I told a story of Abdulla el Raashid, on the way up to Hamra. He had groaned to me of the British sailors coming ashore each day at Rabegh. 'Soon they will stay nights, and then they will live here always, and take the country.' To cheer him I had spoken of millions of English now ashore in France, and of the French not afraid at their menace: whereat he had turned on me scornfully, asking whether I meant to compare France with the land of Hejaz!

Feisal mused a little, and said, 'I am not a Hejazi, by upbringing, and yet, by God, I am jealous for it: and though I know the British do not want it, yet what can I say, when they took the Sudan, also not wanting it? They hunger for desolate lands, to build them up, and so perhaps one day Arabia will seem to them precious. Your good and my good, perhaps they are different, and either forced good or forced evil will make a people cry with pain. Does the ore admire the flame which transforms it? There is no rational ground for offense, but men too weak will be claimant about their little own. Our race will have a cripple's temper, till it has found its feet.'

The ragged lousy tribesmen who had eaten with us astonished me, by their familiar understanding of intense political nationality, an abstract idea they could hardly have caught from the educated classes of the Hejaz towns from those Hindus, Javanese, Bokhariots, Sudanese, Turks, out of sympathy with Arab ideals, and indeed just then suffering a little from the force of local sentiment, springing too high after its sudden escape from Turkish control.

It seemed that it was in part the result of German missions. After their 'Holy War' had failed, instead of letting well alone the Germans had changed over and preached nationality in Turkey. They hoped to make the Empire realize its Ottoman unity: but instead they made Anatolia react against the Armenians, and Arabia react against the Turks. This propaganda on Turanian lines had come very happily in time to reinforce the example and counsels of the Sherifs. Hussein, the leader and noblest of the Sherifs, had had the worldly wisdom to base his precepts on the instinctive belief of the Arabs that they were of the salt of the earth and self-sufficient. Then by his alliance with us he was enabled to back his precepts by arms and money, and the success of his doctrine was assured.

Of course this success was not level throughout. The great body of Sherifs, eight hundred or nine hundred of them, was firmly with him, and understood all the tendency of his argument. They had a number of level-headed men amongst them, successful in their generation, though hardly according to our lights. They lacked experience of administration, but had that great conviction of birth, which gave them the power to hold men's minds, and to direct their courses into willing quietness.

The tribes had followed the smoke of their racial fanaticism: the towns might sigh for the cloying inactivity of Ottoman rule: the tribes were convinced that they had made a free and Arab Government, and that each of them was it. They were independent, and would enjoy themselves:— a doctrine which might have led to anarchy, if it had not meanwhile made more stringent the family tie, and the bonds of kindred responsibility. It entailed a practical negation of central power in internal affairs. The Sherif might have his legal sovereignty abroad, if he liked the high-sounding toy: but home affairs were to be customary. 'Is Damascus to rule the Hejaz, or can we rule Damascus? And it would be hard to say which one was the greatest problem. Only it was sure that they would not have it set: for their idea of nationality was the independence of clans and villages, and their ideal of national union was episodic combined resistance to an intruder. Constructive policies, an organized state, an extended empire were not so much beyond their sight as hateful in it. They were fighting to get rid of Empire, not to win it.

The feeling of the Syrians and Mesopotamians in these Arab armies was very advanced. They believed that by fighting in the Arab ranks, even here in the Hejaz, they were vindicating the rights of all Arabs to a national existence, and without envisaging one state, or even a confederation of states, they were definitely looking northward, wishing to add an autonomous Damascus and Bagdad to the Arab family. They were weak in material resources, and even in success would be, since their world was agricultural and pastoral, without minerals, and so could never be very strong in modem armaments. Were it otherwise, we would have had to weigh more deeply our course in evoking in the Middle East new national movements of such abounding vigor.

Of religious fanaticism there was little trace. The Sherif refused in round terms to give a religious twist to his rebellion. His political creed was pure nationality. The tribes knew that the Turks were Muslims, and thought that the Germans were probably true friends of Islam. They knew that the British were Christians and that the British were their allies. In the circumstances their religion would not have been of much help to them, and they had put it aside. 'Christian fights Christian, so why should not Mohammedans do the same? What we want is a Government which speaks Arabic and will let us live in peace. Also we hate those Turks.'

Chapter 17: The Troops

Next morning I was up early and out among Feisal's troops towards the side of Kheif; by myself; trying to feel the pulse of their opinions in a moment, by such tricks as I had played upon their chiefs the night before. Time was of the essence of my effort, for it was necessary to gain in ten days the impressions which would ordinarily have been the fruit of weeks of observing in my crab-fashion, that sideways-slipping affair of the senses. Normally I went along all day, with the sounds immediate, but seeing in detail nothing, only generally aware that there were things red, or things grey, or clear things about me. Today my eyes had time after time to be switched suddenly on to my brain, that I might note a thing or two the more clearly by contrast with the former mistiness. Such things were nearly always shapes, rocks and trees and men's bodies in repose or movement: not small things like flowers or qualities like color. In this drab war the least irregularity was a joy to all our minds, and I saw that my strongest course was to seize the latent imagination of the General Staff: I believed in the Arab movement, and was confident, before ever I came, that here was the idea to tear Turkey into pieces: but others in Egypt lacked full knowledge and faith, and had been taught nothing intelligent of the Arabs in the field. By noting down some of the character and spirit of these romantics in the hills and valleys about the Holy Cities I might gain the sympathy of Cairo in the further measures necessary to help them.

The men received me cheerfully. They were sprawling like lazy scorpions beneath every great rock or bush, resting from the heat, and refreshing their brown limbs with the early coolness of the shaded surfaces of stone. In my khaki they took me for a Turk-trained officer and a deserter to them, and were profuse in good-humored but ghastly suggestions of how I should be treated. Most of them were young, though the term 'fighting man' in the Hejaz meant anyone between twelve and sixty, sane enough to shoot. They were a tough-looking crowd and dark-colored. Their physical condition was very good. They were thin, but exquisitely made, moving about with a free activity which was altogether delightful to watch.

It did not seem possible that men could be hardier or harder. They could ride immense distances day after day, run through sand and over rocks barefoot in the heat for hour after hour without pain, and climb their hills like goats. Their clothing was just a loose shirt, and sometimes short cotton drawers, with a head shawl, usually of red cloth, which would also act towel or handkerchief or sack as required. They were corrugated with bandoleers, and fired joy shots when they could. Feisal issued each newcomer with fifty cartridges, and did his best to make them precious, but without effect behind the line. When it came to business with the enemy, however, they restrained themselves, thanks to their old practice with single-shot rifles demanding precaution and economy in action. They shot well and carefully but were limited to short ranges, since they had no measure of length, to help them with the sighting. Some were beginning to use their slides by rule of eye and thumb.

They were in wild spirits, as keen and irregular as hawks, quick and intelligent, shouting that the war might last ten years. It was the fattest time the hills had ever known. The Sherif was feeding not only the fighting men, but their families, and paying two pounds a month for a man, four for a camel. Nothing else would have performed the miracle of keeping a tribal army in the field for five months on end. It was our habit to sneer at oriental soldiers' love of pay, but the Hejaz campaign was a good example of the limitations of that argument. The Turks were offering great bribes, and obtaining little service — no active service. The Arabs took their money, and gave gratifying assurances in exchange: yet these very tribes would be still in touch with Feisal, who also spent money freely, on a lesser scale, but got service for his payment.

The Turks cut the throats of their prisoners with knives, as though they were butchering sheep. Feisal offered a reward of a pound a head for prisoners, and had many of them carried to him unhurt. He also paid for captured mules or rifles, and ceded them again to the captors. Such things being equal, the sentimental reasons gave the Arab side a definite preference. The Turks were feared and hated by the Arabs, except in interested cases such as Hussein Mabeirig, and the Sherif was regarded with general pride and veneration as an Arab Sultan of immense wealth and dignity, and Feisal as his warlord. When he fell back from Bir Abbas the Beni Amr asked Sidi Feisal if he now intended to make peace with the Turks, and received an indignant reply, which was endorsed by the other tribes in the field, most of whom would have genuinely regretted an early peace.

The actual forces were continually shifting, in obedience to the rule of flesh. A family would own a rifle, and the sons serve in turn for a few days each. Married men alternated between camp and wife, and sometimes a whole clan would become bored, and take a rest. Consequently the paid men were more than those mobilized, and policy often gave to great sheikhs, as wages of their contingent, money which was a polite bribe for friendly countenance.

Feisal's eight thousand men about him were ten per cent camel corps and the rest hill men. They served only under their tribal sheikhs, and near their homes, arranging their own food and transport. Nominally each sheikh had one hundred followers, but in practice was allowed latitude to keep more or less. The Sherifs acted as common leaders of a group of sheikhs, by virtue of their privileged position, which raised them above the jealousies of the tribes, and by this understanding members of hostile tribes could be made to work together in the field. Blood feuds were nominally healed, and really suspended in the Sherifian area; Billi and Juheina, Harb, Ateiba and Ageyl were living and fighting side by side in Feisal's army.

At the same time the members of one tribe were shy of those of another, and within the tribe, no man would quite trust his neighbor. Each might be, usually was, whole-hearted against the Turks, but perhaps not to the point of failing to work off a family grudge by letting down a family enemy in the field. Consequently they could not be relied on for attack in mass. Indeed probably one company of Turks firmly entrenched in open country could have defied the entire army of them, and defeat, with its casualties, would have put an end to the war by sheer horror.

My conclusions were that the value of the tribesmen was defensive only, and their real element guerrilla warfare. Their intelligent recklessness made them love taking booty, and would have led them to dynamite a railway, plunder a caravan, or steal camels better than anyone, while they were fed and paid by an Arab authority: but they were too individualistic to endure command, or to fight in team, helping one another. A man who would fight well by himself was generally a bad soldier, and these men seemed to me no material for drilling: but if we strengthened them by light automatic guns of the Lewis type, to be handled by themselves (to add to them foreign units like the Egyptian artillery was a mistake), they might be capable of holding their hills, and serving as an efficient screen behind which we could build up, perhaps at Rabegh, an Arab field force of good mobility, capable of meeting a Turkish force, distracted by guerrilla warfare, on their own terms and of defeating it, piecemeal. This force would draw no recruits from the Hejaz. It would have to be formed from the stolid unwarlike Syrian and Mesopotamian towns-folk already in our hands, and officered by Arabic-speaking officers trained in the Turkish army, men of the type and history of Aziz el Masri or Maulud. Such a force alone could finish the war by striking, while the tribesmen skirmished about, and hindered and distracted the Turks by their pin-prick raids.

The Hejaz war meanwhile would be one of dervishes against regular troops, and for the first time the British had found themselves on the side of the dervishes, with their textbooks applying only by contrary. It was the fight of a rocky, mountainous, barren country (reinforced by a wild horde of mountaineers) against an enemy so enriched in equipment by the Germans as almost to have lost virtue for rough-and-tumble war. The hill-belt was a paradise for snipers, and the Arabs very artists in sniping, willing to run or climb any distance for a comfortable shot. Two or three hundred determined men knowing the ranges should hold any section of them; not that the actual peaks were so high, or the water so scarce in the valleys: but because the slopes were too steep. The beds of the valleys were the only practicable roads, and they took the nature of chasms or gorges for miles and miles, sometimes two hundred yards across, but sometimes only twenty, full of twists and turns, one thousand or four thousand feet deep, barren of cover, and flanked each side by pitiless hills of granite, basalt and porphyry: not polished slopes, but serrated and split and piled up in thousands of jagged heaps of fragments as hard as metal and nearly as sharp.

Over these cliffs the Arabs could run barefoot, and they, old gazelle and ibex hunters, knew hundreds of hidden ways from one hilltop to another. It seemed to my unaccustomed eyes impossible that, without treachery on the part of the mountain tribes, the Turks could dare to break their way through. Even with treachery, to pass the hills would be dangerous. The enemy would never be sure that the fickle population might not turn again, and to have such a labyrinth of defiles in the rear, across the lines of communications, would be worse than having it in front. Without the friendship of the tribes the Turks owned only the ground on which their soldiers stood: and lines so long and so complex would soak up all their thousands of men in a night, and leave none in the battle-fronts, for it was not as though the passage of the hills ended their affair. Before them lay the length of the parched Tehama along which their regular army would require great trains of camels to provide its food and water: and if they waited for the winter rain to provide the water they ran a new danger, for the valleys, which were their roads through the hills, might then almost without warning become chest deep roaring torrents, sweeping away everything in their course.

In it all was one disquieting feature, the very real success the Turks were having in the use of their artillery to beat down the determination of the Arabs. The Bedouin had a living terror of the unknown, and the unknown to them yet included airplanes and artillery. Aziz el Masri in the Turk-Italian war had found in Tripoli the same terror of an airplane, but had found also that the terror wore off with deeper acquaintance. We might hope that this might be the case with artillery, but for the moment they thought weapons destructive in proportion to their noise. The sound of the discharge of a cannon sent every man within earshot behind cover. They were not afraid of bullets, or indeed overmuch of dying: just the manner of death by shell-fire was unendurable. It seemed to me that their moral confidence was only to be restored by having guns, useful or useless, but noisy, on their side. In Wadi Safia the theme of all talk was guns, guns, guns, whose power and horror were stark in their wits. From the magnificent Feisal down to the most naked stripling in the army they believed that in their lack of guns lay all the reason of their failure.

When I told them of the landing of the five-inch howitzers at Rabegh they rejoiced, and the news nearly balanced in their minds the check of their last retreat down Wadi Safia. Of course as the Turks had to advance deeper and deeper into the hills artillery would be of less use to them: but its presence would always be a powerful argument, and to fight it we would have to recognize the Arab mania, and lend them enough guns, as amulets, to restore their balance. The guns would be no material use to them, for the Turks were not silly like the Arabs on the point. Indeed it seemed to me that the possession of guns would do the Arabs positive harm, for the virtues of the tribes lay in their mobility and intelligence, and by giving them guns we hampered their movements, and so reduced their efficiency: only if we did not give them guns they would quit service.

Seen from so close, the enormousness of the revolt impressed me. This well-peopled province, from Um Lejj to Kunfida, more than a whole night long in camel-journeying, had suddenly been changed from an area of casual nomad pilferers a deadly enemy of the Turks, fighting them not, certainly, in our manner, but fiercely enough, in spite of the religion which was to raise the East against us in a Holy War. Beyond anything calculable in figures we had let loose a passion of anti Turkish feeling which, embittered as it had been by some generations of subjection might die very hard. There was among the tribes in the fighting zone a nervous enthusiasm common I suppose to all national risings, but strangely disquieting to one from a land so long delivered that the very taste of freedom was unknown in our mouths. It seemed to me that a rebellion on such a scale, on such principles, would do more to weaken a country than unsuccessful foreign wars, and I began to suspect that Turkey had been harmed here more than it would be elsewhere till Constantinople had been occupied, and the Sultan made a puppet of European advisers.

Later I saw Feisal again and once more noted his optimism in the defensive, and his fixed contempt of the chance of a Turkish advance. I ventured to warn him of what I feared might be a real danger: the Turks must know that their weak point was the long and insufficiently defended Hejaz Railway. I thought the late move of Basri Pasha from Medina to Wejh might be a first step towards reinforcing the north. If Basri could trust the Billi, he might come down the coast and straiten the Juheina. They depended economically on the gardens of Wadi Yenbo, as did the Beni Salem on Wadi Safra, and if Basri took them behind Feisal's back the Juheina would have to make their peace with the Turks. The Sherifians would then be pinned in the Hama-Rabegh area, and if the enemy moved from two directions on Wadi Safra, would be broken up, would lose all the defenses of the Rabegh position, and would be thrown back on Mecca, their last resort.

I told him that I saw no means by which the British could assist at Rabegh with troops. The position was too large, and the water at Khoreiba threatened it dangerously. Further, from what I had seen of the temper of the Harb I believed that a foreign landing in Rabegh would send the whole of the tribe sullenly back to their tents. Feisal agreed with me that the moral consequence of an allied landing at any point in the Hejaz would be so disastrous on Arab feeling as practically to put an end to the revolt, but he had little fear that things would ever come to such a pass, that it would be necessary. Nor did he share my anxiety at the prospect of a Turkish diversion from the north down the Juheina coast. He thought that if he were supported in material ways, his chances of success were good.

My concern with the application of the principles of strategy and tactics was only a few days old, and my grasp of them as yet too tentative to enable me to press my instincts in any way. I promised to do my best for him in the matters he had indicated. I would ask my chiefs to arrange for him a base at Yenbo, where the stores and supplies he needed would be put ashore for his own exclusive use. I would try and get him officer volunteers from among the Syrian prisoners of war whom we had captured from the Turkish Army in Mesopotamia or on the Canal. We would try and help them to form gun crews and machine-gun crews from the rank and file in the internment camps with them: and we would try to provide them with such mountain guns and light machine-guns as were obtainable. Lastly I would advise that British Army officers, professionals, be sent down to act as advisers and liaison officers with him in the field.

This time our talk was of the pleasantest, and it ended by warm thanks from him, and a request that I would come back as soon as possible. I explained that my duties in Cairo inhibited me from field work, but that perhaps my chiefs might allow me to pay him a second visit later on, when his present wants were filled, and his movement was going forward prosperously. Meanwhile I would ask him for facilities to go down at once to Yenbo, to embark for Egypt, that I might get things on foot as early as possible. He at once appointed me an escort of fourteen Juheina Sheds, all kinsmen of Mohammed Ali ibn Beidawi, the Emir of the Juheina. They were instructed to guard me down to Yenbo by the Haj road, and to deliver me there intact to Sheikh Abd el Kadii el Abdo, the governor of the town for the Shed. I left Hamra shortly before sunset.

Chapter 18: Return to Egypt

Our march lay back the way we had come, down Wadi Safra, until opposite Kharma, where we turned to the right up the side valley. It was closely grown with stiff brushwood, through which we drove our camels strenuously, after tucking up the long streamers of our saddlebags, to save them from being shredded by the thorns. Two miles later we began to climb sharply, up the narrow pass of Dhiian, and on all hands there was evidence of labor, once expended on the road. It had been artificially smoothed and the stones piled at each side into a heavy wall of defense against the rush of water in the rains. Parts had been graded, and at times even carried on a causeway built seemingly six or eight feet high, of great blocks of uncut stone: but it had been breached at every turn by torrents, and was in tumbled ruin. By now darkness had come down thickly, and the way was so rocky that all my care had to be given to helping my camel and my sight to picking for it the best track to follow.

The ascent lasted perhaps for a mile, or a little more, and the steep descent the other side for about the same. Then we got to the level and found ourselves in a much broken country of ridges, covered by an intricate net of wadis whose main flow was apparently towards the south-west. The going was flat and good for our camels. We rode on for about seven miles in the dark, and then came to a well, Bir el Murra, in a valley bed under a very low bluff on whose head the square courses of a small fort of ashlar stood out against the star-lighted sky. Conceivably both the fort and the causeway in the pass had been built by an Egyptian Mameluke for the passage of the pilgrim caravan from Yenbo to Medina.

We halted nearby for the night and slept for six hours, which was long luxury upon the road, though this night's rest was broken twice by challenges from half-seen parties of mounted men who had stumbled on our bivouac. Afterwards we rose again, and wandered for two hours in and out of small ridges and hills like those of our last few miles before the well. Then dawn broke and showed that we were marching among gentle valleys of sand, with strange hills of lava hemming us in on all sides. The lava here was not the blue-black loose small stones of the fields about Rabegh: rather it was rust colored and piled in huge crags of flowing surface but with a bent and twisted texture, as though it had been played with oddly while yet soft. The sand, which at first had been a carpet about the foot of the rock, gradually gained on it. The lava hills got lower and the sand banked up against them in great drifts, till even the crests were sand-spattered, and at last drowned in it out of sight. So as the sun became high and painfully white we led out upon a rolling waste of dunes, which trended southward, miles away downhill, to the misty sea, grey-blue in the false distance of the heat.

The dunes were only a narrow belt. By half-past seven we were out on a staring plain, of glassy sand mixed with shingle, and overspread with scrub and thorn bushes, with even some good acacia trees. We rode very fast across this. I was a little uncomfortable, for I was not a skilled rider, and the movement exhausted me, while the sweat ran down my forehead and dripped slantingly into my eyelids, which were already crusted with grit and cracked with the burning sunlight. Sweat had only one benefit, when a drop fell from the end of a tuft of hair on to one's cheek, where it struck cold and sudden and unexpected like a splash; and these refreshments were too few to pay for the pain of heat. We pressed on, while the sand yielded to pure shingle, and that again hardened into the bed of a great valley, running down by many shadow interwoven mouths into the sea

We crossed a low rise, and from the far side opened a wide view, which was the delta of Wadi Yenbo, the largest valley of the northern Hejaz. It seemed to be a vivid copse of tamarisk and thorn. To the right, some miles up the valley, showed darkly the palm-groves of Nakhl Mubarak, a country village and gardens of the Beni Ibrahim Juheina. In the distance, ahead of us, lay the high mass of Jebel Rudhwa, which brooded so presently over Yenbo, though more than twenty miles away. We had seen it from Masturah, for it was one of the greatest hills of Hejaz, the more wonderful because it lifted itself in one clear edge from the flat Tehama to its crest. In its protection my companions felt at home, and as the plain was now dancing with unbearable heat we took shade under the branches of a leafy acacia beside the path, and slumbered through the middle day.

In the afternoon we watered our camels at a brackish little water hole in the sand bed of a branch of the main water-course, before a trim hedge of the feathery tamarisk, and then pushed on for two more happy hours. At last we halted for the night in typical Tehama country of bare slowly-swelling sand and shingle ridges, with shallow valleys in between. The Sherifs made a fire of aromatic wood, baked bread, boiled coffee, and then we slept sweetly with a salt wind from the sea blowing over our chafed faces. We rose again at two in the morning, and found that we had a featureless plain of hard shingle and wet sand to cross before we would reach Yenbo, which stood up with walls and towers on a reef of coral rag twenty feet above our level. We raced our camels at their best speed over this open stretch, and entered the gates by six in the morning. They took me straight through the crumbling empty streets (Yenbo was half a city of the dead since the Hejaz Railway opened, and the pilgrim traffic left it for Haifa in the Mediterranean) to the house of Abd el Kader, Feisal's agent, a well-informed, efficient, quiet and dignified person, with whom I had had correspondence when he had been first post-master in Mecca, and we of the Survey in Egypt had been busy making stamps for the new Arab state. He had only just been transferred here, since Feisal had now need of the townsmen, and Mohammed Ali, the Sherif and Emir of the Juheina was none too certain an influence among them.

With Abd el Kader, in his picturesque rambling house looking over the deserted square whence so many Medina caravans had started, I stayed four days; waiting for the ship which it seemed might fail me at the rendezvous. However at last, on the first of November, the Suva appeared, with Captain Boyle on board, and he took me back to Jidda It was my first meeting with Boyle, who had done so much for the beginning of the Arab revolt, and who was to do so much more in the future: but it was not a good first impression which I made. I was travel-stained, and had no baggage with me, and on my head was a native head cloth, which I had put on as a precaution, and as a compliment to the Arabs. Our persistence in the hat (due to a misunderstanding of the ways of heatstroke) had led the East to believe that there was something significant in it, and after long thought their wisest brains concluded that Christians wore the hideous thing in order that its broad brim might interpose between their weak eyes and the uncongenial sight of God. So it reminded them continually how God was miscalled and disliked by Christians. The British thought this offense foolish and reprehensible (quite different in spirit to our dislike of a head cloth), one to be corrected at any price. If the Arabs would not have us hated they should not have us any way: for to wear anything native was not quite 'white'. Unfortunately I had been well educated in Syria before the war, and could wear the entire

Arab outfit when necessary without strangeness, and without any sense of degradation. The skirts were a nuisance running upstairs, but the head cloth was convenient, and well-fitted for the Arabian climate. So I had adopted it when I rode inland, and now had to cling to it under fire of British disapproval, till I should find a shop to sell me another cap.

In Jidda was the *Euryalus* with Admiral Wemyss on board, bound for Port Sudan that the Admiral might visit Sir Reginald Wingate at Khartoum. Sir Reginald as Sirdar of the Egyptian Army had been put in command of the British military side of the Arab adventure, in place of Sir Henry McMahon, who continued to direct its politics: and it was necessary for me to see him, to impart my impressions to him. So I begged the Admiral for a passage over sea, and a place in his train to Khartoum. This he readily granted, after hearing my story, for he, with his active mind and broad intelligence, had taken the greatest interest in the Arab Revolt from the beginning. He had come down again and again in his flagship to lend a hand when things were critical, and had gone out of his way twenty times to help them on shore, where properly it was the Army sphere. He had given the Arabs guns and machine-guns, and landing parties, and technical help, and unlimited transport, and naval co-operation, always making a pleasure of our requests, and fulfilling them in overflowing measure. Had it not been for his good will, and the admirable way in which Captain Boyle gave effect to it, the jealousy of Sir Archibald Murray would have wrecked the rebellion at its start. As it was, Sir Rosslyn Wemyss acted godfather till the Arabs were on their own feet; then he went to London; and Allenby, coming out fresh to Egypt, found the Arabs a factor on his battle front, and put the energies and resources of the Army at their disposal. This was fortunate, for Admiral Wemyss' successor in the naval command in Egypt did all he could to be obstructive to the other services, trying to treat them as ill as he did his own.

In Port Sudan we met two British officers of the Egyptian Amy, waiting to embark for Rabegh. They were to take over command of the Egyptian troops in the Hejaz, and do their best to help Aziz el Masri organize the Arab Regular Force which was going to end the war from Rabegh. This was my first meeting with the two men to whom the Arab cause owed the greater part of its foreign debt of gratitude, for their military success.

In Khartoum I showed Sir Reginald Wigate and Colonel Symes my long reports written in those days of waiting at Yenbo and urged them about matters of equipment and organization I thought lacking in Feisal's army. I said that the situation seemed full of promise. The main need was skilled assistance and all should go prosperously if some regular British officers, professionally competent, and speaking Arabic, were attached to the Arab leaders as technical advisers. Sir Reginald was very keen to do all he could. The Arab Revolt had been his dream for years, and was a policy to which his brain and heart were equally devoted. While I was at Khartoum chance gave him the power to play the only part in it: for the workings against Sir Henry McMahon came to their head, were successful, and obtained his recall to England. Sir Reginald Wingate was ordered down to Egypt in his stead. So when after three or four cool and comfortable days in Khartoum, resting and reading the *Mode D'Arthur* in his hospitable palace, I went down towards Cairo, I felt that the responsible person was in full knowledge of what I had to say.

Egypt was as usual in the throes of a Rabegh question. Some airplanes were being sent down there, and it was a matter whether to send a brigade of troops after them or not. Colonel Bremond, the head of the French Military Mission at Jidda, Colonel Wilson's counterpart, but with more authority for he was a light in native warfare, a practicing success in French Africa, and an ex-chief of staff of a Corps on the Somme, was urging strongly the landing of Allied forces in the Hejaz. To tempt us he had brought to Suez some artillery, some machine-guns, and some cavalry and infantry, all Algerian Muslim rank and file with French officers. These were to be added to the British troops for the Hejaz, and would give the force an international flavor.

My experience of Arab feeling in the Harb country had given me strong opinions on the Rabegh question (indeed most of my opinions were strong) and so I wrote for General Clayton, the chief of the Arab Bureau to which I was now formally transferred, a violent memorandum on the whole subject. Clayton was pleased with my view that the tribes could defend Rabegh perfectly well for months if lent advice and guns, but that they would certainly scatter to their tents again as soon as they heard of the landing of foreigners in force. I further said that the plans were tactically unsound, for the brigade proposed would be quite insufficient to defend the position, to forbid the neighboring water-supplies to the Turks, or to block their road towards Mecca. I accused Colonel Bremond of urging the scheme for motives of his own, not military, not taking account of Arab interests, nor of the success of the revolt, and quoted his words and acts in Hejaz as evidence against him.

Clayton took the memorandum to Sir Archibald Murray, who laid its acidity and force so much that he promptly wired it all home to London, to show how the Arab authorities asking this preposterous sacrifice from him were divided about its wisdom and honesty, even in their own camp. London asked for explanations, and the atmosphere slowly cleared, though in a less acute form the Rabegh question lingered on for two months more. Bremond's motives for urging it became stronger as time passed, and his specious appreciation of the danger of the existing state of affairs made a real dupe of Sir Reginald Wingate, who was constitutionally inclined to his remedy. He was a British general, commander of a nominal expeditionary force, the Hejaz Force, which in reality comprised a few liaison officers and a handful of store men and instructors. If Bremond got his way he would be G.O.C. of a genuine brigade of mixed British and French troops, with all its pleasant machinery of responsibility and dispatches.

My popularity with the staff in Egypt, due to the sudden help I had lent to Sir Archibald's prejudices, was novel and rather amusing. They began to be polite to me, and to say that I was observant, with a pungent style, and character. They pointed out how good of them it was to spare me to help the Arab cause in its difficulties. I was sent for by the Commander-in-Chief, and on my way to him was intercepted by a waiting and agitated aide, and led first into the presence of the Chief of Staff, General Lynden Bell. To such an extent had he felt it his duty to support Sir Archibald in his whimsies that we had confounded the two as one enemy. So I was astonished when as I came in he jumped to his feet, leaped forward, and gripped me by the shoulder hissing, 'now you're not to frighten him: don't forget what I say!' My face probably showed its bewilderment, for his one eye turned bland and friendly, and he made me sit down, and talked nicely about Word, and what fun undergraduates had, and the interest of my report of life in Feisal's ranks, and his hope that I would go back there to carry on what I had so well begun: and mixed in with his kindness were remarks on the frayed nerves of the Commander-in-Chief, and his worry about everything, and the need there was for me to give him a reassuring picture of affairs, and yet not too rosy a picture, since they could not afford excursions either way.

I was hugely amused, inwardly, and promised to be good, but pointed out how my object was to secure the extra stores and arms and officers the Arabs needed and how for this end I must enlist the interest, and if necessary (for I would stick at nothing in the way of duty) even the excitement of the Commander-in-Chief: — but General Lynden Bell at once took me up, saying that supplies were his part, and in them he did everything without reference and he thought he might at once, here and now, admit his new determination to do for us all he could. I must say injustice that I think he kept his word and was fair to us thereafter. I was very soothing to his chief.

BOOK II

Opening the Arab Offensive

My chief was astonished at my favorable news. But promised help, and meanwhile had me bare, a lot against my defeat to Arabia.

I reached Feisal's camp on the day the Turks earned the Defenses of Jebel Subh. By them doing so the entire basis of my old confidence was destroyed.

We haven't been near Yenbo for a while, hoping to return the position: but the tribesmen proved useless failed the assault and we saw that we must at once find a new plan of campaign.

This was hazardous, as the promised military experts had not yet arrived. However, we

Decided that to regain the initiative we must ignore the main body of the enemy and concentrate on his Railway flank.

The first step towards this was to move our base to Wejh: and we proceeded to do this in the grand manner.

Chapter 19: Yenbo

A few days later Clayton told me to return to Arabia. They had decided to make me continue the work begun with Feisal. This was much against my grain and I urged my complete unfitness for the job: how I hated responsibility and how obviously the position of any conscientious adviser would be a responsible one: how in all my life objects had been more grateful to me than persons, and ideas than objects, which made the duty of succeeding with men, of disposing them to any purpose, doubly hard to me. They were not my medium: it was not my practiced technique. I was unlike a soldier, hated soldiering. Of course I had read the usual books, too many books, Clausewitz and jomini, Mahan and Foch, and had played with Napoleon's campaigns, worked at Hannibal's tactics, and followed the wars of Belisarius, like any other man at Oxford: but I had never thought myself into the mind of a real commander compelled to fight a campaign of this own.

All this I told to Clayton, and reminded him that the Sirdar had telegraphed to London for certain regular officers competent to direct the Arab war: but he replied that they might be months arriving, and meanwhile Feisal must be linked to us, and his needs promptly notified to Egypt. So I had to go, leaving the *Arab Bulletin* to others which I had founded, and the maps I wished to draw, and the file of the war changes of the Turkish Army, all fascinating book-activities, for which I was fully qualified: and instead took up a role which I could only half-fill at the best. The credit I gained in it was due to the fortunate chance that there was no artist among the enemy: singularly barren was this Arabian war of men greater than practitioners.

My journey was to Yenbo, now the special base of Feisal's army, where Garland single-handed was teaching the Sherifians how to blow up railways with dynamite, and how to keep army stores in systematic order. The first activity was the better.

Garland was an enquirer in physics, with years of practical knowledge of explosives. He had his own devices for mining trains and felling telegraphs and cutting metals and his knowledge of Arabic and freedom from the theories of the ordinary sapper school enabled him to teach the art of demolition to unlettered Bedouin in a quick and ready way.

Incidentally he taught me to be familiar with high explosive. Sappers handled it like a sacrament; but Garland would shove a fistful of detonators into his pocket, with a string of primers, fuse and fuses, and jump gaily on to his camel for a week's ride to the Hejaz Railway. His health was poor, and the climate made him regularly ill. His heart was weak, and troubled him after any effort or crisis: but he treated these risks as freely as he did detonators, and persisted till he had derailed the first train and broken the first culvert in Arabia.

When I landed I found that things in Hejaz had changed a good deal in the elapsed month. Pursuing his former plan Feisal had moved to Kheif Hussein in Wadi Yenbo and was trying to make safe his rear before going up to Bowat and Bir Nasif to attack the railway in the grand manner. To set him free of the duty of controlling the Harb, his young half brother Zeid was on his way up from Rabegh. Zeid would take over Wadi Safra, and place himself in Hamra or Bir Said, as a subordinate of Sherif Ali. The Harb clans were working well. Those about Bir Denvish and El Sheriufi were active in harrying the Turkish communications between Medina and Bir Abbas. They sent in nearly every day to Feisal a little convoy of captured camels, or rifles picked up after an engagement, or prisoners or deserters. We paid for the other things, but liked the deserters best, for those of Arab blood always joined the Arab army.

The Rabegh force had been shaken by the first appearance of Turkish airplanes over Bir ibn Hassani on the seventh of November, but reassured by the arrival at Rabegh of a flight of British airplanes, B.E.2C. Machines, under Major Ross, an officer who spoke Arabic so well and was so splendid as a pilot that there could be no two minds that have same efficiency than his help. New guns came in nearly every week, till there were twenty-three, of fourteen patterns, mostly obsolete. Ali had about three thousand Arab infantry (two thousand of them regulars in khaki under Aziz el Masri, and the rest irregulars), nine hundred camel corps, and about three hundred Egyptian Army troops. Some French gunners were promised. Sherif Abdulla had at last left Mecca on November the twelfth, and a fortnight later was much where he had meant to be, south, east, and north-east of Medina able to cut off the supplies that trickled in to it from Kasim and Kuwait. Our people in the Persian Gulf had been slow to understand that their ports were really ports of Damascus and Medina, and that their cotton and paraffin, sugar and rice were crossing the desert to the enemy. Abdulla had about four thousand men with him but only three machine-guns, and ten inefficient little guns captured at Taif and Mecca. Consequently he was not strong enough to carry out his further plan of an attack on Medina in conjunction with Ali and Feisal. He could only blockade it, and for this purpose posted himself at Henakiyeh eighty miles north-east of Medina, in Heteym country. There he was too far away to be very useful.

The matter of the stores in the Yenbo base was being well handled. Garland had left the checking and issuing of them to Abd el Kader, Feisal's governor, who was systematic and quick. His excellence was a great comfort to us, since it enabled us to keep our attention on more active things. Feisal was organizing his peasants, his slaves, and his paupers into formal battalions, an irregular imitation of the new model army of Aziz at Rabegh. He envisaged eight battalions, each six hundred strong, with a leading Sherif in command, with a lesser Sherif over every hundred men, and non-commissioned officers for sections of twenty. He hoped they would be dependable collections of undrilled guerrillas. Garland held bombing classes, and fired guns, and repaired machine-guns and harness and made the armors for them all. We were busy and confident.

Feisal had not yet acted on our remarks as to the importance of Wejh, but was imagining an expedition of Juheina to take it. Meanwhile he was in touch with the Billi, the numerous tribes whose headquarters lay in Wejh, and hoped for support from them. Their paramount sheikh Suleiman Rifada was temporizing, or rather hostile, for the Turks had made him Pasha and decorated him: but his cousin Hamid was in arms for the Sherif and had just captured a gratifying little caravan of seventy camels on the way from el Ula with stores for the Turkish garrison of Wejh. As I was starting for Kheif Hussein to press the Wejh plan again on Feisal, news came in of a Turkish repulse near Bir ibn Hassani. A reconnaissance of their cavalry and camel corps had been pushed too far into the hills, and the Arabs had caught it and scattered it. Better and better.

Chapter 20: Nakhl Mubarak — Bad News

So I made a happy start with my sponsor for the journey, Sherif Abd el Kerim el Beidawi, half-brother of Mohammed, Emir of the Juheina but to my astonishment of pure Abyssinian type. They told me later that his mother had been a slave girl married by the old Emir when late in life. Abd el Kerim was of middle height and thin, coal-black but debonair, about twenty-six years old, but young-looking, with only a tiny tuft of beard on his sharp chin. He was restless and active, endowed with an easy salacious humor. He hated the Turks who had despised him for his color (Arabs had little color-feeling against Africans: it was the Indian who evoked their race-dislike) and was very merry and intimate with me. With him were three or four of his men, all well-mounted, and we had a rapid journey, for Abd el Kerim was a famous rider who took pride in covering his stages at three times the normal speed. It was not my camel, and the weather was cool and clouded with a taste of rain in the air. So I had no objection.

After starting we cantered for three unbroken hours. That had shaken down our bellies enough for us to hold more food, and so we stopped and ate bread and drank coffee till sunset, while Abd El Kerim rolled about his carpet in a dog-fight with one of his men. When he was exhausted he sat up, and they told stories and japed till they gained enough of their breath back to get up and dance. Everything was very free, very good-tempered, and not at all dignified. They pleaded with me for a show of boxing, with a little slave as victim, and then wanted to teach me to wrestle.

When we restarted, an hour's mad race in the dusk brought us to the end of the Tehama, and to the foot of a low range of hills, rock and sand, cutting off the coastal plain from Wadi Yenbo. A month ago coming from Hamra, we had passed through its south: now we crossed it, going up Wadi Agida, a narrow winding sandy valley between the hills. It had run in flood a few days earlier, and the soil was firm for our panting camels, but the ascent was steep and we had to take it at a foot's pace. This pleased me, but angered Abd el Kerim, and when in a short hour we had reached the watershed he thrust his mount forward again and we dashed at break-neck speed downhill in the black night (a fair road, fortunately, with sand and pebbles underfoot) for half an hour, when the land flattened out and we came to the outlying plantations of Nakhl Mubarak, the chief date-gardens of the southern Juheina.

As we got near we saw through the palm trees flame, and the flame-lit smoke of many fires, and the hollow ground re-echoed with the roaring of thousands of camels, volleys of shots, and the shouting of men lost in the darkness and looking through the crowd for their friends. In Yenbo we had heard that the Nakhl were deserted, so this tumult meant something strange, perhaps hostile. We crept quietly past an end of the grove and along a narrow street between man-high mud walls, to a silent group of houses. Abd el Kerim forced the courtyard door of the first on our left, led the camels within, and hobbled them down by the walls that they might remain unseen. Then he slipped a cartridge into the breach of his rifle, and stole off on tiptoe down the street towards the noise to find out what was happening. We waited for him, the sweat of the ride slowly drying in our clothes as we sat there in the chill night, watching.

He came back after half an hour to say that Feisal with his camel corps had just arrived from Sueig near Kheif Hussein, and we were to go down and join him at once. So we led the camels out and mounted, and rode in file down another lane on the top of a bank between houses, with a sunk garden of palms on our right

Its end was filled with a solid crowd of Arabs and camels, mixed together in the wildest confusion, and all crying aloud. We pressed through them, and down a ramp suddenly into the bed of Wadi Yenbo, as it ran between the palm-groves of the villages on this side, and the hills dividing it from Wadi Safra on the other.

It was a broad, open space; how broad could only be guessed from the irregular lines of watch-fires glimmering over it to a great distance. Also it was very damp, with slime — the relic of a shallow flood which had passed two days before — yet, in places, covering its stones. Our camels found it slippery going and began to move timidly.

We had no opportunity to notice this just now, or indeed anything, except the mass of Feisal's army, filling the valley from side to side. There were hundreds of fires of thorn-wood burning, and round them were Arabs making coffee or eating, or sleeping muffed like dead men in their cloaks, packed together as closely as they could in the confusion of camels. I had never imagined so many camels together, and the mess was indescribable, as they were couched or tied up here and there along the camping ground, and more were ever coming in, and the old ones leaping up on three legs to join them, roaring with hunger and agitation. Patrols were going out, and caravans being unloaded, and some dozens of Egyptian mules bucking angrily over the middle of the scene.

We ploughed our way through this entire din, and in an island of calm in the very center of the valley-bed found Sherif Feisal, and halted our camels by his side. His carpet was spread over the stones, and on it he was sitting between Sherif Sharraf, Kaimmakam of the Imaret and of Taif his cousin, and Maulud, the rugged slashing old Mesopotamian patriot, now acting as his AD.C. In front of him knelt a secretary taking down an order, and beyond him another reading reports aloud by the light of a silvered lamp which a slave was holding. The night was quite windless, the air heavy, and the unglazed flame burnt up straight and firm.

Feisal was as quiet as ever, and welcomed me with a smile while he finished his dictation. Then he apologized for my disorderly reception, and waved the slaves back to give us privacy. As soon as they had retired with the onlookers a wild camel leaped into the open space in front of us, plunging and trumpeting. Maulud dashed at its head to drag it away, but it dragged him instead, and the load of grass ropes for camel fodder came untied, and poured down over the taciturn Sharraf, the lamp and me in an overwhelming avalanche of hay. 'God be praised,' said Feisal gravely, 'that it was neither butter nor bags of gold', and then he explained to me what had happened.

The Turks had slipped round the head of the Arab barrier forces in Wadi Safra by a side-road in the hills, and had cut their retreat. The Harb in a panic had melted into the ravines on each side, and scaled them in parties of twos and threes, anxious for their threatened families. The Turkish infantry had poured down the empty valley, into Hamra and into Wasta, and had immediately sent some camel corps and mounted infantry over the Dhifran pass to Bir Said, where Ghalib Bey their commander nearly caught the unsuspecting Zeid asleep in his tent. However, warning had just been given and, with the help of Sherif Abdulla ibn Thawab, an old Harith campaigner, Zeid had delayed the enemy attack long enough to get some of his tents and baggage packed on camels and driven away. Then he had escaped himself, but his force which was to cover the Subh hills and Wadi Safra and the Sultani road had melted into a loose mob of fugitives, riding wildly through the night towards Yenbo.

Thereby the road to Yenbo was laid absolutely open to the Turks, and Feisal had rushed down here only an hour ago with five thousand men to protect his base until something properly defensive could be arranged. His spy system was breaking down, since the Harb had lost their wits in the darkness and were bringing in wild and contradictory reports from one side and another about the strength of the Turks and their movements and intention. He had no idea if they would strike straight at Yenbo, or be content with holding the two passes from Wadi Yenbo into Wadi Safra while they threw the bulk of their forces down the coast towards Rabegh and Mecca. The situation would be serious either way: the best that could happen would be if Feisal's presence here attracted them, and caused them to lose more days trying to catch his field army while we strengthened Yenbo. Meanwhile he was doing all he could, quite cheerfully, and I sat down beside him and listened to the news, and the petitions and complaints and difficulties being brought in and settled by him summarily.

This lasted till half-past four in the morning. It got very cold, and the damp of the valley rose up through the carpet, and soaked our clothes, and a white mist collected softly over the whole camp which gradually stilled as the tired men and animals all went one by one to sleep and the fires became slow pillars of smoke. Immediately behind us, rising out of the bed of mist was the southern end of Jebel Rudhwa, more steep and rugged than ever, and brought quite close by the moonlight so that it seemed hanging over our heads. Feisal at last finished the urgent work. We ate half a dozen dates and then curled up on the wet carpet underneath us. As I lay there shivering I saw the Biasha guards creep up and spread their cloaks gently over

Feisal as soon as they were sure he was sleeping. An hour later we got up stiffly in the false dawn (it was too cold for us to go on pretending and lying down) and the slaves lit a fire of palm-ribs to warm us, while Sharraf and me searched for enough food and fuel for the moment. Messengers were still coming in from all sides with evil rumors of an immediate attack, and the camp was not far off panic. So Feisal decided to move to another position, partly because we would be washed out of this one if it rained anywhere in the hills, and partly to occupy men's minds and soothe their restlessness.

When his drum began to beat camels were loaded instantly, and at the second signal everyone leaped into the saddle and drew off to left or right, leaving a broad lane up which he rode. He was on his mare, with Sharraf a pace behind him, and then Ali the standard bearer, a splendid wild man from Nejd, with his hawk's face framed in the long plaits of black hair falling downward from his temples. Ali was dressed garishly, and rode a tall camel. Behind him were all the mob of Sherifs, sheikhs and slaves and myself. There were eight hundred in the bodyguard that morning.

Feisal rode up and down looking for a place to camp, and at last stopped on the further side of a little open valley, the road to Yenbo, which ran down into the main valley just north of Nakhl Mubarak village: though the houses were so buried in the trees that few of them could be seen from outside. On the south bank of this valley were some rocky knolls and beneath them Feisal pitched his two tents. Sharraf had his tent also and some of the other chiefs came and lived by us. The guard put up their booths and shelters and the Egyptian gunners halted lower down on our side and dressed their twenty tents beautifully in line, to look very military. So in a little while we were populous.

I had written to Yenbo a telegram for Rabegh asking them to send a machine over to make an air reconnaissance of Wadi Safra and Bir Said to gain certain news of the enemy. Garland was making an aerodrome at Yenho for their landing, and I decided to have an emergency one here also in case of accident. So we set the Egyptians to clear a large space in the bottom of the valley where there was room to land. They tore up clumps of bushes and small trees, and burned others which were too tough to pull out. There was just one tree which troubled us. It was too big to burn, and we had no dynamite to blast it. We began to dig it out but found this too difficult with the tools we had: and in the end Tewfik Bey, who had succeeded Zeki in the command of the battery, brought up a mountain gun and blew it up by the roots, first shot, with a zero shell.

Chapter 21: Cavil Routine

We stayed here two days, most of which I spent in Feisal's company, and so got a deeper experience of his method of command at an interesting season when the morale of his men was suffering heavily from the scare reports brought in, and from the defection of the northern Harb. Feisal was fighting these two days to make up their lost spirits, and he did it by lending of his own to everyone within reach. He was accessible to all who stood outside his tent and waited for notice, and never cut short petitions, even when they came in chorus with their grief in a song of many verses which they sang around us in the dark. He listened to every case, and if he did not settle it himself, called for Sharraf or Faiz to arrange it for him. This extreme patience was a lesson to me of what headship in Arabia meant.

His self-control seemed equally great. When Mirzuk el Tikheimi, his guest-master, came in from Zeid to explain the shameful story of their rout, Feisal in public just laughed at him and sent him aside to wait, while he saw the sheikhs of the Harb and Ageyl whose carelessness had been mainly responsible for the disaster. These he rallied gently, chaffing them for having done this or that, for having inflicted such losses, or lost so much. Then he called back Mirzuk and lowered the tent-flap, a sign that there was private business to be done. I thought of the meaning of Feisal's name, the sword flashing downward in the stroke, and feared a scene, but he made room for Mirzuk on his carpet, and said, 'Come, tell us more of your knights and marvels of the battle: amuse us.' Mirzuk, a very good-looking clever lad, a little too sharp-featured, falling into the spirit of the thing, began in his broad Ateibi twang to draw us word-pictures of Zeid in flight, of the terror of ibn Thawab and, the ultimate disgrace, of how Sherif el Hussein the Harithi lost his coffee-pots!

Feisal in speaking had a rich musical voice, and used it carefully upon his men. To them he talked in the ordinary tribal dialect but with a curious, hesitant, broken manner as though faltering painfully among phrases, looking inward to his mind for the just word. His thought perhaps moved only by a little in front of his speech, for the phrases at last chosen were usually the simplest, which gave him an effect emotional and sincere. It seemed possible, so thin was the screen of words, to see the pure and very brave spirit shining out.

At other times he was full of humor, that invariable magnet of Arab goodwill. He spoke one night to the Rifaa sheikhs, when he sent them forward to occupy the plain this side of Bir el Fagir, a tangled country of Acacia and Tamarisk thickets on the imperceptible watershed of the long depression uniting Bruka and Bir Said. He told them gently that the Turks were coming on, and that it was their duty to hold them up and give God the credit of their victory: adding that this would become impossible if they went to sleep. The older men, and in Arabia elders matter more than youths, broke out into delighted speech, and after saying that God would give him a victory, and then two victories, prayed that his life might be prolonged for him to accumulate an unprecedented number of victories. What was better, they kept an excellent watch all night, fortified by his example, as were all others who came into direct contact with him. After the first day of this I took heart, believing that in a little while the spirit of the infantry would be good enough to work with. The Juheina camel-riders were less firm: and neither were anything like so cheerful as the Harb and Juheina had been in Hamra the month before.

The routine of our life here in camp was simple. Just before daybreak the army Imam used to climb to the head of the little hill above the sleeping army, and thence utter an astounding call to prayer. His voice was harsh and very powerful, and the hollow acted as a sounding-board, and threw echoes of his call over all the valleys. We were effectually roused, whether we prayed or not, and the most cursed him instead. As soon as he ended, Feisal's own Imam used to cry gently and musically from just outside the tent. A few minutes later one of Feisal's five slaves (all freed men but refusing discharge till it was their pleasure: since it was good and not unprofitable to be my lord's servant) came round to Sharraf and me with a cup of sweetened coffee for each of us. Sugar for the first cup in the chill of dawn was considered fit.

An hour or so later, the gap of Feisal's sleeping tent would be thrown back, an invitation for us to go and call on him. There would be four or five present, and after the morning's news a tray of breakfast would be carried in the staple of this in Wadi Yenbo was dates, but some-times his Circassian grandmother would send him a box of her famous spiced cakes from Mecca, and sometimes Hejris, the body-slave, would give us odd biscuits and cereals of his own trying. After breakfast we would play with bitter coffee and sweet tea in alternation, while Feisal's correspondence was dealt with by dictation to his secretaries. One of these was Faiz el Ghusein, the adventurous, and another the Imam, a sad-faced person conspicuous in the army for the baggy umbrella hanging from his saddle-bow. Occasionally a leading man was given a private audience at this hour but very seldom, for the sleeping tent was kept strictly for the Sherifs own use. It was an ordinary bell tent furnished with a box of cigarettes, a camp bed, a fairly good Kurd rug, a poor Shirazi, and the delightful old Baluch prayer carpet on which he prayed.

At about eight o'clock in the morning Feisal would buckle on his ceremonial dagger and walk across to the reception tent, which was lined with two horrible kilims. We walked after him, and the slaves brought up the rear, and clustered round the open wall of the tent to control the besetting suppliants. Feisal would sit down at the end of the tent facing the open side, and we with our backs against the wall, in a semi circle out from him. The callers lay on the sand in the tent's mouth, or in circles beyond, waiting their turn to come up.

If one was urgent he spoke in a slave's ear, and the slave would ask Sharra for another, who would hand it on to the Emir if he thought fit. Few cases were referred back: none postponed. If possible all business was got through by noon when the Emir liked to rise.

We of the household and any guests then reassembled in the living tent, and Hejris and Salem carried in the luncheon tray, on which were as many dishes as their circumstances permitted. Feisal was an inordinate smoker, but a very light eater, and he used to make believe with his fingers or a spoon among the beans and lentils, rice, spinach and sweet cakes till he judged that we had had enough: and then he would wave his hand and the tray would disappear, while the slaves came to pour water for our fingers at the tent door. Fat men like Mohammed ibn Shefia made a comic grievance of the Emir's quick and delicate meals, and would have food of their own prepared for them when they came away from his dish. After lunch we would talk a little, while snuffing up two cups of coffee, and savoring two glasses full of syrup-like green tea. Then till two in the afternoon the curtain of the living tent was down, sign that meant Feisal was sleeping or reading or doing private business. Afterwards he would sit again in the reception tent till he had finished with all who wanted him. I never saw an Arab leave him dissatisfied or hurt, a tribute to his tact and memory, for he seemed never to halt at a fact nor stumble over a relationship.

If there was time after second audience he would walk with his friends, talking of horses or plants, looking at camels, or asking someone the names of the land-features about him. The sunset prayer was at times public, though Feisal was not outwardly very pious. After it he saw people individually in the living tent, planning the night's reconnaissance and patrols, for most of the fieldwork was done after dark, and for months the enemy had never been more than a few miles away. Between six and seven o'clock they brought in the evening meal to which all present in headquarters were called by the slaves. It resembled the lunch except that many cubes of boiled mutton were sorted through the great tray of rice.

This meal ended our day except for the silent entry of a bare footed slave with a tray of tea-glasses at intervals till bed-time. Feisal did not sleep till very late, and never showed any wish to hasten our going. In the evening he relaxed so far as possible and avoided avoidable work. He would send out for some local sheikh to tell stories of the district and histories of the tribe and its genealogy: or the tribal poets would sing us their war narratives long, traditional forms with stock epithets, stock sentiments, stock incidents grafted afresh on the efforts of each generation. Feisal was passionately fond of Arabic poetry and would often provoke recitations before him, judging and rewarding the best verses of the night. Very rarely he would play chess with the swift unthinking directness of a fencer, but brilliantly well. Sometimes, perhaps for my benefit, he told stories of what he saw in Syria, of Turkish secret history, of family affairs. I learned much of the men and parties in the Hejaz from his own lips.

Chapter 22: Defeat in Wadi Yenbo

On this day Feisal asked me if I would wear Arab clothes like his own while in the camp. I would find it better for my own part since it was a comfortable dress in which to live Arab fashion as we must do besides the tribesmen would then understand how to take me. The only wearers of khaki in their experience had been Turkish officers before whom they took up an attitude of instinctive defense. If I wore Meccan clothes like him or like Sharraf they would behave to me as though I was really one of the leaders and I would be able to slip in and out of his tent without making a sensation which he had to explain away each time to strangers.

I agreed at once very gladly for army uniform was abominable for camel-riding or when sitting about on the ground and the Arab things which I had learned to manage before the war, were cleaner and more decent in the desert. Hejris was pleased too, and exercised his fancy in fitting me out in splendid white silk and gold-embroidered wedding garments which had been sent to Feisal lately (was it a hint?) by his great-aunt in Mecca. I took a stroll in the new looseness of them round the palm-gardens of Mubarak and Bruka, to get used to their feel.

These villages were pleasant little places, all built of mud brick on the high earth mounds encircling the palm-gardens. Nakhl Mubarak lay to the north and Bruka just south of it across a thorny valley. The houses were small mud-washed inside cool and very clean furnished with a mat or two a coffee mortar and food pots and trays. The narrow streets were shaded by an occasional well-grown tree. In the two villages there might have been five hundred houses, though they were scattered and hidden away beyond my power to judge. The earth embankments round the villages were sometimes fifty feet in height for the most part artificially formed from the surplus earth dug out between the trees, from house rubbish and from stones out of the wadi.

The banks were to defend the cultivated area from the floods of Wadi Yenbo, which otherwise would quickly fill the gardens since they to be irrigable, had to be below the level of the valley floor. The narrow plots were divided by fences of palm-ribs or by mud walls, with narrow streams of sweet water flowing in high-level channels round them. Each garden gate was over water, with a bridge to it of three or four parallel palm-logs built up for the passage of donkeys or camels. Each plot had its mud sluice, scooped away when its turn for watering came. The palms, very regularly planted in ordered lines and well cared for, were the main crop; but between the boles were grown barley, radishes, marrows, cucumbers, tobacco and henna. Villages higher up Wadi Yenbo were cool enough to grow grapes.

The views from the little knolls behind our camp were very fine. Rudhwa lay to the north of us, looking about fifteen miles away, with one part or other of it continually wrapped in rain-clouds. It was the biggest feature in sight, and dominated Wadi Yenbo which was a broad scrub-covered plain, relieved by occasional trees and by odd-colored and odd-shaped rocks projecting from its bed at intervals. All the villages in the main bed were on its northern side and their water came out in strongly-running springs, a foot or so below the gravel surface of the valley. The sources had been enclosed in narrow stone-lined channels and led underground from place to place as far as they would carry. The Nakhl Mubarak springs were the last running water in Wadi Yenbo before it reached the sea.

Above Nakhl Mubarak the valley drew in a little, till it seemed less than two miles wide. It ran northeast for some distance to a fork, where the Bugaa branch went off southward from the main stream. Bugaa was half Harb and half Juheina: the villages beyond it, Nijeil and Madsus, with Ain Ali and Shaatha were wholly Harb, like Bir Said. Beyond the fork the country appeared to rise rapidly, and to get mountainous. Buwat itself was said to be on the watershed between Wadi Hamdh and Wadi Yenbo, only twelve miles from the railway.

After the landing ground was finished I felt that I had better get back to Yenbo, to think seriously about an amphibious defense of its port, for Feisal's stand in Nakhl Mubarak could in the nature of things only be a pause. The Navy had promised its every help at Yenbo, and we settled that I should consult Zeid, and act with him as we thought fit. Also by getting back at once I would meet the airplane due next day, and would be able to tell the pilot and observer what I knew of the lie of the country, and where the Turks probably were. In this country of trees and under wood it was seldom that an air reconnaissance yielded an exhaustive report. The hills kept our old machines very high in the air, and the enemy, when not in formed units, had unlimited cover beneath which to remain unseen.

Feisal gave me a magnificent bay camel to take me back, and we marched through the Agida hills by a new road, Wadi Messarih, because of a scare of Turkish patrols on the more direct line. Bedr ibn Shefia was with me, and we did the distance gently in a single stage of six hours, getting to Yenbo before dawn. I was tired after being about for three strenuous days, with little sleep, and with constant alarms and excitements: so I went straight to Garland's empty house (he was living on board ship in the harbor) and fell asleep on a bench: but after a short spell was called out again by the news that Sherif Zeid was coming, and went down to the walls to see the beaten force ride in.

There were about eight hundred of them, quiet but in no other way mortified by their shame. Zeid himself seemed finely indifferent. As he entered the town he turned and cried to Abd el Kader the governor, riding behind him, 'Why, your town is ruinous, I must telegraph to my father for forty masons to repair the public buildings' — and this actually he did. I had telegraphed to Captain Boyle that Yenbo was gravely threatened, and he at once replied that naval help would be there in time.

It was a consolation, very needful, for worse news came next day. The Turks had thrown a strong force forward from Bir Said against Nakhl Mubarak and had caught Feisal's levies while they were yet unsteady. There had been a short fight, and Feisal had broken off, and was retreating here. Things were very serious, and I took my camera and from the parapet of the Medina gate got a fine photograph of the brothers coming in. Feisal had nearly two thousand men with him, but none of the Juheina tribesmen. I looked like treachery and a real defection of the tribes, things which both of us had ruled out of court.

I called at once at his house, and he told me the story. The Turks came forward with three battalions, and a number of mille-mounted infantry, and camels. Their command was in the hands of Ghalib Bey, who handled his troops with great keenness, acting as he did under the eye of the Corps Commander, Fakhri Pasha, who accompanied the expedition. Their chief guide and go-between with the Arabs was Dakhil Allah el Kadhi, the hereditary law-giver of Juheina, a rival of Sherif Mohammed Ali el Beidawi, and after him the second man in the tribe.

They got across Wadi Yenbo into the groves of Bruka in their first onset, and so threatened the Arab communications with Yenbo. They were also able to shell Nakhl Mubarak freely with their seven guns. Feisal was not a whit dismayed but threw out the Juheina on his left to work down the great valley and stand between the enemy and Bir Said. His center and right he kept in Nakhl Mubarak, and he sent the Egyptian artillery to take post in Jebel Agida, to deny that to the Turks. Then he opened fire on Bruka with his own two fifteen ponder guns.

Rasim, a Syrian officer, formerly a battery commander in the Turkish Army, was fighting these two guns, and he made a great demonstration with them. They had been sent down as a gift from Egypt, anyhow, old rubbish thought serviceable for the wild Arabs: just as the sixty thousand rifles supplied the Sherif were condemned weapons, the worn or defective relics of the Gallipoli campaign. So Rasim had no sights or range-finder, no range tables, no high explosive.

His distance might have been six thousand yards, but the fuses of his shrapnel were from the Boer War, full of green mold, and, if they burst, it was sometimes short in the air, and sometimes grazing, as we afterwards realized by experiment in peace at Yenbo, however, he had no means of getting much of his ammunition away if things went wrong, so he blazed off at speed, shouting with laughter at this fashion of making war: and the tribesmen seeing the commandant so merry took heart of grace themselves. 'By God,' said one, Those are the real guns: the importance of their noise!' Rasim said that the Turks were dying in heaps, and they charged forward warmly.

Things were going well, and Feisal had hope of a decisive success when suddenly his left wing in the valley wavered, halted, and finally turned its back on the enemy and retired tumultuously to the camping ground. Feisal was with the center and seeing them coming he galloped back to Rasim, and cried that the Juheina had broken and he was to save the guns. Rasim yoked up the teams, and trotted away to Wadi Agida wherein the Egyptians were taking counsel vapidly with one another. Then he streamed the Ageyl and the Atban, the men of ibn Shefia, the Harb and the Biasha. Feisal and his household composed the rear, and in deliberate procession they moved down towards Yenbo, leaving the Juheina and the Turks on the battlefield.

As I was still hearing of this sad end, and cursing with him the traitor Beidawi brothers, there was a stir about the door, and Abd el Kerim broke through the slaves, swung up to the dais, kissed Feisal's head rope in salutation and sat down beside us. Feisal looked really astonished and said 'Howl', and Abd el Kerim explained their dismay at the sudden flight of Feisal, and how he and his brother and their gallant tribesmen had fought the Turks for the whole night, alone and without artillery, till the palm-groves became untenable and they too had been driven through Wadi Agida.

His brother with half the manhood of the tribe was just entering the gate. The other half had fallen back up Wadi Yenbo, to Kheif Hussein for water. 'And why did you retire to the camping ground behind us during the battle?' asked Feisal. 'Only to make ourselves a cup of coffee: said Abd el Kerim: 'We had fought from sunrise, and it was dusk and we were very tired and thirsty.' Feisal and I lay back and laughed; and then we went out to see what could still be done to save the town.

The first step was simple. We sent all the Juheina back to Wadi Yenbo with orders to mass at Kheif Hussein, and keep up a steady pressure on the Turkish line of communications with Wadi Safra, they were also to push sniping parties down the Agida hills. This diversion would hold up so many of the Turks that they would be unable to bring against Yenbo a force superior in number to the defenders, who in addition had the advantage of a good position. The town lay on the top of a flat reef of coral, rising perhaps twenty feet above the sea, and compassed by water on two sides. The other two sides looked over flat stretches of sand, soft in places, destitute of cover for miles, and with no fresh water upon them anywhere. In daylight if defended by artillery and machine-gun fire, the place should be impregnable.

The artillery was arriving every minute, for Boyle had been better than his word and had concentrated five ships on us in less than twenty-four hours. He put the monitor *M 31,* whose shallow draught made her very fitted for the job, in the end of the southeastern creek of the harbor, whence she could rake the probable direction of a Turkish advance with her six-inch guns: and Crocker her captain, was very anxious to let those guns off again. The larger ships were moored to fire over the town at longer range, or to rake the other flank from the north-eastern end of the harbor. The searchlights of the *Dufferin* and the *M 31* crossed on the plain beyond the town.

To control the shooting according to the map which we had just got ready Boyle landed naval signalers with lamps and telephones. On Feisal's authority they took post in the minaret of the inland mosque, a good observation point. Boyle also lent us machine gunners, and prepared a landing party from the ships. The Arabs were delighted to see the quantity of vessels in the harbor, and prepared to contribute their part to the night's entertainment. They had suffered little hitherto in casualties. They wanted to improve on their late failure and to retake their palm-groves: and Yenbo was a dead end from which they had no retreat. We were in good hope there would be no further panic.

To reassure them fully they needed some sort of rampart to defend, medieval fashion; it was no good digging them trenches, partly because the ground was coral rock, and besides they had no experience of trenches and might not have manned them confidently. So we took the crumbling salt-riddled wall of the place, and doubled it with a second packed earth between the two, and raised them till our sixteenth-century bastions were rifle-proof at least and probably proof against the Turkish mountain guns. Outside the bastions we put barbed wire festooned between the cisterns on the coral plateau beyond the walls. We dug in machine-gun nests in the best angles, and manned them with Feisal's regular gunners. The Egyptians, like everyone else, were given a place in the scheme and all were gratifyingly happy. Garland was engineer in chief and chief adviser.

After nightfall the town hummed with suppressed excitement. So long as daylight lasted there had been shouts and joy shots, and wild bursts of frenzy among the workmen: but when dark came they went back to feed and a hush fell. I think nearly everyone sat up that night. There was one alarm, about eleven pm, and Garland, with a crier, went through the few streets and called the garrison. Every man tumbled straight out and went to his place in dead silence without a shot or a loose shout. The seamen on the minaret sent warning to the ships, whose combined searchlights began slowly to traverse the plain in complex intersections, drawing pencils of wheeling light across the flats which the attacking force must cross. Our outposts had met them only three miles outside the town: but they made no sign, and gave us no cause to open fire.

Afterwards, old Dakhil-Allah told me that he had guided them down to rush Yenbo in the dark and stamp out Feisal's army once and for all: but that their hearts had failed them at the silence, and the blaze of lighted ships end to end of the harbor, and the slow beams of the searchlights revealing the openness of the glacis they would have to cross. So they turned back, and that night, I believe, the Turks lost the war. Personally, I was on the Suva, to be undisturbed and sleeping splendidly at last so I was grateful to Dakhil-Allah for his prudence, since though we might have won a glorious victory I was ready to give much more for just that one night's unbroken rest.

Chapter 23: Recovery

Next day the crisis had passed as the Juheina were active in their flank position up Wadi Yenbo, and Garland's architectural efforts about the town became impressive. The Turks had clearly failed. Sir Archibald Murray, to whom Feisal had appealed for a demonstration in Sinai to prevent further withdrawals of Turks from there for service in Medina, had sent back an encouraging reply, and everybody was breathing easier. A few days later Boyle dispersed the ships, promising another lightning concentration upon another warning, and I took the opportunity to go down to

Rabegh, where I met Colonel Bremond, the great bearded chief of the French Military Mission, and the only real soldier in Hejaz. He was still using his French detachment in Suez as a lever to try to move a British brigade into Rabegh, and as he knew I was not wholly of his party he made an effort now to convert me.

In the course of the argument which followed I said something about the need of soon attacking Medina, for with the rest of the British I believed that the fall of Medina was a necessary preliminary to any further progress of the Arab Revolt. He took me up sharply on the point and said that it was in no wise proper for the Arabs to take Medina. The way he looked at things the Arab Movement had attained its maximum utility by the mere rebellion in Mecca, and military operations against Turkey were better in the unaided hands of Great Britain and France. He wished to land Allied troops at Rabegh because it would quench the ardor of the tribes by making the Sherif suspect in their eyes. The foreign troops would then be his main defense and his preservation would be the issue only of our work: and at the end of the war when Turkey was defeated, the victorious Powers would extract Medina by treaty from the Sultan, and confer it upon Hussein as his reward.

I had not his confidence in our so great strength that we could dispense with small allies and told him shortly that my opinions were opposed to his. I laid the greatest weight on the immediate conquest of Medina and was advising Feisal to move to Wejh, in order to prolong his threat against the railway: and to my mind the Arab Movement would not justify its creation if the enthusiasm of it did not carry the Arabs on their own impulse into Damascus. This was unwelcome to him for the Sykes-Picot Treaty of between France and England had been drawn by Sykes for this very eventuality and stipulated in that condition for the establishment of independent Arab states in Damascus Aleppo and Mosul, districts which would otherwise fall to the unrestricted control of France. Neither Sykes nor Picot had believed that this contingency was really possible: but I knew it was and believed that if it happened the vigor of the Arab Movement would prevent the creation — by us or others — in Western Asia of unduly 'colonial' schemes of imperial exploitation: and I meant to do all in my power to ensure it.

Bremond took refuge in his technical sphere, and assured me on his honor as a staff officer that for Feisal to leave Yenbo for Wejh was military suicide: but I saw no force in the arguments which he threw at me volubly and told him so. It was a curious interview to pass between an old soldier and a young man in fancy dress, and it left a bad taste in my mouth. The individual French were capable sometimes of things heroic, but seldom of the plainly just: and they were incorrigible prose writers, seeing things by the directly-thrown light of reason and understanding, not through the half-closed eye, mistily, by their internal radiance, as was the practice of the imaginative British: so the two races worked ill together on a great work. However, I controlled myself so far as not to tell any Arab of the conversation, but sent a full account of it to Colonel Wilson, who was shortly coming up to see Feisal, to talk the Wejh project over with him.

Before he arrived the center of Turkish gravity changed abruptly. Fakhri Pasha had seen the hopelessness of attacking Yenbo, or of driving after the intangible Juheina in Kheif Hussein. Also he was being violently bombed in Nakhl Mubarak itself by a pair of British seaplanes which did hardy flights over the desert and got well into the enemy on two occasions. They killed and wounded several of the Staff, at an expense to themselves of a float shattered by shrapnel. So Fakhri suddenly decided to fall back on Bir Said, to leave a small force there to check the Juheina, and to move down the Sultani road towards Rabegh with the bulk of his men.

These changes were no doubt partly determined by the unusual vigor of Ali at Rabegh. As soon as he had heard of Zeid's defeat Ali sent him reinforcements and guns, by way of Bedr, and when Feisal himself collapsed he decided to move north with all his army by Bir ibn Hassani to attack the Turks in Wadi Safra and draw them off Yenbo. He had nearly seven thousand men, and Feisal felt that if the move was synchronized with one on his part, Fakhri's force might be crushed between them in the hills. So he wired to Ali, suggesting this, and asking for a delay of a few days till his Juheina and Harb were ready.

Ali however was strung up and would not wait. Feisal none the less decided to co-operate with him, and rushed Zeid out to Masahali in Wadi Yenbo to make preparations. When these were complete he came out himself, and sent Zeid on with the Bisha and Hudheil to rush Bir Said, which they did successfully. He then sent orders to the Juheina to go forward into Wasit, in support of Zeid. They demurred, for ibn Beidawi was jealous of Feisal's growing power among his tribes, and wanted to keep himself indispensable. Feisal left Sharraf in his place, and rode unattended to Nakhl Mubarak. There in one night he convinced the Juheina that he was their leader. Next morning they were all afoot, moving on Hamra, and he went on to collect the northern Harb on the Tasha pass to interrupt the Turkish retreat at Kheif in Wadi Safra,

He had nearly six thousand men, and if he found Ali on the southern bank of the valley they would catch the weak Turks between two fires.

Unfortunately it did not happen. When he was actually on the move he heard from Ali that after a peaceful recovery of Bir ibn Hassani his men had been shaken by false reports of disloyalty among the Subh, and, following the example of Ahmed ibn Mansur, had fallen back rapidly and in disorder to Rabegh. By himself, with a twice-beaten army, Feisal could not risk an assault, so on December the twenty-first the called Zeid and Sharraf back to meet him in Wadi

Yenbo, the united forces camped in Nakhl Mubarak and Bruka for a few days' rest, while the Harb were set on to harrying the Turkish rear on an important scale. In one such effort near Bir Denvish the Rahala took nearly three hundred camels, whose weak mangy condition reassured us as to the Turkish difficulties in maintaining their long lines of supply.

Ali undertook a new effort to counteract the effect of his main failure, sending Sherif Shahad, Emir of Medina before the revolt, with Sherif Fahad up to Mijz, southward of Medina near Bir el Mashi. Their appearance would force the Turks to detach troops from their striking force, in order to defend the southern approaches of Medina, and would fill part of the role for which Abdulla's army had been designed. If only Abdulla had been threatening Medina properly at this time the Turkish expedition against Rabegh would have been prevented; but his men had run short of water and food in their attempted blockade of the town on the east, and he had recalled the bulk of them to his own distant base of Henakiyeh.

In this ominous pause Colonel Wilson came up to Yenbo to persuade Feisal of the necessity of an immediate operation against Wejh. An amended plan had been approved by us all, whereby Feisal would take the whole force of the Juheina, and his permanent battalions, and lead them himself against Wejh with the maximum of naval help. This would make us fairly sure of success, but left Yenbo empty and defenseless behind him, and for the moment he dreaded taking such a risk. He pointed out not unreasonably that the Turks were still mobile in his neighborhood; that Ali's force had proved hollow, unable to rely either on itself or on the Harb; that he had grave doubts whether they would try to defend even Rabegh against serious attack; and that as Rabegh was the bulwark of Mecca, sooner than see it lost he would throw away Yenbo and ferry himself and the Hudtheil and Bisha men thither by sea, to die fighting on the beach.

To reassure him Wilson painted the Rabegh force in warm colors. Feisal checked his sincerity by asking if he would assure him of his personal belief that the Rabegh garrison with British naval help would be able to resist enemy attack till Wejh fell. Wilson looked round the deck of the *Dufferin* (on which we were conferring) for support, and then nobly gave the required assurance, as a wise gamble, since without it Feisal might not move, and his diversion against Wejh was now the only offensive operation in the Arabs' power and the last chance not so much of securing a convincing siege of Medina, as of preventing a Turkish capture of Mecca. He had of course no means of covering his assurance, but a few days later strengthened himself by sending Feisal direct orders from his father the Sherif to proceed to Wejh at once. All this, while the situation in Rabegh grew worse. The enemy in Wadi Safra and the Sultani road were estimated at nearly five thousand men, and in addition the Harb of the north were suppliant to them for the preservation of their palm-groves. The Harb of the south, those in the hands of Hussein Mabeirig, were notoriously waiting for their advance to attack the Sherifians in the rear. At a conference of Wilson, Bremond, Joyce, Ross and others held at Rabegh on Christmas Eve, it was decided to layout a small position on the beach by the aerodrome, capable of being held under the ships' guns by the Egyptians, the Flying Corps and a seaman's landing party from the *Minerva* for the few hours required to embark or destroy the stores. The Turks were advancing steadily, and expected any day to attack the place, which was not in condition to resist one well-handled battalion supported by artillery.

However, they were too slow. They did not pass Bir el Sheikh in any force till near the end of the first week in January, and seven days later they were still not ready to attack Khoreiba, where Ali had an outpost of a few hundred men. The patrols were in touch, and an assault was daily expected, but as regularly delayed. The truth was that the Turks were meeting with increased difficulties. Their headquarters were faced by a heavy sick-rate among their men, and a growing weakness of their animals, both symptomatic of overwork and lack of decent food. Always the activity of the tribesmen behind their back hampered them. Clans sometimes fell away from the Arab cause, but did not therefore become trustworthy adherents of the Turks, who found themselves operating in consistently hostile country. The raids in the first fortnight of January caused them average losses of forty camels and some twenty men killed and wounded every day.

These raids might occur at any point from ten miles this side of Medina for the next seventy miles through the hills. They illustrated the obstacles in the way of the new Turkish Army with its half Germanized complexity of equipment, when it tried to advance through extremely rugged and hostile country with a distant railhead and no made roads. The administrative developments of scientific war had clogged their mobility and destroyed their dash: and their troubles grew in geometrical rather than arithmetical progression each new mile they put between themselves and Medina.

The situation was so unpromising for the Turks that Fakhri was probably half-glad when the sudden moves of Abdulla and Feisal altered the whole strategic conception of the Hejaz war, and hurried the Mecca expedition back from the Sultani and the Fara and the Gaha roads, back from Wadi Safra, after January the eighteenth onwards, until they held only a passive defense of trenches within sight of the walls of Medina — the static position which endured, till the Armistice which ended the war involved Turkey in the loss of the Holy City.

Chapter 24: Read Justment — New Plans

Feisal was a fine hot workman who did a thing whole-heartedly when he agreed to it. He had pledged his word to Colonel Wilson that he would go off at once to Wejh, so he and I sat down together in the afternoon and considered what this new move meant to us and to the Turks. Around us, stretching up and down Wadi Yenbo for miles, in little groups round the palm-gardens, under the thicker trees, and in all the side tributaries, wherever there was shelter from the sun and rain or good grazing for the camels, were the soldiers of our army. The mountaineers, half-naked footmen, had grown few. Most of the six thousand present were camel-men of substance, and their coffee hearths were outlined from far by their camel saddles, pitched in circles for the reclining men to rest their elbows on when talking round the fire between meals. Their physical perfection let them lie relaxed to the stony ground like lizards, molding themselves to its roughness in corpse-like abandon.

Two days among them passed listening to their judgments upon things, drinking their coffee and satisfying their languid curiosity with my travelers' tales of what lay beyond their sight. They were quiet but confident. Some had been serving Feisal for six months or more, and these had lost their first heat of eagerness which had so thrilled me in Hamra: but they had gained experience in return, and the long life of their idea was richer and more important to us than its fierceness. Their patriotism was now conscious, deeply rooted. They still kept their tribal independence of orders, but were less wasteful of ammunition, and had achieved a mild routine in camp life and on the march. When the Sherif came near they fell into a ragged line, and together made the bow and sweep of the arm to the lips, which was the official salute. They did not oil their guns they said then the sand would clog them, and besides they had no oil, and it was better rubbed in to soften the wind-chaps on their skin — but the guns were better kept, and some of them could shoot.

In short they were becoming coherent units under their sheikhs, and attendance became more regular as their distance from home increased. Further, they were tempered to the new idea of leaving their own tribal boundaries, and Feisal had suggested taking them nearly all to Wejh with him; not that we expected formidable opposition, but because we wanted this march, which would be in its way a closing act of the war in northern Hejaz, to send a rumor through the length and breadth of Western Arabia. It was to be the biggest operation of the Arabs in their memory, and so to impress them that there would be no more of those silly defections and jealousies of clans behind us in the future. It was to be a climax which would dismiss all who saw it to their homes knowing that their world had changed indeed.

At last we determined to raise the whole levy of the Juheina, more than had ever before come together for us, and to add to them enough of the Harb and Billi, Ateiba and Ageyl, to give the mass a tribe character. Feisal's great ability and patience in appeasing feuds and blood disputes among his followers had made this mixing possible for us. For technical units we would rely on the newly organized Arab detachments of gunners and machine gunners. After the battle of Nakhl Mubarak we had decided that it was not efficient to brigade Egyptian Army units with the Arabs, and so had embarked the Egyptian officers and men, and turned over all their material and transport and effects, down to their spare shirts, to Rasim, Feisal's gunner. He had collected some Syrians and Mesopotamians out of our ranks, men who had been soldiers in the Turkish Army, and had deserted to us, or volunteered for us out of the prisoners' camps in India and Egypt. They had the elements of drill in them, and he added to them Meccans, freed men and slaves enough to form a battery. Volunteers on a cash basis were secured him from the Egyptian ranks, to make certain the training of the new crews.

In the same way we formed machine-gun companies from the mixed elements available, and armed them with the ten British and captured Turkish Maxims already in Yenbo, They, also, were not so much stiffened as lubricated by bought volunteers from the Egyptian machine gunners. There was a third technical formation created by Maulud Mukhlus, the fire-eating Mesopotamian cavalryman who was Feisal's AD.C. We had got him fifty mules, and he had taken fifty of his infantrymen out of a company of one hundred and fifty men of local material whom he had drilled for guard and escort duty, and had put these astride of the mules, and told them they were mounted infantry.

Maulud was a martinet and a born cavalry officer, and under his strict discipline and Spartan exercises the much-beaten mounted men grew up painfully into excellent soldiers, capable of instant obedience, and of attack in open order, prodigies in the Arab ranks. The new toy pleased us so that after my first inspection we telegraphed for fifty more mules to double it in strength. Of course my help was useless in forming these regular units, but it was obvious that Rasim the gunner, Abdulla el Deleimi the machine gunner, and Maulud the cavalryman, were all experts and enthusiasts in their lines, and we left the working out of their needs to them, merely encouraging their initiative by getting them the materials they lacked.

There were too many pressing details to leave us time to disentangle principle from example, and the dogma of irregular warfare, already present at the back of my mind in cloudy formlessness, expressed themselves as yet mainly in empirical snatching at solutions for attendant difficulties. However in my own impression right and wrong were gradually sorting themselves out. Before the march to Wejh, I had written that the Arab army in mass was not formidable, since it lacked corporate spirit, discipline, mutual confidence. Every Arab man by himself was good: the smaller the unit, the better the performance. A thousand were a mob, ineffective against a company of trained troops, but three or four of them in their own hills would account for a dozen Turkish soldiers. When they sat still they got nerves or melted homeward: even Feisal fell to pieces then: but with plenty to do, riding in small parties, tapping the Turks here and there, retiring when the enemy advanced, to reappear elsewhere: so they were in their element, and must have caused not merely anxiety but bewilderment to their opponents. This was the judgment which Napoleon put into ten words about the Mamelukes: only he was on the other side, and they danced to his tune. My half-memory of his words turned them inside out: and my temper refused to hear the Turkish piping.

We bothered to take this unwieldy mob with us to Wejh in the teeth of efficiency and experience just because there was no fighting in the bill. Our fear was not of what lay before us, but of what lay behind. We were proposing the evacuation of Wadi Yenbo, our only defensive line against the Turkish division in Wadi Safra, only fifteen miles away. We were going to strip the Juheina country of its fighting men, and to leave Yenbo, till then our indispensable base, and the second sea-port of the Hejaz, in charge of the few men unfit for the march north and therefore unfit for anything at all dangerous.

We were going to march nearly two hundred miles up the coast, with no base behind and only hostile territory in front parallel to the railway the enemy's main line of communication along the narrow defile of the maritime plain the only practicable but a waterless road. If the Turks cut in behind us we would be neatly in the void.

However it seemed a safe risk to take since we had intangible assets on our side. In the first place the Turks had now engaged their surplus strength in attacking Rabegh, or rather in prolonging their occupied area so as to attack Rabegh. It would take them days to transfer back north. Then the Turks were stupid and we reckoned on their not hearing all at once of our move and on their not believing it then and not seeing till much later what chances it had given them. If we did our march in three weeks we would probably take them by surprise. Lastly we would develop the sporadic raiding activity of the Harb into a conscious operation. The Rahalah, under

Raba, a most gallant and energetic lad, had set the example of plundering Turk convoys and were getting rich on it with small losses though afterwards Raba himself was killed in a daring effort.

We had applauded these pin-pricks in the Turkish rear: and now began to plan a whole series of such useful plays to be acted in turn by all the clans Mahamid, Fahdah, Subh, Hawazim, Rahalah, Radadah, Sumeidat, Dawahir, Serahah, Hejelah. They were to take booty, if possible, in order to be self-supporting: but primarily they were to lock up large numbers of Turks in defense positions.

To exercise my own hand in this genre I took a test party of thirty-five Mahamid with me from Nakhl Mubarak in the first days of 1917 to Wasit, the old blockhouse well of my first journey from Rabegh to Yenbo. When dark came we dismounted and left our camels with ten men to guard them against possible Turkish patrols. The rest of us climbed the hills north of the Haj road up to Jebel Dhifran: a painful climb for the hills were of knife-sharp strata turned on edge, running in oblique lines from crest to foot. They gave abundance of broken surface but no sure grip, for the stone was so minutely cracked that almost any segment would come away from its matrix in the hand.

The head of Dhifran was cold and misty and time dragged till dawn. We had disposed ourselves in crevices of the rock, and at last saw the tips of three bell tents three hundred yards away beneath us to the right behind a spur at the head of the pass. We could not move round to get a full view, so had to content ourselves with putting bullets through their upper parts. This effort turned out a crowd of Turks who leaped like stags into trenches. We found them very fast targets, and probably they suffered little. In return they opened rapid fire in every possible direction, and between us we made such a terrific row that I expected to see the Hamra force turn out to help. As the enemy was already about ten to one, their reinforcement might have prevented our retreat: so we crawled gently back and then rushed down into the first valley where we fell over two very scared Turks, much unbuttoned, disturbed at their first morning duty. They were ragged, but still something to show, so we dragged them with us for another five hundred yards to the next ridge. There we faced about, and put a hot independent fire into our pursuers. It checked them, and we moved away comfortably to Bir Murra and then home.

Interrogation of these prisoners gave us the disposition of the Turkish Fifty-fifth Regiment and indicated the object of three or four other possible and profitable raids. Feisal arranged these, and ordered all the Harb in his area to go up and snipe every outlying Turkish post and every patrol or convoy at least once a day. We decided that Sidi Zeid could do the same thing from Mijz in Ali's area, against the Turkish communications from the other side, and arranged for him to go in to Yenbo at once to ask the guard-ship to find him a passage to Rabegh in the next patrol-boat going down. Feisal was still nervous at abandoning Yenbo, and when casting about for a new expedient we suddenly remembered Sidi Abdulla in Henakiyeh. He had now some five thousand irregulars, and a few guns and machine-guns, and the reputation of his successful (if too slow) siege of Tall. It seemed a shame to leave him wasting in the middle of the wilderness. I suggested that he might come to Kheibar, to threaten the railway north of Medina: but Feisal improved vastly on this suggestion by remembering Wadi Ais, the historic valley of springs and palm-villages flowing through the impregnable Juheina hills north-eastward from behind Rudhwa to the Hamdh valley near Hedia. It laid just one hundred kilometers north of Medina, within sight of the railway, a direct threat on Fakhri's communications with Damascus. In easy touch with it across the line were Kheiber, Teima, and Henakiyeh; from it Abdulla could keep up his arranged pressure upon Medina from the east, and prevent the ingress of caravans from the Persian Gulf also it was near Yenbo, which could easily feed him there with munitions and supplies.

The proposal was so obviously an inspiration that we sent off Raja el Khuluwi at once to put it to Abdulla: and we were so sure that he would adopt it that we urged Feisal to move away from Wadi Yenbo northward on the first stage of his journey to Wejh, without waiting for the reply.

Chapter 25: Evacuating Yenbo

Feisal agreed and we struck tents on January the third, taking the upper road, through Wadi Messarih for Owais, a group of wells about fifteen miles to the north of Yenbo. The hills were beautiful today. The rains of December had been abundant and the warm sun after them had deceived the earth into believing it was spring. So a thin grass had come up in all the hollows and flat places. The blades (single, straight and very tender) shot up between the stones.

If a man bent over from his saddle and looked downwards he would see no new color in the ground: but by looking forward, and getting a distant slope at a flat angle with his eye, he would feel a lively mist of pale green here and there over the surface of slate blue and brown-red rock. In places the growth was strong and our painstaking camels had become prosperous, grazing on it.

The starting signal went but only for us and the Ageyl. The other units of the army, standing each man by his couched camel, lined up beside our road and, as Feisal came near, saluted him in silence. He called back cheerfully, 'Peace be upon you', and each head sheikh returned the phrase. When we had passed they were told to mount, taking the time from their chiefs so the forces behind us swelled constantly till there was a moving line of men and camels winding up the narrow pass towards the watershed for as far back as the eye reached. Feisal's greetings had been the only sounds before we reached the crest of the rise where the valley opened out and became a gentle forward slope of soft shingle and flint, bedded in sand.

There ibn Dakhil, the keen and intelligent sheikh of Russ who had raised this contingent of Ageyl two years before to aid Turkey, and had brought it over with him intact to the Sherif when the revolt came, dropped back a pace or two, marshaled our following into a broad column of ordered ranks and made the drams strike up. Then the march became rather splendid and barbaric. Feisal in front, in white: Sharraf on his right in red head cloth and henna-dyed tunic and cloak: myself on his left in white and scarlet: behind us three banners of faded crimson silk with gilt spikes: behind them the drummers playing a march and behind them again the wild mass of twelve hundred bouncing camels of the bodyguard, packed as closely as they could move, the men in every variety of colored clothes and the camels nearly as brilliant in their trappings. Everyone suddenly burst out singing with full throat a war song in honor of Feisal and his family. We filled the valley to its banks with our river of camels, and poured down in a flashing stream.

At the mouth of Messarih a messenger rode up with letters to Feisal from Abd el Kader in Yenbo. Among them was one three days old for me from Captain Warren, to say that he would not embark Zeid till he had seen me and heard details of the local situation. He was in the Sherm, a lonely creek eight miles up the coast from the port, and a place where he liked to lie since he could there play cricket on the beach, and was saved from the plague of flies which invaded any ship lying in Yenbo harbor: but of course he cut himself off news by staying so far away, and it was a point of old friction between us. Warren was well-meaning but had not the breadth of Boyle, the fiery politician and constitutionalist, or the brain of Linberry of the *Hardinge* who filled himself with the shore gossip of every port he touched, and who took a personal interest in the life of all classes on his beat. Warren looked on the land as a thing sometimes tied up to, sometimes run into, and its inhabitants as people out to exploit the Navy.

I felt I had better leave the march at once, and race off to Yenbo to regulate affairs. Zeid was a nice fellow, but would assuredly do something quaint in his enforced holiday: and we needed peace just then. Feisal sent some Ageyl with me, and we made speed for Yenbo: indeed, I got there in wee hours, leaving my disgusted escort (who said they would wear out neither their camels nor their bottoms for my impatience) halfway on the road, across the plain so wearily well-known to me. The sun which had been delightful over our heads in the hills now in the evening shone straight into my face with a white fury before which I had to press my hand as shield over my eyes. Feisal had given me a powerful racing camel, a present from the Emir of Nejd to his father, and the finest and roughest animal I had ridden. Later I killed her by overwork on the road to Akaba.

On arrival in Yenbo things were not as I expected. Zeid had been embarked, and the *Duffferin* had started that morning for Rabegh: so I sat down to take count of what we needed of naval help on the way to Wejh. Feisal had promised to wait at Owais till I reported everything prepared. My first check was a conflict between the civil and military powers. Abd el Kader, the energetic and temperamental governor, had been cluttered up with duties as our base grew in size, till Feisal added to him a military commandant, Tewfik Bey, a Syrian from Horns, to care for ordnance stores. Unfortunately, there was no arbiter to define ordnance stores, and that morning they fell out over empty arms chests: Abd el Kader locked the store and went off to lunch. Tewfik came down to the quay with four men, and a machine-gun and a sledge hammer, and opened the door. Abd el Kader got into a boat, rowed out to the British guard-ship, the tiny *Espiegle,* and told her embarrassed but hospitable captain that he had come to stay. His servant brought him food and he slept that night in a camp-bed on the quarter-deck.

I wanted to hurry, so began to solve the deadlock by making Abd el Kader write to Feisal for his decision and by making Tewfik hand over the store to me. We brought the *Arethusa* near the sloop, that Abd el Kader might direct the loading of the disputed chests from his ship: and lastly I brought Tewfik off to the *Espiegle* for a temporary reconciliation. It was made easy by an accident, for as Tewfik saluted his guard of honor (not strictly regular, this guard, but politic) at the gangway his face lit up and he beamed and said 'this ship captured me at Kuma', pointing to the trophy of the name plate of the Turkish gunboat *Marmans* which the *Espiegle* had sunk in action on the Tigris. Abd el Kader was as interested in the tale as Tewfik, and the trouble ceased.

Sharraf came in to Yenbo next day as Emir in Feisal's place. He was a powerful man, perhaps the most capable of all the Sherifs in the army but devoid of ambition acting out of duty not for pleasure. He was rich and had been chief justice of the Sherifs own court, for years. He knew and handled tribesmen better than any man alive and they feared him, for he was severe and impartial, and his face was sinister with a left eyebrow which drooped, the effect of an old blow and which gave a forbidding hardness to his expression. The surgeon of the *Suva* operated on the eye and repaired much of the damage: but the face remained one to rebuke liberties or weaknesses. I found him good to work with, very clear headed wise and kind with a pleasant smile — his mouth became soft then while his eyes remained terrible — and a determination to do fittingly always.

We agreed that the risk of the fall of Yenbo while we hunted Wejh was great and that it would be wise to empty it of stores so far as possible. Boyle gave me an opportunity, by signaling that either *Dufferin* or *Hardinge* would be made available for transport: so I replied that as the difficulties would be very severe. I preferred *Hardinge* Captain Warren whose ship intercepted the message regarded it as superfluous but it brought in the *Hardinge* two days later in the best of tempers. She was an Indian troop-ship and her lowest troop-deck had great square ports all along above water level. Linberry opened these for us and we stuffed straight into them off lighters eight thousand rifles three million rounds of ammunition thousands of shells quantities of rice and flour a shed full of uniforms, two tons of high explosive, and all our petrol, pell-mell. It was like posting letters in a box. In no time she had taken over a thousand tons of stuff.

Boyle came in for the news as eager as possible for the expedition. He promised the *Hardinge* should act as depot ship throughout, to land food and water whenever needed and this solved the main difficulty. The Navy was already collecting. We would have half the Red Sea Fleet presently. The Admiral was expected and landing parties were being drilled on every ship.

Everyone was dyeing white duck khaki-colored, or sharpening bayonets or practicing with rifles. I hoped there would be no fighting for Feisal had nearly ten thousand men and these were enough to fill the whole Billi country with armed parties and carry off everything not too heavy or too hot. The Billi knew it and were now profuse in their loyalties to the Sherif, and completely converted to Arab nationality. They saw that the Turks were too few to resist us.

I was sure we would take Wejh, but was really afraid that numbers of Feisal's host would die of hunger or thirst on the way. Supply was my business, and I felt it rather a responsibility.

However, to Urn Lejj, half-way, it was friendly country, and nothing much could happen so far as that: and therefore I sent word to Feisal that all was ready, and he left Owais on January the twelfth, the very day that good news came from Abdulla, welcoming the Ais plan, and promising an immediate start thither. The same day came news of my relief Newcombe, the regular officer being sent to Hejaz as chief of our military mission had arrived in Egypt, and his two staff officers, Cox and Vickery, were actually on their way down the Red Sea. Feisal, in welcoming the proposal to attach Cox to Yenbo and Newcombe to himself, had asked Clayton to retain me also for service with his forces.

Boyle took me up to Urn Lejj on his ship the *Suva* and there we went ashore to get the news. The sheikh told us that Feisal would arrive that day, not in the village, but at Bir el Waheidi, the water supply, four miles inland. We sent up a message for him, and then walked over to see the fort which Boyle had shelled some months before with the *Fox,* in dislodging the Turkish garrison. It was just a rubble barrack, and Boyle looked at the ruins and said, 'I'm rather ashamed of myself for smashing such a potty place.' He was a very professional officer, as alert as any man could be, both business like and official, sometimes a little intolerant of easy-going things and people. Red-haired men are seldom patient, and 'Ginger Boyle' as the men called him was a warm man. While we were looking over the ruins four ragged grey-bearded elders of the village came up and asked leave to speak. They said that some months before a sudden two tunneled ship had come there and destroyed their fort. They were now required to rebuild it for the police of the Arab Government, and wished to ask the generous captain of this peaceable one-funneled ship for a little timber or help towards the restoration. Boyle was restless at their long speech, and snapped at me, 'What is it? What do they want?' I said, 'Nothing, they were only describing the terrible effect of the *Fox* 'bombardment.' Boyle looked round him and smiled grimly and said, 'It's a fair mess.'

Next day Vickery arrived. He was a gunner, and in ten years' service in the Sudan had learned Arabic — both literary and colloquial — perfectly. He had come straight from the Somme, full of knowledge of technical war and of artillery, and was rather sore at the job which lost him his chances of distinction in France. However, he looked forward to meeting Feisal, and we arranged to go up next day with Boyle, to make the timetable for the attack proper. The governor got us camels, and we rode up the valley behind the town, turning first to the north and then to the east up a stony track to a stiff watershed, over granite. Then we rode down gently over sandy slopes to a soft plain, and through a thicket of good thorn-trees, beyond which Feisal was camped. It was an amusing trip for me, for Vickery (always a little delicate towards himself) had retained his helmet, but put an Arab head cloth and rope over it, so that from behind his was the most enormous head in the world: and he was out of practice in camel riding, and Boyle was new to it. The Arabs had never seen red hair before, and knew it must be false: so they called him the 'Ancient', one who hid the whiteness of his aged locks with henna.

During lunch, at which Feisal had done his best by various modes of sheep and rice to conceal the bareness of camp cookery, there was an unfortunate lapse when Vickery pulled out a great flask of whiskey and mixed himself a hearty drink. We were not alone as guests, and it was tactless; but long residence in the Sudan, which had no educated class, or press, or public opinion, took the fine edge off some Englishmen. However, after lunch we got to work and discussed the march to Wejh. We had already decided to break the army into sections, and to proceed independently to our meeting place of Abu Zereibat in Hamdh, where there was abundant water: but for the intervening stretch we could get little information from our Juheina guides. Few of them could count, and they had not the capacity to estimate if the known wells were enough to water our thousands, or not. In the end we decided to risk it. There had been a shower the night before which might give us casual pools, and if we did run short the worst effect would be two days' delay at the end. After Abu Zereibat there was no water before Wejh, but Boyle agreed that the *Hardinge* should take station in Sherm — Habban supposed to be a possible harbor — and land twenty tons of water for us on the beach. So that was settled.

It was decided to issue the army with eight days' ration of flour and rice from the *Hardinge* now: and to put ashore something extra for Abdulla's army when he arrived in Ais, to which this was the nearest port. Boyle would see to this and for the shore organization Feisal decided that he would have to leave behind Sheikh Yusuf Khusheirim, a Medina townsman who had been his father's business agent in Medina for many years, and who had been admitted a member of the Juheina tribe, though of Indian origin. To leave him here was necessary perhaps, but a loss to us, for Sheikh Yusuf had been our Adjutant-General, and invaluable in supply and transport work. However, the eight days' food he would now give us would carry us to Wejh, and after that we might make new arrangements.

For the actual attack on Wejh we offered Boyle an Arab landing party of several hundred men, Harb and Juheina peasantry and slaves, under Saleh ibn Shefia, Mohammed's young son. He was negro, but a pleasant boy, of good courage, with the faculty of friendliness. He kept his men in reasonable order by conjurations and appeals, and never minded how much his own dignity was outraged by them, or by us. Boyle accepted them, and decided to put them on another deck of the all-embracing *Hardinge,* whose stomachs seemed as plentiful as a camel's. We agreed that they with the naval party should be landed to the north of the town, where the

Turks had no post to block a landing, and from which flank Wejh village and harbor were best turned. Boyle would have at least six ships, carrying fifty guns to occupy the Turks' minds, and a seaplane ship to direct the guns. We said we would be at Abu Zereibat on the twentieth of the month, at Habban for the *Hardinge's* water on the twenty-second, and that the landing party should go ashore at dawn on the twenty-third, by which time our mounted men would have closed all roads of escape from the town. Boyle was nervous the Turks might escape sooner, but I knew that their factor of transport would make this difficult for them: nor did I much care if they did, for it was Wejh we wanted, as a new base, and the fate of the few Turkish soldiers in it concerned themselves more than it did us. The French motto of 'Killing Germans' translated into 'Killing Turks' would not have excused a single casualty in Arabia.

The news from Rabegh was good: and the Turks as yet had made no attempt to profit by the nakedness of Yenbo. These were our hazards, and when Boyle set them at rest we were mightily encouraged. Abdulla was almost in Ais, we were half-way to Wejh: the initiative had again passed to the Arabs. I was so joyous that for a moment I forgot my self-control and, counting Vickery one of us, said exultantly that in a year we would be tapping on the gates of Damascus. A chill came over the feeling in the tent and my hopefulness died. Later I heard that he had gone to Boyle and vehemently condemned me as a braggart and a visionary: but though the outburst was foolish, as I saw when I had made it, yet it was not an impossible dream for five months later I was in Damascus, and a year after that I was its governor.

I had angered him and he had disappointed me. He knew I was militarily incompetent and thought I was politically absurd. I knew he was the trained soldier our cause needed and yet he seemed blind to its power. The Arabs nearly made shipwreck on this blindness of their European advisers, who had learned the iron military language, and thought in terms of discipline and salutes, battalions, attacks, mass, strategic points, areas of occupation, and who could not or would not forget it in the new jargon of a popular movement. It was already clear to me that rebellion was not war: indeed it partook more of the nature of peace — a national strike perhaps.

The conjunction of Semites, an idea, and an armed prophet held illimitable possibilities and had the direction been in skilled hands it would not have been Damascus but Constantinople which we reached in 1918. The half was not made of us.

My only assets for the position in the Arab movement that I at last unwillingly assumed were goodwill and an open mind and hope. I had no sense of command, no instinct for tactics no mastery of Arabic: and at every step and glaringly in every crisis my raw methods made our progress hesitant and dangerous. I knew it (the self-knowledge itself unfitted me for leadership) and again and again I tried to find a master from among the qualified: but they would not lend themselves, and so the adventure had to suffer. It had been my fault often to hold places for which I was ten years too young and the penalty of youth was heavy. I myself paid it cheerfully, but in this war the Arabs paid it for me. For youth to have ability was no palliation since, to men, ability without years was like the cutting edge of a chisel, necessary, indeed perhaps the main justification of the chisel, but a nuisance without the uncouth and irresponsive handle. Vickery had the age of me and beside him I felt miserably wrong. It was difficult to resist the man with a strong point of view who showed his belief that he was right.

Chapter 26: The Order of March

In the morning, having seen that the unloading of the *Hordinge* into open dhows at sea was proceeding without friction, I went ashore to Sheikh Yusuf, and found him flurried. He was helping his Bisha police and the frightened villagers and some of the Maulud's men quickly to throw a barricade across the near end of the main street. He told me that fifty wild mules, without halter or bridle or saddle had been loosed on shore that morning from a ship. By luck rather than skill they had been stampeded into the marketplace, and the exits were now all barred, and there they must remain ramping about the stalls till Maulud, to whom they were addressed, had invented saddlery in the wilderness. This was the second batch of fifty mules for the mounted infantry, and by the chance of our fear at Yenbo we fortunately had spare ropes and enough bits for them on board of the *Hordinge*. So by noon the shops were again open, and the damage paid for.

I went up to Feisal's camp, which was busy. Some of the tribes were drawing a month's wages, all were getting eight days' food: tents and heavy baggage were being stored here and the last arrangements for the march being made. I sat by his staff and listened to their chatter. Among them were Faiz el Ghusein, Bedouin sheikh, Turkish official chronicler of the Armenian massacres, now secretary; Nesib el Bekri, Damascene land owner, and Feisal's host in Syria, now exiled from his country with a death-sentence over him; Sami, Nesib's brother, graduate of the Law School, and now assistant paymaster; Tewfik el Halabi, ex-journalist, now assistant secretary, a little white-faced man and furtive, with a whispering manner, honest in his patriotism but perverse in life and so a nasty colleague.

Hassan Sharaf the headquarters' doctor, a noble man who had put not merely his life but his purse to service in the Arab cause, was plaintive with excess of disgust at finding his phials smashed and their drugs confounded in the bottom of his chest. Tewfik rallying him said, 'Do you expect a rebellion to be comfortable and the contrast with the pale misery of his manner delighted us. In moments of hardship the comfort and humor of triteness outweighed a world of wit.

With Feisal in the evening we talked of the coming marches. The first stage was short: to Semna where were palm-groves and wells of abundant water. After that there was choice of ways, to be determined only when our scouts returned with their report of pounded rainwater. By the coast, the straight road, it was sixty dry miles to the next well, and our multitude of footmen would find that long. In the foothills lay water, at Khaff and Towala, making three easy stages of twenty-five miles each: but the wells were seepages in valley beds, and there had been little rain last year and the year before. So they might be too small for us.

The lack of rain would mean a lack of grazing, and we had no means of carrying barley with us from the *Hardinge.* The local fodder was in the form of grass-ropes, so rare and expensive (three days' camel feed would cost a sovereign) that the soldiers could not buy it. Feisal's hired camels were got for four pounds a month, the owners to feed them, and because of this prohibitive cost of hay all were weak and thin. Quite a number died of exhaustion. The Arabs cared for them, more or less, and there was little mange or sickness: but the carrying capacity even of the best was low.

Also we had too few of them. Feisal's own baggage train had been driven down towards Rabegh when Zeid was cut off at Bir Said, and the Juheina camels were not abundant. Our army at Bir el Waheida amounted to five thousand one hundred camel riders, and five thousand three hundred men on foot with four Krupp mountain guns and ten machine-guns, and for the transport of all of these we had three hundred and eighty baggage camels. Some had to take water for the gun-mules. We carried five hundred shells, one hundred thousand rounds of rifle ammunition: and only the balance of the train was available for stores. Everything was cut to the lowest point, far below the standard of the Turks, or of the British, or of the Egyptians, the latter army being perhaps the most elaborate in existence For example, our mountain battery, in its Egyptian days, had required three hundred and sixty camels for its proper transport. In Rasirn's hands it marched out of Wejh with less than eighty, for a like journey of fourteen days, carrying as much ammunition as of old.

Next day we were to start just after noon, and punctually by lunchtime Feisal's work was finished. We were a merry party, Feisal himself, relaxed after responsibility, Abd el Kerim, never very serious, Sherif jabar, Nasib and Sami, Tewfik, Hassan Sharaf and myself. After lunch Feisal's, the last tent, was struck. We all went to our camels where they were couched about in a circle, saddled and loaded, each held short by a slave standing on its doubled fore-leg. The kettle drummer waiting beside ibn Dakhil, the commander of the bodyguard, tapped his drum four or five times, and everything became still. We watched Feisal. He got up from his rug, on which he had been saying a final word to Abd el Kerim, and walked to his camel. There he caught the two pommels in his hands, put his knee on the side of the saddle and said aloud, 'Make God your agent' the slave instantly released the camel, which sprang up. When it was on its feet Feisal passed his other leg across its back, swept his skirts under him by a wave of the arm and settled himself in the saddle.

As his camel rose we had jumped for our saddles and the whole mob rose together, some of the camels roaring but the most quiet, as trained she-camels should be. Only a young animal, a male or ill-bred would grumble on the road, and self-respecting Bedouin would not ride such, since the noise might give them away in night marches or surprise attacks. The camels took their first steps hastily, and we the riders had quickly to hook our legs round the front cantles, and pick up the headstalls to check the pace. We then looked where Feisal was and tapped our mounts' heads gently round, and pressed them on the shoulders with our bare feet till they were in line beside him. Afterwards ibn Dakhil came up into station with us, and after a glance at the country and the direction of march passed a short order for the Ageyl to arrange themselves in two equal wings, spreading out to right and left of us for two or three hundred yards, camel marching by camel, in line as near as the accidents underfoot permitted.

These Ageyl were Nejd townsmen, the youth of Aneyza, Boreida or Russ, who had contracted either with the Turks or with the Sherif for service as regular camel corps for a term of years. They were young, usually from sixteen to twenty-five, and nice fellows, large-eyed, cheery, a little educated, catholic, very intelligent and good companion on the road. There was seldom a heavy one. Even in repose, when most Eastern faces emptied themselves of life, these lads remained keen-looking and handsome. They talked a delicate and elastic Arabic, and were well-mannered, often foppish in habit. There was a docility and reasonableness in their town-bred minds which made them good servants, and they were unrivaled travelers, who looked after themselves and their masters without reiterated instructions. Their fathers bred or sold camels and they had followed the trade from infancy; consequently they handled camels as familiarly as did any Bedouin, and the decadent softness in their nature made them biddable, tolerant of the harshness and physical punishment which in the East were the outward proofs of discipline. They were essentially submissive, good soldiers who fought with courage when well led.

Not being a tribe, they had no blood enemies and passed everywhere in the desert freely; the carrying trade and chaffer of the interior lay in their hands. Yet the opportunity of gain there was scanty, and they had been tempted abroad partly for money, partly from love of adventure, partly by dissatisfaction with their home conditions. The Wahabis, a fanatical Muslim heresy, had imposed their strict rales on the easy and civilized Kasim. In Kasim there was little coffee hospitality, much prayer and fasting, no tobacco, no artistic dalliance with women, no silk clothes, no gold and silver head ropes and ornaments. Everything was pious or puritanical; the Kasim townsmen who were merchants and concupiscent men of the world found it irksome, while their less patient sons went abroad to find fortune and indulgence.

It was a natural phenomenon, this periodic rise, a little more than a century apart, of ascetic creeds in central Arabia. The votaries found all the beliefs of their neighbors cluttered with inessential things, which became impious in the hot imagination of their preachers. Again and again they had arisen, had taken possession, soul and body, of the tribes, and had dashed themselves to pieces on the comfortable possessions of the urban Semites. They ebbed and flowed like the tides or the changing seasons each movement with the seeds of death in it through its excess of Tightness: and doubtless they must recur so long as the causes: sun, moon, and wind acting in the emptiness of open spaces, weighed without check on the unhurried and encumbered minds of the desert dwellers.

However, this afternoon the Ageyl were not thinking of God but of us and as ibn Dakhil ranged them to the right and left of us they fell neatly into ranks. There came a warning patter from the drums and the poet of the right wing burst suddenly into strident song a single invented couplet, of Feisal and the pleasures he would afford us at Wejh. The right wing listened to the verse intently and then took it up and sang it together once, twice, and three times at each repetition more provokingly throwing into it pride and self satisfaction and derision. However, before they could brandish it a fourth time the poet of the left wing broke out in his solo, an extempore reply to the couplet of his rival on the right in the same manner, in answering rhyme, and completing or capping his sentiment. The left wing took it up in a roar of triumph, and then the drums tapped again, the standard bearers threw out their great crimson banners, and the whole guard right left and center broke together into the rousing tune of their regimental chorus.

> 'I've lost Britain and I've lost Gaul.
> I've lost Rome and worst of all.
> I've lost Lalage!'....

only it was Nejd they had lost and the women of the Maabda, and their future lay from Suez to Jidda — but it was a good song with a rhythmical beat in it which the camels loved so that they put down their heads and stretched out their necks and with lengthened pace shuffled forward musingly while the song lasted.

Our road today was easy for them, since it was over firm sand slopes, long slowly-rising waves of dunes, bare-backed, but with scrub in the folds, and sometimes a barren palm tree solitary in a damp depression. Afterwards we reached a broad flat and there were two horsemen, catching us up, came cantering across from the left to greet Feisal. I knew the first, dirty old blear-eyed Mohammed Ali el Beidawi, third son of Beidawi the great dead Emir of the Juheina and his father's successor, despite the two brothers senior to him by birth:— but Abd el Aziz and Abd el Mejid, these two, were soft-witted, and Ghalib, the fourth brother, though more presentable than Mohammed Ali, was unpopular. Abd el Kerim, my old road-fellow, was the quickest of the family, but his slave-mother barred him from the Emirate, to which besides his feather-head hardly aspired.

The second horseman, the companion of Mohamed Ali looked strange, and when he came nearer I saw he was in khaki uniform, with a cloak to cover it and a silk head cloth and head rope, much awry, over all. He looked up and there was Newcombe's red and peeling face, and his vehement mouth, between his straining eyes and strong, humorous chin. He had arrived at Urn Lejj this morning and, hearing we were only just off, had seized Sheikh Yusufs horse and galloped after us. I offered him my spare camel, and introduced him to Feisal. Newcombe greeted him like an old school friend, and at once they plunged into the middle of things, suggesting, improving, debating and planning at lightning speed. Newcombe's initial velocity was enormous and here the freshness of the day and the life and happiness of the army gave an inspiration to the march and brought the future bubbling out of us without pain.

In the middle of the flat we passed Ghowashia, a ragged grove of cultivated palms, and on its far side marched over sand to a lava field, gradually ascending but easy to move across since its roughness was all drowned in sand, deep enough to smooth them, but not deep enough to be too soft. The topmost stones of the highest piles of lava blocks showed through. An hour later we came abruptly to the crest of this bed, where it dropped in a sand slope, so abrupt and swept and straight as to be called a sand-cliff, down to a broad, splendid valley of rounded pebbles. This was Semna and our road went down the steep, through terraces of palms and through palm-groves at its foot into the open valley which ran towards the sea in a steady fall from the hills to the north-east.

The wind had been following our march and so it was very still and warm in the bottom of the valley in the lee of the great bank of sand. Here was our water, and here we would halt till the scouts returned from seeking rain-pools in front of us — for so Abd el Kerim our chief guide had advised. We rode the four hundred yards across the valley and up the further slopes till we were safe from floods, and there Feisal tapped his camel lightly on the neck till she sank to her knees with a scrape of shingle pushed aside and settled herself. Hejris spread the carpet for us. and with the other Sherifs we sat and jested while the coffee was made.

I maintained against Feisal the greatness of Ibrahim Pasha Milii, leader of Kurds in North Mesopotamia. When he was to march his, women rose before dawn and running noiselessly overhead on the stretched tent-cloth untied the strips of it while others beneath held and removed the poles till all was struck and divided into camel-loads and loaded. Then they drove off, so that when the Pasha woke he was alone on his pallet in the open air where at night he had lain down in the rich inner compartment of his great tent.

He would get up at his leisure and drink coffee sitting like ourselves on his carpet: and afterwards the horses would be brought and they would ride towards the new camping ground. But if on his way he wanted coffee he would crisp his fingers to the servants and the coffee man would ride up beside him with his pot ready and his brazier burning on a copper bracket of his saddle and serve the cup on the march without breaking stride: and at sunset they would find the women waiting and the erected tent standing furnished for them as it had been on the evening before.

Today had a grey weather so strange after the many thronging suns that as I walked with Newcombe about the valley we were always stooping aside to look where our shadows had gone. We talked of what I knew and hoped and of what he wanted. They were the same thing so we had brain leisure to note Semna and its fine groves of cared-for palms enclosed by their little hedges of dead thorn with here and there huts of reed and palm-rib to shelter the owners and their families at times of fertilization and harvest. In the lowest gardens and in the valley bed were the wood-lined wells whose water rose sometimes till only four feet from the surface and was they said, fairly sweet and never-failing: but the wells were so small that to water our host of camels took the night.

Feisal wrote letters from Semna to twenty-five leaders of the Billi and Howeitat and Beni Atiyeh, saying that with his army he would be instantly in Wejh, and they must see to it. Mohammed Ali el Beidawi bestirred himself and, since almost all our men were of his tribe, was useful in arranging the detachments and detailing them their routes for the morrow. Our water-scouts had come in, reporting shallow pools at Gelib and Dhulm, two points well-spaced on the coast road. After cross-questioning them we decided to send four sections that way, and the other five by Khuff: so we thought we should arrive soonest and safest at Abu Zereibat. It was a point not easy to decide, and again we marked the poor help of the Musa Juheina, our guides and informants. They seemed to have no unit of time smaller than the half-day, or of distance between the span and the stage: and a stage might be from six to sixteen hours according to the man's will and camel.

Intercommunication between our units was hindered because often there was no one in them who could read or write, and it became difficult not to lose touch as lack of water upset our program. Much of the delay, confusion, and actual danger of hunger and thirst which marred this expedition would have been avoided had time allowed us to examine the route beforehand. The animals were without food for nearly three days, and the men marched the last fifty miles on half a gallon of water, with nothing to eat. Yet it did not in any way dim their spirit, and they trotted

into Wejh gaily enough, hoarsely singing, and executing mock charges: but Feisal said that another midday of the sort would have broken both their speed and their energy.

When business ended, Newcombe and I went off to sleep in the tent Feisal had lent us, as a special luxury. Baggage conditions were so hard and so important for us that we made a pride of faring like the men who could have no means of transporting unnecessary things: and never before had I had a tent of my own. We pitched it at the very edge of a bluff of the foothills, a bluff no wider than the tent and rounded so that the slope went straight down from the pegs of the door-flap. There we found sitting and waiting for us Abd el Kerim, the Beidawi Sherif, wrapped up to the eyes in his head cloth and cloak, since the evening was chill and threatened rain. He had come to ask me for a mule for himself with saddle and bridle complete. The smart appearance of Maulud's little company in their British breeches and puttees, and the fine new animals they had been wrestling with in the market at Urn Lejj, had roused his desire.

I played with his eagerness, and put him off, advancing a condition that he should ask me only after our successful arrival at Wejb, and with this he was content. Like many shallow cheerful people he had a streak of false melancholy in him, and this evening he felt full of unspecified longings, and talked about one rare subject and another while we hungered for sleep. At last he rose to go but chancing to look across the valley saw the hollows beneath and about us winking with the faint camp-fires of the scattered contingents. He called me out to look and swept his arm round saying half-sadly. 'We are no longer Arabs but a people.'

He was half-proud too, for the advance on Wejh was their biggest effort, the first time in their memory that the manhood of a tribe with transport, arms and food for two hundred miles had left its district and marched into another's territory without the hope of plunder or the stimulus of blood-feud. Abd el Kerim was glad that his tribe had shown this new spirit of service, but also sorry, for to him the joys of life were a fast camel the best weapons and a short sharp raid against his neighbor's herd and these joys, the gradual success of Feisal's ambition were less and less easy to achieve for a responsible person.

Chapter 27: Marching

In the morning it rained persistently, till near midday, and we were so glad to see more water coming to us, and so comfortable in the tents at Semna that we delayed our start till the sun shone again in the early afternoon. Then we rode westward down the valley in the fresh light.

Behind us the Ageyl came first. After them Abd el Kerim led his Gufa men, about seven hundred camels with more than that number of men following afoot. They were dressed in white, with large head-shawls of red and black striped cotton, and they waved green palm branches instead of banners. Next to them was Sherif Mohammed Ali Abu Sharrain, an old patriarch with a long curling grey beard and an upright carriage of himself His three hundred riders were Sherifs, of the Aiaishi (Iuheina) stock known Sherifs, but only acknowledged in the mass since they had no inscribed pedigrees. They wore rusty-red tunics of henna with black cloaks, and carried swords. Each had a slave crouched behind him on the crupper of his camel, to help him with rifle and dagger in the fight, and to watch his camel and cook his food for him on the road. The slaves, as befitted slaves of poor masters, were very little dressed, and exposed their strong black legs which gripped the camel's woolly sides in a vice to lessen the shocks inevitable on their bony perches: while they had knotted up their ragged shirts into the plaited thong about their loins to save them from the fouling of the camels and their staling on the march. Semna water was medicinal and our animals' dung flowed like green soup down their hocks that day.

Behind the Ashraf came the crimson banner of our last tribal detachment, the Rifaa, nomad Juheina, under Auda ibn Zuweid, the old wheedling sea-pirate who had robbed the Stotzingen mission and thrown their wireless and their Indian servants into the sea at Yenbo. The sharks presumably refused the wireless, but we had spent fruitless hours dragging for it in the harbor. Auda still wore a long rich fur-lined German field-officer's greatcoat, a garment little suited to the climate but, as he insisted, magnificent booty. He had about a thousand men, three-quarters of them on foot, and next to him marched Rasim, the gunner commandant, with his four old Krupp guns on the pack-mules, just as we had taken them, without authority, from the Egyptian Army.

Rasim was a Damascene, a sardonic fellow, who rose laughing to every crisis and slunk about like a sore-headed bear, with grievances, when things went well. On this day there were dreadful murmurings, for alongside him rode Abdulla el Deleimi, the dapper Mesopotamian in charge of the machine-guns, a quick, clever, rather superficial but attractive officer, much of the professional type, whose great joy was to develop some rankling sorrow in Rasim till it discharged, full blast, on Feisal or myself. Today I helped him by telling Rasim that we were moving at intervals of a quarter-day in echelon of sub-tribes. Rasim looked over the new washed under wood, which glistened at each raindrop in the light of the evening sun setting, out across the waves, below a ceiling of red clouds, and he also looked at the wild mob of Bedouin racing here and there by foot after birds and rabbits and lizards and jerboas and after each other, and assented sourly, saying that he too would shortly become a sub-tribe, and echelon himself half a day to one side or another, and be quit of flies.

We rode over the flat sand, winding among the thorn trees, which here were plentiful and large, till we came out on the sea beach and turned northward along a broad well-beaten track, the Egyptian pilgrim road. It ran within fifty yards of the sea, and we could go up it thirty or forty singing files abreast. A little later an old lava bed half-buried in sand jutted out from the hills four or five miles away to the cast, and made a promontory to the left of us. The road cut across this, but by the near side were some mud flats, on which shallow reaches of water burned in the last light of the sun out to sea: and as this was Gelib, and our expected water, Feisal signaled the halt. We got off our camels and stretched ourselves and walked before supper to the sea by hundreds, and bathed, a screaming splashing mob of fish-like naked men of all earth's colors.

Supper was to look forward to, as a Juheini had shot a fat gazelle that afternoon, and had given it to Feisal: and gazelle meat was better than any other found in the desert, because of its fatness, however barren the land and dry the water-holes. At first starting a man in the crowd had shot a hare from the saddle, but for the risk of much wild shooting Feisal had then forbidden it, and the succeeding hares, jerboas and lizards put up by our camels' feet had been chased with sticks. We laughed at these sudden commotions in the marching companies, cries and camels swerving violently, their riders leaping off and laying out wildly with their canes, to kill and to be pickers-up of the kill Feisal was happy to see the army win so much meat, but disgusted at the shameless Juheina appetite for lizards and jerboas, The lizards were the *dhab:* beasts two feet long and as thick as a man's calf

Supper was the expected success, and after it we retired early and supine: but soon after Newcombe and myself had stretched out in our tent, we were quickened by a wave of excitement traveling up the lines running camels, shots and shouts. A breathless slave thrust his head under the flap, crying. 'News, news, Sherif Bey is taken!': I jumped up and ran through the gathering crowd to Feisal's tent, which was already filled and beset by a wild mob of mends and servants. Beside Feisal, portentously and unnaturally collected in the din, sat Raja ibn Khuluwi, the Temimi (Ben; Mohammed Harb) tribesman, who had kept to Abdulla Feisal's word to move from Henakiyeh into Wadi Ais. Feisal was radiant, his eyes swollen with joy, and he jumped up and shouted to me through the other voices, 'Abdulla has captured Eshref Bey', and then I knew how big and good the event was.

Eshref was a notorious adventurer in the lower levels of Turkish politics. In his boyhood near his Smyrna home he had been just a brigand: but with years he became a revolutionary, and when he was finally captured Abd el Hamid exiled him to Medina, where he spent five colored years. At first he was imprisoned by the governor, but one day broke the privy window and escaped to take refuge with Shekad, the bibulous Emir, in his suburb of Awali. Shekad was as usual at war with the Turks and gave him sanctuary, but Eshref found life dull there, and one day seeing a fine mare in the stable, borrowed her and rode to the Turkish barracks. On its square was the officer-son of his enemy the governor drilling a company of unarmed gendarmes. He galloped him down, slung him across the saddle in front of him and made away before the astonished police could protest.

He took off to Jebel Ohod, an uninhabited place, driving his prisoner before him, calling him his ass, and lading upon him the thirty loaves and the skins of water he provided for their nourishment. To recover his son the Pasha gave Eshref liberty on parole and five hundred pounds. He invested the money in camels, a tent, and a wife, and wandered like an Arab among the tribes till the Young Turk movement came. Then he reappeared in Constantinople and became a bravo, doing Enver's murders. His services earned the appointment of inspector of refugee relief in Macedonia, and he retired a year later with an assured income from landed estate. When war broke out he was in Egypt, and after some adventures on the Suez Canal went down to Medina, with the mission to open communications with the isolated Turkish garrison in Yemen.

For this cause he was allowed to enroll volunteers from the army in Medina, was given funds, and letters from the Sultan to all neutral notables in Arabia. He determined to proceed by way of Hail, the capital of ibn Rashid. His track on this first stage of the journey had happened to cross Abdulla's, on his way to Wadi Ais, near Kheibar, and some of the Arabs, watching their camels during a midday halt, had been stopped by Eshref's men and questioned. They said they were Heteyrn and Abdulla's army was only a supply caravan going to Medina Eshref released one of them with orders to bring up the whole party for examination: and this man told Abdulla of the soldiers up there on the hill.

Abdulla was puzzled and sent horsemen to investigate. A minute later he was startled by the sudden chatter of a machine-gun. He leaped to the conclusion that the Turks had sent out a fighting column to cut him off; and ordered all his mounted men to charge them, desperately. They galloped over the machine-gun with few casualties, and scattered the Turks. Eshref fled on foot to the hilltop. Abdulla offered a reward of a thousand pounds for him, and near dusk he was found, wounded, and captured by Sherif Fauzan el Harith.

In the baggage were twenty thousand pounds in coin, robes of honor, costly presents, some interesting papers, and camel-loads of rifles and Mauser pistols. Abdulla wrote an exultant letter to Fakhri Pasha, telling him of the capture, and left it nailed to an uprooted telegraph pole, between the metals of the railway where he crossed it next night on his unimpeded way to Wadi Ais, Raja had left him there, camped in quiet and in ease. The news was a double fortune for us.

Between the joyful men slipped the sad figure of the Imam, till he stood in front of us and raised his hand. Silence fell for an instant: he said, 'Hear me', and intoned an ode in praise of the event, to the effect that Abdulla was specially favored, and had attained quickly to the glory which Feisal was winning slowly but surely by hard work. The poem was creditable as the issue of only sixteen minutes, and the poet was rewarded in gold. Then Feisal saw a gaudy jeweled dagger at Raja's belt; Raja stammered it was Eshref's. Feisal threw his own across and pulled off the other, to give it in the end to Colonel Wilson. 'What did my brother say to Eshref?' 'This is your return for our hospitality', and Eshref had replied like Suckling... 'I can fight, whether I am wrong or right.

'How many millions did the Arabs get?' asked old Mohammed Ali when he heard of Abdulla to the elbows in the captured chest flinging gold by handfuls to the tribes. Raja's story was everywhere in demand, and he slept a richer man that night. His news deserved it, for Abdulla's march to Ais made the Medina situation sure. Murray was pressing in Sinai, Feisal nearing Wejh, and Abdulla half-way between Wejh and Medina, within striking distance of the line: consequently the position of the Turks in Medina became defensive only. They must reinforce the railway guards, and could only draw the necessary men from the field army which had been striking at Yenbo and Rabegh. The tide of ill fortune in the Arab Revolt had turned: we were made happy in the knowledge and the camp was noisy until dawn.

On the next day we rode easily, first across the lava bed which was only a quarter of a mile wide, and not rough, and then over ordinary Tehama till about time for breakfast, when we found some more little water-pools. By them we made a halt, and afterwards in the noon warmth marched a few more miles, and camped in the bed of a valley flowing down from el Sukhur, a group of three extraordinary hills which protruded from the low masses of Jebel Heiran like three granite bubbles blown through the earth by someone as a violent joke. The journey was a pleasant one, for we had a success to look for in front, and a success continuing behind us, and our stages were short and comfortable.

It was cool, there were a lot of us, and we two Englishmen had a tent in which we could shut ourselves up and be alone for a while. A weariness of the desert was the living always in company, each of the party hearing all that was said, and seeing all that was done by the others day and night. Yet the craving for solitude seemed part of the delusion of self-sufficiency, a fictitious making rare of the person to enhance his own strangeness in his own eyes. To have privacy, as Newcombe and I had, was ten thousand times more restful than the open life, but the work suffered by that erection of a bar between us and the men on whose goodwill and obedience the success would rest. Among the Arabs there was no distinction except the unconscious power which accomplishment gave a famous sheikh, and they taught me that no man could be their leader except he ate the ranks' food, and wore their clothes, and lived level with them, and yet appeared better in himself

In the morning they told us that the Arwa had fallen behind, since we had exhausted the pools at Gelib, and they had had to make a side-march to untouched water. However, we pushed on towards Abu Zereibat regardless, in a day that we felt burning hot after the cold and wet weather of the winter. Today the sun was incandescent in a cloudless sky, and the old eye-racking dazzle and dance of sunbeams on polished sand and polished flint again bewildered me. Our path rose slightly, and we looked over a sweeping fall of bare black gravel between us and the sea, which now lay about eight miles to the westward. On our right, Heiran and its fellow ranges in ridge after ridge of ascending degrees built up the great Shefa, the littoral escarpment of the Red Sea watershed.

We stopped once, and afterwards began to feel that in front of us soon must be a point from which a great depression would lie open: but it was not till two in the afternoon that we crossed a low basalt outcrop to this crest. From it we looked out over a trough fifteen miles across, which was Wadi Hamdh escaped from the hills. On the north-west spread the great delta through which Hamdh spilled itself by twenty mouths into the sea: and we saw the dark lines which were thickets of scrub in the flood channels of the dried beds twisting in and out across the flat from the hill-edge beneath us, till they were lost in the sun-haze thirty miles away beyond us to our left, near the invisible sea.

Behind Hamdh rose sheer from the plain a double hill jebel Raal, hog-backed, only for a gash which split it in the middle. Later we found that in the very heart of the hill the gash widened out to make a setting for a shingle-strewn, white, tree-covered plain, Magrah Raal. To our eyes, sated with small things, it was a fair sight, this end of a dry river longer than the Tigris, the greatest valley in Arabia, first understood by Doughty, and as yet unexplored: and though Rudhwa behind Yenbo was greater and cleaner cut, still Raal was a great hill, sharp and distinctive, and did honor to the Hamdh.

Full of expectation, we rode down over the gravel slopes, on which tufts of grass became more frequent, till at three o'clock we entered the wadi itself It proved to be a bed about a mile wide, filled with clumps of *Oslo* bushes, round which clung sandy hillocks each a few feet high. The sand was not pure, but seamed with lines of dried and brittle clay, the indications of old flood levels. These divided the sand hills sharply into layers, and they were rotten with salt in their dried mud, and flaking away, so that our camels sank fetlock-deep into them with a crunching noise like breaking pastry. The dust rose up in thick clouds, thickened yet more by the sunlight held in them.

The ranks behind could not see where they were going, which was difficult for them, as the hillocks became closer together, and split the bed into a maze of shallow channels, the work of partial floods year after year. Before we came to the middle of the valley everything was overgrown by the brushwood, which sprouted out from the mounds and laced one to another and its twigs were dry and dusty, and brittle as old bone. We tucked in the streamers of our gaudy saddlebags, to save their being jerked off by the bushes, drew our cloaks tight over our clothes, bent our heads down to save our eyes and crashed straight through like a storm through reeds. The dust was blinding and choking, and the snapping of the branches, grumbles of the camels, shouts and laughing of the men made a rare happening of it all.

Chapter 28: In Billi Country

When we in front had almost reached the far bank the ground suddenly cleared, and we rode across a clay bottom, in which stood a deep brown water pool, eighty yards long and about fifteen yards wide. This was the flood-water of Abu Zereibat, our goal. We went a few yards further, through the last scrub, and reached the open north bank of Wadi Hamdh, where Feisal had appointed the camp. It was a huge plain of sand and flints, running open to the very feet of Raal, with room on it for all the armies of Arabia. So we stopped our camels there, and the slaves unloaded them and set up the tents, while we walked back to see the mules thirsty after their long dry march since the previous day, and the foot soldiers rushed into the pond kicking and splashing with pleasure in the sweet water. The abundance of fuel was an added happiness, and in whatever place they chose to camp every little group of friends had a roaring fire, very welcome, as a wet mist rose eight feet thick out of the ground and with it our woolen cloaks stiffened and grew cold.

It was a black night, moonless, but above the fog very brilliant with the stars and it was strange to stand on a little mound near our tents and look over the rolling white sea of fog, out of which stood tent-peaks and tall spires of melting smoke, luminous underneath where the flames licked up into the clean air, and to listen to the noises of the unseen army. Old Auda ibn Zuweid corrected me gravely when I said this to him, telling me, 'It is not an army, it is a world which is moving on Wejh', and I rejoiced at his insistence, for it had been to create this very feeling that we had hampered ourselves with the unwieldy crowd of men in so difficult a march.

That evening the Billi began to come in to us shyly, and swear fealty, for the Hamdh valley was the boundary between them and the Juheina. Soon after Hamid el Rifada rode up with a numerous company to pay his respects to Feisal. He told us that his cousin Suleiman Pasha, the paramount of the Billi, was at Abu Ajaj, fifteen miles to the north of us, trying desperately for once to make up the mind which had chopped and balanced profitably throughout a long life. Then without warning or parade Sherif Nasir of Medina came in to us. Feisal leaped up and embraced him, and led him over to me.

Nasir made a splendid first impression, all and more than we had hoped, much as we had heard, and much as we were expecting of him. He was the opener of roads, the forerunner of Feisal's movement, the man who had fired the first shot in Medina, and who was to fire the last shot at Musleimieh beyond Aleppo on the day that Turkey asked for an armistice: and from beginning to end all that could be told of him was good. Our thoughts of him were of an honest simple man serving his country for love of it, and never grudging anything, however hard, which seemed to its advantage.

He was a brother of Shehad, the Emir of Medina. Their family was descended from Hussein, the younger of Ali's children, and they were the only descendants of Hussein considered Ashraf and not Saada. They were Shias, and had been since the days of Kerbela, and in Hejaz were respected only second to the Emirs of Mecca. Nasir himself was a man of gardens, whose lot had been unwilling war since boyhood. The spirited attack upon Medina seen by Wavell on his first pilgrimage was to save Nasir who had been wounded in the foot and captured by the Turks: and had the rescue not succeeded the course of this revolt of the Sherifs might have been different. He was now a man of twenty-seven, with a low broad forehead and sensitive eyes. His weak pleasant mouth and small chin were clearly seen through his clipped black beard.

For the last two months he had been up here in Wadi Hamdh, containing Wejh, and Feisal asked him for the last news. He replied that the company of Turkish camel corps posted near us at Wadi Miya had been withdrawn that morning towards Wejh. Also Hamaad el Mangara had raised the Moahib and some of the Billi of the mountain for the Sherif in spite of the appeals of Dakhil-Ailah, the Kadhi of the Juheina who implored them to remain pro-Turk or at least neutral. He had no word of our other detachments coming up by Towala and Khuff from Urn Lejj.

We slept late the following day, to brace ourselves for the necessary hours of talk. Feisal carried most of this upon his own shoulders: Nasir supported him as second-in-command, and the Beidawi brothers sat by to help. The day was bright and warm, threatening to be hot later, and Newcombe and I wandered about looking at the watering and the men, and the constant parties of newcomers. When the sun was high a great cloud of dust from the east heralded a larger party and we walked back to the tents to see Mirzuk el Tikheimi, Feisal's sharp, mouse-featured guest-master, ride in. He led his force of Hameida, Samarra and Foweida clansmen of the Juheina past the Emir at a canter to make a show. They stifled us with their dust, for the dozen horsemen in his van, carrying a large red flag and a large white flag, drew their swords and charged round and round our tents. We admired neither their riding nor their mares: but this may have been because they were a nuisance.

At noon the Wuld Mohammed Harb and the mounted men of the ibn Shefia battalion came in, three hundred men, under Sheikh Salih and Mohammed ibn Shefia. Mohammed was a tubby vulgar little man of about fifty-five, common-sensible and energetic, rapidly making a name for himself in the Arab army, for he would get any sort of manual work done by his men, who were the sweepings of Wadi Yenbo, landless and without family, or else the laboring class of Yenbo townsmen, hampered by no inherited dignity or prejudices. They were more in hand than any other of our troops except the gentlemanly Ageyl.

Just before the afternoon prayer we had another dust-bath, when Mifleh el Hansha brought in the Zuweida, and Sherif Mohammed ibn Jebarra brought in the Beni Ibrahim. These two contingents of two thousand strong made up the tail of our tribal forces except for Saad el Ghoneim, head of the Marawin of Urn Lejj, and he did not arrive till the work was over. We were already two days behind our program and Newcombe decided to ride ahead this night to Habban with Mohammed Ali el Beidawi and Hamid Rifada. There he would meet Boyle and explain that we would fail the *Hardinge* at the rendezvous, but would be very glad if she could return there on the evening of the twenty-fourth when we would arrive much in need of water. He would also see if the naval attack could be delayed till the twenty-fifth to preserve the joint scheme.

After dark there came a message from Suleiman Rifada, with a gift camel for Feisal and a message asking him to keep it if he was friendly or to send it back if hostile. Feisal was vexed and protested his inability to understand so feeble a man. Nasir replied at once. 'Oh, it's because he eats fish. Fish swells the head and then this follows: The Syrians and Mesopotamians and men of Jidda and Yenbo laughed loudly to show that they did not share this belief of the upland Arab that a man of his hands was disgraced by tasting the three mean foods — chickens, eggs and fish. Feisal said with mock gravity. You insult the company we like fish: Others said, 'We abandon it. and take refuge in God': and Mirzuk to change the current said. 'He is an unnatural birth neither raw nor ripe: However we eventually left Suleiman alone, for Feisal was careful to avoid the semblance of conflict in order that his rebellion might keep its boast of having never fired a conscious shot at an Arab nor been fired at by an Arab. This record gave it a surface of universality and protected it against the entry of tribal feuds into its texture.

We left Abu Zereibat on the morning of Tuesday the twenty-third of January early and marched for three hours in a straggle down Wadi Hamdh. Then the valley went away to the left, and we struck out across a hollow plain which seemed to extend from the tooth-like peak of Abu Ajajon the right, to the Hamdh, and on its far side to Jebel Kurkrna, the southern pillar of the delta. This desolate featureless region today was cold and the hard north wind drove down the grey coast into our faces. As we marched we heard intermittent heavy firing from the direction of Wejh, and feared that the Navy had lost patience and were acting without us. However we could not make up the days we had wasted, so we pushed on for the whole dull stage crossing affluent after affluent coming down from the Abu Ajaj direction. The plain was striped with these wadis, all shallow and straight and bare, as many and as intricate as the veins in a leaf at last we re-entered Hamdh, at Kesir: about half-past four in the afternoon; we had meant to halt there for water, but the pools were dry. So we went on for another half-hour to Kuma, and though its clay bottoms also held only mud, decided to camp, rather than to search further in the dark.

While we were camping there was a sudden rush. Camels had been seen pasturing away to the east, and the energetic of the Juheina streamed out, captured them and drove them in. Feisal was furious, and shouted to them to stop, but they were too excited to hear him: so he snatched his rifle, and shot at the nearest man, who was about two hundred yards away. He missed him but the man was frightened and tumbled off his saddle, and the others seeing this checked themselves. Feisal had them all up before him, laid about the principal with his camel-stick, and impounded the stolen camels and those of the thieves till the number was complete. Then he handed the beasts back to their Billi owners, who had by now run in as suppliants. Had he not done so it would have involved the Juheina in a private war with the Billi, our hoped-for allies of the morrow, and might have checked the extension of the Arab Movement beyond Wejh.

The next morning we made for the beach, and up it, along the Egyptian pilgrim road to Habban at four o'clock. The *Hardinge* was duly there, to our relief, and already landing water, although the small bay gave little shelter, and the rough sea rolling in made boat-work hazardous. Many captains would have said that as we had not kept our timetable we should have no water, but Linberry's humanity recognized our goodwill and fight against circumstance, and that our mules and men might die of thirst if he did not afford relief, He was able to land about a third of the proper quantity before night and the waves stopped work. We reserved first call for the mules, and gave what was left to the more thirsty of the footmen, but it was a difficult night, and crowds of suffering men lingered jostling about the tanks in the rays of the searchlight, hoping for a last attempt.

I went on board, and heard that the naval attack had been carried out on the Um Lejj plan as though the land army were present, since Boyle feared the Turks would run away if he waited.

As a matter of fact the day we reached Abu Zereibat, Ahmed Tewfik Bey, Turkish governor, had called in his camel corps, and addressed the garrison, saying that Wejh must be held to the last drop of blood. Then at dusk he had got on to his camel and ridden off to the railway with the few mounted men fit for the journey. The two hundred infantry determined to do his abandoned duty, and put up a good fight against the landing party: but they were outnumbered three to one, and the naval gunfire was too heavy to let them make proper use of their positions. So far as the *Hardinge* knew, the fighting was not ended, but Wejh town had been occupied by us.

Chapter 29: Wejh

The news excited the army, which began to trickle off northward soon after midnight. At dawn we rallied the various contingents in Wadi Miya, twelve miles south of the town, and advanced on it in order, sending one detachment eastwards to Kalaat el Sebeil, the pilgrimage station six miles east of Wejh, and the Turks' way of retreat towards el Ula. This force found a remnant of the Wejh infantry there, and scattered them into the hills. The Billi, seeing them defenseless, captured them, and to maintain an absolute impartiality delivered half to Feisal and the other half to Basri Pasha, the Turkish commandant in el Ula. The fort at Sebeil was stocked with Turkish rifles, far more than could ever have been required for the few troops at Wejh our men shared them out, with the ammunition, the little food, and the clothing also there.

We in the main body went on straight towards el Wejh, meeting a few scattered Turks, of whom one party put up a short resistance. They said the ridge, or rather the coral reef at the end of the long valley down which we rode, was still held. The Ageyl dismounted, and stripped off their cloaks and head cloths and shirts, and went on in brown half-nakedness, which they said would ensure clean wounds if they were hit: also the clothes would not be damaged. Ibn Dakhil took command, and I admired the quietness and regularity of their obedience. They advanced by alternate companies, in open order, at intervals of four or five yards, with even-numbered companies in support, making good use of the poor cover which existed.

It was pretty to look at the neat little brown men in the sunlit sandy valley with the blue pool of salt water in their midst to set off the crimson banners which two standard bearers carried in the van. They went along in a steady lope, covering the ground at nearly six miles an hour, dead silent, and reached and climbed the ridge without a shot fired. So we knew the work had been finished for us and trotted forward, to find the boy Saleh, son of ibn Shefia, in possession of the town. After us from all points of the desert the army came racing in.

Saleh told us that the casualties had been nearly twenty killed, and later we heard that a lieutenant (R.F.C.) had been mortally wounded in a seaplane reconnaissance. One British seaman was wounded in the foot. Vickery, who had directed the battle, was satisfied, but his satisfaction annoyed me. The whole fight seemed to me unnecessary; and his conduct of it a proof of his misconception of the tactics of the revolt. For us to win an unnecessary action, or to fire an unnecessary shot or to suffer an unnecessary casualty, was wrong.

Our men were not materials, like soldiers, but friends of ours, trusting in our leadership. We were in command not professionally, but by favor, and our men were volunteers, individuals, local men, relatives so that a death was a personal sorrow to many in the army. It was silly with tribesmen to play the Turks according to 'Army' rules, and yet hope for advantage. The two hundred Turks in Wejh had no transport and no food, and if left alone a few days would have surrendered in the usual way.

Even had they escaped, the value of a single Arab life wouldn't have mattered. We wanted Wejh as a base against the railway and to extend the Arab front, and the smashing and killing in it had been wanton.

The place was inconveniently smashed. Its townspeople had been warned by Feisal of the coming attack, and advised either to forestall it by revolt, or to clear out: but they were mostly Egyptians from Kosseir, preferred the Turks to us, and decided to wait the issue. So when the ibn Shefia men and the Biasha entered, fighting, they found the houses packed with fair booty, and made a sweep of it. They robbed the men, broke open doors, searched every room, smashed chests and cupboards tore down all fittings and slit open every mattress and pillow for hidden treasure: while the fire of the fleet punched large holes in every prominent wall or building. In short the town was in a woeful mess almost uninhabitable when its people returned from the hills.

Our main difficulty was the landing of stores. The Fox had sunk the local lighters and rowing boats and there was no sort of quay: but the resourceful *Hardinge* thrust herself into the harbor which was wide enough but much too short and landed our stuff in her own cutters. We got up a tired working party of ibn Shefia followers and with their clumsy or languid help got enough food into the place for the moment's needs. The townspeople had returned only to bother us for they were hungry and furious at the state of what had been their property and began to take it out by stealing everything of ours unguarded even slitting open the rice-bags on the beach and carrying away quantities in their held-up skirts. Feisal corrected this by making the pitiless Maulud town governor. He brought in his rough-riders and in one day of wholesale arrest and summary punishment had convinced half the able-bodied males to leave our things alone.

Two days later I went up on the *Hardinge* to Cairo with Colonel Wilson to ask Egypt for the fuller assistance which we felt we might expect now we had shown ourselves an investment worthy of confidence: and we received it. In other respects, the capture of Wejh, which had been a foregone conclusion when the Navy showed itself so willing to help, gave us what we wanted. The moral greatness of the march up-country left the Arab Movement without an active opponent in Western Arabia: and there could be no question of its failing whatever happened afterwards. In particular the vexed Rabegh question died.

The cheap price we paid for these benefits was our trouble on the march and even from this we drew profitable lessons in tactics and the organization of raids. Feisal had been quite alone during the operation for Sharraf his Chief of Staff in Wadi Yenbo, had been left there as district Emir, and Sheikh Yusufhad stayed in Urn Lejj. Feisal had shown a large indifference to detail sound enough if he had had good assistants but dangerous when dealing with very ordinary sheikhs; and the confusion taught me how low the limit of efficient number in Bedouin warfare was, and how even the best of the Arab leaders could not successfully exceed it. His Syrian staff lost grip, or rather never grasped at all the nature of the Bedouin about them: and this taught me not to mix sedentary Semite and nomad Semite in one pack. As I realized all these things, the deaths of those twenty men in the Wejh streets seemed not to matter much.

BOOK III

A Railway Diversion

Our taking Wejh had the desired effect upon the Turks, who gave up their advance towards Mecca, and took on a passive defense of Medina and its railway. We prepared to attack these according to our experts' plans.

The Germans saw the danger of envelopment, and persuaded Enver to order the instant evacuation of Medina. Sir Archibald Murray begged us to put in such a sustained attack: as should destroy the retreating enemy.

Feisal was soon ready to do this: so I went off to Abdulla to get his co-operation. On the way I fill sick and while lying alone with empty hands was driven to think about the campaign. I saw that our practice was better than our theory.

So on recovery I did little to the railway, but returned to Wejh with new ideas. I tried to make the others admit them to their minds, to adopt deployment as our ruling principle, to put preaching before fighting.

They preferred the limited and direct objective of Medina. So I decided to leave them, and to slip off by myself to Akaba to test my own theory.

Chapter 30: Rewards and Squabbles

In Cairo the yet-hot authorities promised us more money for Feisal, mules and machine-guns and mountain guns: but these last of course we never got. The gun question was an eternal torment. Because of the hilly trackless country field guns were no use to us: and the British Army had no mountain guns, except the Indian ten-ponder which was serviceable only against an unarmed enemy. The War Office might have borrowed or bought guns from her allies: but did not. Bremond had some excellent Schneider sixty-fives at Suez, with Algerians to man them, but he regarded them only as a lever by which to move Allied troops into Arabia. When we asked him to send them down to us even without the men, he would reply first that the Arabs would not treat their crews properly, and then that they would not treat the guns properly. His price was a British brigade for Rabegh, and we would not pay it.

He feared to make the Arab army too formidable: which was an argument one could understand: but the case of the British Government was incomprehensible. It was not ill-will, for they gave us all else we wanted; nor was it niggardliness, for their total help to the Arab Movement in materials and money was over ten millions. I believe it was sheer stupidity: but it was maddening to be unable to attempt many enterprises, and to fail in many others which we did attempt, for the merely technical reason that we could not keep down the Turkish artillery, since its guns outranged ours by three or four thousand yards. In the end, fortunately, Bremond overreached himself, after keeping his batteries idle for a year at Suez. Commandant Cousse, his successor, ordered them down to us, and by the help of one of them we entered Damascus: but for the preceding year they had been, to each Arab officer who entered or left our base in Suez, silent incontrovertible witnesses of French malice towards the Arab Movement.

We received a great reinforcement to our cause in Jaafar Pasha, a Bagdadi officer from the Turkish Army. After distinguished service in the German and Turkish armies he had been chosen by Enver to organize the levies of the Sheikh el Senussi, and sent to Tripoli in a submarine. There he had made a decent force of them, and had shown good tactical ability against the British in two battles. Then he was captured and lodged in the Citadel at Cairo with the other officer prisoners of war. He escaped out of it, one night climbing down a blanket rope towards the moat: but the blankets fell under the strain of him and in the fall he hurt his ankle and was retaken helpless. In this state he gave us his parole, and was enlarged after paying for the torn blanket. But one day he read in an Arabic newspaper of the revolt of the Sherif, and of the execution by the Turks of prominent Arab nationalists his friends and realized all at once, that he was on the wrong side.

Feisal had heard of him of course, and wanted him as Commander-in-Chief of the regular troops. The main direction of our efforts now was to strengthen these units in his army. His need of gunners, machine-gunners, mounted infantry and trained infantry was hampering Feisal in every way. Those he had were good. They came by desertion or as volunteers from the prison-camps of the British forces in Mesopotamia and Sinai, and they were therefore enthusiasts, men fighting with ropes about their necks: but this made them difficult to command and by common agreement we knew that Jaafar was one of the few men alive with the ability, reputation and personality to weld them into an army. King Hussein would not have it. He was old and narrow, and disliked Syrians and Mesopotamians by instinct. He wanted Mecca to deliver Damascus and refused the services of Jaafar. Feisal then accepted him, on his own responsibility, for he knew that the North could only be freed by its own men, serving in the Arab ranks, and adding to the strength as they went forward, their kinsmen in the provinces they entered. Feisal was much wiser than the father, and had courage to follow his instincts.

In Cairo were Hogarth and George Lloyd and Storrs and Deedes, and many old friends: and beyond them the Arab circle of well-wishers was now strangely increased. In the Army our shares rose steadily, as we showed profits on our previous account. Lynden Bell stood firmly our friend, and swore that method was coming out of the Arab madness. Sir Archibald Murray had realized with a sudden shock that more Turkish troops were fighting the Arabs than were fighting him and began to remember how he had always favored the Arab Revolt. Admiral Wemyss was as ready to help now as he had been in our hard days around Rabegh. Sir Reginald Wingate, High Commissioner in Egypt, was happy in the success of the work he had advocated for years. I grudged him this a little, for McMahon had taken the actual risk of starting it and had been broken just before its luck turned. However, that was hardly Wingate's fault.

In the midst of my touching the slender stops of all these quills there came a rude surprise. Colonel Bremond called to felicitate me on the capture of Wejh, saying that it confirmed his belief in my military talent and encouraged him to expect my help in an extension of our success. He wanted to occupy Akaba with an Anglo-French force and naval help. He pointed out the importance of Akaba, the only Turkish port left in the Red Sea, the nearest to the Suez Canal the nearest to the Hejaz Railway, on the left flank of their Beersheba army. He suggested its occupation by a composite brigade, which should advance up Wadi Itm and deliver a crushing blow at Maan; and began to enlarge on the nature of the ground.

I replied that I knew Akaba, from before the war: and his scheme seemed to me militarily impossible. We could take the beach of the Gulf, but our forces there would be under observation and gunfire from the coastal hills as unfavorably placed as on a Gallipoli beach, and these hills were granite masses thousands of feet high, impracticable for heavy troops, and the passes through them were formidable defiles, very costly to assault or to cover. We would require thousands of the best hill-troops from India, and they would be occupied mainly in combating the local Arabs who would certainly resist a British invasion. In my opinion Akaba, whose importance was all and more than what he said, would be best taken by an irregular force of Arabs, descending from the east without naval help.

Bremond did not tell me (but I knew) that his real wish to take Akaba was to head off the Arab Movement, to get a mixed force in front of them (as at Rabegh) so that they might be confined to Arabia, compelled to waste their efforts against Medina. The Arabs always feared that the Sherifs alliance with us was based on a secret agreement to sell them at the end, and a Christian invasion would have confirmed their fears, and destroyed their co-operation.

I did not tell Bremond (but he knew) that I meant to defeat his efforts, and to take the Arabs soon into Damascus. He did not know the impossible coast between Wejh and Akaba, and feared that I would go forward again in such a march as that from which he had tried to dissuade me before Yenbo. It amused me, this childishly-concealed rivalry: but he ended his talk by saying that he was going down to Wejh anyhow to put the scheme to Feisal. Now I had not warned Feisal that Bremond was a crook. Newcombe was there, with his friendly desire to get moves on. We had not talked over the problem of Akaba. Feisal had not been there, and so knew neither the terrain nor the tribes. It seemed best for me to hurry down and put them on their guard against the notion: so I left the same afternoon for Suez, and sailed that night. Two days later in Wejh I explained myself satisfactorily.

Bremond came after ten days and opened his heart, or at least part of it, to Feisal, who returned him his tactics with improvements. Bremond began by presenting him with six Hotchkiss automatic rifles, complete with instructors to explain them to the Arabs. This was a noble gift, but Feisal took the opportunity to ask him to increase his bounty, and to give him one of the two batteries of quick firing mountain guns waiting at Suez. He explained that he was sorry to have had to leave Yenbo for Wejh, since Wejh was so much further from his objective, Medina: but it was really impossible for him to attack the Turks (who had quick-firing French guns) with rifles, or with the old weapons supplied him by the British Army. His men had not the technical excellence which made a bad tool prevail over a good one. As it was, he had to exploit his only advantages — numbers and mobility — and unless his equipment could be improved there was no saying where this protraction of his front might end!

Bremond tried to turn it off by belittling guns. They were useless for his form of warfare. On the other hand it would end the war at once if he would make his men climb about the country like goats and tear up the railway. Feisal was angry at the metaphor, which was impolite in Arabic, and, looking at Bremond's six feet of comfortable body, asked if he had ever tried to 'goat' himself. The argument was getting worse and worse, but Bremond stuck to him gallantly and introduced the question of Akaba, saying there was real danger to the Arabs in the Turks' possessing it, and how he should press the British to take it over. Feisal in reply gave him a geographical sketch of the land behind Akaba (I recognized the less dashing part of it myself) and explained the tribal difficulties and the food problem, all the points which made it a serious obstacle. He ended by saying that after the cloud of orders and counter-orders, and confusion over Rabegh, he had not really the face to approach Sir Archibald Murray with another request for an excursion.

Bremond had to retire from the battle, in good order, with a Parthian shot at me by telling Feisal to insist that the British armored cars in Suez be sent down to Wejh for service there: but even this was a boomerang since they had started! It was very silly in dealing with an Easterner whose wits had been tempered and sharpened by living in a viva-voce world, to attempt finesse or deceits unless they were superlatively well done: and Bremond cannot but have known that he was clumsy. After he had gone I returned to Cairo for a cheerful week, in which I gave my betters much good advice. Murray, who had had to earmark Tullibardine's brigade for Akaba, approved me still further when I declared against that side-show also.

When I got back again to Wejh I found Vickery just leaving for Egypt. In one way it was a pity, for he was a soldier to his fingertips, with great irregular experience and knew Arabic through and through in the way we all should have known it: but we got on better without him for he had never accepted our conditions. He was too worldly to like the Arab Revolt — indeed no one but an enthusiast could have seen the ideal that lay behind its unpleasantness and puerilities: — and the cold-blooded making use of an enthusiasm my fashion was equally beyond his understanding. So his advice was not rooted deep enough, either in thought or character, to help us: and he felt always cynical and ashamed in talk with the leaders. Then he was ambitious. His mind ran on decoration and promotion, and as he saw no public for the Arab campaign he called service in it professional suicide.

He was at once too critical with us, and too familiar with the Arabs. I imagined that the legend of our greatness would soon fade if the people knew us well and so always held a little apart in spirit, though not in manner. Vickery tended to be a regal boon-companion and risked earning their contempt by showing an unconscious condescension. To this society of Sheikhs and Sherifs with their sense of personal dignity he came fresh from years in government circles where he had experienced servility and rebellious insolence, but never friendship. His examples of native authority had been clerks or officials not men born to power and the veil of office as subtle and impermeable as our veil of flesh lay between him and the people. For this difficulty the East preferred stupid Englishmen as governors. The brilliant sometimes guessed and then were dangerous but it salved a little the hurt native self respect to fool the others. The first meeting in native dress with an Englishman, witnessing that awful blankness in his eye which saw, not a fellow man but landscape or local color had illuminated my dark places. Use would either have impressed his opinion, to the ruin of my self-respect or it would have brought resentful violence, in assertion of a common humanity. It led me to constant reading of the Houyhnhnm, whether I was dressed Arab or English fashion: but that grace was because I inhabited the same body under either envelope and could always laugh.

Chapter 31: Reorganisation

Life in Wejh was interesting. After the first troubles when stores were so difficult to land, and when landed so difficult to keep, things quieted down and the details of arms and food ran easily. We began to set our camp in order. Feisal pitched his tents (now an opulent group living tents, reception tents, staff tents, guest tents, servants') about a mile from the sea, on the edge of the coral shelf which ran up gently from the beach till it here ended in a steep drop facing east and south over the broad sandy valleys which radiated star-like from the land-locked harbor. The tents of the soldiers and tribesmen grouped themselves about these valleys, leaving the chilly height for ourselves and very delightful in the evening we northerners found it when the breeze came in from the sea and carried us the beat of the waves faint and far off like the echo of invisible traffic up a by-street in London.

Immediately beneath us were the Ageyl, an irregular close group of tents. South of these were Rasirn's artillery, and by him for company Abdulla's machine-gunners, in regular lines, with their animals picketed out in those formal rows which were incense to the professional officer, and convenient where space was precious. Out further in the valley lay the market, with a boiling swell of men always about the goods, which they set out plainly on the ground without any pretense of shops. Beyond it in all directions were the scattered tents and shelters of the tribesmen, running up every gully and windless place, and to the east the open valley full of camel-parties coming in and out past the few straggling palms which marked the nearest too-brackish well. In the background were the foothills, reefs, and clusters like ruined castles, thrown up craggily to the great horizon of the coastal range.

It was the custom in Wejh to camp wide apart, very wide apart, and my life was moving back and forth, to Feisal's tent, to the English tents, to the Egyptian Army tents, to the town, the port, the wireless station, tramping all day, restlessly up and down these coral paths in my sandals or barefoot, hardening my feet, getting by slow degrees the power to walk with little pain over sharp burning ground, tempering my already trained body to greater efforts.

The Arabs wondered why I did not ride a mare on these occasions, and I forbore to puzzle them by incomprehensible sayings such as that I was hardening myself, or that I would always rather walk than ride for hatred of animals: yet the first was true and the second was true. For me there was something disagreeable and hurtful to my pride in the sight of these lower forms of life. Their mere existence seemed a servile reflection upon our human kind, the sense with which a god would look on us: and to make use of them, or to lie under an avoidable obligation to them seemed to me shameful. It was as with the Negroes, tom-tom-playing themselves to red madness each night under the ridge: one did not mind their faces, clearly so different from our own: but it hurt that they should possess exact counterparts of all our bodies.

Inside the tents Feisal was working day and night, at his political work in which so few of us could lend him help. Outside them the crowd employed and diverted us with their parades, joy-shooting, and marches of victory. Also there were accidents. One day a group of Arabs, playing with an unexploded seaplane bomb which they had found behind our tents, set it off: and their scattered limbs were blown about the camp, marking the white canvas with red splashes which soon turned a dull brown and then faded pale. Feisal had the tents changed, and ordered the bloody ones to be destroyed: but the more frugal slaves washed them. Another day a tent took fire, and three of our guests were part-roasted. The camp crowded round and roared with laughter at them till the fire died down: and then rather shamefacedly, we cared for their hurts. A third day, a mare outside the tents was wounded by a falling bullet: and many tents were pierced. In the three years of the revolt, the Arabs for joy fired in the air millions of shots, yet by them was never a man killed. Feisal forbade the shooting twenty times, but it was good manners in Arabia, and he could not afford to reprove each new group of adherents as they joined him.

One night the Ageyl occupied us, by mutinying against ibn Dakhil their commandant, for that he fined them too generally and flogged them too often and too severely. They rushed his tent but he had taken refuge somewhere else. So they threw his things about and beat his servants, while howling, shooting in all directions, and rushing about like mad. Since there was not enough there to blunt their fury they began to remember Yenbo, and went off to kill the Ateiba. Feisal from his bluff saw their move, snatched up his sword and ran down barefoot ahead of us amongst them in the dark, laying about him to right and left with the flat of it like four men.

He delayed them a little, and meanwhile the slaves and horsemen called for more help, and we all dashed downhill and helped to break them up by rushes and shouts, and blows of sheathed swords. Mirzuk rode up and gave Feisal a horse. On it he charged down some of the ringleaders while we dispersed groups by firing Very lights into their clothing. In the end they were got back to camp with only two killed and thirty wounded. Feisal came through it quite unhurt. It was after this that we sent ibn Dakhil off to Nuri Shalaan, since though he was a splendid rider, the best man in Arabia for a long journey on camel-back, and a smart officer, yet his life would no longer have been safe from his own men.

The army in Egypt had given us two armored cars, Rolls-Royce's, released from the campaign in German East Africa. Newcombe brought them down to Wejh for trial up-country. In charge of them were Gilman and Wade, and their crews were British, men from the A.S.C. to drive and from the Machine Gun Corps to shoot. Having them in Wejh made things more difficult for us, since all the food we had been eating and the water we had been drinking were at once medically condemned: but the company of decent English people was a balancing pleasure, and the amusement of pushing cars and motor bicycles through the desperate sand in Wejh was great. The difficulty was heart-breaking, and at first we thought insurmountable: but eventually Gilman found that by taking all the armor off the Rolls, and by putting double wheels fore and aft, he could get them fairly well over the better ground, and could rush them at speed over soft places. One of these soft places was the last twenty miles of plain in front of Jebel Raal, and the cars used to cross it in little more than half an hour, leaping from ridge to ridge of the dunes, or swaying dangerously round their curves.

Driving across country was fierce labor, and the men grew arms like boxers, and used to swing their shoulders professionally as they walked. As time passed they became skilled, developing a particular style and art of sand-driving, able to get their cars over country which at first we had thought impossible. Our best drivers became wonderfully expert, and it was thanks to their breaking-in at Wejh that afterwards they did so easily at Akaba. Had we worked longer at Wejh we would have got the cars up country in fighting trim and in action against the Turks, for after passing the coastal plain the going improved, along the valleys and over the rock debris of the hills of the interior. However, as it was, they and we both learned the business. The Rolls were most useful across country, but the Crossly tenders of the Royal Flying Corps ran them close: for they had box-bodies and could carry more than our stripped armored cars. We tried some Talbots but they had too little clearance and were geared too high. The Fords ran well over the hard ground, but ploughed to a standstill wherever the sand was deep, unless we hitched them behind the Rolls or Crosslies and towed them, two or three in a string, at speed. The Arabs loved the new toys. Bicycles they called devil-horses, and thought the children of cars, which themselves were the sons and daughters of trains: it gave us three generations of mechanical transport.

The Navy added greatly to our interests in Wejh. At first, the *Hardinge* was our constant friend, but her great cargo space made her in demand everywhere along the coast till she became as fleeting a visitor as her sisters, the *Differin* and the *Northbrook.* The *Espiegle,* however, was then sent by Boyle to Wejh to stay with us, because of her general usefulness, as station ship. She had the delightful orders to 'do everything in her power to co-operate in the many plans which would be suggested to her by Colonel Newcombe, while letting it be clearly seen that she was conferring a favor'. Her captain, Fitzmaurice (a good name to bear in Turkey), was the soul of hospitality, and found some quiet amusement in our work on shore. He helped us in a thousand ways and above all in signaling, for he was a wireless expert, and one day at noon the *Northbrook* came in and landed an Army wireless set, on a light lorry, for us. There was no one to explain it, and we were at a loss: but Fitzmaurice raced ashore with half his crew, ran the car out to a good place, rigged the masts professionally, started the engine, and connected the gear to such effect that before sunset he had called up the astonished *Northbrook* and held a long conversation with her operator. The station increased the efficiency of the base at Wejh, and was busy day and night, filling the Red Sea with messages in diverse keys.

Chapter 32: Conversion

The enemy was still playing our game. Feisal's eccentric march to Wejh and Abdulla's to Wadi Ais had cut short their advance on Rabegh, and by the middle of February 1917 they had almost finished the re-arrangement of their forces. They held an entrenched line round Medina, just far enough out to make it impossible for the Arabs to shell the city (though such an attempt was never made or imagined by us) and yet confined enough to demand only a small force. Their other troops were being distributed along the railway, in strong garrisons at all water stations between Medina and Tebuk, and in smaller posts between these garrisons, so that daily patrols might guarantee the entire track. In short they had fallen back on as dull and stupid a defensive as could be conceived, and Garland had gone south-east from Wejh, and Newcombe north-east, to pick holes in it with high explosive. They would cut rails and bridges and had automatic mines to blow up running trains.

The Arabs had passed from a state of doubt to a state of violent optimism, and were promising exemplary service. We enrolled most of the Billi, though Suleiman Rifada had at last brought a vacillating mind down upon the more profitable Turkish side, and gone in to el Ula, leaving us a brother and two sons as bridges to favor if his expectations proved false. Hamaad el Mangara and Abu Shaama brought Feisal the Moahib, and made him master of Arabia between the railway and the sea. He then sent the Juheina to their homes, or to Abdulla in Wadi Ais, and washed his hands of responsibility south of Wadi Hamdh. His northern neighbors were the Abu Tageiga Howeitat, who had shown their good will just after Wejh by chasing out the small Turkish garrisons from Dhaba and Moweillah. This success cleared the coast of the Red Sea from Jedda to the mouth of the Gulf of Akaba from the enemy, and left Feisal free from all anxiety about his peace in Wejh.

He could now prepare to deal solemnly with the Hejaz Railway; but with a practice better than my principles I begged him first to delay in Wejh, and set marching an intense movement among the tribes beyond us, that in the future our revolt might be extended, and the railway threatened from Tebuk (our present limit of influence) northward as far as Maan. My vision of the course of the Arab war was still purblind, and I had not seen that the preaching was victory and the railway a delusion. For the moment I roped them together, and fortunately Feisal liked the working on men's minds better than the breaking of their railway, and so the preaching went the better.

With his nearest neighbors, the coastal Howeitat, he had already made a beginning: but we now sent to the Beni Atiyeh, stronger people lying to the north-east of us: and among them on February the twelfth, we gained a great step when Asi ibn Atiyeh came in and swore allegiance. His main motive was jealousy of his brothers, so that we did not expect from him active help: but the bread and salt with him gave us freedom of movement across his tribe's territory. To exploit this we sent up old Mohammed Ali ibn Beidawi, the lazy and popular, to Dhaba, where he confirmed the Abu Togeiga, and could work upon Beni Atiyeh. I visited him at Dhaba and found him doing well, but unable to bring in the other sons of Harb from their village of Tebuk to join us. We had not expected that he would.

If we wanted to get beyond Tebuk, towards Maan or Akaba (and we did. badly) it was clear that we must find a way round by the east, and for this we should require the favor of the nomads there. Our route would run first through the Billi and Moahib country so far as the railway: and would then cross part of the district of the Fejr. We had the Fejr. Beyond them lay the various tribes owing obedience to Nuri Shaalan, the great Emir of the Rualla, who, after the Sherif and ibn Saud and ibn Rashid, was the fourth figure in the desert.

Nuri was an old man, probably over seventy, who had ruled his Anazeh tribesmen for more than thirty years. The Shaalans were the chief family of the Rualla, but Nuri had no precedence among them by birth: nor was he loved, nor a great man of battle. His headship had been acquired by sheer force of character, and on the way to it he had had to kill two of his brothers. Since then he had added Sherarat and some sets of the other Anazeh to the number of his followers, and in all his desert his word was absolute law. He had none of the wheedling diplomacy of the ordinary sheikh: a word and there was an end of opposition or of his opponent. The Bedouin feared and obeyed him, and to use his roads we must have his friendly countenance.

Fortunately this was easy. Feisal had secured it years ago. Nuri was an Arab nationalist who had suffered exile once for his assumed convictions, and in '95 he and Feisal had made an accord, by means of Faiz el Ghusein, then a Turkish official and Feisal's secret representative. When the Arab Revolt began next year Feisal's followers and friends who had remained to allay suspicion till the last moment with Jemal in Damascus, took horse according to his instructions and galloped out twenty miles into the desert. There they met their guides, who eventually took them to jauf Nuri's desert capital, and thence to the Arab army by Medina. Since that date we had remained in touch with Nuri. Ibn Sheddad, a Beni Wahab sheikh had visited him with presents in November last, and we had received the return messages and presents while we were still in Yenbo.

Now early in February Faiz el Ghusein went up to him with ibn Dakhil from Wejh, and on the way crossed ibn Dughmi, one of the chief men of the Rualla, coming down to us with the desirable gift of a drove of some hundreds of good baggage camels. Nuri of course still kept friendly with the Turks: Damascus and Baghdad were his markets and they could have half starved his tribe in three months had they suspected: but it was understood between us that when the moment came we should have his armed help: and till then anything that would not cause an open breach with Turkey.

His favor would open to us Wadi Sirhan, the famous roadway camping ground and chain of water holes that in a series of linked depressions extended from jauf Nuri's capital in the south-east northwards to Azrak, which lay opposite Amman and Deraa, near Jebel Druse in Syria. It was the freedom of this Wadi Sirhan we needed to get from our Fejr friends to the tents of the eastern Howeitat, the famous Abu Tayi, of whom Auda, the greatest fighting man in all Arabia, was chief. Only by means of Auda Abu Tayi could we swing the tribes from Maan to Akaba so violently in our favor that they would help us take Akaba and its hills from their Turkish garrisons: only with his active support could we come from Wejh to Maan. Since our Yenbo days we had been longing for him, and trying to win him.

We made a great step forward soon after we got to Wejh, for ibn Zaal his cousin and one of the four war-leaders of the Abu Tayi, came in to us on February the seventeenth which was in all respects a fortunate day. At dawn there came in five chief men of the Sherarat, from the deserts east of Tebuk, bringing a present of eggs of the Arabian ostrich plentiful in their little frequented desert. After them, the slaves showed in Dhaif Allah. Abu Tiyur, a cousin of Hamd el Arar ibn jazi, who was paramount of the central Howeitat of the Maan plateau. These were numerous and powerful, splendid fighters and blood enemies of their cousins the nomad Abu Tay; because of an old-grounded quarrel between Auda and Hamd: we were proud to see them coming thus far to greet us, but not yet content for they were less fit than the Abu Tayi for our purposes about Maan, and so less to be regarded.

On the heels of the ibn Jazi came a cousin of Nawwaf, Nuri Shaalan's eldest son, with a mare sent by Nawwaf to Feisal. The Shaalan and the Jazi were hostile, and made eyes at one another, so we hastily improvised a new guest-camp, segregating the parties. After the Rualla, was announced Ahmed Abu Tageiga, chief of the sedentary Howeitat of the coast, bringing his tribe's respectful homage, and their spoils of Dhaba and Moweilleh. Room was made for him on Feisal's carpet, and the warmest thanks rendered him for his opportune action against the northern garrisons.

In the afternoon ibn Zaal arrived, bringing with him ten other of Auda's chief followers. He kissed Feisal's hand, once for Auda and then once for himself and, sitting back, declared that he came from Auda, to present salutation, and to ask for orders. Feisal, with policy, controlled his outward joy, and introduced him gravely to his blood-enemies the Jazi Howeitat Ibn Zaal acknowledged them distantly. Later, we held great private conversations with him and dismissed him with rich gifts and richer promises, and Feisal's message to Auda that his mind would not be happy till he had seen him face to face in Wejh.

Auda was an immense chivalrous name, but an unknown quantity to us, and in so vital a matter as Maan we could not afford a mistake. He must come down and see us, so that we might weigh him, and frame our future plans actually in his presence. After ibn Zaal came Hamed and Jezaa Abu Shaama, with Billi and Wuld Ali sheikhs, to report progress against the railway, and the gradual hemming in of the Turks in their station-garrisons.

This was one day, a fortunate day indeed but, except that all its events were happy, not essentially unlike Feisal's every day, which made fat my diary. The roads leading down to Wejh were full of envoys and volunteers, and great sheikhs riding in to swear allegiance. The contagion of their constant passage made the lukewarm Bilti always more profitable to us. Feisal swore the new adherents solemnly on the Koran between his hands, to wait while he waited, march when he marched, to give obedience to no Turk, to do kindness to all who spoke Arabic whether Bagdadi, Aleppine and Syrian, or pure blooded, and to put independence above life, family, or goods. He also began to confront them at once in his presence with their tribal enemies, and to compose their feuds. An account of profit and loss would be struck between the parties with Feisal modulating and interceding between them and often paying the balance or contributing towards it from his own funds to hurry on the pact.

For two years Feisal so labored daily putting together and arranging in their natural order the innumerable tiny pieces that made up Arabian society and combining them into his one design of war against the Turks. There was at this moment no blood feud behind him in all the districts through which he had passed and he was court of appeal for Western Arabia. I think he showed himself very worthy of this office. He never gave a partial decision or a decision so impracticably just that it must lead to disorder. No Arab ever impugned his judgments or questioned his wisdom and competence in tribal business.

By patiently sifting out right and wrong by his tact his wonderful memory he gained an ascendancy over the nomads from Medina to Damascus and beyond. He was recognized as a force transcending tribe something greater than their own blood-chiefs or jealousies. The Arab Movement became in the best sense national. Something within which all Arabs were at one and for which private interests must be set aside: and in this movement the chief place by right of application and by right of ability, properly belonged to the man who filled it for those few weeks of triumph and disillusion after Damascus was set free.

Chapter 33: A Railway Offensive

While all this cheerful work was going on an urgent message from Cairo told me to wait in Wejh for two days to meet the *Nur el Bohr,* an Egyptian patrol ship coming down with news. I was not well and so waited with an excellent grace. She arrived on March the tenth and disembarked MacRury who gave me a copy of long telegraphic instructions from Jemal Pasha to Fakhri in Medina. These were transmitted from Enver Pasha and the German staff in Constantinople, and ordered the instant abandonment of Medina, and evacuation of the troops there by route march in mass to Hedia first: thence to el Ula: thence to Tebuk: and finally to Maan where a new railhead would be constituted.

This move would have pleased the Arabs excellently, but the army of Egypt was seriously perturbed at the prospect of twenty-five thousand Anatolian troops, with far more than the usual artillery of a corps, descending suddenly on the Beersheba front. Clayton in his letter told me it was to he treated with the utmost concern, and every effort made at any cost to capture them in Medina, or to destroy them when they came out. Newcombe was away on the line doing a vigorous demolition-series about Muadhdham in the north so that the immediate responsibility fell on me. I feared that little could be done in time for the message had been some days on the way and the evacuation was to begin at once. However we went up to Feisal to talk of it.

I told him frankly the position, and that allied interests in this case demanded the sacrifice or at least the postponement of immediate advantage to the Arabs. Feisal always rose to a proposition of honor and agreed instantly to do his best. We worked out our possible resources and arranged to move them into contact with the railway at once. Sherif Mastur, an honest quiet old man, and Rasim with the Rifaa, Merawin, the mule-mounted infantry, and a gun were to proceed at once to Fagair in Wadi Hamdh. It was the first good water-base north of Wadi Ais, and Mastur's duty would be to hold up the part of the railway immediately in front of him, which was the first section north of that which Abdulla was engaging.

We sent Ali ibn el Hussein tojeida, a good spring north of Fagair, to attack the next section of line northward from Mastur. We told Abdulla ibn Mahanna to get it to el via and watch it. We sent orders to Sherif Nasir to stay out near Kalaat el Muadhdham and to keep his men in hand for an effort. I wrote asking Newcombe to come in for news. Old Mohammed Ali was to move from Dhaba to Khoreita, near Tebuk, so that if the evacuation got so far we would be ready for them. All our hundred and fifty miles of line was thus beset with parties, and we agreed that Feisal himself should stay at Wejh, ready to bring help to whatever sector most needed him.

My part was to go off at once to Sherif Abdulla in Wadi Ais, to try and find out why he had done nothing against the Turks in the last two months, and to persuade him if the Turks came out, to go straight for them. I hoped personally that we might deter them from moving at once by making so many small raids on this long length of line that traffic would be seriously disorganized and the collection of the necessary food-dumps for the army at each main stage be made impracticable. The Medina force had little animal transport and so could carry little with them. Enver had instructed them to put their guns and stores on trains and to enclose these trains in their columns, and march up the railway covering them. It was an unprecedented maneuver and I thought if we gained ten days to get in place and if they then attempted anything so silly that we would have a fair chance of destroying them all.

Next day I left Wejh, feeling very unfit for a long march while Feisal in his haste and many preoccupations had chosen me a traveling party of queer fellows. These were four Rifaajuheina, and one man of the Merawin as guides: and for myself I had the Syrian soldier-servant of Dr Hassan Sharraf, Arslan, a good fellow who made the bread and rice for me on the trip and acted besides as butt to the Arabs; also four Ageyl, a Moor and an Ateiba, Suleiman. The camels were all thin with the bad grazing of this dry Billi territory and so we would have to go slowly.

Delay after delay took place in our starting which was not till nine at night and then unwillingly: but I was determined to get clear of Wejh somehow before morning. We went four hours and then slept. Next day we did two stages of five hours each and so camped at sunset next Abu Zereibat, in our old ground of the winter. The great pool had shrunk little in the two months but was noticeably more salt. A few weeks later it was unfit to drink. It seemed there was a shallow well near by which when open afforded just tolerable water nearly all the year, I did not look for it since boils were beginning on my back and made the jolting of the camel painful and I was tired.

We rode away long before dawn and having crossed Wadi Hamdh got confused in the broken surfaces of Agunna, an area of low hills to the south of the valley. When day broke we recovered direction and went over a low watershed and down steeply into el Khubt, a hill-locked plain extending from us across to the Sukhur, the granite bubbles of hills that had been prominent on our road up from Urn Lejj. The ground was luxuriant with colocynth whose runners and fruits looked festive in the early light. The Juheina said the leaves and stalks were excellent food for the horses which would eat them and defended them from thirst for many hours. The Ageyl said that the best appetizer was to drink camel-milk from cups of the scooped-out rind. The Ateibi said that he was sufficiently moved if he just rubbed the juice of the fruit on the soles of his feet. The Moor Hamed said that the dried pith made good tinder. Anyway, they agreed that the whole plant was useless for camels.

This talk carried us across the Khubt, a pleasant three miles and through a low ridge into its second half, called el Darraj. We now saw that, of the Sukhur, two stood together to the northeast great grey striated piles of volcanic rock, reddish-colored where protected from the burning of the sun and the bruising of sandy winds. The third Sakhara, which stood a little apart, was the bubble-rock that had most roused my curiosity. Seen from nearby, it more resembled a huge football half-buried in the ground. It too was brown in color: the south and east faces were quite smooth and unbroken, and its regular domed head was polished and shining and had fine cracks running up and over it like stitched seams: — altogether one of the strangest hills in

Hejaz, a country of strange hills. We rode gently towards it looking at it across a thin shower of rain which came slanting beautifully across the sunlight. On our right were some tents of Waish Billi, taking advantage of their peace with the Juheina to move from their own draught land into the abundant pasture of their neighbors. They were watering from Heiran.

Our path took up between the Sakhara and the Sukhur by a narrow gorge with sandy floor and steep bare walls. Its head was rough. We had to scramble for fifteen minutes up shelves of coarse-faced stone and along a great fault in the hillside between two tilted red reefs of hard rock. The summit of the pass was a knife-edge and from it we went down an encumbered gap, half blocked by one fallen boulder which had been hammered over with the tribal marks of all the generations of men who had used this road. Afterwards it opened into tree-grown spaces, collecting grounds in winter for the sheets of rain which poured off the glazed sides of the Sukhur. There were granite outcrops here and there and fine silver sand underfoot in the still damp water-channels that took us down into Wadi Heiran.

We then entered a wild confusion of granite shards, piled up haphazard into low mounds, in and out of which we wandered any way we could find practicable going for our hesitating camels. Soon after noon it gave place to a broad wooded valley, up which we rode for an hour till our troubles began again, for we had to dismount and lead our animals up a narrow hill-path with broken steps of rock so polished by centuries of passing feet that they were dangerous in this wet weather. They took us over a great shoulder of the hills and down among more small mounds and valleys, and afterwards by another rocky zigzag descent into a torrent-bed. This soon became too confined to admit the passage of laden camels, and the path then left it to cling precariously to the hillside with a cliff above and a cliff below. After fifteen minutes of this we were glad to reach a high saddle on which former travelers had piled little cairns of commemoration and thankfulness.

We stopped to add one to the number, and then rode down a sandy valley into Wadi Handbag, a large well-wooded tributary of Hamdh. After the broken country in which we had been prisoner for hours, the openness of Handbag was refreshing. Its clean white bed swept on northward through the trees in a fine curve under precipitous hills of red and brown, and it gave views for a mile or two up and down its course. There were green weeds and grass growing on the lower sand-slopes of the tributary by which we had come down into it, and we stopped there for half an hour to let our camels eat the juicy healthy stuff.

They had not so enjoyed themselves since Bir el Waheidi, and tore at it ravenously, swallowing it and stowing it away — unchewed — in their stomachs pending a fit time for reposeful digestion. We then crossed the valley and up a great branch which opened opposite our entry. This Wadi Kitan was also beautiful. Its shingle face was without loose rocks and was grown over with plentiful trees. On the right were low hills: but on the left it was bounded for perhaps six miles by great heights, called the Jidhwa, in parallel ridges of steep broken granite very red just now in the sunset.

We camped at its rise, and I lay down at once under the rocks and rested, so soon as the camels were unloaded and driven out to pasture. My body was very sore, and I had headache and high fever, the accompaniments of a sharp attack of dysentery which had been troubling me along the march and had laid me out twice in short fainting fits, when the more difficult parts of the climb had asked too much of my strength. Dysentery of this Arabian coast sort used to fall like a hammer blow, and crush its victim for a few hours: after which the extreme effects passed off, but it left men curiously tired, and subject for weeks to sudden breaks of nerve.

My followers had been quarreling all day, and while I was lying by the rocks a shot was fired near at hand. I paid no attention, for there were hares and birds in the valley, but a little later Suleiman roused me and made me follow him across the valley to an opposite bay in the rocks where one of the Ageyl, a Boreida man, was lying dead with a bullet through his temples. He was stone dead, and the shot had been fired from close by, for the skin was burnt about one wound. The other Ageyl were running about frantically, and I asked what it was, and Ali their head man said that Hamed the Moor had done the murder. I suspected Suleiman, because of the feud between the Atban and Ageyl which had burned up in Yenbo and Wejh, but Ali assured me that Suleiman had been with him three hundred yards further up the valley gathering sticks, when the shot was fired. I sent out the Juheina also to search for Hamed, and crawled back myself to the baggage, feeling that this need not have happened this day of all days when I was in pain.

As I lay there I heard a rustle near me, and opened my eyes slowly to see Hamed's back as he stooped over his saddlebags which lay just beyond my rock I covered him with a pistol, and then spoke to him. He had put down his rifle to lift his gear and was at my mercy: and I kept him there till the others came. We held a court at once, and after a little Hamed confessed that he and Salem had had words and he had shot him in a mad moment. This settled the doubt which had lain in my mind; but not Hamed's fate. The Ageyl acting as relatives of the dead man demanded blood for blood. The others supported them, and I tried in vain to talk Ali round: my head was aching with the fever and I could hardly think, but probably not even in health, with any eloquence could I have begged Hamed off, for Salem had been a friendly fellow and the crime wanton.

They raised the difficulty which would make civilized man shun justice like a plague if he had not the needy to serve him as hangmen for wages. There were other Moroccans in our army, and to let the Ageyl kill one in feud would have meant reprisals by which our unity would have been endangered. It must be a formal execution, and at last desperately I told Hamed that he must die in punishment, and laid the burden of his killing on myself Perhaps they would count me not qualified for feud. At least I was a stranger and a kinless man, and no revenge could lie against my followers.

I made him enter a narrow gully of the spur, a dank twilight place overgrown with weeds. Its sandy bed had been pitted by trickles of water down the cliffs in the late rain. At the end it shrank to a crack a few inches wide. The walls were vertical. I stood in the entrance and gave him a few moments' delay, which he spent crying on the ground. Then I made him rise and shot him through the chest. He fell down on the floor shrieking with the blood coming out in spurts over his clothes, and jerked about till he rolled nearly to where I was. I fired again but was shaking so that I only broke his wrist He went on calling out less loudly, now lying on his back with his feet towards me, and I leaned forward and shot him for the last time in the thick of his neck under the jaw. His body shivered a little, and I called the Ageyl who buried him in the gully where he was. Afterwards the wakeful night dragged over me, till long before dawn I had the men up and made them load, in my longing to be out of Wadi Kitan. They had to lift me into the saddle.

Chapter 34: To Abdulla

At dawn we found ourselves crossing a steep, short pass out of Wadi Kitan into the basin of Amk, the main drainage valley of these succeeding hills. Amk flowed past Khaff, and into the sea by Gelib, where we had camped on our second night out from Urn Lejj. We turned aside to the right into Wadi Reimi, one of its tributaries, to get water. There was no proper well, but rather a seepage hole in the stony bed of the valley, and we found it partly by our noses: though curiously enough the taste, while as foul was quite unlike the smell. We refilled our water skins, and Arslan baked me bread, and we rested for two hours. Then we went on through Wadi Amk, an easy green valley which made comfortable marching.

When the Amk turned westward we crossed it and went up a small sandy tributary, between piles of the warped grey granite (like cold toffee) which was common up-country in the Hejaz. The valley became a defile, and ended at the foot of a ridge up which went a natural ramp and staircase, badly broken, twisting and difficult for camels, but short. At the head we were in an open valley for an hour, with low hills to the right and mountains to the left. There were water pools in the crags, and many Merawin tents were pitched under the fine trees that studded the flat. The fertility of the slopes was great, and on them grazed plentiful flocks of sheep and goats.

We got milk from the Arabs: the first milk which my Ageyl had seen for two years, since the drought began. The track out of the valley when we reached its head was execrable, and the descent beyond into Wadi Marrakh almost dangerous, but the view from the crest compensated us. Wadi Marrakh, a broad peaceful avenue, ran quite straight before us, between two regular walls of hills, and descended rapidly to a circus where valleys from left and right, and from the front, seemed to meet together. We rode down towards this spot, which might be four miles away: and nearing it passed a piled circle of uncut stones forty feet in diameter, and a few feet high, with a central cairn like an island within the ring, and with small square heaps round about, outside the circle. Afterwards there were frequent cairns and heaps, and rude walls in every flat place of the valley. Some looked like house-ruins, and the broken walls of garden-terraces. The Juheina ascribed them to the Beni Hillal, for their own greatest constructions were the little stone box-houses put up by the shepherd boys on cold days in winter to shelter the newborn kids or lambs from the wind.

When we entered the amphitheater it became a double sweep of the grey hill walls, back on each side in a semi-circle. Before us, to the south, the curve was barred across by a straight wall or step of blue-black lava, at whose foot was a little grove of thorn trees. We made for these and halted, and lay down in their thin shade, grateful for what cool there was. Today was very hot, and my weakness had so much increased that my head hardly held up against it. The puffs of feverish wind pressed like scorching hands against our faces, burning our eyes. My pain made me breathe in gasps through the mouth, and the wind cracked my lips and seared my throat till I was too dry to talk, and drinking became sore: and yet I always needed to drink, for the thirst would not let me lie still and get the peace I longed for. The flies were a plague.

The bed of the valley was of fine quartz gravel and white sand, whose glitter thrust between our eyelids and the level of the ground, seemed to dance as the wind moved to and fro the white tips of the stubble grass. The camels loved this grass which grew about sixteen inches high, in tufts, on slate-green stalks: and they gulped down great quantities of it until the men drove them in and couched them by me. At the moment I hated the camels, for the much food had made their breath stinking, and they belched up a new mouthful from their stomachs each time they had chewed and swallowed the last, till the green slaver of it ran out between their loose lips over the side-teeth, and dripped down their sagging chins.

In my anger from where I lay I threw a stone at the nearest which got up and wavered about behind my head near me for a time: finally it straddled its back legs and staled in wide bitter jets and I was so far gone with the heat and weakness and pain that I just lay there and cried about it un helping. The men had gone off to make a fire and cook a gazelle one of them had fortunately shot, and I realized that on another day this halt would have been pleasant to me also, for the hills were very strange and their color vivid. The base was the deep warm grey of old stored sunlight: but about their crests ran sharp veins of granite-colored stone, generally in pairs, following the contours of the sky line, like the rusted metals of a forgotten scenic railway. Arslan said they were combed like cocks, a better observation.

After the men had fed we remounted and easily climbed the first wave of the lava flood that had run down from Wadi Gara towards the hollow. This first step was short, and then we had a second, equally straight and level, on the top of which lay a broad terrace with a little alluvial plot of sand and gravel in its midst. The lava was a nearly clean floor of iron-red rock-cinders, over which were scattered great fields of loose stone. The third and other steps continued to the south of us: but we turned east, up Wadi Gara, one of the main sources oft he flow. It had perhaps been a deep granite valley before the lava came, and the lava had flowed slowly down the middle, gradually filling it, but arching itself up in the center in a heap. On each side was a trough, down which between the lava and the hillside poured the rain water as often as storms burst in the hills. The flow proper, as it coagulated, had been twisted like a rope, cracked into all possible sliver and bent back irregularly upon itself. The surface was buried in small loose fragments through which generations of camel-parties had painfully worn an inadequate track.

We struggled along for nearly two hours, going slowly, our camels wincing at every stride as the sharp edges slipped beneath their tender feet. The paths were only to be seen by the droppings along them, and by the slightly bluer surfaces of the rubbed stones. The Arabs said they were impassable after dark, which was to be believed, for we risked laming our beasts each time our impatience made us urge them on Just before five in the afternoon, however, the way got a little easier. We seemed to be near the head of the valley, which grew narrow. Two or three side streams of lava came down from the south. Before us on the right an exact crater with tidy furrows scoring it from lip to foot gave us good going for it was made up of black ash as clean as though sifted, with here and there a bank of harder soil, and cinders. Beyond it was another lava field, but one which looked older than the valley, for its stones were smoothed, and between them were stats of flat earth overgrown with rank weeds. In among these open spaces was a large group of Bedouin tents whose men ran out to us, when they saw us coming, and taking our head stalls led us in.

They proved to be Sheikh Fahad el Hansha and his men, old and garrulous warriors who had marched with us to Wejh and had been with Garland on his raid with Abd el Kerim, that great occasion when the first automatic mine had succeeded under a troop train near Toweira station. Fahad would not hear of my resting quietly outside his tent, but with the reckless equality of the desert men urged me inside into an unfortunate place amongst all his own vermin, and plied me with bowl after bowl of diuretic camel milk between questions about Europe, and my home tribe and the extent of the English camel pasturages, and the war in the Hejaz and the wars elsewhere, and Egypt and Damascus, and how Feisal was.

So passed the long hours till ten at night when at last the guest sheep was carried in, dismembered royally over a huge pile of buttered rice. I ate as much of this as manners demanded, twisted myself up in my cloak, and slept like a log, the lice and fleas unable to distract me because of my bodily exhaustion after those hours of the worst imaginable marching. The illness however, had stimulated my ordinarily sluggish fancy, which ran riot this night in dreams of wandering naked for an eternal night over interminable lava, looking like scrambled eggs gone iron-blue, and very wrong, sharp as insect bites underfoot as often as we had to climb across it, and with some horror, perhaps a dead Moor, always climbing after us.

In the morning we woke early and refreshed, with our clothes stinging-full of fiery points feeding on us. After one more bowl of milk pressed on us by the eager Fahad I was able to walk over to my camel unaided and mount her actively. We rode up the last piece of Wadi Gara to the crest, which lay among cones of black cinders from a huge crater to the south. The watershed was marked by a larger ruin, but still of dry stone, perhaps a fort to block attack from the east. Thence we turned to the right across the Gara to a branch, passing remains of old settlements, with low walls built along the edges of the basalt flows, and halted for a few moments at the tents of Musleh, Fahad's cousin, but, to his chagrin, refused hospitality. The valley ended in a chimney, up which we pulled our camels, and beyond it we had an easy descent into Wadi Murrmiya, an important tributary of Hamdh.

The middle of the valley bristled with harra like galvanized iron, but on each side there were smooth sandy beds, affording good going. After a while we came to a fault in the lava, in which was a track from our side to the other; by this we crossed, and found the lava full of patches of soil apparently of extreme richness, for in them were green trees and grassy lawns of real grass, starred with flowers, the best grazing of all our ride, and looking the more wonderfully green against the blue-black twisted crusts of rock about. The lava had changed its character. Here were no piles of loose stones, as big as a skull or a man's hand, rubbed and rounded together: but bunched and crystallized fronds of metallic rock, impassable.

Another watershed conducted us to an open place where the Juheina had ploughed some eight acres of the thin soil below a thicket of scrub. They said there were other fields like it in the neighborhood, silent witnesses to the courage and persistence of the Arabs. They called it Wadi Chetf and after it was another broken river of lava, the worst going of all that we had yet encountered. A shadowy zigzagged path across it. We lost one camel with a broken foreleg; the result of a stumble in a pot-hole: and the many bones that lay about showed that we were not the only party to suffer misfortune in the passage. However, this was the end of our lava, according to the guides, and we went along easy valleys with finally a long run up a gentle slope till dusk. The going was so good and the cool of the day refreshed me that we did not halt at nightfall after our habit, but pushed on for an hour till we had crossed from the basin of Murrmiya into the basin of Wadi Ais, and there, by Tleih, we stopped for our last camp in the open.

I rejoiced that we were so nearly in, for fever was heavy on me, and I was afraid that perhaps I was going to be really ill: and the prospect off align into the well-meaning hands of the tribesmen in such a state was not pleasant. Their only treatment of every sickness was to bum a hole or many holes in the patient's body at some other spot believed to be the complement of the part affected. It was a cure tolerable to such as had faith in it: but torture to the unbelieving, and to incur it unwillingly would be silly, and yet very probable, for the Arabs' good intentions were sometimes as selfish as their good digestions.

In the morning we had an easy ride over open valleys and gentle ridges into Wadi Ais, and arrived at Abu Markha, the nearest watering-place, just a few minutes after Sherif Abdulla had dismounted there, and while he was ordering his tents to be pitched in an acacia glade beyond the well. He was leaving his old camp at Bir el Amri lower down the valley, as he had left Murabba his camp before, since the ground had become fouled by the careless multitude of his men and animals. I gave him the letters from Feisal, and explained the situation in Medina, and the need we had of haste to block the railway. I thought he took it coolly, but without argument went on to say that I was a little tired after my journey and with his permission would lie down and sleep for a while. He pitched me a tent next his great marquee, and I went in to it and rested myself at last. It had been a struggle against faintness the day long in the saddle, to get here at all: and now the strain was ended. I felt that another hour would be the breaking point.

Chapter 35: Strategy and Tactics

I spent about ten days lying in that tent suffering a bodily weakness which made my animal self crawl away and hide till me shame was passed. As usually in such circumstances my mind cleared and my senses became more acute and I began at last to mink continuously of me Arab Revolt as an accustomed thing to rest upon against me pain. It should have been thought out long before but at my first landing in Hejaz there had been a crying need for action and we had just done what seemed to instinct best, without probing into the why. or formulating what we really wanted at the end of all. Instinct so abused without its basis of past knowledge and reflection had grown merely feminine and was now destroying my confidence: so I snatched me opportunity of this forced idleness to look for me equation between my book-reading and my movements and spent the intervals of my uneasy sleeps and dreams plucking at the tangle of our present.

As I have shown. I was unfortunately as much in command of me campaign as I pleased, and was untrained. In military theory I was tolerably read my Oxford curiosity having taken me past Napoleon to Clausewitz and his school to Caemmerer and Moltke, Goltz and the recent Frenchmen. They had seemed partial books and after looking at Jomini and Willisen I had found broader principles in Saxe and Guibert and the eighteenth century. However Clausewitz was intellectually so much me master of them all and his book so logical and fascinating that unconsciously I had accepted his finality until a comparison of Kuhne and Foch had disgusted me with soldiers made me weary of their officious glory critical of all their light. In any case my interest had been abstract concerned with the philosophy and theory of warfare, especially from its metaphysical side.

Now in me field everything had been concrete especially the tiresome problem of Medina, and to distract myself from that, I began to recall suitable maxims on the conduct of warfare: but they would not fit and worried me. Hitherto Medina had been an obsession for us all: but now that I was ill whether it was that we were near to it (one seldom liked the attainable) or whether it was that my eyes were misty with too constant staring — but anyway its image was not clear. One afternoon I woke out of a hot sleep, running with sweat and pricking with flies, and wondered what on earth was the good of Medina to us? Its harmfulness when we were at Yenbo had been patent — the Turks in it were going to Mecca: but we had changed all that by our march to Wejh, Today we were blockading the railway and they only defending it. The garrison of Medina was reduced to an inoffensive size, were sitting in trenches, destroying their own power of movement by eating the transport they could no longer feed. We had taken away their power to harm us, and yet wanted to take away their town. It was not a base for us like Wejh, or a threat like Wadi Ais. What on earth did we want it for?

The camp was bestirring itself after the long torpor of the midday hours, and noises began to filter in to me from the world outside, through the yellow lining of canvas, whose every hole and tear was stabbed through by a long dagger of sunlight. I heard the stamping and snorting of the horses plagued with flies where they stood in the shadow of the trees, the complaint of camels, the ringing of coffee mortars, distant shots. To their burden I began to drum out the aim in war. The books gave it to me pat — the destruction of the armed forces of the enemy by the one process — battle. Victory could be purchased only by blood. This was a hard saying for us, as the Arabs had no organized forces. A Turkish Foch would have no aim? The Arabs would not endure casualties... how would our Clausewitz buy his victory? Von der Goltz had seemed to go deeper when he said that it was necessary not to annihilate the enemy but to break his courage, only we showed no prospect of ever breaking any body's courage.

However, Goltz was a humbug and these wise men must be talking metaphors, for we were indubitably winning our war: and as I pondered, it dawned on me that we had won the Hejaz war. Out of every thousand square miles of Hejaz nine hundred and ninety-nine were now free, and it came yet clearer to me that this was rebellion: more like peace than like war, as Vickery had provoked me to say. Perhaps in war the absolute did rule: but for peace a majority was good enough. If we held the rest, the Turks were welcome to the tiny fraction on which they stood till peace or Doomsday showed them the futility of clinging to our window pane.

I brushed off the same flies from my face patiently content to know that the Hejaz war was won and practically finished with: had been won from the day we took Wejh if we had had the wit to see it. Then I broke the thread of my argument again to listen. Those distant shots had grown and tied themselves into long ragged volleys. They ceased. I strained my ears for the other sounds which I knew would follow: and sure enough across the silence came a rustle like the dragging of a skirt over the flints all round the thin walls of my tent then a moment's pause while the camel-riders drew up: and then the soggy tapping of their canes on the thick of their beasts' necks to make them kneel.

They knelt without noise and I timed it in my memory: first the hesitation as the camels looking down felt the soil with one foot for a soft place: then the muffed thud and the sudden loosening of breath as they dropped on their foreleg since this party had come far and their camels were tired: then the shuffle as the hind legs were folded in. and the rocking as they tossed from side to side thrusting outward with their knees to bury them in the cooler subsoil below the burning flints while their riders with a quick soft patter of bare feet like birds over the ground were led off tacitly either to the coffee hearth or to Abdulla's tent, according to their business. The camels would rest there uneasily switching their tails across the shingle till their masters remembered and looked to them.

I had made a comfortable beginning of doctrine but was left still to find an alternative end and means of war. Ours seemed unlike the ritual of which Foch was priest and I recalled him to see a difference in kind between him and us. In his modern war, *absolute* war he called it — two nations professing incompatible philosophies put them to the test of force. Philosophically it was idiotic, for while opinions were arguable convictions to cure them, needed shooting: and the struggle could end only when the supporters of the one immaterial principle had no more means of resistance against the supporters of the other. It sounded like a twentieth century restatement of the early wars of religion whose logical end was the final destruction of one creed.

This might do for France and Germany but did not represent the British attitude. Our army was not intelligently maintaining a philosophic conception in Flanders or on the Canal. Efforts to make our men hate the enemy usually made them hate fighting. Indeed Foch had knocked out his own argument by saying that such war depended on levy in mass, and was impossible with professional armies: while the old army was still the British ideal and its manner the ambition of our ranks and our files. To me the Foch war seemed only one variety, no more absolute than another. One could as explicably call it 'murder war'. Clausewitz had enumerated all sorts of wars... personal wars, joint-proxy duels, for dynastic reasons... expulsive wars, in party politics... commercial wars, for trade objects.... Two wars seemed seldom alike. Sometimes the parties did not know their aim, and blundered till the march of events took control. Victory often leaned to the clear-sighted, though fortune and superior intelligence had sadly muddled nature's inexorable law.

So I wondered why Feisal wanted to fight the Turks, and why the Arabs helped him, and saw that their aim was geographical, to extrude the Turk from all Arabic-speaking lands in Asia. Their peace ideal of liberty could exercise itself only in that condition after that process. On the way we might kill Turks: we disliked them very much: but the killing was an accidental. If they would go quietly the war would end. If not we would urge them, or try to drive them out, In the last resort we would be compelled to the desperate course of blood, and the maxims of 'murder war', but as cheaply as could be for ourselves, since the Arabs fought for freedom, and that was a pleasure to be tasted only by a man alive. Posterity was a chilly thing to work for, however a man happened to love his own, or other people's already-produced children.

At this point a slave slapped my tent-door and asked if the Emir might call. So I struggled into some clothes, and crawled over to his great tent to sound the depth of motive in him. It was a comfortable place, kept luxuriously shaded and carpeted deep in bad rugs the aniline-dyed spoils of Hussein Mabeirig's house in Rabegh. Abdulla passed most of his day in it, laughing with his friends, and playing wild games with Mohammed Hassan the court jester. I set the ball of conversation rolling between him and Shakir and the chance sheikhs, among who was the fire-hearted Ferhan ej Aida son of Doughty's friend, Motlog: and was rewarded, for Abdulla's words were definite. He emphasized his hearers' present independence compared with their past servitude to Turkey, and roundly said that this talk of Turkish heresy or of the immoral doctrine of *Yeni Turan* or of the illegitimate Caliphate was beside the point. It was Arab country and the Turks were in it: that was the one issue. My argument preened itself.

The next day a great complication of boils showed itself, to conceal my lessened fever, and to chain me down yet longer in impotence upon my face in this stifling tent. When it grew too hot for dreamless dozing I picked up my tangle again, and went on raveling it out, considering now the whole house of war in its structural aspect, which was strategy, in its outward arrangements, which were tactics and in the sentiment of its inhabitants which was psychology: for my personal duty was command and the commander, like the master architect, was responsible for all.

The first confusion was the false antithesis between strategy, the aim in war, the synoptic regard seeing each part in relation to the whole, and tactics the means towards the strategic end the particular steps of the staircase. They seemed only two points of view, from which to consider the elements of war the algebraically element of things the biological element of lives, and the psychological element of ideas. The algebraically element looked to be a pure science subject to mathematical law, inhuman. It dealt with known invariables, fixed conditions space and time inorganic things like hills and climates and railways, with mankind in type masses too great for individual variety, with all artificial aids and the extensions given our faculties by mechanical invention. It was essentially formidable.

Here was a pompous beginning, and my wits, hostile to the abstract, took refuge in Arabia again. In the Arab case the algebraic factor would first take practical account of the area we wished to deliver and I began idly to calculate how many square miles... sixty, eighty, one hundred... perhaps one hundred and forty thousand square miles. And how would the Turks defend all that?... no doubt by a trench line across the bottom, if we came like an army with banners... but suppose we were (as we might be) an influence. An idea, a thing intangible, invulnerable without front or back, drifting about like a gas? Armies were like plants, immobile as a whole, firm-rooted, and nourished through long stems to the head. We might be a vapor blowing where we listed. Our kingdoms lay in each man's mind, and as we wanted nothing material to live on, so we might offer nothing material to the killing. It seemed a regular soldier might be helpless without a target, owning only on what he sat and at what he could poke his rifle.

Then I figured out how many men they would need to sit on all this ground, to save it from our attack in depth, sedition putting up her head in every unoccupied one of those hundred thousand square miles. I knew the Turkish Army exactly, and even allowing for their recent extension of faculty by airplanes and guns and armored trains (which made the earth a smaller battlefield) still it seemed they would have need of a fortified post every four square miles, and a post could not be less than twenty men. If so they would need six hundred thousand men to meet the ill-wills of all the Arab peoples, combined with the active hostility of a few zealots.

How many zealots could we have? At present we had nearly fifty thousand: sufficient for the day. It seemed the assets in this element of war were ours. If we realized our raw materials and were apt with them, the climate the railways, deserts, and technical weapons could also be attached to our interests. The Turks were stupid, the Germans behind them dogmatically. They would believe that rebellion was absolute like war, and deal with it on the analogy of war. Analogy in human things was fudge any how: and to make war upon rebellion was messy and slow, like eating soup with a knife.

This was enough of the concrete so I sheered off *erionium* — the mathematical element — and plunged into the nature of the biological factor in command. It seemed to be the breaking point, life and death, or less finally, wear and tear. The war-philosophers had properly made an art of it and had elevated one item, 'effusion of blood', to the height of a principle. It became humanity in battle, an act touching every side of our corporal being, and very warm. There was a line of variability, man running like leaven through all its estimates, making them irregular. The components were sensitive and illogical, and generals guarded themselves by the device of a reserve, the significant medium of their art, Goltz had said that if you know the enemy's strength, and he was fully deployed, then you could dispense with a reserve: but this was never. The possibility of accident, of some flaw in materials, was always in the general's mind, and the reserve unconsciously held to meet it.

The 'felt' element in troops, not expressible in figures had to be guessed at by the equivalent of Joa in Plato, and the greatest commander of men was he whose intuitions most nearly happened. Nine-tenths of tactics were certain to be taught in schools: but the irrational tenth was like the kingfisher flashing across the pool, and there was the test of generals. It could only be ensued by instinct so sharpened by thought often practicing the stroke that at the crisis it came as naturally as a reflex. There had been men whose Yoga a so nearly approached perfection that by another road they seemed to reach the certainty of *erionium*. The Greeks might have called such genius for command *vonau;* had they been bothered by an Arab Movement.

My mind see sawed, to apply this theory to ourselves; and at once saw that it went beyond mankind. It should apply also to materials. In the Turkish Army things were scarce and precious, men less esteemed than equipment. Our cue was to destroy not his army but his minerals. The death of a Turkish bridge or rail, machine or gun or charge of high explosive was more profitable to us than the death of a Turk. In the Arab army at the moment we were chary both of materials and of men. Governments saw men only in mass: but ours being irregulars were not formations but individuals. An individual death was like a pebble dropped in water. Each might make only a brief hole, but rings of sorrow widened out from them. We could not afford casualties.

Materials were easier to replace. It was our obvious policy to be superior in some one branch, guncotton or machine-guns or whatever could be made decisive. Foch and others had laid down the maxim, applied to men of being superior at the critical point and moment of attack. We might apply it to materials, and be superior in equipment in one dominant moment or respect: and for both things and men we might give the doctrine a twisted negative side, for cheapness' sake, and be weaker than the enemy everywhere except in that one point or matter.

Most wars were wars of contact both forces striving into touch to avoid tactical surprise. Ours should be a war of detachment. We were to contain the enemy by the silent threat of a vast unknown desert not disclosing ourselves till the moment of attack. This attack might be nominal, directed not against him but against his stuff: so it would not seek either his strength or his weakness, but his most accessible material. In railway-cutting it would usually be an empty stretch of rail: and the emptier, the greater the tactical success. We might turn our average into a rule, though not a law, for war was antinomian, and develop a habit of never engaging the enemy. This would chime with the numerical plea never to afford a target. Many Turks on our front had no chance all the war to fire at us, and correspondingly we were never on the defensive except accidentally, and in error.

The corollary of such a rule must be perfect 'intelligence', so that we could plan in complete certainty. The chief agent must be the general's head, and his knowledge must be faultless, leaving no room for chance. Morale seemed to be built on knowledge and to be broken by ignorance. If we knew all about the enemy we would be comfortable. We should take more pains in the service of news than any regular staff ever took.

I was getting through my subject. The algebraically factor had been translated into terms of Arabia, and fitted us like a glove. It promised victory. The biological factor had dictated to us a rational development of the tactical line which was most in accord with the genius of our tribesmen. There remained the psychological element to build up into an apt shape. It seemed to lack a Greek name, so I went to Xenophon, a temporary soldier like myself, and stole his word dietetics, which had been the art of Cyrus before he struck.

Our propaganda was its stained and ignoble offspring. It was the pathetic, almost the ethical in war. Some of it concerned the crowd, the adjustment of its spirit to the point where it became fit to exploit in action, the prearrangement of its changing spirit to a certain end. Some of it concerned the individual, and then it became a rare art of human kindness, transcending, by purposeful emotion, the gradual logical sequence of the mind. It was more subtle than tactics, and more worth doing, since it dealt with uncontrollable, with subjects incapable of direct command. It considered the capacity for mood of our men, their complexities and mutability, and the cultivation of what in them profited our intention.

We had to arrange their minds in order of battle, just as carefully and as formally as other officers would arrange their bodies: and not only the minds of our own men, though naturally they came first. We must also arrange the minds of the enemy, so far as we could reach them: and then those other minds of the nation supporting US behind the firing line, since more than half the battle passed there in the back: and the minds of the enemy nation waiting the verdict, and of the neutrals looking on....

There were many humiliating material limits, but no moral impossibilities: so that the scope of our dietetic activities was unbounded. On it we should mainly depend for the means of victory on the Arab front: and the novelty of it was our advantage. The printing press, and each newly-discovered method of intercommunication, favored the intellectual above the physical, civilization paying the mind always from the body's funds. We kindergarten soldiers were beginning our art of war in the atmosphere of the twentieth century, able to estimate our weapons without social prejudice. To the regular officer with the tradition of forty generations of serving soldiers behind him, the old arms were the most honored. We had seldom to concern ourselves with what our men did, but always with what they thought, and for us the dietetic would be more than half command. In Europe it was set a little aside, and entrusted to men outside the General Staff. In Asia the regular elements were so physically weak that the irregulars could not let the metaphysical weapon rust unused. A province would be won when we had taught the civilians in it to die for our ideal of freedom. The presence or absence of the enemy stood only on a secondary plane.

I had now been eight days lying in this remote tent, keeping my ideas general," till my brain became sick of unsupported thinking and had to be dragged to its work by an effort of will, and went off into a doze whenever that effort was relaxed. The fever passed: my dysentery ceased and with the restored strength the present again became actual to me. Facts concrete and pertinent intruded themselves into my reveries, and my inconstant wit bore aside towards all these roads of escape. So I hurried into line my shadowy principles, to have them once precise before my power to evoke them faded.

Not perhaps as successfully as I have written down. I thought my problems out mainly. In terms of Hejaz, illustrated by what I knew of its men and its geography. These would have been too long here: so the argument has been compressed into an abstract form.

It seemed to me proven that rebellion must have an unassailable base, guarded not only from attack but from the fear of attack. These bases we had in the Red Sea ports: in the desert, in the spirits of our men. It must have a sophisticated alien enemy, disposed as an army of occupation in an area greater than it could dominate effectively from fortified posts. It must have a friendly population, of which some two per cent must be active, and the rest quietly sympathetic, to the point of not betraying the movements of the minority. The active rebels must have the virtues of secrecy and self-control: and the qualities of speed, endurance and independence of arteries of supplies. They must have the technical equipment to paralyze the enemy's communications, by destroying them where the enemy was not.

I asked myself if we had these qualities, and enjoyed these conditions, and believed that we did. The endurance of the Bedouin and their camels gave us mobility. The desert gave us security, the power of denying targets to the enemy. Time was on our side to create a striking force. In Feisal's creed of nationality we had the doctrine to make every Arab ours. Final victory seemed certain.

Chapter 36: Attacking Aba El Naam

Obviously I was well again, and began to remember why I had come to Wadi Ais. The Turks were intending to march out of Medina, and in that case Sir Archibald Murray wanted us to attack them on formal lines. It was irksome that he should come butting in to our show from Egypt, asking from us alien activities.

Battles in Arabia were a mistake since our contest was not physical but material. We only profited in them by the ammunition the enemy fired off. Our successes were square miles of country occupied. Napoleon had said it was rare to find generals willing to fight battles, but the curse of this war was that so few could do anything else. Saxe had told us that irrational battles were the refuges of fools: rather they seemed to me imposition, on the side which believed it weaker, hazards made unavoidable either by lack of land room or by the need to defend a material property dearer than the lives of soldiers. We had nothing material to lose so our best line was to defend nothing and to shoot nothing. Our cards were speed and time, not hitting power. The invention of bully beef had profited us more than the invention of gunpowder but gave us strategically rather than tactical strength. As to strategy, range was more than force.

Yet the British were the bigger, and the Arabs lived only by grace of the shadow they cast. We were yoked to Sir Archibald Murray, and must work with him, and if necessary sacrifice our interests for his, if they could not be reconciled. At the same time we could not possibly act alike. Feisal might be a free gas; Sir Archibald's army, perhaps the most cumbrous in the world, was a thing which had to be laboriously pushed forward on its belly. It was ridiculous to suppose it could keep pace with ethical conceptions so nimble as the Arab Movement: doubtful even if it could understand them. However, perhaps by hindering the railway we could frighten the Turks off their plan to evacuate Medina, and give them an excuse to remain in the town: a conclusion serviceable both to the Arabs and to the English.

Accordingly I wandered into Abdulla's tent, announced my complete recovery, and ambition to do something to the Hejaz Railway. Here were men, guns, machine-guns, explosives and automatic mines: enough for a main effort; but Abdulla was apathetic. He wanted to talk about the royal families of Europe, or the battle on the Somme; the slow march of his own war bored him. However, Sherif Shakir, his cousin and second-in-command, was fired to enthusiasm, and secured us license to do our worst. Shakir loved the Ateiba, and swore they were the best tribe on earth: so we settled to take mostly Ateiba with us. Then we thought we might have a mountain gun, one of the Egyptian Army Krupp veterans, which had been sent by Feisal to Abdulla from Wejh as a present. There was also a weird little mountain howitzer given to us off a Nile gunboat, and which I wanted very much to try. It looked like a vegetable marrow on wheels, and lay back on the ground to be fired. I could not conceive that it was of any us.

Shakir promised to collect the force and we agreed that I should go in front, gently as befitted my weakness, and search for a good target. We thought it would be best to attack a railway station, and the nearest and biggest was Aba el Naam. It sounded the most probable, or at any rate we would look at it first; so off we set. With me went Raho, an Algerian, now officer in the French Army and part of Bremond's mission, a very honest and hard-working fellow. Our guide was Mohammed el Kadhi, whose old father Dakhil-Allah, hereditary lawman of the Juheina, had guided the Turks down to Yenbo last December, and had not joined us till after Abdulla had occupied Ais. Mohammed was eighteen, solid and silent-natured. Sherif Fauzan el Harith, the famous warrior who had captured Eshref that night at Janbila, and Suleiman el Judi, a white-bearded Sherif, escorted us, with about twenty Ateiba and five or six Juheina.

We left on March the twenty-sixth, while Sir Archibald Murray was attacking Gaza, and rode down Wadi Ais: but after three hours the heat proved too much for me, and we stopped by a great sider tree (Iote or jujube, but the fruit was scarce) and rested under it the midday hours. Sired trees were very shady; there was a cool east wind, and few flies. Wadi Ais was luxuriant with thorn trees and grass, and its air with white butterflies and the scents of wild flowers: so that we did not remount till late in the afternoon, and then did only a short march, leaving Wadi Ais by the right, after passing in an angle of the valley a ruined terrace and cistern. Once there had been villages in this part, and the underground waters had then been carefully employed in their frequent gardens: but now it was waste.

We struck our camp in Wadi Seram, where there was water, early the following morning, and had two hours' rough riding around the spurs of Jebel Serd, till we got into Wadi Turaa, a historic valley, which linked itself by an easy pass to the Kheif in Wadi Yenbo. We spent this midday also under a tree, near Bir Fueis and by some Juheina tents, where Mohammed guest while we slept. Then we rode on rather crookedly for two more hours, and camped after dark in a side valley of Wadi Meseij. By ill luck this evening a very early spring scorpion bit me severely on the left hand, when I lay down to sleep. The place swelled up, and my arm was stiff and sore for several days.

At five the next morning, after a long night, we started again, and passed through the last hills, and out into the jurf an undulating open space which ran up southward to Jebel Antar, the strange crater whose split and castellated top made it a landmark from afar. We turned half-right in the plain, to get under cover of the low hills which screened it off from Wadi Hamdh, in whose bed the railway lay: and behind these hills we rode southward almost to their end which was opposite Aba el Naam. There we halted to camp quite close to the enemy and quite in safety.

The hill top above us commanded them and we climbed it at sunset for a first view of the station. The hill was perhaps six hundred feet high and steep and I made many stages of it resting on my way up: but the sight from the top was good. The railway was very clear about three miles off. The station had a pair of large two-storied houses of basalt a circular water tower and other buildings. There were bell tents and huts in the station yard and trenches but no sign of guns and we could see only about three hundred men in all. A large bridge of some twenty white limestone arches across Hamdh north of the station had its own post of a dozen tents and some shelters on a black knoll behind it. Mohammed pointed these out with satisfaction for a few weeks ago he and his father had gone down there and destroyed an arch of it as proof that their conversion to the Arab cause was real.

We had heard that the Turks patrolled their neighborhood actively at night. It seemed undesirable, so we sent off two men to lie by each blockhouse, and fire a few shots after dark. This was done and the enemy thinking it a prelude to attack, stood to under arms in their trenches all night while we were comfortably sleeping: but the cold woke us early to find a restless dawn wind blowing across the jurf and singing in the great trees round our camp. As we climbed the hill to our observation point the sun came above the clouds and an hour later it had grown very hot.

We lay like lizards in the long grass round the stones of the foremost cairn upon the hill top. and saw the garrison parade. There were three hundred and ninety infantry little toy men who ran about when the bugle sounded and formed up in stiff lines below the black building till there was more bugling and then they scattered, and in a few minutes the smoke of cooking fires went up from all sides. A herd of sheep and goats issued from the station and moved towards us in charge of a little ragged boy. Before he reached the foot of the hills there came a loud whistling down the valley from the north and a tiny train ground slowly into view across the hollow-sounding bridge and halted in the station, panting out white puffs of steam.

The shepherd lad held on steadily, driving his goats with shrill cries up our hill for the better pasture on the western side. We sent Hussein with two of our Juheina down behind a ridge where he must pass, and as soon as he was surely invisible from the enemy, they ran out from each side and caught him. The lad was a Heteymi, one of those outcasts of the desert, whom some called aborigines, though their type was Semitic only a little better fleshed and ruddier than the Bedu. However, they were members of no recognized Arab stock, and their poor children commonly hired themselves out as herds to the tribes about them. This one cried continually, and made efforts to escape as often as he saw his goats straying uncared-for about the hill. In the end the men lost patience and tied him up roughly, when he screamed for terror that they would kill him. Fauzan had great ado to make him quiet, and then questioned him about his Turkish masters. But all his thoughts were for the flock, and he stared at them miserably while the tears made edged and crooked tracks down his dirty face.

These shepherds were a class apart. For the ordinary Arab the hearth was a university, about which their world passed and where they heard the best talk and news of their tribe, its poems, histories, love tales, law suits and bargains By such constant sharing in the hearth councils they grew up masters of expression, dialecticians, orators, able to sit with dignity in any gathering and never at a loss for moving words. The shepherds missed all this. From infancy they followed their calling, which took them in all seasons and weathers, day and night, into the hills and condemned them to loneliness and brute company. In the wilderness, among the dry bones of nature, they grew up natural, knowing nothing of man and his affairs, hardly sane in ordinary talk, but very wise in plants, wild animals, and the habits of their own goats and sheep, whose milk was their chief sustenance. As they got older they got sullen, and often became dangerously savage, more animal than man, haunting their flocks, and finding the satisfaction of their appetites in them, to the exclusion of more normal affections.

The long restful day on the hilltop gave me back something of the sense-interests which I had lost since I had been ill. I was able to note once more the typical hill scenery with its hard stone crests the sides of bare rock, and the lower slopes of loose-sliding screens, whose fragments packed solidly at their base with a thin dry soil. The stone itself was glistening, yellow sunburned stuff metallic in ring, and brittle, splitting red or green or brown as the case might be. From every soft place sprouted thorn-bushes. And there was frequent grass, usually coming up from the one root in a dozen blades growing knee-high and straw colored, the heads were empty ears between many-feathered arrows of silvery down with these, and with a shorter grass whose bottle brush heads of pearly grey reached only to the ankle, the hillsides were furred white and danced in the wind.

It was hardly verdure but excellent pasturage and in the valleys were bigger tufts of grass, coarse, waist-high, and bright green when fresh, though they soon faded to the burned yellow of ordinary life.

They grew thickly in all the beds of water-ribbed sand and shingle, between the occasional thorn-trees, some of which stood forty feet in height. The sider trees with their dry sugary fruit were rare: but bushes of browned tamarisk, and broom other varieties of coarse grass, some flowers, and everything that had thorns flourished about our camp, and made it a rich sample of the vegetation of the Hejaz highlands. Only one of all the plants profited us, and that was the *hemeid,* a sorrel with fleshy heart-shaped leaves, and a spike of red or pale blossom its pleasant acidity allayed our thirst today on the hilltop, for we had forgotten to carry up water.

At dusk we climbed down again to our party bringing with us the goatherd prisoner and what we could gather of his flock. We learned that Shakir would come in the night, and so with Fauzan wandered out across the darkening plain towards the station till we found a pleasant gun-position in some low ridges not two thousand yards from the trenches. When we came back, very tired fires were burning among the trees. Shakir had just arrived, and his men and ours were roasting goat-flesh contentedly. The shepherd was being tied up behind my sleeping place for he had gone frantic when he saw his charges unlawfully slaughtered. He refused angrily to taste any of the supper and we only forced bread and rice into him by the threat of dire punishment if he longer insulted our hospitality. They tried to convince him that we would take the station next day and kill his masters, but he would not be comforted and afterwards had to be lashed to his tree again.

After supper Shakir told me that he had brought only three hundred men instead of the agreed eight or nine hundred. However , it was his war, and therefore his tune, so we hastily modified the plans. We would not take the station; we would fight it by a frontal artillery attack, while we mined or cut the railway to the north and south, in the hope of entrapping that halted train. Accordingly we chose out a party of Garland-trained men to blow up something just north of the bridge at dawn, to seal that direction, while I went off with high explosive and a machine-gun and its crew to lay a mine to the south of the station, the probable direction from which the Turks would seek or send help.

Mohammed el Kadhi guided us very well up to a deserted part of the line just before midnight I dismounted, and fingered its rails for the first time since the war, thrillingly. Then in about an hour's busy work we laid the mine, which was a trigger action to fire into twenty pounds of blasting gelatin when the weight of the locomotive overhead deflected the metals. Afterwards we posted the machine-gun in a little bush-screened watercourse, fully commanding the spot where we hoped the train would be derailed. They were to hide there all night, while we went on and cut the telegraph in an unsuspicious spot.

So we rode another half-hour, and then turned in to the line, and again were fortunate to strike yet another unoccupied place. Unhappily then it appeared that none of the four remaining Juheina could climb a pole, and eventually I had to struggle up it myself.

It was all I could do, after my illness, and when the third wire was cut the flimsy pole shook so that I lost grip, and came slipping down the sixteen feet with a crash upon the stout shoulders of Mohammed, who had run in to break my fall , and got nearly broken himself also. We took a few minutes to breathe, but afterwards were able to walk off together to our camels, and eventually got back to camp just as the others had saddled up to go forward, that they might be in place by dawn.

We let them go, and fell down under our trees for an hour sleep, without which I felt I would collapse utterly. It was only just before daybreak, that hour when uneasiness was in the air, a affecting trees and animals and making even men sleepers turn over slightingly, it woke Mohammed who wanted to see the fight. To get me up he came across and cried the morning prayer-call in my ear. I sat up and rubbed the sand out of my red-rimmed aching eyes and we disputed vehemently of prayer and sleep. However he pleaded that there was not a battle every day and showed the cuts and bruises he had sustained during the night in helping me. By my own blackness and blueness I could feel for him and being now fully awake I pardoned him and we rode off to catch up the army after letting loose the still unhappy shepherd boy with advice to wait there for our return.

A band of trodden untidiness in a sweep of gleaming water rounded sand showed us the road they had taken and we reached them just as the guns opened fire. The howitzer was as odd as we had expected and made only lateral or direct brackets. They seemed to be a class of gun which required learning: but the mountain gun did excellently and crashed in the top of one building damaged the second holed the water tank, and hit the pump room. One lucky shell caught the front wagon of the train on the siding and it took fire furiously. This alarmed the locomotive which uncoupled and went off southward. We watched her hungrily as she approached our mine: and when she was on it there was a soft cloud of dust and a report and she stood still. The damage was to the front part. As she was reversed and the charge had exploded late: but we waited and waited in vain for the machine-gun to open fire while the drivers got out and jacked up the front wheels and tinkered at them. Then we learned that the gunners had become afraid at their loneliness and had packed up and marched to join us when we opened fire. It was too late to replace them and half an hour later the repaired engine went on towards Antar, going at a foot pace and clanking loudly but going.

Meanwhile the wood and tents and trucks in the station were burning and the smoke was too thick for us to shoot: so we ventured up to see our results. On the way an outpost of nine Turks tried to surrender but the Arabs mistook their signs and killed them with a volley. Further on we found twenty-four men hiding in a ditch and took them. We found the train interesting since the last truck was double-skinned and the interstice packed for a crude armoring with shingle, as protection against rifle fire: but it was burning too hotly, and the Turks were too close and we dared not be very curious.

Shakir came away with us, and we broke off the action. The Ateiba might have rushed the place but with loss, and its possession for a few hours seemed to us not worth a casualty. We had taken thirty prisoners, and a mare, two camels and some more sheep, and had killed and wounded seventy of the garrison, at a cost to ourselves of one man slightly hurt. So the experiment had justified itself so far, especially as traffic was held up three days, while the Turks recovered confidence.

Chapter 37: Mining for Trains

We left two parties in the neighborhood to do damage to the line on the next day and the next, while we rode straight back to Abdulla's camp, which we reached on April the first His horsemen came galloping out to meet us, Mohammed el Nasir, Dhib and the rest, good-looking youths splendidly mounted on the Emir's blood mares, and splendidly dressed. Their silk skirts fluttered out over the backs of their animals. Shakir, who was splendid in habit, held a grand parade on entry, and had fired thousands of joy shots in honor of his partial victory.

We found the Heteymi lad a billet as shepherd to Dakhil-Allah, Mohammed's father; this consoled him at last, and he laughed when we gave him a new shirt and a scarlet head cloth. He asked at once for a rifle to make him a full man. In the evening I went wandering in the thorn-grove behind the tents, and as I wandered began to see through the thick branches a wild light burning up in bursts of flame, and across the flame and smoke came the rhythm of drums and hand clapping and the deep roaring of a tribal chorus. I crept up quietly, and saw an immense fire in a ring of hundreds of Ateiba, sitting on the ground one by the other, gazing intently on Shakir upright and alone in their midst, and the leader of their song and dance. He had put off his cloak, and stood up only in his white head-veil and his white robes: and the powerful firelight reflected on these and on his pale, ravaged face. As he sang he threw back his head, and at the close of each phrase raised his hands, and let his full sleeves run back on to his shoulders, while he waved his bare arms weirdly. The tribe around him beat time with their hands and bayed out the refrains at his nod. Outside the circle of light, the trees where I stood were alive with Arabs of stranger tribes whispering to one another, and listening to the war dance and song of the Ateiba.

In the morning we determined on another visit to the line, to make fuller trial of the automatic mine-action that had half failed at Aba el Naam. Old Dakhil-Allah said that he would come with me himself on this trip since the project of looting a train tempted him. With us went some forty of the Juheina, who seemed to me stouter men than the high-bred Ateiba. However, one of the chiefs of the Ateiba, Sultan el Abbud, a boon friend of Abdulla and Shakir, refused to be left behind. He was a good-tempered hare-brained fellow, sheikh of his section of the tribe, and had had more horses killed under him in battle than any other Ateibi warrior. He was about twenty-six, and a great rider, full of quips and fond of practical jokes, very noisy: tall and strong with a big, square head wrinkled forehead, deep-set bright eyes, and a young mustache and beard which hid his strong jaw and the wide straight mouth, with white teeth like a wolfs.

We took a machine-gun and its thirteen-soldier crew with us, to settle our train if we caught it. Shakir, with his grave courtesy to the Emir's guest set us on our road for the first half hour. This time we kept to the Wadi Ais almost to its junction with Hamdh, finding it very green and full of grazing, since it had flooded twice already in this winter. At last we bore off to the right over a ridge on to a flat where there were Harb tents. Dakhil-Allah halted among them, expecting to be entertained, but they and he were old enemies, and they refused him. He was angry, and at once sent word of this breach of the Sherif's peace to Abdulla, who later corrected them.

However, they gave us a sheep, so we had a proper meal and then slept in the sand, rather distressed by a shower of rain which sent little rills over the ground about midnight: but the next morning was bright and hot, and we rode into the huge plain which was Wadi Hamdh, or here rather the confluence of four great valleys, Tubj a, Hamdh, Ais and Jirzil. The course of the main stream was full of Asia wood, just as at Abu Zereibat, with the same leprous hummocky bed covered with sand-blisters: but the thicket was only about two hundred yards broad, and beyond it the plain with its shallow torrent-beds stretched for further miles, till at noon we halted in Wadi Tubja, at a place like a wilderness garden, waist-deep in juicy grass and flowers, upon which our happy camels gorged themselves for an hour and then sat down, full and astonished.

The day grew hotter and hotter, and the sun seemed to draw close to us, and scorched us without intervening air. The clean sandy soil was so baked that my bare feet could not endure it, and I had to walk in sandals, to the amusement of the Juheina whose thick sales were proof even against slow fire. As the afternoon passed on the sun became dim, but the heat steadily increased with an oppression and sultriness which took me by surprise, so that I was always turning my head to see if something was not standing just behind me, shutting off the air.

There had been long rolls of thunder all morning in the hills, and the two peaks of Serd and Jasim were wrapped in folds of dark blue and yellow vapor which looked motionless and substantial. After we had marched a few minutes I looked back at them, and saw that part of the yellow cloud off Serd was coming slowly in our direction against the wind, raising scores of dust-devils before its feet. The cloud was nearly as high as the hill. While it approached it put out two dust-spouts, tight and symmetrical columns like chimneys, one on the right and one on the left of its front. Dakhil-Allah looked ahead and to each side for shelter, but saw none. He warned me that the storm would be heavy.

When it got near, the wind which had been scorching our faces with its hot breathlessness fell suddenly and, after waiting a moment, blew bitter cold and damp upon our backs. It also increased greatly in violence, and at the same time the sun disappeared, blotted out by thick mists of yellow air over our heads. We stood in a horrible faint light, dim and fitful. The brown wall of cloud from the hills was now very near, rushing changeless upon us with a loud grinding sound, and three minutes later it struck us, wrapping us in a blanket of dust and stinging grains of sand, twisting and turning in violent eddies, and yet advancing eastward at the speed of a strong gale.

The internal whirling winds had disquieting effects. We had put our camels' backs to the advancing storm, to march before it: but these side blasts tore our tightly held cloaks free from our hands filled our eyes, and robbed us of all sense of direction by turning our camels right or left from their course. Sometimes they were blown completely round: once we were clashed together in a vortex, while large bushes, tufts of grass, and even a small tree was torn up by the roots in dense waves of the soil about them, and were driven against us, or blown over our heads with dangerous force. We were never blinded — it was always possible to see for seven or eight feet to each side — but it was risky to look out, since beside the sandblast we never knew if we would not meet a flying tree, a rush of pebbles, or a spout of dust.

This storm lasted for eighteen minutes, and then leaped forward from us as suddenly as it had come. Our party was scattered over a mile or more, and before we could rally, while we and our clothes and our camels were all smothered in dust, yellow and heavy with it from head to foot, down burst torrents of thick rain and muddied us to the skin. The valley began to run in plashes of water, and Dakhil Allah urged us across it quickly. The wind chopped once more, this time to the north, and the rain came driving before it in great sheets of spray. It beat through our woolen cloaks in a moment, and molded them and our shirts to our bodies, and chilled us to the bone.

We reached the hill-barrier to the east about three o'clock, but found the valley of our road bare and without shelter, and colder than ever. After riding up it for three or four miles we halted, and climbed a great crag in front of us to see the railway which Dakhil-Allah said lay just beyond. The wind was so terrible at the height that we could not cling on to the wet and slippery rocks, against the slapping and bellying of our cloaks and skirts. I took mine off, and climbed the rest of the way naked, more easily, and hardly colder than before. But the effort proved entirely useless. The air was too thick for me to distinguish anything, so I worked down, cut and bruised, to the others, and dressed thankfully. On our way back to get her we had an accident, the only casualty this trip. Sultan had insisted on coming with us, and his Ateibi servant, who must follow him, although he had no head for heights, slipped or grew dizzy in one bad place, where there was a fall of forty feet on to the stones, and plunged down headlong.

When we got back my hands and feet were too numbed to serve me longer, and I lay down and shivered for an hour or so while the others buried the dead man in a side-valley. On their return they met suddenly face to face an unknown rider on a camel, crossing their track. He fired a shot at them. They fired back, snap-shooting through the rain, and then the evening swallowed him up to the westward. This was disquieting, for surprise was our main ally, and now we could only hope that he would not return to give warning to the Turks.

After the heavy camels with the explosives caught us, we mounted again to get closer to the line and find out where we were: but we had hardly started when down the visible wind in the misty valley came brazenly the food-call of Turkish bugles. Dakhil-Allah thrust his head sideways forward in the direction of the sound, and understood that over there lay Madahrij, the small station below which we meant to work, and so we steered on the noise, rather riled again, for it spoke of supper and of tents, and we were without shelter, and on such a night could not hope to make ourselves a fire and bake bread from the flour and water in our saddle bags, and consequently would go hungry.

At last we reached the railway after ten o'clock at night, in conditions of invisibility which made it futile to look for a machine gun position. At random I pitched on Kilo. 1121 from Damascus, and laid the mine there. It was a complicated mine, whose central trigger was to fire simultaneously two charges thirty yards apart: and we hoped in this way to get the locomotive whether it was going north or south. Burying the mine took four hours, for the rain had caked the surface and rotted it. Our feet made huge tracks, on the flat and on the bank, as though a school of elephants had been dancing there. To hide these marks was out of the question, so we did the other thing, trampling the line to the north and to the south for hundreds of yards, even bringing up our camels to help until the ground looked as though half an army had crossed the valley, and the mine-place was no better and no worse than the rest. Then we went back to a safe distance, behind some mounds, and cowered down miserably in the open, waiting for daylight. The cold was intense, and our teeth chattered and we trembled and hissed involuntarily, while our hands drew in like claws.

The clouds had disappeared by dawn, and a red sun came up over the very fine broken hills facing us east of the railway. Old Dakhil-Allah had been an active guide and leader to us in the night, and he now took general charge and sent us out singly and in pairs in all directions, to watch the approaches to our hiding place. He himself crawled up the ridge before us, with his glasses, to report what happened on the railway. I was praying that nothing would happen till the sun had gained power and warmed me for the shivering fit still jerked me about. However the sun was up and unveiled, and things quickly improved. Soon I felt that my clothes were drying. The Arab shirt was almost the lightest dress possible but was clammy in rain and gave little defense against the weather. By noon it was nearly as hot as on the day before, and we were gasping for shade and wishing we had thicker clothes to keep the sun out.

First of all though at six in the morning Dakhil-Allah reported a trolley, which came from the south, and passed over the mine harmlessly: — to our satisfaction for we had not laid a beautiful compound charge for just four men and a sergeant. Then sixty men sallied out from Madahrij. This disturbed us till we saw that they were to replace five telegraph poles blown down by the storm of the afternoon before. Then at seven-thirty a patrol of eleven men went down the line, two inspecting each rail minutely three marching each side of the bank, out on the flat looking for cross tracks, and one, presumably the N.C.O in charge, walking grandly along the metals with nothing to do.

However today they found something, when they got to our footprints about Kilo. 1121, and they concentrated there on the permanent way, and stared at it, and wandered up and down it, and scratched the ballast and thought exhaustively. The time of their search passed slowly for us: but the mine was well hidden, so eventually they gave up and wandered on towards the south, where they met the Hedia patrol and both parties sat there together in the cool shadow of a bridge arch and rested after their labor. Meanwhile the train, a heavy train came along from the south. Nine of its laden trucks were full of women and children from Medina, civil refugees being deported to Syria with their bales of household stuff. It ran right over the charges without exploding them. As an artist I was furious as a commander deeply relieved for women and children were not the spoils we dreamed of the Juheina had all raced to the crest where Dakhil-Allah and I lay hidden when they heard the train, to see it blown to pieces. Our stone head work had been built for two, so that the hilltop a conspicuous bald cone just opposite the working party, became suddenly and visibly populous. This was too much for the nerves of the Turks who fled back into Madahrij and thence at about five thousand yards, opened a brisk rifle fire on us. They must also have telephoned to Hedia, for it too came to life: but since the nearest outpost on that side was about six miles off they held their fire, and contented themselves with selections on the bugle played all day. The distance made it musical and beautiful.

Even the rifle shooting did us no harm but still this disclosure of ourselves was unfortunate. At Madahrij were two hundred men, and at Hedia eleven hundred, and our retreat was by the plain of Hamdh on which Hedia stood. Their mounted troops might sally out and cut our rear. The Juheina had good camels like mine, so we were all right but the machine-gun was a captured German sledge Maxim a heavy load for its tiny mule. The servers were on foot, or on other mules, and their top speed would be about six miles an hour, and their fighting value with a single gun not high. So after consulting Dakhil-Aijah we rode back with them half-way through the hills, and there dismissed them with fifteen Juheina, towards Wadi Ais.

This made us safe, and Dakhil-Allah, Sultan, Mohammed and I rode back with the rest of our party to have another look at the line. The sunlight now was terrific with faint gusts of scorching heat blowing up at us out of the south. We took refuge about ten o'clock under some large trees and there we baked bread and lunched in nice view of the line and shaded from the worst of the sun. About us, over the gravel circles of pale shadow from the crisping leaves ran to and fro like grey indeterminate bugs, as the slender branches dipped reluctantly in the hot wind. Our presence annoyed the Turks, who shot and trumpeted at us incessantly through the middle of the day, and till near evening. The line was held up while they wondered who we were and what we wanted. We slept by watches.

About five they grew quiet and then we mounted and rode slowly across the open valley towards the railway. Madahrij revived in a paroxysm of fire and all the trumpets of Hedia blared again. The monkey-pleasure of pulling large and impressive legs was upon us, and so when we reached the line we made our camels kneel down neatly beside it, and led by Dakhil-Allah as our Imam we performed a sunset prayer quietly between the rails. It was probably the first prayer of the Juheina for a year or so, and I was a novice, but from a distance we passed muster, and the Turks stopped shooting in bewilderment. After the prayer we sat round smoking till dusk, and then I tried to go by myself to dig up the mine, to learn why it had failed.

However, the Juheina were as interested in that as I was, and came along in a swarm and clustered all about the metals while I searched for it. They brought my heart into my throat, for it took me an hour to find just where the mine was hidden. Laying a Garland mine was shaky work, but scrabbling in pitch darkness up and down a hundred yards of line, feeling for a hair-trigger buried in the ballast of the bank, seemed an almost uninsured occupation. The two charges connected with it were so powerful that they would have rooted up fifty yards of track, and I saw visions of blowing up, not only myself but my whole force, every moment. To be sure, that would have completed the bewilderment of the Turk!

At last I found it, and discovered by touch that the lock had sunk about one sixteenth of an inch, due to my bad setting, or to the ground having subsided after the rain. I replaced it firmly, and then to explain ourselves plausibly to the enemy, we began blowing up things to the north of the mine. We found a little four-arched bridge and put it into the air, cleanly. Afterwards we turned to rails and cut about two hundred: and while the men were laying and lighting these charges, I taught Mohammed how to climb a splintery pole, and together we cut wires, and by their aid dragged down poles. All was done at speed, for we feared the Turks might still come after us: and as soon as our explosive was finished we ran back like hares to our camels, and mounted them, and trotted through the windy valley to the plain of Hamdh.

There we were in safety, but old Dakhil-Allah was too pleased with the mess we had made of the line to go soberly. When we were on the sandy flat he beat up his camel into a canter, and we all pounded madly after him through the colorless moonlight. The going was perfect, and we never drew rein for three hours, till we over rode our machine-gun and its escort camping in el Fershah. The soldiers heard our yelling rout coming through the night, thought us enemies of sorts, and let fly at us with their Maxim: but it jammed after half a belt and they were tailors from Mecca unhandy with it so no one was hurt and we captured them mirthfully.

In the morning we slept lazily long, and breakfasted at Rubiaan, the first well in Wadi Ais. Afterwards we were smoking and talking, before bringing in the camels, when suddenly we heard the distant boom of a great explosion behind us on the railway. We wondered if the mine had been discovered or had done its duty. Two scouts had been left to report, and we rode slowly to wait for them. Besides, the rain of two days ago had brought down Wadi Ais once more in flood and its bed was all flecked over with shallow pools of soft grey water, lying between banks of silvery mud, rippled by the current into scales like a fish. The warmth of the sun made the surface like fine glue, on which our helpless camels sprawled comically, and went down with a force and completeness surprising in so dignified a beast.

The sunlight, the easy march and the expectation of the scouts' news made everything gay, and we developed unexpected virtues: but our limbs were still stiff from the exertions of yesterday and determined us to fall short of Abu Markha that night. So, near sunset, we chose a dry terrace in the valley to sleep upon. I rode up to it first, and turned and looked at the men reined in just below me, standing, they and their bay camels, in a group like copper statues, so fierce was the red light of the setting sun upon their faces. They seemed to be burning with an inward flame.

Before the bread was baked the scouts arrived, and told us that at dawn the Turks had been very busy round our damages: and a little later a locomotive with trucks of spare rails, and a crowded labor gang on top, had come up from Hedia and, when it had got over the mine, had exploded it both in front and behind itself This was everything we had hoped and we rode back to Abdulla's camp on the morning of April the seventh, in a singing company. We had proved that a well-laid mine could fire, and that a well-laid mine was difficult even for its maker to discover. These points were of importance, for Newcombe, Garland and Hornby were now all up upon the railway, harrying it: and mines were our best weapon to make the working of trains costly and dangerous for the enemy.

Chapter 38: Abdulla and Friends

Despite his kindness and charm I could not like Abdulla or the life of his camp; perhaps because I was unsociable, and these people had no personal solitude: perhaps because their good humor showed me the futility of my more than Palomidcs' pains, not merely to seem better than myself, but to make others better: whereas nothing looked futile in the atmosphere of high thinking and strenuous responsibility which ruled at Feisal's, Abdulla passed his merry day in the big cool tent accessible only to his friends, limiting suppliants or new adherents or the hearing of his followers' disputes to one short public session in the afternoon. For the rest he read the papers, ate very carefully, slept, and especially played games, either chess with his staff, or practical jokes with Mohammed Hassan, a Yemeni from Taif, nominally muedhdhin in the camp but really court fool; and a tiresome old fool I found him, though my illness left me less even than usual in the jesting mood.

Abdulla and his friends Shakir and Fauzan and the two sons of Hamza among the Sherifs, with Sultan el Abbud and Hoshan from the Ateiba, and Abdulla ibn Mesfer the guest-master, would spend much of the day and all the evening hours tormenting Mohammed Hassan. They stabbed him with thorns, stoned him, and dropped sun heated pebbles down his back: or set him on fire. Sometimes the jest would be elaborate, as when they laid a powder trail under the rugs, and persuaded Mohammed Hassan unwittingly to sit on the inner end of it. Once Abdulla set a coffee-pot on his head, and shot it off three times with his rifle at twenty yards — and then rewarded his long-suffering servility by three months' pay.

Abdulla would sometimes ride a little, and sometimes shoot a little, and would then return exhausted to his tent for massage, and afterwards recites from the camp would be introduced to soothe his aching head. He was fond of Arabic poetry and exceptionally well read in it. The local poets found him a profitable audience. He was also interested in history and letters, and would have grammatical disputations in the tent before him, and adjudge prizes.

His accounts and secretarial work were in the hands of Sheikh Othman, a Yemeni scholar from Zebid, a mild white-faced man of thirty-five, a storehouse of Arabic verse, but not of much character. He was paymaster and chief justice and supply officer to the entire army, and painfully overworked, without even a clerk to help him. Abdulla exercised little supervising care. He affected to have no concern for the Hejaz situation; he regarded the autonomy of the northern Arabs as assured by the promises of Great Britain to his father and was inclined to rest quietly on this security. I longed to tell him that the half-witted old man had obtained from us no concrete or unqualified undertaking of any sort, and that their ship might founder on the rock of his political stupidity: but that would have been to give away my English masters, and the mental tug of war between honesty and loyalty, after swaying for a while, settled again expediently into a deadlock.

Abdulla found the basis of Arab strength in Yemen, not in Syria, and was only waiting for the boredom of these northern operations to cease before turning his attention thither. He professed great interest in the war in Europe, and studied it closely in the Egyptian press. He was also acquainted with many points in Western politics and knew about the courts and ministries of Europe, even to the name of the Swiss President! I remarked again how much the comfortable fact that we still had a King made for England's reputation in this world of Asia. Old artificial societies like the Arab found a sense of honorable security when dealing with us, in such a proof that the highest place in our state was not a prize for mere merit or ambition.

Time slowly depressed my first favorable opinion of Abdulla's character. His constant ailments, which once aroused compassion, became fitter for contempt when their causes were apparent in laziness and self-indulgence, and when he was seen to cherish them as occupations of his too-great leisure. His casual attractive fits of arbitrariness now seemed feeble tyranny disguised as whim: his friendliness became caprice, his good humor, love of pleasure. Even his simplicity appeared false upon experience and, because it was less trouble to him than uncharted thought, inherited prejudice or religious belief was allowed unchallenged rule over the keenness of his mind. His brain betrayed an intricate pattern; idea twisted tightly into or over idea till the whole was a strong cord of design: and yet his indolence marred his scheming too. His web was constantly unraveling through his carelessness in leaving it unfinished: but it never separated into straight desires. Always he watched out of the comer of his bland and open eye our returns to his innocent questions, reading an insect-subtlety of significant meaning into every hesitation or uncertainty or mistake honestly made.

One day I entered to find him sitting very upright and wide-eyed, with a spot of red in either cheek. He told me that Sergeant Prost, an unaffected friendly learned Frenchman, his old tutor from Constantinople, had just come from Colonel Bremond, the innocent bearer of a letter which pointed out how the British were wrapping up the Arabs on all sides, at Aden, at Gaza, at Bagdad, and hoped that Abdulla realized his situation. He asked me rather hotly what I thought of it, and I was put about to answer the plausible charge. In the end I fell back on artifice, and replied in a pretty phrase that I hoped he would suspect our honesty when he found us back-biting our allies in private letters. The delicately poisoned Arabic pleased him, and he paid us the keen compliment of saying that he knew we were sincere, since otherwise we would not be represented by a man like Colonel Wilson at Jeddah.

Therein, typically, his subtlety hanged itself, for judging others by himself he did not see the double-subtlety which negatives him. Perhaps our ends were crooked: he did not grasp that honesty was the sharpest tool and means of rogues, and that Wilson might be too downright to suspect evil in those above him. Wilson never told even a half-truth. If instructed to inform the King diplomatically that the subsidy of the month could not at present be increased he would ring up Mecca and say, 'Lord, Lord, there is no more money this month.'

As for lying, Wilson was incapable of it, and most of all incapable of practicing the art upon Arabs whose whole life passed in a mist of deceits, and whose intuitions were of the finest. The Arab leaders showed a completeness of instinct, reliance upon intuition, the something fore-known, which left our centrifugal minds gasping in the distance. They understood and judged quickly effortlessly, unreasonably, like women: it almost seemed as though the Oriental exclusion of woman from political activity had conferred her particular gifts upon man-kind: and some of the speed and secrecy of our victory, and its regularity, might perhaps be ascribed to the fact that from end to end of it there was nothing female but from our camels in the Arab Movement.

The outstanding figure in Abdulla's entourage was Sherif Shakir a man of twenty-nine a personal favorite of the old King and the companion since boyhood of the four Emirs. His mother was Circassian, and his grandmother and from them he obtained his very fair complexion: but all the flesh of his face was torn away by smallpox, which had left only a few places in which could grow the occasional hairs of his thin beard and mustache. From this white ruined face, two dark restless eyes looked out, very bright and big for the faintness of his eyelashes and eyebrows made his stare directly disconcerting. His figure was tall, slim, almost boyish from the continual activity of the man and his athletic life. His sharp decided, but pleasant voice frayed out if he shouted. His manner was abrupt and imperious, but delightfully frank with a humor as cracked as his laugh.

His bursting freedom of speech seemed to respect nothing on earth except King Hussein: but towards himself he exacted respect, more so than did Abdulla who was always playing undignified tricks with his companions, or with the bevy of silk-clad young fellows who stood about him when he would be easy. Shakir joined wildly in the sport but would punish a liberty taken smartly. He dressed simply but very cleanly and like Abdulla spent public hours using the toothpick and tooth stick. He took no interest in books. The great library of Arabic manuscripts formed by Zeid, his father had been destroyed in Taif by the Turks who poured petrol over the books and set fire to them during the siege: but this worried Shakir less than anyone. He never wearied his head with meditation but was intelligent and interesting to talk to. He was devout, but hated Mecca, and played backgammon while Abdulla read the Koran.

In war he was the man-at-arms, not the general, and showed a headlong dash and courage. Twice he had saved Abdulla's life in action. His feats made him the darling of the tribes who loved him and obeyed him implicitly tomorrow or the next day, to the confusion of their own chiefs. He returned this liking described himself as a Bedawi and an Ateibi, and imitated them. He loved their manners, spoke their dialects, and was happy sitting with them telling tales. He wore his black hair in plaits streaming down each side of his face, and kept it glossy with butter and strong by frequent washings in camel urine. He encouraged nits, in deference to the Bedouin proverb that a deserted head showed an ungenerous mind, and wore the *brim,* a plaited girdle of thin leather thongs wrapped three or four times round the loins to confine and support the belly. He owned splendid horses and camels, was considered the finest rider in Arabia, and was always ready for a match with anyone.

He seemed capable rather of fits of energy than of sustained effort, but there was balance and shrewd depth behind his wild manner, and Hussein had used him on embassies to Constantinople, Damascus and Cairo in days before the war. He met Hogarth, Storrs and Cornwallis south of Jidda at that first meeting in Arabia, when the date of the Arab rising was definitely fixed: and this was only a logical outcome of the former intricate dealings between the Emir of Mecca and the Khedive of Egypt, generally through him as intermediary. His figure must have looked strange in the stucco splendor of the Abdin.

Abdulla admired Shakir, and tried to imitate his attitude of gay carelessness, out of weakness whereas Shakir's was the outcome of strength. So without meaning it Shakir complicated my mission. Most of the men in camp were Atban, who seemed not anxious to fight. They knew nothing of the country they were in, and their sheikhs were nonentities. Abdulla had only a handful of Juheina, the local people with him and, led away by Shakir's love for the Ateiba, hardly desired more. Of his machine-guns only two were efficient. His regulars on whom he depended for the use of these and of his artillery were some seventy in number, but raggedly dressed and deficiently equipped, and no one but Raho the Algerian seemed to take interest in them.

Abdulla made very little of the tactical situation, pretending pettishly that it was Feisal's business. He had come to Wadi Ais to please Feisal, his younger brother, and there he would stay. He would not go on raids himself, and hardly encouraged those of his men who did. I detected jealousy of Feisal's successes in this, as if he wished ostentatiously to neglect military operations to prevent unbecoming comparison with his brother in their performance. Had Shakir not helped me in the first instance I might have had delay and difficulty in getting work started : though Abdulla would have ceded in time, and permitted graciously anything that did not call directly upon himself For action one had to depend on Shakir or on Dakhil-Allah.

Dakhil-Allah deserved well of us, for he was forceful and did his best. He was about fifty years old, short and stout and squalid with a hard-bitten weathered face, and about him something of the squatness of a harsh-skinned grey toad. His wrinkled forehead, deep-set eyes down-sloping at the outer comers, without eyebrows and generally screwed up to mere slits, his broad low hooked nose, sliced to a point by an old wound, his wide curly mouth, thin-lipped and generally locked, his stringy grey beard showing his long jaw very broad under the ears, together made up a whole as striking as it was unlike the ordinary Arab.

In spite of his tiny feet and hands he was physically powerful and active. He was rich and as famous for his hospitality as for his four wives, one fixed and three floating, but each with her separate tent and flock in a separate camp. He wore few and filthy old clothes, was a great poet and genealogist, eloquent, impenetrable, authoritative, suspicious. His common speech was amusingly indecent. His inherited office of chief justice of the Juheina gave him courtesy precedence, and with the eastern clans he had real power, accepting only meek suggestions from ibn Beidawi, his Emir. He spoke Turkish fluently, and had been in receipt of fifty-six pounds a month, as subsidy for keeping the Hejaz Railway intact, and it was like him, when he had decided to join the Sherif, to draw his next month in advance, and then to ride off and blow up the Aba el Naam bridge on his journey in to Abdulla's camp.

He was especially attentive to me, since he feared Feisal's grudge for his having led the Turks down to Yenbo in December 1916, on the occasion when both Feisal and Zeid were signally discomfited. My visit to Wadi Ais was a golden opportunity for him to make a friend in Feisal's camp, and he asked if, when I returned, he might send his son Mohammed with me, to make his peace. I liked Mohammed, a curly, dark-faced, sturdy lad of perhaps eighteen, who had helped me good-temperedly on the railway, and had earned this reward: for by nature he was sulky, and the willingness had been compelled upon him by his father's stringent threatening. So I told the grateful Dakhil-Allah that I would be his surety in Wejh.

Chapter 39: Returning to Wejh

Abdulla had now two parties on the railway, with relieves arranged for their constant maintenance. They promised to do a demolition of some sort every day or two. Much less interference than this would suffice to wreck the working of its trains, and by making the maintenance of the garrison at Medina just a shade less difficult than its evacuation, would serve the interests of British and Arabs alike. So I judged my work in Wadi Ais done well enough to let me go.

I longed to get north again, quit of the railway and of this relaxing camp. Abdulla might let me do all I wanted, but would do nothing of his own, whereas Feisal was the working enthusiast with the one idea of making his ancient race again justify its renown by winning freedom with its own hands, and for me the best value of the Revolt lay in the things which the Arabs attempted without aid. When I was with Feisal they could do no more, for he had already persuaded them to do their utmost, and his lieutenants Nasir or Sharra for Ali ibn el Hussein seconded his plans with all their heads and hearts: but my part was synthetic. I combined these loose showers of sparks into a firm flame, transformed their series of unrelated incidents into a conscious operation.

We left on the morning of April the tenth, after pleasant farewells from Abdulla, a most generous host. He sent Shakir with us for the first few miles, on a glorious mare: yellow the Arabs called it, white being an ill-omened word of an animal. Then we rode off alone on our journey. The three Ageyl who had done so well on the trip up from Wejh were with me, and Arslan, the little Syrian Punch-figure, very conscious of Arab dress, and of the droll outlook and manners of all Bedouin. He rode disgracefully and endured sorrow the whole way, at the uneasy steps of his camels: but he saved his self-respect by pointing out that in Damascus no decent man would ride a camel and his humor by showing that in Arabia no one but a Damascene would ride so bad a camel as that under him. Mohammed el Kadhi was our guide, and he brought about six of his followers with him.

We marched up Wadi Tleih as we had come, but then branched off to the right, so that we might miss the lava, and struck into Wadi Osman which would lead us into

Hamdh. We had forgotten to take any food with us, so stopped after nine o'clock in Wadi Saura at some Erwa tents, and took hospitality of their rice and milk. This spring time in the hills was the time of plenty for the Arabs, whose tents were full of sheep milk and goat milk and camel milk, and everyone well-fed and well-liking. Afterwards we rode, in weather like a summer's day in England, for five hours down Wadi Osman, a narrow flood-swept valley which turned and twisted in the hills but gave an easy road. The last part of the march was after dark, and when we stopped we found Arslan was missing. We fired volleys and lit fires in the hope that he would come upon us: but till dawn there was no sign, and the Juheina ran back and forward along our road in doubting search. However, he was only a mile behind us, still fast asleep under a great tree.

A short hour afterwards we found ourselves at tents of a wife of Dakhil-Allah. We stopped for a meal, and Mohammed allowed himself a bath, and a fresh braiding of his hair, and clean clothes. They took very long about the food, and it was not till near noon that it came at last, a great bowl of saffron-rice with a broken lamb littered over it. Mohammed, who felt it his duty in my honor to be dainty in service, arrested the main dish, and took from it the fill of a small copper basin which he set between himself and me. Then he waved the rest of the camp on to the large supply. It was pleasanter so, for some of the Juheina were rough feeders.

Mohammed's mother was an oldish woman, who felt herself old enough to be curious about me, and to ask questions about the women of the tribe of Christians, and to marvel at my white skin, and my horrible blue eyes, which looked like sky shining through empty eye-sockets. She begged me to take great care of Mohammed, and to protect him against Feisal's anger: and chose out of the herd a much-fired riding camel which she said should be a present from the Kadhi to the Emir.

Wadi Osman today was less irregular in course, and broadened slowly. After two hours and a half it twisted suddenly to the right through a gap in a low reef, and we found ourselves in Hamdh, which here flowed in a narrow cliff-walled gorge. As usual the edges of the bed were bare, of hard sand and the middle bristled with hamd-hasla trees in grey salty bulging patches. Before us were flood-pools probably filled from Wadi Osman of sweet and good water the largest pool being nearly three hundred feet long and two feet deep. Its bed was deep cut into the soil of light clay and Mohammed said that its water would remain till the year's end but would soon turn salt and useless.

After we had had our drinks we bathed in it and found it full of little silver fish like sardines and that they were ravenous. We lingered about prolonging our bodily pleasure for two hours after bathing, and remounted in the dark and rode down a good track along the south bank of the valley for about six miles till we felt sleepy. Then we turned away to the left up on to higher ground for our night's camp. Wadi Hamdh differed from the other wild valleys in the Hejaz, by the chill air which struck up from it. This was. Of course most obvious at night when a white mist lifted itself some feet up from the ground and stood over it motionless and everything glistened with a salt sweat: but even in daytime and when the sun was shining the valley felt damp and raw and unnatural.

Next morning we started early and passed large pools in the valley but few of them were fit to drink and the rest gone green and brackish with the little white-fish floating dead and pickled in them. Afterwards we crossed the bed, and left it to the south while we struck over the plain of Ugila, where Major Ross had lately chosen an aerodrome. Arab guards were sitting by his petrol and we breakfasted from them, and then went along Wadi Methar to a shady tree where we slept four hours.

In the afternoon everyone was fresh, and the Juheina began to match their camels against one another. At first it was two and two but the others joined till they were six abreast, and the road was bad. Finally one lad galloped his animal into a heap of stones, and she slipped, and he crashed off and broke his arm. This was a misfortune but Mohammed got off coolly tied him up with rags and camel-girth and left him at ease under a tree to rest a little before riding back to Ugila for the night on his way home. The Arabs were casual about broken bones. In Wadi Ais I had seen a youth whose forearm had of old set crookedly, and he had now dug away at himself with a dagger till he had bared the bone, and re-broken it, set it straight, and there he lay philosophically enduring the flies in his tent, with his left forearm huge under healing mosses and clay on stick-splints, waiting for it to be well.

Our camp this night was under a cliff which the Bedu climbed to a rock pool they knew of, and where they filled a skin of delicious clear dark water, very cool and soft. Arabs traveling without food tried so far as possible always to camp near water: and at this time of year just after the rains there were so many casual pools that a man who knew his district had no difficulty anywhere. In the morning we pushed on to Khauthilla, where Suleiman Rifada had cleaned out an old well and fitted it with a pump (long broken) and laid himself out a vegetable garden nearby. It was all deserted now, as he had finally thrown in his lot with the Turks, so we made free with his barren plants while we watered the camels. The water was impure, and purged them.

Khauthilla was not unbeautiful, for there were sharp hills about the valley, especially Raal, the greatest, to the west, and near the well were tall trees, and some dam palms, always good to look at. We rode again in the evening, for another eight miles, finally camping on the soft white plain that lay hidden in the cleft dividing Raal in two.

We intended to push straight through to Wejh in the last day, so got up soon after midnight, and before daylight were coming down the long slope from Raal into the plain that extended across the mouths of Hamdh into the sea. The ground was scarred with motor tracks, which excited a lively ambition in the Juheina to hurry on and see the new wonders of Feisal's army. So we did a straight march of eight hours, unusually long for these Hejaz Bedouin.

We were then near Jebel Murra and reasonably tired, both men and camels; as we had had no food since breakfast the day before. Therefore it seemed fit to the boy Mohammed to run races. He jumped from his camel, took off nearly all his clothes, and challenged any of us to race him to the clump of trees up the slope in front, for a pound English. Everyone took the offer, and the camels set off in a mob. The distance proved about three-quarters of a mile, uphill, over heavy sand, which was probably more than Mohammed had bargained for. However, he showed surprising strength and won, but by inches only and promptly collapsed on the ground under the shade, bleeding from his mouth and nose. Some of our camels were very good and they went their fastest when so matched against one another.

The air was very hot down here and heavy for men who had been long in the hills, and I feared there might be consequences of Mohammed's exhaustion: but after we had rested an hour or two, and made him a cup of coffee, he got going again all right, and marched the six remaining hours into Wejh as cheerfully as ever, continuing to play the little jests which had brightened our march from Abu Markha. If one man rode quietly behind another's camel, poked his stick suddenly up its rump, and screeched, it mistook him for an excited male, and plunged off at a mad gallop, very disconcerting to the rider. A second good game was to cannon one galloping camel with another, to crash it into a near tree. If it succeeded either the tree went down (valley trees in the light Hejaz soil were notably unstable things) or the rider was scratched and torn, or best of all he was swept quite out of his saddle, and left impaled on a thorny branch, if not dropped violently on the ground. This counted as a bull, and was very popular with everyone else.

The Bedu were odd people. Sojourning with them was unsatisfactory for an Englishman unless he had patience wide and deep as the sea. They were absolute slaves of their appetite, with no stamina of mind, drunkards for coffee, milk or water, gluttons for stewed meat, shameless beggars of tobacco. A cigarette went round four men in a tent before it was finished, and it would have been intolerable manners to have smoked a whole one through. They dreamed for weeks before and after their rare sexual exercises, and spent the intervening days titillating themselves and their hearers with bawdy tales. Had the circumstances of their lives given them greater resources or opportunity they would have been just sensualists. Their strength was the strength of men geographically beyond temptation: the poverty of Arabia made them simple, continent, and enduring. If forced into civilized life they would have succumbed like any savages to its diseases, meanness, luxury, cruelty, crooked dealing, artifice, and like savages they would have taken these diseases in grave and exaggerated form for lack of old inoculation.

If they suspected that we wanted to drive them, either they were mulish, or they went away. If we knew them, and had the time and gave the trouble to represent things to them in a manner which appealed, then they would go to great pains for our pleasure. Whether the results achieved were worth the effort required, no man could tell. Englishmen, accustomed to greater returns, would not, and indeed could not, have spent the time and thought and tact lavished each day by their sheikhs and emirs for such meager ends. Their processes were clear, their minds moved logically as our own, with nothing incomprehensible or radically different, except the premise: there was no excuse or reason except ignorance whereby we would call them inscrutable or Oriental, or leave them misunderstood.

They were mentally European, and would follow us, if we could endure with them and play the game according to their rules. The pity of it was that we often began to do so, and then broke down with exasperation and threw them over, blaming them for what was a fault in our own selves. Such strictures were like a general's complaint of his bad troops, in reality a confession of our own lack of foresight. Often we made them out of mock modesty to show that, though mistaken, we had at least the wit to see our mistakes. If we had thought a little longer we would have seen that such wit, sooner used, would have taught us our material, and saved us from the need of confession. To have been at fault in our own men was to condemn ourselves beyond pardon.

CHAPTER 40: AUDA AND AKABA

We stopped just outside Wejh for long enough to change our filthy clothes, and then rode straight to Feisal's tent. The guest-master took charge of Mohammed and the Juheina, while Feisal led me into the inner tent to talk about what had happened. It seemed that everything was well. More cars had arrived from Egypt. Yenbo was now emptied of its last soldiers and stores, and Sharraf himself had come up. With him was an unexpected unit, a new machine-gun company of amusing origin. We had left thirty sick and wounded men in Yenbo when we marched away. There were also broken weapons, and two British armor-sergeants repairing them. The sergeants had found time hang heavy, and so had taken three mended Maxims and the patients and combined them into a machine-gun company and had trained them by dumb show so perfectly that they were our best gunners.

Rabegh was also being abandoned. The airplanes from it had already flown up here, and were established. Their Egyptian troops had been shipped after them, with Joyce and Goslett and the Rabegh staff, who were now in charge of things at Wejh. Newcombe and Hornby were up-country, tearing at the railway day and night, almost with their own hands for lack of helpers. The tribal propaganda was marching forward: all was for the best, and I was about to take my leave when Suleiman the guest-master hurried in and whispered to Feisal, who turned to me with shining eyes, trying to be calm and said, 'Auda is here.' I shouted, 'Auda Abu Tayi', and at that moment the tent-flap was drawn back and a deep voice boomed salutations to our lord, the Commander of the Faithful: and there entered a tall strong figure with a haggard face, passionate and tragic. This was Auda, and with him his young son, Mohammed, a child of eleven years old.

Feisal had sprung to his feet. Auda caught his hand, and kissed it warmly, and they drew aside a pace or two, and looked at each other: a splendid pair, as unlike as possible, but typical of much that was best in Arabia, Feisal the prophet, and Auda the warrior, each looking his part to perfection, and each immediately understanding and liking the other. Then they sat down and spoke. Feisal introduced us one by one, and Auda with a word seemed to register each. We had heard a great deal of Auda, and I had been banking, as a result of what I knew, to open Akaba with his help: and when I had listened to him for a few moments, and felt the force and directness of the man, I knew that we had attained our end. He had come down to us like a knight-errant, chafing at our delay in Wejh, anxious only to be up and acquiring merit for Arab freedom in his own lands. If his performance was one-half his desire, we would be fortunate and rich. That being seen and a weight off all our minds, we went in to supper.

We were a cheerful party, Nesib el Bekri, Faiz el Ghusein, Mohammed el Dheilan, Auda's politic cousin, Zaal his nephew, and Sherif Nasir, resting in Wejh for a few days between expeditions. I told Feisal odd stories of Abdulla's camp, and the joys of breaking railways. Suddenly Auda scrambled to his feet with a loud 'God forbid', and flung from the tent. We stared at one another and there came a noise of hammering outside. I went after him to learn what it meant, and there was Auda bent over a great rock pounding his false teeth to fragments with a stone. 'I had forgotten,' he explained, Jemal Pasha had these made for me. I was eating my lord's bread with Turkish teeth!' Unfortunately he had very few teeth of his own, so that to eat the meat he loved was great difficulty and after-pain for him, and he went about half-nourished for three months, till we had taken Akaba, and Sir Reginald Wingate had sent him a dentist from Egypt, who made him an Allied set.

Auda was very simply dressed in white cotton, northern fashion, with a red Mosul head cloth. He might be over fifty, and his black hair was streaked with white, but he was still strong and straight, loosely built, spare, and active as a much younger man. His face was magnificent, even to its lines and hollows, and showed how true it was that the death of Annad, his favorite son, in battle with his jazi cousins, had cast sorrow over all his life, by the bitter failure of his dream to hand on through him the greatness of the name of Abu Tayi to future generations. He had large eloquent eyes, like black velvet in richness. His forehead was low and broad, his nose very high and sharp, powerfully hooked: his mouth rather large, and his beard and mustaches trimmed to a point, in Howeitat style, with the lower jaw shaven underneath.

The Howeitat came some centuries ago from the Hejaz, and their yet-nomad clans prided themselves on being true Bedu, and Auda was the master-type of the Abu Tayi. His hospitality was sweeping, inconvenient except to very hungry souls. His generosity kept him always poor, despite the profits of a hundred raids. He had married twenty-eight times, had been wounded thirteen times, and in the battles he provoked had seen all his tribesmen hurt, and most of his relations slain. He himself had killed seventy-five men, all Arabs, by his own hand in battle, and had never killed a man except in battle. Of the number of dead Turks he could give no account: they did not enter his register. The Toweiha in his hands had become the first fighters of the desert, with a tradition of desperate courage, and a sense of superiority which never left them while there was life and work to do... but which had reduced them from twelve hundred men to less than five hundred, in thirty years.

Auda raided as often as he had opportunity, and as widely as he could. He had seen Aleppo, Basra, Wejh, and Wadi Dawasir on his expeditions: and was careful to be at enmity with nearly all tribes in the desert, to give proper scope for raids. In his robber-fashion he was as hard-headed as he was hotheaded, and in his maddest exploits there would be a cold factor of possibility to lead him through. His patience in action was extreme, and he received and ignored advice, criticism, or abuse with a smile as constant as it was very charming. If he got angry his face worked uncontrollably and he burst into a fit of shaking passion only to be assuaged after he had killed: then he was like a wild beast, and men escaped from his presence. Nothing on earth would have made him change his mind or obey an order or do the least thing of which he disapproved: and he took no heed of men's feelings when his face was set.

He saw life as a saga, and all events in it were significant, and all personages in contact with him heroic. His mind was stored with tales of old raids, and epic poems of fights, and he overflowed with them on the nearest listener. If he had no listener he would very likely sing them to himself in his tremendous voice, deep and resonant and loud. He had no control over his lips, and was therefore terrible to his own interests, and hurt his mends continually. He spoke of himself in the third person and was so sure of his fame that he loved to shout out stories against himself, At times he seemed taken by a demon of mischief, and in public assembly would invent appalling tales of the private life of his hosts or guests: and yet with all this he was really modest, as simple as a child, direct, honest, kind-hearted, and warmly loved even by those to whom he was most embarrassing — his mends.

Afterwards I went down near the beach where Joyce lived beside the spread lines of the Egyptian troops, in an imposing array of large tents and small tents, and we talked over things done and things to do. All efforts were still being directed against the railway. Newcombe and Garland were near Muadhdham with Sherif Sharraf and Maulud. They had many Billi, the mule-mounted infantry, and guns and machine-guns, and hoped to take the fort and railway station there. Newcombe meant then to move all Feisal's men forward, to some point very close to Medain Salih or el Via and, by taking and holding a part of the line, to cut off Medina once and for all and compel its early surrender. Colonel Wilson was coming up to help in the actual operation, and Colonel Davenport would take as many of the Egyptian Army as he could transport and feed, and would use them to reinforce the Arab attack.

This entire program was what I had believed necessary for the further progress of the Arab Revolt, when we took Wejh. I had planned and arranged some of it myself: but now that happy fever and dysentery in Abdulla's camp had made me think about the real strategy and tactics of irregular war, and it seemed to me that not merely its details but the essence of it were wrong. It became my business to explain my changed ideas, and to persuade my chiefs to follow me.

So I began with the three propositions: first, that irregulars would not attack places, and so they were incapable of forcing a decision: secondly, that they were as unable to defend a line or point as they were to attack it: thirdly, that their virtue lay in depth, not in face.

The Arab war was geographical, and the Turkish Army an accident, not our target. Our aim was to seek its weakest material link and bear only on that till time made the mass of it fall. Our largest resources were the Bedouin, on whom our war must be built. They were unused to formal warfare, but had assets of mobility, endurance, individuality, knowledge of the country, intelligent courage. With them dispersal was strength, and consequently we must extend our front to its maximum, to impose on the Turks the largest possible passive defense, since materially that was the most costly form of war.

Our duty was to attain our end with the greatest economy of life, since life was more precious to us than money or time. If we were patient and superhuman-skilled we could follow the direction of Saxe and reach victory without battle by pressing our advantages mathematical and psychological. Fortunately our physical weakness was not so great as to demand this. We were richer than the Turks in transport, machine-guns, cars, high explosive: in everything except men and guns. We could develop a highly-mobile, highly equipped striking force, of the smallest size, and use it successively at distributed points of the Turkish line to make them strengthen their posts beyond the defensive minimum of twenty men. Such would be a short cut to success.

It would be no more than a short cut, for these regular troops could never win the war. We could use them only to precipitate the Turkish crash. In our success the ruling factor would always be the favor of the population earned and cemented by the preaching of Feisal. Only by grace of the tribes could the soldiers march: and the soldiers might be very few for their power was not reckoned in figures. With five times the mobility of the Turks we could face them with one-fifth their number.

Accordingly we must not take Medina. The Turk was harmless there; in Egypt he would cost us food and guards. We wanted him to stay in Medina and every other distant place, in the largest numbers. Our ideal was to keep his railway just working, but only just, with the maximum of loss and discomfort. The factor of food would confine him to the railways, but he was welcome to the Hejaz Railway, and the Trans-Jordan Railway, and the Palestine and Damascus and Aleppo railways for the duration of the war, so long as he gave us the other nine hundred and ninety-nine thousandths of the Arab world. If he showed a disposition to evacuate too soon as a step to concentrating in the small area which his numbers could dominate effectually then we would have to restore his confidence, by reducing our enterprises against him. His stupidity would be our ally for he would like to hold, or to think he held as much of his old provinces as possible. This would keep him in his absurd position all Banks and no front.

In detail I criticized the Newcombe scheme. To hold a middle point of a railway would be expensive, for the holding force might be threatened from each side. The mixture of Egyptian troops with tribesmen was weak. If there were professional soldiers present, the Bedouin would stand aside and watch them work, glad to be excused the leading part. Jealousies would be the outcome. Further the Billi country was very dry, and the maintenance of a big force up by the line would be very difficult. However, neither my general reasoning nor my particular objections had much weight.

Meanwhile I was working out, with Auda Abu Tayi, a march to the Howeitat in their spring pastures about Jebel Tubaik or in the Sirhan as the case might be. From them we might raise a mobile camel force with Rualla and Sherarat contingents and rush Akaba by their help alone without guns or machine-guns. Auda thought that with dynamite and money all things were possible and promised that the smaller clans about Akaba, the Niadat, the Dhibat and the Arnran, would join us. Feisal was already in touch with them and we believed that they would support us if we won a preliminary success up by Maan, and then moved in force against the port. The Navy raided it while we were thinking and their captured Turks gave us such useful information that I became eager to go off at once.

The desert route was so long and so difficult to Akaba that we could take no guns or machine-guns, or stores or men. Accordingly the element I would withdraw from the railway scheme was only my single self: and this in the circumstances was a negligible amount, for I felt so strongly against it that my help there would have been only half-hearted. Therefore I decided to go my own way with or without orders. I wrote a letter full of apologies to General Clayton telling him that it was with the best intentions: and went.

BOOK IV

Extending to Akaba

The port of Akaba was naturally so strong that it could be taken only by surprise from inland: but the adherence to Feisal at this juncture of Alida Abu Tayi made us hope to enroll the tribes in the eastern desert such a descent upon the coast.

Nasir, Auda and I set off together on the long ride. Hitherto Feisal had been the public leader but his remaining in Wejh threw an ungrateful primacy of this northern expedition upon myself I accepted It and its dishonest implication as our only means of victory.

We tricked the Turks and entered Akaba with good fortune.

Chapter 41: Geography of Akaba

Akaba, the much discussed, was of peculiar concern both to the Arabs and to the British, who were each anxious to get it away from the Turks. A first effect of its capture would have been the closing down through completion of purpose of the Northern Red Sea Patrol, whose ships had fathered our revolt stage by stage as we crept slowly up from Jidda: but Akaba was more than the last Turkish Red Sea port. It had a military importance, as the key to the only road fit for wheels between the enemy and Egypt, to the south of the Dead Sea.

The great depression of the Red Sea northward of Akaba prolonged itself through the Dead Sea, the Jordan valley and Galilee to between the Lebanon, and, by cutting Syria in two longitudinally, made movement from east to west always painful, and sometimes impossible. Between the Red Sea and the Dead Sea this depression took a peculiarly forbidding shape, in the deep and narrow Wadi Araba, a soft-bedded hollow one hundred miles long, four or five miles wide, and sunk often four thousand feet below the steep walls of hills that confined it on either side.

In the length of this Wadi Araba there was only one carriage road out of it westward towards Sinai and Egypt, and that just three miles from Akaba, where the old road of the Egyptian Pilgrimage climbed up in scarped curves of forbidding steepness from the beach to the level plateau which extended nearly to the Suez Canal; and likewise eastward there was only one great track up from Wadi Araba to the plateau of eastern Syria by Maan on the Hejaz line, and that just four miles from Akaba, where the Wadi river, after its deep and winding passage of the hills, finally broke out to sea-level.

Its special value to the Turks was that in their hands it might, when they pleased, be constituted a threat on the right flank of the British army. At the end of 1914 their higher command had thought to choose it as their main route to the Canal, and to this end had made a second pass from the Maan heights into Wadi Araba fit for wheeled transport: but afterwards they found the food and water difficulties too great for their large forces, and in preference adopted the Beersheba route. Now, however, the British had left the Canal positions, and had thrust forward to Gaza and Beersheba. This made the feeding of the Turkish army in front of them easier by shortening their line.

Consequently the Turks had surplus transport. Akaba was also of greater geographical value, since it now lay behind the British right, and a small force operating from it would threaten either el Arish or Suez effectively. The British Staff felt the inconvenience of this uncontained enemy base in all their efforts to prolong their right wing against Beersheba.

The Arabs needed Akaba, firstly to extend their front, which was their tactical principle, and secondly to link up with the British. If they took it, the act gave the Allies all Sinai, and made a positive junction between them and Sir Archibald Murray in front of Gaza. Then they would be really useful and then they would obtain the material help they needed to let them expand. The human frailty of the British Staff was such that nothing less than physical contact with us would persuade them of our importance. Murray was friendly to us: but if we became his right wing he would equip us properly, almost without the asking. Allenby did so later. Accordingly, for the Arabs, Akaba spent plenty in food, money, guns advisers. It was also the nearest Red Sea port to the Hejaz Railway, only seventy miles away compared with the hundred and thirty of Wejh. So both new and old schools could agree upon its advantages. Indeed we were now three schools of thought in Arabia. I wanted to hurry the Arabs northward, disregarding the Turkish garrisons in Arabia. I wanted them to join up with the British, to act as the right wing of the Allies in the conquest of Palestine and Syria, to assert the Arabic-speaking peoples' desire and desert of freedom and self-government In my view, if they did not reach the main battlefield against Turkey, they would have to confess failure, to remain a side-show of a sideshow, on a level with the Aden field force, or the army in Mesopotamia. I had preached this to Feisal from our first meeting in Wadi Safra.

Our second school wanted to take Medina, by assault, or failing that by cutting the railway and making it starve. They believed that the fall of Medina was a necessary preliminary to the northern extension I envisaged. The third school, of Bremond and his government, wanted to keep the Arabs in Arabia, away from the British and the Palestine front. They had wider views of what was undesirable in the Middle East. They were contented if the British defended Egypt with minimum forces. They had no wish to see a British offensive into Syria, or a British victory over the Turkish Empire.

My friends saw the war double. France, England and Russia were fighting Germany in Europe: England and Russia were fighting Turkey in Asia. Our victory in the first would bring about peace with the second: but a peace which we could not afford, for it would be a bargain peace, in which we would be swindled, and Turkey would come out stronger than before. The British Empire rested on a foundation of illusion (unlike French North Africa, which was held by force), and if Turkey was allowed so to challenge us and to escape scot-free, the illusion would end. For the life of Britain we must beat Germany in Flanders: for the life of Britain's Empire we must beat Turkey in Syria: and those military critics, who honestly said, 'Afterwards, afterwards,' to the Eastern pleading lost sight of the psychology of the English, who would not have embarked in a new war to end Turkey when Germany had fallen. If Turkey was to be defeated it must be before Germany broke.

So we wanted to get to Akaba at once, while it was yet lightly held. Early in the war there had been a big force there: but they had been drawn off for Palestine and Hejaz, and the new troops who would be sent there when the Turkish Staff decided to perturb Murray by threatening his right, had not yet begun to arrive. Murray himself (and before him Maxwell) had wished to take the place, but had not dared. The British force in Egypt was small, Akaba was difficult, and nothing less than Akaba would serve the purpose. Murray had lately raided Nekhl, in the middle of the Sinai desert, to try to draw the Turks' teeth before their contemplated expedition to Suez: but though he destroyed the well at Nekhl this only made more obvious that they would advance by Themed and Sudr, two surface water-supplies on the same road.

To take Akaba meant a naval expedition, and a landing. The landing would not be difficult, but afterwards there was no logical objective. There was no covering position to the beach, which could be shelled always from the hills. The enemy garrison was posted in these hills in elaborate prepared positions, constructed one behind the other in a series, as far as the mouth of Wadi Itm. If the British advanced to this point they would have affected nothing material and would be exposed to continual flank attack from the hills. The Turks would be quite secure, for their line of communication with their railway base seventy miles away from the Wadi Itrn, and so they would be able to increase their defending force or to change its disposition at their will.

The British would be able to deliver themselves from these attacks only by forcing the twenty-five miles of the gorge in the teeth of the enemy, to deny them access to the coastal range. Now the Wadi Itm was from two to five thousand feet in depth, and often less than one hundred yards in width, and ran between fretted hills of granite and diorite whose sides were precipices hundreds of feet in height. The hundred-yard width of the bed was so encumbered by rocks that in places camels could pass only two abreast. It was winding and blind, afforded innumerable natural positions for defense, and hiding places not merely among the cliffs, but in the boulder-masses of the floor. The many side-ravines allowed easy retirement to forces knowing the country. There was water in these side-ravines but none in the main valley; another advantage to the defense.

The Turks had organized the valley in position after position prepared to cover every foot of these twenty-five magnificently defensible miles. Then the granite valley ended in a sandstone plain, which was open and not difficult to cross, but dry. Beyond the plain was another range of heights the tilted edge of the limestone plateau of Syria, rising two thousand feet in a single heave up a twisting hill road to a crest over four thousand feet in height. On the head of this lay great springs, enough to supply some thousands of men. From them the land ran down gently, across involved valleys separated by rolling wormwood-covered slopes for twenty more miles into Maan, a main station on the Hejaz Railway four hundred kilometers from Damascus and eight hundred from Medina.

The approach Akaba-Maan thus formed a natural defensive position of almost unequaled strength, and the Staff in Egypt estimated that to carry it against a weak enemy might take three divisions almost the complete strength of Sir Archibald Murray's army: but success would depend on the speed of the operation, and the Turks might be able to reinforce by rail and route march faster than we could disembark, for the Akaba water-supply was inconvenient, and to land so great an expedition in a harbor less gulf would not be easy. In fact, a British landing there was out of the question, and the same arguments applied to an Arab landing. The local people would have stood by and watched, like the Billi, but with disastrous results, for without their active help the Sherifians would be as ill off as the British, and would also require three divisions to clear Wadi Itm and the crest of the Maan escarpment.

Accordingly my discussions with Auda had been on how to invent a surprise for the Turkish defenders: how to ensure the armed co-operation of the local tribesmen on our side during this surprise: in fact how to advertise it among the Arabs without telling the Turks! Also, how to get access to the Itm gorge either in rear or in flank, by some method less costly than by disembarkation and frontal attack, in which there could be no hope of success for a weak or irregular force. Fortunately I knew Akaba and Wadi Itm and Maan well enough to check what he told me, and to think with certainty.

It was obvious that from Wejh we had only one road: to march inland through the Billi hills: to cross the railway, and pass through the Fejr desert to Wadi Sirhan by Jauf: and then to march up Wadi Sirhan and westwards to Jefer, in front of Maan. There we could concentrate, and either strike at Maan or slip round it, and marched down the Turkish line of defenses to Akaba. This was the unguarded way, the line of least resistance, and the only possible one for us. It would be an extreme example of a turning movement, since it would involve us in a desert march of perhaps six hundred miles to capture a trench within sight of our ships: but there was no alternative, and it was so entirely in the spirit of my sick-bed principles that its issue might well be fortunate, and would certainly be instructive, for us. We plumped for it.

Chapter 42: From Wejh to El Kurr

In our preparations Feisal thought and planned and worked for everybody. We decided that only Sherif Nasir could be our leader: his dear goodness provoking an answering devotion even from the depraved would be like a benediction on the forlorn hope. We broke our wishes to him, and he sighed a little, for he was body-weary after months of service in the vanguard and mind-weary as the time drew on and his careless years seemed past. He feared the maturity coming upon him with its ripeness of thought, the skill, and the finished art: but which, for lack of the poetry informing his youth, might make mere living not a full end of life. He was physically young yet, but his changeable and mortal soul was growing old before his body: going to die before it, as with most of us.

To deal with the semi-nomad and sedentary elements of the northern population, we needed a Syrian of brains and position, and this too was a difficulty: there were few Syrians capable of adventure in the desert. Finally Feisal spared to us Nesib el Bekri, incomparably the best of those in the Arab camp. He was political-minded, able, and persuasive, he had a good mood and his patriotism sometimes overcame his native passion for the indirect. His long desert journey to join us proved that he had it in him to endure hardship. He chose an officer, Zeki, of Damascus, as his companion: for Syrians, unlike Englishmen, could not make friends of the Bedouin.

For escort we had seventeen Ageyl (half of ibn Dgheithir's company), and Auda with his kinsmen would march with us. Feisal made up a purse of twenty-two thousand pounds in gold, all that he could afford, and more than we asked for, to pay the wages of our party, and of the new men we enrolled, and to make such advances as should stimulate the Howeitat to swiftness. We shared it out between us, against the chance of accident upon the road. Sherif Yusuf now back in charge of supply, gave us each a half-bag of flour, whose forty-five pounds were reckoned a man's pinched ration for six weeks. This went slung on the riding saddle and Nasir as well took enough on baggage camels to distribute a further fourteen pounds per man when we had marched the first fortnight out from Wejh, and had eaten enough room for it in our bags.

We had a little spare rifle ammunition, and some spare rifles, as presents, and loaded six camels with light packs of blasting gelatin for rails or trains or bridges in the north. Nasir, a great Emir in his own place also carried a good tent in which to receive visitors and a camel-load of rice for their entertainment: but the last we ate between us, with huge comfort, for the unrelieved diet of water-bread and water, week after week, grew uninspiring. We were beginners in this style of traveling, not understanding that dry rice, as the lightest food which could be carried, was the best for a long journey. Six months later, neither Nasir nor I wasted transport on rice-luxury.

All things were ready on the ninth of May, and in the full heat of that afternoon we set out from Feisal's tent at Wejh, with his good wishes sounding after us from the hilltop as we marched across the valley beneath. The first short stage Nasir did upon his mare, whose head-trappings were gaudy clanking Turkish medals. In a raid with Newcombe against the line he had captured a box of enemy decorations on their way down to please the army in Medina: and he had used them to adorn his horse. We went only so far as the fort at Sebeil, inland of Wejh, where the Egyptian Pilgrimage used to halt for water from the abundant wells. The castle lay in a rocky valley, and was all a ruin within. We camped by the great dry brick tank from which the caravans watered, and busied ourselves under the shade of the curtain wall, or of the trees, in putting to rights such deficiencies as this little march had shown.

My Ageyl — Mukheymer, Meljan and Ali — had been supplemented for the trip by Mohammed, a blowzy, obedient peasant boy from a village in the lava field of Kiswe in the Hauran near Damascus, and by Gasim of Maan, a fanged and yellow-faced outlaw, who lied into the desert and joined the Howeitat after killing a Turkish official in a dispute over cattle-tax. Crimes against tax-gatherers had a sympathetic side to all of us, and this gave Gasim a specious rumor of geniality which, we discovered later, was actually far from the truth.

However, I left him with the others to repack my saddle, and wandered through the broken fort till I got a view of our party at ease beneath the palms, shielding itself from the blazing sun. It seemed a small party to win a new province, and so apparently others thought, for shortly Lamotte, Colonel Bremond's representative with Feisal, rode up on a horse in great good humor, to take a last photograph of us. A little later Yusuf arrived with the good doctor and Tewfik el Halabi and Nesib's brothers, to wish us well on our march, and we joined in a spacious evening meal, whose materials the prudent Yusuf had brought with him. His not-slender heart perhaps mislead him at the notion of a bread supper; or was it the beautiful desire to give us a last feast before we were lost in the wilderness? Anyway it was good.

After they had gone back in the early evening we loaded up once more, and started about midnight to do another stage of our journey to KUIT, the Billi oasis in the hills where we would next water. Nasir was our guide, for he had grown to know this country as well as he did his own, Medina. While we rode through the moonlit and starry night his memory was dwelling very intimately about his home, and he told me of their stone-paved house and the sunk halls with their vaulted roofs against the summer heat, and of the gardens planted with every kind of well-bearing fruit tree, in shady paths, about which they could walk at ease mindless of the position of the sun. He told me of the wheel at the bottom of the garden, over the well, with its machinery of leather trip-buckets, raised by oxen walking down an inclined path of hard-trodden earth, and how the water from its high reservoir slid in little concrete channels about the borders of the paths, or worked fountains in the courts. Even there was enough for a great vine-trellised swimming tank, lined with shining cement, in whose green depth he and his brother's household used to plunge at midday.

Nasir, though usually merry, had a quick vein of suffering in him, and tonight he was wondering why he, an Emir of Medina, rich and powerful and at rest in his garden-palace, had thrown up all to become the weak leader of desperate adventures in the desert. For two years he had been outcast, always fighting beyond the front line of Feisal's armies, chosen for every particular hazard, as the pioneer in every advance: and meanwhile the Turks were in his house, wasting his fruit trees and chopping down his palms. Even, he said, the great well, which had sounded with the creaking of the bullock wheels for six hundred years, had fallen silent, and the garden, cracked with the summer heat, was becoming waste, as the blind hills over which we rode.

After four hours we lay down and slept for two hours, and rose up again with the sun. The baggage camels with us were weak with the mange that cursed all Wejh, and moved slowly. We riders, light-mounted, might have passed them easily, but Auda, who was regulating our marches, forbade. We must think of the difficult marches in front, for which our animals would need all the fitness we could conserve in them. So we plodded on soberly for six hours, through easy valleys between low rocky ridges, in a great heat. The summer sun in this country of white sand behind Wejh had great power of dazzle in the eyes: and the bare rocks on each side of our path held its full force. They were too hot to touch and threw off waves of heat in which our heads ached and reeled.

At eleven in the forenoon we were mutinous against Auda's wish still to hold on. So we halted and lay under trees till half-past two, each of us trying to make a patch of solid shadow for himself beneath a doubled blanket caught across the thorns of overhanging branches: and then we rode on again and, after another three hours' gentle going over the level bottoms, passed between walls of a great valley, a first outlier from the foothills of the Shefa, the coastal ridge and backbone of Arabia. This was the valley of el KUIT, and its green garden lay just in front of us.

Here we seemed fortunate, for white tents peeped from among the palms. While we dismounted, wondering whose they were, Rasim and Abdulla, Mahmud the doctor and even old Maulud the cavalryman came out to welcome us. Auda too found friends with news of the north and of the well-being of his tribe, for here were ibn Mijlad, a chief from Mesopotamia, and Sagr ibn Shaalan, a relative and messenger of the great Nuri Shaalan, Auda's friend and ally. They were on their way to greet Feisal (not without expectation of advantage to themselves from his bounty and gratitude) and told us that Sherif Sharraf whom we wished to meet at Abu Raga, our next stopping-place, was up at the railway raiding for a few days. This meant that there was no hurry about our marching: so we stopped at el KUIT and made holiday for two nights.

It contented me, for the old trouble of boils and fever that had shackled me in Wadi Ais was come back strongly upon me, making journeying a pain, and each day of rest was a blessed relaxation of my will strung to go on, a chance to add patience to my thin reserve. So I lay still, and received into my mind the sense of peace and greenness and the presence of water which made this garden in the desert so beautiful and haunting, as though pre-visited: yet it was merely that long ago I had seen fresh grass growing in the spring.

The one inhabitant of KUIT, the only sedentary Belluwi, and an old hoary Wabsi named Dhaif-Allah, labored day and night with his daughters in the little terraced plot which he had received from his ancestors. It was built out of the south edge of the valley in a bay defended against flood by a massive wall of unhand stone, and in its midst was the well of clear cold water. Above it stood a balanced cantilever of mud and rude poles after the Egyptian model. By this Dhaif-Allah, in the morning and evening when the sun was low, drew up great bowls of water and spilled them into the clay runnels that were contrived through his garden among the tree-roots. He grew low palms, that their spreading leaves might shade his plants from the sun, which otherwise might in that stark valley wither them, and had young tobacco (his most profitable crop) and beans and melons, cucumbers and egg-plants in their season.

The old man lived with his women in a brushwood hut beside the well, and was scornful of our politics, asking what more to eat or drink all these efforts and sacrifices would bring us. We gently teased him with notions of liberty and free possession of the Arab countries for the Arabs. However, he would not understand, but got up and struck himself proudly on the chest crying, 'I, I am Kurr.' He was free and wanted nothing for others and nothing for himself but his garden, and did not know why others should not become rich in a frugality like his. His skullcap, greased with sweat to the color and consistence of lead, he boasted had been his grandfather's, who had bought it when Ibrahim Pasha was in Wejh a century before: his other necessary garment was a shirt, and when he went annually to Wejh with his tobacco he would buy there a shirt for the new year for himself, and one for each of his daughters, and one for the old woman — his wife.

Still we were grateful to him, for besides that he showed an example of contentment to us slaves of unnecessary appetites, he sold us vegetables and on them and on the tinned bounty of Rasim and Abdulla and Mahmud we lived richly. Their entertainment was warm and generous, and each evening they with Nesib and Zeki used to have music round the fires: not the monotonous open throated roaring of the tribes, or the exciting harmony of the Ageyl, but the strange falsetto quarter-tones and trills of the cities of Syria. Maulud had musicians in his unit, and bashful soldiers were brought up each evening to play guitars and sing banal café-songs of Damascus and the love verses of their villages. I lay some distance away in Abdulla's tent where I was lodged and the ripple of the flowing water and the tree-leaves softened the music, so that it became dully pleasant to the ear.

Often too Nesib el Bekri would take out his manuscript of the songs of Selim eljezairi, that fierce unscrupulous revolutionary who, in his leisure moments between campaigns with the Turkish Army, studies in the Staff College, and the bloody missions he fulfilled for the Young Turks his masters, had made verses in the common speech of the people about the freedom which was coming to his race. Nesib and his mends had a swaying rhythm in which they would chant these songs, putting all their hope and passion into the words, their round Damascus faces moon-large in the firelight, sweating. When they began, the soldier camp would grow dead silent till the stanza ended, and then from every man would come a deep sigh and echo of the last sound as proof of agreement. Only old Ohaif-Allah went on splashing out his water, sure that, after we had finished with our silliness, someone would yet buy his green stuff.

Chapter 43: In Abu Raga

To the townsmen this garden was a memory of the world before we went mad with war and drove ourselves into the desert: to Auda there was an indecency of exhibition in the plant-richness, and he longed for an empty view. So we cut short our second night in paradise, and at two in the morning went on up the valley. It was very dark, with only the stars in the sky, and they unable to cast much light into the depths where we were wandering. Auda was guide, and to make us sure of him he lifted up his voice in an interminable 'ho, ho, ho' song of the Howeitat, an epic chanted on three bass notes, up and down , back and forward, in so round a voice that the words were indistinguishable. After a little we thanked him for the singing, since the path went away to the left in Wadi Arnoua, and our long line followed his turn by the echoes of his voice rolling about the torn black cliffs in the moonlight.

The Howeitat speech was a strong dialect of ancient Arabic which marked them out as people of a migration. Sometimes they were difficult to follow. One day in Wejh a mixed group of us had been sitting together, the town Arabs all scholars and lovers of their language, talking of Akaba and Itm and the Araba. Mohammed el Dheilan, Auda's sour-smiling cousin, when I ended, breathed thoughtfully, *'Naam, yerawazun el tleimeh, hatta yukhemmunla:* It was beyond me, and I looked round and asked doctors and Hejazis, editors and lawyers and poets in turn what it meant. They confessed they did not understand. Feisal, who had understood, rejoiced at the discomfiture of the staff of the Arabic revival, happy in his supremacy, since for him Arabic was an acquired language, laboriously grafted by the full effort of the man over his boyhood's Turkish.

Mohammed also had enjoyed our temporary eclipse, and on this long journey he and Sherif Nasir took pains with my Arabic, giving me in turn lessons of the classical Medina tongue and of the vivid desert language. In the beginning my Arabic had been a halting command of the tribal dialects of the Middle Euphrates (a not impure form) but now it became unrecognizable as the product of any district, a fluent mingling of

Hejaz slang and north tribal poetry, with household words and phrases from the limpid Nejdi, and book forms from Syria. The fluency hid a total absence of grammar, which made my talk a perpetual adventure for my hearers. Newcomers imagined I must be from some unknown part, a shot-rubbish ground of Arabic parts of speech, moods, tenses, genders, numbers cases.

However, as yet I understood not three words of Auda's song, and after half an hour the chant tired me, while the old moon climbed slowly up the sky till it sailed over the topmost hills, and threw a deceitful light, less sure than darkness, into our valley. We marched on till day broke and afterwards till half-past eight in the morning, while the early sun, very trying to those who had ridden all night, opposed us. Then we breakfasted off our own flour, lightening at last, after days of hospitality, the food-load our poor camels carried. Since Sharraf was not yet due in Abu Raga we were determined to make no more of haste than the water-difficulties compelled. So after food we put up again our blanket roofs, and lay there till two in the afternoon fretfully dodging about the ground in their fleeting shadow, getting very moist with the heat and the constant pricking of the flies.

At last Nasir gave the marching signal, and we went up the defile with slightly pompous hills each side of us, for four hours, when we agreed to camp again in the valley bed. There was abundant brushwood about us for fuel and up the cliff on our right lay Ain Arnoua, pools of fresh water from the rock, which gave us a delicious drink with our evening meal. Nasir was wrought up by it and commanded rice for supper and called the friends to feed with us. Our rule of march was odd and elaborate. Nasir. Auda and Nesib were separate houses, knowing one another, but admitting the supremacy of Nasir only because I lived with him as a guest and furnished them with the example of respect. They all needed to be consulted on the details of our going, and where and when we should halt or march. This was inevitable with Auda, a child of battle who had never known a master since when as a tiny boy he had first ridden his own camel. It was necessary with Nesib, a Syrian of that queer race very jealous hostile to merit or to the acknowledgement of it. To combine such people demanded a war cry and a banner from the outside world, and a stranger to lead them, one whose supremacy should be based on a foundation illogical undeniable empiric which instinct might accept and reason could find no rational basis to deny or approve. Such a basis was the working idea of this army of Feisal's, the conceit that an Emir of Mecca a descendant of the Prophet, a Sherif, was an otherworldly dignitary, whom sons of Adam might reverence without shame. This was the binding assumption of the Arab Movement: that which gave it unanimity: the imbecile god whose worship was imbecility in us.

In the morning we rode away at five and in a few minutes our valley pinched together and we went round a sharp spur ascending steeply. The track became only a bad hill-path, zigzagging pettily up and up a hillside too steep to climb except on all fours. We dropped off our camels and led them by the headstalls. Soon we had to help one another urging the camels from behind pulling them from the front, encouraging them over the worst places adjusting their loads to ease them. Parts of the track were dangerous where rocks bulged out and narrowed it, so that the near half of the load struck, and forced the animal to the cliff-edge. We had to unload and repack the food and explosives, and in spite of all our care, lost two of our feeble camels in the pass. The Howeitat killed them where they lay broken, stabbing a keen dagger into the throat artery near the chest while the neck was strained tight by pulling the head round to the saddle. The wound soon made them collapse from loss of blood they were at once cut up and shared out as meat.

We reached the head of the pass at half-past seven and were glad to find it not a range but the edge of a plateau which sloped slowly before us to the east. The first yards were rough and rocky overgrown with low mats of thorns like heath: but afterwards it was easier country and we came to the sources of a valley of white shingle in the midst of whose bed a Bedouin woman was filling her water skin with a copper cup by which she ladled milky water, quite pure and sweet from a little hole a foot wide scraped elbow-deep in the pebbles. This was Abu Saad, and for its name's sake and for its water, and the joints of red meat bumping on our saddles, we settled we would stay here one night, passing yet more of the time which must be passed before Sharraf came back from the railway.

So we rode on four more miles, looking for a camping place, and came to a place of green spreading trees, standing in thickets of low thorn-scrub, very close grown above, but hollowed out underneath like booths. By day these made tent-ribs for our blankets stretched against the masterful sun. At night they were walls to our sleeping places. We had got used to sleeping abroad, with nothing overhead except the moon and stars, and nothing either side to keep distant the winds and the noises of the night, and by contrast it was strangely novel but quieting to rest within walls, and with a roof on top even though the walls and roof were only screens of interlacing twigs making a blacker mesh against the star-scattered sky. So we could not resist the comfortable temptation of the thorn bowers.

For myself I was ill again a fever increasing upon me, and my body very sore with boils and the rubbing of my sweaty saddle. When Nasir, without my prompting halted at the half-stage I turned to him and thanked him warmly to his astonishment It was a good camping ground on the limestone of the Shefa crest, but before us we could see a great dark lava field and short of it ranges of red and black banded sandstone cliffs with conical tops. Auda told me this was Wadi Jizil, the southern end of Hesma, the hollow place of a forest of square-built platform mountains, as Doughty described them, near their north point in Petra. It was the territory of the Nabateans, who had made their homes among these strange islands and turrets of wind-chiseled rock. At Abu Raga, which lay before us in jizil, Newcombe had found a Nabatean inscription.

The air up here on the high tableland was not so warm, and morning and evening there blew across us a free current which was refreshing after the suspended stillness of the valleys. We had a meat meal from off our dead camels, and started more gaily the next morning down a gently falling plateau of red sandstone for an hour. Then we came to a first break of surface, descending a sharp passage to the bottom of a shrub-grown sandy valley, on each side of which sandstone precipices and pinnacles, gradually growing in height as we went down, detached themselves sharply against the morning sky. It was shadowed in the bottom, and the air tasted wet and decayed, as though sap was drying out into it. The edges of the cliffs about us became clipped strangely, like fantastic parapets. Half an hour later we turned a sharp corner and entered Wadi jizil, the main gutter of these sandstone regions.

Jizil flowed southward till it fell into Hamdh opposite Wadi Ais, at the northern end of the great plain over which Dakhil-Allah and his men had galloped so freely with me some weeks ago. Here it was a deep gorge some two hundred yards in width, full of tamarisk sprouting from its bed of red drifted sand, with soft banks, perhaps twenty feet high, wherever an eddy in the flood or wind had heaped up and left the heavier dust under the returns of cliffs. The walls on each side were of regularly laid bands of sandstone, red in many shades, and streaked with dark seams. Their bases were protected by a talus of debris from the heights above, and over this had sprouted loose grass and bushes. The union of dark cliffs, pink sand floors and pale green shrubbery was beautiful to our eyes sated with months of sunlight and black shadow: when evening came the low sun made one side of the valley a dull purple and the other a hot crimson, as though consuming in a furnace of its rays. We felt that our path had brought us to good places, and half hoped that Sharraf would dally longer on the line.

Our camp was on some swelling dunes of weedy sand by the great pool of brackish water in a cliff-edged elbow of the valley, where a narrow cleft had set up a backwash and scooped out the basin in which this remnant of the flood was caught. When we had settled ourselves we sent a man up the valley to where we saw the white peaks of Sharraf's tents above an oleander thicket, to ask for news of him. They expected him next day, so we agreed that we might spend at least two nights in this strange-colored, echoing place. The brackish pool was fit for our camels, and in it we bathed at noon. Then we ate and slept generously, and such other time as I had was spent wandering in the nearer valleys seeing the horizontal stripes of pink and brown and cream and red which made up the general redness of the cliffs, and delighting in the varied patterns of thin penciling of a lighter or darker tint which were drawn over a plain body of rock. The broom and tamarisk were there for fuel, and our camels went daily to pasture up by Abu Saad.

In the afternoon I was lying behind some shepherd's fold of sandstone blocks in soft warm air and sunlight, with a low burden of the wind plucking at the rough wall-top above my head. The valley was instinct with peace, and the continuing noise of the wind made even it seem patient, waiting there. My eyes were shut and I was dreaming when a youthful voice spoke to me, and I looked up to see an anxious Ageyli squatting by me. He said that he was a stranger, and his name was Daud, and he appealed for my compassion. His friend Farraj was in trouble for burning their tent in a frolic, and Saad, captain of Sharraf's Ageyl, was going to beat him in punishment. At my intercession he would be released.

As it happened, just then Saad came to visit me, and I put it to him while Daud sat by, watching us, with his mouth slightly, eagerly open, his eyelids narrowed over his large, dark eyes and his straight brows deeply furrowed with anxiety. Daud's pupils were set a little in from the center of his eyeballs, and this subtle defect gave him an air of acute readiness. Saad's reply was not comforting. The pair was always in trouble, and of late so outrageous in their tricks that Sharraf the severe had noticed, and ordered an example made of them. All he could do for my sake was to let Daud bear half the ordained sentence. Daud leaped at the chance, kissed my hand and

Saad's and ran off up the valley, while Saad laughing told me stories of the famous pair. It seemed they were an instance of the boy and boy affection which in the East the lack of female companionship made common. They often led as in this case to manly love of a depth and force beyond our flesh-steeped conceit, since among the Arabs the warmest were innocent, and, if sexuality entered, the intensity passed into a give and take, unspiritual relation, like their marriages.

Next day Sharraf did not come. Part of the morning passed in Nasir's tent, with Auda talking of the march in front, while Nasir with his forefinger and thumb flicked spluttering matches from a safety box across the tent at us. In the midst of our merriment two bent figures, with pain in their eyes, but crooked smiles upon their lips, hobbled up and saluted. They were Daud the quick tempered and his love-fellow Farraj, a most beautiful soft-framed girlish creature, with innocent smooth face and swimming eyes. They said they were for my service. I had no need of them and objected that they were crippled after their beating and could not ride. They replied they had now ridden bare-backed to the camp, to answer that expected remark. Sharraf was not coming for two days, and by then they would be fit as ever. I said our march was hard: they said their camels were good. I said I was a simple man, who disliked servants about me. Daud turned away, defeated and angry: but Farraj said that at least I needed men, and they would come with me only for company and out of gratitude. While the harder Daud revolted, he went over to Nasir and knelt in despairing appeal, all the woman of him evident in his longing. In the end on Nasir's advice I took them both, mainly because they looked so young and clean.

Sharraf delayed to come until the morning of Wednesday, but then we heard him loudly, for the Arabs of his raiding force fired slow volleys of shots into the air, and the echoes were thrown about the windings of the valley till even the barren hills seemed to join in the salute. We had decided to take from him the other nineteen Ageyl of ibn Dgheithir's company as additional escort to our gold-sacks on the desert traverse: so we dressed in our cleanest to go and call on him with the news, and taste his hospitality. Auda put on the splendors he had bought at Wejh: a mouse-colored greatcoat of broadcloth with velvet collar, and yellow elastic-sided boots. These below his streaming hair and ruined face made him like a tired tragedian. Sharraf was kind to us, for he had captured prisoners on the line, and blown up rails and a culvert.

We lunched off mutton and rice, drank much coffee and sweet tea, and inspected our recruits. Nasir's joy in them was broken when he found their pay three months in arrears and had to make it up from his hoarded treasure: however, we had had good food and a pleasant talk, and the company complete would face the unknown roads and danger, and the long journey on short rations, with greater courage while their chief ibn Dgheithir promised to be a good helper to us. He was a man much walled into his own temperament, remote and abstracted, but self-sufficient. When he heard that from here we would cross the barren marches of the Fagir, from the railway to Wadi Sirhan, a thirsty journey with only one well, Fejr, in the midst at which to drink, he made no remark, except to tell a laconic story of his last fight with the Shammar, in which he had been worsted. It was a famous raiding area, and though we would now be fifty rifles (among them great men like Auda and his kinsmen), yet with our food and gold we would be in no trim for the speedy battles of the desert, and if we lost only the gold we would yet cripple Feisal's northward extension. Every reason made us cautious.

Sharraf gave us one piece of very grateful news. In Wadi Diraa, west of Muadhdham, almost on our road, were great rock-pools of rainwater, new-fallen and sweet, enough for us and all with us. This would shorten our waterless march to Fejr by fifty miles, and remove its danger of thirst, which was of great benefit, for we were short of water-skins, and there were none to be obtained in Wejh or in all the Billi country for love or money. Our total water carriage came to about twenty gallons, for our fifty men, and accordingly we had to hurry from source to source, hoping that no delay or accident would befall us on the road.

Chapter 44: Harrat El Aweirid

Next day we left Abu Raga near mid-afternoon, not sorry to be again on the road, for this so-beautiful place had not been healthy for us and we had much fever during our three days' rest in its confined bed. Auda led us up a tributary which flowed down into Wadi Jizil from the east. Soon it widened into the plain of the Shegg, a sand flat. About it in scattered confusion sat small islands and pinnacles of red sandstone grouped like the seracs of a glacier, wind-eroded at their bases till they looked very fit to fall and block the road which wound in and out between them through narrows seeming to give no passage, but always at the end of their crevasses opening by a new turn into yet another bay among the rocks. Through this maze Auda led unhesitatingly, digging along on his camel, elbows out, hands poised swaying up in the air by his shoulders. I marveled how he found his singing way through the thousands of blind alleys.

There were no footmarks on the ground, for each wind that blew swept like a great brush over the sand-surface, stippling the prints of the last travelers till the surface was again a virgin pattern of innumerable tiny waves. Only the dried camel droppings, which were lighter than the sand and round like walnuts, escaped its covering. They rolled about between the ripples, and were heaped up in every comer-pocket by the driving wind. It was perhaps by them, as much as by his unrivaled road-sense, that Auda knew his way. We enjoyed the march, for the rock shapes were a constant speculation and astonishment, and their granular surfaces and red color and the curved chiseling of the sand-blast upon them softened the sunlight, and gave our streaming eyes relief

In the mid-march we perceived a little party of five or six riders coming from the railway and aiming towards Sharraf's camp at Abu Raga. I was in front with Auda, and we had that delicious thrill: — 'friend or enemy?' — of meeting strangers in the desert, while we circumspectly drew across to our vantage side, to keep the rifle-arm free for a snap shot, but when they came nearer we saw they were of the Arab forces, and that one, riding loosely on a hulking camel with the unwieldy Manchester-made saddle of the British Camel Corps, was a fair-haired shaggy-bearded man in tattered uniform. This we guessed must be Hornby, Newcombe's pupil, the wild engineer who vied with him in smashing the railway. As we passed we exchanged greetings, and he said that Newcombe was gone down to Feisal at Wejh, to talk over his difficulties and make fresh plans to meet them.

Newcombe had constant difficulties from his excess of zeal, and his habitual doing four times what any other Englishman would do, and ten times what the Arabs thought needful or wise. Hornby spoke little Arabic and Newcombe not enough to persuade the Bedouin, though enough to give orders: but orders were not in place inland. The persistent pair would cling for weeks to the railway edge, almost without helpers, often without food, till they had exhausted either their explosives or their camels, and had to return for more. The barrenness of the hills made their trips hungry for their camels, and they wore out Feisal's best animals in turn. In this Newcombe was chief sinner, for his journeys were done at the trot: also as a surveyor by trade he could not resist looking from each high hill over the new country he crossed, to the exasperation of his escort who had either to leave him to his own courses (a lasting disgrace to abandon a companion of the road) or to founder their own precious and irreplaceable camels in keeping pace with him. 'Newcombe is like fire,' they used to complain: 'he burns friend and enemy', and they admired his amazing energy with a nervous shrinking lest they be his next friendly victims.

The Arabs told me Newcombe would not sleep except with his head on the rails, and that Hornby would worry the metals with his teeth when guncotton failed. These were legends, but behind them lay a sense of their savagery, of their insatiable thirst to go on and on with the work of destruction till there was no more to destroy. Between the two of them, four Turkish labor battalions were kept busy, patching culverts, relaying sleepers, jointing new rails: and guncotton had to come in increasing bulk to Wejh to meet their appetite. They were wonderful: but their too great goodness discouraged our feeble teams, making them ashamed to exhibit their inferior talents: and so always Newcombe and Hornby remained individualists, barren of the fruits of imitation. It seemed to me that it might have been better for them to have held their eagerness in check, while developing the meaner efforts of their men, since the half-taught combination of the thousands of Arabs would in the end outweigh the brilliance of single genius.

At sunset we reached the northern limit of the ruined sandstone land, and rode up to a new level sixty feet higher than the old, no longer red and sandy, but blue-black and volcanic, with a scattered covering of worn basalt-blocks, small as a man's hand, neatly bedded in a single layer like cobble paving over a floor of fine hard black cinder-debris of themselves. The rain in its age long pelting seemed to have been the agent of these stony surfaces by washing away the dust from above and between them, till the stones, set closely side by side and as level as a carpet, covered all the face of the plain, and shielded from direct contact with the weather the salty mud that filled the interstices of the lava flow beneath. It grew easier going as we went further, and Auda ventured to march after dark, due north towards the Pole Star.

It was very dark: a clear night enough, but the black stone underfoot swallowed the light of the stars, and at seven o'clock, when at last we halted: we found only few of our party with us. We had reached a gentle valley, entirely free of basalt, with a yet damp soft sandy bed, in which grew thorny brushwood of a sort unhappily useless as camel food. We ran about tearing up these bitter bushes by the roots and heaping them together in a great pyre, which Auda lit when the fire grew hot, a long black snake wormed slowly out into our group from the heap of fuel: we must have gathered it with the twigs as it lay torpid. The flames went shining across the dark flat, a beacon to the heavy and tired camels which had lagged so much today: but it was two more hours before the last group arrived, the men singing Sherifian marching songs in their loudest voices, partly to encourage themselves and their hungry animals over the ghostly plain, partly so that we might know them friends, and neither challenge nor shoot.

In the night some of our camels strayed away, hunting vainly for pasturage, and our people in the morning had to go up and down the country looking for them: so that it was nearly eight o'clock and we had baked bread and eaten, before again we started. Our track lay across more of the lava field of yesterday, but to our morning strength the stones seemed rarer, and waves or hard surfaces of laid sand often drowned them smoothly with a covering as good to march on as a tennis court. We rode fast over this for six or seven miles, but then the trodden road turned towards Muadhdham, and we left it, and went just west of a low cinder crater, and across the flat dark stony watershed that divided the Wadi Jizil from the basin in which the railway ran. Up here at their springing, these great water-systems were shallow sandy beds, scoring involved yellow lines across the blue-black plain.

We marched steadily till noon, and then stopped and sat out on the bare ground till three o'clock, an uneasy halt made necessary by our fear that the hungry camels, so long accustomed only to the sandy tracks of the coastal plain, might have their soft feet scorched by these sun-baked stones, and go lame with us on this first stage of the road. After we mounted, the going became worse, and we had continually to twist in our course to avoid large fields of piled basalt, or deep yellow water courses which cut through the crust into the soft stone beneath. After a while, red sandstone again cropped out in crazy chimneys from which the harder layers projected knife-sharp in level shelves beyond the softer degraded rock. At last these sandstone ruins became plentiful in the manner of yesterday and stood grouped about our road in such checked yards of light and shade.

They passed and we entered again on volcanic ground. Quantities of little pimply craters stood about, often two or three together and from them spines of high, broken basalt led down like disordered causeways across the barren ridges: but these craters looked old, not sharp and well-kept like those of Ras Gara near Wadi Ais, but worn and soft-curved, sometimes opened nearly to ground level by a great bay broken into their central hollow. Many of them were only a hundred feet high. The basalt which ran out from them was a coarse bubbled rock like the Syrian dolerite, and on its exposed surfaces the sand-laden winds had ground it to a pitted smoothness like orange-rind and the sun had faded it to dull blue-grey.

Away from the craters the basalt was strewn in small tetrahedral, with angles rubbed and rounded, stone set close to stone like a mosaic upon an under soil of pink-yellow mud. The ways worn across such flats by the constant passage of camels were very evident since the slouching tread had pushed the blocks to each side of the path, and. in the wet weather thin mud had run into the hollow tracks so worn and had inlaid them in white against the blue. Less-used roads for hundreds of yards were like narrow ladders laid across the stone-fields, for the tread of each foot was filled in with clean yellow mud, and ridges or bars of the blue-grey stone remained between each stepping place lying across the direction of the way. After a stretch of such stone-laying would be a field of jet-black basalt cinders, firm as concrete in the sun-baked mud: and afterwards a valley of soft black sand with more crags of weathered sandstone rising from the blackness, or from waves of the windblown red and yellow grains of their own decay.

Nothing in the march was normal or reassuring. We felt we were in an ominous land incapable of life hostile even to the passing of life except painfully along the sparse roads that time had laid across its face. Our march was deadly slow, for we were forced into a single file of weary camels, picking a hesitant way step by step across the loose boulders for hour after hour. At last Auda told me that we were nearly at an end of the lava-troubles, and pointed ahead to a fifty-foot ridge of large twisted blocks, lying coursed one upon the other as they had writhed and shrunk in their cooling. There was the limit, and he and I rode on together, and from its head saw in front of us an open rolling plain (Wadi Aish) of fine scrub and golden sand, with green bushes scattered here and there. In it we found a very little water in holes which someone had scooped, probably after the rainstorm of three weeks ago. We camped by them for the night, and drove our unladed camels out till sunset to graze for the first adequate time since Abu Raga.

While they were scattered over the land, mounted men appeared on the horizon to the east, making towards the water in the bed of our valley under the steep cliffs. They might have been Shammar and a raiding party, for they came on too quickly to be honest, and fired at our herdsmen: but the rest of us ran at once upon the scattered reefs and knolls and shouted and shot. Hearing us so many they drew off as fast as their camels would go, and from the ridge in the dusk we saw them, a bare dozen in all, scampering far away towards the line. We were glad to see them avoid us so thoroughly, for we had no mood to fight luxury-battles, or to lie awake all night defending our animals. However, as a precaution we did drive them together into a gulf of the cliff and slept across the mouth of it in line ourselves, with a sentry to give warning of a rush: but nothing happened and at dawn we had saddled up for the short remaining stage to Diraa, the water pools of which Sharraf had given us word.

The first few miles were through the grateful sand and scrub of Wadi Aish, and afterwards we crossed a simple lava-flat. Then came a shallow valley, fuller of sandstone pillars and mushrooms and pinnacles than anything of yesterday. It was a mad country, like nothing but a field of ninepins, set as close as might be, and from ten to sixty feet in height. The sand paths between them were wide enough for one only, and our long column wound blindly through them, seldom a dozen of us having common sight at once. This ragged thicket of stone was perhaps a third of a mile in width and stretched like a red river to right and left across our path. Beyond it was a sharp broken cliff, up which led a graded path over black ledges of rotten stone. At the top we halted and looked back and down over the heads of sandstone, fifty feet below us, and saw, beyond, the peaceful black and yellow flats of our early march.

Then we turned again forward over a plateau strewn with small loose blue-black basalt shards, but easy going, and not dazzling to the eyes, and after a while entered Wadi Diraa and marched down its bed for an hour or more, sometimes over loose grey stone , sometimes along a sandy bottom between low rock sides. There we found a deserted camp, with empty sardine tins, proof of Newcombe and Hornby. A little way behind were the limpid pools, and we halted there till the afternoon, for we were now quite near the railway, and had to drink our stomachs' full and fill our few water skins, all ready for the long dash to Fejr.

We decided to start again at four o'clock, in order to reach the line by sunset: and spread ourselves out over the stones of the valley for the long and insufferably hot delay. Auda came down to me to see Farraj and Daud dress my camel with butter, for relief against the intolerable itch of the mange which had broken out severely on its face. The dry pasturage of the Billi country and the infected ground of Wejh had played havoc with our beasts. In all Feisal's stud of riding camels there was not one healthy: in our little expedition every camel was weakening daily, the best being mine and Auda's and ibn Dgheithir's. Nasir was full of anxiety that many of them would break down in the forced march before us and leave their riders stranded without water or relief in the desert.

We had no medicines for mange, and could do little for it in spite of our desire. However, the rubbing and anointing did make my animal more comfortable, and we repeated it as often as Farraj or Daud could find butter in our party. These two boys were giving me great satisfaction. They were brave and cheerful, and unlike the average of mankind. As their aches and pains wore off they showed themselves active, good riders, and willing workmen. I liked their free conduct towards myself and the instinctive understanding they had with one another, against the rest.

Chapter 45: The Railway and El Haul

At a quarter to four we were in the saddle, going down Wadi Diraa. We left it after two miles and struck off north-eastward, out of the rocky country into steep and high ridges of shifting sand, sometimes with a cap of harsh red rock jutting from them. We wandered between these, going slowly and irregularly: and after a while three or four of us went forward in advance of the main body, and climbed on hands and knees to a sand-peak, to spy out the railway.

There was no air, and the exercise was more than we required: but our reward was immediate, for the line showed itself quiet and deserted-looking, on a green flat at the mouth of the deep valley, down which the rest of the company was marching circumspectly with ready weapons.

We checked the men, who drew together into groups at the bottom of their narrow sand-fold, while we climbed to the last outcrop and studied the railway. Everything was indeed peaceful and empty, even to the abandoned blockhouse square in front of us. The greenness was due to a rich patch of rank grass and weeds between us and the line. We ran to the edge of the rock-shelf under our feet, and leaped from it out on to the sliding slope of fine dry sand, and rolled down in a magnificent slide till we came to an abrupt and rather bruising halt on the level ground beside the column. We mounted, and hurried our camels out to the grazing ground and leaving them there, ran over to the railway and shouted to the others to come on.

This unmolested crossing was blessed, for Sharraf had warned us repeatedly and seriously against the provoked activity of the enemy patrols of mule-riding infantry and camel corps, reinforced from the entrenched posts by infantry on trolleys mounting machine-guns. Our riding beasts we chased into the grass to feed for a few minutes, while the heavy camels marched over the valley and the line and the farther flat, till they were in the shelter of the sand and rock mouths of the similar valleys beyond the railway. Meanwhile the Ageyl amused us by fixing guncotton and gelatin about our crossing-place to as many of the rails as we had time to reach: and, when our munching camels had been dragged away and into safety on the far side, we began to light the fuses one by one, and filled the hollow valley with the echoes of our repeated bursts.

Auda had not known dynamite before, and with a child's first pleasure was moved to a rush of hasty poetry on the glory of the noise. We also cut the three telegraph wires, and fastened the free ends to the saddles of six riding camels of the Howeitat. The astonished beasts struggled far into the eastern valleys with the growing weight of the twanging, tangling wire and the bursting poles dragging after them. At last they could no longer move, and we cut them loose and rode laughing after the caravan. The railway had been our first anxiety, and it was triumphantly passed and left in ruins behind us, while we marched with filled water-skins across the open desert, having nothing fixed or certain before us, except the well of Fejr, till we reached the Howeitat, or the water in the Sirhan near jauf the headquarters of Nuri Shaalan, our secret ally.

For five miles more we proceeded in the growing dusk, up the valleys beyond the line, between ridges which seemed to run down like fingers from some knuckle-ridge in front of us. At last their rise and fall became too sharp to be crossed with safety by our weak animals in the dark: and there we halted in an open place. The baggage and the bulk of our riders were still ahead of us, keeping the advantage they had gained while we played with the railway, and we could not find them in the night, for the Turks were shouting hard and shooting at shadows from their stations on the line behind us, and as we did not know their force we judged it prudent to keep quiet ourselves, and not light fires or send up signals to attract attention.

However, ibn Dgheithir, who was in charge of the main body, had left a connecting file behind him and, in consequence, before we had fallen asleep, two men came in to us, and reported that the rest were securely camped in the hidden fold of a steep sandbank a little further on. So we threw our saddlebags again across our camels, and plodded after our guides in the murky dark (tonight was almost the last night of the moon) till we reached their hushed picket on the ridge, and beyond them found the others camped, and bedded ourselves down by them without words. In the morning Auda was afoot before four o'clock, and just as day broke we started off on our long journey toward Wadi Fejr.

For half an hour the way led uphill, till at the end we climbed a ridge, and plunged over down a sand slope. Into it our camels sank knee-deep, held upright despite themselves by its clinging. They were able to make way only by casting themselves on and down its loosen face, breaking their legs out of it by their bodies' weight. At the bottom we assembled once more, and found ourselves in the head-courses of a valley system which appeared to run southward towards Muadhdham. Another half-hour took us to the springing of this, and we breasted the low edge of the plateau which was the watershed between Hejaz and Wadi Sirhan.

There we found ourselves suddenly on a great plain, with an illimitable view out downhill to the east, where one gentle level after another slowly modulated into a distance only to be called distance because it was a softer blue, and more hazy, than the land before it. The rising sun flooded this falling plain with a perfect level of light, throwing up for us long shadows of almost imperceptible ridges, and the whole life and play of a complicated ground-systems — but a transient one, for a few minutes later, as we looked at it, the shadows drew in towards the dawn, quivered a last moment behind their mother-bank and then went out as though at a common signal. The full morning had begun, and the blaze of sunlight poured impartially on every stone and unevenness of the desert over which we had to go.

Auda struck out north-eastward, aiming for a little saddle that joined the low ridge of Jebel Ugula to a spur from the truncated cone of Selhub or Sellum (our Howeitat were not sure upon the name), a lofty hill on our left about three miles away. We crossed the saddle, after a march of about four miles, and found beneath our feet little shallow runnels in the ground. Auda pointed to them saying that they ran to Nebk in the Sirhan, and that we would follow them till we met the Howeitat in their summer camp; and then we went on northward with these shallow water-courses twining to right and left of our path in the loose ground.

A little later we were marching over a low ridge of slivers of sandstone with the nature of slate, sometimes quite small, but sometimes great slabs ten feet each way and perhaps four inches thick. Auda ranged up beside my camel, and pointing to each side with his riding stick, told me to write down on my map the names and nature of the land. The valleys on our left were the Seil Abu Arad rising in Selhub, and fed by many successors from the great divide as it was prolonged northward to Jebel Rufeiya by Tebuk. The valleys on our right were the Seil el Kelb from Ugula, Agidat el jemelein, Lebda and the other ridges which bent round us in a great bow eastward and north-eastward. These two water systems united fifty miles before us in Fejr, the valley of the old well which made possible our march over this parched region. I cried Auda mercy of his names swearing I was no writer-down of unspoiled countries to pander idle curiosity and the old man much pleased began to tell me personal notes and news of the chiefs with us, and of those in the tents we were aiming for. His wise talk whiled away the passage of desolation.

The Fejr Bedouin, whose property was called our plain, el Houl, because it was desolate, today we rode in it without seeing any sign of life, no tracks of gazelle, no lizards no burro wings of rats not even any birds. There seemed no activity animal or vegetable, and we ourselves felt tiny in it and our urgent progress all day across its immensity stillness and immobility of futile effort. The only sounds were the hollow echoes, like the shutting down of pavements over vaulted places, of rotten stone slab on stone slab when they tilted under our camels' feet and the slow but piercing rustle of the sand, as it crept slowly westward before the hot wind of the open desert along the sides of the worn sandstone, under the overhanging caps of harder layer which gave each ridge its shape.

It was a breathless wind, with the furnace taste sometimes known in Egypt when a hamsin blew, and as the day went on and the sun rose in the sky it became stronger, and more filled with the dust of the Nefudh, the great sand-desert of Northern Arabia close by us over there but invisible behind the haze. By noon it was a half-gale and so dry that our shriveled lips cracked open and the skin of our faces chapped while our eyelids gone granular seemed to creep back and lay bare our shrinking eyes. The Arabs drew their head cloths tightly across their noses, and pulled the brow-folds forward, so that they became visors for them with only a narrow loose-flapping slit of vision.

At this stifling price they kept their flesh unbroken for they feared the sand particles which would wear open the chaps into a painful wound... but for myself I always rather liked a hamsin, since it was a wind of an ordered conscious malevolence, which seemed to fight to destroy mankind with its torment: and it was pleasant to out pace it so directly, challenging its strength, and conquering its extremity, and there was pleasure also in the salt sweat-drops which ran singly down the long hairs over my forehead, and dripped like ice-water with a shock of refreshment on my cheek. At first I played at catching them in my mouth, but as we rode further into the desert and the hours passed, the wind became stronger, thicker in dust, more terrible in heat My camel's pace became sufficient increase to the irritation of the choking waves, whose dryness broke upon my skin and made my throat so painful that for long I could eat little of our bread. When evening came I was content that my burned face still felt the other and milder airs of darkness.

We plodded on all the day (even without the wind forbidding us there could have been no more of our luscious halts under the shadow of blankets in these marches, if we would arrive unbroken men with strong camels at el Fejr), and nothing made us open an eye or think a thought till after three in the afternoon. Then we came to a cross-ridge swelling at last into a noticeable hill, a proper reason for the divorce of Abu Arad from Seil el Kelb, which now drew to itself the more part of the tributaries, and as Seil Gelib cut through the Dhakiyeh hills on our right, aiming northward. At the foot of the rise stood two pyramids, Tulul el Shebb, small sharp regular remains of what had been perhaps once a ridge before the rain and the wind undercut the cap, and left only these two artificial-seeming mounds.

Beyond the rise we dropped to a long slope, slow degrees of a washed gravel surface, with striplings of an occasional torrent bed going down into Wadi Abu Arad, which hugged a course at the foot of the Rufaiyir hills to the westward. Auda and I trotted together down this slope, to get some relief from the intolerable slowness of the caravan. Near sunset, a low wall of hills became clear, barring across our way to the north, and shortly after I saw that Seir Abu Arad turned eastward this side of it, and swept along our front we entered its bed a few minutes later, finding it a mile wide, and thickly covered, inches deep, in a scrub which was dry and parched like dead wood , and crackled and split with little spurts of dust when we began to gather it into a fire to show the others where we had made the halt

They did not arrive for an hour or more, when the wind had altogether died away, and the evening, calm and black and full of stars, had come down on us. Auda set a watch through the night, for this district was in the line of raiding parties, crossing between Jebel Shammar, Teima, Tebuk, Maan, Tubaik, el Ula and Jauf, and in the hours of darkness there were no friends in Arabia We had covered about fifty miles this day, all we could do at a stretch, and enough according to our program. So we halted the night hours, partly because our camels were weak and ill, and partly because the Howeitat were not intimate in this country, and feared to lose their way if they should ride too boldly without seeing.

Chapter 46: Wadi Fejr

The following day we started before dawn, going down the bed of Seil Abu Arad till the white sun came up over the Zibliyat hills ahead of us. Then we turned more north to cut off an angle of the valley, and rode across its left bank in a few minutes, and down a flint slope over limestone into Riet el Khel, a great tributary from the hills of Urn Regaiba on the west. It joined Abu Arad where Wadi Gelib flowed in, and their joint stream became the Fejr valley. We halted for half an hour till we saw the main body corning, and then Auda, Nasir and myself, unable longer to endure passively the hammer strokes of the sun upon our bowed heads, pushed forward at a jerky trot Almost at once we lost sight of the others, blotted out by the lymph-like heat vapor throbbing across the flat: but this was of no concern, for the road was evident, down the scrubby bed of Wadi Fejr.

At the height of noon we reached the well of our desire. It was about thirty feet deep, stone-stoned, and seeming ancient: but we left it and rode to the bank, and halted in the shade. The valley here was only five hundred yards across, and was bounded by low ridges, straight-topped with sandy bases. It had flooded in some burst of rain the year before, and therefore contained much dry and thirsty pasture: to this we loosed our camels, and then the rest came up, and drew water and baked bread. The water was abundant, slightly brackish, but not ill-tasting when drunk fresh: though it soon grew foul if kept in a skin. We let the camels crop industriously till nightfall, then watered them again, and pounded them under the bank a half-mile from the water , for the night: thus we left the well unmolested in case any raiders should need it in the dark hours. We were now half-way across the open country to the Sirhan, with half our danger and trouble freely passed. Our spirits rose, and we spoke of news of the Howeitat at the reported flood-pool of Abu Ajaj on the morrow.

As usual we were off before dawn, though we had an easy march before us: but the heat and glare of the desert was so painful that we designed to pass the midday in some shelter. After two miles the valley spread out, and somewhat later we came to a low broken cliff on the east bank opposite the mouth of Seil Raugha. Here the country looked greener, and we asked Auda to fetch us game. He sent Zaal one way and rode westward himself across the open plain which stretched beyond view, while we turned in to the cliffs and found beneath their fallen crags and undercut ledges abundant shady places, cool against the sun, and restful for the eyes. The hunters returned before noon, each with a good gazelle. We had filled our water-skins at Fejr, and could use them up, for Abu Ajaj in front of us was still fit to drink: so there was great feasting on bread and meat in our stone dens. These indulgences amid the exertion and slow fatigue of long unbroken marches gave grateful moments to the delicate townsfolk among us: to myself, and to Zeki and Nesib's Syrian servants, and in a lesser degree to Nesib himself.

We rested till two in the afternoon and reached our stage, Khabr Ajaj, just before sunset, after a dull ride over the great plain that extended Wadi Fejr to the eastward for many miles. The pool was of this year's rain, already turned thick, and brackish, but good for camels and just possible for men to drink. It lay in a shallow double depression by Wadi Fejr, whose flood had filled it about two feet deep over an area two hundred yards across. At its north end was a low sandstone tamp. We had thought to find some Howeitat here, but the ground was grazed bare and the water fouled by their animals, while they themselves were gone. Auda searched for their tracks, but could find none. They had probably decamped ten days ago, when the water became too salt for household use: and the windstorms since had swept the sand face into clean new ripples. However, since they had come down here from Tubaik, they must have gone out into Sirhan : so if we went on northward we would find them.

The following day, Wednesday, May the twenty-third, was our fourteenth from Wejh, and when its sun rose we were again marching along the Fejr valley, which was here called Seil Hawia. However, in the afternoon we left it at last to steer for Arfuja in Wadi Sirhan, a point rather east of north from our position. Accordingly we inclined to the right, over flats of limestone and sand, and saw a few miles farther east a comer of the Great Nefudh, the famous belt of sand-dunes which cut off Jebel Shammar from the Syrian Desert. Palgrave, the Blunts, and Gertrude Bell amongst the great travelers had crossed it, and I begged Auda to bear off a little and let us enter it... but he replied that men went to the Nefudh only of necessity, when raiding, and that the son of his father did not raid on a tottering mangy camel. Our business was to reach Arfaja alive.

So we were wise and marched on, over monotonous glittering sand and over those worse stretches, *Giaan,* of hard unbroken polished mud, nearly as white and smooth as laid paper, and often whole miles square. They blazed back the sun into our faces with glassy vigor, so that we rode with the light raining its arrows upon our heads, and its reflection glancing up from the ground through our inadequate eyelids. It was not a steady pressure, but a pain ebbing and flowing, at one time piling itself up and up till we nearly swooned, and then falling away coolly in a moment of apparent shadow, which was in reality a black web crossing the retina: and which, like the struggles to the surface of a drowning man, gave us a moment's breathing space only to store new capacity for suffering.

We grew short-answered to one another, but relief came in the evening when the sun sank low behind our left shoulders, and then came six o'clock when we halted for supper, and pleased ourselves with bread I gave my camel what was left over of my share, for the poor animal was tired and hungry in these bad marches. She was the pedigree camel given by ibn Saud of Nejd to King Hussein and by him to Feisal, a splendid beast, rough but sure-footed on hills, and great-hearted. Arabs of means rode none but she-camels, since they went smoother under the saddle than the males and were better tempered, and less noisy: also they were more patient, and would endure to march long after they were worn out, indeed until they tottered with exhaustion and fell in their tracks and died: whereas the coarser males grew angry, and flung themselves down when tired, and from sheer rage would die there unnecessarily.

After dark we crawled on again for three hours to the top of El jaala, a sand ridge, and there we slept thankfully after a bad day of burning wind, and dust blizzards full of drifting sand which stung our inflamed faces, and at times in the greater gusts wrapped the sight of our road from us and drove our complaining camels up and down. But Auda was anxious about the morrow, for another hot head-wind would delay us a third day in the desert, and we had no water left: so he called us early in the night, and we marched down the slope into the plain of the Biseita (so called in derision, for its huge size and flatness) before day broke. It was a bare and barren place, as flat as a table for two days' march each way of us, and covered with a fine litter of sun-browned flints. These made the surface restfully dark but were hot and hard-going for our camels, some of which were already beginning to limp with sore feel.

The sandy plains of the coast, or of south-central Arabia, being soft to the feet, made delicate the pads of the camels brought up on them, and if these animals were taken suddenly inland for prolonged marches over flints or other hard and heat-retaining ground their soles would burn until at last perhaps the outer hide cracked off, and a blister of bare flesh, two inches or more across, would appear in the center of the pad. In this state they could march as well as ever over sand, but if by chance the foot came down on a pebble they would stumble, or flinch as though they had stepped on fire and in a long march under such conditions might break down altogether unless they were very brave. We began today to be nervous of our mounts, for though we had doctored them regularly with tar and turpentine, yet many of them were showing rawness, and an extra day over flint might put them out of action afterwards for weeks. So we rode forward carefully picking the softest way, Auda and I in front.

As we went some little puffs of dust scurried into the eye of the wind across the flat ahead: Auda said they were ostriches: and a few minutes later a man ran up to us with two great ivory eggs. We settled that we would breakfast on this bounty of the Biseita, and looked for fuel to cook them: but in twenty minutes had only a wisp of dry grass. The barren desert was defeating us. The baggage train passed and my eye fen on the blasting gelatin. We broached a packet, shredding it carefully into a fire beneath the eggs propped on stones, till the experts pronounced the cookery complete. Nasir and Nesib dismounted to scoff at us, really interested. Auda drew his silver-hilted dagger of Jauf smiths' work, and chipped the top of the first egg. A stink went across our party like a pestilence. We fled to a clean spot, rolling the second hot egg before us with gentle kicks, and opened it, it was fresh enough and hard boiled, and we dug its contents out with the dagger on to the flint flakes which were our platters, and ate it piecemeal, persuading even Nasir, who in his life before had never fallen so low as egg-meat, to take his share. The verdict was tough and strong, but good in the Biseita.

When this was finished Zaal saw an onyx, and hunted it on foot, stalked it, and killed it. The best joints were tied upon the baggage camels for the next halt, and our march continued. Afterwards the greedy Howeitat saw more onyx in the distance and went after the foolish beasts, which ran a little, and then stood still and stared till the men were near, and too late ran away again. Their white bellies betrayed them, for in the magnification of the mirage they shone out from afar, winking strangely as the animals stirred themselves to look at us.

Chapter 47: the Biseita

I was too weary and too little sporting to go out of the straight way for all the rare beasts in the world; so I rode after the caravan, which my camel overhauled quickly with her longer stride. At the tail of it were my men, walking on their feet They feared that some of their animals would be dead before evening, if the wind blew stronger, but would lead them all day, in the hope of getting them in. I admired the contrast between them, Mohammed the peasant, lusty and heavy-footed, and with him the lithe and graceful Ageyl, among whom Farraj and Daud were dancing along, barefoot, delicately built like thoroughbreds. Only Gasim was not there: they thought he was behind with the Howeitat, for his surliness kept him commonly with the little-spoken Bedouin.

I knew there was no one behind so rode forward to see him and ask how his camel was: and at last I found his camel, saddled but rider less: one of the Howeitat was leading it. His saddlebags were there, and his rifle and his food, but he himself was nowhere to be found and gradually it dawned on us that the miserable man was lost. This was a dreadful business, for in the haze and mirage the caravan could not be seen two miles, and on the iron ground it made no tracks: alone he would never overtake us.

Everyone had marched on thinking he was with some friend elsewhere in our scattered line, but much time had passed and it was nearly midday, so that he must be miles back. It was a mystery to know what had happened to him. That his camel was loaded was proof that he had not been forgotten asleep at our night halt. The Ageyl ventured that perhaps he had dozed off in the saddle, and fallen in the dark and stunned or killed himself: or perhaps someone of the party had borne him a grudge. Any way they did not know. He was an ill-natured stranger, no charge on any of them, and they did not greatly care.

This was true, but it was true also that Mohammed whose countryman and fellow he was, and who was technically his road companion, knew nothing of the desert, had a foundered camel, and could not turn back for him. It would be murder if I sent him, and that shifted the difficulty to my shoulders. The Howeitat who would have helped us were away in the mirage out of sight hunting or scouting forward along our advance. Ibn Dgheithir's Ageyl were so clannish that they would not put themselves about except for one another. Besides, Gasim was my man, and as by desert law there could be no desertion between us it was clearly marked that on me lay the responsibility for him.

I looked weakly at my men trudging along, and wondered for a moment if I could change with one of them, and send him back alone on my camel to the rescue. My shirking the duty would be understood, since I was a foreigner: but that was precisely the plea I did not dare set up while I yet presumed to lead these Arabs in their own revolt. It was hard anyway for a stranger to influence another people's national movement, and doubly hard for a Christian and a sedentary person to lead muslim nomads. I would make it impossible for myself if I claimed the privileges of both societies.

So I turned my unwilling camel round without saying anything, and forced her grunting and moaning for her camel friends, back past the long line of men, and past the baggage into the emptiness behind. My temper was not at all heroic, for I was furious with my other servants, and with my play-acting as a Bedouin, and most of all with Gasim, a gap-toothed grumbling fellow, scrimshank in all our marches bad-tempered, suspicious and brutal a man whose engagement I had much regretted, and of whom I had promised to rid myself, so soon as we reached a possible discharging-place. It seemed absurd that I should have to peril my weight in the Arab adventure for a single worthless man.

My camel seemed to feel it also, by her deep grumbling but that was a constant resource of ill-treated camels. They had been accustomed from calf-hood to go about in droves, and some got so conventional that they would not march alone: while even the best of them would never leave their habitual party without loud grief and unwillingness such as mine was showing. She kept on turning her head back on her long neck, and lowing to the rest, and walked very slowly and bouncingly needing careful guidance to keep her on the road and a tap from my stick at every pace to keep her moving. However, after a mile or two she felt better and began to go forward less constrainedly, but still too slowly. I had been noting our direction all these days with my oil compass and hoped by its aid to arrive back nearly at our starting place: which lay, by my reckoning about seventeen miles south-west by south of us.

After twenty minutes the caravan was out of sight, and it was borne in on me how really barren the Biseita was. Its only marks were the old sanded *samh* pits across all possible of which I rode because my camel pads would show in them, and they would be so many blazes to me of the way back. This *samh* was the hour of the Sherarat, who were poor in all but camel-stocks and made it their pride to find the desert sufficient for their every need. When mixed with dates, and loosened with butter, it was good food: but this year there was none, nor had been since the great season of six years ago.

The pits, little threshing floors of the Sherarat women, were hollowed in the ground by the simple means of pushing aside the flints over the area of a circle ten feet across. The flints heaped themselves up round the rim of the pit, and made it inches deep, and in this hollow place they collected and beat out the small red seed so abundantly carried in the heads of the plant.

The constant winds sweeping since over them could not indeed put back the flint surface (that would perhaps be done by the rain in thousands of winters) but had leveled them up with blown sand, pale in color, so that the pits looked like grey eyes in the blackness of the stony surface.

I had ridden for about an hour and a half, easily for the breeze was behind me, and I had been able to wipe the sandy crust from my red eyes and could look forward almost without pain for so long as I pleased, when I saw a figure or a large bush or at least something black ahead of me. Of course there was a mirage, which made everything shift, and destroyed all sense of height or distance: but this thing seemed to be moving a little to the east of our proper direction, and on chance I turned my camel's head that way, and in a few minutes saw that it was Gasim. When I called he stood still confusedly, and I rode up to him and saw that he was nearly blinded, and silly, standing there with his arms held out to me, and his black mouth gaping open. The Ageyl had put our last water in my skin before I started, and this he poured madly over his face and breast in his haste to drink. He stopped babbling incoherently, and instead began to wail out his sorrows. I sat him on the camel's rump, and made him hold the back of the saddle, then stirred her up and mounted.

When we turned in the old direction to follow our party, the beast seemed much relieved, and moved forward willingly. With the compass I was able to set an exact course, so exact that again and again I found our old tracks, in the shape of little spurts of paler sand scattered over the brown-black flint. The way ran gently downhill, and in spite of the double weight on her back the camel began to stride out, and even at times she put her head down, and for a few paces developed that fast and most comfortable shuffle to which the best animals while yet young were broken by skilled riders. This proof of spirit in her in reserve rejoiced me, and the little time we had lost in search meant that we were nearly sure to overtake the rest.

Gasim was a nuisance, weeping and moaning about the great pain and terror of his thirst: Arab villagers were sometimes almost like Turks in their complete surrender to an illness of which they felt convinced. I told him to stop, but he went on, and began to sit loosely until at each step of the camel he bumped down on her hindquarters with a crash which like his crying spurred her to greater pace. There was danger in this, for we might easily founder her so, and again I told him to stop: and when he only screamed louder than ever, I hit him and shouted that for another sound I would throw him off and ride away by myself: after which he was quiet.

Probably not four miles had been passed when again I saw something like a black bubble, lunging and swaying in the mirage ahead. There were three of them, and I wondered if they were enemy, being sure that it was not the caravan so soon. A minute later the haze unrolled from them with the disconcerting suddenness of all illusion, and it was Auda with two of Nasir's men come back to look for me, I yelled jests and scoffs at them for abandoning a mend in the desert. Auda pulled his beard and grumbled that he had not been present when I had ridden back or I would not have gone. Meanwhile Gasim was transferred to a better rider's saddle-pad, and we ambled forward together gladly.

Auda pointed to the wretched hunched-up figure and denounced me, 'For that thing, not worth a camel's price....' I interrupted him with 'Not worth a florin, Auda', and he was delighted in his simple mind, and rode near Gasim, and struck him sharply, trying to teach him to repeat like a parrot his price. Gasim grinned with rage, and afterwards sulked silently. In another hour we were on the heels of the baggage camels, and as we passed up the line Auda repeated my joke to each pair, perhaps forty times in all, till I had seen to the full its feebleness.

Gasim was transferred with insults to his own saddle. He explained that he had dismounted to ease nature, and had missed the party afterwards in the dark: but obviously he had gone to sleep, where he dismounted, with the fatigue of our slow hot journeying. We rejoined Nasir and Nesib in the van. Nesib was vexed with me, and blamed me to Nasir for periling the lives of Auda and myself on a whim: for it was dear to him that I reckoned they would come back for me. Nasir was shocked at his ungenerous outlook, and Auda was glad to rub into a townsman the paradox of tribe and city, the collective responsibility and group-brotherhood of the desert, contrasted with the isolation and competitive living of the crowded districts.

However, this little affair had passed away some hours of March, and the rest of the day seemed not so long, though the heat became worse and worse, and the sand-blast stiffened in our faces till the air could be seen and heard whistling past our camels on each side like a stream of smoke. The ground was flat and featureless as ever till near five o'clock when we saw low mounds ahead of us and a little later found ourselves in comparative peace, amid sand-hills coated slenderly with tamarisk. These were the Kaseim of Wadi Sirhan. The bushes and the dunes broke the wind, and it was sunset, and the day mellowed and reddened on us from the west, and I wrote in my book that the place was beautiful.

Palestine became a land of milk and honey to those who had spent forty years in Sinai: Damascus had the name of an earthly paradise to the tribes which could only enter it after weeks and weeks of painful marching across the flint and limestone of this northern desert: and so the Kaseim of Arfaja in which we spent that night after five days across the blazing Houl in the teeth of a sandstorm looked fresh and countrified. They were raised only a few feet above the Biseita, and from them valleys seemed to run down towards the east where lay the wells we wanted: but now that we had crossed the desert and reached the Wadi Sirhan safely, the terror of thirst had passed and we knew better our fatigue. So we agreed to camp for the night where we were, and to make great fires in case the slave of Nuri Shaalan, who also had wandered from our caravan today should be looking, lost, for us in the Biseita in the dark.

We were not greatly perturbed about him. He knew the country and his camel was under him. It might be that he had intentionally struck out east of our line towards Maigua, or the more direct way to Jam. Nuri's capital, to bring him advance news of our coming and of our messages and presents for him. However it was, he did not come that night nor on the next days, and when months after I asked Nuri of him, he replied that his dried body had at last been found, lying beside his camel's, both unlaundered, far out in the wilderness. He must have lost himself in the sand-haze and wandered about till his camel broke down: and there died of thirst and heat. Not a very long death — even for the strongest man a second day in summer was all but very painful, for thirst was an active malady, a fear and panic which tore the brain and reduced a brave man to a stumbling babbling maniac in an hour or two and then the sun killed him. Auda's instinct for the road saved us this danger. I checked him by my compass, and even when the dust was thickest and the direction of the sun was lost, he kept steadily on, steering perfectly.

It was indeed a continent night, for we had not a mouthful of water, and so of course ate nothing: yet the certainty that we would drink on the morrow let us sleep easily, lying on our bellies, for that prevented the inflation of foodlessness. The sand and the dry winds caused the Arabs to drink freely all their lives. They had little power of restraint over water, and it was useless to suggest their rationing it: indeed it would have been presumptuous for us to have made the suggestion, for we were strangers, and they had spent their lives coping with thirst. Probably they would have resented the idea that we could teach them. Their habit was to fill themselves full to vomiting point at each well, and either to go dry to the next, or if they carried water, to use it lavishly at the first halt, drinking and bread making, and then to go on unprovided.

As my ambition was always to avoid comment upon my difference I copied their example in traveling with them, trusting with reason that their physical superiority was not great enough to trap me into serious harm. Actually I only once went ill with thirst.

Chapter 48: Wadi Siriian

Next morning we rode down a series of slopes, and over one ridge, and a second, and a third, each three miles from the other, and at eight o'clock dismounted at the wells of Arfaja, the sweet smelling bush from which they were named being fragrant all about us. We found the Sirhan not so much a valley as a long fault in the desert, draining the country on each side of it, and collecting the waters into the successive depressions of its bed. The ground-surface was off linty gravel, alternating with soft sand, and the aimless valleys seemed hardly able to trace out their slow and involved levels between the loose sand-dunes over which blew the feathery tamarisk with its whipcord roots, binding their slopes together.

The *imshosh* of Arfaja were unlined wells, dug about eighteen feet through gravel to water which was creamy in texture, with a powerful smell and a brackish taste. We found it delicious and, as there was some green stuff about, good for camel-food, decided to stay here the day while we searched for the Howeitat. There was no trace of them about the wells, or in the pasture grounds, and by sending a man back to Maigua, the southernmost well of the Sirhan, we would establish whether or not they were behind us: and if they were not, would be able to march towards the north with confidence that we were on their track.

Hardly, however, had the man ridden off when one of the Howeitat saw riders hiding in the scrub to the north of us, and there was an instant call to arms. Mohammed el Dheilan, Auda's politic cousin, was the first into the saddle, and with the other Toweiha he galloped out against the supposed enemy while Nasir and I mustered the Ageyl, whose virtue was not in fighting Bedouin-fashion with Bedouin, and placed them in knots about the dunes so as reasonably to defend the baggage. However the enemy got off: Mohammed returned after half an hour to say that he had not made relentless pursuit for pity of the condition of his camel. He had seen only three tracks in the sand, and supposed that the men we saw had been the scouts of a Shammar raiding party in the neighborhood.

In the dunes and tangled thickets of the Sirhan raiding parties could lie or wander for days undetected, watering at one or other of its many wells: and somewhere in its great length they would be sure to light on a camp of Rualla, or Sherarat, Howeitat, Beni Sakhr or Serahin, whose grazing herds of camels would give them a chance of booty. The Shammar were habitual enemies of all these northern tribes and able to make head against them, for in themselves they were a powerful confederation, and they lived in a strong place, fenced from retaliatory raids by the Nefudh, the sand desert, and by great lava fields. In Jebel Shammar, their headquarters, they had, thanks to the power and wealth of ibn Rashid, their prince a market center of their own at Hail, which served also as capital of their nomad state, and armor, and court of justice.

The acting Emir of the Rashids, Saud ibn Abd el Aziz, a young fellow, leaned to the hereditary friendship of his family with the Turks, and depended on them for his food, since the British would not admit him to Basra, and the Sherif could not reach him for the bar of the Hejaz Railway in between. The Turks had decorated him, and given him twelve thousand Mauser carbines, to arm his tribesmen: and encouraged him to attack the British in Mesopotamia. However, the Emir was only half-hearted in his efforts in the east, and soon returned west again to the Hejaz line, nominally to protect it against Abdulla. In reality he temporized, and before the end of the war was in friendly relations with Mecca.

Yet, whatever their lord's politics, there was no doubt that Shammar parties regarded all in Wadi Sirhan as fair game: and so it behooved us to be careful. Auda called up Zaal his nephew, the keenest eye of all the Howeitat, and asked him to go out and examine the enemy tracks, to discover their numbers and intention. Zaal was a lithe metallic man, with a bold, open, appraising look, cruel lips and a thin laugh, full of the brutality which these nomad

Howeitat had caught from the peasantry. He went off as we wanted, and searched, but found that the whole ground in the thicket of brushwood about us was full of tracks, and the tamarisk kept the wind off the sandy floor, so that it was impossible to distinguish particularly the footprints of today.

The rest of the daylight passed peacefully, and we lulled ourselves, though we kept a sentry posted on the head of the great dune behind the water-holes. At sunset I went down to the well edge and washed myself with its smarting water, and on my way back halted at the Ageyl fire to take coffee with them, while listening to their Nejdi Arabic. They began to tell me long stories of Captain Shakespeare, who had been received by ibn Saud in Riyadh as a personal friend, and had crossed Arabia from the Persian Gulf to Egypt, and had been at last killed in battle by the Shammar, in a set-back which the forces of Nejd had suffered in one of their periodic wars.

Many of these Ageyl of ibn Dgheithir's had traveled with him, as escort or followers, and had tales of his magnificence and of the strange seclusion in which he kept himself day and night. The Arabs who usually lived in heaps suspected some ulterior reason for the too-great privacy: and to remember this and to forswear all selfish peace and quiet while wandering with them was one of the least pleasant lessons of the desert war: and humiliating too for it was a part of pride with us to hug solitude ourselves finding ourselves to be remarkable men when there was no competition present.

While we talked the coffee was roasted and dropped with three grains of cardamom into the mortar. Abdulla then brayed it for us pounding it with the dring-drang, dring-drang pestle strokes of village Nejd, two pairs of staccato beats of equal value. Mohammed el Dheilan heard them and came over to us silently across the sand and sank down camel-like on the ground next to me to taste their drink; for the Ageyl coffee was our best. He was a companionable fellow Mohammed a powerful thinking man with a wry humor and an affectation of sour craft, sometimes justified by his acts, but generally concealing a friendly cynical nature. In appearance he was unusually strong and tall not much under six feet in height a man of perhaps thirty-eight, broad and active, with a high-colored face ruggedly lined and very crafty eyes.

He was the second man of the Abu Tayi, with far more followers than Auda, far richer than him and more luscious in his habits. He had a little house in Maan, and landed property (and. it was whispered cattle) near Tafileh. Under his influence the war-parties of the Abu Tayi rode out delicately with sunshades to defend them from the fierceness of the sun and with bottles of mineral water in their saddlebags to relieve their toil upon the journey. He was the brains of the tribal councils and directed their politics. He had risen against the Turks ten years before but had been captured and condemned, and only the intervention of Nuri Shaalan pardoned him. Then he became the sober lawyer of the tribe and their advocate with the Government. Auda had now led him into rebellion again and his sore-headed critical spirit pleased me, and generally I used his intelligence and greed to convert him to my party before approaching Auda with a new idea.

The long ride in company had had its effect upon us all, tempering both our minds and our bodies. The hazard of our goal was always in our thoughts: day and night consciously and unconsciously we were training and exercising ourselves reducing our wills to suit our single purpose. To this end these odd moments of talk about the evening fire were most often dedicated, and we were so thinking, while the coffee-maker was boiling up his coffee, and tapping it down again, making a palm-fiber mat to strain the grounds before he poured, since grounds in the cup were evil manners, when there came a sudden burst of fire from the shadowy dunes to the east of us, and one of the Ageyl toppled forward into the center of the fire-lit circle with a screech.

Mohammed with his powerful foot thrust a wave of sand over the fire, and in the quick blinding darkness we rolled behind banks of tamarisk and scattered for our rifles, while the men ready in the outlying groups began to return the fire, aiming hurriedly towards the flashes. We had unlimited ammunition, and showed it. The enemy, astonished perhaps at our preparedness or disappointed in his hope of surprise, gradually slackened his efforts. At last his fire stopped, and we held our own lying there listening for a rush, or for attack from a new quarter. Perhaps for half an hour we lay perfectly still except for the groans and at last the death struggle of the man wounded by the fireside at the first volley.

Then we were impatient of waiting longer, and Auda sent out Zaal, his head scout on all the expeditions of the clan, to search round carefully and find out what was happening to the enemy. After another half-hour his voice called to us from a mound a little way outside our line. He reported that there was no enemy left within reach of us. They had mounted their camels and ridden away: apparently about twenty of them.

Despite Zaal's assurances we passed a restless night, and in the morning before dawn we buried Asaaf our first casualty, and moved off northward keeping in the bottom of the hollow, with the sand hills mostly on our left. We rode for five hours, and then halted for breakfast, on the south bank of a great spill of torrent-beds running down into the Sirhan from the south-west.

Auda told me these were the mouths of Seil Fejr, the valley whose head we had seen at Selhub, and down whose bed we had marched right across the Houl.

The grazing here was better than at Arfaja: and so we allowed our camels the four hours of noon to fill themselves: a poor proceeding, for the midday grazing was not so profitable: but we enjoyed ourselves, under the shadow of our blankets, sleeping out the sleep we had missed the night before. Here in the open, away from all possibility of hidden approach, we had no fear of disturbance: and it was our ambition by displaying our strength and confidence to dissuade the invisible enemy from the attack. Our camels were too weak for mounted battle, unfit either to charge or to escape. We were hampered by loads of gold totaling five hundredweight, and by seven hundredweight of high explosives, and if we lost either our hopes were dashed. Our desire was to fight Turks, and this inter-Arab business was sheer waste.

In the afternoon we rode on twelve miles, and there found a sharp group of firm sand hills, the Kaseim of Maiseri, a name properly given to a well three miles further on. These hills enclosed an open space big enough for us, and commanded the country round about. So we halted there, in expectation of another attack in the night. From the crest we looked over a complete desolation, a sandy waste of tamarisk and scrub, and open flint fields between the dunes, while away to the north-east, across the Sirhan bed, was Mismah, the first crater of the volcanic belt which ran continually along by the east of the Sirhan from here to Azrak and to the Druze mountains, cutting off the Hiseita and the Suwan, the country of Tebuk and Maan and Amman, from the open plains of the great Syrian desert that stretched from Damascus to Kerbela.

That night of course passed peacefully after such preparations, and next morning we did a fast march of five hours, our camels being full of life after their feed of yesterday, to Awaisit, an oasis-hollow a mile and a half across of grown or stunted palm-trees, with tamarisk clumps here and there. To the west it went out in a long depression of a day's march towards Hausa and Tubaik. Our end of the hollow was rotten with salt, but pits in the ground reached plentiful water about seven feet underground everywhere. It tasted sweeter than the water of Arfaja. The Sirhan was full of salt, and nearly all its wells were tainted. A first drink was tolerable but if kept enclosed in a vessel the water developed a foul smell and taste, and ruined coffee, tea and bread, and refused to lather with soap.

In fact we were tiring of Wadi Sirhan, though Nesib and Zeki still planned works of plantation and reclamation here by the Arab government when by them established. Such vaulting imagination was typical of Syrians who easily persuaded themselves of possibilities, and as quickly reached forward and laid the responsibilities elsewhere. 'Zeki,' said long day, 'your camel is very full of mange.' He agreed mournfully, and that he would rub her skin with ointment in the evening. On the next day he outlined to me the scheme of an official veterinary service, in Syria when Damascus was taken. It would have a staff of skilled surgeons and assistants, in a central hospital, or rather central hospitals, for horses and for camels and for donkeys and cattle, even (why not?) for sheep and goats. There must be a scientific and bacteriological department, to make researches into new cures for the disease. Did I advise a library? There must be district hospitals too, and traveling inspectors and he carved up Syria into areas of convenient sub-division.

Next day he returned to his labor upon the new department after sleeping over it and told me that nothing less than perfection satisfied him. He regretted that I was always snatching after the merely opportune, I answered in his vein that I thought perfection in the least of things would end our world, and I had not finally made up my mind on that. When I was angry I prayed God to swing it into the fiery sun, and prevent the sorrows of the yet unborn: but when I was contented I wanted to lie there in the shade forever, and be absorbed in it. Uneasily he shifted the talk to stud farms, and on the fifth day his poor camel died, very truly because, as he pointed out. I had not dressed her. Auda, Nasir and the rest of us kept our beasts going by constant care. We could just stave the mange off till we should reach camp and be able to buy medicines and doctor them properly.

We started again at one o'clock, when it was still too hot, but these morning halts were not for our comfort but for our camels' grazing. For us it was better to be in the saddle, where the motion gave US air and change and occupation, than to sweat in the shadow of a blanket chasing flies while pretending to sleep. We rode for three hours, and then saw a mounted man bearing down fast on us. There was a momentary tension, but then the Howeitat hailed him. He was one of their herdsmen, and warm greetings were exchanged in an unhurried voice as was proper in the desert, where noise was a lowbred business at the best and urban at its worst.

He told us the Howeitat were camped up the valley in front, from Isawiya to Nebk, anxiously waiting our news. All was well with them and their tents. Auda's anxiety passed and his eagerness kindled. We rode fast for an hour, to Isawiya, and found there amongst others the tents of Ali Abu Fitna, chief of one of Auda's clans. Ali was an old unkempt man with red eyes and a large dripping nose, whose untended beard jutted forward from his jaw.

He greeted us warmly and urged us to accept the hospitality of his tent. We excused ourselves as too many and camped nearby under some thorns, while he and the other tent holders made estimate of our numbers, and prepared feasts for us in the evening, to each group of tents a little batch of visitors. The meal took hours to produce, and it was long after dark when they called us to it. I woke and stumbled across and ate: and as soon as it was over we made our way back to our couched camels and slept again.

Chapter 49: Howeitat Feasting

Our march troubles were over. We had found the Howeitat: our men were in excellent fettle: we had our gold and our explosives still intact, and had lost only two of our number on the road. So we drew happily together in the morning to a solemn council and discussed the future. There was agreement that our first act should be to make a present of six thousand pounds to Nuri Shaalan, by whose benevolent sufferance we existed in Wadi Sirhan. We wanted from him the further grace of liberty to stay there while making our preparations, and enrolling our fighting men; and when we moved off we wanted him to look after the safety of the families and tents and herds of those who marched with us.

These were great matters, and so it was determined that Auda himself should ride up to Nuri on embassy to explain the gift, since Auda and Nuri were old friends. The Rualla were too near and too big a tribe for Auda to fight, however lordly his delight in war: and so self-interest had prompted the two great men to an alliance: and between these strongest personalities in the desert, acquaintance had induced a whimsical regard, by virtue of which each suffered the other's oddities with patience.

With Auda would go ibn Muslim, Nasir's secretary, to convey Feisal's personal messages, and to explain to Nuri what we hoped to do, and our desire that he remain neutral, or rather that he make a public demonstration of adherence to Turkey. Only in this way could he cover us.

Meanwhile we would stay with Ali Abu Fitna, moving gently northward with him towards Nebk, where Auda would tell all the Abu Tayi to collect, on the plea of tribal business. He would be back from Nuri before we were united to meet him. This was the business, and we loaded the six bags of gold into Auda's and ibn Muslim's saddlebags, and off they went. Afterwards the chiefs of the Fitenna waited on us, and said that they were honored by the chance to feast us twice a day, forenoon and sunset, so long as we remained with them; and they meant what they said. Howeitat hospitality was unlimited (no three-day niggardliness of the nominal law of the desert) and importunate, and left no honorable escape for us from the entirety of the nomad's dream of well-being.

Each morning between eight and ten a little group of blood mares under a strange assortment of imperfect saddling would come up to our camping place, and on them Nasir, Nesib, Zeki and I would mount, and with perhaps a dozen of our men on foot would move solemnly across the valley by the sandy paths between the bushes. Our horses were led by our servants since it would be immodest to ride free or fast. So eventually we would reach the tent which was to be our feast-hall for that time, each family claiming us in turn, and bitterly offended if Zaal the adjudicator preferred another out of just order.

As we arrived the dogs would rush out at us, and be driven off by some of the onlookers always a crowd had collected round the chosen tent and we stepped in under the ropes of the tent to its guest half, made very large for the occasion, and carefully dressed with its wall-curtain on the sunny side to give us shade. There the bashful host would receive us with a murmur and vanish again out of sight. The tribal rugs, lurid red things from Beirut, were ready for us, arranged down the partition curtain, along the back wall, and across the dropped end, so that we sat down on three sides of a square with an open dusty space between us. We might be fifty men, perhaps.

The host would reappear standing by the pole and our local fellow-guests. Mohammed el Dheilan, Zaal and the other sheikhs would reluctantly let themselves be placed on the rugs between us sharing our elbow-room on the pack-saddles padded with folded felt rugs against which we leaned. The front of the tent was cleared and the dogs were frequently chased away from before us by excited children who ran across the empty space pulling yet smaller children after them. Their clothes were less as their years were less, and their pot-bodies rounder. The smallest of all would stare gravely balanced on spread legs stark-naked sucking their thumbs and pushing out their expectant bellies towards us.

Then would follow an awkward pause which our friends would try to cover, by showing us on its perch the household hawk (when possible a sea bird taken young on the Red Sea coast) or their watch-cockerel or their greyhound. Once, a tame ibex was dragged in for our admiration, another time an onyx. When these were exhausted they would try and find a small-talk to distract us from the household noises and the urgent whispered cooking directions wafted in from beyond the curtain with a powerful smell of boiled fat and drifts of tasty smoke.

After a silent space the host or a deputy would come forward and whisper 'Black or white', an invitation for us to choose coffee or tea. Nasir would always answer 'Black', and the slave would be beckoned forward with the beaked coffee pot in one hand and three or four clinking cups of white ware in the other. He would dash a few drops of coffee into the uppermost cup, and proffer it to Nasir; then pour the second for me and the third for Nesib and pause while we turned the cups about in our hands and sucked them carefully to get appreciatively from them their last richest drop.

As soon as they were empty his hand was stretched out and clapped them noisily one above the other and tossed out with a lesser flourish for the next of us in order and so on round the assembly till all had drunk. Then back to Nasir again. This second cup would be tastier than the first, partly because the pot was yielding deeper from the brew partly because of the heel taps of so many previous drinkers present in the cups and the third and fourth rounds if the meat delayed so long would be of surprising flavor.

However, at last two men came staggering in through the thrilled crowd carrying between them the rice and meat on a tinned copper tray or shallow bath, about five feet across, set on a high foot like a great egg cup's. In the tribe there was only this one food-bowl of the size, and it had an incised inscription worked round it in florid Arabic characters: 'To the glory of God, and in hope of forgiveness, the property of His suppliant Auda Abu Tayi.' It was borrowed by the host who was to entertain us for the time, and since my urgent brain and body made me sleepless, from my blankets in the first light I would see the bowl going across-country, and by marking down its destination would know where we were to feed that day.

The bowl was now brim-full ringed round its edge by white rice in an embankment a foot wide and six inches deep, filled with legs and ribs of mutton till they toppled over. It took two or three victims to make in the center a dressed pyramid of meat such as honor prescribed. The center-pieces were the boiled heads, upturned, propped on their stumps of neck deep-buried in the food, so that the ears, browned like old leaves, flapped out on the rice-surface. The jaws gaped emptily upward, pulled wide open, to show the hollow throat, with the tongue, still pink, clinging to the lower teeth; and the long incisors whitely crowned the pile, very prominent above the nostrils' prickly hair and the lips which sneered away blackly from them.

This load was set down on the soil of the cleared space between us, where it steamed hotly, while the procession of minor helpers carried in the small cauldrons and copper vats in which the cooking had been done. From them, with much-bruised bowls of enameled iron, they ladled out over the main dish all the inside and outside of the sheep, little bits of yellow intestine, the white tail-cushion of fat, brown muscles and meat and skin, all swimming in the liquid butter and grease of the seething. The bystanders watched the work anxiously, with muttered satisfactions when a very juicy bit plopped out.

Pouring these bowls-full of scrap over the heap was warm labor, for the fat was scalding. Every now and then a man would drop his baler with an exclamation, and plunge his burnt fingers, not reluctantly, in his mouth to cool them: but they persevered till at last their scooping rang loudly on the bottoms of the pots, and with a gesture of triumph they fished out the intact livers from their hiding place in the gravy and topped the yawning jaws with them. Then two raised each cauldron and tilted it over the mass, letting the liquid splash down upon the meat till the crater of the rice was full, and the loose grains at the edge swam in the abundance, and yet they poured till amid exclamations of astonishment from us it was running over and a little pool congealing in the dust. That was the final touch of splendor, and the host called us to come and eat.

We feigned a deafness, as manners demanded; at last we heard him, and looked surprised at one another, each urging his fellow to move first: till Nasir rose coyly, and then we all came forward , and sank on one knee round the tray wedging in and huddling up till the twenty-two for whom there was space were grouped around the food. We turned back our right sleeves to the elbow, and taking lead from Nasir with a low, 'In the name of God the merciful, the loving-kind', we dipped together.

The first dip for me at least was always cautious, since the liquid fat was so hot that my unaccustomed fingers could seldom bear it: and so I would toy with an exposed and cooling lump of meat till others' excavations had drained my rice-segment. We would knead between the fingers, not using the palm, neat balls of rice and fat and liver and meat, all cemented by gentle pressure, and project them by leverage of the thumb from the crooked forefinger into the mouth.

With the right trick and the right construction the little lump held together and came clean off the hand: but when surplus butter and old fragments clung cooling to the fingers they had to be licked carefully, to make the next effort slip easier away.

The host stood by the circle encouraging the appetite with pious ejaculations, and we worked at top speed twisting, tearing, cutting and stuffing, never speaking since conversation at a meal would be an insult to its quality, though it was proper to smile thanks when one of the more intimate guests passed across a select fragment or when Mohammed el Dheilan or Farraj gravely handed over a huge barren bone with a blessing. On such occasions I would return the compliment with some hideous and impossible lump of guts, a flippancy which rejoiced the Howeitat, but which the gracious and aristocratic Nasir saw with disapproval.

As the meat pile wore down (nobody really cared about the rice: the flesh was the luxury) one of the chief Howeitat eating with us would draw his dagger, silver-hilted, set with turquoise, a signed masterpiece of Mohammed ibn Zari of jauf and would cut crisscross from the larger bones long diamonds of meat easily torn up between the fingers; for it was necessarily boiled very tender, since it had all to be disposed of with one hand.

At length some of us were nearly filled, and these began to play and pick, glancing sideways at the rest, till they grew slow, and at last ceased eating, elbow on knee, and the hand hanging down from the wrist over the tray edge to drip, while the fat and butter and scattered grains of rice cooled and stiffened into a white grease which gummed the fingers together. When all had stopped Nasir cleared his throat meanly, and we rose up together in haste with an explosive, 'Our host, God requite it you', and grouped ourselves outside among the tent-ropes while the next twenty guests came forward and inherited our leaving.

Those of us who were nice would go to the end of the tent where the flap of the roof-cloth beyond the last poles drooped down as an end curtain, and on to this, the clan handkerchief (whose coarse goat-hair mesh was pliant and glossy with much use) would scrape the thickest of the fat from their hands. Then we would make back to our seats, and retake them slightingly, while the slaves of the tent, leaving aside the skulls of the sheep which were their share, would come round our ranks with a wooden bowl of water and a coffee cup as dipper and pour water over our fingers, while we rubbed them on this side and on that of the tribal soap-cake.

Meantime the second and third sittings by the dish were having their turn, and then there would be one more cup of coffee, or a glass of syrup-like tea, and at last the horses would be brought, and we would slip out to them, and mount them, with a quiet blessing to the hosts as we passed by. As our backs were turned the children would run in disorder upon the ravaged dish, and tear the gnawed bones

The most famous sword-smith of my time was ibn Bani of Hail. He rode once on foray with the Shammar against the Rualla, and was taken. When Nuri Shaalan knew him, he shut him up in prison with his own smith, ibn Zari, swearing they should stay there till their work was indistinguishable. So ibn Zari, already the greater artist, bettered his skill by means of the craft-secrets of his rival from one another, and escape into the open with valuable fragments to be devoured in security behind a distant bush: while the dogs prowled round snapping and the master of the tent fed the choicest of all to his greyhound.

This fashion of rising up all at once from the food was of the central deserts of Arabia. In the north and about Damascus each guest slipped aside like a peasant as he was filled. In the far north by Aleppo the Anazeh set the guest to eat by himself and in the darkness, that he might be not ashamed of his appetite before the host: all these were modes, but among the most considerable men the manner of Nasir was generally praised.

Chapter 50: With the Tribes

On the first day we feasted once, on the second twice on the third twice, at Isawiya; and then on the thirtieth of May we saddled and rode easily for three hours past an old sanded lava field on the east to Abu Tarfeiyat, a valley in which seven-foot wells of the usual brackish water lay all about us. The Abu Tayi struck camp when we struck, and journeyed at our side, and camped around us: so today for the first time I was spectator and actor of the march of an Arab tribe: and my mind went making pictures of them on the road, or rather tried always to discover what effect upon myself their pictures made.

It was strangely unlike the usual desert-constancy. Today the grey-green expanse of stones and bushes quivered like a mirage with the movement of men on foot, and horsemen, men on camels, camels bearing the hunched black loads which were the goat-hair tent-cloths, camels swaying curiously like butterflies under the winged and fringed howdahs of the women, camels tusked like mammoths or tailed like birds with the cocked and dragging tent poles of silvery wood. There was no order or control or routine in their march, other than the wide front, the self-contained parties, and the simultaneous start, which the insecurity of countless generations had made instinctive.

Just it was that the desert usually so sparse that it gave value to every man, seemed with their numbers to come suddenly alive.

The pace was very easy and we who had been guarding our own lives for weeks found it a relaxation beyond feeling to know ourselves so escorted as to share the light liability of danger with a host. Even our most solemn riders let themselves go a little and the wilder ones became licentious. First amongst these of course were Farraj and Daud, my two imps whose spirits not all the privations of our road had quelled for a moment. Today about their riding places in our line, centered a constant swirl of activity or accident, as their irrepressible mischief found new forms of expression.

They grated on my dry patience a little, because the plague of snakes which had been with us since our first entry into the Sirhan, here rose to its height, and became memorable, almost a terror to me. In ordinary times the Arabs said snakes were a little worse here than elsewhere because of the water in the desert: but this year the valley seemed creeping with homed vipers, and puff adders cobras and black snakes. At night movement was dangerous from the number of them in the bushes: and at last we found it necessary to walk with sticks, beating on each side while we stepped warily through the scrub with our bare feet.

We could not lightly draw water after dark for there were snakes swimming in the pools, or clustering in thick knots around their brinks. Twice puff adders came twisting along the ground into the open ring of our debating coffee-circle. Three of our men died of bites, but four recovered after enduring great fear and pain and a swelling of the poisoned limb. The Howeitat treatment was to bind up the part with a snake skin plaster and to read some chapters of the Koran to the sufferer until he died. They also pulled thick ankle boots red with blue tassels and horseshoe heels, of Damascus work over their homy feet when they went late abroad.

A strange thing was the snakes' habit at night, when we slept, of lying beside us, probably for warmth, under or on the blanket. When we learned this our rising was with infinite care and the first up would search round the fellows with a stick till he could pronounce them unencumbered. Our party of fifty men killed perhaps twenty snakes daily in these places, and at last they got so on our nerves that the boldest of us feared the ground day and night, and those who like myself had always had a shuddering horror of them longed that our stay in Sirhan might end.

Not so Farraj and Daud. To them this was a new and splendid game, and they troubled us continually with false alarms, and furious beatings upon the head of every harmless twig or root that caught their fancy. At last, in our noon-halt, I charged them strictly never to let the name of snake again pass their lips aloud, and for a while, sitting down by our traps upon the sand, we had peace. To live on the floor, whence it was so far to rise up and walk, disposed me to inaction, and there was much to think about: so that it may have been an hour afterwards before I noticed that the offending pair were smiling and nudging one another. My eyes idly followed their eyes to the neighborhood bush, under which a brown snake lay coiled, glittering at me.

I moved myself in time, and cried to Ali, who jumped in with his riding-cane and settled it then I told him to give the two boys a swinging half-dozen each, to teach them not again to be literal at my expense. Nasir heard where he was slumbering behind me, and with joy shouted to add half a dozen from himself Nesib copied him and then Zeki and then ibn Dgheithir, till half the men were clamoring for revenge on them. The culprits were abashed when they saw that all the hides and all the sticks in the party would hardly expiate their account: however, I saved them the weight of it, and instead we proclaimed them moral bankrupts, and set them under the Howeitat women to gather sticks and draw water for the tents.

So they labored shamefully for the two days we spent at Abu Tarfeiyat; where on the first day we feasted twice and on the second day twice. Then Nesib broke down, and on plea of illness took refuge inside Nasir's tent, and ate dry bread thankfully. Zeki had been ailing on the road, and his first effort in the Sirhan at the Howeitat sodden meat and greasy rice had prostrated him. He also lay within the tent, breathing disgust and dysentery against us. Nasir had had long experiences of tribal ways and stood the test grandly. It was incumbent on him, for the honor of our guesses to answer every call, and for greater honor he needed me to come with him, and we two represented the camp each day, with a proportion of the Ageyl.

Of course it was monotonous, but in return the crystal happiness of our hosts was a visual satisfaction, and to have shattered it a crime. Our education had been to cure us of prejudice and superstition, our culture to make us understand the simple. These people were achieving for our sake the height of nomadic ambition, a continued orgy of seethed mutton and it was our duty to live up to it. My heaven might have been a lonely soft armchair a book rest, and the works of poets hand-set in Caslon, hand-printed on the best paper: but I had been for twenty-eight years well-fed and if Arab imagination ran on food-bowls, so much the better for them. They had been provident expressly on our account. A few days before we came, a drover bringing fifty sheep from Nejd towards his market in Damascus had stayed with them, and by Auda's order they had bought the flock to entertain us worthily. In fifteen meals (a week) we had consumed them all, and the hospitality guttered out.

On the first of June we left Abu Tarfeiyat in the morning, and after an hour reached the lava field of Muhaidir, to which we rose by an easy path from the sandy plain. Its barren top was strewn with worn blocks of line-grained dolerite just showing through the wind borne sand that covered all the roughness and gave us good going for the camels. The volcanic rock here about six miles wide, barred right across the Sirhan from the east till it met the Suwan, a flint ridge that was the western bank. North of it was a valley in which lay Um el Fenajin, unlined pits live or six feet deep holding brackish water. We passed them, and the lava fell back on each side, leaving a great plain of tamarisk and wormwood, miles and miles across. We rode over it for an hour, to Jemajem, another well and for some miles further till we crossed a low limestone ridge to Bir el Adheimat, beside some well-grown palms.

There we halted for a while, and I climbed the sharp end of the ridge above the well. Three snakes disputed it with me but afterwards I was able to see that we were on the very western edge of the Sirhan. This ridge joined the Suwan, which here came close in to the depression eastward was a hollow country of limestone, and grey scrub and grey lava and sand for miles as far as a bald white patch that was part of the salt marshes of Hadhodha, the lowest level of Sirhan, constant lagoons of salt water with quick shores, impassable for camels except by known paths to the salt-gathering places.

The only green things in sight were a few palms about Ain el Beidha, three miles away but after that, for the twenty miles to Jebel Urn Idhn beyond the eastern lava, the landscape was of a hopelessness and sadness deeper than all the open deserts we had crossed. A sand desert, or a flint desert, or one of bare rocks was sometimes exciting, and in certain lights had the beauty of sheer sterility and desolation: but there was something sinister, something actively evil in this snake-devoted Sirhan waste, so pregnant with salt water, fruitless palms, and unprofitable bushes which served neither for grazing nor for firewood. We hated it so much that we made a fight march to be out of it the sooner.

Accordingly we went eight or nine miles after dark and reached Wadi Bair, a very broad estuary of tamarisk with the delightful bitter scent of worm wood in its air: and there we lay down in the open, with a clean wind blowing on us from the cool north, and slept with no fear of puff-adders as our bedfellows. It was only for the one night, and we knew that next day and for many days the Sirhan would be our lot: but the craving for an open place was too heavy on us, and we fled to it.

In the morning we started at dawn making for Ageila, and rode through Ghutti, whose weak well was nearly sweet. When we got near we saw that it was held by many tents, and presently a troop came out to meet us. They were Auda Abu Tayi and ibn Muslim, safely back from Nuri Shaalan, with the one-eyed Durzi ibn Dughmi, our old guest at Wejh. His presence proved Nuri's favor, as did their strong escort of Rualla horse, who, bareheaded and yelling, welcomed us to Nuri's empty house there in Ageila with a great show of spears, and wild firing of rifles and revolvers in the dust at full gallop.

This modest manor had some fruitful palms, enclosed, and they had pitched ready for us beside the garden a Mesopotamian tent of white canvas. Here also stood Auda's tent, a huge hall seven poles long and three wide, so that in all he had twenty-one in his house, and Zaal's tent was near it, and many others, and through the afternoon proceeded fusillades of honor, and deputations, and gifts of ostrich eggs, and Damascus dainties, and camels, and scraggy horses, while the air was loud about us with the cries of Auda's volunteers demanding service, immediate service, against the Turks.

Affairs looked well, and we set on three men to make coffee for the visitors, who came in one by one to Nasir, or group by group, swearing allegiance to Feisal and to the Arab Movement in the Wejh formula, and promising to obey Nasir, and to follow after him with their contingents. Besides their formal presents each new party deposited on our carpet their privy accidental gift of lice, and long before sunset Nasir and I were in a fever with relay after relay of irritation. Auda had a stiff arm, the effect of an old wound in the elbow joint, and so could not scratch all of himself: but time had taught him a way of thrusting a cross-headed camel stick up his left sleeve, and turning it round and round inside against his ribs: and that relieved him, more than our claws did us.

We only stayed the one night, and in the morning moved to Nebk Abu Gasr, so named from another palm-grove and mud house of Nuri Shaalan's; here there was plentiful water, with some grazing, and Auda had appointed it our rallying place, because of the convenient nearness of the Blaidat, or 'salt hamlets', Kaf, Ithara,

Wishwasha, Jetjer, where a few hundred Syrian peasants, clients of the Rualla Emir, looked after his palm-groves and salt-pans, and kept a scanty market for his tribes.

Chapter 51: Excursions

At Nebk, Sherif Nasir and Auda sat down for many days, to consider wages, to enroll the men, and to prepare the road along which we would march by approaching the tribes and the sheikhs who lived along it. Leisure remained for Nesib, Zeki and myself As usual, the Syrian unstable judgment, not able to consist in the narrow point of virtue, staggered to the circumference. In the heady atmosphere of first enthusiasm they ignored Akaba, despised the plain purpose which had led us here. Nesib knew the Shaalans and the Druses, and in his mind enrolled them, and not the Howeitat, struck at Deraa, not at Maan, occupied Damascus, not Akaba, He pointed out that the Turks were all unready. We were sure to gain our first objective, by sheer surprise: and therefore that objective should be the highest. Damascus was indicated inevitably.

I pointed him in vain to Feisal yet in Wejh, to the British yet the wrong side of Gaza, to the new Turkish army massing in Aleppo to recover Mesopotamia, and showed how we in Damascus would be unsupported, without resources or organization, without a base, without even a line of communication with our mends; but Nesib was now soaring above geography, and beyond tactics, and only sordid means would bring him down. So I went to Auda, and said that with the new objective the cash and credit would go to Nuri Shaalan and not to him: and I went to Nasir, and used my influence and our liking for one another to keep him on my plan, and fanned the jealousy easily lit between a Sherif and a Damascene, between an authentic Shia descendant of Ali and Hussein, and a reputed descendant of Abu Bekr.

The matter was one of life and death for our movement. I believed that if we took Damascus we would not hold it six weeks, for Egypt would not in that time be ready to plunge at the Turks in front of them, nor would sea transport be available at the moment's notice to land a British army at Beirut: and when we lost Damascus we would have lost our supporters (only their first flush was profitable: a rebellion that stood still or went back was lost) and would not have gained Akaba, which was the last base in safe water, and in my judgment the only door, except the middle Euphrates, from which we could unlock Syria without risk.

Fortunately both Nasir and Auda answered sensitively to my whisperings, and after recriminations Nesib left us, and rode off with Zeki to the Druse mountain, under safe-conduct of Hussein el Atrash, the Druse master of Anz by Salkhad. There he meant to do the preliminary work necessary to launch his great Damascus scheme. I knew his incapacity to create, but it was not in my mind to have even a half-baked rising there, to spoil our future material, so I was careful to draw his teeth before he started, by taking from him most of the money Feisal had shared out to him. The fool made this easy for me, as he knew he had not enough for all he wanted, and measuring the morality of England by his own pettiness, came to me for the promise of more if he raised a Syrian movement independent of Feisal, under his own leadership. I had no fear of so untoward a miracle, and instead of calling him a rat, gave my ready promise for the future, if he would for the present give me his balance to help us to Akaba, where I would make funds available for the general need. He yielded to my condition with a bad grace, but Nasir was delighted to get two bags of money unexpectedly.

However, the optimism of Nesib had had its effect upon me (giants being easier to imagine than were pygmies) and while I still saw the liberation of Syria happening in steps of which Akaba was the indispensable first, I now saw the steps coming very close together, and as soon as Nesib was out of the way planned to go off myself rather in his fashion on a long tour of the north country to sound its opinion and learn enough to lay definite plans. My general knowledge of Syria was fairly good, and some parts I knew exactly: but I felt that one more sight of it would put straight the ideas of strategic geography given me by the crusades and the first Arab conquest, and enable me to adjust them to the two new factors in my problem, the railways in Syria, and the allied army of Murray in Sinai. .

Also I wanted an excuse to get away from the long guiding of people's minds and convictions which had been my part since Yenbo six months before. It should have been happiness, this lying out, free as air, with life about me striving its uttermost whither my own spirit led: but its unconscious serving of my purpose poisoned everything for me. A man might clearly destroy himself: but it was repugnant that the innocence and the ideals of the Arabs should enlist in my sordid service for me to destroy. We needed to win the war, and their inspiration had proved the best tool out here. The effort should have been its own reward: — might yet be, for the deceived — but we the masters had promised them results in our false contract, and that was bargaining with life, a bluff in which we had nothing wherewith to meet our stake. Inevitably we would reap bitterness a sorry fruit of heroic endeavor.

My ride was long and dangerous, no part of the machinery of the revolt, as barren of consequence as it was unworthy in motive. I met some of the more important of Feisal's secret friends, and saw the more important of our campaigning grounds: but it was artistically unjustifiable. At the time I was in reckless mood, not caring very much what I did, for in the journey up from Wejh I had convinced myself that I was the only person engaged in the field of the Arab adventure who could dispose it to be at once a handmaid to the British Army of Egypt, and also at the same time the author of its own success.

The abyss opened before me suddenly one night upon this ride, when in his tent old Nuri Shaalan bringing out his documents asked me bluntly which of the British promises were to be believed. I saw that with my answer I would gain or lose him: and in him the outcome of the Arab Movement: and by my advice that he should trust the latest in date of contradictory pledges, I passed definitely into the class of principal. In the Hejaz the Sherifs were everything and we were accessory: but in this distant north the repute of Mecca was low and that of England very great. Our importance grew: our words were weightier indeed, a year later I was almost the chief crook of our gang.

So already I knew that when we had taken Akaba I would have to lead the movement either directly or indirectly, and as I was little a man of action the prospect appeared hateful. So many men craved action, detested thinking: it was an irony I should fill one of their places unwillingly. I had never coveted a greater office than the one I held: never envied a greater man than the self I was: but always I would have given all my soul for something less, because of a certain sluggishness of sense which demanded immediacy of contact for the attainment of sharp perception: it was sensation for me when the turn meant food or hunger: but in the category of food dry bread and a feast seemed alike. Accordingly, on this march I took risks with the set hope of proving myself unworthy to be the Arab assurance of final victory. A bodily wound would have been a grateful vent for my internal perplexities a mouth through which my troubles might have found relief

When I returned it was June the sixteenth, and Nasir was still laboring in his tent. He and Auda had been seeing too much of one another for their good and lately there had been a breach; but this was easily healed and after a day the old man was as much with us as ever, and as kind and difficult. We stood up always when he entered, not for his sheik-hood, for we received Sitting sheikhs of much older rank: but because he was Auda, and Auda was such a splendid thing to be. The old man loved it, and however much we might wrangle, everyone knew that in reality we were his friends.

We were now five weeks out from Wejh: and had spent nearly all the money we had brought with us: we had eaten all the Howeitat sheep we had rested or replaced all our camels: and nothing hindered the start. The freshness of the adventure in hand consoled us for everything, and Auda gave a farewell feast, the greatest of the whole series, in his huge tent the eve before we started. Everyone was present, and five of us of the great tray were eaten up in relay, as fast as they were cooked and carried in, by the crowd.

It was a delightful red evening, and after the feast the whole party sat on rugs or lay in the sand lingering round the outside coffee hearth under the stars while Auda and the others told us stories. The guest space of the tent held two hundred, and there were perhaps six hundred present. In a pause I remarked casually that I had looked for Mohammed el Dheilan in his tent that afternoon, to thank him for a milk camel he had given me, but had not found him. Auda shouted for joy, till everybody looked at him and then, in the silence which fell that they might learn the joke, he pointed to Mohammed sitting dismally beside the coffee mortar, and said in his huge voice:

'Ho! Shall I tell why Mohammed for fifteen days has not slept in his tent?' and everybody chuckled with delight, and conversation stopped, as they stretched out on the ground, chin in hands, to hear the story which they had heard perhaps twenty times, prepared to take its good points. The women, Auda's three wives, and Zaal's wife, and some of Mohammed's, who had all been helping to cook, came across, straddling with their pot-bellies and the curious billowy walk which came of carrying burdens on their heads, till they were near the partition curtain and there they leaned and listened like the rest while Auda told at length how Mohammed had bought in the bazaar at Wejh a costly string of pearls, before all of us, and had not given it to any of his wives, and so they were at odds with one another, except in their common rejection of him.

The story was of course a pure invention of Auda's selfish humor, and the luckless Mohammed who had dragged through the fortnight staying casually with one or other of the tribesmen, called upon God for mercy, and upon me for witness that Auda lied. I cleared my throat solemnly, and Auda asked for silence, and begged me to confirm his words.

I began with the introducing phrase of a formal tale: 'In the name of God the merciful, the loving-kind. We were six in Wejh. There were Auda, and Mohammed, and Zaal, Gasim el Shimt, Mufaddhi and the poor man [myself]: and one night just before dawn Auda said, "Let us make a raid against the market": and we said, "In the name of God": and we went, Auda in a white robe and a red head doth and sandals of Kasim pieced leather work, Mohammed in *seven flings* of silk and barefoot, Zaal... I forget Zaal: Gasim wore cotton, and Mufaddhi was in silk of blue stripes and an embroidered head doth. Your servant was as your servant.'

There was a pause of astonishment. All this was a dose parody of Auda's epic style, and I mimicked also his wave of the hand, his round voice, and the rising and dropping tone which emphasized the points, or what he thought were points of the pointless stories.

The Howeitat listened as silent as death, twisting the it full bodies inside their sweat-stiffened shirts for joy, and staring hungrily at Auda, for they all recognized the original, and parody was a new art to them and to him. The coffee man, Mufaddhi, himself a character, forgot to pile fresh thorns on his fire, for fixity of listening to the tale.

I told how we left the tents, with a list of the tents, and how we walked down towards the village, describing every camel and horse we saw, and all the passers-by, and the ridges, 'all bare of grazing, for by God that country was barren .

'And we marched: and after we had marched the time of a smoked cigarette, we heard something, and Auda stopped and said, "Lads, I hear something." And Mohammed stopped and said. "Lads, I hear something." And Zaal, "By God, you are right." And we stopped to listen and there was nothing, and the poor man said, "By God, I hear nothing": and Zaal said, "By God. I hear nothing": and Mohammed said, "By God, I hear nothing": and Auda said, "By God, you are right."

And we marched and we marched and the land was barren, and we heard nothing. And on our right hand came a man and he was a Negro mounted on a donkey. The donkey was grey, with black ears, and one black foot, and on its shoulder was a brand like this [a scrabble in the air] and its tail moved and its legs: and Auda saw it, and said, "By God, a donkey": and Mohammed said, "By the very God a donkey and a Negro." And we marched. And there was a ridge, not a great ridge: but a ridge as great as from here to the what-do-you-call-it that is yonder: and we marched to the ridge and it was barren. That land is barren.

'And we marched: and beyond the what-do-you-call-it there was a what-is-it, as far as hereby from thence, and thereafter a ridge: and we came to that ridge, and went up that ridge: it was barren, all that land was barren: and as we came up that ridge: and were by the head of that ridge: and came to the end of the head of that ridge, by God, by my God, by very God, by my very God, the sun rose upon us!'

It ended the session. Everyone had heard that sunrise twenty times in its immense bathos, after an agony piled up of linked phrase upon linked phrase, repeated and repeated by Auda, as his favorite trick to carry over for hours the thrill of a raiding story in which nothing happened: and the trivial rest of it was exaggerated, the degree which made it like one of Auda's tales, and yet also the history of the walk to market at Wejh which many of us had taken. The whole tribe was in waves of laughter on the ground.

Auda laughed the loudest and longest, for he loved a jest upon himself, and the fatuousness of my epic had shown him his own sure mastery of descriptive action. He embraced Mohammed, and confessed that the invention of the necklace was a fraud to bring upon him family disasters which would all be merged in happiness and a joyous pardon when the truth was known. In gratitude Mohammed invited the camp to breakfast with him in his regained tent on the morrow an hour before we would start out for the swoop on Akaba.

That last meal was good, partly because it was the last, partly because Mohammed had killed a suckling camel-half for us and it had been boiled in sour milk by his wives who were famous cooks. Mohammed was a peasant in his rich standard of living, and a nomad in manner and force of character, and the combination made an admirable host. Afterwards we sat under Nuri's clay house, and saw the three women take the great tent down, and the serving men pack it on camels. It was greater than Auda's tent, eight-fold, of twenty-four poles, longer and broader and loftier than any in the tribe, and new, like all his household goods.

Nothing could be handier than an Arab tent. In shape an oblong of cloth, with ropes and pegs at the ends and in the sides by the pole-gussets, it was pitched always by a woman. She would spread it out flat upon the ground, strain out the cords, and hammer in the pegs. Then she would insert the light poles one by one under the cloth, and lever it up by them, till the whole was in place, and the tent pitched, single-handed, however strong the wind.

Then a side curtain was skewered to the edge of the roof-cloth, on the desired side and the partition curtain was skewered across the middle between the guest-space and the family space and the home was finished.

If it rained some of the side poles were drawn in at the foot so slanting the roof-cloth down that the rain drops might fall obliquely against it Then it remained reasonably watertight In summer it was much less hot than our canvas tents for the loose-woven fabric of hair and wool did not absorb the sun-heat because of its nature and of the air spaces and currents existing between the threads.

Chapter 52: Bair

We started about an hour before noon Nasir led us riding his Chazala, a camel built like an antique ship grand and huge towering a good foot above the next in size of all our animals; and yet perfectly proportioned and with a stride like that of an ostrich: a lyrical beast the noblest and best bred of the Howeitat camels a female of nine remembered dams Auda was beside him and I skirmished about their gravities on Naama, a racing camel and my last purchase. Behind me rode my Ageyl, with Obeyd my spare camel and Mohammed the clumsy peasant who was now companioned by Ahmed a new follower also a peasant but for six years living among the Howeitat by his thews and wits a knowing eager ruffian.

In a few minutes we came to a rise of sixty feet, which took us out of the Sirhan, on to the first terrace of the Ard el Suwan, a country of black flints over pale limestone, not very solid but hard enough in the little tracks which the weight of the passing feet of centuries of camels had worn down an inch or two into the surface. At half-past one, we entered Wadi Hasaida, flowing eastward towards the Sirhan and later came in sight of the Wakf the ridge of flint downs which went up towards Hazim, and deflected the water-channels from the Thlaithukhwat, northward into the Azrak depression.

Our aim was Bair, a historic group of Ghassanid wells and ruins thirty or forty miles out in the desert east of the Hejaz Railway and now a well-known Beni Sakhr watering place. It laid some six miles from us, and there we would camp a few days while our scouts brought us flour from Kerak or Tafileh, hill villages above the Dead Sea beyond the line. Our food from Wejh was nearly finished (except that Nasir still had some of the precious rice for great occasions) and we could not yet forecast the date of our arrival in Akaba. It was not possible to rush straight for it. We had written to the Howeitat clans between Maan and the coast, and must have their replies before we entered their hills.

In all we had enrolled at Nebk five hundred and sixty men, and had left one hundred of them behind us to safeguard the Howeitat tents in the Sirhan. With our own fifty the present party totaled more than five hundred strong, and the sight of these hardy confident northerners moving about us, gaily chasing gazelle over the face of the desert took from us momentarily all sorry apprehension of the issue of our enterprise. Nasir had left his tent with the Arabs so that our camp that evening in the open was easily pitched. We felt it was a rice night, and the chiefs of the Abu Tayi came to sup with us and afterwards with the dying fire pleasantly red between us in the cool of this upland north-country, we sat about on the carpets chatting of this thing and that, remote from our purpose.

Nasir presently rolled over on his back with my glasses and began to study the stars, counting aloud first one known group and then another, crying out with surprise when he discovered little ones not noticed by the unaided eye. Auda set us on to talk of telescopes, of the great ones, and of how man in three hundred years had so far advanced from his first essay that now he built glasses as long as a tent, through which he counted thousands of unknown stars. And the stars, what are they?' We slipped into talk of worlds beyond world sizes and distance beyond wit. 'What will now happen with this knowledge?' asked Mohammed. 'We will set to, and the combined efforts of many learned and some clever men will in the next centuries make glasses as more powerful than ours, as ours are than Galilee's; and yet more hundreds of astronomers will distinguish and reckon yet more thousands of now unseen stars. When we see them all, there will be no night in heaven:

'Why are the Westerners always wanting more?' said Auda provocatively. 'Behind our few stars we can see God who is not behind your million.' 'We want the world's end: 'But that is God's' complained Zaal, half angry. Mohammed would not have the subject turned. 'Are there men on all these greater worlds?' he asked. 'God knows'. And has each the Prophet and heaven and hell?' Auda broke in on him. 'Lads, we know our districts and our camels and our women. The excess and the glory are to God. If the end of wisdom is to add star to star our foolishness is pleasing': and then he spoke of money, and distracted their minds till they all buzzed at once. Afterwards he turned to me, and whispered that I must get a worthy gift from Feisal for him when he gave us Akaba.

We marched at dawn, and in an hour topped the Wagf and rode down its far side into Wadi Ausaji. The ridge was only a bank of chalk, flint-capped, a couple of hundred feet high. We were now in the hollow between the Snainirat on the south, and the three white heads of the Thlaithukhwat on the north. Soon we entered Wadi Bair, and marched up and across it for hours. There had been a flood there in the spring, and it was green and pleasant, to the eye and to our camels' palates, after the long hostility of the Sirhan.

About noon Auda told me he was going to ride ahead of us to Bair, and would I come? The old man was on a young and unbroken camel, hardly worthy his reputation, and he found her difficult to keep at an orderly speed. So we went off at a fast trot, and in two hours came upon it quite suddenly, below a knoll to which we had crossed over an elbow of the valley. Auda had hurried on to visit the tomb he had built over the grave of his son Annad, whom five of his Motalga cousins had killed near Bair, in revenge for Abtan, their champion, slain by Annad in single combat. Auda told me how Annad had ridden at them, one against five, and had died as he should: but it left only the little Mohammed between him and childlessness, and was the grief of his life. He had brought me with him to hear him greatly lament his dead.

However, as we rode down the short slope towards the graves we were astonished to see smoke going up from the ground about the wells. We changed direction sharply, and began warily to approach the ruins to find out what it was. It seemed there was no one there, but the thick dung-edge round the well brink was charred, and the well itself all shattered at the top. The ground was torn and blackened as if by an explosion, and when we looked down the shaft we saw its stoning stripped and split, and many blocks thrown down the bore half choking it and the water in the bottom. I sniffed the still air and thought the smell was dynamite.

Auda ran down to the next well, built in the bed of the valley below the graves, and that too was ragged about the head, and choked with fallen stones above the water. This: said he 'is Jazi work.' We walked across the valley to see the third, the Beni Sakhr well, and found it only a crater of white chalk. Zaai arrived, grave at the sight of the disaster. Together we explored the ruined khan, there were traces of a camp of perhaps a hundred horse the night before. There was a fourth well, lying to the north of the ruins in the open flat, and to it we went hopelessly, wondering what would become of us now Bair was all destroyed: but to our joy it was uninjured.

This was a Jazi well, and its immunity gave a strong color to Auda's theory: so we looked for the tracks of the destroyers and found that they had come from and returned towards the railway. They must have only a short start of us, and when the first of our party came up Auda sent them on with Zaal to give chase. However, it was fruitless.

We were disconcerted to find the Turks so ready, and began to fear that perhaps they had raided el Jefer also the Howeitat wells to the east of Maan where we had planned to make a last concentration before we attacked the Turkish posts. This would be a real embarrassment for us.

Meanwhile our situation was not dangerous, thanks to the fourth well, but uncomfortable, since its water facilities were insufficient for five hundred camels.

Accordingly it became imperative to try to open the least damaged of the other wells that in the ruins, about whose lip the turf was smoldering: and Auda and I went off with Nasir to look again at it.

An Ageyli brought us an empty wooden box of Nobel's gelignite, evidently the explosive that the Turks had used. From the scars in the ground it was clear that several small charges had been fired simultaneously, probably by electricity, around the head of the shaft, and perhaps others lower down, though if so these had been ineffective, since not enough stone had fallen in completely to block the water in the bottom. We were staring down it and when our eyes were adjusted to its dark suddenly we saw many little chambers cut in the shaft less than twenty feet below. These were still tamped, and some had wires hanging down.

Evidently there was a second series of explosions prepared and either inefficiently wired or with a very long time-fuse. Hurriedly we unrolled our bucket-ropes and twined them together into something thick enough to climb, and hung them clear down the middle of the well from a stout pole laid across the top; for the sides were tottering, so that had the rope scraped them, blocks of the stoning might have been dislodged. I then went down and looked and found to my pleasure that it was a case of bad work. The charges were small, not above three pounds each, and had been wired in series with field telephone cable: but something had gone wrong and the Turks had either scammed the job, or their scouts had seen us coming before they had had time to re-connect,

So soon we had two fit wells, and a clear profit of thirty pounds of enemy gelignite and we determined to stay a week in this fortunate Bair. A third object — to discover the condition of the Jefer wells was now added to our needs for food, and for news of the state of mind of the tribes between Maan and Akaba. We sent a man to Jefer; and we prepared a little caravan of pack-camels with Howeitat brands, and sent them across the line to Tafileh with three or four obscure Howeitat clansmen, people who would never be suspected of association with us. They would buy the flour we needed, and bring it back to us in five or six days' time.

As for the tribes about the Akaba road, we wanted their active help against the Turks, to carry out the provisional plan we had made at Wejh. This plan was based on the ground conditions and the probable dispositions of the enemy, and we hoped not to change it. Its essence was surprise. The Turks administered the Akaba road from Maan, their main base where they had posted a battalion and some details. These sent a weekly caravan of supplies to Akaba where the garrison was only about three hundred men: and in intermediate posts at points along the road they had about three hundred more.

Our idea was to advance suddenly from el jefer, across the railway, and to occupy the head of the great pass, Nagb el Shtar, down which the road dipped from the Maan plateau to the red Guweira plain. To hold this pass we would have to capture Aba el Lissan, the large spring at its head, about sixteen miles from Maan; but the Gunnison was small, and we hoped to overrun them with a rush. We would then be astride the road, which at the end of the week would fall from hunger: though probably before that the hill tribes, hearing of our success at Aba el Lissan, would have joined us and wiped out their local posts.

The only risk in the plan after the capture of the first garrison was that the force in Maan might sally out and fight us while we sat near them at the head of the Shtar descent. If as at present they were only a battalion they would hardly dare it and before reinforcements could arrive on our alarm from Palestine or Damascus. Akaba would have surrendered to us, and we would have the advantageous position of the gorge of Wadi Itm between us and the enemy: and that would take them weeks to carry against a spirited and mobile defense. So our insurance for the success of our plan was to keep Maan careless and weak: and for that it would be best that they should not suspect our presence in their neighborhood.

It was never easy for us to keep our movements secret as we lived by preaching to the local people, and the unconvinced would tell the Turks. Our long march into Wadi Sirhan was known to the enemy and the most civilian owl could see that the only object of such a proceeding was to take Akaba. The demolition of Bair (and Jefer too, for we had it confirmed that the seven wells of Jefer were destroyed) showed that the Turks were on the alert to that extent.

However there was no measuring the stupidity of the Turkish Army which fact helped us now and again, and harmed us constantly, since we could not avoid despising them (Arabs were a race gifted with uncommon quickness of mind and over-valuing it) and an army suffered when unable to yield honor to its enemy. For the moment, it might be helpful, and so we had undertaken a prolonged campaign of deception intended to make them believe that our objective lay nearer to Damascus.

They were susceptible to pressure in that neighborhood, for the railway between Damascus and Deraa and Amman was the communication not merely of their Hejaz army, but of Palestine also: and if we attacked there we would do double damage. So in my long trip round Baalbek and Damascus and the Hauran I had dropped hints of our near arrival in Jebel Druse: and had been glad to let Nesib go up there, noisily but with small resources. Nuri Shaalan had warned the Turks in the same sense: and Newcombe down near Wejh contrived to lose official papers on the railway, among them a plan for marching from Wejh by Jefer and the Sirhan to Tadmor to attack Damascus and Aleppo. The Turks took the documents very seriously, and chained up an unfortunate garrison in Tadmor till the end of the war, much to our advantage.

Chapter 53: A Raiding Party

It seemed wise to make some further concrete effort in the same direction, during the week that we must spend in Bair, and Auda decided that Zaal was the best man to ride with me in command of a party to attack the line as near as we could get to Deraa. The Turks would then believe that from Nebk we had moved to Azrak, on our way to the Hauran. Zaal, a noted raider, chose one hundred and ten men, individually, from those present in our force, and we went off early on June the twenty-first.

We rode hard, in six-hour spells day and night, with one or two hours' interval between the spells. For me it was an interesting and eventful trip, for the reasons which made it dull to the Arabs namely that we were an ordinary tribal raiding party, riding on their conventional lines, in the formation and after the pattern which their generations of practice had shown them were most efficient. In the afternoon of Saturday we reached the railway just above Kalaat el Zcrga, the Circassian village north of Amman. The hot sun and day and night fast riding had tried our camels, and Zaal had decided to water them at a ruined village of the Roman period, whose cemented underground water cisterns had been filled by the late rains.

It lay within a mile of the railway, and we had to be circumspect, for the Circassians hated the Arabs, and would have been hostile had they seen us, and also there was a military post of two tents on a tall bridge just down the valley to our right. While the men looked after the camels Zaal and I climbed to the top of a mound south-west of the ruins, and watched the life along the railway and in Zerga village behind it.

After the watering we rode north for another six miles, and in the early dark turned in towards the line to examine Dhuleil bridge which Zaal reported as a big one, good to destroy the men and camels stayed on the high ground east of the railway to cover our escape if anything untoward happened, while Zaal and I went down to the bridge to look it over. There were Turks just beyond it, quite a large camp with many tents and cooking fires, about two hundred yards away and we were puzzled to explain their strength, till we reached the bridge and found it being rebuilt. The spring flood had washed away four of its arches and the line was temporarily laid on a deviation. One of the new arches was finished, one had the vault just turned, and the centering was being placed for a third.

It was of course no use bothering to destroy a bridge in such a state, so we drew off quietly (not to alarm the workmen), walking over the loose stones which turned under our bare feet in a way imposing care, if we would avoid the risk of sprain. Once I put my foot on something moving, soft and cold, and stepped heavily, on the chance it was a snake: but no harm followed. The brilliant stars cast about us a false light, no real illumination, but rather a transparency of air lengthening slightly the shadow below each stone, and making a faint grayness of the ground, which hardly showed us where depressions lay.

We consulted together, and decided to go a few miles further north, towards Minifir, where Zaal thought the land would be propitious for mining a train. This would be better than a bridge for we had only the gelignite of Bair, and our real need was just for a demonstration to make the Turks think that we were based on Azrak, fifty miles away to the east. We rode a little, and came out on a flat plain, crossed by a very occasional shallow bed of fine shingle. Over this we were going easily when we heard a long rumble, and then came a dancing plume of flame, bent low by the wind of its speed. It seemed to light us, extending its fire-tagged curtain of smoke over our heads, so near were we to the railway, and we shrank back a little, while the train rushed on. Two minutes' warning of it, and I would have blown its locomotive into scrap.

Afterwards our march was quiet till dawn, when we found ourselves riding up a narrow valley in the low hills. At its head was a sharp turn to the left, into an amphitheater of the rock where the hill went up by step after step of broken cliff to a crest on which stood a massive cairn. Zaal said that the railway was visible from that, and if true the place was an ideal ambush, for the camels could be herded without guardians into the pit where the pasture was excellent.

We dismounted, and I climbed at once up to the cairn with Zaal. We found it to be the ruin of an Arab watch tower of the Christian period, and it commanded a most gracious view of rich pastoral hills beyond the line, which here ran round the foot of the hill in a lazy curve, open to our sight for perhaps five miles. Below on our left was the square box of the coffee house, a railway halt, about which a few little soldiers were slouching peacefully. We lay where we were, alternately watching and sleeping, for many hours, during which a train came along from the south, and ground slowly past up the stiff gradient. We made plans to mine the line that night.

However, in the mid-morning we saw a dark mass moving towards us from the north, down the valley of the railway. As they approached we made out that they were mounted men, about one hundred and fifty, and they were riding directly for our hill. It looked as though we had been seen and reported, which was quite possible since all this area was grazed over by the sheep of the Belga tribes, and their shepherds, when they saw our steeliness, would have taken us for robber-enemies.

Our position was an admirable one from which to attack the railway: but a death-trap in which to be caught by superior mobile forces: so we sent down the alarm at once, and as soon as the camels were ready, mounted, and slipped across the valley of our entry, and over its eastern ridge into a small plain. Here we could canter our animals, and we made speed to the low mounds marking its further side, and got behind them before the enemy was in a position to see us.

There the terrain better suited our tactics and we waited for them: but they were at least imperfectly informed, for they contented themselves with riding past our old hiding place, and along each side of our entrance valley. Then they went away quickly towards the south, leaving us puzzled. There were no Arabs among them: all were regulars in uniform — so we had not to fear being tracked: but it certainly looked as though the Government had taken alarm. This was according to my wish, and I was glad, but Zaal, who has the military responsibility felt diffident. He held a council with those others who knew the country and eventually we remounted and jogged off to another hill rather north of our old one, but satisfactory.

This was Minifir proper a round-headed grass-grown hill, made up of two shoulders with a high neck joining them. We rode up from the east between the spurs which were the prolongations of the shoulders, by a broad track perfectly covered from north and south and west affording a safe retreat back into the mass of small downs which there filled the desert. At the top the neck was cupped and the collected rain had made the soil rich so that the grazing was sumptuous but the camels required constant care since if they wandered two hundred paces in that direction they became visible from the railway, which ran about four hundred yards from us low down on the western face of the hill.

Our control of the railway was good. On each side the shoulders pushed forward in spurs smaller than those on the eastern face and the line passed through them in shallow cuttings. The material from the cuttings had been thrown across the hollow in a bank, pierced at the center by a lofty culvert which let the little zigzag gully running down from the neck pass through it into a larger transverse valley-bed beyond.

To the northward the line curved away in a three-hundred meter curve, hard uphill to a deep white cutting which led through to the great plain of If dein reaching right up to Deraa. We could see the line running across this for seven or eight miles to Mafrak station to the east of which the wide level of the southern Hauran spread out, like a grey sky flecked with small dark clouds, which were the dead basalt towns of Byzantine Syria. Southward we could see only a mile or two but there was a cairn on that shoulder from which we could look for six miles or more, nearly to Sumra station by Dhuleil Bridge.

The high land facing us to the west was the Belga, all spotted with the black tent-villages of the peasants in their summer quarters. They could see us too in our hill-cup so we sent word over that we were Howeitat and Sherarat friends, intending harm only to the Turks. Our messengers came back with a bag of flour and we had a day's bread a luxury since the lowness of our food-supply in Bair had reduced us to parched com, and, for lack of cooking opportunity on the forced march, the men had been chewing it raw.

This was a trial too steep for me and mostly I had ridden fasting. We took a risk, telling them of us but betrayal was an unlikely act of an Arab in the circumstances. When trusted with important information they usually respected the confidence: whereas if they discovered a thing hidden they seemed to feel bound to profit by their knowledge. On this occasion they kept silent about us till we had gone and then were fervid and eloquent in helping the Turks to prove that we fled away eastward, by the road that led to Azrak.

Chapter 54: A Blank

We buried that night a great Garland mine automatic-compound, to explode three charges in parallel by instantaneous fuse, on top of the culvert, and then lay down to sleep, sure that we would hear if a train came along in the dark and fired it. However, nothing happened and at dawn I went down to the line again, and removed the detonators which (additional to the trigger action) had been laid out on the face of the metals. Afterwards we sat there all day fed and comfortable, cooled by a powerful wind which hissed like surf as it ruffed up the stiff-grassed hill.

For hours nothing came along: but at last there was a flutter among the Arabs, and Zaal with the Hubsi and some of the more active men dashed down towards the line. We heard two shots under us in the dead ground, and after half an hour the party reappeared, leading two ragged Turkish soldiers deserters from the mounted column of the day before who told us their headquarters were Deraa, and that the battalion of five hundred in two detachments, had just been ordered to Amman. They, tired of ill-treatment, had deserted by Samra in the dark, and were on their way back to Anatolia on foot.

One was badly wounded, shot by a Rualla lad while attempting to escape up the line, and in the aileron he died, most miserable about himself and his fate. Exceptionally, for when death became certain most men felt the quietness of the grave waiting for them, and went to it not unwillingly. The other man was hurt also, a clean gunshot in the foot, but he was very feeble and collapsed when the wound grew cold and painful. His thin body was so covered with old bruises, tokens of army service, that he could lie only on his face. We offered him the last of our bread and gave him a drink, and did what else we could for him: but it was little.

In the middle of the afternoon came a fresh thrill from the south when we saw the mule-mounted infantry reappear heading up the line towards us. They would pass in the valley of the railway below our ambush, and Zaal and the men were urgent with me to attack them on the sudden. We were one hundred, they little over two hundred. We had the upper ground, could hope to empty some of their saddles by one first unexpected volley, and then it would be a camel charge upon them Camels especially down a gentle slope would overtake mules in a few strides, and their moving bulk would send spinning the lighter animals and their riders. Zaal gave me his word that no regular cavalry let alone mere mounted infantry could cope with tribal camels in a running fight. We would take not only the men, but their precious animals.

I asked him how many casualties we might incur ourselves, and he guessed five or six and then I decided to do nothing; to let them pass unheeding. We had one objective only the capture of Akaba, and had come up here solely to make it easier by persuading the Turks that we were at Azrak. To lose five or six men in a demonstration however profitable financially would be fatuous or worse since we might want one last rifle to take Akaba, and Akab was vital to us. After it we might waste men but not before.

I told Zaal, who was not content: while the furious Howeitat threatened to run off downhill at the Turks willy-nilly. They wanted a booty of mules: and I particularly did not. for it would have diverted us. Commonly tribes went to war to gain honor and wealth; the three noble spoils were arms riding animals, and clothes, and if we took these two hundred mules the proud men would have thrown up Akaba and gone home by Azrak to the tents to triumph before their women. Also we could not take prisoners to Bair, since Nasir would not be grateful for two hundred useless mouths. Arab rules of war forbade killing men in cold blood: we would have had to let them go again and something of our real numbers and intention would have been revealed to the enemy. So we sat and gnashed our teeth at them, and let them pass. This was a severe ordeal from which we only just emerged with honor Zaal did it Auda had charged him, and he was on his best behavior, expecting tangible gratitude from me later: and glad meanwhile to show me his authority over the Bedouin. They respected him as Auda's deputy with me, and as a famous fighter: and in one or two little mutinies he had shown a self-conscious mastery. Now he was tested to the utmost. The Hubsi, Auda's cousin, a fine spirited youth of perhaps seventeen, while the Turks were defiling innocently not three hundred yards from our itching rifle muzzles, sprang suddenly to his feet and ran forward shouting to attract their attention and compel a battle: but Zaal caught him in ten strides, threw him down like a child, and hit him savagely time and again till we stopped him for fear lest the lad's now very different cries might fulfill his former purpose.

It was sad to see a sound and pleasant little victory pass voluntarily out of our hands, and we were gloomy till the evening came down, and confirmed our sense that once more there was no hope of a train. This was the final occasion, for thirst was hanging over us, and on the morrow the camels must be watered. So after nightfall we returned to the line, and laid some thirty charges of gelignite against the most curved rails, and fired them leisurely. The curved rails were best, for the Turks would have to bring down new ones from Damascus. Actually this took them three days and then their construction train stepped on our Garland mine (which we had carefully left as hook beyond the demolition's bait) and hurt its locomotive, and they held up traffic for three other days while the line was picked over for fresh traps.

For the moment of course we could anticipate none of these good things. We did the destruction, returned sorrowfully to our camels, and were off for the south soon after midnight. The man we had taken prisoner was left behind on his hilltop, for he could neither walk nor ride, and we had no carriage for him. We feared he would starve to death where he lay and indeed already he was very ill: so on a telegraph pole felled across the rails by the damaged stretch we put a letter in French and German to give news of where he was, and that we had captured him wounded after a hard fight.

We hoped this might have saved him the tortures which the Turks inflicted on red-hand deserters, or from being shot if they thought he had been in collusion with us: but when we came back to Minifir six months later to mine a second train, the picked and scattered bones of the two bodies were lying out on our old camping ground. One felt sorry always for the men of the Turkish Army, The officers, volunteer and professional, had caused the war by their ambition: — almost by their existence — and we wished they could receive not merely their numerical deserts, but all that their conscript men suffered through their fault.

Chapter 55: Blood

In the night we lost our way among the stony ridges and valleys of Dhuleil, but kept moving until dawn, so that half an hour after sunrise, while the shadows were yet long across the green hollows, we had reached Khau, the old ruin, our former watering place, where it broke from its hilltop against Zerga like a scab. We were working hard at the two cisterns, watering our camels for the return march to Bair, when a young Circassian came in sight, driving three cows towards the ruins whose rich green stuff afforded good pasture.

This would not do, so Zaal sent off his too-energetic offenders of the day previous to show their proper mettle in stalking him: and they brought him back, unharmed but very frightened, a few minutes later, Circassians were swaggering fellows, inordinate bullies in a clear road: but if firmly met they cracked, and so this young fellow was in an unpleasant extremity of terror, offending all our senses of respect. We drenched him with water till he recovered, and then set him to fight at daggers with a young Sherari who had been caught stealing on the march: but after no more than a scratch on each side the prisoner gave in and threw himself down weeping.

Now he was a nuisance, for if we left him be would give the alarm, and send the horsemen of the village out against us. If we tied him up in this remote place he would die of hunger or thirst, and besides we had no rope which we could spare. It seemed we might have to kill him, but this seemed wasteful, unworthy of a hundred men. At last the Sherari boy said that if we gave him leave he would settle his account and leave him living. When we agreed he looped his wrist up to his saddle and trotted him off with us for the first hour, till he was dragging breathlessly. We were then still near the railway, but four or five miles from Zerga.

There he was stripped of his presentable clothes, which fell to his owner, by point of honor. The Sherari threw him on his face and picking up his feet drew his dagger and like a flash chopped him with it deeply across the soles. The Circassian howled with pain and terror, thinking he was being killed. It was an odd performance, but effective and more merciful than death for while the cuts would do no permanent harm they would make him travel to the railway on hands and knees, a work of perhaps an hour, and his nakedness would keep him in the shadow of the great rock by which we laid him, till the sun was low. His gratitude was not very coherent but we could not delay to teach him manners: so we gave him water, and rode on.

Afterwards we marched steadily till sunset across undulating country in whose bottoms the grazing was very rich. Through it the camels with their heads down snatching plants and grass, moved with a strange gait, trying for us who were always looking down the chute of their long sloped necks: but we were marching eighty miles a day, and halted only in the gloaming, when we let the camels breathe a little. Today I fell asleep, but after two hours we rode again across Wadi Hamman in front of Dhaba station. Zaal gave us another short rest about midnight, and soon after daylight we turned to the west towards Atwi station.

We meant to do something inexpensive here, to make the Turks believe that more than one band was out from Azrak: so we dismounted some way off the railway which ran between broken reefs of limestone, and crept carefully forward till we saw the station beneath us. It was composed of two stone houses (the first only one hundred yards away) in line from us and therefore obstructing one another. Men were walking about obviously without disquietude. Their day was beginning, and from the guardroom thin blue smoke curled up into the air, while a soldier drove out a flock of young sheep to crop the rich meadow between the station and the valley which gave the place its name.

The sight of this flock sealed the business, for after the horse-diet of dry com, meat appealed with a craving. The Arabs' teeth gritted as they counted ten, fifteen, twenty, twenty-five, twenty-seven in all. Zaal, with a hard light in his eye, led them quickly down to the valley just south of the station where the line crossed it by a bridge. They dropped into the bed, and in single file behind Zaal crept along beneath its five-foot bank till they faced the station eighty yards away across the meadow.

We watched them from our cairn, covering the guard room and station yard with our rifles, to aid in the retreat if an alarm was sounded. However, all remained silent and we saw Zaal stop, and lean his rifle on the near bank, shielding his head with infinite precaution behind some grasses growing near the brink. He took slow aim at the party of officers and officials sitting on their chairs shaded from the morning sun outside the ticket office. Then he pressed the trigger, and there came almost together the report and the crash of the bullet striking the stone wall behind the group, while the fattest man bent slowly forward in his chair and sank upon the ground under the frozen stares of his companions.

An instant later Zaal's men poured in their volleys, broke out of the valley, and rushed over the field in a few strides: but before they came the door of the northernmost house clanged to, and rifles began to speak from behind its steel window shutters. We replied at first, but soon saw our impotence, and in a few minutes everyone ceased fire. The Sherari came past our mound driving off the guilty sheep eastward into the hills where the camels were; and the other men ran down into the station to join Zaal who was busy about the door of the nearer and undefended building.

In the very height of their plundering there was a pause and a panic : for the Arabs were such accustomed scouts that almost they felt danger before it came to them, their senses taking the precautions before their minds were persuaded. Swinging down the line towards us from the south was a trolley, with four men on it, to whose ears the grinding of the wheels had deadened our shots. The Rualla ran down the line in a compact party, crept under a culvert, and waited, while the rest of us crowded silently by the bridge. The trolley came on unsuspectingly, and rolled over the heads of the Rualla ambush. They came out and lined the bank behind, while we filed solemnly out across the green in front The Turks slowed in horror and then jumped off to each side and ran into the rough: but our rifles cracked once more and they were dead.

The trolley rolled to our feet with coils of copper wire and tools to mend the telegraph, and we took their materials to put concealed earths in the long distance wire at three or four places.

Others fired the railway station whose woodwork caught freely after petrol had been splashed on it. The planks and doth hangings were soon twisting and jerking convulsively as the flames licked them up. Meanwhile the Ageyl were measuring out the gelatin, and as soon as the wiring was finished we lit the charges and destroyed a culvert, many rails, and some furlongs of telegraph.

At the roar of the first explosion our hundred knee-haltered camels rose smartly to their feet and at each following burst hopped more madly on three legs till they had shaken off the hitch about the fourth and drove out every way like a scattered flock of starlings into the void. Chasing them and chasing the sheep took us three hours, for which fortunately the Turks gave us law, or some of us would have had to walk home. Then we put a few miles between us and the railway before we sat down and had our free feast of mutton. We were short of knives: and having killed the sheep in relay had recourse to flints to cut them up. It interested me to see that, as men unaccustomed to such expedients we used them in the Eolithic spirit: and it came to me that if steel had been constantly rare we would have chipped our tools skillfully as paleontologists: while, had we had no metal whatever, all our art would have been lavished on perfect and polished stones. The one hundred and ten men of our raiding force ate the best parts of twenty-four sheep at the sitting while the camels browsed about, or ate what we left over, for the best riding camels were taught to like cooked meat. When it was all over we mounted and rode through the night towards Bair, which we entered without casualty, successful, well-fed, and enriched, at dawn.

Chapter 56: Away to Take Akaba

Nasir had done great work during the interval. A week's flour for all of us had just come from Tafileh, in exchange for the gold we sent, and so our freedom of movement was restored. We might well take Akaba before we starved again. He had received good letters from the Dhumaniyeh, the Darausha, and the Dhiabat, which three Howeitat clans lived on or about Nagb el Shtar, the difficult pass we wished to occupy first, of the entire Maan-Akaba road. They were willing to help us, and if they struck soon and strongly there seemed reason to hope that the great factor of surprise would mean success to their effort.

As my party rode in from the north there came from the east a messenger post-haste from Nuri Shaalan at Hazim near Azrak. He brought greetings, and Nuri's news that the Turks, being sure we were in Wadi Sirhan on our way to Jebel Druse, had called upon Nuri for his son Nawaf as guide-hostage to take four hundred of their cavalry from Deraa down the Sirhan in search of us. Nuri had sent his nephew Trad, a leader of importance, but better spared than Nawaf if an accident should happen. Trad was at this moment guiding them along the valley by devious routes in which the men and horses were suffering terribly from thirst.

They were now near Nebk, our old camping ground. Nuri was not letting their news get back to Deraa, so that the Turkish Government should believe us still in the wadi till their cavalry returned, and he promised that the return should be by the same way, to give us the clear run of Bair. Accordingly we might reassure ourselves about the enemy. About Maan especially they were not in the least anxious, since they believed that the desert roads to it were doubly blocked. The engineers who had blown up Bair reported every source of water utterly destroyed: so we could not be there, while the wells of Jefer had been dealt with a few days earlier.

It might be that Jefer really was denied to us: but though convenient, its water was not absolutely necessary, for we were now in such training that we could endure thirst for a time without losing activity. Also we were not without hope that at Jefer too we would find the technical work of demolition ill done by these pitiful Turks. Dhaif-Allah Abu Tiyur, after Hamd el Afar a leading man of the Jazi Howeitat, one who had come down to Feisal at Wejh and sworn allegiance, had sent from Maan a secret message to Mohammed el Dheilan here in Bair.

He had been present in Jefer when the King's well was fired by dynamite placed about its lip and had seen and heard the upper stones clap themselves together, and key over the mouth of the well. He told us this, and his conviction that the rest of the masonry was intact, and that we would be able to reopen it again in a few hours' work. We hoped so, and rode away from Bair all in order, on the twenty-eighth of June in the morning, for Jefer to find out.

We marched all day, and slept in Rijit el Herar, further out on the weird plain of Jefer; next day by noon we were at the ruins of the wells. They seemed, after all, most thoroughly destroyed, and the fear grew that we might find in them the first check to our elaborate scheme of operations, and the scheme was so much too elaborate that the effect of a check might be far-reaching.

However, we went to the well, Auda's family property, of which Dhaif-Allah Abu Tiyur had told us secret things, and began to sound about it. The ground rang hollow under the tent mallet, and much encouraged we called for volunteers able to dig and build. Some of the Ageyl came forward, led by Abdulla the Mirzugi, a capable camel boy of Nasir's, from the Bugum tribe. They started with the few tools we had. The rest of us formed a ring and watched them work, singing to them, and promising them gold when they found the water.

It was a hot task in the full glare of the summer sun in that blinding place, for the Jefer plain was of pure hard mud — flat as the hand, white with salt, and twenty miles across: but time pressed us, since if we failed we must ride fifty miles in the night to the next well. So we pushed the work by relays at full speed through the midday heat. It made easy digging, for the explosion that had shifted the stones had cracked and loosened the soil about them. As they dug and threw out the earth on all sides, the core of the well rose like a tower of rough stones in the center of their pit, proving that the damage was indeed superficial.

Very carefully we began to take away the ruined head of the pile. Some of it was difficult work, since the stones had become interlocked in their fall: but this was all the better sign, and our spirits rose. Before sunset they shouted that there was no more packing soil, that the interstices between the blocks were clear, and that they heard the mud-fragments which slipped through splashing many feet below.

Half an hour later came a rush and rumble of stones in the mouth, followed by a heavy splash and yells. We rushed down to see and by the Mirzugi's torch saw the well yawning open, no longer a tube, but a deep bottle-shouldered pit, twenty feet across at the bottom, which was black with water, and white with spray in the middle where the Ageyli who had been clearing away the blocked stones when the key slipped was striking out lustily in the effort not to drown. Everybody laughed down the well at him, till at last Abdulla lowered him a noose of rope, and we drew him up, very wet and angry but in no way damaged by his fall.

We rewarded and feasted the diggers on a weak camel that had been near death in the march today, and watered our animals all night, while a second squad of Ageyl with a long chorus steeped up to the mouth again in an eight-foot throat of mud and stones. At dawn the earth was stamped in round it, and the well stood complete to the surface of the desert, as fit in appearance as it had ever been. Only the water was not very much. We worked it the twenty-four hours without rest, and ran it to a cream: and there were still some of our camels not satisfied. They went to other wells, away south of us across the flat.

Here from Jefer we took action. Riders went forward into the Dhumaniyeh tents at Batra to lead their promised attack against the Turkish garrison of Fuweilah, the fort that covered the head of the pass, and the spring of Aba el Lissan, and the crest of the Maan road where it dropped in steep waves into the Guweira plain. Our attack was planned to take place two days before the weekly food caravan started out from Maan to replenish the stocks of its client garrisons.

The Akaba road struck out south-west from Maan, and ascended gradually through ridges of bare flint to Waheida, the first large spring and blockhouse, about seven miles from Maan. After Waheida it went on through down country, ever more clothed with wormwood, to Mreigha, the second blockhouse and spring, about five miles further. Thence another three miles of easy track up a valley led to Aba el Lissan, a great spring only two miles from the edge of the plateau.

So far as this crest the road was, in fine weather a tolerable motor road, and the surrounding country open, advantageous to the more regular army. Accordingly we wanted to get possession first of the head of the pass and to clear the Turks back from it towards Maan, and forward into Akaba; as this manner of proceeding would make the reduction of the more distant places easier by impressing on their garrisons the hopeless manner in which they were cut off from their friends.

We sat in Jefer meanwhile waiting for the evening of the first, when we should hear of the fortune of the attack. On its success or failure would depend the direction of our next march. The halt was not unpleasant, in the knowledge that for once others were going to do the fighting. In addition our place had its comic side. We were within sight from Maan, for those few minutes of the day in which the mirage did not make eyes and glasses useless and yet we were strolling about admiring our new well-lip in complete security, because the Turkish garrison believed life impossible either here or at Bair, and ourselves that day engaged with their cavalry at Kaf.

I lay under some bushes near the well for hours against the heat, very lazy, pretending to be asleep, with the wide silk sleeve of my pillow arm drawn over my face as veil against the flies. Auda sat up and talked like a river telling his best stories in great form. At last I reproved him with a smile for talking too much and doing too little. He smacked his lips with pleasure of the work to come.

At dawn on July the first a tired horseman rode into our camp, with the news that the Dhumaniyeh had fired on the Fuweilah post the afternoon before, as soon as our men had reached them. The surprise had not been quite complete and the Turks had manned their stone breastworks and driven them off The Arabs had fallen back into cover, and the enemy believing they had only an ordinary tribal affray to cope with had made a sortie on their horses and swept down the valley towards the Dhumaniyeh encampment beyond the ridge.

The Turkish commanding officer was Dhurrnush, the half-bred Arab from Kunfida, who had sworn fealty to Feisal a year before in Damascus, but who had not realized that this was a first move of the cause to which he was pledged, At the head of his men he burst into the Arab tents to find them deserted except for an old man, six women and seven children. In anger at finding nothing hostile or able-bodied, the troopers smashed up the camp and its contents, and cut the throats of its helpless ones.

Dhurrnush was thrown in the *scuffle* trying to restrain his men and maddened by the scene he had witnessed, pulled his horse round and with only two or three men galloped off towards Maan. The Dhumaniyeh on the hilltops heard and saw nothing till it was too late: but then in their fury they dashed down across the return road of the murderers and cut them off to the last man. To complete their vengeance they later assaulted the now weakly garrisoned fort, carried it in the first rush, and took no prisoners.

We were ready saddled and within ten minutes had loaded up and marched, bearing west-south-west, for Ghadir el Haj, the first railway station south of Maan, on our direct road for Aba el Lissan Simultaneously we detached a small party of Abu Tayi northwestward, to cross the railway just above Maan and create a diversion against the Turkish guards on that side, about Aneyza. Especially they were to try to capture the great herds of sick camels that the Turks pastured in the Shobek plains till once more fit for service.

We calculated that the news of their Fuweilah disaster would not have reached Maan till this morning, and that they could not drive in their camels (even supposing our northern party missed them) and fit out a relief expedition before nightfall: and if by then they heard us attacking the line at Ghadir el Haj they would probably divert this relief force in the first instance thither, and so give us complete leisure to move on Akaba unmolested.

With this hope we rode steadily through the flowing mirage till the afternoon. Then we descended on the line with little opposition, and having delivered a long stretch of it from guards and patrols began to use all our remaining explosive on the rails and many bridges of the captured section. The little garrison of Ghadir el Haj sallied out with the valor of ignorance from their trenches against us: but the heat haze blinded them, and we drove them off with loss.

They were on the telegraph, and would notify Maan, who besides could not fail to hear the repeated bursts of our explosions. It was our aim to bring the enemy down upon us in the night: or rather down here where they would find nobody, but many broken bridges: for we worked fast and did great damage. For the first time we used as mine-chambers the drainage holes in the spandrels. They held from three to five pounds of gelatin each were fired by short fuses, and brought down the arch, shattered the pier, and stripped the side walls, in no more than six minutes' work. So quickly and cheaply we ruined ten bridges and many rails, and finished our explosive. Afterwards at dusk, when our departure could not be seen, we called the force together and rode five miles westward of the line till we were in a covered place. There we made fire and baked bread.

However, our meal was not yet cooked when Darausha horsemen rode up and said that before sunset a long column of fresh troops, infantry with guns, had appeared at Aba el Lissan from Maan. The Dhumaniyeh, disorganized with victory, had had to abandon their ground without fighting. They were now at Batra waiting for us.

We learned afterwards that this unwelcome and unwanted vigor of the Turks was an accident. A relief battalion of new troops from Zunguldak by way of the Caucasus had arrived at Maan by train on that very day from Damascus. The news of an Arab demonstration against Fuweilah arrived simultaneously and the battalion, which was formed up ready in the railway station with its transport, was hurriedly strengthened by a section of pack artillery and some mounted men and moved straight out as a punitive column to rescue the garrison of the supposedly besieged post.

So they had left Maan in the mid-morning and marched gently through Waheida and Mreigha along the motor road, the men on foot, sweating in the heat of this south-country after their long sojourn in the northern snows, and drinking thirstily of all its springs. From Aba el Lissan they climbed uphill towards the old post, which was deserted except for the silent vultures, flying above the stone walls in slow uneasy rings. The battalion commander feared the sight might be too much for his young troops, and led them back to the spring of Aba el Lissan, in its steep narrow valley, where they camped all night in peace about the water.

Chapter 57: A Fight

The news shook us into quick life. We threw our baggage across our camels on the instant and rode off with the Darausha over the rolling downs of this end of the table land of Syria. Our hot bread was in our hands and we ate it as we went, and there mingled with it the taste of the dust of our large force as it crossed the valley bottoms, and something of the strange keen smell of the wormwood that overgrew the slopes.

In the still air of these hot evenings in the hills, after the long breathless days of summer, everything struck very sudden on the senses: and when marching in a great column, as we were, the front camels pacing cautiously in the dark kicked about the aromatic dust-laden branches of the shrubs, raising their scent particles into the air where they hung in a long mist, scenting the road of those behind.

On the slopes it was the sharpness of wormwood, and in the hollows the oppressive richness of their stronger and more luxuriant growths. Our night-passage might have been through a planted garden, and the rich part of the unseen beauty of successive banks of flowers. Even the noises were very clear, and to be heard from far. After a while Auda broke out singing, away in front, and the men joined in from time to time, with something of the thrill of greatness, the catch at heart, of an army moving into battle.

We rode all night and when dawn came were dismounting on the crest of the hills between Batra and Aba el Lissan, with a wonderful view westwards over the green and gold Guweira plain, and beyond it to the ruddy mountains hiding Akaba and the sea. Gasim Abu Dumeik, the head of the Dhumaniyeh, was waiting anxiously for us, surrounded by his hard-bitten tribesmen, their grey strained faces flecked with the blood of their fighting yesterday. There was a great greeting for Auda and Nasir; we made hurried plans, and scattered to the day's work: since we could not go forward to Akaba with this battalion in undisputed possession of the head of the pass. Unless we dislodged it our two months' hazard and effort would fail before we had seen even first-fruits.

Fortunately the poor handling of the enemy gave us an unearned advantage. They slept on, down in the valley, while we split into sections and crowned the hills in a wide circle about them unobserved. Then we began to snipe them steadily in their positions under the slopes and rock-faces by the water hoping to provoke them out and up the hill in a charge against us. Meanwhile Zaal rode off with our horsemen, and cut the Maan telegraph and telephone in the plain behind Mreigha

This went on all day. It was terribly hot hotter than ever before I had felt it in Arabia, and the anxiety and constant moving made it hard for us. Some even of the tough tribesmen broke down under the cruelty of the sun and crawled or had to be thrown under rocks to recover in their shade. We had to run up and down, supplying our lack of numbers by mobility, ever looking over the long ranges of hill for a new spot from which to counter this or that Turkish effort. The hillsides were steep and exhausted our breath, and the plants and grasses twined like little hands about our ankles as we ran and plucked us back. The sharp ground tore our feet, and before evening the more energetic men were leaving rusty prints upon the ground with their every stride.

Our rifles grew so hot with the sun and shooting that they seared our hands and we had to be grudging of our rounds considering every shot, and setting great pains to make it sure. The rocks on which we flung ourselves to get our aim were burning with the sun, so that they scorched our breasts and arms, from which later the skin peeled off in ragged sheets. For the time they were painful and made us thirst. Yet even water was short with us as we could not spare men to fetch enough from Batra, and they said if all could not drink it was better that none should.

We consoled ourselves knowing that the enemy in their enclosed valley would be hotter than we were in the open hills and also they were Turks men of white meat little apt for warm weather. So we clung tightly to them, and did not let them move or mass or sortie out against us cheaply. They could do nothing valid in return. We were no targets for their rifles since we moved with speed eccentrically. Also we were able to laugh at the little mountain guns which they fired up at us. The shells passed over our heads and burst hundreds of feet behind us in the air; and yet of course, for all they could see fairly above the hostile summit of the hill.

In the afternoon I had a heat-stroke myself, or pretended to, for I was dead-tired of the weariness of it all, and cared no longer how it went. So I crept down into a hollow on the south-east where there was a trickle of thick water in a muddy cup of the hills, and strained to suck some moisture off its dirt through the filter of my sleeve. Nasir joined me, panting like a winded animal, with his cracked and bleeding lips shrunk apart in his distress: and then old Auda appeared, striding down powerfully, his eyes bloodshot, and staring, his knotty face working with excitement.

He grinned with malice when he saw us lying there, spread out trying to find coolness under the bank, and croaked to me harshly, 'Well, how is it with the Howeitatl All talk and no work!' 'By God indeed: said I back again, for I was angry with everyone and with myself, 'they shoot a lot and hit a little.' Auda turned almost pale with rage, and trembling tore his head cloth off and threw it on the ground beside me. Then he ran back up the hill like a madman, shouting out to his men on this side and the other in his dreadful strained and rustling voice.

They came together to him, and after a moment scattered away downhill. I feared things were going wrong, and struggled up to Auda where he stood alone on the hilltop, glaring at the enemy: but all he would say to me was, 'Get your camel, if you wish to see the old man's work.' Nasir called for his camel and we mounted.

The Arabs passed in front of us into a little sunken place, which rose to a low crest, and we knew that beyond the crest the hillside went down in a facile slope to the main valley of Aba el Lissan, somewhat below the spring. All our four hundred camel men were here collected, on our side of the ridge, holding together in a tight mass, just out of sight of the enemy. We rode to their head, and asked the Shimt what it was and where the horsemen had gone.

He pointed over the ridge to the next valley above us, and said, 'With Auda there': and as he spoke there were yells and shots in a sudden torrent from beyond the crest, and we kicked our camels furiously to the edge to see. There were our fifty horsemen coming down the last slope into the main valley like a runaway, at full gallop, shooting from the saddle. As we watched two or three went down, but the rest thundered forward at a marvelous speed, and the Turkish infantry who had been huddled together under the cliff, ready to cut their desperate way out towards Maan in the first dusk, began to sway in and out, and finally broke before their rush.

Nasir screamed at me, 'Come on' with his bloody mouth, and we all plunged our camels madly over the hill, and down towards the head of the fleeing enemy. The slope was not too steep for a camel-gallop but steep enough to make their pace terrific, and their course uncontrollable: indeed it was very difficult to sit the wildly-plunging animals at all. Yet the Arabs were able to extend to right and left when the ground widened, and to begin to shoot from the saddle into the Turkish brown. The Turks had been too bound up in the terror of Auda's furious charge against their rear to notice us as we came over the eastward slope: so we also took them by surprise and in the flank: and a charge of ridden camels going nearly thirty miles an hour would sweep away everything in the track

My camel was the Sherari racer, Naama, which I had bought off a widow in Nebk the month before, at a great price: and she stretched herself out, and hurled downhill with such might, that we soon out distanced the others. The Turks fired a few shots, but mostly only shrieked and turned to run: and the bullets they did send at us were not very harmful, since it took much to bring a charging camel down in a heap.

I had got among the first of them, and was shooting, with a pistol, of course, for only an expert could use a rifle at the gallop, when suddenly my camel tripped and went down emptily upon its face, as though it had been pole-axed. I was torn completely from the saddle, and went sailing grandly through the air for a great distance, and landed with a crash which seemed to drive all the power and feeling out of me. I just lay there passively, waiting for the Turks to kill me, continuing the verse of a half-forgotten poem whose rhythm something, perhaps the long stride of the camel, had brought back to my mind as we leaped down the hillside: —

'For Lord I was free of all Thy flowers, but I
chose the world's sad roses, and that is why my
feet are torn and mine eyes are dim with sweat;
But at Thy terrible judgment seat, when this my
tired life closes, I am ready to reap whereof I
sowed, and pay my righteous debt.'

And at the same time another part of my mind thought what a poor squashed thing I would look when that following cataract of men and camels had poured over me.

However, after a long time I finished my poem, and no Turks came, and no camel trod on me: a curtain seemed taken away from my ears, and there was a great noise in front. So I sat up and saw the battle over, and our men driving together and cutting down the last broken remnants of the enemy. Behind was my camel's body, which had lain there like a rock and divided the charge into two streams past me: and in the back of its skull was the heavy bullet of the fifth shot I had fired.

Mohammed brought me Obeyd, my spare camel: and Nasir came back leading the Turkish commander, whom he had rescued, wounded, from Mohammed el Dheilan's wrath. The silly man had refused to surrender, and was trying to restore the day for his side with a pocket pistol. The Howeitat were very fierce, for the slaughter of their women on the day before had been a new and horrible side of warfare suddenly revealed to them. In all their history were only two remembered instances of a woman intentionally harmed in life or body, and they had been brought up to execrate the authors of these outrages in passionate songs.

Besides, these murders had reminded them of the blood-debt they owed the Turks, since the abortive Kerak rebellion before the war, when the Turks had punished the leaders mercilessly, and inflicted upon the condemned most painful sufferings before they let them die. So there were in all only one hundred and sixty prisoners, many of them wounded; and some three hundred dead and dying were scattered over the open valley each side of the road.

A few of the enemy got away, the gunners on their teams, leaving the guns, and some mounted men and officers, with their Jazi guides. Mohammed el Dheilan chased them for three miles into Mreigha, hurling insults at them as they rode, that they might know him, and keep out of his way, for the feud between Auda and his Motalga kinsmen had never applied with great force to Mohammed the political-minded, who showed friendship to all men of his tribe when he was alone and at liberty to do so. Among these fugitives was Dhaif-Allah Abu Tiyur, who had done us the good turn about the King's well at Jefer.

Auda came swinging up to us on foot, his eyes glazed over with the rapture of battle, and the words bubbling with incoherent speed from his mouth. 'Work, work, where are words, work, bullets, Abu Tayi....' and he held up his shattered field-glasses, his pierced pistol-holster, and his leather sword-scabbard cut to ribbons. He had been the target of a volley, which had killed his mare under him, but the six bullets through his equipment had left him scar less.

He told me later in strict confidence that he had bought a miniature Koran for one hundred and twenty pounds, thirteen years before, and had not since been wounded. Indeed Death had avoided his face, and gone sturdily about killing his brothers and sons and followers at his side. The book was one of the little Glasgow reproductions, costing eighteen pence in England, but the Arabs were too afraid of Auda's deadliness to laugh at his superstition (unworthy in a grown Bedouin), or to explain to him his bad bargain.

He was wildly pleased with the fight, most of all because he had confounded me and shown what his tribe could do. Mohammed was wroth with us for a pair of fools, calling me worse than Auda, since I had only insulted him by words like flung stones in order to provoke him to the deed of folly which had nearly killed us all: though as a matter of fact it had only killed two of us, one of the Rualla and one Sherari: and of the wounded the only one hard hit was the brother of Sheikh Durzi, Benaiah ibn Dughmi, a head man of the Rualla, whose leg was shattered. However, he recovered and six months later was walking about with a limp.

It was of course a pity to lose anyone of our men, but time was of importance to us between Maan and Akaba, and so imperative was the need of dominating Maan, in order to shock the little Turkish garrisons between us and the sea into surrender, that I would have willingly consented, for this once, to lose even more than two. The book-philosophers had called war a passionate and tragic drama, but to me it was essentially scientific and numerical, and the officer who allowed his sentiment to obscure for an instant his consciousness of the priceless value of his men's lives would have shown himself unfit for his office. Yet there were occasions like this when Death justified himself and was cheap.

I made haste to question the prisoners about themselves and their movements, and if more troops were in Maan, since their own prompt appearance at Fuweilah made me fear that the garrison had perhaps been heavily increased. But the nerve crisis had been too severe for them, and some gaped at me, and some gabbled unintelligibly, while others with helpless weeping embraced my knees, protesting that they were Moslems and my brothers, without listening for an instant to my queries or replying a sane word.

Finally I got angry and took one of them aside and was rough to him, shocking him by new pain into a half-understanding, when he answered to simple questions well enough, and very reassuringly, for I learned that their battalion was the only reinforcement, and it merely a reserve battalion; the two companies who remained in Maan were not enough to defend its perimeter.

This meant we could take it easily, and the Howeitat clamored to be led there, lured by the dream of unmeasured loot, though what we had taken here was a rich prize. However, Nasir, and afterwards Auda, helped me stay them. We could not keep Maan, and to lose a good life on a mere plundering raid was not our morality. We had no support, no regulars, no guns, no base nearer than Wejh, no communications, no money even, for our gold was exhausted, and we were issuing our own notes, promises to pay 'when Akaba is taken', for daily expenses. Besides, one did not change a strategic scheme to follow up a tactical success. We must push straight on to the coast, and reopen our sea contact with Suez, if we were not to suffer disagreeable surprises from Sinai.

However, it would be good to alarm Maan further: so we sent mounted men to Mreigha and took it, as the Turks were leaving it: and to Waheida and took it this news, and the loss of their camels on the Shobek road, the demolition of el Haj, and the massacre of their relieving battalion all came to Maan together, and caused a very proper panic. The Staff wired for help, the civil authorities loaded the archives into trucks, and left, hot-speed, for Damascus.

Chapter 58: Akaba Taken

Meanwhile our Arabs had plundered all there was to be found on the Turks, in their baggage train, or at their camp, and then soon after moonrise Auda came to us and said that we must move. This angered Nasir and myself Tonight there was a dewy west wind blowing, and at Aba el Lissan's four thousand feet, after the heat and burning passion of the day, the damp chill of it struck very sharply on our wounds and bruises. The water-spring was a thread of silvery water flowing in a runnel of pebbles across delightful turf green and soft, and on it we were lying wrapped in our cloaks, wondering about something to eat; and if it were worth preparing: for we were subjects at the moment of the physical shame of success, a reaction of victory when it became clear that nothing was worth doing, and that nothing worthy had been done.

However, Auda insisted. Partly it was superstition again: he feared the newly-dead around us: partly lest the Turks return on us in force from somewhere: partly lest other clans of the Howeitat take us, lying there broken and asleep. Some of them were his blood-enemies: others might say they came to help our battle, and in the darkness thought we were the Turks and fired at us blindly. So we roused ourselves, and jogged the sorry prisoners into line. They had to walk, for the most part. Some twenty of our camels were dead or dying from the charge, and for spares we had only the old camels that had carried dynamite, they hardly carried us, and many of our animals were too weak to take a double burden. Those that could were loaded with an Arab and a Turk:

but some of the Turkish wounded were too hurt to hold themselves on, pillion. We possessed no other means, and in the end had to leave about twenty of them behind on the thick grass beside the rivulet, where at least they would not die of thirst, though there was little hope of life or rescue for them.

Nasir set himself to beg blankets for these abandoned men who were half-naked, and while the Arabs packed I went off down the valley to where the fight had been to see if the dead had any clothes which they could spare. But the Bedouin had been beforehand with me, and had stripped them to the skin. It was their point of honor, as part of the triumph of victory, to wear the clothing of a dead enemy: and next day we saw our force transformed as to the upper half into a Turkish force, each man in a soldier's tunic: for it was a battalion straight from home, very well found and dressed.

The dead men looked wonderfully beautiful. The night was shining gently down, softening them into new ivory. Turks were white on the clothed parts of their bodies, much whiter than the Arabs among whom I was living, and these soldiers had been very young. Close round them lapped the dark wormwood, now heavy with dew, in which the ends of the moonbeams sparkled like sea-spray. Dead men seemed flung so pitifully on the ground, huddled anyhow in low heaps that one wished to straighten them to lie comfortably at last. So I put them all in order, one by one, very wearied myself in mind and body, and longing to be of these quiet ones, not of the restless noisy aching mob up the valley, quarrelling over the plunder, boasting of their speed and strength, to endure God knew how many toils and pains of this sort, till death, whether we succeeded or failed, wrote the last chapter in our history.

In the end our little army was ready, and we wound slowly away up the height and beyond into a hollow which was a little sheltered from the wind, and there, while the tired men slept, we chiefs sat down together, and wrote letters to the heads of the coast Howeitat, telling them of the victory, that they might invest their nearest Turks, and hold them busy till we came. We had been kind to one of the captured officers, a policeman despised by his regular colleagues, and him we persuaded to be our Turkish scribe to tell the commandants of Guweira and Kethera and Hadra, the three posts between us and Akaba, that if our blood was not hot we took prisoners, and that a prompt surrender would ensure their good treatment, and safe delivery in rich Egypt.

This lasted till dawn, and then Auda marshaled us in order for the road , and led us up the last mile of soft heather-clad valley between the rounded hills. It was all intimate and home-like: till we neared the last green bank, and realized suddenly that it was the last, and beyond lay nothing but clear air. The abrupt change this time checked me with amazement at its loveliness: and afterwards however many times we came that way there was always a little catch of eagerness in the mind, a pricking forward of the camel, and straightening up to see again over the crest into openness.

The hillside swooped down below us for hundreds and hundreds of feet, and broke away on each side in curves like bastions, against which summer morning clouds were breaking: and from its foot opened the new earth of the Guweira plain. Aba el Lissan was made of rounded limestone breasts covered with earth and heath, green, well watered. Guweira was a map of pink sand, brushed over with the streaks of water-courses, and elsewhere clothed in acres of scrub: and, out of this and bounding this, rose islands and cliffs of the glowing sandstone, scarped by the winds, and furrowed by rain, colored celestially by the early sun.

To have wandered for days on the plateau imprisoned in its valleys, climbing one ridge only to meet another, and then to have come without introduction to this brink of freedom was a rewarding vision, like a sudden window in the wall of life, and we walked down the zigzag pass of Shtar, to feel its loveliness, for on our camels we rocked too much with sleep to dare see anything. At the bottom the animals found a matted thorn which gave them great pleasure of eating, and we in front made a halt, and rolled off our saddles on to sand, soft as a couch and like the desert in its comfort, and went at once to sleep.

Auda came, and we pleaded that it was not because we were tired, but to be merciful to our broken prisoners. He replied that if we rode they alone would die of exhaustion, but that if we dallied both they and we would die of hunger or thirst: for truly there was now little water and no food. However, we could not help ourselves, and stopped that night short of Guweira, after going only fifteen miles.

At Guweira we knew lay ibn Jad, balancing his policy to come down with the stronger: and today we were the stronger, and the old fox was ours. He met us full of honeyed speeches, and led us to the three little stone houses which were all the post. He had one hundred and twenty Turks, the garrison, his prisoners, and wished to hand them over to us here: but we agreed with him to carry them at his leisure and their ease to us at Akaba. Today was the fourth of July and we must make haste for we were hungry, and Akaba was still far ahead behind two defenses. The nearer, Kethira, under the height of Heiran, was stubborn, and would not answer our messages or parley with our flags. They were on a cliff, commanding the valley, a strong place which it might be costly to carry by open assault

We assigned the honor, in irony, to ibn Jad and his unwearied men, advising him to attempt it in the hours of darkness. He shrank, made difficulties, and pleaded the full moon: but we cut hardly into the excuse, promising that tonight for a while there should be no moon. By my diary there was an eclipse, and it came duly, and in the confusion the Arabs got around the post and forced it without loss, while the superstitious Turkish soldiers were firing rifles and clanging copper pots to rescue their threatened satellite.

In the morning we set out early across the strand-like Guweira plain, making for the watershed into Wadi Itm, We had made Niazi Bey, the Turkish battalion commander, our guest to excuse him the humiliation of being a subject of Bedouin contempt, and now he sidled up by my camel, and with his swollen eyelids and long nose betraying the moroseness of the man, began to complain that an Arab had insulted him, by a gross Turkish word.

I apologized, but said no more was called for since the term used could only have been learnt on some old occasion, from the mouth of one of his Turkish fellow-countrymen in authority. The Arab was repaying Caesar.

He was not satisfied and, changing his grumble, pulled from his pocket a wizened quarter of bread, and asked me if that was fit breakfast for a Turkish Staff officer. The truth was that the heavenly twins, foraging in Guweira, had bought or found or stolen a Turkish soldier's ration loaf, and I had divided it between them and Niazi and myself I said it was not breakfast, but lunch and dinner too, and perhaps tomorrow's meals as well. I, a Staff officer of the British

Army, which was not less well fed than the Turkish, had eaten mine with the relish of victory. It was the defeat, not the bread which stuck in his gullet, and I hoped he was not going to blame me for the issue of a battle imposed on both our honors.

No more was said, and we marched down the wild narrows of Wadi Itm, whose intricate ruggedness increased as we penetrated deeper and deeper into the hills. After Kethira we found one empty Turkish post after another. Their men had been drawn in to the Khadra garrison, to the entrenched position at the mouth of the Itm, which covered Akaba so well against the risk of a fruitful landing from the sea. Unfortunately for the enemy, they never imagined attack from the interior and of all their great works not one trench or post faced inland. Our advance from so new a direction threw them into panic, and wisely they did not progressively resist us. The attempt if made would have availed them nothing, for we had the hill tribes with us, and by their help we could occupy the sheer peaks with riflemen whose plunging fire would render the gorge untenable for troops without overhead cover.

In the afternoon we were in contact with this main position, and heard from the Heiwat Arabs who flocked in to us from the west that the subsidiary posts about Akaba had been called in or reduced so that only these last three hundred men lay between us and the free use of the sea. We dismounted from our camels and called a council to hear that the enemy was resisting firmly dug into trenches with bomb-proof shelters and with a new artesian well which watered them sufficiently. Only it was rumored that they had little food.

It was a deadlock, and our council wrangled this way and that with arguments and plans and bickering between the prudent and the bold. Tempers were short and bodies restless in the incandescent gorge whose shimmering granite peaks radiated the sun in a myriad point of light and down whose deep and tortuous bed no wind could come to relieve in any way the slow saturation of its air with heat. Our numbers had swollen till we were much more than a thousand strong, and so many crowded in the narrow space filled it and pressed about us, and broke up our council twice or thrice partly because it was not good they should overhear us wrangling, partly because in the sweltering confinement our own unwashed smells offended us. Through our heads our heavy pulses throbbed like clocks.

We sent the Turks summonses, first by Arabs with white flags but they shot at them, and then by Turkish prisoners in uniform but they shot at them also. This inflamed our Bedouin, whose endurance too was worn thin, and while we were yet deliberating a sudden wave of them burst up on to the rocks and sent a hail of bullets spattering down against the enemy. Nasir ran out barefoot to stop them , but halted after ten steps on the burning ground and screeched for sandals, while I crouched in my atom of shadow too wearied of these men whose minds all wore my livery to care who regulated their febrile impulses.

However, Nasir brought quiet again on them and came back to me with Farraj and Daud, who had been the ringleaders. For correction they were set on scorching rocks till they begged his pardon. Daud yielded immediately but Farraj who for all his soft form was of whipcord and by much the masterspirit of the two, laughed from his first rock, sat out the second sullenly, and gave way with a bad grace only when ordered to a third.

His stubbornness should have been stringently visited: but the only punishment possible to our hands in this vagrant life was corporal which had been tried upon the pair so often and so uselessly that I was sick of it. If confined this side of cruelty the surface pain seemed only to irritate their muscles into activities wilder than those for which they had been condemned. Their sins were an selfish gaiety and the thoughtlessness of unbalanced youth being happy when we were not: and for such silliness to hurt them mercilessly like criminals till their self-control gave way in despair and their manhood was lost under the animal distress of their bodies, seemed to me degrading, almost an impiety towards two sunlit beings on whom the shadow of the world had not yet fallen, the most gallant, the most enviable I knew.

We had a third try to communicate with the enemy by means of a little Turkish conscript who said that he understood how to reach them. When we gave him leave he undressed himself and went down the valley in little more than his boots and his countrymen out of curiosity and their Turkishness let him in. An hour later he proudly brought us a reply, very polite, to the effect that in two days if help did not come from Maan, they would surrender.

This was folly, for we could not hold our men indefinitely and a general engagement would have meant the massacre of every Turk. I held no great brief for them but it was better that they be not killed, if only to spare myself the pain of seeing it. Besides we might have suffered loss on the way. There was no second eclipse to exploit, and night operations in the now staring fullness of the moon would be nearly as exposed as day. It would be dear to kill one hundred Turks at the price of an Arab: for this was not, like Aba el Lissan, an imperative battle. We gave our little man a sovereign as earnest of his reward, and walked down with him till quite close to the enemy, and sent him in for an officer to speak with us. After some hesitation this was achieved, and to him we explained fully the situation on the road behind us, and our growing force, and our short control over their tempers. The upshot was that he promised to surrender his post at daylight. So we had another sleep (an event now rare enough to chronicle) in spite of our thirst, for the wretched prisoners had climbed in a horde up to the Resafe wells and drained them dry without leaving us a drop to drink.

Next day at dawn fighting broke out on all sides, for hundreds more hill men, again doubling our number, had come about us in the night and, not knowing the arrangement, began shooting at the Turks, who defended themselves. Nasir and I went out with ibn Dgheithir and his Ageyl marching in fours to the open bend of the valley below our men, who ceased fire not to hit us. The Turks also stopped at once, for they had no more fight or food left in them, and thought that we were well supplied. So the surrender went off quietly after all.

As the Arabs rushed in to plunder the camp I noticed one of the prisoners in field-grey uniform, with a red beard and puzzled blue eyes, and spoke to him in German. He was the well-borer, and knew no Turkish and was amazed at the doings of the last two days. He begged me to explain what it all meant, since he had not understood the officers. I said that we were a rebellion, of the Arabs against the Turks. This took him time to appreciate. He wanted to know who was our leader and I said the Sherif of Mecca. He supposed he would be sent to Mecca. I said rather to Egypt, and he enquired the price of sugar there, and when I told him it was cheap and plentiful he was glad

The loss of his belongings he took philosophically, but was sorry for his well, which a few more days' work would have finished as his monument. He showed me where it was, and by pulling on the sludge bucket we drew enough delicious water to quench our thirsts. Then we mounted our camels and raced through a driving sand-storm down to Akaba, only four miles further, and splashed into the sea, on July the sixth, just two months after our setting out from Wejh.

BOOK V

Marking Time

Our capture of Akaba closed the Hejaz campaign, and laid on us the new task of helping the British to invade Syna. The Arabs working found Akaba turned into a virtually right wing of Allenby's army in Sinai

To mark the changed relation Feisal was transferred as an Army Commander, to Allenby's command. Allen by undertook responsibility for his operations and his proper equipment

Meanwhile we organized the Akaba position as an unassailable base, and went on to hinder train traffic on the Hejaz Railway.

Chapter 59: A Cross Sinai

Through the whirling dust we perceived that Akaba was all a ruin. Repeated naval bombardments had degraded the place to its original rubbish and the poor remains of the houses stood about in a litter with none of the dignity of ancient buildings, of which the durable bones face with a great defiant gesture that inevitable Time whose advancing years have already devoured their accidents. Akaba was dirty and contemptible and the wind howled miserably across it.

We wandered into the shadow of the cool groves of palms, lining the beach to the very break of the splashing waves, and sat down there and watched our men streaming past in a line of flushed vacant faces which seemed to hold no message for us. For months Akaba had been the horizon of our minds the goal to which all efforts turned: we had had no thought, we had refused thought of anything beside. Now we had achieved the end and we despised a little the life which had bestowed so much effort on an object whose attainment changed nothing either in our minds or in our bodies.

In the strange blank sunlight of victory we were scarce able to feel ourselves. We spoke with surprise sat down emptily fingered our white skirts doubtful if we could understand or learn who we were. Others' noise was an unreality a singing in the ears dreamlike or as if drowned in deep water. The astonishment of continued life was upon us and we did not know how to turn the gift to account. Especially for me was it hard, since though my sight was sharp I never saw men's features: always I peered for their living truth imagining for myself the spirit-reality of this or that: and today each man owned his desire and was fulfilled in it, and became meaningless.

Hunger called us out of our trance. We had now seven hundred prisoners in our train in addition to our own five hundred men and our two thousand allies: and we had not any money (or indeed a market near): and the last meal had been two days ago. In our riding camels we possessed meat enough for six weeks but it was a poor diet and a dear one which would bring future immobility upon us. Besides them, in the sea were fish though we had no boat, no net, no hooks, nothing to catch them with except a last few ounces of blasting gelatin. We set about bombing them, however, as a first measure, while we looked through the gardens.

The palms were heavy with dates, but unhappily these were yet small and green. To eat them raw was nearly as nasty as the ones they were intended to allay. Cooking made them better in the taste but still deplorable afterwards, and we and our prisoners went about sadly, faced with the dilemma of constant hunger or of violent diurnal pains. However, it was good to be sparing, a great aid to continence, and the grosser forms of gluttony fell away from us.

The assiduous food-habit of a lifetime had trained the English body to the pitch that it could produce a punctual nervous excitation in the upper belly a few minutes before the fixed hour of each meal: and we sometimes gave the honored name of hunger to this sign that our gut had cubic space for more stuff. Arab hunger was not a pain but the cry of a long-empty laboring body fainting with weakness. They lived on a fraction of our bulk food, and their systems made exhaustive use of what they got. A nomad army did not dung the earth richly with by-products.

Meanwhile Nasir and I slept. We tried to signalize each stage accomplished by this little extra peace and quiet, for in the desert we were only left alone by men and flies when lying on our backs, with a cloak as a shield over our faces, asleep or pretending to sleep. In these days our forty-two officer prisoners were an intolerable nuisance. They were disgusted when they found how ill-provided we were: indeed for long they refused to believe it was not a fraud done to annoy them, and plagued us day and night for delicacies, as though we had all Cairo hidden in our saddlebags. We had made them guests of our bare hospitality to save them the petty spitefulness of the Arabs: for this garrison had been long in Akaba, and few men in our force had not suffered abuse or injury at their hands.

In the evening, our first reaction against success having passed off, we began to think how we should keep Akaba, having gained it: and our supper taught us that the urgent need was food. We must as soon as possible open communications with the British. At dawn there had been an armed tug, H.M.S. *Slieve Fay,* off the town, but she had not seen our signals, and after firing a few shots at the hills had steamed away again. That meant no other patrol visit for a fortnight, so that we must send news overland the one hundred and fifty desert miles to Suez. For many reasons I decided to go across myself, that I might arrange direct in Cairo the needful shipment of supplies and money to keep Nasir alive.

There was little fear of a crisis at Akaba meanwhile, so far as the enemy was concerned. Maan would still be living under the dread of our attack, more eager to dig trenches and machine-gun pits in their perimeter than to stir up again our hornets of the Howeitat: and also they had ten days' work to repair their railway. It was inevitable that after the pause, if we remained supine, they would prepare an advance to Akaba to crush us: but not with less than seven or eight thousand troops, and to collect these and their transport would require two months.

It would give me time to go and come, and indeed in Egypt I might make the two months longer. The seven thousand reinforcements could only be drawn from the Beersheba front. Since we had not heard of Murray and his efforts, if he pressed the Palestine Turks as vigorously as he had done in March, he would straiten them of men, and dissuade them from spending many in so remote a purpose as retaking Akaba. I could probably arrange it with him.

Altogether it seemed fit to ignore the enemy, and yet to be quite safe we discussed defenses. Aba el Lissan was no more use to us for it lay in a country of all arms, and therefore unfavorable to the irregulars who desired irregular ground-surfaces. We settled that Auda with the mass of the Howeitat should return, when food came, to Guweira. In the hills west of it was water enough for him, and he would there be nearly forty miles from Maan, and well covered by the natural difficulties of the descent of Shtar, and the crossing of the arid Guweira sands. In fact as safe as safe need be.

And we would make him safer yet, in excess of precaution. We would put an outpost twenty miles to his north, in the impregnable fastnesses of Wadi Musa, among the rock-ruins of Nabatean Petra: and link them to him by a half-way post at Delagha, covering the Gharandel road from Maan to Wadi Araba, the route in relay to Itm manufactured by the enemy in 1914. Auda should also send men to Batra, southward of Aba el Lissan, so that the Howeitat would be disposed in a semi-circle of four positions round the edge of the Maan highlands, covering every way towards Akaba, for each of these places had its own road line back to our port.

They lacked good lateral intercommunication, but that hampered us little, for the internal jealousies of our tribes made it unwise to support one by the other; our Divisions were mutually incompatible. It was even an advantage, for it meant that these four positions existed independently, and no one was necessary to another. This would fox the enemy, who had swallowed whole Goltz's rather impertinent half-truths and generalities about the art of war. They thought him not an unintelligent parody of Clausewitz, but final authority. He told them that to take one point of a defensive position crashed down the lot: and we looked to their delivering a spirited drive against one of our four places and sitting afterwards in it dazed for an uncomfortable month, unable to advance for the threat of the remaining three, and scratching their heads and wondering why the others did not fall.

With such assurances in my mind it was easy to leave Akaba, and Nasir bade me farewell in the early afternoon of July the seventh. We were eight in number, mostly Howeitat, mounted on the eight best camels in the force: one even was the famous jedhah, the seven-year-old for whom the Nowasera had fought the Beni Sakhr. The other seven were not in prime condition, for reasons easily understood. The distance to Suez was one hundred and fifty miles: the road barren and only one point of water on it. As we rode round the head of the bay we discussed the manner of our journey. If we went gently, sparing the animals, they and we would go weak with hunger. If we rode hard we might break them down in mid-desert.

Finally we agreed to keep to walking pace, however tempting the surface, and to keep to it for so many hours of the twenty four as our endurance would allow. On such tests the man, especially if he happened to be foreign, usually collapsed before the beast: in particular I had been riding fifty miles a day for the last month, and was near my limit of strength. If I held out we should reach Suez in fifty hours of a march: and to excuse us cooking-halts upon the road we carried lumps of boiled camel, and some broiled dates tied up in a rag behind our saddles: also two skins (about eight gallons) of water.

After passing the gulf we rode through the first granite foothills of the Sinai escarpment into Wadi el Masri, and over the Egyptian bridge up the great engineered road with its gradient, in places, of one in three and a halt. The climb was severe in our haste, and we reached the crest before sunset with both men and camels trembling and breathless with fatigue. One camel we sent back as unfit for the trip; with the others we pushed out across the mud plain, an excellent aerodrome, till we came to some thorn-scrub. There we slipped down from our saddles while the animals cropped about the bushes for an hour.

Near midnight we reached Themed, the only wells on our route, in a clean valley-sweep below the deserted but unbroken guard house where the Sinai police had lived before the war. We let the camels breathe and gave them water and drank much ourselves in preparation for the one hundred and twenty dry miles still before us. Then up and on again, plodding through a silence of night so intense that continually we turned round in the saddles listening for fancied noises away there by the cloak of stars; but all the activity lay in ourselves, and the crackling of our passage through the undergrowth, which scattered a perfume like ghost-flowers about us.

Dawn came very slowly, and we marched on, till the sun was well up. By now we were far out in the plain through which sheaves of shallow water-courses flowed northward towards the gorge in the Hellal Mountain made by Wadi Arish, the central water-system of all Sinai, as it cut its way into the sea: and we stopped to breakfast ourselves, and to give our camels a few minutes' mockery of pasture. Then again in the saddle till noon, and past noon when through the mirage we came quite suddenly on the lonely ruins of Nekhl.

This we left on our right, for we knew that there were neither Turks nor Arabs nor British in it. Murray had pushed a raiding party out so far, and they had shattered the fort and blown in the wells to deny the enemy this useful concentration post from which to plot against the safety of the Canal. So we continued steadily till sunset along the derelict telegraph which pointed us the straight road to Suez. At sunset we halted again for an hour.

The camels were getting sluggish now, and we were utterly wearied: but Motlog the one-eyed the owner of the Jedhah, called us to action, and we remounted, and rode steadily at a mechanical walk up the slopes of Heidan into the Mitla hills. As we reached them the moon came out suddenly and all their tops, strangely contoured in form-lines of the limestone strata, shone out as though crystalline with snow. We turned a little towards the right, aiming for the pass of Wadi el Haj down into the valley of the Canal.

In the early dawn we were well into the Haj descent, and passed a melon field sown by some adventurous Arab in this no man's land between the rival annies. We halted for another of our precious hours, and loosed the disgusted camels to search round the sand-valleys for something to eat while we cracked the unripe melons and cooled our chapped lips on their pith . Then again forward, in the heat of the new day, though the canal valley at this end of the Suez gulf was constantly refreshed from the breezes of the Red Sea, and never too oppressive. We were passing down the narrow winding bed of Wadi el Haj, between its sandy cliffs.

Around us appeared here and there mottled places, where rusted tins of bully-beef, scattered remains of the tactical marches and operations of Young husband's troops from the Canal L. By midday we were through the easy dunes, after an enjoyable switchback ride up and down their waves, and out on the flatter plain which extended round the Mabeiuk hills on all sides. Suez was to be guessed at, as the frise of indeterminate points moping and bobbing in the mirage of the canal hollow far in front.

We reached the great trench lines, with their forts and barbed wire, roads and railways which the competitive pride of sectional engineers acting on a faulty theory of the defense had imposed upon the sweating British army throughout the whole eighty miles of the Canal's length However, now they were falling to decay, and we passed them without difficulty, meeting no one. Our aim was the Shatt, a post opposite Suez on the Asiatic bank of the Canal, and we reached it at last near three in the afternoon, forty-nine hours after we had ridden out of Akaba. For a tribal raid this would have been fair time, and we were tired men before even we started.

It was pleasing for an unknown native party coming in to the British defense area from enemy desert to be able to reach the Canal bank within three hundred yards of Suez unnoticed by any sentry: but actually Shatt was in unusual disorder since plague had appeared there two or three days before, and the old camps had been hurriedly cleared, left standing while the troops bivouacked out in the clean desert. Of course we knew nothing of this but hunted in the empty offices till we found a telephone. Then I rang up the Suez headquarters and said that I wanted to come across to Suez.

They regretted that it was not their business, as the Inland Water Transport managed transit across the Canal, according to their own methods. There was a sniff of implication that these methods were not those of the General Staff. This did not daunt me, for I was never a partisan of my branch of the service. So I rang up the Inland Water Transport and explained that I had just arrived in Shatt from the desert with news for General Headquarters, and wanted to come across to Suez. They were sorry but they had no free boats just then. They would be sure to send for me first thing in the morning, to carry me over to the Quarantine Department: and rang off.

Chapter 60: Allenby

Now I had been four months in Arabia: and for most of them continually on the move. In the last four weeks I had ridden some fourteen hundred miles by camel, not sparing myself anything necessary to advance the war: but I was not going to spend one unnecessary night with my familiar vermin. I wanted a bath and something cold with ice in it to drink: and to change these clothes, all sticking to my saddle-sores in filthiness: and to eat something more tractable than green date and camel sinew. I got through again to the Inland Water Transport, and talked to them like Chrysostom. It had no effect, so I got more vivid: but then once more they cut me off I grew very vivid to the instrument, and a broad sympathetic northern accent from the military exchange came down the line: It's no bluidy good, Sir, talking to them fucking water boogars: they're all the same.'

It expressed the apparent truth, and the good operator worked for me till I got through to the Embarkation Staff at Port Tewfik. This was generally Lyttleton, a major of the busiest, who had added to his innumerable labors the trifling one of catching the Red Sea warships one by one as they entered Suez roads, and persuading them (how some of them loved it!) to pile high their decks and magazines with stores for Wejh or Yenbo. In this way he ran our thousands of tons of cargo and our men free of charge as a by-play in his routine work, and always found time to smile at the curious things we did, and the curious folk we were.

He had never failed us, and so also this time. As soon as I told him who and where I was, and what was not happening in the Inland Water Transport, the difficulty was over. His launch was ready: he would be at the Shatt in half an hour. I was to come straight to his office, and not explain (till perhaps now, after the war) that a common harbor launch had entered the sacred waters of the Canal without permission of the water directory. All fell out as he said. The launch came and I embarked, sending my men and camels northward to Kubri, where by telephone from Suez I would prepare them rations and shelter in the animal camp on the Asiatic shore. Later of course they received their reward of a few hectic and astonishing days in Cairo.

Lyttleton saw my weariness, and sent me at once to the hotel Long ago I had thought it poor, but by now it was become splendid: and after getting over its first impression of an odd customer in an odder dress it produced the hot bath, and the cold drinks (six of them) and the dinner and the bed of my dreams. All was made easy for me by a very willing intelligence officer who was warned by his spies of a disguised European in the Sinai Hotel and came across to prove me. He was good enough to charge himself with the care of my men at Kubri, and to prepare me tickets and passes to Cairo next day.

The strenuous control of civilian movement in the Canal zone entertained a dull journeying to Ismailia. A mixed body of Egyptians and British soldiers came round the compartments of the train interrogating us and scrutinizing passes. It was proper to make war on all permit men, so when they came to me I replied in fluent English, 'Sherif of Mecca, Staff, to their Arabic inquiries. They were astonished. The sergeant begged my pardon: he had not heard. So I repeated that I was in the Staff uniform of the Sherif of Mecca. They looked at my bare feet, and white silk robes, and gold head rope and dagger. It was impossible! 'What army, sir?' 'Meccan.' 'Never heard of it; don't know the uniform.' 'Would you know a Montenegrin dragoon?'

This question was a home-thrust. All Allied troops in uniform could travel without pass, on warrant only, like mine. They did not know all the Allies, much less their uniforms. Mine might really be some rare army. They fell back into the corridor, and watched me while they wired up the line. Just before Ismailia a perspiring intelligence officer in wet khaki boarded the train to check my statements. He too seemed doubtful of the right of the Meccan army to wander about in fancy clothes: so as we had almost arrived I gave him also the special pass with which my friend at Suez had been careful to provide me. The officer was not pleased. The merit of that journey in the heat to catch me on the train seemed not to be its own reward to him.

In Ismailia, Suez passengers changed for Cairo. When the other train arrived, I saw in it an opulent saloon. From it descended Admiral Wemyss and Burmester and Neville with a very large and superior general. A terrible tension grew up along the platform, as the party marched up and down it in weighty discourse. Officers saluted once: twice: they went on walking up and down. Three times was too much. Some withdrew to the fence and stood permanently to attention. These were the mean sows. Some fled. These were contemptible. Some turned to the bookstall and studied the book backs avidly. These were shy. Only one was blatant.

I caught Burmester's eye. He wondered who I was, for I was burned crimson and very worn with travel: later I knew that my weight was less than seven stone just now. However, he answered, and I explained myself and the history of Akaba. It excited him. I said I wanted the Admiral to send a store ship there at once. Burmester said the *Dufferin* came in that day, and he would promise she should load all the food in Suez, go straight to Akaba, and bring back the prisoners immediately. This was splendid. He would do it himself, since he did not wish to interrupt the Admiral and Allenby.

'What's Allenby doing here?' said I. 'Oh, he's in command....' 'And Murray?' 'Gone home.' This was news of the biggest, concerning me narrowly, and I fell to wondering if this heavy rubicund man was like ordinary generals and if we would have trouble for six months teaching him. Murray and Belinda had begun so tiresomely that our thought those first days had been not to defeat the enemy, but to persuade our own chiefs to let us live. Such fighting was the least grateful form, and every new departure had a sickening plenty of it.

The peace Army had prepared for war by forming a caste habit, which tried all ideas by the King's Regulations and rejected such as transgressed in matter or even in manner. So they secured an iron individuality of the soldier, whatever his self as a man, and *ex cathedra* they became intolerant of exception. By time and performance we had converted Murray and Lynden Bell, and between the Gaza battles they had written to the War Office commending the Arab venture, and especially Feisal in it. This was generous of them and our secret triumph, for they were an odd pair in one chariot : — Murray all brains and claws, nervous, elastic, changeable,

Lynden Bell so solidly built up of layers of professional opinion, glued together after Government testing and approval, and later trimmed and polished to standard pitch.

However, the train was starting, so I climbed back and reached Cairo at noon and after lunch went to the Savoy, and walked past the sleeping sentry up the quiet corridors to Clayton's room, knowing that he cut his lunch hour to a scanty half, to cope with the multitudinous questions of his daily work. As I came in he glanced up from his desk and muttered, *'Mush fadi* (Anglo-Egyptian for 'engaged') but I spoke and got a very hearty welcome. In Suez the night before I had scribbled a short report, and so we were able to talk only of what next needed doing. Before the hour ended, the Admiral had rung up to say that the *Dufferin* was even then loading flour and getting in coal for her emergency trip to Akaba.

Clayton drew sixteen thousand pounds in gold from the Bank and got an escort to take it to Suez by the three o'clock train. This was urgent, to let Nasir meet his debts. The notes we had issued at Bair, Jefer and Guweira were penciled promises on army telegraphs forms to pay so much to bearer in Akaba. It was a great system of payment on delivery, but no one had dared issue notes before in Arabia as Beduin had no pockets in their shirts or strong-rooms in their tents for paper storage, and notes could not be buried. So there was an unconquerable prejudice against them, and for our good name it was essential that they be early redeemed.

Afterwards in the hotel I tried to find some clothes less exciting than my Arab get-up: but the moths had corrupted all I had and it was three days before I became normally ill-dressed. Meanwhile I heard of how good Allenby was, and of the last tragedies of Murray, the second attack on Gaza which London forced on him, and which he was too weak or too politic to resist, and how we went into it, everybody, generals and Staff officers, even soldiers convinced that we would be beaten, while Murray in headquarters worked for a perfectly safe defeat, losing enough men to show he had tried, and not enough to be disastrous : five thousand eight hundred was the casualty bill run up among them wantonly. They said Allenby was getting thousands of fresh men, and hundreds of guns, and all would be different.

Before I was clothed the Commander-in-Chief sent for me, curiously. In my report, thinking of my more direct models Saladin and Abu Obeida, I had stressed the strategic importance of the tribes between Akaba and Damascus, and their proper use as a threat to the railway communications of the Turks in Palestine. This jumped with his ambitions, and he wanted to weigh me further. It was a comic interview, for Allenby was physically large and confident, and morally so great that the comprehension of our littleness was not easy to him. He sat in his chair looking at me — not straight, as his custom, but sideways, puzzled.

He was newly come from France, where for years he had been a tooth of the great machine grinding the faces of the enemy. He was full of Western ideas of gun-power and weight, the worst training for our war, but as a cavalryman was already half-persuaded to throw up the new school and in this different world of Asia to follow Guy Dawnay and Chetwode along the worn road of maneuver and movement: yet he was hardly prepared for anything so odd as myself, a little bare-footed skirted person preaching a Willisen strategy of communications, offering to hobble the enemy by preaching, if given stores and arms and a fund of two hundred thousand sovereigns to convince and control the converts.

Allenby could not make out how much was genuine actor and how much charlatan: the problem was working behind his eyes and I left him to its difficulties. He did not ask many questions, or talk much, but studied the map and listened to my explanation of the nature of eastern Syria and the inhabitants. At the end he put up his chin and said quite directly, 'Well, I will do for you what I can', and that ended it. I was not sure how far I had caught him, but in the future we learned that he always meant exactly what he said, and that what Allenby could do was enough for the very greediest of his subjects.

Chapter 61: Rearrangement

To Clayton I opened myself completely. Akaba had been taken on my plan by my own effort. The cost of it had fallen on my brains and nerves. There was much more I felt inclined to do, and capable of doing: if he thought I had earned the right to be my own master. The Arabs said that each man believed his ticks to be gazelles: and I did, strenuously.

Clayton agreed that at least they were spirited and profitable ticks: but objected that the actual command could not be given to an officer younger than the rest. He asked if Joyce would not do as commanding officer at Akaba: and this suited me perfectly.

Joyce was a man in whom one could rest against the world, a serene, unchanging comfortable spirit. His mind was like a green landscape, with four comers to its view, cared-for, friendly, limited, and displayed.

He had won golden opinions at Rabegh and Wejh, repeating that very labor of building up an army and a base which would be necessary at Akaba. He was rather Clayton-like, himself, a good cartilage to set between opposing joints, but with more laughter than Clayton, for he was broad and much over six feet in height. His nature was to be devoted to the nearest job without straining on his toes after longer horizon. So each of us would have a sphere, and he was not likely to run loosely up-country in search of the more joyful adventures in the hills. Also he was more patient than any recorded archangel, and only smiled that jolly smile of his, whenever I came in with a revolutionary scheme, and threw new ribbons of fancy about the neck of the wild thing he was slowly rearing.

The other staff was easy. For supply officer we would have Coslett, the businessman whose orderly mind had made chaotic Wejh so prim. The airplanes could not yet be moved: but the armored cars might come straight away, and a guard-ship, if the Admiral was generous. We rang up Sir Rosslyn Wemyss, who was very generous: he said his flagship, the *Euryalus,* should sit there for the first few weeks. This was genius for in Arabia ships were esteemed by the number of their funnels and the *Euryalus,* with four was something exceptional in ships. Her great reputation confirmed all the mountains in their belief that we were indeed the winning side: and her huge crew, with the help of Everard Feilding for fun built us a good pier while they were stationed there.

On the Arab side I said that the expensive and difficult Wejh should be closed down and Feisal came to Akaba with his full army. This seemed sudden to Cairo, who checked a moment. So I went further than I hoped to get, and pointed out that the Yenbo Medina sector also became a back-number, and advised the transfer to Akaba of the stores, money, and officers now devoted to Ali and Abdulla. This seemed to them plainly impossible and they granted me my wish regarding Wejh at once in compromise.

Then I showed that Akaba was Allenby's right flank, only one hundred miles from his center but eight hundred miles from Mecca. The map showed that Akaba faced northward: as we prospered the Arab work would be done more and more in the Palestine sphere. So it was logical that Feisal be transferred from the command of his father King Hussein in Mecca, to become an army commander under Allenby in Syria.

This idea held difficulties. First, would Feisal accept? However, I had talked it over with him in Wejh months ago, and knew that he was willing. Then there was the feeling of the High Commissioner. Feisal's army had been the largest and most distinguished of the Hejaz units: there was little doubt that its future would not be dull. General Wingate had assumed responsibility for the Arab Movement at its darkest moment, to his own great risk in reputation: dare we ask him to relinquish its best part on the threshold of a loud success?

Clayton knew Wingate very well and was not afraid to broach the idea to him: and Wingate said promptly that Allenby could make more direct and larger use of Feisal than he could: and for the good of the show he was delighted to give him anything from his command which seemed desirable. So this delicate side of the affair was arranged without friction, indeed with honor to both sides: on Allenby's for asking, on Wingate's for cheerfully giving up the credit of the Arab Movement which had for years been his dream, and whose reproach he had borne since McMahon left.

A third difficulty of the transfer of command might be the feelings of King Hussein. He was an obstinate, narrow-minded suspicious character little likely to sacrifice his vanity to forward a unity of control His opposition would wreck the scheme: and therefore I offered to go down myself to Jidda to persuade him, calling on the way to see Feisal and to get from him such recommendations of the change as should fortify the powerful letters that Wingate was writing to the King. This they accepted.

We sent emergency shipments of food and arms to Akaba, to fill the gap till the new organization took over. Nasir replied cheerfully to our telegrams. All was very well and the Turks had not yet pushed out from Maan to take Aba el Lissan from our Howeitat watching post. The *Differin* came back to Suez with the prisoners from Akaba and the sick and wounded for treatment. She was detailed to take me down to Jidda on the new mission and I joined her on the morning of July the seventeenth.

She took two days to reach Wejh: and going ashore early in the morning I was told that Feisal with Joyce and Newcombe and all the army was at Jeida, a little palm-garden and rivulet nearly one hundred miles inland where they had made an advance base for attacking the railway somewhere near el Via the *Differin* wanted to stay only one night, so I went to the aerodrome, and Captain Stent, who had succeeded Ross in command of the Arabian flight, sent me up by air to the camp. It was comfortable to fly over the head of Raal, and to cross at sixty miles an hour the hills which we had learned so toilsome on camel-back.

Feisal was eager to hear the details of Akaba, and laughed at our apprentice-wars. We sat and worked the whole night after. He wrote the necessary letters to his father, and made the first arrangements towards getting Jaafar Pasha and his army back to Wejh, ready to be ferried to Akaba in the long-suffering *Hardinge.* Such of the Ageyl and Ateiba as were still fit for active service he ordered to set out by land up the coast towards Akaba immediately. Some French gunners and machine-gunners should go on as an advance party.

At dawn they flew me back safely to Wejh, and an hour after again in the *Differin* we were making for Jidda where things became easy for me with Wilson's powerful help. He agreed that Akaba was our most promising sector, and to make it strong as soon as possible sent up a shipload of his reserve stores and ammunition, and offered us any of his officers on loan. It was pleasant to find these two people, Wilson and Wingate, still preserving to the fourth year of the war the spirit which adopted as a matter of course the expedient promising best for the public interest.

Especially he helped me with the King, who came down from Mecca and talked discursively to us. Wilson had a wonderful influence in his counsels because the Arabs always trusted him, sure of his single eye to their best interests. He was the King's touchstone, by which to try doubtful courses. Thanks to him the proposed transfer of Feisal to Allenby's command was accepted at once, King Hussein taking the opportunity to stress his complete loyalty to our alliance. Then changing his subject, as usual without obvious coherence, he began to expose his religious position, neither strong Shia nor strong Sunni, aiming rather at a simple pre-schism interpretation of the faith, to reduce the influence of the new sects and orders grown up since in the provinces of Islam. In foreign politics he betrayed a mind as narrow as it had been broad in unworldly things, with much of that destructive tendency of little men, by turning public principle into private prejudice, to deny always the honesty of their opponents. I grasped something of the fixed jealousy which made the modernist Feisal suspect always in his father's court: and how easily mischief-makers could persuade the King that in spirit we were disloyal to Mecca.

While we lived so interestingly at Jidda, playing with new ideas on the faces of these men not in our state, watching their minds, two abrupt telegrams came from Egypt and shattered our peace. The first reported on certain evidence that the Howeitat were in treasonable correspondence with the enemy at Maan. The second connected Auda with the plot. This dismayed us. Wilson had traveled from Wejh to Fagair with Auda, and had formed the inevitable judgment of his perfect sincerity: and the Arab Movement had not yet had its traitor. However, we knew Mohammed el Dheilan was capable of double-play, and ibn jad and his friends were still uncertain: so we prepared to leave at once for Akaba. Treachery was as rare among the Arabs as among English, and had not been taken into account when we built a plan for defending Akaba. If it came to a head our movement would crash, as nothing but too little land-room, or treachery, could crash a rebellion.

Fortunately the *Hordinge* was in harbor, and Boyle sent her off at once northward with us. On the third afternoon we were in Akaba, where Nasir had apparently no notion that anything was wrong. His news was that the Turks were back in Aba el Lissan, and Auda near Guweira. I told him of my wish to greet Auda: he lent me a swift camel, and a guide, and at dawn we found Auda and Mohammed and Zaal all in a tent there. They were astonished when I dropped in on them, but protested that all was well. After compliments we fed together.

Others of the Howeitat came in, and there was gay talk about the war. I distributed the King's presents to the chief sheikhs of the tribe, and told them, to their laughter, that Nasir had got his month's leave to Mecca. The King was an enthusiast for the revolt, and believed that his servants too should work manfully. So he would not for any pretext allow a Sherif to visit Mecca, and they, poor men, found the continual military service heavy banishment from their wives. We had jested a hundred times that Nasir would deserve a month's holiday if he took Akaba: but he had not actually believed in it, and had rejoiced when I gave him Hussein's letter the evening before. In gratitude he sold me his Ghaza Ja, the regal camel he had won from the Howeitat in Nebk: and as her owner I became an object of new-interest to the Abu Tayi.

After lunch, by pretence of sleep, I got rid of most of the visitors, and then abruptly asked Auda and Mohammed to take a walk with me to visit the ruined fort and reservoir marking Roman, Nabatean and Arabic Guweira. When we were alone I mentioned their correspondence with the Turks. Auda began to laugh, Mohammed to look disgusted. Finally they explained that Mohammed had taken Auda's seal and written to his friend the Governor of Maan offering to lead the Howeitat away from the Sherifs cause. The Turks had replied gladly, promising great rewards if it happened, and Mohammed had asked for something on account.

Auda only then heard of it. He waited till the messenger with presents was on his way, and then caught him and robbed him to the skin, and was denying Mohammed any share of the spoils. This was a farcical story, and we laughed richly over it: but there was more behind. I discovered gradually that they were angry that no guns or troops had yet come to their support, and that no rewards had been given them for taking Akaba. They were very anxious to know how I had learnt so much of their secret dealings, and how much more I knew. I played on this fear by my unnecessary amusement, and by quoting in careless laughter actual phrases of the letters exchanged.

This created the impression desired, and then I told them Feisal's entire army was coming up as transport became available, and how Allenby was sending more rifles and guns and high explosive and food and money to Akaba. Finally I suggested that Auda's present expenses in hospitality must be great, and would it help if we give him in advance him something now in anticipation of the great gift Feisal would make him personally, when he came from Wejh? Auda saw that the immediate moment would not be unprofitable: that Feisal would bring greater good: and that the Turks would be always with him if other resources failed. So he agreed in a very good temper to accept my advance, and with it to keep the Howeitat well-fed and cheerful.

It was near sunset. Zaal had killed a sheep and we ate again in great amity. Afterwards I remounted, with Mufaddih, who was to draw Auda's allowance, and Abd el Rahman, a servant of Mohammed's, who, he whispered to me, would receive any little thing I wished to give him separately. We rode all night towards Akaba, where I roused Nasir from his sleep to talk a last business. Then I paddled out in a derelict canoe from the new Euryalus jetty to the Hardinge just as the first light of dawn was creeping down the western peaks.

I went below and bathed, and slept till mid-morning. When I came on deck the ship was rushing grandly down the narrow gulf under full steam for Egypt. My appearance caused a sensation, for they had not dreamed I could reach Guweira, assure myself upon the situation and get back in less than six or seven days to catch a later steamer: and had wireless to Cairo that everything possible was being done to confirm the Arabs in their allegiance.

As it was, we rang up Cairo and announced that the situation at Guweira was thoroughly good, and no spirit of treachery abroad. This may have been hardly true but the deception was mine and I regularly reduced impolitic truth in my communications as it was Egypt which kept us alive by favor of stinting herself To make her continue in sacrifice we must keep her confident and ourselves a legend — since the crowd wanted book-heroes and the so-simple Staff would not understand how much more human old Auda was because after the battle and murder his heart yearned towards the enemy at length subject at his free choice to be spared or to be killed and therefore never so lovely.

Cairo was a refreshment to the eyes, and I lazed away a week there in holiday during which General Salmond of the Royal Flying Corps promised to help me if necessary by bombing Maan from Arish, before we had our own flight of machines allotted to us for Akaba. The Howeitat were still in the callow stage about air attack, and feared it unreasonably, and the Turkish airplanes were active against them. Maan was within bombing-radius from Kuntilla, an old Egyptian frontier post north of Therned, and I agreed to put there a post of men, to transport thither bombs and petrol and spares and to mark out a suitable landing ground. So after my rest in Cairo I went up twice from Akaba to Kuntilla by camel and saw to it that everything was ready.

Chapter 62: On the Threshold of Syria

Meanwhile I was thinking hard and performing these mechanical duties without care, unconsciously. Till Feisal and Jaafar and Joyce and the army came we could do little but plan: but that for our own credit was an essential thing. There had been in our war till now only one studied operation — the march on Akaba; and the other haphazard playing with the men and movements of which we had assumed the leadership disgraced our minds. I had vowed if possible to know always where I was going and by what road in future before I moved. Today this meant a change of direction for our thoughts.

After Wejh it had been borne in upon me that the Hejaz war was won: after Akaba all of us saw that it was ended. Feisal's army had cleared off its Arabian liabilities and stood now with

Seven Pillars of Wisdom its back to the friendly Hejaz; and in alliance with the troops under Allenby, the joint Commander-in-Chief contemplated the invasion and conquest, or deliverance, of Syria from the Turks. The successful close of our first campaign opened to us the gate for understanding our second.

The difference between Hejaz and Syria was the difference between the desert and the sown. The problem that faced us was one of character: no less than the change-over from the nomad to the townsman: the learning to become civil. Wadi Musa village was our first peasant recruit, and unless we became peasants too, the movement would go no further.

It was good for the Arab Revolt that so early in its growth this change imposed itself we had been trying a hopeless thing, laboring to plough the waste lands, to make nationality grow in a place full of the certainty of God, that up as certainty which forbade all hope. Among the tribes our creed and its success could be only like the desert grass — a beautiful swift seeming of spring which, after a day's heat, fell to brown dust. Aims and ideas could be translated into tangibility only by expression in material things. The desert and the desert men were too detached to express the one, too poor in goods, too remote from complexity to carry the other. If we would prolong ourselves we must win into the ornamented lands, to the townsmen and villagers whose roofs and fields held their eyes downward and near.

The planning began, as it had begun in Wadi Ais, by a study of the map, and a recollection by myself of the nature of this our battle ground of Syria, as it had stood before the war. Our boundaries on the south were the Maan line, and on the east the nomadic portion of the desert. To the west Syria was limited by the Mediterranean, which made its coast from Gaza to Alexandretta on the north, the Turkish populations of Anatolia gave it an end. Within its limits the land was much parceled up by natural divisions. Of them the first and greatest was longitudinal, caused by the mountains that ran like a rugged spine from north to south, dividing a narrow coastal strip from a wide inland plain. These areas had climatic differences so marked that they made two countries, two races almost, with their respective populations. The shore Syrians lived in different houses, fed and worked differently, and used an Arab different in inflexion and intonation from that of the inlanders. They spoke of the interior unwillingly as of a wild land full of blood and terror.

The inland plain was again subdivided geographically into further long strips by its rivers. The valleys of the Jordan, Litani and Orontes were the most stable, most prosperous villages of the country, and reflected themselves in the natures of their inhabitants. Beyond them, on the desert side, lay the strange shifting populations of the border-land, wavering eastward or westward with the season, living by their wits, wasted by drought and locusts, by Bedouin raids, and, if these failed them, by their own incurable blood-feuds.

Nature had so divided the country into zones: and man had elaborated nature, and given to her compartments additional complexity. Each of these main north-and-south strip divisions was crossed and walled off artificially into communities mutually at odds. We had to reckon up their classes and causes, to see how best to gather them into our hands for offensive action against the Turks. Feisal's opportunities and difficulties lay in the political complications of the face of Syria, and in our minds we classified and arranged them in geographical order, like a moral map.

In the very north, furthest from us, the language-boundary followed not inaptly, the coach road from Alexandretta to Aleppo, until it met the Bagdad Railway, and then went up the line to Jerablus on the Euphrates, the northernmost Arab village in the Euphrates valley: but an enclave of Turkish speech lay to the south of this general line, in the settlements of Turkoman villages north and south of Antioch, and in the Armenians who were sifted in among them.

Otherwise, a main component of the coast population was the community of Ansariya, disciples of a strange cult of a principle of fertility, sheer pagan, anti-foreign, distrustful of Islam but drawn at moments towards Christians by the attraction of their common persecution. The sect was vital in itself, and as clannish in feeling and politics. One Nosairi would not betray another, and would not betray an unbeliever. Their villages lay in patches down the main hills from Missis to the Tripoli gap. They spoke Arabic only, and had lived there since the beginning of Greek letters in Syria. Usually they stood aside from affairs, and left alone the Turkish Government, in hope of reciprocity.

Mixed among the Ansariya were colonies of Syrian Christians, and in the bend of the Orontes had been some firm blocks of Armenians who could not agree with the Turks. Inland near Harim were settlements of Druses, Arabic in origin, and some Circassians from the Caucasus. These had their hand against all North-east of them were Kurds, speaking Kurdish and Arabic settlers of some generations back, who were marrying Arabs and adopting their politics. They hated Christians most, and after them Turks and Europeans.

Just beyond the Kurds existed a few Yezidis, Arabic-speaking, but in thought affected by the dualism of Iran and in their worship prone to placate the spirit of evil, and warped with an admiration of four crude bronze birds Christians, Mohammedans and Jews, peoples of revelation united only to spit upon Yezid. Inland of them stood Aleppo a town of two hundred thousand people and an epitome of all these races and religions. Eastward of Aleppo for sixty miles were settled Arabs whose color and manner became more and more tribal as they were nearer the fringe of cultivation where the semi-nomad ended and the Bedawi began.

A section across Syria from sea to desert, a degree further south, began in colonies of muslim Circassians near the sea. In the new generation they spoke Arabic, and they were an ingenious race, but quarrelsome, much opposed by their Arab neighbors. Inland of them were districts of Ismailia. These Persian immigrants had turned Arab in the course of centuries but worshipped among themselves a king, Mohammed, who in the flesh was the Agha Khan. They believed him to be a great and wonderful sovereign honoring the English with his friendship. They hated Moslems, and looked for the crumbling of the Turks. Meanwhile they were trampled on and were driven to hide their beastly opinions under a veneer of orthodoxy. Everyone knew how thin that was. They had signs by which to recognize one another and, though miserably poor paid yearly tribute towards the princely living of the Agha.

Beyond them were the strange sights of villages of Christian tribal Arabs, some of semi-nomad habit under their own sheikhs. They seemed very sturdy Christians, quite unlike their sniveling brethren in the hills. They lived like the Sunni about them, dressed and spoke like them, and were on the best of terms with them. East of the Christians lay semi-pastoral muslim communities, and east of them again some villages of Ismailia outcasts, on the extreme edge of cultivation, whither they had retired in search of the peace men would not give to them. Beyond, there was nothing but Bedouin.

A third section through Syria another degree lower down, fell between Tripoli and Beirut. At first, near the coast, were Lebanon Christians, for the most part Maronites or Greeks. It was hard to disentangle the politics of the two churches. Superficially one should have been French and one Russian: but a part of the Maronites to earn their living had been in the United States, and had developed there an Anglo-Saxon vein, not the less vigorous for being spurious. The Greek Church prided itself on being old Syrian, autochthonous, of an intense localism which might send it to the arms of the Turks rather than endure irretrievable domination by a Roman Power.

The adherents of the two sects were at one in unmeasured slander, when they dared, of Mohammedans and their religion. Such verbal scorn seemed to salve their consciousness of inbred inferiority. The families of Mohammedan Sunni lived among the Christians, Arabic-speaking like them, and identical in race and habit, except for their less mincing dialect and less parade of emigration and its results.

On the higher slopes of the hills clustered settlements of Metawala, Shia Mohammedans who came from Persia generations ago. They were dirty, ignorant, surly and fanatical, refusing to eat or drink with infidels (holding the Sunni as bad as the Christian) following only their own priests and notables. They spoke Arabic, but disowned in every way the country and people about them. Strength was their virtue, and a rare one in garrulous Syria. Over the hills were villages of Christian yeomen, living in free peace with their Sunni neighbors, as though they had never heard the grumbles of their fellows in Lebanon. East of them were semi-nomad Arab peasantry, and then the open desert.

A fourth section, a degree southward, would have fallen near Acre. There, the inhabitants from the sea-shore were first Sunni Arabs, then Druses, then Metawala. On the banks of the Jordan valley lived bitterly suspicious colonies of Algerian refugees, facing villages of Jews. The Jews were of varied sorts. Some were Hebrew scholars of the traditionalist pattern: but they spoke Arabic with their neighbors, and had developed a standard and style of living befitting the country while yet better than the Arab ways.

The later comers among them many of whom were German inspired had introduced strange manners of cultivation and strange crops, and European houses (erected out of charitable funds) into this land of Palestine which seemed too small and too poor to repay in kind their efforts: but they were at least honest attempts at self-support and deserved honor, in contrast with the larger settlements of sentimental remittance-men in Jerusalem. Manually they tended to rely on Arab labor and the land tolerated them. Galilee did not show the deep-seated antipathy to Jewish colonists and their aims which was an unlovely feature of the Judean area.

Across the Arab eastern plains, lay the Leja, a labyrinth of crackled lava, where all the loose and broken men of Syria had forgathered for unnumbered generations. Their descendants lived there in rich lawless villages, secure both from the Turk and Bedouin, and worked out their internecine feuds at leisure. South of them opened the Hauran, a huge fertile land, thickly peopled in its western half with Arab peasantry, warlike and as self-reliant and prosperous an element as any in Syria.

East of them were the Druses, Arabic-speaking but heterodox Moslems, who revered a mad and dead sultan of Egypt, and hated Maronites with a bitter hatred which, when encouraged by the Ottoman Government and the Sunni fanatics of Damascus, found expression in great periodic killings. None the less the Druses were disliked by the muslim Arabs and despised them in return: they were at feud with the Bedouin obeyed only their own leaders and preserved in their mountain fastnesses a hollow show of the chivalrous semi-feudalism in which they had lived in the Lebanon in the days of their great Emirs.

A fifth section in the latitude of Jerusalem would have begun with Germans, and with German Jews, speaking German or German-Yiddish more intractable even than the Jews of the Roman era, unable to endure contact with others not of their race, some of them farmers most of them shop-keepers in the main the most foreign and uncharitable part of the whole population of Syria. Behind them lay their enemies, the sullen Palestine peasants, more stupid than the yeomen of North Syria, materialist as the Egyptians, and bankrupt.

East of them lay the Jordan depths, inhabited by a charred race of serfs, and across it group upon group of self-respecting village or town Christians who were, after their co-religionists of the Orontes valley, the least timid examples of their faith in the country.

Among them and east of them were tens of thousands of semi nomad Arabs, holding the creed of the desert, living on the fear and bounty of their Christian neighbors. Down this debatable land the Ottoman Government had planted a long line of Circassian immigrants. They held their ground only by the sword and the favor of the Turks, to whom they were necessarily devoted.

Chapter 63: Syrian Towns

The tale of the inhabitants of Syria was not ended in this count of odd races and religions. Apart from the country-folk, in our summing of the land, we had to consider the six great towns: Jerusalem, Beirut, Damascus, Horns, Hama and Aleppo as entities each with its own character, direction and opinion of itself.

Jerusalem was a squalid town, which all Semitic religions had made holy. Christians and Mohammedans came there on pilgrimage to the shrines of its past, and the Jews looked to it for the political future of their race: and in it these united forces of the past and the future were so strong, that the city almost failed to have a present. Its people, with the rarest exceptions, were characterless as hotel servants, living on the crowd of visitors passing through. Questions of Arabs and their nationality were very far from them, though familiarity with the differences among Christians at their moment of most poignant expression had Jed the classes of Jerusalem to despise foreigners generally.

Beirut was altogether new. It would have been bastard French in feeling as in language but for its Greek harbor and American college. Public opinion in it was made by the Christian merchants; fat men living by exchange, for Beirut itself produced nothing. The next strongest component was the class of returned emigrants, happy on their invested savings in the town of Syria which to them most resembled the Washington Avenue where they had made good. Beirut was the door of Syria, a Levantine screen through which shop-soiled foreign influences flowed in, and represented Syria as much as Soho represented the Home Counties.

Yet in Beirut, because of its geographical position of its schools of the freedom engendered by intercourse with many foreigners there had been before the war a nucleus of people, Mohammedans, talking and writing and thinking like the doctrinaire cyclopredists who paved the way for revolution in France, and whose words permeated to parts of the interior where action was in favor. For their sake (most of them were martyrs now, in Arab eyes), and for the power of its wealth and for its exceeding loud and ready voice. Beirut was to be reckoned with. Damascus, Horns, Hama and Aleppo were the four ancient cities in which Syria took pride. They stretched like a chain along the fertile valleys of the interior between the desert and the hills. Because of their setting they turned their backs upon the sea and looked eastward. They were Arab and knew themselves such. Of them and of Syria, Damascus was the inevitable head the seat of lay government, and the religious center. Its sheikhs were leaders of opinion and more 'Meccan' than others elsewhere. Since they took only three days from Medina by the railway the citizens were fresh and turbulent always willing to strike as extreme in thought and word as in pleasure. Damascus boasted to move before any part of Syria. The Turks made it their military headquarters just as certainly as the Arab Opposition or Oppenheim or Sheikh Shawish there established themselves. Damascus was a lodestar to which Arabs were naturally drawn and a city which would not easily be convinced that it was unwillingly subject to an alien race.

Horns and Hama were twins disliking one another. All in them manufactured things. In Horns generally cotton and wool in Hama silks and brocades. Their industries were prosperous and increasing their merchants quick to find new outlets or to meet new tastes. North Africa, the Balkans, Asia Minor, Arabia, Mesopotamia used their stuffs. They demonstrated the productive ability of Syria unguided by foreigners as Beirut proved its understanding of distribution. Yet while the prosperity of Beirut made it Levantine, the prosperity of Horns and Hama reinforced their localism, made them more entirely native and more jealously native than other Syrian towns. Almost it seemed as though familiarity with plant and power had taught people that their fathers' manners were the best.

Aleppo was a great city in Syria, but not of it, nor of Turkey nor of Mesopotamia. Rather it was a point where the races, creeds, and tongues of the Ottoman Empire met and knew one another in a spirit of compromise. The clash of varied characteristics which made its streets a kaleidoscope imbued the Aleppine with a lewd thoughtfulness which corrected in him what was blatant in the Damascene. Aleppo had shared in all the civilizations that had turned about it and the result seemed a lack of zest in what its people did. Even so they surpassed the rest of Syria. They fought and traded more, were more fanatical and vicious and made most beautiful things: but all with a dearth of conviction which rendered their great strength barren.

It was typical of Aleppo that there, while yet Mohammedan feeling ran high more fellowship should rule between Christian and Mohammedan. Armenian, Arab, Turk, Kurd and Jew than in perhaps any other great city of the Ottoman Empire, and that more friendliness though less license should have been accorded to Europeans. Politically the town would have stood aside altogether, but for the influence of the unmixed Arab quarters which like overgrown half-nomad villages, scattered over with priceless mosques of the early period extended east and south of the mural crown of its great citadel. These after the maiden of Damascus were the most national of any parts of towns and the intensity of their patriotism tinged the rest of the citizens with a color of locality which was by so much less vivid than the unanimity of Damascus.

Chapter 64: Syrian Politics

All these peoples of Syria were open to us by the master-key of their common Arabic language. Their distinctions were political and religious: morally they resembled one another, with a steady gradation from neurotic sensibility on the sea-coast to reserve inland. They were alike quick-minded, admirers but not seekers of truth self-satisfied not, like the Egyptians helpless before abstract ideas, but unpractical and very lazy in mind as to be habitually superficial. Their ideal was to be left alone to busy themselves with others' affairs.

From childhood they were lawless, obeying their fathers only from physical fear, and their government later for the same reason: and yet there were few races with the respect of the upland Syrian for customary law. All of them wanted something new, for with their superficiality and their lawlessness was combined a passion for politics, the science of which it was fatally easy for the Syrian to gain a smattering, and too difficult to gain a mastery. They were discontented always with what government they had, but few of them honestly thought out an alternative, and fewer still agreed upon what they needed.

Many cried for autonomy for Syria, having knowledge of what autonomy was, but not knowing what Syria was, for in Arabic there was no such word, nor any word for all the country any of them meant. In Turkish, 'Syria' was the administrative province of Damascus: but in Arabic they called this Sham after the town. Aleppines called themselves Aleppines, and the Beirutis, and so down to the smallest villages, and this verbal poverty indicated their political disintegration. Between town and town, village and village, family and family, creed and creed existed intimate jealousies, sedulously fostered by the Turks to render their spontaneous union impossible.

In settled Syria there was no indigenous political entity larger than the village, and in patriarchal Syria was nothing more complex than the clan under its leader: and these units were informal and voluntary, with heads indicated from the entitled family only by the slow cementing of expressed public opinion. The constitution above them was the imported bureaucracy of the Turk, maintained by force, and impossible if carried out to the letter; but in practice either fairly good or very bad according to the less or greater frailty of the human instruments, generally the gendarmes, through which it worked.

Time seemed almost to have proclaimed the impossibility of autonomous union for such a people. In history Syria had been a corridor between sea and desert, joining Africa to Asia, Arabia to Europe. It had been a prize-ring of the empires lying about it, a vassal now of Anatolia, now of Greece, or Rome, or Egypt, or Arabia, or Persia, or Mesopotamia. When given a momentary independence by the weakness of its neighbors it had at once resolved itself fiercely into discordant northern and southern and eastern and western 'kingdoms', with the areas and populations at best of Yorkshire, at worst of Rutland for if Syria was by nature a vassal country it was also by habit a country of agitations and revolts.

Other elements in Syria cried aloud for an Arab kingdom. These were usually the Moslems, and the Catholic Christians would counter them by demanding European protection of an altruistic thalamic order, conferring privileges without obligation. Both proposals were of course far from the hearts of the autonomy groups, but the spectacle of their internal division, and suspicion that Syria's future neighbors would not be of the weak sort which enabled it to snatch a fearful independence had reconciled them to having such words constantly on their lips.

The people even the best-taught of them, showed a curious lack of proportion, an ignorance of the smallness and unimportance of their country and a misconception of the selfishness of great powers who would normally consider their own interests to the exclusion of those of unarmed races. They trusted that their opinions would be taken by England or France before their destiny was fixed and for years after these two powers had signed a treaty dividing Asiatic Turkey into spheres, they gravely debated the direction of their suffrage.

This blindness was the opportunity of the advocates of an Arab kingdom, and enabled that solution to come forward like a third candidate, as though the powers had not determined: and the nature of the treaty settlement allowed the Englishmen on the spot to support it without qualm. The Franco-British solution took no account of local wishes, or of history, or of geography and while it endured would hamper the commercial and political growth of the country: but the framers of the agreement were not of equal caliber, and the weaker was put, by gallant irony, in the exact position of its prototype that medieval Kingdom of Jerusalem which had fallen before the alliance of Egypt and Mesopotamia.

The control of the Arab Movement was left lying, like a golden apple between the contestants, but the charm was cogged. One of the two powers was given all the deserts — the sources of originality, all the holy places — the sources of fervor, all the great rivers — the sources of power, in the Arabic-speaking world. With these assets it might safely invest for the future whose outlines revealed themselves so inevitably a client growth: though the time of fruit had not nearly come.

As the master-key of these peoples' opinion lay in their common language, so the key of their imagination lay likewise in the word 'Arab', which struck a chord in some of the least likely minds. The Moslems whose mother tongue was Arabic looked upon themselves for that reason as a chosen people. The heritage of the Koran and the classical poets held Arabic-speaking peoples together. The patriotism which ordinarily attached itself to soil or race was warped to fit a language.

A second buttress of a polity of Arab motive was a distortion of the dim glories and conquests of the Arab Caliphate whose memory yet endured among the people through centuries of Turkish misgovernment. The accident that these traditions savored rather of the Arabian Nights than of sheer history maintained them in the conviction that their past was more splendid than the present of the Ottoman Turks.

Yet we had to admit that we were running too far and too fast ahead of time with these our dreams. An Arab government now in Syria, though buttressed on Arab prejudices, would be nearly as much imposed as the Turkish Government, or a foreign protectorate, or the historic Caliphate. Syria remained today as vividly colored a racial and religious mosaic as ever in the past. Any wide attempt at unity would make a patched and parceled thing, ungrateful to a people whose instincts had been forever and ever towards parochial home rule.

Our only excuse for over running time was war-necessity. The reaction would not come till after victory, and for that victory everything material and moral might be pawned. Syria's general discontent with the Turks might be made to seethe up into a fleeting common movement, if a new factor appeared offering to realize the centripetal nationalism preached by the Beirut eyclopredists. A new factor it must be and an outside factor, since only disinterested authority could restrain the jarring sects and classes from mutually destructive anarchy: and within our sight the only independent factor with a prepared groundwork and many adherents would be a Sunni prince Arabic speaking pretending to revive the Ommayads or Ayubids.

Concretely we estimated that the Syrians were ripe for spasmodic local revolt: that they were too jealous to combine and too conceited to adhere to a foreign cause: but that Feisal, foretelling the glories of a new kingdom of Damascus might persuade most of the inland ones (the men worth having in a fight) to follow him for a time until he succeeded and tried to transfer their debauched enthusiasm to the side of ordered government: and the more loose informal inchoate this new government the less would be the inevitable disillusionment following its institution.

Chapter 65: Irregular War

So my mind reviewing the country of Syria from the palm-garden of Akaba, had decided that in its complex dissatisfactions lay the possibility of revolt: and that in the personality of Feisal we had a rallying point at which to turn this revolt into victory. There remained for me to repeat the example of my sick-bed theorizing of Wadi Ais, and to make clear for myself and others the technique and direction of the new revolt

The direction a blind man could see. The critical center of Syria in all ages had been the Yarmuk valley whose owner owned the whole country strategically. Our direction was the Hauran, the railway from Damascus to Deraa, and either of those towns. It was convenient for us that just here lived the best people the self-reliant eastern tribes and villages of the desert edge. When the Hauran joined us our campaign would be well ended.

The process should be to set lip another ladder of tribes comparable to that by which we had climbed from Wejh to Akaba: only this time our ladder would be made of steps of Howeitat, Beni Sakhr, Sherarat, Rualla and Serahin, to raise us to Azrak, the desert oasis nearest Hauran or Jebel Druse. We needed to reach more than three hundred miles, a long stride without railways or roads but one which would be made safe and comfortable for us by an assiduous cultivation of desert power, the control by camel parties of the desolate and unmapped wilderness of mid-Arabia, from Mecca to Aleppo and Bagdad.

In character our operations of development for the final stroke should be like naval war, in their mobility, their ubiquity, their independence of bases and lack of communications, their ignoring of ground features, of strategic areas, of fixed directions, of fixed points. 'He who commands the sea is at great liberty, and may take as much or as little of the war as he will': and we who commanded the desert might be equally fortunate. Camel raiding-parties, self contained like ships, might cruise without danger along the enemy's cultivation-frontier, and tap or raid into his lines where it seemed easiest or fittest or most profitable, with always a sure retreat behind them into the desert-element which the Turks could not explore.

With the favor of the tribes we would be fortified in our freedom of movement, by their intimate knowledge of the desert edge of Syria, a country peculiarly and historically indefensible against attack from the east. Discrimination of what point of the enemy army organism to disarrange would come to us with experience. I had a ground work since I had traversed most of the country many times on foot before the war, working out the movements of Saladin or Ibrahim Pasha. Deeper war practice would make us adepts in that geographical intuition of wedding unknown land to known in a mental map.

Our fighting tactics should be always tip and run: not pushes, but strokes. We should never try to maintain or improve an advantage, but should move off to strike again somewhere else. We should use the smallest force in the quickest time, at the furthest place. If the action continued till the enemy had changed his dispositions to resist it, we would be breaking the spirit of our fundamental rule of denying him targets. If the enemy brought us to action we would be disgraced technically, even if victorious in the issue.

The necessary speed and range at which to strike, if we were to make war in this distant fashion, would be attained through the extreme frugality of the desert men, and their high efficiency when mounted on their female riding camels. The camel, that prodigious piece of nature, was an intricate animal, but in expert hands yielded a remarkable return. We had found that on camels we were independent of supply for six weeks if each man left the sea-base with a half-bag of flour, forty-five pounds in weight, slung on his riding saddle: and for shorter marches luxurious feeders might also have rice.

Of water we would not want to carry more than a pint each. The camels needed to drink perhaps every third day, and there was no gain in making ourselves richer than our mounts. Some of us never drank between wells, but those were hardy men: most drank fully at each well, and carried a drink for the intermediate dry day. In summer the Arab camels would do about two hundred and fifty miles after a watering: and this would be three days' vigorous march. An easy stage was fifty miles: eighty was good: in an emergency we might do one hundred and ten miles in the twenty four hours. Twice I did one hundred and forty-three, alone on the Ghaza Ja. Wells were seldom a hundred miles apart, so the pint-radius was more than we really needed.

Our six weeks' food would give us capacity for a thousand miles out and home, which would be, like the water-figure, more than ever we required. The endurance of our camels made it possible (for me, the camel-novice in the army, 'painful' would be the fitter word) for us to ride fifteen hundred miles in thirty days, without ever a fear of starvation however much we exceeded in time, since each of us sat on two hundred pounds of potential meat. If food lacked, we halted and ate our worst camel. Probably it would be poor eating, but fat camels were precious, since our power depended on the number we had. On the march they had to exist on grazing, and after each raid they would be worn thin, and be sent to pasture for some months' rest, while we called out a relay tribe, or found fresh animals.

The equipment of the raiding parties should aim at simplicity, with nevertheless a technical superiority over the Turks in the most critical department. I sent to Egypt demands for great quantities of light automatic guns, Hotchkiss or Lewis, to be used not as machine guns but as repeating rifles, snipers' tools. The men should be kept deliberately ignorant of their mechanism, so that the speed of action shouldn't be hampered by efforts at repair. We should fight battles of minutes, at eighteen miles an hour. If a gun jammed, the gunner should throw it aside and go on with his rifle. So we would not lavish ammunition: and this would deliver us from led camels. On the saddle could hang an automatic and a rifle and a hundred cartridges, supplies for at least two actions. We would sleep in our cloaks, with perhaps a blanket for luxury. All depended on our riding light.

Another special feature might be high explosive, a weapon of the attack. Nearly every man in the Revolt should be qualified by rule of thumb lessons in demolition work. Eventually we evolved special methods of our own for rapid destructions under fire, in the course of our months of practice: and before the end of the war were dealing with any quantity of track and bridges with effect, economy and safety. It was only guns we never got until the last month, and the pity of it in maneuver war, one long-range gun outweighed the value of ninety nine short.

The distribution of the raiding parties should be unorthodox. We could not mix or combine tribes, because of their dislikes and distrusts. Likewise we could not use the men of one, in the territory of another. In compensation we might aim at the widest dissipation of force, to have the most raids on hand at once: and might add fluidity to their speed by using one district on Monday, another on Tuesday, a third on Wednesday. So their natural mobility would be reinforced. It would give us priceless advantage in pursuit, since our ranks would refill with fresh men at each new tribe, and maintain always their pristine energy. In a real sense maximum disorder would be our equilibrium.

The internal economy of our raiding parties should be equally curious. We aimed at irregularity and maximum articulation. For one thing our circumstances would not be twice similar, so no formal system of units could ever fit them twice: and for another we would throw the enemy intelligence off the track. It was by the identical battalions and divisions, and by their numbers, that information built itself up: an army could be inferred on the evidence of prisoners from three companies. Our strengths should depend on a whim.

We were serving a common ideal, without tribal emulation; and so we could hope for no esprit de corps to reinforce our motives. Ordinary soldiers were made a caste either by great pay and rewards in dress and privilege, or as in England by being outcasts, low fellows cut off from life by contempt. We could not so knit man to man, for our tribesmen were in arms willingly, by conviction. Many armies had been enlisted voluntarily: few had served voluntarily through a long war in conditions as hard as ours. Any of the Arabs could go home without penalty whenever the conviction failed him: our only contract was honor.

Consequently we had no discipline in the sense in which it was restrictive, submerged of individuality, the lowest common denominator of men. In peace-armies it meant the limit of energy attainable by everybody on parade, the hunt not of an average but of an absolute, the hundred-per-cent standard in which the ninety nine were played down to the level of the weakest. The aim was to render the unit a unit, the man a type, that their effort might be calculable, and the collective output even, in grain and bulk. The deeper the discipline, the lower the individual's efficiency and the better the performance.

It was the difference between a job and a masterpiece, a deliberate sacrifice of capacity in order to reduce the uncertain element, the bionomic factor, in enlisted humanity, and its necessary accompaniment was compound or social war, that form in which the man in the fighting line had to be the product of the multiplied exertions of the long hierarchy, from workshop to supply unit, which maintained him in the field.

The Arab war should react against this. Our conditions laid it upon us to make our war simple and individual. Every enrolled man should serve in the line of battle, and be self-contained there. We must have no communication or labor troops. The efficiency of our forces must be the personal efficiency of each single man. It seemed to me that in our articulated war the sum yielded by single men would be at least equal to the pro duct of a compound army of the same strength: and the one system was possible to adjust to tribal life and manners, given elasticity and insight among the commanders: and the other impossible.

For these commanders we should rely mainly on the tribal chiefs. Arab townsmen, professionally trained in the Turkish Army, had the numerical attitude too ingrained in them to lead irregulars. They thought of their troops as so many, not as so-and-so and so-and-so. Few of them could mix smoothly and by name with Bedouin. In Englishmen we were more fortunate. Most young Englishmen had the roots of eccentricity in them, and so should get on well enough. Of course we must use very few of them in the field, not more perhaps than one per thousand of the Arab troops. More, however precious, would have caused irritation, just because they were foreign bodies: and those who did function would do so by influence and advice, by their superior knowledge: not by any accident of authority.

In practice we should not employ in the firing line the greater numbers which the adoption of a simple system put theoretically at our disposal. We had better use them in relay, for otherwise our attack (as contrasted with our threat) would become too extended. Each man in action must have liberal workroom: in irregular war, of two men together one was being wasted. Our ideal should be to make battle a series of single combats, our ranks an assembly of commanders-in-chief, the neglected tactics which let Napoleon beat the Mamelukes.

Our value would depend entirely on our single quality. The moral strain of isolated fighting made the Simple war very hard upon the soldier, exacting from him special initiative, endurance and enthusiasm. He must keep always cool, for the excitement of a blood lust would impair the science of a combatant, and our victory would depend on our just and expert use of speed, concealment and technical advantage. Irregular war was far more intellectual than a bayonet charge.

The illiteracy of our forces should do good rather than harm, since it would ensure our working always in these small numbers, explaining our plan verbally to every man: and it had trained their minds to a longer memory and a closer hearing of the news. Nor should our tactics be very subtle, since they had to be translated into independent action through the muddle-heads of our followers, and success would not follow unless a majority of them used their intelligence to forward our conception against the moral and material accidents of the path: but this dilution of tactical ability to the level of the lowest interpreter, though regrettable, should not be all loss, since the alternative was independent enterprise and we knew that even a mediocre design persisted in, was grander than the most brilliant expedient, and would prevail in the end.

These irregular tactics were means to carry our movement to its final moment, when by the last shot fired we would attain our climax, and the Turkish Army would pass suddenly out of activity. Our offensive, our advance, our development all lay in the use of tribes, and more tribes, and still more tribes: but we should remember that if we would keep what the tribes won for us it must be by following the maxim of the armed prophet. In other words Feisal's regular troops (jaafar's lumpy men) were our static side, the means of securing the fruits of tribal opportunity. They were no more than the subsidiary means: a bullet shot from the tribal gun: but they were yet unfit even for such a role: and it was clear that our first and greatest need at Akaba was to increase them and their efficiency.

The armored cars could not act this garrison-purpose. They were weapons of attack and pursuit. Upon special occasions we might strengthen the raids with them, for once their British drivers had learned to drive and knew the track, they could keep up with a camel party, and even pass them for a short space. Supply difficulties, however, made them cumbrous and shorter-ranged, so that we seldom used them beyond a hundred miles from home. They were magnificent fighting machines, decisive whenever their crews put them into action in favorable conditions; but not good to use with camel-parties in joint fighting. Each had the same tactical principle of fire in movement, but to yoke armored and unarmored cavalry together took the dash out of each. The cars saw the camel-men wincing from the sting of bullets: the camel-men lost heart seeing the privilege of the invulnerable cars.

Chapter 66: Distractions

While these notions were clearing slowly in my head, the bay filled with ships; Feisal landed, and with him Jaafar Pasha and his staff and Joyce, the fairy godmother. Then came the armored cars and Goslett and the Egyptian laborers, and thousands of troops. The things we needed were quickly set in train to our best ability. The Turks had made good use of their six weeks' peace. Falkenhayn had been down to advice them, and it had put new intelligence into their doings, and made them much worthier of our work. Maan had been made a special command and put under Behjet, the old G.O.C Sinai, from Beersheba. He had been given six thousand infantry and a regiment of cavalry and one of mounted infantry and had entrenched Maan till it was impregnable according to the standard of maneuver war. Great supply dumps had been collected and a flight of airplanes operated daily from Maan.

By now the Turkish preparations were nearly complete, and they began to move in satisfactory style, disclosing that their main objective was Guweira, the biggest and on the whole the best road by which to retake Akaba from Maan. They pushed out two thousand infantry to Aba el Lissan, and fortified it. Cavalry kept the outskirts clear, and depots there and at Waheida freed them of any danger of siege. Posts were set at Basta and at Hisha, over the railhead of the timber-cutting gangs , to contain a possible Arab counter-stroke from Wadi Musa against the flank of Aba el Lissan.

This nervousness they showed about Wadi Musa was our cue. We would play with them a little and reassume the initiative without expense, disturbing their orderly development. There was no fear about Akaba, or even Guweira, for we had moved a thousand of our Arab Regulars forward under Rashid Medfai, and were strong enough to deal with any snap attack: but it seemed inartistic to incur an unnecessary battle with its risk of accident since the Arab regulars were untried, and might be too crude for a big affair.

It would be more like ourselves to weaken them by distant distraction, that they might fritter away their Aba el Lissan striking force on petty defense: but perhaps best of all we might tempt them, as preliminary to their assault on Guweira, to go for us in Delagha or Wadi Musa with a view to turning us out of these threats to their flank and rear. Of the two, Wadi Musa was from our point of view the most desirable as their target, since its natural obstacles were so tremendous that the human factor might behave as badly as it liked and yet win a noble victory.

To bait the hook the men of Delagha were told to get busy. The Turks were full of spirit, and at once put in a counter-stroke from which they themselves suffered sharply. We were pleased and rubbed in the lesson to the peasantry of Wadi Musa, stressing the rich booty now enjoyed by their rivals of Delagha To encourage them Maulud the old war-horse went up with a strong detachment of his mule-mounted regiment and quartered himself among the famous ruins of Petra. The Liathena, under the dashing leadership of their one-eyed sheikh, Khalil, began to foray out across the plateau, and to snap up by twos and threes Turkish riding or transport animals, together with the rifles of their occasional guards. This went on for weeks while the irritated Turks grew hotter and hotter.

We could also prick the Turks into discomfort by air attack. We were to have machines of our own at Akaba when an aerodrome was cleared for them : but meanwhile the enemy machines were worrying the Howeitat, and so we found it necessary to ask General Salmond for his promised attempt at a longdistance raid on Maan from Kuntilla. The preliminaries for this had been arranged in July from Egypt, so that all he had to do was to order off the machines.

The rest of the trouble would fall upon the pilots, and as it was a very difficult job Salmond chose out Stent and some of our tried pilots of Rabegh and Wejh, from his men in Sinai, and told them to do their best. They had all had experience of forced landing on any kind of surface, and could pick out an unknown destination across unmapped hills instinctively: and Stent spoke Arabic well. Their machines were old B.E.2s and 12S, none too good: Kuntilla was a bad landing ground, and the flight would have to be air contained since there was no road thence to Egypt; but we had sent up a hundred bombs from Akaba, and some petrol and spares, under guard of a dozen Ageyl, so that little more than mechanics need be brought.

The three machines left the desert railway near Arish on August the twenty-seventh, and duly arrived at Kuntilla, and landed with success between the large holes on the aerodrome. They slept that night under their wings and at dawn loaded up with sixteen bombs (twenty-ponders) apiece, and set off eastward. One engine failed, but soon after the start, and just got back unhurt. The other two reached Maan, and dropped their thirty two bombs in and about the unprepared station. Two bombs fell into the barracks, and killed thirty-five men, and wounded fifty.

Eight others struck the engine shed, doing heavy damage to the plant and stock within. Another bomb in the general's kitchen finished his cook and his breakfast: four fell on the aerodrome, among the enemy machines.

Stent was a bundle of nerves, who to punish himself used to do outrageous things. On this occasion he flew too low, to make sure of his aim, and profited though the machines were badly starred by shrapnel and machine-gun fire while they wandered over the camp. However, the pilots and engines were unhurt, and returned safely to Kuntilla. That afternoon they patched all the machines, and after dark ceased work and slept again, under them.

In the following dawn they were off once more, the three this time and flew to Aba el Lissan, where the great camp seen the day before had made Stent's mouth water.

They bombed the horse lines and stampeded the animals, and then visited the tents and scattered the Turks in great confusion. As on the day before they flew low and were much hit, but not fatally. Long before noon they were back in Kuntilla. Stent looked over the remaining petrol and bombs, and decided that they were enough for one more effort: so he gave directions to everyone to look for the battery that had troubled them in the morning.

They started in the midday heat Kuntilla lay two thousand feet up, so this was possible: from Akaba on the hot sea-level they would never have got off the ground. Their loads were so heavy they could get no height, and therefore they came blundering just over the great crest behind Aba el Lissan, and down the valley at about three hundred feet. The Turks were always somnolent at noon, and were taken completely by surprise. Thirty bombs in all were dropped: one direct hit silenced the battery: the others killed dozens of the men and the scarcely-recovered animals. Then the machines were light again, and soared up and home to Kuntilla. Stent and his party packed their things, and returned to el Arish satisfied. The Arabs rejoiced: the Turks were seriously alarmed. Their men were set to digging shelters, and their own repaired machines were disposed about the plateau for camp defense.

We had perturbed the Turks at home by air attack: we were luring them towards a wrong objective by irrigative raids: our third resource to ruin their offensive disposition was to go for their railway, whose need would make them split up their striking force on defensive duties. Accordingly we arranged for demolition attacks on the old Wejh model to happen in mid September at many points.

Auda would supervise a big one on top of the plateau between Maan and Shedia. Other Howeitat would take up just below the plateau edge, near Ramleh. We called up the Beni Atiyeh and directed them to blow up rails south of Ramleh, next to the Howeitat. Others were to cut culverts near Tebuk. We even sent men south of Tebuk to find Mirzuk el Tikheimi, the intelligent youth who had proved himself before Wejh. He was still operating from Wejh, but we summoned him to march northward from Dizad, attacking posts and line and bridges, until he reached the Akaba area and needed to come in to refill. He had a considerable force of Ateiba with him, and if the Beni Atiyeh helped properly might do something important.

There remained to me the personal need to justify the new prominence and authority I had assumed in the Arab Movement, in accordance with my decision during the march to Akaba. To cut a figure and do nothing was to sink to the level of a Nesib el Bekri: to prove my fitness as a leader I must be active after the manner of a Bedouin champion; something dramatic was called for.

This was also desirable tactically. We must develop a new line if we were to keep the Turks guessing. My notion was to mine a train. This was an old idea attempted many times by means of automatic mines with varying success. Something more vigorous and certain was indicated, and I had imagined a direct firing by electricity of a charge under the locomotive. The British sappers encouraged me to try: especially General Wright, the chief engineer in Egypt, who took a sporting interest in my irregularities, and had given me the help of his great experience. He sent me the recommended tools: an exploder and some insulated cable.

With them I went on board H.M.S. Humber, the monitor that had succeeded the Euryalus as our guard-ship, and introduced myself to Captain Snagge in command. He was fortunate in his ship, which had been built for Brazil, and was much more comfortably furnished than British war-vessels: and we were very fortunate in him and in this, for he was the spirit of hospitality, and she gave him power to indulge himself. His inquiring nature took interest in the shore, and he saw the comic side of even our disasters, in a way which was the best comfort and example to ourselves.

To tell him the story of a failure was to laugh at it, and always for a good story he gave me the prize of a hot bath, and a tea with civilized trappings and without blown sand in it. His kindness and help to all the British in Akaba served us in lieu of visits to Egypt for repairs, and enabled us to hammer on against the Turks through month after month of disappointment.

The exploder turned out to be a formidable locked white box, very heavy. We split it open and found a ratchet handle, and pushed it down without blowing up the ship. Then we examined the wire, which was very heavy rubber-insulated cable. We cut it in halt: fastened the ends to two screw terminals on the box, and transmitted shocks to one another most convincingly. It worked.

I fetched a box of detonators, and we stuffed the free ends of the cable into one and pumped the handle: nothing followed. We tried again and again ineffectually, and grieved over it. At last Snagge rang his bell, and produced a gunner warrant officer who knew all about circuits. The machine needed special electric detonators. The ship carried six, and Snagge gave me three of them. We joined one up with our box and when the handle was crashed hard down it blew up beautifully. So I felt that I knew all about it and turned to arrange the details of the raid.

For place, the most promising and easiest-reached part seemed about Mudowwara, the great water station in the desert eighty miles south of Maan. A smashed train there would be an unwelcome nuisance to the enemy. For men I would rely on the Howeitat, whose courage was fully tried, and at the same time the expedition would test my new recruits, three Haurani peasants whom I had added to my personal followers, in view of the new importance of the Hauran in our scheme of things, and the need for us to learn its dialect and feelings, and the construction and jealousies of its clan-framework, and to be familiar with its names and roads. These three new fellows, Rahail and Assaf and Hemeid, would teach me imperceptibly about their home districts, as we rode to and from, on business, chatting.

To make sure of the arrested train I needed my own section of guns and machine-guns. For the first I decided on trench-mortars: for the second, Lewis guns. Accordingly Egypt selected me two forceful sergeant-instructors from the army school at Zeitun, to come to Akaba and teach squads of Arabs how to use such things. Snagge gave them quarters in his ship since we had no English camp on shore where they could live.

Their names may have been Yells and Brooke but everyone called them Lewis and Stokes after their jealously-loved tools. Lewis was an Australian long and thin and sinuous his active body curving in unmilitary fashion. His hard face arched eyebrows and predatory nose gave him the peculiarly Australian air of reckless willingness and capacity to do something very soon. Stokes was a stoutly built placid English yeoman workmanlike always silently watching for an order to obey.

Lewis was full of suggestion and bursting with delight at what had been well done whenever a thing happened. Stokes never offered an opinion up until after action when he would stir his cap up reflectively and take pains to recount the mistakes he would a second time avoid. They were both admirable men. Egypt had lent them for a month and in this short time, without language or interpreter they got on terms with their classes and taught them to use their guns with reasonable precision. More was not required: for an empirical habit would better agree with the spirit of our haphazard raids than complete scientific knowledge. Your specialist was so often a lop-sided thing.

As we worked away at the organization of the raid we discovered that Mudowwara was the boundary-line between the Howeitat and Beni Atiyeh: so we must have men from each tribe in our party. Three sheikhs of the Ageilat, the clan to which Mudowwara belonged happened to come in to Feisal then. He lent me two as guides and sponsors, and kept the third with him as our surety.

As we talked with them our appetites rose. Mudowwara station sounded weak and vulnerable. If we could raise three hundred men with our mortars and guns we might rush it suddenly. That would be an achievement for its deep well was the means by which the Turks kept working the dry section between Maan and Dhat el Haj. If we blew in the well they would have to add so many more water-wagons to their trains that the service across the gap would become unprofitable almost impossible for load-carrying.

Chapter 67: Attitudes

At such an ambitious moment came Lewis the Australian, and said that he and Stokes would like to be of my party. This was a new idea, and attractive. With their aid we would feel sure of our technical detachments, and might confidently attack a garrisoned place. Also the sergeants wanted to go so very much, and their good work in training deserved reward: and it would be interesting to see their reflection in the Arabs' talk, and hear their opinion of the Arabs. It was true that their loaned month was nearly up: but that was not a promised date, and anyway, even if Egypt remembered them so soon, it would have no means of recalling them from the interior. It seemed a move worth trying.

They were warned that their experience might not at the moment seem altogether joyful. There were no rules, and could be no mitigations of the marching, feeding, and fighting inland. If they went they would have to agree to give up their British Army comforts and privileges. They would share and share with the Arabs (except in booty!) and would have to be treated, even by me, exactly as the Arabs in matters of food and discipline. If anything went wrong with me they, not speaking Arabic, would be in a tender position. If they understood all this, and yet wanted to come along, they might.

Lewis replied that he was looking forward to just this very strangeness of life. Stokes supposed that if we did it he could. So they were fitted with clothes, and were lent two of my best camels, and stuffed their saddle-bags tight with bully-beef and biscuits, and off we went together on the seventh of September, riding up Wadi Itm, to collect our Howeitat from Auda in Guweira.

For the sergeants' sake, to harden them gently to camel-riding, things were made a little better than my word, and we marched very easily for today while we were our own masters. They had neither of them ever been on a camel before, and there was a little risk that the fearful heat of the naked granite walls of Itm might knock them out before the trip had properly begun. September was a bad month, and a few days before even in cool Akaba, in the shade of the palm-gardens of the beach, the thermometer had September Attitudes shown one hundred and twenty-three degrees. So we halted for midday under a cliff a few miles up the valley and in the evening rode another ten miles and camped for the night by a brushwood thicket at the watershed near Khaldi.

We were comfortable with cans of hot tea, and rice and meat, and it was covertly enjoyable to see the percussion of the unusual surroundings on the two men. Each reacted to the type expected. The Australian from the first seemed quite at home, and behaved freely towards my men and the Arabs: but when they fell into his spirit and returned his fellowship, he was astonished, almost resentful, since he had never imagined that they would be misled by his kindness to forget the difference between a white man and a brown.

It added humor to the situation that he was browner by far than my new followers. Of these Rahail interested me most. He was quite a lad, but a free-built sturdy fellow, too fleshy for the life we were to lead, but for that the more tolerant of pains. His face was high colored, his cheeks a little full, and low-pouched, almost pendant. The mouth was budded and small, and the chin very pointed. This with the high strong brows and the antimony-enlarged eyes gave him a mixed air of artifice and petulance, of weary patience self imposed, and even a little pride. He was blowsy-spoken (mouthing his Arabic, vulgar in dialect), forward and impudent in speech, always thrusting, flaunting, restless and nervous. His spirit was not as strong as his body, but mercurial. When exhausted or crossed he broke into miserable tears, chased away by any interference and leaving him then fit for more endurance. This recovery was so immediate that in the end he wore down our constant effort by his chain of fresh starts. The others Mohammed and Ahmed, my old followers and Rashid and Assaf, the two probationers, gave Rahail much license of behavior partly because of his animal attractiveness and of his tendency to advertise his person. Into this it was not wise to let myself enquire too closely: but he had to be checked sharply once or twice as regards the sergeants.

Stokes the Englishman felt the Arab strangeness keenly and was driven to become more himself, more insular. He behaved with perfect manners, but with a shy correctness which reminded them in every movement that he was unlike them and English. This careful consideration elicited a return of respect. To them he was 'the Sergeant' while Lewis was 'the long one'. The Australians, a race new, narrow, unreserved, hurt themselves by lack of measure both in their friendliness and in their correction.

These were matters of instinct, and all classes followed them in their degree. It was sometimes humiliating to find that wide reading and thinking, book-experience of all countries and ages of the world had yet left in us prejudices like those of washerwomen, and no such verbal ability as theirs in getting on terms with strangers. The English in the Middle East divided into two great sorts: one, a subtle insinuating type, studied and seized the characteristics of the people of the country about them. They adapted themselves to their speech, to their conventions of thought, very often almost to their manner. They directed the people in their own courses, gliding them almost without touch into the lines they would have. They held a frictionless habit of influence in which their own nature hid unnoticed.

The other type was the John Bull of the book, who became the more rampantly English the longer and further he was away from England. In the end he invented an Old Country for himself, a home of all remembered virtues so splendid in the distance that when at length he did return he found the reality a sad falling off and often withdrew his muddle-headed self into a fractious advocate of the good old times. Abroad he was a rounded sample of our traits, a deep influence on his surroundings, through his armored certainty. He showed them how individual the complete Englishman could be, and while there was friction in his track, and his direction was less smooth than that of the intellectual type, yet it looked as though his example, being cleaner-cut, was more conspicuous and his effect wider.

Both sorts agreed in the direction of this example, one by assent, the other by implication. Each in his way assumed the Englishman a chosen being inimitable. They felt the copying him a kind of blasphemy, or at least an impertinence to be put down with the contemptuous name of fraud. In this conceit they urged on their people the next best thing. God had not given it to them to be English; therefore their duty remained to be as good of their own type as possible. Consequently we admired native dress studied their language, wrote books about their architecture, their folklore, their dying industries.

One day we woke up to find this chthonic spirit turned political and always shook our heads with sorrow over their ungrateful nationalism — though it was the fine flower towards whose blooming our innocent efforts had all turned. Such things were inevitable anyhow with a sheepish humanity as education in the outside world widened imitatively down from class to class: and if we had not the fortune often to find a Durham to help us down constitutional staircases we at least as seldom fell with a North. The French seemed oddly unlike ourselves: for though they started with a similar doctrine that the Frenchman was the perfection of mankind (not merely acting so, but saying it) they went on contrarily to encourage their foreign subjects to imitate them as near as might be for even if they could never attain the level of the true article yet their virtue would be greater as they resembled the prototype. We found imitation a parody: they read it as a compliment.

On the next day in the early heat we were near Guweira, riding comfortably along the sanded plain of restful pink with its grey green undergrowth when all at once there came a droning through the air. Quickly we drove the camels off the open road into the bush-speckled ground where their irregular coloring would not be marked by the enemy airmen; for our loads of blasting gelatin my favorite and most powerful explosive and the many ammonal filled shells of the Stokes gun would be ill neighbors in a bombing raid. So we waited there sitting soberly in the saddle while our camels grazed the little that was worth eating in the scrub till the airplane had circled it's twice about the rock of Guweira in front of us and planted three loud bombs.

Then we collected our little caravan again on the path and paced on gently into the camp now flooding with life as the Arabs issued from their refuges in the long undercut ledges of the red island of sandstone which gave Guweira its name. As we rode up we met Sherif Mastur, the Emir in charge and old Auda walking quietly back to their unhurt tents. They welcomed us with full hospitality: but the sergeants, more for the Arabs' sake than for their own were excused the full ordeal of polite eating with the fingers. Instead they passed their time watching over the piles of explosives and ate their bully-beef in peace and alone except for the buzzing myriads of flies which swarmed in the available air for a belt of a solid mile about the place.

Guweira was very thronged with life, for all the Howeitat of the hills and the highlands were attracted to its new booth-fair and shops, and to the coffee-hearths of their greatest men under the cliff. As far as the eye reached, the plain was softly moving with their herded camels, and their multitude drained the near water-holes each morning even before dawn so that the late risers had to travel many miles to drink.

This was little matter, for the Arabs had nothing to do all morning but wait for the daily airplane, and afterwards had nothing but talk to fill their time till it was dark enough for sleep.

The talk and the leisure were too plentiful, and revived the old jealousies which had been stilled for the taking of Akaba. Auda was ambitious to take advantage of our commitments to him, and of our reliance on his help to assort the tribes. He drew the bulk wages for the Howeitat, and by paying or withholding the money sought to compel the smaller free-sections to his leadership. They resented it and clan after clan of these independent folk had revolted against him, threatening either to retire into their hills or to reopen touch with the Turks. There were thousands of Howeitat in hundreds of sections, the most uncompromising, hard-headed, greedy land-lawyers. To hold them content without angering Auda was a task delicate enough for the most fastidious mind, for the pride of war-wages had made among them almost as many sheikhs as followers, and combined action — or indeed any action at all — became less probable even than usual. Also it was one hundred and twenty degrees in the shade, and the shade was a surge of flies.

The three southern subsections on which we had been counting for our raid were among the dissidents, and they were more interested in politics than in going off to the railway in doubtful search of hard blows. Mastur spoke to them, and the chiefs of the Abu Tayi spoke, and we all spoke to them, without effect. It seemed as though our plans were about to break down at the start.

One day, going along before noon under the rock. Mastur met me and said that they were mounting to desert our camp and movement. Full of vexation I swung round and burst into Auda's tent. He was sitting on its sand floor feeding on boiled bread with his latest wife, a jolly, good humored girl whose brown skin was all stained blue by the indigo dye from her new smock. When I appeared suddenly, the little woman whisked out through the back-flap like a rabbit. I laid aside my purpose in order to gain ground with Auda, and began to jeer at the old man, provokingly, for being so old and yet so foolish like the rest of his race, who regarded our comic reproductive processes not as merely an unhygienic pleasure, but as a main business of life.

He retorted with his desire for children, and I asked him if he had found life good enough to thank his parents for bringing him into it or wantonly to confer the doubtful gift upon an unborn spirit?... but he maintained himself. 'Indeed, I am Auda,' said he firmly 'and you know Auda. My father (God be merciful to him) was master, and greater than Auda, and he would praise my grandfather. So indeed the world gets greater as we go back.'

'But Auda, we say honor our sons and our daughters, for they are heirs of our accumulated worth, fulfillers of our broken wisdom, since with each generation the earth is older, mankind more removed from its childhood...: But the old thing, not today to be teased, looked back at me through his narrowed eyes with a benign humor, and pointed to Abu Tayi, his son, out on the plain before us trying a new camel, banging it on the neck pettishly with his stick in a vain effort to make it put its head down and pace like a thoroughbred. 'O world's imp: said he, using his common name for me, 'if God please he has inherited my worth, but thank God not yet my strength and if I find fault with him, I will redden up his tail. No doubt you are very wise: I did not tell Auda that the earliest man of property, when archaeology first found him, displayed in his use of materials as much acuteness of brain as had we, the latest fruits.

However, the upshot of the talk was that he was powerless to give effect to his goodwill to help me, and I told him that I would go off to a clean spot, to see if I could do anything by my independent self We hired twenty camels to carry the explosives, and the morrow, two hours after the airplane, was appointed as the hour for our start southward to Rum, a rumored camp of Arabs six hours away from us.

The airplane was the quaint regulator of time in the Guweira camp, and public business built itself about its come and go. The Arabs, up as ever before dawn, waited for it: and Mastur would set a slave on the crag's peak to look or listen for the first warning. When its constant hour drew near, he and the other Arabs would leave their standing tents, and saunter in chatting groups with a great parade of carelessness towards the rock. Arrived beneath it, each man climbed to the ledge he favored. After Mastur would climb the bevy of his slaves, with his coffee on the brazier, and his carpet. This would be set out in a shaded nook, and there he and Auda would sit and talk till the little shiver of excitement tightened up and down the crowded ledges when first was heard the song of the engine over the pass of Shtar.

Then everyone pressed back against the rock wall and waited stilly while the enemy machine overhead circled vainly about the strange spectacle of this crimson rock banded with thousands of gaily-dressed Arabs sitting in nests like eagles within every cranny of its face. The airplane dropped three bombs or four bombs or five bombs according to the day of the week. Their bursts of dense yellow smoke sat on the sage-green plain compactly like cream-puffs, writhing in the windless air for many minutes till they slowly spread and faded. Though we knew there was no menace in it, yet we could not but catch our breath when the engine was loud over us, and the sharp-growing cry of the falling bombs hurt our ears.

Chapter 68: Rum

Even though empty-handed, we were glad to leave the noise and heart-burnings of Guweira, and vigorously we chased the flies from one another's backs, to be comparatively alone upon the march. As soon as we reached shade we halted: indeed there was no need of haste, and the two unfortunate fellows with me were tasting of such heat as they had never known, for the day was stifling, and the air was like a glowing metal mask pushed over our faces. It was admirable to see the sergeants struggle not to complain, that they might keep the spirit of their Akaba undertaking to endure what came upon them as firmly as the Arabs: but by this silence they went far past their bond, and it was their ignorance of Arabic which made them so superfluously brave. The Arabs themselves were loud against the tyrannous sun and the breathlessness: but the test-effort was wholesome, and for effect I played about, seeming to enjoy myself

In the late afternoon we marched a little further, and stopped the night under a thick screen of tamarisk trees. The camp was very beautiful, for behind us was a cliff perhaps four hundred feet in height, a deep red in the level sunset. Under our feet was spread a floor of buff colored mud, as hard and muffled as wood-paving, flat like a lake for half a mile each way: and on a low ridge to one side of it stood the grove of tamarisk, stems of brown wood, edged with a sparse and dusty fringe of green, which had been faded by the drought and sunshine till it was nearly of the silver grayness under the olive leaves about Les Baux, when a puff of wind from the river-mouth had rustled up the valley-grass and made all its trees turn pale.

We were riding for Rum, the northern water of the Beni Atiyeh, and a place which stirred my thought since even the unsentimental Howeitat had told me it was lovely. The morrow would be new with our entry to it: but very early while the stars were yet bright I was woke up by Aid, the humble Harithi Sherif accompanying us from Guweira. He had crept to me, and said in a chilled voice, 'Lord I am gone blind.' I made him lie down, and felt that he shivered as if cold: but all that he could tell me was that in the night, waking up, there had been no sight, but only pain in his eyes. No doubt the sun-blink had burned them out.

This had roused us, and it was yet early as we rode across the mud-flat between two great pikes of sandstone to the foot of a long, soft slope, poured down from the domed hills in front of us. It was tamarisk-covered; the beginning of the valley of Rum, they said. We looked up and saw on the left a long wall of rock, a sheer face one thousand feet high, swinging in like a great wave towards the middle of the valley, whose other side, to the right, was an opposing line of steep broken red hills. We rode forward up the slope, sometimes crashing a way through the brittle undergrowth.

As we went, the brushwood grouped itself into thickets whose massed leaves took on a stronger tint of green, the purer for their contrasted setting in plots of open sand of a delicate pink, very clear and cheerful. The ascent became gentle till at last the valley was no more than a confined tilted plain. The hills on the right grew taller and sharper, and ranged into a fair counterpart of the immense wall on the other side, which had now straightened itself to one massive rampart of redness. The walls drew together till only two miles apart: and then , towering gradually till their parallel parapets must have been nearly two thousand feet above us, ran forward in an avenue for miles.

They were not unbroken walls of rock, but were built up in sections in crags like giant buildings, along the two sides of the street. Deep side-alleys, fifty or sixty feet across, divided the crags whose planes were smoothed and rounded by the weather into huge apses and bays and enriched with much surface fretting and fracture, like design. Caverns high up on the precipice were round like windows; others near the foot gaped like doors, and dark stains ran down their faces for hundreds of feet like accidents of use. The cliffs were striated vertically, in the granular layers of their rock; and their main order stood on a plinth of a level broken stratum of stone deeper in color and harder in texture, which did not, like the sandstone hang in folds like cloth but chipped itself to lose courses of screed like the horizontal footings of a wall.

The crags were capped in many nests of domes, less hotly red than the body of the hill, rather grey and shallow. They gave the last semblance of Byzantine architecture to this irresistible place, this processional way greater than any imagination. Our whole armies would have been lost in the length and breadth of it and within these walls a squadron of airplanes could have wheeled in formation. Our little caravan grew ashamed, and we fell dead quiet and slipped secretly between the tamarisk bushes afraid either of attracting the notice of others, or of flaunting our own smallness in the presence of the hills.

The silence and bigness of the valley was like a childish dream, and we looked backward through our minds for its prototype, wondering if or when it had been that we had walked with all the men of earth up between these walls towards that open square in front where the road seemed to end; and this, with the inimitable medicine of learning the slender achievement of our hands, made each visit to Rum memorable. Later on, when we were going often to and from the railway, my mind, always ready to go hostage for the enchantment of things, used to turn me aside from the direct road, and clear my senses by a night in Rum, and by the ride down its valley in the dawn towards the shining plains, or up its valley in the sunset towards that glowing square which my timid anticipation never let me reach.

Today we rode up it for hours, while its perspectives grew greater and more magnificent in their ordered design, till in the afternoon we came to a gap in the cliff-face on our right, and through this we turned into a new wonder. The gap was perhaps three hundred yards across, a crevice in such a wall, and led us to an amphitheatre, oval in shape, shallow in front and long-lobed right and left. The walls of it were precipices like all the walls of Rum, but to the eye greater almost than any, for it lay in the very heart of a ruling hill, and its smallness made the height seem overpowering.

The sun had sunk behind the western wall, leaving all the pit in shadow, but when we looked back its setting glare had stained to a startling red the wings each side of the entry: which framed between them the fiery bulk of the further wall across the great valley. The pit-floor was of smooth damp sand, and it was thickly wooded with dark shrubs, while about the feet of all the cliffs lay immense boulders greater than houses, indeed sometimes like fortresses which had crashed down from the sheer heights above. In front of us a path, pale with use, zigzagged up the plinth of the wall, to the point from which the main face rose, and there it turned precariously southward along a shallow ledge outlined by occasional leafy trees. From between these trees, in hidden crannies of the rock, came strange cries, the echoes, turned into music, of the voices of the Arabs watering their camels at the springs which flowed out here, three hundred feet above the ground.

The rains, falling on the grey domes of the mountain top, seemed to have been caught in its hollows, and to have soaked slowly into the porous rock, and my mind followed them for slow centuries, filtering downward through those hundreds of feet of sandstone till they came against the impervious horizontal layer of the plinth and ran along the top of it under pressure in jets which burst out on the cliff-face at the junction of the two layers. They afforded the strangest and the most beautiful watering-places but were difficult because of the rocky nature of the path and of the danger of the slope beneath.

We turned into the left-hand lobe of the amphitheatre. At its far end Arab ingenuity had formed a clear camping place out of a tiny platform under an overhanging rock: and there we unloaded our animals and settled down. The dark came upon us quickly in this high and imprisoned place and we felt the damp and the mist of the water-laden air cold against our sunburned skin. The Howeitat explosive-carriers collected their drove and led them with echo testing shouts up the hill path to water in the night for their early return to Guweira. We lit fires and cooked rice to add to the sergeants' bully-beef, while my coffee-men prepared for the visitors who would come to us.

The Arabs in the villages of tents outside the hollow of the springs had seen us enter and were not slow to learn our news. In an hour we had the head-men of the Darausha, Zelebani, Zuweida and Togatga clans about us and there rose great talk, none too happy. Aid the Sherif

was so cast down in heart at the blindness which had come upon him that he was incapable of lifting the burden of entertainment from my shoulders and a work of such special requirements for each occasion was not to be well done by me alone. The men were all angry with the Abu Tayi, and suspected us of abetting Auda in his ambitions. They were unwilling to serve the Sherif in any way till assured of their liberty and a favorable settlement of their past claims.

Gasim Abu Dumeik, the fine horseman who had led the Dhumaniyeh on the day of Aba el Lissan, was particularly vicious. He was a dark man with a proud petulant face and a thin-lipped smile good enough usually at heart but crusted, however today he flamed with inner jealousy of the Toweiha. Alone I could never win him for he suspected foreigners so to make patent his hostility I took him as adversary and fought him so fiercely with my tongue that he was silenced and in shame his relatives deserted him and rallied ever so little to my side. I made clear how much stronger their voice with Feisal would be if they went to him after the service of my successful raid against the line.

Some saw the truth of this, and their flickering judgments began to murmur at their chiefs, to advocate marching off with me. I took the chance to say that Zaal would be here in the morning from Guweira with his followers of the Abu Tayi as nucleus of the expedition, and that he and I would accept the help of them all, except the Dhumaniyeh, who had been made impossible by Gasim's words. They would be erased from Feisal's book of service, and would forfeit all their earned good will and due rewards. Gasim withdrew from the fireside in great anger, saying he would join the Turks at once.

Chapter 69: Repairs

Next morning there he was, with all his men, ready to oppose our move or to join us, as the whim went. While he hesitated, Zaal arrived, and the pair had high words. Fortunately we got between them before a fight could start, but enough passed to overthrow the weak arrangement of the night, The other clans were disgusted at this fierceness of the Dhumaniyeh, and in secret were alarmed at their proposed return to the Turkish side. In twos and threes they came to me quietly, as volunteers, but begged me to make it right with Feisal before we started, that they might be known as loyal.

Their doubts determined me to communicate at once with Akaba, partly that this trouble might be composed, and partly to raise a baggage train from the army camels to carry the explosives to the line. It would not be fitting to hire Dhumaniyeh camels, in the circumstances; and there were no others here. We tried to find a messenger to Feisal, but failed, as they said that Gasim would not let him through. The best way was to go myself, since no one would dare to hinder me. Accordingly the two sergeants were commended to Zaal, who swore to watch them day and night and to answer for their lives himself, with his twenty-five picked braves of the Abu Tayi: and off Ahmed and I rode for Akaba, on stripped camels, meaning to hurry.

We knew only the way by Guweira and Wadi Itm, and it was very long. We had heard that a short-cut existed out westward from Wadi Rum, but could find no guide to show it us. At first we tried vainly up and down the valley for it, and were giving up in despair when we chanced on a little camel-boy who blurted out that we should go along the next valley to our right by it, after a ride of only an hour, we were on a watershed from which valleys trended away westward. They could lead only into Itm and Akaba, for there was no other drainage through the hills: and we raced down them, ever and again cutting at a venture across ridges of hills on our right into parallel tributaries, to shorten the assumed line.

In the beginning it was clean sandstone country, with pleasant rock-shapes all about: but as we went we were glad to see spines of granite, the material of the shore, in front of us, and after thirty miles of favorable surface, on a gradient good for trotting down, we passed by a very winding valley, the southern Itm, into the main pass above the well where the Turks had made their last stand in July. The journey took us only six hours.

In Akaba we rode straight to Feisal's house, and found him just ready to eat. My sudden return scared him with the fear of a disaster, but a word explained the little drama being played at Rum, and after we had fed we took the necessary steps. The twenty camels should start up in two days. Meanwhile to salve the troubles he would lend me Sherif Abdulla el Feir, his best man present, the same who had ridden in Dakhil-Allah's party to Madahrij from Wadi Ais six months before. We also arranged that the families of the men who rode with me to the railway should draw provisions from his stores on my certificate, as soon as the raiding force had actually set out.

Abdulla and I went off before dawn, and in the afternoon after a friendly ride reached Rum and found all safe: so an anxiety was lifted. It was a risk to leave the sergeants there alone in the mutiny, but there had been no good alternative, since their riding with me would have made the trip so slow that the Arabs might have scattered before our return with Feisal's news. However, as it was, Sherif Abdulla at once got to work and, collecting the Arabs including the recalcitrant Gasim about him, began to smooth over their grieves with that ready persuasiveness which all Arab leaders naturally possess.

In his two days' idleness Lewis had explored the cliff, and reported the springs very good for washing in: so I went off up the hill to get rid of some of my dust and strain from the long rides. The quick path from our camp was not by the way of the camels, but straight up the gully into the face of the hill, using the help of the ruined wall formerly carrying the open stone conduit in which a spout of water had run down the ledges to a Nabatean well-house on the valley floor. It was a climb of fifteen minutes to a tired person, and not difficult. At the top, el Shellala, the waterfall, as the Arabs named it, was only a few yards away.

Its rushing noise came from my left, by a jutting bastion of cliff over whose face trailed long runners of green leaves. The path skirted it in an undercut ledge, and on the bluff above was deep cut Nabatean inscriptions, and a sunken panel incised with a monogram or symbol. Around and about were many Arab cuttings including tribe-marks, some, no doubt, unknown witnesses of old forgotten migrations; but for the moment all my attention was for the splashing of the water in its crevice under the shadow of the overhanging rock.

From this rock a silver runlet of water issued out into the sunlight. I stepped across and looked in to see a spout of dark-red water, a little thinner than my wrist, jetting out firmly from a fissure in the roof, and falling with that clean sound into a shallow frothing pool, dammed up behind the step that served as entrance to the spring. The walls and roof of the crevice dripped with moisture, and were hung with thick ferns and grasses of the finest green. It was a paradise of five feet square, just big enough for me, and had waited all the years to give me pleasure.

At once I threw aside the clothes which had been clinging about my soiled body and stepped into the little pool under the spouting water, to taste at last a freshness of moving air and water against my tired skin. It was deliciously cool, the first great comfort for weeks. I lay there quietly for a long time, letting the clear dark water run over me in a rabble stream: and then began to rub the travel dirt away. While I was so busy, a grey-bearded ragged man with a hewn face of great power and weariness came slowly along the path till he was opposite the spring, and there he let himself down with a sigh on to my clothes spread on a rock beside the path.

He heard me and leaned forward, peering with his red eyes into the hollow, to see what was this white thing splashing in the pool. After a long stare he seemed content, and closed his eyes, groaning, 'The love is from God, and of God, and towards God.' This stopped me suddenly. I had believed Semites unable to use love as a sign of the link between themselves and God, indeed unable to conceive of such a relation except with the intellectuality of Spinoza, who had loved so rationally and sexless and transcendently that he had not sought, indeed had not permitted, a return. It had been

Christianity which first let love into the upper world from which the desert and the Semite, from Moses to Zeno, had shut it out: and Christianity was a hybrid, except in its first root not essentially Semitic, largely as it had persisted among the descendants of its founders in Syria.

Its birth in Galilee had saved it from being just one more of their innumerable revelations. Galilee in Syria was the one non-Semitic province, contact with which was almost uncleanness for a perfect Jew. Like Whitechapel to London, it lay alien to Jerusalem, doing and thinking no good for the adopted land. Christ by choice passed his ministry in its intellectual freedom , not among the simple mud huts of a Syrian village, but in polished streets, among for a and pillared houses and rococo baths, products of an intense if very exotic and provincial and corrupted Greek civilization.

The people of this strange colony were not Greek — at least in the majority — but Levantines of sorts, aping a Greek culture to their best ability, and in a strange revenge producing, not the correct and banal Hellenism of the exhausted homeland, but a fierce tropical rankness of idea, in which the rhythmical balance of Greek art and Greek ideal eroticism blossomed into strange flowers with something of the tawdry and passionate colors of the East. In the Gadarene poets a mirror was held up to the sensuality and disillusioned fatalism, passing into disordered lust, of their age and place, and perhaps from this earthiness the ascetic Semite religiosity caught that gleam of humanity and real love which made the distinction of Christ's music, and fitted it to sweep across Europe in a fashion of which Judaism and Islam were incapable.

And then Christianity had had the fortune of later architects of genius, and in its passage from time to clime had suffered sea-changes incomparably greater than Islam or the unchanging Jewry, out of the colored language of Alexandrian bookishness into the Latin character for the mainland of Europe: and, last and most terrible passing of all, when it became Scandinavian with a metaphysical synthesis to suit our chilly disputatious north. So remote was the Presbyterian from the Orthodox faith of its first or second appearance that we used to send missionaries to persuade these softer and warmer Oriental Christians to our presentation of a logical God.

Islam too had changed in moving from continent to continent. It had avoided metaphysics except in the introspective mysticism of Iranian devotees: but in Africa it had taken on colors of fetishism (so to express in a loose word the varied animalisms of the Dark Continent) and in India it had had to stoop to the legality and literal representation of the Hindu mind. Islam, six hundred years younger than Christianity, still had life to draw apart into alienated provinces, but yet wanted the terrible outbursts of internecine fury which flowed of a jangle of modernism and tradition.

In Arabia, however it had kept its Semitic character or rather the Semitic character had endured through the phase of Islam expressing the monotheism of open spaces, the passed through infinity of pantheism and its everyday usefulness of a household God. So that my aid man became portentous and seemed to overturn all my theories of their Arab nature. In fear I leaped out of my bath after a moment's thought and advanced to recover myself in my clothes.

He closed his eyes with his hands and groaned heavily. It was with pain that I persuaded him to let me dress and to lead him tenderly along the crazy path, and down the steep windings that the camels had made when they daily climbed to water. He sat down by our coffee-place, and Mohammed blew up the fire and prepared him drink while I sought to make him utter doctrine.

When the evening meal was ready we fed him, but his sounds were only groans or broken words. Finally, late at night, he rose painfully and slowly to his feet and tottered off deafly into the night, taking his beliefs, if he had any, with him. The Howeitat told me he wandered always among them muttering strange things, not knowing day or night, not troubling himself for food or work or shelter. He was given bounty of them all, as an afflicted man: but never replied a word or talked aloud, except when by himself, or with animals.

Chapter 70: A Fresh Start

Abdulla made steady progress with his settlement, Gasim was no longer defiant, but sulky, and would not leave his tent or give public counsel how his followers should act: so about a hundred men of the smaller clans dared to defy the Dhumaniyeh, and sent for their camels to ride with us. We talked it over with Zaal, and decided to call such a number enough. With them we would start for the railway and try our fortune to the utmost of this power. By longer delay we risked some of the adherents whom we now had, with little hope of getting others anywhere, in the present temper of the tribes.

It was a tiny party, only a third of what had been hoped, and probably our weakness would modify our plans regrettably: also we lacked an assured leader. Zaal, as ever, showed himself capable of being chief Thinking in advance, most active in all concrete preparations, he was a man of great mettle, but too close to Auda to suit the book of the rest, and his sharp tongue and the sneer hovering on his blue wet lips fanned their distrust and made them reluctant to obey even his good advice.

On the next day the baggage camels came from Feisal, twenty of them in charge of ten freedmen, and guarded by four of his body-slaves. These last were the most trustworthy attendants in the army, with a quite particular reading of the duties of personal service. They would have died to save their master hurt, or have died with him if he were hurt, and we had thought it wise to attach two to each of the sergeants so that, whatever happened to me, their safe return to the coast would be assured to our best ability. We sorted out the loads needed for the reduced raid which still lay within our scope, and arranged to start early on the morrow.

Accordingly at dawn on the sixteenth of September we rode out from Rum. Aid the blind Sherif insisted on coming with me despite his lost sight, saying that he could ride, if he could not shoot, and if God was good to us he would, in the flush of the success, take leave from Feisal and go home, not too sorry, to the blank life which would be left. Zaal led his twenty-five Nowasera, the sub-section of Auda's Arabs who called themselves my men, and were famous the desert over for the excellence of their two stocks of riding camels. My hard riding appealed to them, and tempted them to my company. Old Motlog el Awar, the owner of el Jedhah, the finest she camel in north Arabia, rode her in our van. We all looked at her with proud or greedy eyes as the case was.

My Ghazal a was taller and more grand, with a faster trot, but too old to be galloped far. However, she was the only other animal in the party, or indeed in the desert, to be matched with the Jedhah in her class, and my honor was increased by her dignity. Stokes rode her a great part of the day, as the Manchester-made saddles (of the British Camel Corps) which the sergeants had chosen to ride had galled them both, and the Englishman, less surface-hard than the Australian, felt the new life heavy upon him. The two sheikhs of the Beni Atiyeh rode with my men, and the rest of our party strayed like a broken necklace.

There were small groups of the Zuweida, the Darausha, the Togatga, and the Zelebani clans: and it was on this ride that first the virtue of Hammad el Tagtagi was brought to my mind. Half an hour after we started, there rode out from a side-valley and joined us some shamefaced men of the Dhumaniyeh, unable to endure the sight of others riding off in pursuit of merit while they idled with the women. No one group would ride or speak with another: and I passed back and forth all day like a shuttle, talking first to one lowering sheikh and then to another, striving to draw them together by stages of the less ungrateful, so that before a cry to action came there might be at least a show of solidarity. As yet they agreed only in not hearing any word from Zaal as to the direction and purpose of our march, though he was admitted the most intelligent warrior of us all, and the most experienced. For my private part he was the only one to be trusted further than eye-sight: the others for the least cause would have deserted. Neither their words nor their counsels nor their rifles were sure.

Poor Sherif Aid's uselessness even as nominal leader forced me to assume the direction myself, against both principle and judgment, as the special arts to lead a tribal raid, and the details of food halts and pasturage, road-direction, pay, disputes, division of spoil, feuds and march order, were unknown to me and much outside my training. The attempt to vamp these matters kept me too occupied to see the fresh country we were passing through, and prevented my worrying out in my slow way how we must modify to suit this little force our plans for assaulting Mudowwara, and what were the best uses of our explosive in a surprise attack.

We put our midday halt in a fertile place, where the late-spring rain, falling on a sandy talus had brought up a thick tufting of silvery grass which our camels loved. The weather was mild and perfect as an August in England, and we lingered in great content, set free at last from the bickering appetites of Rum, and from that slight rending of nerve inevitable when leaving even a temporary settlement. Man in our circumstance took root so soon. Late in the day we rode again, tending downhill in a narrow valley between sandstone heights: till before sunset we were out on Wadi Dumna, another strange flat of laid yellow mud like that which had been to us so wonderful a prelude of Rum's glory. By its edge we camped for the night.

My care all day had borne fruit, and our camp settled in only three parties, round three bright fires of crackling flaring tamarisk. At one supped myself and my men: at the second Zaal and the Nowasera : at the third all the other Howeitat together: and late at night, when we had well adjusted ourselves with gazelle meat and hot bread, it became possible to bring the chiefs of the other two groups together at my neutral fire, and by it to discuss sensibly our course for the morrow.

It seemed that about sunset we should water at Mudowwara well which lay two or three miles this side of the railway station, in a covered valley. Then in the early night we might go forward to examine the station closely and see if in our weakness we might yet attempt some stroke against it. I held strongly to this still, against the common taste, for it was by so much the most critical point on the line for the Turks that our effort there would outweigh many times those on other points. The Arabs did not see it, but their minds did not hold a picture of the entire long Turkish front with its necessitous demands. However, we had reached harmony for the moment, and scattered to sleep more confidently.

In the morning we delayed to eat again having only six hours of march before us and then pushed out across the mud-flat , being so fortunate at one point of our road as to find barley straw in heaps the remains of a snatched crop of com here by the Beni Atiyeh in the summer. Our camels filled themselves on it ravenously and later we went on over a plain of firm limestone rag carpeted with a single layer of brown weather-blunted flint this we crossed, to low hills of limestone and flint with occasional soft beds of sand under their steeper slopes where the eddying winds had dropped their dust. Through these we rode up shallow valleys to a crest and then by like valleys down the far side till we issued abruptly from the dark tossed stone-heaps into the wideness of a sun-steeped plain across which an occasional low and drifting dune flung a doubtful line.

The Beni Atiyeh sheikhs now guiding us over their own district changed direction and led us to the left skirting the foot of the ridges along a hard strip of ground between them and the glaring plain. We had made our noon-halt at the first entering of the broken country and rightly in the late afternoon came to the well we wanted. It was an open pool a few yards square in a hollow of a valley of large stone slabs and flint and sand. The stagnant water looked uninviting, for over its face was a thick mantle of green slime, from which swelled curious bladder-like islands of floating fatty stuff.

The Arabs explained that the Turks had thrown dead camels into the pool to make the water foul but that months had passed and the effect was now grown faint. It might have been fainter for my taste but it was all the drink we would get in the neighborhood unless we took Mudowwara station so we set and filled our water skins at once. One of the Howeitat while doing this slipped off the wet ledge into the pool. The green carpet closed homily over his head and hid him for an instant: but then he gasped up vigorously and scrambled out amid our laughter leaving behind him a black hole in the water from which a stench of old meat rose up almost like a pillar, visible, and hung about us and him and the valley disconcertingly.

At dusk Zaal and I with the sergeants and some of the other leaders crept forward quietly over the mounds that separated us from the sight of the railway. In half an hour we were at the head of the last, in a place where the Turks had dug trenches and built up with stones, an elaborate outpost of engrailed sangars: but on this black night of the new moon while we had chosen for our raid they were empty and desolate.

In front and below us lay the station, with its doors and windows sharply marked by the yellow cooking-fires and lights of the garrison. It seemed about five hundred yards away, and completely under our observation, but the Stokes gun would carry only three hundred yards, so that we needed a nearer place of equal advantage. Accordingly we went on slowly, hearing the noises of the enemy, and afraid that their barking dogs would uncover us. Sergeant Stokes made a cast out to left and right but found no gun-position in which he would be at once safe from the enemy fire, and furnished with a reasonable retreat into the hills behind if the thing miscarried.

Meanwhile Zaal and I crawled across the last flat to the station, till we could count even the unlighted tents and hear the men talking. One of them came out a few steps in our direction, and hesitated. Then he struck a match to light a cigarette, and the bold light flooded his face, so that we saw him plainly, a young, hollow faced sickly officer. He stood there busy for a moment, and returned.

We moved back to our hill and consulted in whispers. The station was very long, of stone buildings so solid that they might be proof against our time-fused shell. The garrison seemed about two hundred. They had no trenches, and were scattered. On the other hand we were only one hundred and sixteen rifles, and not a happy family. Had we been united we could have dared a rush and taken the place with a few casualties: but, as it was, each man would have feared lest the others abandon him suddenly, or even shoot into him from the back, for no Arabs were so rancorous as these Howeitat in their internal feuds.

Therefore, we would have to lay formal siege, and shell the garrison out: and there was no fitting spot where the guns would be safe if the enemy made a rush. Nor was it sure that the Arabs would face a rush solidly. So in the end I voted that we leave it alone, unalarmed, for a future occasion. Everyone agreed with relief: but it was a sad decision for the place was practically in our power, and its capture would cripple the railway for very long.

However, our first tactical principle was safety-play, and as the station would obviously always be easy to attack by night I resolved to reserve it till we could return with guns and enough margins of men to attempt it without risk. This might be at an early date, but actually one accident after another saved Mudowwara, month by month, so that it was not till August 1918 that it at last met the fate so long overdue, when Buxton with his Imperial Camel Corps surprised it in the dawn.

Chapter 71: An Ambush

We returned quietly to our camels, and slept above the well in a side place where the Turks would not see us, in case they had a habit of patrol. Next morning we returned a little on our tracks till a fold of the plain hid us from the railway and then marched off southward across the sandy flat, which was full of tracks of gazelle, onyx and ostrich, with in one spot the pad-marks of a leopard. We were making for the low hills bounding the far side, intending to blow up a train, for Zaal had said that where these touched the railway was such a curve as we needed for the mine-laying, and that the spurs commanding the bend would give us an ambush and a good field of fire for our rifles and machine-guns.

So we went straight across to the cover of these southern ridges, and turned east in them till within half a mile of the line. There we halted our camels in a thirty-foot valley, and told the men to wait, while a few of us walked down to the line, which here bent a little eastward to avoid the point of the higher ground under our feet. The point ended in a flat table, fifty feet above the track, and as many feet wide: while half-way down its slope ran a terrace-step facing north across the depression that was the mouth of the valley wherein our men were hiding.

The metals crossed this hollow on a high bank, pierced in the center by a two-arched bridge, about ten feet high, for the passage of the occasional rainwater. This seemed an ideal spot to lay the charge. It was our first try at electric mining, and we had not an idea of what would happen: but it stood to our reason that the job would be more sure if there was an arch under the explosive, since then, whatever was the effect on the locomotive, the bridge would certainly go and the succeeding coaches be derailed.

It was about three hundred yards from the bridge to the ledge, which would make an admirable gun position, exactly right for the Stokes. For the automatics it was too high, but the enfilade because of the curve would be masterful whether the train was going up or down the line: and so we determined to put up with the disadvantage of plunging fire. It was good to have the two British responsibilities in one place, safe from surprise and with an independent retreat into the rough if the worst came to the worst, for to risk their lives for a train would have been criminal. Our purpose and ambition was to bother the Turks by hampering the railway traffic, an object not serious enough to justify a single deliberate casualty, least of all an English one: and we were beginning badly, for today Stokes was in great pain with dysentery. Few Englishmen seemed to have been given organic resistance to diseases by their way of upbringing.

We walked back to our camels, dumped the loads, and sent the animals away behind a few more ridges to pasture in safety near some undercut limestone rocks from which the Arabs could scrape salt. The free men carried down the Stokes gun and its shells, and the Lewis guns, and gelatin, and insulated wire and magneto and tools to the chosen place. The sergeants set up their toys on the terrace while we went down to the bridge to dig out a bed between the ends of two steel sleepers, wherein to hide my fifty pounds of gelatin. We had stripped off the paper wrapping of the plugs, and kneaded them all together by the help of the sun-heat into a shaking lump of jelly in a sandbag. It made a convenient package for one man to handle.

The burying of it was not easy. The embankment was steep, and had sheltered in the pocket by the hillside a great wind laid bank of sand. No one crossed this but me, stepping very carefully, and yet I left unavoidable great prints all over it. To scatter the ballast dug out from the track over this sand would have been to risk drawing further attention to the spot: so I had to gather all the stones in my cloak, and lade them in repeated journeys to the culvert, and there tip them naturally over the shingle bed of the old water course.

It took nearly two hours to finish the digging and cover up the charge, and then came the difficult job of unrolling the heavy wires from the detonator to the hills behind, from which we would fire the mine. The top sand of the hollow was crusted, and had to be broken through to bury the wires. They were stiff wires which scarred the wind-rippled surface of the sand with long lines like the belly marks of preposterously narrow and heavy snakes. When pressed down in one place they rose into the air in another. At last, to make them lie still, they had to be weighed down with rocks which in turn had to be buried at the cost of great disturbance of the ground.

Afterwards it was necessary to go back over the area to brush off the marks with a sandbag used like a stipple to get a wavy surface: and finally with a bellows and long funning sweeps of my cloak to simulate the smooth laying of the wind. In all it took five hours to finish, but then it was well-finished, and neither myself nor any of us could see where the charge lay, or that double wires led out underground from it to the firing point two hundred yards off in the rocky ground westward, below the guns.

The wires were just long enough to cross a first ridge into a depression a yard deep there we brought their ends to the surface and connected them with the electric exploder. It was an ideal place for it, and for the man who fired it, except that from it the bridge was not visible. However, this meant only that someone would have to press the handle when a signal was given him from a point fifty yards ahead which commanded a view of both bridge and firing point. Salem, Feisal's best slave, leader of the four he had lent me, asked for this task of honor and was yielded it by acclamation. The end of the afternoon was spent in showing him, on the disconnected exploder, what to do till he was act-perfect, and banged down the ratchet precisely as I raised my hand when the imaginary engine was on the bridge.

Then we walked back to camp together, leaving one man on watch by the line. We reached our baggage to find it deserted, and stared about in a puzzle for the rest, whom we saw suddenly where they sat in a line against the golden light of sunset along the crest of a high ridge just south of us. We yelled to them to lie down and come down, but they sat up there on their perch like a school of hooded crows in full view of anyone to north and south.

At last we ran up and threw them off the sky-line but it was too late. The Turks in a little hill-post by Hallat Ammar four miles south of us had seen them, and had already opened fire in their alarm into the long shadows which the declining sun was pushing gradually up the slopes towards them. The Beduin had an abiding contempt for the stupidity of the Turks, and took no care in fighting them. Against other Arabs they were past-masters in the art of using country: but they regarded the Turks as unworthy of refinements. This ridge on which they had sat was visible at once from Mudowwara and Hallat Ammar, and they had frightened both posts by their sudden ominous expectant watch.

However, it was too late to do anything but fume inwardly, and rile them outwardly by a lecture on the elementary principle of surprise in attack — a lesson they took smartly from a novice in raid-warfare. Then the dark closed on us, and we knew that we must sleep away the night patiently in hope of new activity on the morrow. Perhaps the Turks would not imagine our purpose, but would reckon us gone if our place looked desert in the morning. So we lit our fires in a deep hollow, and baked bread and were comfortable. The common tasks had made our three one party, and the hilltop folly had shamed everyone on reflection into agreement that Zaal should be our leader.

Day broke quietly, and for hours we watched the empty railway with its peaceful camps. The constant care of Zaal and of his lame cousin Howeimil kept us safely hidden, though with great difficulty, because of the insatiate restlessness of the Bedouin. They would never sit down and be still for ten minutes, but must fidget and do or say something. This defect made them very inferior to Englishmen for the long slow strain of a waiting war, and accounted somewhat for their impatient uncertainty in defense. Today they made us very angry.

Perhaps, after all, the Turks saw us: for at nine o'clock some forty men came out of the tents on the hilltop away to the south, and advanced in open order towards us. If we left them alone they would turn us off our mine in an hour: if we opposed them with our superior strength and held them or drove them back, the railway would take notice and traffic be held up till they knew all clear. It was a quandary, and eventually we settled it to our best by sending against them thirty men with orders to check them gradually, and if possible to draw them lightly aside by retiring away from us and the line into the broken hills where regular troops would not dare to follow far. This might hide our main positions from them.

For some hours it worked as we hoped: the firing grew desultory and distant. A patrol came confidently up the line from the south, and walked past our hill and over our mine and on towards Mudowwara without noticing us or the traces of our work. There were eight soldiers, and a stout corporal, who mopped his brow against the heat for it was now after eleven o'clock and really warm. When he had passed us by a mile or two the fatigue of the tramp became too much for him. He halted his party and marched them down the bank into the shade of a long culvert, under whose arches a cool draught from the east was gently flowing: and there in comfort they lay down on the soft sand, drank water from their bottles smoked, and at last slept a little.

Chapter 72: Loot

Noon brought a fresh care. Through my powerful glasses we saw a large patrol of perhaps a hundred men issue from Mudowwara station and make straight across the sandy plain towards our place. They were coming very slowly and no doubt unwillingly, for every good Turk in Arabia liked his midday sleep: but they could hardly take more than two hours to reach us. The situation was become intolerable.

Accordingly we began to pack up preparatory to moving off, having decided to leave the mine and its leads in place, on the chance that the Turks might not find them, and we return on some better occasion and take advantage of all the careful work the day before when we had buried them so exactingly. When we were ready we sent messengers to our covering detachment on the south telling them to meet us further up.

Just as they had gone, the watchman cried out that smoke in clouds was rising from Hallat Ammar. Zaal and I rushed up hill and saw that indeed there must be a train waiting in that station. As we were trying to see it over the hill with our glasses, suddenly it moved out in our direction. We yelled to the Arabs to get down to our prepared position as quick as possible, and there came a wild scramble over sand and rock into place. Stokes and Lewis in their boots could not win the race, but came well-up, all their pains and dysentery now forgotten. They were in luck, for the train, being from the south, would leave them astern of it and in quite the best place when it blew up.

The Arabs posted themselves in a long line behind the spur running north from the guns past the exploder to the mouth of the valley of the bridge. From it they would fire directly into the derailed carriages from the flank at less than one hundred and fifty yards. An Arab stood up on high behind the guns, and shouted to us what the train was doing: — a necessary precaution, for if it carried troops and detrained them behind our ridge we would have to face about like a flash and retire fighting uphill for our lives. Fortunately it held on at all the speed the two locomotives could make on wood fuel.

As it drew near the place where we had been reported, it opened a hot random fire into the desert where we were supposed to be. I could hear the racket coming, as I sat on my hillock by the bridge waiting to give the signal to Salem, who was dancing round the exploder on his knees, crying with excitement, and calling urgently on God to make him fruitful. The Turkish fire sounded very heavy and I wondered with how many men we were going to have affair, and if the mine would be advantage enough for our eighty to meet them properly. The range was so short that any way would be desperate, and I feared the Arabs were not wholehearted. It would have been better if the first experiment had been simpler.

However, it was too late for prudence and at that moment the engines, looking very big, rocked whistling into view round the bend, traveling their fastest. Behind them were ten box-wagons, all crowded, and rifle muzzles were sticking out of the windows and doors, and there were little sandbag nests on the flat roofs in which Turks held on precariously while they shot out at us. I had never thought of two engines, and decided on the moment to fire the charge under the second, so that, however little its effect, the uninjured one would not be able to uncouple and drag the carriages away.

So when the front driver of the second engine was on the bridge, I raised my hand to Salem, and there followed a terrific roar, and the line vanished from sight behind a jetted column of black dust and smoke a hundred feet high and as many wide. Out of the darkness came a series of shattering crashes, and long loud metallic clanging of ripped steel, while many lumps of iron and plate, with one entire wheel of a locomotive, whirled up suddenly black out of the cloud against the sky, and sailed musically over our heads to fall slowly and heavily into the desert behind. Except for the flight of these there came a dead silence, with no cry of men or shot, as the now-grey mist of the explosion drifted from the line towards us, and over our ridge until it was lost in the hills.

I took advantage of this lull to get off my exposed position, out of the coming line of fire, and ran southward to join the sergeants, my main preoccupation. As I passed Salem he picked up his rifle and charged out into the murk Before I had climbed up to the guns the hollow was alive with shots and with the brown figures of the Bedouin leaping forward to get to grips with the enemy. I looked round to see what was happening so quickly, and saw that the wagon sides were jumping under the bullets that riddled them, and the Turks were falling out from the far doors to gain the shelter of the railway embankment.

As I watched, our machine-guns chattered out from over my head, and the long rows of Turks on the carriage roofs rolled over and were swept off the top like bales of cotton, before the shower of bullets which stormed along the roofs, and splashed clouds of yellow chips from the planking as it furiously cut into them. The dominant position of the guns had been an advantage to us so far.

When I reached Stokes and Lewis the engagement had taken another turn. The Turks — such of them as yet lived — had got into the shelter behind the bank here about eleven feet high, and from the safe cover of the wheels were firing back point-blank at the Bedouin only twenty yards away from them across the sand-filled dip. The enemy, now in the crescent of the curving line, were secure from the machine-guns: but Stokes at once slipped into his gun the first shell, and a few seconds later there was a crash as it burst behind the bank and beyond the train in the flat desert east of the line.

He touched the elevating screw and slipped in his second shot. This burst just by the trucks in the deep hollow below the bridge where the remaining Turks were taking refuge. It made a shambles of the group and the survivors broke out eastward in a panic into the desert throwing away their rifles and equipment as they ran. This was the opportunity of the Lewis-gunners. The sergeant grimly traversed with drum after drum into their ranks till the open sand was littered with dead bodies. Mushagraf the Sherari boy behind the second gun saw the battle was over threw aside his weapon with a yell and dashed down at full speed with his rifle to join the others, who were beginning like wild beasts to tear open the carriages and fall to plunder. It had taken nearly ten minutes.

I looked up-line through my glasses and saw the Mudowwara patrol breaking back uncertainly towards the railway to meet the train-fugitives who were running their fastest northwards. Then I looked south and saw that our thirty men had ceased their action and were cantering their camels neck and neck in this direction to share our spoils. The Turks in contact with them saw them go and were beginning to move after them with infinite precaution, firing heavy volleys as they came.

Evidently we had a clear half-hour and then a double threat against us and I ran down to the ruins to see what the effect of the mine had been. The bridge was all gone and into its gap was fallen the front wagon which had been filled with sick. The smash had killed all but three or four and had rolled dead and dying into a bleeding heap against the splintered end. One of those still alive, half deliriously called out to me something which contained the word typhus. So I wedged shut the door and left them there alone.

All the succeeding wagons were derailed and smashed and some had their frames irreparably buckled. The second engine was a blanched pile of smoking iron. Its driving wheels had been blown off and upward, taking the whole side of the boiler away, and the cab and tender were twisted about and torn into strips among the piled stones of the bridge-abutment. It would never ran again: but the front engine had got off better. Though heavily derailed lying half-over with its cab burst, the steam was still at pressure and the driving gear intact.

Our greatest aim was to destroy the locomotives, and, to make sure such a case, I had kept in my arms a box of guncotton with a fuse and detonator ready fixed, for emergency. I put them in position on the outside cylinder and prepared to fire them. It would have been better on the fire box but I knew nothing of locomotives, and its sizzling steam made me fear that the boiler might explode generally and sweep my men (who were swarming like ants over the booty) with a blast of jagged steel fragments. It was impossible to wait till they had finished for they would loot until the Turks came. So I lit the fuse, and in the half-minute for which it would burn got between it and the plunderers, and drove them a little backward with great difficulty. Then the charge burst, blowing the cylinder to smothers, and the axle too, without harming anyone. At the moment I was distressed with uncertainty whether it was enough: but we had no more explosive. Afterwards we heard that the Turks found the wreck beyond use and broke it up.

The valley was a weird sight. The Arabs had gone raving mad and were rushing about at top speed bare-headed and half-naked screaming shooting in the air clawing one another nail and fist, while they burst into trucks and staggered back and forward with immense bales of goods. The train was packed with troops and refugees sick men volunteers from the Medina garrison for boat service on the Euphrates, and families of Turkish officers being returned to Damascus. The booty was enormous. The Arabs ripped open the bundles and tossed the contents over the ground, smashing everything they did not like.

There were sixty carpets spread about, dozens of mattresses and flowered quilts, blankets in heaps, clothes for men and women in all variety, clocks, cooking pots food, ornaments and weapons. To one side stood thirty or forty hysterical women, unveiled, tearing their clothes and hair, shrieking them distracted. The Arabs never regarded them but went on wrecking the household goods looting their absolute fill for the first time in their lives. Camels had become common property. Each man frantically loaded the nearest with what it could carry and then shooed it off westward into the void while he turned to his next fancy. Everybody was snatching everybody else's pet treasures.

The women saw me tolerably unemployed, and rushed yelling at me, and caught at me with howls for mercy. I assured them that it was all going well, but they would not get away till their husbands delivered me; they were in yet stronger panic and knocked their wives about and seized my feet themselves in a very agony of terror of instant death. A Turk broken down so was a nasty spectacle, and I kicked them off in disgust as well as I could with my bare feet, and finally broke free of them.

Next was a group of Austrians, officers and non-commissioned, who appealed to me quietly in Turkish for quarter. I replied in halting German, whereupon one broke into fluent English, and begged a doctor for his wounds. We had none: not that it mattered, for he was mortally hurt and dying. I told them the Turks would return in an hour and care for them: but he was dead before that, as were most of the others (instructor-sergeants, who had been in Tebuk teaching the use of the new Skoda mountain howitzers that Austria had supplied to Turkey for the Hejaz war), for some dispute broke out between them and my own bodyguard, and one of them fired a shot at

Rahail from his pistol. My infuriated men cut them down, all but two or three, before I could return to interfere.

Chapter 73: Escape

Lewis and Stokes had come down to help me, and I was a little anxious about them, for the Arabs had lost their wits and were as ready to assault friend as foe. Three times I had had to defend myself against them, while they pretended not to know me and snatched at my things. However, the sergeants' war-stained khaki presented fewer attractions to the Bedouin: but to be on the safe side I told them not to collect loot in the Arabs' sight. Lewis went out east of the railway to count the thirty men he had slain, and incidentally to find a little Turkish gold and other trophies in their haversacks. Stokes strolled through the wrecked bridge there he saw twenty Turks torn to pieces by his second shell, and retired hurriedly.

So far as I could see in the excitement, we had suffered no loss. Among the ninety military prisoners, to my astonishment, were five Egyptian soldiers in their underclothes. They knew me, and explained that in a great raid of Davenport's near Hedia they had been cut off by the Turks and captured in the night. They seemed glad to be excused a long sojourn in Turkey by the good fortune of a railway accident. I sent them to lead the prisoners away by themselves to our appointed rallying place by the salt rocks, a mile or two to the west of us in the desert.

Just then Ahmed came up to me with his arms full of booty, and shouted (no Arab could speak normally in the moment of victory) that an old woman in the last wagon but one wished to see me. I sent him off at once, empty-handed, to get my camel and some of the baggage camels to remove the guns, for the enemy's firing was now plainly audible, and the Arabs, sated with spoils, were beginning in panic to escape one by one towards the hills, driving their tottering camels before them into safety.

In the end of the wagon sat an ancient and very tremulous Arab dame who asked me what it was all about. I explained: she said she was too infirm to travel, and must wait her death there.

I replied that she would not be harmed. The Turks were almost arrived and would recover what remained of the train. She accepted this, and begged me to find her old black servant, to bring her water. The slave woman was with the rest: we filled a cup from the spouting tender of the first engine (delicious water from which Lewis was already slaking his thirst) and then I led her back to her mistress. The old lady seemed grateful, and months after came to me secretly from Damascus a note and a quite pleasant little Baluch carpet from the lady, Ayesha, daughter of Jellai el Lei, of Medina, in memory of an odd meeting.

Ahmed never came back with the camels, and my other men, possessed by greed, had dispersed over the countryside with the Bedouin. There had been money in the train, and they were hugging bags of silver coin, intent only on getting away with them alive. The sergeants and myself remained alone on the line, which had a strange silence now. We began to fear that we must abandon the guns and run for it: but just then saw two camels dashing towards us. Zaal and Howeimil had missed me and had returned to look.

We were rolling up the insulated wire, since we had no more, and if we lost it must abandon hope of another train soon. Zaal dropped from his camel and would have me mount on it and ride: but instead we loaded it with the wire and the exploder. Zaal found time and breath to laugh at our quaint booty, after all the gold and silver in the train. Howeimil was dead lame from an old wound in the knee, and could not be made to walk: but we got him to couch his camel reluctantly, and hoisted the Lewis guns, tied butt to butt like scissors, across behind his saddle. There remained the trench mortars without transport: but Stokes reappeared, leading unskillfully by the nose a baggage camel he had found straying untended in the hollow. We packed them on this in great haste; put Stokes (who was weak with dysentery) on Zaal's saddle, and sent them out with Howeimil at their best pace.

Meanwhile, Lewis and Zaal and I made a fire of cartridge boxes and petrol and waste and banked round it all the Lewis drums, and the spare small-arms ammunition, and gingerly, on the top, some loose Stokes shells. Then we ran. As the flames reached the cordite and ammonal there was a famous noise. The thousands of cartridges went out in series like massed machine guns and the shells roared off in thick columns of dust and smoke. The outflanking Turks felt that we were in strength and strongly posted. They halted their rush, took cover, and began to move carefully eastward to surround our position, and reconnoiter it according to rule. Through the five hundred yard gap so left on the west we sped panting away into concealment in the ridges.

It seemed a happy ending to the affair, and we were glad to get off with no more loss than my camels and baggage: though the sergeants had lost their kits and were sorry about them. However, there was food at Rum, and Zaal thought that perhaps we would find some of our property with the others who were waiting for us behind the appointed rocks ahead. We came, and my men were there, loaded with booty, and with them all our camels. The saddles were being suddenly delivered of spoils to look as if ready and waiting for our mounting.

I explained softly to them what I thought of the two who should have brought up the camels according to my order, when the firing ceased. They pleaded that the noise of the explosion had scattered the animals in fright, and that afterwards the Arabs had appropriated each man any animal he saw. This was probably true, but they also were able-bodied and might have helped themselves. We asked if anyone were hurt: and a voice said that the Shimt's boy, a very dashing fellow, had been killed in the first rush forward at the train. This rush was a mistake, done without instruction, as the Lewis and Stokes guns were sure to end the business if the mine worked properly. So I felt that his loss was not directly my reproach.

Three men had been slightly wounded... but then one of Feisal's slaves came up and said that Salem was missing. We called everyone together, and questioned them, and at last an Arab said that he had seen him lying hit just beyond the engine. This reminded Lewis, who had seen, unknowing that he was one of us, a negro on the ground there badly hurt. I had not been told and was angry, for Salem was in my charge, and here for the second time I had left a friend behind.

I asked for volunteers to come back and find him. After a little, Zaal agreed, and then twelve other of the Nowasera, and we mounted and trotted fast across the plain towards the line. As we topped the last ridge but one, we saw the wreck and the Turks clambering over it in swarms. There must have been one hundred and fifty of them, and our attempt was hopeless. Salem would have been dead, for the Turks did not take Arab prisoners. Indeed they used to kill them in horrible ways so that out of mercy we were now finishing those of our badly wounded who would have to be left on ground abandoned to the Turks.

We had to give up Salem: but instead I said to Zaal that we might slip up-valley and recover the sergeants' kits. He was willing, and we rode till the Turks saw us, and drove us to take cover behind a bank. Our camp had been in the next hollow, across a hundred yards of flat, so watching our time, one or two of the quicker youths ran across with me to drag back the saddlebags. We made two easy journeys, for the Turks were very distant and their long fire always bad: but for our third trip they had got up a machine-gun, and the dusty splashes of the bullets on the dark flint ground let them range well about us.

So I sent the Howeitat boys away, picked out the only things light and worth having of the remaining baggage, and rejoined them safely. We mounted, and pounded in cover down the slope and across the valley. On the open other side the Turks saw us, and counted our fewness. They grew bold: and ran forward on both flanks to cut us off Zaal threw himself from his camel, and climbed with five men to the head of the ridge and fired back at them. He was a marvelous shot, who could bring down a running gazelle from the saddle at three hundred yards, and his fire checked them.

He called to us laden men to hurry across the next hollow and hold it while he fell back on us: and in this fashion we retired from ridge to ridge putting up a good delay action at short range, hitting thirteen or fourteen Turks, at an expense on our side of only four camels wounded. At last when we were only two ridges from our supports, feeling sure that we would do it easily, a solitary rider appeared coming up. It was Lewis with a Lewis gun held efficiently across his thighs. He had heard the rapid fire of our retirement, and thought he would come and see if we needed help.

It changed our strength very much, and my mind, for I was angry with the Turks who had got Salem, and had chased us breathless so far in dust and heat and streaming sweat. Therefore I called to Zaal: and we took place to give our pursuers a knock, but they must have suspected our silence, or been afraid of the distance they had come; anyway we heard and saw no more of them. We waited a few minutes and then, becoming wise and cool again, rode off after the others.

They had marched away very heavy laden . We had ninety prisoners, of whom ten were friendly Medina women electing to go to Mecca by way of Feisal: and there had been twenty-two unridden camels for them all. The women had climbed on to the pack-saddles, and most of the thirty wounded were in pairs on the rest. It was four-thirty in the afternoon. We were exhausted: the prisoners had drunk all our water, and it was imperative we should refill from the old well at Mudowwara that night to sustain ourselves so far as Rum.

As the well was close to the station it would be best for us to get to it and away from it as soon as possible, lest the Turks come out and find us there defenseless. Victory always made an

Arab force cease to exist, and now we were no longer a raiding party but just a baggage caravan stumbling along, loaded to breaking point with all the household goods needed to make rich an Arab tribe for years. In the history of the Howeitat there had never been such loot, and the men were burning to get back intact to their tents to tell there the story of the most toothsome warfare which had ever been.

We broke up into a long column of little parties, and struggled northward. The sergeants had asked me for a sword and a rug each, as souvenirs of their first private battle, and I went down the whole line to look out something for them. On this errand, suddenly I came to Feisal's three slaves, and saw to my astonishment that on the crupper behind one of them, strapped to him, was Salem, the missing man, unconscious, with his clothes soaked in blood.

I trotted up to Ferhan and asked where he had been and how he had found Salem. He told me that when the Stokes gun fired its first shell, Salem had rushed past the locomotive, and one of the Turks on the train had shot him in the back. The bullet had gone in at one side, and come out near his spine, without in their judgment hurting him mortally. He had lain there till the train was taken, and then the Howeitat had stripped him of cloak and dagger and rifle and headgear. Mijbil, one of the freedmen, had found him so and had lifted him straight to his camel and trekked off homeward alone, without waiting for us, or telling us. Ferhan had overtaken him on the road, and had relieved him of Salem, who, when he recovered, as later he did, perfectly, bore me always a little grudge for having left him behind when he was of my company and wounded. My habit of sheltering behind a Sherif was to avoid measuring myself against the pitiless Arab standard, with its no mercy for foreigners who wore its clothes and aped its manners. It was not often that I was caught with no more shield than poor blind Sherif Aid.

We reached the well in three hours and watered without interruption. Afterwards we moved off, still in a loose mob, for another ten miles or so, when we were beyond possible pursuit. There we lay down and slept, and in the morning found ourselves happy and tired. Stokes had had his dysentery rather heavy upon him the night before, but sleep and the ending of anxiety made him well. He and I and Lewis, the only unburdened ones, went on in front by a new road across one huge mud-flat after another, till just before sunset we were at the bottom of Wadi Rum where we had entered it from Guweira.

This was important, for our armored cars were making themselves a road from Akaba to Guweira, and these twenty miles of hard mud might enable them to reach the line by Mudowwara quickly and easily. If they could, and if the ground about Mudowwara was fit for cars at speed, then we could at a day's notice always hold up the circulation of trains for as short or long a time as we pleased. When the cars were through to Guweira we must test this idea. Thinking of it, we wheeled into the avenue of Rum and picked our way towards the wide valley between the cliffs. Again we felt how Rum inhibited excitement by its serene beauty. Such greatness made our littleness a shame, and stripped off the cloak of laughter in which the three of us had wrapped our individualities as we rode over the jocund flats. We reached the bottom of the valley when it was still gorgeous in its sunset color, the cliffs as red as the clouds in the west, and like them in size, and in the level bar they rose against the sky.

The night came down as we rode towards the springs, and the valley became a mind-landscape. The cliffs on each side were not visible, but felt in the imagination, which tried to piece out the plan of their battlements by following the dark patterns they cut out of the lower edge of the canopy of stars. The blackness in the depth with us was very real — it was a night to despair of movement. We felt only our camels' labor, as hour after hour smoothly and monotonously they shouldered their puny way along the unfenced level with the wall in front no nearer and the wall behind no further than at the beginning.

About nine at night we were in front of the pit in which lay the water and our old camp. We knew its place because the deep darkness about us there grew pitch dark. We turned our camels to the right and walked towards the rock, which reared the domes of its crested hills so high over us that the head ropes slipped back round our necks as we stared up at them. It felt as though we would touch the wall if we stretched out even our camel-sticks in front of us: and yet we walked in under their horns for many paces more.

At last we were in the tall bushes and we shouted. An Arab shouted back, and the echoes of my voice rolling down again from the cliff met his cry rising, and the sounds wrapped themselves together and wrestled among the crags. A pale flame showed up on the left, and we marched to it, and found Musa, our watchman there. He lit a fire of powerfully-scented wood, and by its light we broke open a box of bully-beef and biscuits, and fed ourselves ravenously, gulping down through our food one bowl after another of the delicious water, ice-cold and almost heady after the foul and aged drink of Mudowwara which had poisoned our throats for so many days.

We slept through the coming of the rest. In the morning we washed and mended ourselves and in the afternoon all collected, with our sixty eight prisoners for some had died and some had slipped away from Mudowwara well in the night confusion, and with Zaal as guide, marched gently across the hills in the direction of my ride the week before, into the southern Itm, where we slept a comfortable night. In the morning of September the twenty second we were back in Akaba, entering in glory, laden with all manner of precious things. We boasted to Feisal and Joyce that the trains were now at our mercy.

From Akaba the two sergeants took hurried ship to Egypt. Cairo had remembered them and was peevish over their non-returning. However, they could pay this penalty of their delay cheerfully, without reason to regret Arabia. They had had a strange trip, and had won a battle, single-handed, and had had dysentery on the march, and lived on camel-milk and rice, and learned to ride fifty miles a day without pain... also Allenby gave them a medal each.

Chapter 74: Raiding

The first two days in Akaba passed talking politics and strategy and army organization with Feisal, while preparations for a new operation went forward. The story of our luck quickened the camp, and the mining of trains promised to become as popular with the Arabs as it was harmful to the Turks. It might happen frequently, if we trained men in the technical side of the work: and this would have the further advantage of delivering me from such adventures, which accorded with only half my function: as the tribal leader: not as Feisal's chief staff officer.

So we cast about for a party Captain Pisani was the first volunteer. He was the very experienced commander of the French detachment at Akaba, an active soldier who burned for distinction: and distinctions. His chiefs wanted their nation to take a prominent place in the records of the Arab Revolt, and had hinted to Pisani that a Croix de Guerre might be added to his eighteen medal-ribbons if he did something against the railway. By talking vaguely of a British Military Cross we secured that his effort should be supplementary to ours, rather than competitive. Feisal also found me three young Damascenes of family, who were ambitious of leading tribal raids in the near future. We took only Lewis guns with us, since last time had proved them formidable enough for so easy a target as a train: and their being entrusted to my own bodyguard ensured that the whole party would be as mobile as the riding camels.

We went to Rum and announced that this raid was reserved for the Dhumaniyeh, who had treated us scurrilous and threatened us the week before. Such coals of fire scorched them, but their greed would not let them refuse even this deepest insult of a too-ready pardon. Only we rejected Gasim Abu Dumeik in favor of Salem Alayan, his cousin, as our leader. Everyone for days around flocked to join, and were generally denied: nevertheless we started out with fifty men above the hundred which was the desirable number. We also levied a huge train of empty pack-camels to carry off the intended spoils.

For variety we determined to work quite close to Maan. So we rode over the mud-flat and up the pass that led to the plateau under Batra, climbing out of heat into cold, out of Arabia into Syria, from a land of tamarisk and mirth into a land of wormwood. As we topped the pass and saw the red stain like blood on the hills, below which lay the leech-infested wells, there met us the first breath of the northern desert wind, that air too fine to describe, almost too fine to think about, which told of perfect loneliness, dried grass, and the sun on burning flints.

Salem said that Kilometer 475 would be good for mining: perhaps it had been, but when we walked down to it at sunset we found ourselves beset on all sides by enemy blockhouses, and had to creep away shyly. We marched down the line till midnight, when we discovered a possible place, where the line crossed a wide valley October Raiding on a high straight bank, pierced by bridges on each side and in the middle: for we meant of course to vary from our method of last time. The nearest Turkish posts were distant four kilometers on the north, and two and a half on the south.

There we laid an automatic mine of a new and very powerful Lyddite type, as an experiment. The burying took hours, and dawn came unseen upon us as we worked. There was no perceptible lightening, but we knew suddenly that we could see, and when we stared round to know why the dark was no longer dark we discovered that the day had no evident source. It was not till long minutes afterwards that the sun disclosed itself high above the earth over a vignette bank of edgeless mist.

We retired a thousand yards up the valley, round the first bend, where it was a scrubby bed confined between thirty-foot banks, and there we made our ambush throughout the intolerable day. The sun grew powerful as the hours passed, and shone so closely upon us in our radiant trench that we felt crowded by its rays. The camels strayed continually into danger, and the men were a mad lot, sharpened to distraction by hope of success; they would listen to no word but mine, and brought me all their troubles for judgment. In these six strained days there came to a head and were settled twelve cases of assault with weapons, four camel lifting, one marriage, two thefts, a divorce, fourteen feuds, two evil eyes, and a bewitchment.

These decisions had to be arrived at by me unaided, without experience, with my very imperfect knowledge of the Arabic language. The fraudulence of the whole business stung me deeply. Here were more fruits — very bitter fruits — of that decision on the way to Akaba, that I must become not an instigator but a principal of the Arab Revolt. It had been made openly after days or rather months of hesitation, and it involved me primarily in a constant attitude of deception, of raising the Arab Revolt on false pretenses, and secondarily in an assumption of false authority over the lives and habits of my dupes. Today, with my imperfect Arabic, I was judging their suits on little more evidence than their faces, as visible to my eyes weakly watering and stinging after this year's exposure to the throb, throb of the sunlight.

We waited that day, and all the night. At sunset a scorpion scuttled out of my saddlebags under the bush by which I had lain down to make note of the day's weariness, and fastened on my left hand and stung me — it seemed repeatedly. The pain was very great, and my arm swelled up, and kept me uneasily awake until the second dawn. It checked thought, and so was a not unwelcome relief to my overburdened mind, for seldom was the body clamant enough to interrupt my self-questioning, and then only by the help of some such surface injury sweeping all the sluggish nerves like fire.

Nor did pain of this quality ever endure long enough really to be a cure. On this occasion, after distracting me for the night, it gave way to that unattractive and not honorable internal ache which, after a little, in itself provoked thought, and left me yet weaker to endure it unharmed. In such conditions the war seemed to me a folly as great as the crime of my sham leadership, and sending for Salem I was about to resign myself and my pretensions into his puzzled hands when the watcher announced a train.

It came down from the direction of Maan, a water-train, and passed over the mine without accident. The Arabs thanked me, for a booty of water did not enter their dreams, though it would have been useful to us for the moment since tonight we would be attacked by thirst. However, it passed over, and proved the mine action a failure, and at noon with my pupils I went down to the line, and laid an electric mine over the heads of the lyddite charges, so that the detonation of the one would fire the other. For concealment we trusted to the mirage, and to the midday drowsiness of the Turks; justifiably, for there was no alarm in the hour we spent digging and hiding the charge.

We laid it over the southernmost bridge, and brought the electric leads along the track to the middle bridge, which we had pitched on as the best firing point. The man who worked the exploder there would be perfectly concealed by the arch from the guards in the train overhead. The Lewis guns we would put under the northern bridge, also to hide when the train passed along, but to come out on the lee side and rake the length of the train when the Turks jumped out from our rifle fire, after the mine had exploded. The Arabs would line the bushes of a cross-channel of the valley three hundred yards our side of the railway track.

We waited afterwards for the rest of October the fifth, a day of sunlight and flies, and the slow discomfort of the scorpion bite, and thirst and foolish disputes to be appeased. Enemy patrols marched actively up and down the line, morning, afternoon and evening. In the night we sent all our camels along with a part of our men, to go to Fasoa for water from the old pilgrim tank. It lay under the rifles of a Turkish post, but in the darkness they could see nothing, and Dheilan, the head man of the Darausha, who was with us as my friend, supervised our waters in such a way that they gave no warning of themselves while they drew for the animals, and drank and filled the common water-skins for us.

In the morning our reunited party mounted eagerly to the watching place, and looked northward for the train, which was two days overdue. At last, about eight in the morning, we saw the smoke of it on the horizon as it left Maan. At the same time we saw the first patrol of the day approaching. There were only a half-dozen men in it, but their warning would deter the train, and we watched them and it straining, in wonder which would win the race to us. The train was very slow, and the patrol sometimes halted for a little.

We calculated they would be yet two or three hundred yards short of us when the train came. So we ordered everybody to their stations. There were twelve loaded wagons, and the engine panted on the upgrade. However, it held on steadily. I sat by a bush in the stream bed, a hundred yards from the bridge on which lay the mine, in view of it and of the exploder-party and of the machine-guns, ready to give them the signal at the moment. It was strange to see the unconscious train, rumbling carelessly over the fidgeting Ahmed and Lutfi el Asili, and the gunners.

When Faiz and Bedri el Azm, the exploders, heard the engine pass over their arch they got up and danced a war-dance round their little box. The Arabs behind lying in the ditch were hissing and calling softly to me that it was time to fire: but they were well hidden, and kept still till the engine was exactly over the first arch. Then I jumped up and waved my cloak round my head. Faiz instantly pressed his handle, and the great noise and dust and blackness burst up as at Mudowwara a few days before.

It enveloped me where I sat close to it, for some minutes, and the green-yellow sickly smoke of lyddite hung sluggishly about the wreck. The Lewis guns rattled out suddenly, three or four short bursts: then there was a yell from the Arabs' ditch, and headed by Pisani with their vibrant battle-cry they rushed past me in a wild torrent for the train. I walked slowly after them, and saw them flood over and take its first part in a moment.

A Turk appeared upon the buffers of the fourth truck from the end, and a few seconds later the gap of daylight widened slowly between it and the taken half The couplings had been loosed or broken by the shock, and the tail of the train was slipping back down the gradient. I made a languid effort to get behind it with a stone, but scarcely cared enough to do it well. It seemed fair and witty that this much of the booty should escape. A Turkish colonel on the staff came to the coach window and fired at me with a Mauser pistol, cutting through the flesh of my hip. I laughed at his too-great energy which thought, like a regular officer, to promote the war by killing an individual. Rahail shot back at him, and he fell out of sight into his compartment, which gathered speed as it ran off downhill. We walked up to look at what we had done.

The mine had taken out the near arch of the bridge and destroyed the locomotive. The fire box was torn open, and many of its tubes burst. The cab was cleared out, a cylinder gone, the frame buckled, two driving wheels and their journals shattered. The tender and first wagon had telescoped. Some twenty Turks were dead, and others prisoner, including four officers who stood by the line weeping for the life which the Arabs had no mind to take.

The contents of the trucks were foodstuffs, some seventy tons of them, 'urgently needed', according to the waybill, in Medain Salih, for ibn Rashid, the Emir of Hail, who had come in to the railway with a force of Shammar auxiliaries, nominally to help Fakhri Pasha, but really to see how the Turks were placed. We found duplicates of this waybill, sent one to Feisal as detailed report of our success, and left the other properly receipted in the van. We also kicked back some dozen civilians who had thought they were going to Medina by this train.

Pisani superintended the carrying off or destruction of as much as possible of the booty; we worked in haste, for the Turks from the blockhouses north and south put in a dashing attack, which no one of us felt any inclination to resist. As before, the Arabs were now merely camel-drivers, walking behind their pack animals, urging them westward. Farraj held my camel while Salem and October Raiding Dheilan helped with the exploder and the too-heavy wire. The Turks were four hundred yards away when we had finished, and we rode off without a man killed or wounded.

My pupils were fully satisfied with their experience. They practiced the art of mining afterwards, by themselves and taught others with increasing success. Their fortune and the rumor of me rolled about the tribes in a growing wave: not always intelligently. 'Send us a lumens and we will blow up trains with it', wrote the Beni Atiyeh to Feisal. He lent them Saad el Sikeini, a cut-and-thrust Ageyli who had worked with me, and by his help they got an important train carrying Suleiman Rifada, our old nuisance of Wejh, and other chiefs, with twenty thousand pounds in gold, and precious trophies. There were many such efforts.

In the next four months our force from Akaba had destroyed seventeen locomotives between Deraa and Abdulla's section by Wadi Ais. Running over the line became an uncertain terror for the enemy. At Damascus the people scrambled for the back seats in the trains, and willingly paid extra for them. Twice the engine-drivers struck. Civilian traffic nearly ceased, and we extended our threat to Aleppo by the simple device of posting a notice one night on the town hall in Damascus, announcing the forthcoming opening of mine attacks against the Syrian railway, and warning good Arabs that they traveled by it at their own risk. We also sent high explosive up to Hama to afford the Turks tangible proof of our intention.

The loss of the engines was sore upon the Turks. The rolling stock south of Damascus was pooled for the Palestine and Hejaz Railways, and our destructions not merely so reduced the enemy carrying capacity that the mass evacuation of Medina became impossible, but began to pinch them about Jerusalem just when the British were getting formidable, and General von Kress required the most adequate provision to hold them up.

Chapter 75: Harvest

Meanwhile Egypt had wired for me. An airplane from Suez carried me back there in two hours, and then I went by train beyond el Arish to G.H.Q., where Allenby, by the splendor of his will, was recreating the broken British army. First he asked me what our railway efforts meant — or rather if they meant anything beyond the obvious rather melodramatic advertisement they gave Feisal's cause.

I explained my hope to leave the line just in working order — but only just — to Medina, where Fakhri's corps fed itself and cost less than if in prison at Cairo. The surest way to limit the line without killing it was by attacking the trains: — an operation honorable, easy, and profitable for us. The Arabs put into mining a zest and dash absent from their pure demolitions of material, rails or bridges. We could not yet afford to break the line finally, since that meant railhead at Maan. Railhead was the strongest point of a railway, and we preferred weakness for a neighbor, till our regular army was trained and equipped and numerous enough to invest Maan. Not till then would we definitely stop the trains by Mudowwara: for investment was neither a fit nor a possible role for Beduin to play.

He asked next about Wadi Musa, for he had intercepted Turkish messages which showed that they meant to attack it very shortly. I explained the openness of our Guweira camp, and that we had tried to decide the Turks to attack Wadi Musa in preference, as Wadi Musa was impregnable. We had provoked them again recently by raiding Shobek and the Turkish wood cutting depot in the forest near it. They had laid down a branch-line to collect this wood, on which they mainly relied for their railway fuel, and we infuriated jemal, whose temper was always dangerous, by burning his depot, and capturing his labor and his guards. We also gained for our own ranks Subhi el Omari, a machine-gun officer from Damascus, pressed into the Turkish army. He deserted to us, and his nobility was a star to our junior officers afterwards.

At the same time we reduced the Wadi Musa garrison, to make it not too evidently strong, and were about to be rewarded by jemal's falling into our trap. He was, so Allenby said, massing troops here and there before it, in heavy numbers. The truth was that the Turks acted in complete fog with regard to us. We went about in parties, not in stiff formation, and so their airplanes failed to estimate us. No spies could count us either, and we ourselves had not the smallest idea of what our own strength at any given moment was, so that treachery, if any there happened to be, was unfruitful.

On the other hand we knew them exactly, each single unit, and every man they moved. They treated us as regulars, to save themselves the pain of innovation, or because they misunderstood guerrilla war. Before venturing a move against us they calculated what, in any circumstance, was the total force we could meet them with. We were less orthodox (we might have been called gamblers, only that we staked on certainties) and when we moved knew exactly what they would meet us with. This was our balance, and for these years the Arab Movement lived on that exhilarating but slippery tableland which lay between 'could' and 'would'. We allowed ourselves no margins anywhere for accident: indeed, 'no margins' was the Akaba motto, continuously in the mouths and minds of us all.

At G.H.Q. I spent the one night getting informed of their designs of a last attack on the Gaza line, in order that we might co-operate intelligibly, and then went straight back to Akaba to prepare our part. This took time and trouble, and excited us so that jemal's great attack on Wadi Musa made hardly any noise. Maulud presided beautifully. He opened his center, and with the greatest humor let the Turks in till they broke their faces against the vertical cliffs of the mountain which was the Arab refuge. Then, while they were yet puzzled and hurt, he came down simultaneously on both flanks.

They drew off dazed, and never ventured another attack on a prepared Arab position. Their losses had been heavy, but their loss of nerve at finding us invisible and yet full of backlash cost them more than the killed and wounded. Thanks to Maulud our situation about Akaba became entirely easy, and we no longer had to plan at all for the safety of our base.

BOOK VI

The Raid upon the Bridge

By November 1917 Allenby was ready to open a general attack against the Turks along his whole front. The Arabs should have done the same in their sector: but I was afraid to put everything on a throw, and designed instead the specious operation of cutting the Yarmuk valley railway, to throw into disorder the expected Turkish retreat. This half measure met with the failure it deserved.

Chapter 76: Potentialities

Accordingly October 1917 could be a month of free anticipation for us, knowing that Allenby, with Bois and Guy Dawnay, was working out his plan against the Turkish fortified line of Gaza-Beersheba: while the Turks, a comparatively small army in a strong position with excellent lateral communications, had been puffed up to a heady confidence by their victories over Sir Archibald Murray, and imagined that the succeeding British generals would be equally incompetent in tactics, equally unable to keep what their troops won for them by sheer fighting. So they were careless in their first-line dispositions and muddled their reserves.

They much deceived themselves. Allenby's coming had remade the English. As soon as he landed in Egypt his open breadth of personality swept away the mist of private and departmental jealousies behind which Murray and his men had worked. The noise of the grinding of axes in GH.Q became so low that staff officers were able to think about the enemy.

Some changes of personnel helped. General Lynden Bell found the new atmosphere too bracing and made way for General Bois, Allenby's Chief of Staff in France, a little, quick, brave, pleasant man, a tactical soldier, perhaps, and in most ways an admirable and effaced foil to Allenby, who used to relax himself on Bois. Unfortunately neither the one nor the other had the power of choosing men, but Chetwode's wisdom supplied this lack by completing them with General Guy Dawnay as third member of the staff.

Bois had never an opinion, nor any knowledge. Dawnay was mainly intellect. He lacked the eagerness of Bois, and the calm drive and human understanding of Allenby, who was the man the men worked for, the graven image all of us worshiped. Dawnay was a cold shy mind, gazing on our efforts with a bleak eye, always thinking, thinking. Beneath this mathematical surface were hidden passionate many-sided convictions, a reasoned scholarship in higher warfare, and a brilliant bitterness of judgment. He was disappointed with us and with life, which had not gone with him as he wished.

He was the least professional of soldiers, a banker who read Greek history, a strategist unashamed, and a burning poet with strength to deny the littleness of daily things. During the war he had had the grief of planning the attack at Suvla (spoiled by incompetent tacticians) and the battle for Gaza. With each work of his they ruined, he withdrew further into the hardness of his frosted pride, for he was of the stuff of fanatics. Allenby broke into him by not seeing his dissatisfaction, and Dawnay replied by giving for the Jerusalem advance all the genius that was in him. A cordial union of two such men made the Turks' position hopeless from the outset. Their divergent characters were mirrored in the intricate plan. Gaza had been entrenched on a European scale, with line after line of defenses in reserve. It was so obviously the enemy's strongest point that Murray had twice chosen it for frontal attack. Allenby, fresh from France, insisted that his assault must be delivered by overwhelming numbers of men and guns, and the thrust maintained by enormous quantities of all kinds of transport. Bois nodded his assent.

Dawnay was not the man to fight a straight battle. He sought to destroy the enemy's strength with the least fuss, not by hitting it directly, but by studying his moral weaknesses and developing them: like a master politician he would use the bluff Chief as a cloak for the last depth of justifiable slimness. He advised a drive at the far end of the Turkish line, near Beersheba. To make his victory cheap he wanted the enemy main force behind Gaza, which would be best secured if the British concentration was hidden, so that the Turks persuaded themselves that the flank attack was only a shallow feint. Bois nodded his assent.

Consequently the movements were made in great secrecy: but Dawnay found an ally in his intelligence staff who advised him to go beyond these merely negative precautions and to take still greater pains in giving the enemy speciously wrong information of the plans. The author of this positive policy, and the actual inventor of the frauds, was Major Meinertzhagen, a student of migrating birds drifted into soldiering, whose hot immoral hatred of the enemy expressed itself as readily in trickery as in violence. He persuaded Dawnay of the value of his suggestions. Allenby reluctantly agreed. Bois nodded assent: and the work began.

Meinertzhagen knew no half-measures. He was logical, an idealist of the deepest, and so possessed by his convictions that he was willing to harness all evil to Good's chariot. He was a strategist with wide views, a geographer, and a silent laughing masterful man, who took as much pleasure in deceiving his enemy (or his friends) by an unscrupulous jest, as in spattering the brains of a cornered mob of Germans one by one with his African knobkerri. His instincts were abetted by an immensely powerful body, and a savage brain not hampered by doubts or prejudices, habits or rules of game.

He prepared false army papers, elaborate and very confidential, which, to a trained staff officer, would indicate wrong positions for Allenby's main formations, a wrong direction of the coming attack, and a date some days too late. This information was led up to by careful hints given in code wireless messages, things which we knew the enemy picked up and deciphered: and then Meinertzhagen mounted his horse and rode out with his notebooks and private papers on a forward reconnaissance. He pushed too far until the enemy saw him, and nearly surprised him. In the ensuing gallop he lost all his loose equipment and very nearly himself as well: but was rewarded a little later by seeing the enemy reserves moving unhurried towards Gaza, and their whole preparations swung towards the coast and made less urgent. An army order by Ali Faud Pasha cautioned his staff against carrying documents into the line, by the horrible example of a British officer who had given away matters very useful to his enemy, in carelessness.

We on the Arab front were very intimate with this enemy. Our Arab officers had all been Turkish officers, and knew every leader on the other side, personally. They had suffered the same training, thought just as they did, took their point of view. By practicing modes of approach upon the Arabs we could see how the Turks were thinking, and could understand, almost get inside, their minds. Further, there was constant touch between us and them, for the whole population of the enemy-occupied area was for us without pay or need of persuasion. In consequence, our intelligence service was the widest and fullest and most certain imaginable.

We knew better even than Allenby the hollowness of the enemy. We knew the magnitude of the British resources, and we under-estimated the crippling effect of too-plentiful an artillery, and the general cumbrous intricacy of the British infantry and cavalry, which moved only with rheumatic slowness. We hoped that Allenby would be given a month's fine weather, and in that case expected to see him take not merely Beersheba and Jerusalem, but Haifa also, sweeping the Turkish Army in one shapeless ruin through the hills.

Such would be our moment, and we needed to be ready for it in the spot where our weight and tactics would be most unexpected and most damaging in the attack. For my eyes the center of attraction, since the spring reconnaissance with the Abu Tayi, had been Deraa. It was the junction of the Jerusalem-Haifa, Damascus Medina railways, the navel of the Turkish armies in Syria, the only common point of all their fronts: and by chance an area in which lay great untouched reserves of Arab fighting men, educated and armed by us, and in regular traffic with our markets at Akaba. We could there use the Rualla, the Serahin, the Serdiyeh, the Khoreisha and, far stronger than these tribes, the settled peoples of the Hauran and Jebel Druse.

I pondered for a while whether we should not call up all these adherents, and tackle the Turkish communications in force. We were certain, with any management, of twelve thousand men, enough to rush Deraa, to smash all the railway lines in the Hauran, even to take Damascus itself by surprise. By doing one of these things we would make the position of the Beersheba army critical: perhaps close its avenues of direction and supply. The effort was well within our power: the people would rise if we told them to: and the temptation was very sore to stake all now on the issue.

It was not the first or last time that service to two masters irked me. I was one of Allenby's officers, in his confidence; and in return he expected us to do the best we could for him. I Was Feisal's adviser and knew that he relied so far on my advice being competent and honest as to take it often without question or argument. Yet I could not explain to Allenby the whole Arab situation, and was not empowered to disclose the full British plan to Feisal. It was strange and often difficult to choose between the two voices that were trusting me.

Of course we were fighting for an Allied victory and if in the end the sake of the English, the leading partner, was to be forwarded only by sacrificing the Arabs on the field of battle, then it would have to be done unhesitatingly: but it was hard to know just when it was the end, and necessary: and in this case to cast the die and lose meant to have ruined Feisal's cause from the nature of these followers of ours in Hauran, since they were sedentary.

They were writing to us, begging us to come. The leader of the hollow country about Deraa, Sheikh Taiai el Hareidhin, sent to me urgent messages that with the help of a few of our riders, as proof of Arab support, he would undertake to give us Deraa. Such an exploit would have done the Allenby business: but was not one which Feisal should afford unless he had a fair hope of retaining it. Its sudden capture, followed by a retreat, would have involved horrible massacres of all the splendid peasantry of the district.

They would have formed the bulk of our forces in the operation, and were not Bedouin, able to fall back into the desert when the raid ended or miscarried. They were prosperous townsfolk and villagers who lay open themselves, their families, and their property to the revenge of a peculiarly barbarous enemy. Accordingly they could only rise once, and their effort on that occasion must be decisive. To call them out now was to risk the best asset Feisal held for eventual success, on the speculation that Allenby's first attack would sweep the enemy before it, and that the month of November would be rainless, favorable to a rapid, successful advance.

I weighed the English again and again in my mind and could not honestly say that I was sure of them. They were often gallant fighters, but their generals as often gave away in stupidity what they had gained in ignorance. A year later I would have judged differently: but for the moment Allenby was quite untried, sent to us with a not-blameless record from France, and his troops had broken down in and been broken by the Murray period. Had his affairs looked desperate it would have been another matter: but the war generally was going neither very well nor very ill, and it seemed as though there might be time for another try next year. To declare now would put the responsibility of success upon my head, and the risks seemed to me unjustifiable. So I decided to postpone the hazard for the Arabs' sake.

Chapter 77: A Foray

However, the Arab Movement lived for bread on Allenby's good pleasure, and so it was needful to look about for some operation less than a general revolt in the enemy rear, one which could be achieved by a raiding party of nomads, without involving the settled peoples, and which would yet please him by being of material help to the British pursuit of the enemy. These conditions and qualifications pointed to an attempted cutting of one of the great bridges in the Yarmuk valley.

It was up the narrow and precipitous gorge of the River Yarmuk that the railway from Palestine climbed to the plateau of the Hauran, on the way to Damascus and central Syria and Turkey proper. The depth of the Jordan depression, and the abruptness of the plateau-face, made this section of the line most difficult to build. The engineers in the end had laid the track in the very course of the winding river-valley: but this was too narrow and too steep, and to gain development the line had to curve about, crossing and re crossing the stream-bed continually, on a series of identical steel bridges each fifty meters, one hundred and sixty-two feet, in span. Of these bridges the furthest west and the furthest east, numbers two and thirteen, were incapable of quick deviation.

The Turks were pinched for pack-transport, and therefore to cut one of these bridges would isolate their army in Palestine from its food and ammunition base in Damascus, and destroy its power of escaping from Allenby's advance. To raid the Yarmuk we would have to ride from Akaba by way of Jefer to Azrak, some three hundred and twenty miles by the best route: and from Azrak, which would be our desert base, it was more than a hundred miles to the bridges. The Turks thought the danger from us so remote that they ignored it: and guarded the bridges so insufficiently that they seemed fair objects for a Bedouin raid.

Accordingly we suggested the scheme to Allenby, who asked that it be done on November the fifth, or one of the three following days. If it succeeded and the weather held up afterwards for another fortnight, the odds were that no surviving unit of von Kress' army would get back to Damascus. The Arabs would then have a splendid opportunity to carry their wave forward into their own capital, taking up from the British just at the half-way point, when the original impulse was nearly exhausted. The betting would be safe enough for us to call everybody out, and they would rise readily and quickly, as the magnitude of the Turkish disaster would be generally evident.

For such an eventuality we needed to hold there at Azrak the authority to lead all these new adherents of ours, if the moment came. Taiai we knew was ready: with the southern Druses we were in sufficient touch by means of Hussein Abu Naif, the Atrash overlord of the district about the fortress town of Salkhad. The northern Druses we neither knew nor cared for: they were over winningly greedy braggarts whose help would have been dear at their price. Of the tribes, the Beni Sakhr were at this time very close to Feisal. He had entrusted the care of them to Ali ibn el Hussein, the youthful and attractive Harith Sherif who had so distinguished himself in the early desperate days about Medina, and later had out Newcombed Newcombe about el Ula.

Ali had been Jemal's guest in Damascus through 1915 and 1916, and had then learned something of Syria: and so I asked him from Feisal to lead this present enterprise. His courage, his resource, and his energy were proven. There had never been an adventure since the beginning too dangerous for Ali to attempt, nor a disaster too deep for him to face with his wild high yell of a laugh. That he had not been killed predicated astonishing coolness in the tight places he enjoyed so much.

He was physically splendid — not tall nor heavy but so strong that he would kneel down, resting his forearms palm-up on the ground, and rise to his feet with a man standing on each hand. It required his full strength, and his arms wobbled so that the men being lifted only maintained their balance by gripping his luxuriant black hair: but few people could have done so much, and in addition Ali could outstrip a trotting camel on his bare feet, keep his speed over half a mile, and then vault with one hand into the saddle, holding his rifle in the other. He was impertinent, headstrong, conceited, as reckless in word as in deed, impressive (if he pleased) on public occasions, and fairly educated for a person whose ambition was to excel all Bedouin in war and sport. He was the ideal many-sided leader who could turn to effect any mad situation as it arose.

Ali would bring us the Beni Sakhr. We had good hopes of the Serahin, the tribe then at Azrak. I was in touch with the Beni Hassan. The Rualla of course at this season were down away in the south of the Wadi Sirhan at their winter quarters, so that our greatest card in the Hauran could not be played: but anyhow we had ample resources. Faiz el Ghusein had gone into the Leja to prepare his Sulut tribesmen (whose strategic position gave them a value quite disproportionate to their number) for action against the Hauran railway if the signal came. Explosives were stored in the desirable places, to wait this moment. Our friends in Damascus were warned that things might happen, and Ali Riza Pasha Rikabi, whom the innocent Turks thought was their military governor, and whom we knew to be Sherman chief agent and conspirator, took quiet steps to get control if the emergency needing help arose.

My detailed plan was to rush from Azrak across the Khoreisha country under guidance of Rafa (that most gallant sheikh, who had convoyed me in June) to Urn Keis, in one or two huge marches with a handful of perhaps fifty men. Urn Keis was Gadara, very precious with its memories of Menippus, and of Meleager, the hot Greek Syrian whose self-expression marked the highest point of Syrian letters. It stood just over Hemme, the westernmost and best of all the Yarmuk bridges, a masterpiece whose destruction would fairly enroll me in the Gadarene school. The people there were prepared not to see us.

There were only half a dozen sentries actually on the girders and abutments, which I had carefully reconnoitered. My hope was to persuade some of the Abu Tayi under Zaal to come with me. These men-wolves would make certain the actual storming of the bridge. To prevent enemy reinforcements coming up at once from Hemme station we would put a machine-gun on the high ground this side of the bridge to sweep the approaches. For the other flank we would have a Lewis gun. These would be handled by the Indian machine-gun section that Captain Bray had formed of volunteers from the cavalry division in France. They were under Jemadar Hassan Shah, a firm and experienced man, and had been months up-country from Wejh. So they could be fairly assumed experts on camel-back, fit for the forced marches in prospect.

The precise demolition of the girders demanded a necklace of blasting gelatin, fired electrically. The Humber made us canvas straps and buckles, to simplify the fixing. Nonetheless, the job remained a difficult one to do under fire, and for fear of a casualty C. E. Wood, the base engineer at Akaba, the only sapper available, was invited to come along and help. He immediately agreed, though condemned medically for active service as the result of a bullet through the head in France, a fact which made him privately suspect both his strength and his nerve in emergency. Also he had never yet in his life been on a camel. George Lloyd, who was spending a last few days in Akaba before going to Versailles on a regretted inter-Allied commission, said that he would ride up with us as far as el jefer: and, as he was one of the best fellows and most unobtrusive travelers alive, his coming added greatly to our pleasant anticipation.

As we were making our last preparations, an unexpected ally arrived in the Emir Abd el Kader el Jezairi, grandson of the chivalrous defender of Algiers against the French. The family had lived in Damascus for a generation, taking a leading position in the town. One of them, Omar, had been hanged by Jemal for treason disclosed in the Picot papers. The others had been deported, and Abd el Kader told us a long story of his escape from Brusa, and his journey with a thousand adventures across Anatolia and Syria to Damascus. There he had learned for certain of the Arab Revolt and had come down by way of Jebel Druse to see what it offered.

In reality he was an Islamic fanatic, half-insane with religious enthusiasm, and a most violent belief in himself He had been released from confinement at the request of Abbas Hilmi, and sent down by him on his private business to Mecca. He went there, saw King Hussein, and came back to Akaba with a crimson banner, and noble gifts, his crazy mind half-persuaded of our right, and glowing jerkily with excitement.

To Feisal he offered the bodies and souls of his villagers, sturdy hard smiting Algerian exiles living compactly in the Jaulan region along the north bank of the Yarmuk. We seized at the chance this would give us to control for a little time the middle section of the valley railway with two or three of the main bridges, and without the disability of raising the countryside, since the Algerians were hated strangers and the Arab peasantry would not join them.

Accordingly we put off calling Rafa to meet us at Azrak, and said not a word to Zaal, centering instead all our thoughts on Wadi Khalid and its bridges. While we were in this train of mind arrived a telegram from Colonel Bremond, warning us that Abd el Kader was a spy and traitor in Turkish pay. It was disconcerting, and we watched him narrowly, but found no proof of the charge, which was not to be accepted blindly as Bremond was more a politician than a colleague, and his military temper might have carried away his judgment when he heard Abd el Kader's outspoken denunciation of France and things French. The French habit of conceiving of their country as a fair woman had given them a national spitefulness against those who scorned her charms.

Feisal told him to ride with Ali and myself, and said to me: 'I know he is mad: I think he is honest. Guard your heads and use him.' We carried on and showed him our complete confidence, on the principle that a crook would not credit our honesty, and that an honest man was made a crook soonest by suspicion. As a matter of fact his muslim susceptibilities were outraged by my Christianity: his pride was hurt by our companionship, since the tribes greeted Ali as greater and treated me as better than him. His bullet-headed stupidity broke down Ali's self-control twice or thrice into painful scenes: and in the end he left us in the lurch at a critical moment, after hindering our march and upsetting our plans as far as he could.

Chapter 78: Forward

It was as difficult as ever to get started. Amongst my own preparations were the careful picking of my bodyguard, and the adding to it of new men for the special line of country we would cross.

As usual there were plenty of applicants from whom to choose: and in the end I took six recruits on trial. One of these was Mahmud, a native of Turra, on the Yarmuk, the nearest village to the upper bridge. He was an alert and hot-tempered lad of about nineteen, with the petulance which often goes with curly hair. Another was Abd el Aziz of Tafas, an older fellow, who had spent three years with the Bedouin avoiding military service. He was capable with camels, a shallow spirit, almost rabbit-mouthed, but proud of himself A third was Mustafa, a gentle boy from near Deraa, very honest, who went about always sadly by himself (he was deaf and ashamed of his infirmity, as though it were wrongdoing). One day on the beach, in a short word, he had asked to be admitted to my bodyguard. So evidently did he expect to be refused that I took him, and it was a good choice for the others, since he was a mild peasant, and they could bully him and put upon him all the menial tasks. Yet he too was happy, for he was among desperate fellows, and the world would think him desperate. To balance his inefficiency on the march I enrolled Showakh and Salem, two Sherari camel-herds, and Abd el Rahman, a runaway slave from Riyadh, now freedman of Mohammed el Dheilan, the Toweihi.

Of the old bodyguard I gave Mohammed and Ali a rest. They were tired after the train-wrecking adventures and, like their camels, needed to go out to pasture quietly for a few weeks. This left Ahmed to become the inevitable head man of the party. He deserved it, for his ruthless energy, but the obvious choice was seldom good and, as I half-expected, he misused his power and became oppressive. So it was his last march with me. I took Kreim for the camels, and Rahail, the lusty conceited Haurani lad, for whom overwork was the grace which kept him continent. Matar, a parasitic fellow of the Beni Hassan, attached himself to us. His fat peasant's body filled all the seat of his camel saddle, and took nearly as large a share in the lewd or lurid jokes necessary on the march to pass the guards' leisure. We might enter Beni Hassan territory, and he had some influence. His obvious greed made us easily sure of him, and of his helpfulness till his great expectations failed. My service was now profitable, for I knew my worth to the movement, and spent freely to keep myself safe in it. Rumor, for once in a helpful mood, gilded my open hand. Farraj and Daud, the two favorite Ageyl, and Khidr and Mijbil, two Biasha, completed the party.

Farraj and Daud were capable and merry always on the road, which they loved as all the lithe Ageyl loved it, but in camp their excess of spirit seemed riotous, and led them continually into affairs. From these I had to extricate them, with more or less of trouble and expense. This time they surpassed themselves, by being missing on the day of our departure until noon, when there came a message from Sheikh Yusuf that they were in his prison, and would I talk to him about it? I went up to his house and found his bulk shaking between rage and laughter. He had just bought and not yet branded a cream colored riding camel, of the purest blood. The beast had strayed in the evening into the palm-garden where my Ageyl were camped. They never suspected she was the Governor's, and had amused themselves till dawn by dyeing her head bright red with henna, and her legs bright blue with indigo, before turning her loose. Akaba was immediately in an uproar about this circus-beast. Yusuf recognized her with difficulty and hurled all his police abroad to find the criminals. The two friends were dragged before the judgment seat, stained to the elbows with dye, and loudly protesting their entire innocence. The circumstances were, however, too strong for them, and Yusuf, after doing his best with a palm-rib to hurt their feelings, put them in irons for a slow week's meditation. I made good his damage by the loan of a camel from my stud till his own should be respectable to ride. Then I explained that there was instant need of the sinners and appealed to his humor by a solemn promise of another dose of his treatment for them when their skins were fit; so he ordered their release. They were delighted to escape the vermin prison on any terms, and rejoined us singing.

This business had delayed us, and so we had an immense final meal in the luxury of the camp at Akaba, and started in the evening of October the twenty-fourth. We marched slowly for four hours, and camped two miles down the right branch of Wadi Itm after midnight. The first march was always slow, for both camels and men hated the moment of setting out on a new hazard. The loads slipped, saddles had to be re-girthed, and riders changed. Beside my own camels (Ghazala, the old grandmother, now far gone in foal, and Naama, a full-pointed Sherari camel which the Sukhur had stolen from the Rualla) and the bodyguards' camels, I had mounted the Indians and lent camels to Wood (who was delicate in the saddle and rode a fresh animal nearly every day) and to Thome, Lloyd's yeomanry-trooper, who sat his camel almost like an Arab, and looked workmanlike in a head cloth with a striped cloak over his khaki. Lloyd himself was on a thoroughbred Dheraiyeh which Feisal lent him: a fine fast animal, but clipped after mange and a little thin.

Our party straggled badly. Wood fell behind, and my men being fresh and having much work to keep the Indians together, lost touch with him. So he found himself alone with Thome, and they two missed our turn to the east, in the blackness that always fills the depths of the gorge by night except when the moon is directly overhead, and went on up the main track towards Guweira. They rode for hours but, of course, saw no signs of us, and at last decided to wait for day in a side-valley of the hills. Both were new to the country, and not sure of the Arabs, and so they took turns to keep awake watching their camels. We guessed what had happened to them when they never came, and before dawn sent back Ahmed, Abd el Aziz and Abd el Rahman, the three of my men who knew this country, with orders to scatter up all the available roads and bring the missing pair after us or before us to Rum.

I stayed with Lloyd and the main body as their guide, to take them up the curved slopes of Hawara and over the pink and green valleys of Nejd to Rum. The air and light were so wonderful that we wandered round and round without thinking in the least about today or tomorrow: also I had Lloyd to talk to, and the world seemed very good. There had been a faint shower in the evening, which had brought earth and sky together in the mellow day. The colors in the cliffs and trees and soil were so pure and vivid that we ached for real contact with them and for our tethered inability to carry anything of them away. We were full of leisure. The Indians proved bad camel-masters and could only move slowly and clumsily, while Farraj and Daud pleaded a new form of saddle-soreness, called Yusufiyeh', which made them walk most of the journey.

We entered Rum at last with the crimson sunset burning on its stupendous cliffs, and throwing long beams of hazy fire down the walled avenue towards Guweira. Wood and Thome were there already in the sandstone amphitheater of the springs. Wood was ill, and lying down on my odd camping platform under the great red boulders of the south side. Abd el Rahman had caught them before noon, and after a good deal of misunderstanding, for their few words of Egyptian did not help much with his clipped Aridh dialect or the Howeiti slang with which he eked it out, had persuaded them to follow him. He had cut across the hills by the difficult path from 'bel Hiran to Rum, to their great discomfort. Wood had been hungry and hot and worried, angry to the point of refusing the native mess which Abd el Rahman contrived for them in a Njadat tent on the way. He had begun to believe that he would never see anything of us again, and was ungrateful when we did arrive, too overcome with the awe that Rum compels on all her visitors to sympathies deeply with his sufferings. In fact we staled at him and said, 'Yes,' and left him lying there while we wandered off and talked in whispers about the wonder of the place. Fortunately Ahmed and Thome thought more of food, and, with supper, friendly relations were restored.

We slept that night in the chill air which drops down the hill-face with the waterfall, and next day, while we were saddling, Ali ibn el Hussein and Abd el Kader appealed. Lloyd and I had a second lunch with them, for they were quarreling, and to have guests held them in check for a while. Lloyd was of the rare sort of traveler who can eat anything with anybody, anyhow and at any time. Then, making pace, we pushed after our party down the chasm of Wadi Rum through the tamarisk. It was Lloyd's first sight of Rum, whose giant hill-shapes ale full of design and as fur above Nature as great architecture, but beautiful too, as though God had built them ready for some great pageant to which the sons of men were insufficient.

At the bottom of the valley we crossed the flat Goa, where we pleased Wood by matching our camels in a quick burst over its velvet surface, till we overtook the main body, and scattered them with the excitement of our gallop. The Indians' soberly laden camels danced like iron mongers till they had shed their burdens, and then we calmed ourselves, and plodded all together gently up Wadi Hafira, the narrow gash which runs like a sword-cut into the plateau. At its head lay the stiff pass (on to the height of Batra) that we had used for the second railway-raid but today we fell short of this, and out of laziness and a craving for comfort stopped in the sheltered bottom of the valley at our old camping ground, where the camels grazed their fill for the first time since Akaba. We lit great fires of brushwood, which were cheerful in the cool evening, and reveled in abundance of food.

Farraj had prepared rice in his manner for me as usual. Lloyd and Wood and Thome had brought with them bully beef and biscuits. So we joined ranks and feasted. Afterwards I talked late to Lloyd about my Bagdad plan. The war was not looking too well, and I thought the spare Englishmen in Mesopotamia and Palestine might soon be called away to France, if so, the Arabs would be left alone on the offensive in Turkey; and the offensive was theirs without choice, since a rebellion can be no otherwise. Our present march was taking us to Jebel Druse. It was my hope to make a base there: and while the Turks were guarding Damascus against us, to slip into Bagdad. In Mesopotamia were one hundred thousand Arab fighting men, better in small packets than the Turk small packets, for the flower of Turkey had died in Gallipoli and the Caucasus. Bagdad was lighter held than Syria, and as easy for us. To be sure, the Mesopotamians were not yet nationalists, and the British there said they would not fight: but it was our day's work to turn new provinces into fighting men, and we had little fear that our cry and creed of freedom would ever find one Arab deaf to it.

Next day we pushed up the zigzag broken path to the crest, stopping on each new face to look down the grassy street of the Hafira valley behind us, with one regular cone-hill in its center, and in the background the fantastic: grey domes and glowing pyramids of the mountains of Rum, prolonged today into even wider fantasies by the cloud-masses brooding over them. Lloyd's fresh eyes sharpened all the known sight for me: while we watched, our long train wound upwards, till before noon all the camels, Arabs', Indians', and baggage, had reached the top without accident. Very pleased, we plumped ourselves down in the first green valley over the crest, in shelter from the wind and warmed by the faint sunshine, which tempered the autumn chill of this high tableland. Someone began to talk again about food.

Chapter 79: Night Marching

I went away north scouting with Awad, a Sherari camel-boy whom I had engaged in Rum at short notice and without much investigation. There were so many baggage camels in our party, and the Indians such novices at loading and leading them, that much work was falling on my bodyguard and they were being diverted from their proper duty of riding with me. So when Showakh came up and introduced his cousin, a Khayal Sherari who would serve with me on any conditions, I had accepted him at the glance, and now thought it wise to test him a little before a crisis came on us.

We circled round Aba el Lissan and Fuweilah, to make sure that their Turkish garrisons were in seemly idleness, for they had had an inconvenient habit of rushing a mounted-infantry patrol over the Batra sites at sudden notice, and I had no mind to put my party into unnecessary action yet. Awad was a ragged brown skinned lad of perhaps eighteen, splendidly built, with the muscles and sinews of an athlete in fine training, active as a cat, alive in the saddle (he rode magnificently) and not ill-looking, though with something of the base appearance of the Sherarat, and in his savage eye an air of constant and rather suspicious expectancy, as though he looked any moment for something new from life, and that something not wholly grateful.

These Sherarat were an enigma in the desert. To look upon, they were Arab, only perhaps better made, and stronger of body. They were harder-living and more ascetic than any Bedouin.

Often they spent years in the open without once visiting a market, existing on samh and dates, and camel-milk from their prolific herds. They bred the best camels of north Arabia, and had a profound understanding of their care and treatment. They were brave fighters, though not for their own hand, for they had no blood-enemies or tribal organization, but were split up all over the northern desert as helots among the Arabs. Chasib el Lehawi, counted a sheikh among them, was the grandson of a peasant in Tafileh, and eminent only for his wealth. In truth they were not a tribe, but a race, cousins of the Heteyrn, and like them were despised by their Arab neighbors, thought too base to breed with, denied humane consideration, and treated in public with a loud contempt. All this they took uncomplainingly.

I used many of them during my rides from Akaba and found them useful. They were as Arabic as Arabia itself, and yet stood outside its society, and had no common feeling with its tribes. They were outcasts, and their consciousness of extreme degradation was a positive base on which to build a trust. Other men had hopes or illusions. The Sherarat knew that nothing better than physical existence was permitted them by mankind in this world or another. I treated them, however, exactly like the others in my bodyguard. This they found astonishing and yet pleasant, when they came to believe it, and learned that my protection while they served me was active and sufficient. On such material terms they would become wholly my property, and good slaves they were, for nothing in the desert was beneath their dignity or beyond their strength.

Awad was still doubting and before me showed himself confused and self-conscious, though I had seen that with his fellows he could be merry and full of japes. His engagement was a sudden fortune beyond dreams, and he was pitifully determined to suit my mind. For the moment this was to wander across the Maan highroad in order to draw the Turks' notice. When we had succeeded and they trotted out in chase we returned back, doubled again, and so tricked their mule-riders towards Aba el Adham. Awad took a gleeful concern in the game, and handled his new rifle well.

Afterwards I climbed with him to the top of the hill near Ageila, overlooking Batra and the valleys that sloped to Aba el Lissan, and we lay there lazily by the cairn till afternoon, watching the Turks riding in a vain direction, and our fellows asleep, and their pasturing camels, and the shadows of the low clouds seeming like gentle hollows as they chased themselves in the sunlight over the grassy levels. It was peaceful, chilly, and very far from the fretting of the world. The austerity of these great heights had shamed back the vulgar baggage of our daily cares. In the place of Consequence, it set Freedom, power to be alone, to slip the escort of our manufactured selves; a rest and complete forgetfulness of being.

But Awad could not forget his appetite and the new sensation of power in my caravan to satisfy it regularly each day: so he fidgeted about the ground on his belly chewing innumerable stalks of grass, and talking to me of his animal life in jerky phrases with averted face, till we saw Ali's cavalcade beginning to lip over the head of the pass on to the plateau. Then we ran down the green slopes to meet them, and heard how he had lost four camels on the pass, two broken by falls, two others just failed for weakness in mounting the rocky ledges. Also he had fallen out again with Abd el Kader, from whose defeat and conceit and boorish manners he prayed God to deliver him.

We left him there to follow us after dark, and since his would be an all-night march, and he had no guide with him, I loaned him Awad, who knew the country to the railway and beyond to jefer, where we would meet again in Auda's tents. Then we loaded up and moved forward over the shallow valleys and cross-ridges till the sun set, when we were at the last high bank, from the top of which we could have a wide view across the great depression, from Aneyza to Shedia, On whose western edge the railway ran. In the furthest distance we saw the square box of the station at Ghadir el Haj, breaking out artificially in the blue level, miles and miles away. Behind us in the valley were broom bushes, so we called a halt, and with their branches made our supper-fires. This evening Hassan Shah devised a pleasant notion (which later became a habit) of winding up our meal by an offering of his Indian tea. We were too greedy and grateful to refuse, and to our shame we eventually exhausted all his tea and sugar before fresh rations could be sent up to him from the base.

I knew this same country very poorly, but before dark Lloyd and I went up and marked the bearing of the railway, in the place where we proposed to cross just below Shedia. As the stars rose we agreed that we must march upon Orion. So we started, and marched on Orion for hour after hour with the effect that Orion seemed no nearer and there were no signs of anything between us and him. We had debouched from the ridges upon the plain, and the plain was never-ending, and monotonously striped by shallow wadi-beds, with low flat straight banks which in the milky star-light looked always like the earthwork of the expected railway. The going underfoot was firm, and the cool air of the desert in our faces made the camels swing out freely. Lloyd and I went on in front to lead the party and spy out the line, that the main body might not be involved if chance put us against a Turkish blockhouse or night-patrol. Our fine camels, lightly ridden, set too long a stride, so that without knowing it we drew more and more ahead of the laden and laboring Indians. Hassan Shah the Jemadar threw out a man to keep us in sight, and then another, and after that a third, till his whole party was only a hurrying string of connecting files. Then he passed up an urgent whisper, which reached us unintelligible after passing through three languages, to go slow that the men might once more get together.

We halted in an open place; and so knew that the quiet night was full of sounds; while the scents of the withering plants about us ebbed and flowed in our faces with the dying wind. Afterwards we marched again more slowly, as it seemed for hours, and the plain was still barred with deceitful dykes, which kept our attention at full stretch unprofitably. We felt that the stars were shifting, and that we were steering wrong. Lloyd had a compass somewhere, and we halted and groped for it in his deep saddlebags unsuccessfully. Thome rode up and found it in some cranny of his own. We stood around calculating on its luminous arrow-head, and deserted Orion for a more auspicious northern star.

Then again forward interminably till, as we climbed a larger bank, Lloyd reined up with a gasp and pointed right ahead. Fair in our track on the horizon were two cubes blacker than the sky and by them a smaller pointed roof We were bearing straight for Shedia station, and nearly into it. At once we swung off to the right, and jogged hastily across an open space, a little nervous lest some of the caravan strung out behind us should miss the abrupt change of course: but all was well, and when we collected a few minutes later in the next hollow we exchanged greetings on our thrill in English and Turkish, Arabic and Urdu. Behind us broke out a faint clamor of dogs in the Turkish camp.

We now knew our place, and took a fresh bearing to the southward, to avoid the first great blockhouse below Shedia, with which we had had affair when blowing up our second train. We led off confidently, expecting to cross the line in a little. Yet again the time dragged and nothing showed itself It was midnight, and we had marched for six hours, and Lloyd began to speak bitterly of reaching Bagdad in the morning. There could be no railway here. Thome saw a row of trees, and saw them move; the bolts of our rifles clicked: but they were only trees.

We gave up hope and rode on carelessly, nodding in our saddles, letting our tired eyes lid themselves. Again the Indians lagged far behind our hasty camels; but after an hour the last bank of the night loomed differently in front of us. It took straight shape, and in its length grew darker patches which might be the shadowed mouths of culverts. We spurred our minds to a fresh interest, and drove our animals swiftly and silently forward to see. When we were near, the bank put up a fencing of sharp spikes along its edge. These were the telegraph poles. A white-headed figure standing there checked us for a moment, but he never stirred, and so we judged he was a kilometer post.

Quickly we halted the party, and rode to one side and then straight in to challenge what lay behind the quiet of the place, expecting the darkness to spout fire at us suddenly, and the silence to volley out in rifle-shots. But there was no alarm. We reached the bank and found it deserted. We dismounted and ran up and down, each way two hundred yards — nobody; there was room for us to cross.

We sent back to order the others immediately over into the empty friendly desert on the east, and then sat down side by side on the metals and listened to the singing of the wires above our heads, while the long line of shadowy bulks wavered up out of the dark, shuffled a little on the bank and its ballast, and passed down behind us into the dark in that strained noiselessness that is a night march of camels. The last one crossed, and the little group of us on foot collected about the nearest telegraph post. There was a short scuffle out of which Thome rose slowly up the pole till he caught the lowest wire, and swung himself on to its insulator bracket. Then he reached up to the top, and a moment later there was a loud metallic twang and shaking of the post as the cut wire leaped back each way into the air, and slapped itself free from ten or more poles on either side. The second and third wires followed it, twisting noisily along the stony ground, and yet no answering sound came out of the night, showing that we had crossed rightly in the empty distance of two blockhouses. Thome with his splintery hands slid down the now tottering pole into our arms. We walked back to our kneeling camels beside which stood my impatient guards and trotted out till we caught up the company. Another hour and we ordered a camp for the short rest till dawn, but before then were roused by a brief flurry of rifle fire, and the tapping of a machine-gun far away to the north. Ali ibn el Hussein and Abd el Kader were not making as clean a crossing of the line as we had done.

Next morning in a cheerful sunshine we marched up parallel with the line a little, till we had saluted the first train from Maan, and then struck inland over the strange Jefer plain. The day was close, and the sun's power increased, making mirages on all the heated flats. Riding in front or behind or on the side of our long straggling party we saw parts of them drowned in the silver flood, parts of them swimming high over its changing surface, as it stretched and shrank with each swaying of the camel, or inequality of ground.

Early in the afternoon we found Auda Abu Tayi, camped unobtrusively in the broken bushy expanse south-west of the wells. He received us with some constraint. His large tents, with the women, had been sent away beyond reach of the Turkish airplanes into Tubaik. He was living in the lining of an E.P. tent with half the wall, while Zaal lived next him in the cover of the tent (propped up on two looted railway-poles) and the other side of the wall.

There were only a few Toweiha present, and those in the midst of a violent money dispute with Auda, over the distribution of tribe-wages. The old man was sad we should find him in this weakness. I did my best tactfully to smooth out the troubles by giving their minds a new direction and fresh interests, and succeeded so far that they smiled, which with Arabs was often half the battle. It was all the gain prudent for the time, and we rose up together and went off to eat with Mohammed el Dheilan, in his tent about half a mile to the north of Auda's. He was a better diplomat, because less open than most Arabs, and would look cheerful, if he thought it proper, whatever the truth. So we were made very welcome by him, and given a luscious platter of rice and meat and dried tomatoes. Mohammed was a villager at heart, and fed too well.

After the meal, as we were wandering back over the sharp dry ditches, like mammoth wallows, that the collected flood-water of two years ago had hacked deeply into the grey fibrous mud of the Jefer plain, I broached to Zaal my plans for an expedition to the Yarmuk bridges, with alternative object Hemme, Wadi Khalid, or Tell el Shehab. He disliked the idea very much. Zaal in October was not the Zaal of August. Success was changing the hard-riding gallant of spring into a prudent man, whose new wealth made life precious to him. In the spring he would readily have led me anywhere — but the Hallat Ammar raid had tried his nerve, and he now said that on this errand he would only mount if I made a personal point of it.

I asked what party we could make up and he named three of the men in the camp as good fellows for so desperate a hope. The rest of the tribe were away, dissatisfied. To take three Toweiha would be worse than useless, for their just conceit would inflame all the others in the party while they themselves would be too few to suffice for anything alone. It seemed to me better to be quit of them: so I said that I would try elsewhere. Zaal showed his relief

While we were still discussing it and what we ought to do (for I needed the advice of Zaal, one of the finest raiders alive and most competent, in his cool courage, to judge my half-formed scheme) a scared lad rushed to our coffee-hearth in Auda's tent and blurted out that riders in a dust-cloud were coming up fast from the side of Maan. The Turks there had a mule-regiment, and a cavalry regiment. It was only twenty-five miles across a level plain. They often sent their airplanes to bomb el jefer, and were always boasting that they would someday raid the Abu Tayi. So we all jumped up to receive them as well as possible.

Auda had fifteen men, of whom five were able bodied and the rest grey-beards or boys, but we were about thirty strong, and I pondered on the hard luck of the Turkish commander who had chosen for his surprise the day on which there happened to be staying with the Howeitat a section of Indian machine-gunners who knew their business. We couched and knee-haltered the camels in some of the deeper water ruts, and placed the teams with their Vickers' and Lewis' in others of these natural trenches, admirably screened with alkali bushes, and commanding a flat field eight hundred yards each way. Auda dropped his tents, and threw out his riflemen to supplement our fire, and then we waited easily till the first horsemen rode up the bank on to our level, and we saw they were Ali ibn el Hussein and Abd el Kader, who had gone away too far to the north, and so were coming into Jefer from the enemy direction. We forgathered merrily and Mohammed produced a second edition of his tomato-rice for Ali's immediate comfort. They had lost two men and a mare in the shooting on the railway in the night.

Chapter 80: the Beni Sakhr

Lloyd was to go back from here to do duty at Versailles, and we asked Auda for a guide to take him across the line to Rum and Akaba. About the man there was no difficulty, but great difficulty of how to mount him. The Howeitat had not a camel in their tents. There were some horses, but the riding camels were all out at pasture a full day's journey to the south-east. Arabs laid their property open to surprise by their fashion of pasturing the camels at a distance. It was a choice of evils for them, since Bedouin life was a struggle between the need of water for the household, and of grazing for the camels, and the household generally won, as it was easier to send the camels away for their four days' dry pasturage than to carry drinking-water daily a great distance to the tents. It meant, however, that it was hopeless to expect sudden mounted help or the quick start of an expedition from a tribal camp, and relay riding on loaned camels in the desert was impossible.

Auda offered to send a man to bring a camel, but that would have meant too long a wait: so I cut the difficulty by providing a mount for the new guide from my own camels. Choice fell on the old Ghazala, whose pregnancy had proved more heavy than we thought. Before our long expedition ended she would be unfit for fast work. So in honor of his good seat and cheerful spirit Thome was transferred to her and duly photographed, while the Howeitat stared open-mouthed. They esteemed Ghazala above all the camels of their desert, and would have paid much for the honor of riding her, and here she was given to a soldier, whose pink face and eyes swollen with ophthalmia made him look feminine and tearful; a little, said Lloyd, like an abducted nun. As escort were added Khidr and Mijbil, the two Biasha, who would suffer more than my other men from the cold in store than us. To mind their camels on the way down went Salem the Sherari: and after these preparations they rode off in the afternoon. It was a sorry thing to see Lloyd go. With him one could discuss any book or thing in heaven or earth: he was the one fully-taught man with us in Arabia, and in these few days together our minds had ranged abroad . Also he was so understanding, helped so wisely, and wished our cause so well. When he left I was given over again to war and tribes and camels without end.

The night began with a surfeit of such work. The matter of the Howeitat must be put right. After dark we drew in round Auda's hearth and for hours I was reaching out to this circle of fire-lit faces, playing on them with all the tortuous arts I knew, now catching one, now another (it was easy to see the lash in their eyes when a word got home) and again taking a false line and wasting minutes of my precious time without response. The Abu Tayi were as hard minded as they were hard-bodied, and the heat of conviction had burnt out in all of them long since. Their climax had been our taking Akaba: then they had been supreme, riders of the spirit before whom material bars shattered and fell away. They still had in them fiber for another effort, if there was time and a preacher to arouse them: but this waiting game they hated, and yet they were a link in our chain and must hold for our sakes.

Gradually I won my points and felt easier: but the argument was yet marching near midnight when Auda suddenly held up his stick and called for silence. We listened wondering what the danger was, and after a little while heard a creeping reverberation, a cadence of blows too dull, too wide, too slow easily to find response in our ears. It was like the mutter of a distant, very lowly thunderstorm, and Auda raised his haggard eyes towards the western sky, and said, 'The English guns.' Allenby was leading off: and his sounds closed my case for me beyond dispute.

Next morning the atmosphere of the camp was serene and cordial. Old Auda, his difficulties over for this time, embraced me warmly, again and again saying farewell, and wishing peace upon me. At the last, while I was standing with my hand on my couched camel he ran out once more, and took me in his arms and strained me to him. I felt his harsh beard brush my ear as he whispered to me windily, 'Beware of Abd el Kader.' There were too many men about us to say more. We pushed on, over the interminable but weirdly beautiful Jefer flats. The night fell on us, in a valley near the Shomari, at the foot of the flint scarp which rose like a sea-cliff above the level plain. We camped there in a pocket of under wood, very rich in snakes. The next day we rode forward again without any incidents towards Bair.

Our marches were short and very leisurely. The Indians were novices on the road. They had been with Newcombe for weeks inland from Wejh, and I had rashly understood that they were riders: but now, on good animals, and trying their best, they did only thirty or thirty-five miles a day. Some of Sherif Ali's Bisha guards were little better, since the Bishi is a lubber on a camel, and theirs were rotten with mange. My own animals, thanks to the care of Farraj and Daud, the Aglan, were splendid. The Ageyl loved camels, and they felt it a shame to their corps if their own mounts and those of their masters were not always in the best condition.

So we found each day an easy movement, without effort, quite free of bodily strain. A golden weather, the misty dawns, mild sunlight, and an evening chill added a strange peacefulness of nature to the peacefulness of our march. This week was a St Martin's summer, which passed like a remembered dream. I felt only that it was very gentle, very comfortable, that the air was happy, the earth virgin, and my friends content. Conditions so perfect must needs presage the ending of our time, but this certainty of death in store for us, being unchallenged by any rebellious hope, deepened the quiet of the autumnal present. There was no thought or care at all. My mind was as near stilled those days as ever in my life.

Near the Mertaha we camped for lunch and for a midday rest: the soldiers had to have three meals a day. Suddenly there was an alarm. Men on horses and camels appeared from the west and north, and closed quickly on us. We jumped up and snatched our rifles. The Indians were getting used to short notices, and carried their Vickers' and Lewis' stripped for action. After thirty seconds we were in complete posture of defense, though in this shallow country our position held little of advantage. To the front on each flank was my bodyguard in their brilliant clothes, lying spread out between the grey tufts of weed, with their rifles lovingly against their cheeks. By them were the four neat groups of khaki Indians, crouched about their guns. Behind lay Sherif Ali's men, with himself standing in their midst, bareheaded and keen, leaning easily upon his rifle. In the background were the camel men, driving in our grazing animals to be under cover of our fire.

It was a picture that the party made, and I was still admiring ourselves, and Ali was exhorting us to hold our fire till the attack became real: when Awad sprang up and ran out towards the enemy, waving his full sleeve over his head as a sign of friendliness.

They fired at or over him, ineffectually. He lay down and shot back, one shot, aimed just over the head of the foremost rider. That and the ready silence of the rest of us perplexed them. They pulled off, collected together in a hesitant group, and after a minute's discussion flagged back their cloaks in reply to our signal.

One of them rode out alone towards us at a foot's pace. Awad, protected by our rifles, went on some two hundred yards to meet him in the open, and saw that he was a Sukhuri, who appeared very sorry when he learned our names. We walked back together to Sherif Ali, followed at a distance by the rest of the newcomers after they had seen our peaceful greeting. They were camel herds and a raiding party from the Zebn Sukhur, who camped at Bair, as we had expected.

Ali was furious with them for their treacherous attack on us, and threatened all manner of pains. They accepted his tirade sullenly, saying that it was a Beni Sakhr manner to shoot over all strangers. Ali accepted this as their habit, and a good habit in the desert, but protested again at their unheralded appearance against us from three sides, since this showed a premeditated ambush. The Beni Sakhr were a dangerous gang, not pure enough nomads to hold the nomadic code of honor, or to obey the desert law in spirit, and not villagers enough to cease the business of loot and raid. Anyone who passed through their camps did so at his own risk: had we been another tribe, or a caravan of merchants, they would have plundered us without mercy.

We went on resting there while our late assailants went into Bair to tell the Arabs of our coming. Mifleh el Gomaan, chief of the clan, and head-man in the camp, thought it best to efface our memory of the ill-reception by a public show in which all the men, horses and camels in the place turned out, and welcomed us along Wadi Bair to the wells with wild cheers and galloping and curveting, and much firing of shots, and shouting. They whirled round and round us at a desperate pace, chasing one another, clattering over the rocks with reckless horsemanship, and with small regard for our staidness, since they broke in and out of the ranks, and let off their rifles under our camels' necks continually. Clouds of fine chalk dust arose, parching our throats with heat like lime, and making them hoarse as ravens.

Eventually the parade eased off, but then Abd el Kader, thinking the flattery even of fools desirable, felt it upon him to assert his virtue. They were shouting to Ali ibn el Hussein, 'God give victory to our Sherif, and were reining back on their haunches beside me with, 'Welcome Aurans, harbinger of action.' So he climbed up his mare, into her high Moorish saddle, and, with his seven Algerian servants behind him in stiff file, began to prance about delicately in slow curves, crying out, 'Houp, Houp,' in his throaty voice, and letting off a rifle unsteadily in the air.

The Bedu, astonished at this spiritless performance, gaped silently, till Mifleh came up to Ali and myself, and said in his wheedling way, 'Lord pray call off your servant, for he can neither shoot nor ride, and if he hit someone he will destroy our good fortune of today' Mifleh did not know, but there was finally precedent for his nervousness. Abd el Kader's brother, the Emir Mohammed Said, held what might well be a world's record for three successive fatal accidents with automatic pistols in the circle of his Damascus mends. This history made Ali Riza Pasha say, 'There are three things notably impossible: one, that Turkey win this war; one, that the

Mediterranean become champagne; one, that I be found in the same place with Mohammed Said, and he armed.'

We off-loaded in the flat place between the ruins and the northern well. Beyond us the ground was picketed by the black tents of the Beni Sakhr, like a herd of goats scattered in the valley. A messenger came down to bid us to Mifleh's tent, which stood up on the knoll above the grave-yard, in the best place of all. First, however, we had work to do. The camels had to be watered, for the next stage was a long one; and Ali had an enquiry to make. At the request of the Beni Sakhr, Feisal had sent up to Bair a party of Bisha masons and well-sinkers, to clear out the well from which we had taken the dynamite, and to reline its shaft to the ground level. This had been months before, and still they reported the work not finished: so Feisal, in answer to the complaint he had received, deputed Ali ibn el Hussein to examine their work.

Ali found evident signs of slackness, and that the Bisha men had been forcing the Arabs to provide them with meat and flour, to get even this little result. He charged them with it. They prevaricated, but the Sherifs had a trained judicial instinct, and Mifleh was preparing a great supper for us. My men whispered to me excitedly that sheep had been seen to die behind his tent. So Ali's justice moved on wings. He heard and condemned the blacks all in a moment, and had justice executed on them by his slaves inside the ruins before the food-bowls were carried up. Then they returned, a little self-conscious, kissed hands in sign of amenity and forgiveness, and a reconciled party knelt together to meat.

Howeitat feasts had been wet with butter: the Beni Sakhr were overflowing. Our clothes were splashed, our mouths running over, the tips of our fingers were scalded with its heat. As the sharpness of hunger was appeased, the hands dipped more slowly, but the meal was still far from the just end when Abd el Kader grunted suddenly and rose to his feet, wiped his hands on a handkerchief and sat back in his place on the carpets by the tent-wall. The rest hesitated, but Ali muttered, 'The fillah', and the work continued till all were filled, and the more frugal of us began to lick the stiffening fat from between our smarting fingers.

Then Ali cleared his throat, and at the sound we rose rhythmically to our feet, while he said, 'God be generous to you, a host.' The servers washed our hands under dippers of water and afterwards we returned to our carpets to wait with coffee till the second and third relays round the pans were satisfied. One little thing of five or six in a filthy smock sat there stuffing solemnly with both hands from first to last, and at the end, with swollen belly and face glistening with grease, staggered of hugging a huge unpicked rib in triumph in his arms.

In front of the tent the dogs cracked the bones loudly, and Mifleh's slave in the corner split open th sheep's skull, and sucked out the brains. Meanwhile Abd el Kader sat there spitting and belching, an picking his teeth. Finally he sent one of his servants for his medicine chest, and poured himself out draught, grumbling that tough meat was bad for his digestion. He hoped by this unmannered to make himself a reputation for grandeur hardly of this world. His own villagers could no doubt be brow beaten in such a way, but the Zebn were unfortunately too near the desert to be measured by the peasant-measure. By the more courteous standard of the nomad his behavior was vulgar and ignorant and he had the further misfortune at the moment to be contrasted with the perfect dignity of Ali ibn el Hussein, a real lord in his own country, and an exquisite on all public occasions. So poor Abd el Kader was not understood.

He took himself off, and we sat there with the company in the tent-mouth, looking across the dark hollow, now set out in little constellations of tent-fires, seeming to mimic or reflect the sky above. It was a calm night, except when the dogs provoked one another to choral howling, and as these grew rarer we heard again the quiet steady thudding of the guns in Palestine.

To this accompaniment we told Mifleh that we were about to raid the Deraa district, and would be glad to have him with us, and some fifteen of his tribesmen, all on camels. After our failure with the Howeitat, we had decided not to announce the plain object of our hopes, since the forlorn character of the expedition might prevent others joining. As a matter of fact he agreed at once, apparently with haste and pleasure, and promised to bring the fifteen best men in the tribe, and his own son with him. This Turki was an old love of Ali ibn el Hussein: the animal in each called to the other, and they wandered about inseparably everywhere taking pleasure in a touch and silence. He was a fair open-faced boy of perhaps seventeen, short but broad and powerful, with a round freckled face, upturned nose, and very short upper lip, showing his strong teeth, but giving his full mouth rather a sulky look, belied by his happy eyes.

We found him a plucky, faithful lad, who served us well on two critical occasions. His good temper atoned for his having inherited or adopted a shade of the begging habit of his father, whose face was all eaten up with greed. However, Turki was so simple and friendly about it that we easily pardoned him, and generally rewarded his persistence. His great anxiety was to be sure that he was reckoned a man among the men, and he was looking to do something bold and wonderful which would gain him the right also to flaunt himself before the girls of his tribe. He rejoiced exceedingly in a new silk robe I gave him, and walked twice through the tent-village without his cloak, railing at laggards for the meet, to show everyone that he was conveniently dressed.

Chapter 81: The Serahin

Our caravan left Bair at dark, after their watering. We chiefs waited while the Zebn got ready. Mifleh's preparations included a visit to Essad, the supposed ancestor of the clan, in his bedecked tomb near Annad's grave. The Beni Sakhr were settled-Semite enough already to have dressed themselves in the village-superstitions of holy places, sacred trees, and the shrines of ancestors. The fewness of the generations which brought this to pass was another proof of the mighty land-change lying between the desert and the sown. Mifleh thought the occasion warranted his adding another head-cord to the ragged collection looped round the sheikh's headstone, and characteristically he asked us to provide him with the offering. I handed over one of my gaudy red-silk and silver Meccan ornaments, remarking that the virtue lay with the donor. The thrifty Mifleh pressed upon me one half-penny in exchange, that he might plead fair purchase: and when I came past a few weeks later and saw that it was gone, he cursed loudly in my hearing the sacrilege of some godless Sherari, who had robbed his ancestors. Turki would have told me more.

An hour or two later we pulled out for Ammari in Wadi Sirhan, the nearest water-hole, some ninety miles away: but this evening we did only an easy stage. We rode out of Wadi Bair, by a steep old pathway up the bank, and thence towards the plateau of the Erha, across the sources of the great valleys, Bair and Ausaji, which ran down from the south face of the Erha Hadi Thlaithukhwat water parting and, after a long journey eastward, at last reached the Sirhan. Near the crest of the ridge we found the others and at once camped for the night. There was a late moon, and we made a fire: but there passed no talk or coffee-making round it for this time. We lay close together, hushed and straining the ears to catch all the throbbing of Allenby's guns. It spoke more eloquently of our support than anything that we could say: and there was sheet lightning in the west, which made gun-flashes.

Next day we passed the crest just to the left of the Thlaithukhwat, the three sisters whose clean white peaks were landmarks on their lofty water-shed for a day's journey all about; and went down the soft rolling slopes beyond them into Wadi Dherwa, which was our route. The exquisite November morning had softness in it like the air of an English summer: but I was spending all the halts and riding all the stages in the ranks of the Beni Sakhr, teaching my ear their dialect, and storing in my memory for future use the tribal, family or personal notes they let drop about themselves. It was easy to make tribesmen talk about their friends and enemies, and one another; and profitable, since without this information no one could hope to handle them freely.

To have shown in an unguarded statement, or by direct question, ignorance of such matters would have been fatal to me, for every competent Arab was familiar with them by instinct or experience. In the small and little-peopled desert every worshipful man knew every other, and instead of books they studied their own generation. To have fallen short in this knowledge would have meant being branded either as ill-bred, or as a stranger, and strangers were not admitted to familiar intercourse, and were shut out from councils and friendly confidences. There was nothing so wearing in all Arabia as this constant mental gymnastic of apparent omniscience at each time of meeting a new tribe. An effort to grasp unknown allusions, and to take an intelligent share in a half-intelligible conversation, would be hard in England, where only politeness was at stake, but how much more in the Arab Revolt, where one bad failure not merely in etiquette or in imagination, but in understanding a new dialect, might have wrecked the whole endeavor.

At nightfall we camped in an affluent of Wadi Jesha, by the shelter of some bushes of faint grey-green foliage, which pleased our camels, and gave us firewood. That night the guns were very clear and loud, perhaps because the hollow of the Dead Sea lying between us and them threw the echoes of the sound over our high plateau. The Arabs whispered to one another: 'They are nearer than last night: the English are advancing: God deliver the men under that rain of blows.' They were thinking compassionately of the Turks, so long their weak oppressors, whom for their weakness, though oppressors, they loved more than the strong foreigner, with his stony justice.

The Arab respected force a little: he respected craft more and often had it in an enviable degree: but most of all he respected that blunt sincerity of utterance, so easily assumed by many Englishmen and nearly the only weapon God had excluded from the

Arabian armament. The Turk showed all these things by turn and so as a race commended himself to the Arabs for such a while as he was not corporately feared. There lay much in this distinction of the corporate and the personal. There were Englishmen they knew whom individually the Arabs preferred to any Turk or other foreigner: but to have presumed on it and have said that therefore the Arabs were pro-English, would have been rank folly. Each stranger made his own bed among them: and some of us would be ashamed to say what poor beds ours were.

Next morning we were up early, meaning to push the long way to Ammari by sunset. We crossed ridge after carpeted ridge of sunburned flints grown over with a saffron plant a few inches high, but so bright and close that all the view was golden yellow. Safra el Jesha, the Sukhur called it. The valleys were only inches deep, their beds grained like morocco leather in an intricate pattern of meshed curves by the passage of innumerable rills of water after the last rain.

The swell of each curve was a grey breast of sand set hard with mud sometimes glistening with salt-crystals sometimes rough with a projecting brush of half-buried twigs. Here and there in the watercourses were long troughs with brown clay banks and stony bottoms twenty or more feet wide and perhaps three hundred long sites of the flood-pools left by the scour of the short-lived torrent.

These tailings of valleys running from the Muheiwir and Buaisiri water-shed into Um Mahrug or the Sirhan were always rich in grazing of rods and fine grass, nusshiand khamis. When there was water in these hollows the tribes collected about them, and the ordinarily empty wilderness became peopled with tent-villages. The Beni Sakhr with us had so camped a few years before, and as we passed over the monotonous downs they pointed first to one indistinctive hollow with its oblong gutter-trenches and its scattered fire stones and then to another saying There was my tent and there lay Hamdan el Saih. Look at the dry stones for my bed-place, and for Tarfa's next to it. God have mercy upon her: she died the year of samh, in the Snainirat, of a puff adder:

About noon a party of trotting camels appeared over the ridge between us and the Ghadaf, and moved fast and openly towards us. Little Turki cantered out on his old she-camel with cocked carbine across his thighs to find out what they meant 'Ha,' cried Mifleh to me while they were still a mile off, 'that is Fahad, on his Shaara, in the front These are our kinsmen': and sure enough it was. Fahad and Adhub, chief war-leaders of the Zebn, had been camped west of the railway by Zizia, when a Comani came in to Mithgal with news of our march. They had saddled at once, and by hard riding across the Atatir had caught us only half-way on the road. Fahad chided me gently in his courteous fashion for presuming to ride their district on an adventure, while he lay in his tent.

These sons of Trad, the desert-famous champion of the Beni Sakhr, could not miss an opportunity of following up their father's deeds. Fahad was a melancholy, soft-voiced, little-spoken man of perhaps thirty with a white face, trim beard and tragic eyes. His young brother Adhub was taller and stronger, but yet not above middle height. Unlike Fahad he was active and noisy and uncouth looking with his snub nose, his hair-less boy's face, and his gleaming green eyes always flickering restlessly and hungrily from object to object His commonness was pointed by his disheveled hair and dirty ragged clothes. Fahad was neater, but still very plainly dressed and the pair, on their shaggy home-bred camels, looked less like great sheikhs of their reputation than can be conceived. However, they were famous fighters, and so keen and ready for any quantity of trouble that they and their few followers were very welcome.

We spent a poor night at Ammari. A high cold wind was stirring the ashen dust of the salt-ground round the wells into a fine haze which gritted everything as with the breath of an eruption: and we were ungrateful for the water. It was practically on the surface, like so much of the water in the Sirhan , but most of the pools were too bitter to drink. One notable one, however, called Bir el Emir, was thought very good by contrast. It lay in a little floor of bare limestone among the sand-hummocks. The water (opaque and tasting of mixed brine and ammonia) was just below the level of the rock-slab in a little stone bath with ragged undercut lips. Yet it was fairly deep, as Daud proved by hurling Farraj fully dressed into it. He sank completely out of view in its yellowness, and afterwards rose quietly (on the surface under the rock edge where he could not be seen in the dusk. Daud waited a strained minute, and when his victim still did not appear tore off his cloak and plunged in feet-first after him — to find him smiling at him in shallow water under the overhanging ledge. When they had been got out they had a wild struggle in the sand beside the water-hole. Each sustained hurt, and they returned to my fire dripping wet, in rags, bleeding, with their hair and faces and legs and arms and bodies covered with mud and thorns, more like the devils of a whirlwind than their usual suave delicate presences. I asked what had happened, and they said they had been dancing, and had tripped over a bush and bruised themselves. They would like a gift of new clothes. Their hopes were blasted, and I sent them off to repair damages. They turned up smiling half an hour after, bringing me a peace drink of coffee, made from the local water, and so a miserable brew, for all the strength and spice in the pot did not conquer either the foul taste or the stink of it, Possibly the diversions of the bathers had not much purified the source, for being like fishes in the water (Daud had been a pearl in the Persian Gulf) they had begun their battle there, and had only been dragged up on land when choked and breathless and exhausted.

My bodyguard, and especially the Ageyl in it, were by nature foppish, and spent much of their wages on dress and ornament, and much of their leisure time washing themselves and their clothes, and braiding their long plaits of shiny black hair. Butter gave it the polish, and to keep down the vermin they dragged the scalp frequently with a fine-toothed comb, and sprinkled it with camel staling. A German doctor at Beersheba in their Turkish days (these were the men who one misty dawn had rushed our Yeomanry in Katia and wiped out a post) had taught them to be clean by imprisoning the lousy ones in army latrines and making them swallow their lice. His lesson seemed to have been permanent, though their effort after cleanliness could not, in the nature of the desert, be more than a pursuit, without hope of happy ending.

The wind became faint at dawn, and we moved forward for Azrak, only half a march ahead. Hardly, however, were we clear of the drifts beside the wells when there was an alarm. Mounted men had been seen in the brushwood overgrowing the bed of the depression to the north. This country was a Tom-Tiddler's ground of raiding parties, and the Beni Sakhr got wildly excited. We drew together in the best place and halted. The Indian section chose a tiny ridge hacked about with narrow ruts of water-channels, couched their beasts in the hollow behind, and had their guns mounted in due order in a moment. Ali and Abd el Kader threw out their great crimson banners in the intermittent breeze. Our skirmishers, headed by Ahmed and Awad, ran out to the right and left and long shots began to be exchanged.

It all ended suddenly. The enemy broke cover, and marched in line towards us waving their cloaks and sleeves in the air, and chanting songs of welcome. They were the fighting men of the Sirhan tribe on their way to swear allegiance to Feisal. When they heard our news they turned back with us, rejoicing to be spared the road. They made some little pomp over the entry to their tents at Ain el Beidha, a few miles east of Azrak, where the whole tribe was gathered, and our reception was loud because there had been fear among the women that morning when their men marched away.

The tribe was nomadic but of very limited range, and stood usually on the defensive. Few of them had ever been as far as Bair, and none of them knew the Howeitat district, so that the journey to Akaba had seemed a great undertaking. However here they were, returning the same day, with a Sherif of their own, and Arab banners, and machine-guns, marching a ragged hundred men abreast, and singing as merrily as when they started out. My eyes were on a notable red camel, perhaps a seven year old, under a Sir hani in the second line. The tall beast would not be put upon but, with a long swinging pace of which there was no equal in the crowd of us, forged to the front, and kept there despite all challenge. Ahmed went off to get acquainted with her owner.

In the camp the chief men distributed our party among the tents for the privilege of entertainment. Ali, Abd el Kader, Wood and myself were taken in by Mteir, the paramount sheikh of the tribe, an old toothless friendly thing, whose loose jaw sagged in his supporting hand all the while he talked. He gave us a fussy greeting and abundant hospitality of seethed sheep and bread. Wood and Abd el Kader were perhaps a little squeamish, but Ali and I behaved beautifully. The Serahin were primitive in food discipline and in the common bowl there was more splashing than was proper in the best tents or families. Afterwards, by constraint of Mteir's urgency, we lay on his rugs for the one night. I did not dare to sleep. Round our fresh bodies for a change of food had collected all the army of local fleas, lice and ticks, who were sick of unmitigated Sirhan diet. In their delight they were so ravenous that with the best will in the world I could not go on feasting them. Nor apparently could Ali, for he too sat up and said he felt wakeful. So we roused Mteir, and sent for Milleh ibn Bani, a sub-chief and a young active man accustomed to command their battles. To them we explained what we wished to do.

They would not hear of it Hemme they said was quite impossible. The Turks had just lately filled the Irbid country with hundreds of sections of military woodcutters, and no hostile party could hope to slip through undetected. They professed great suspicion of the Moorish villages in the Jaulan, and of Abd el Kader, and said that nothing would persuade them to visit the one under guidance of the other. For Tell el Shehab they feared lest the villagers, their inveterate enemies, attack them in the rear. They also pointed out that if it rained the camels would be unable to trot back across the muddy plains by Remthe, and then the whole party would be cut off and killed.

We were now in deep trouble. The Serahin were our last resource, and if they refused to come with us we would be unable to carry out Allenby's project by the appointed time. Accordingly Ali and myself collected about our little fire more of the better men of the tribe, and fortified the part of courage by bringing in Fahad, and Milleh, and Adhub. Before them we began to combat in words this crude prudence of the Serahin, a view which seemed all the more shameful to us after our long sojourn in the wilderness, in the light of its clear vision.

We put it to them, not abstractly, but concretely for their case, how life in the desert was sensual only, to be lived and loved just in its extremity. There could be no rest-houses for us, no dividend of joy paid out. Its spirit was accretive, to endure as far as the senses would endure, and to use each such advance made good as a base for further adventure, deeper privation, sharper pain. Sense could never look backward. A felt emotion was for us a conquered emotion, an experience gone dead which we buried by expressing it. Yet the empty shell might add to the stature of the pedestal of our minds, giving us longer sight towards more distant riches.

To be of the desert was to wage unending battle with an enemy who was not the world or life or anything, but just hope itself, and failure seemed God's freedom to mankind. We might only exercise this, our freedom by not doing what it lay within our power to do, for then life would belong to us, and we would have mastered it by holding it cheap. Death would seem best of all our works, the last liberty within our grasp, our final leisure: and of these two poles of our being, death and life, or rather leisure and subsistence, we should shun subsistence (which was life) in all save its faintest degree, and cling close to leisure. So we would serve the not-doing rather than the doing.

Some men there might be, uncreative, whose leisure would be barren: but the activity of these would have been material only, and better they did nothing than just tangible things. If our purpose in the world was to bring forth immaterial things, things creative, partaking of our spirit, not of our flesh, then we must be jealous of our physical demands, since in most men the soul grew aged long before the body. Mankind had been no gainer by its drudges.

There could be no honor in a sure success, but much might be wrested from a sure defeat. Omnipotence and the Infinite were our two worthiest foemen, indeed the only ones eligible for a full man to meet, for they were monsters of our own minds' making, and the stoutest enemies were of the household. In fighting Omnipotence, honor was to throw away the poor resources that we had, and dare Him empty-handed, to be beaten not merely by more mind, but by better tools. To the clear-sighted, failure was the only goal to seek. We must believe through and through that there was no victory, except to go down into death fighting and crying for failure itself, calling in excess of despair to Omnipotence to strike harder, that by His very striking He might temper our tortured selves into the weapon of His own ruin.

This was a halting, half-coherent speech, struck out desperately moment by moment in our extreme need, upon the anvil of those white minds round the dying fire, and hardly its sense remained with me afterwards; for once my picture-making memory forgot its trade, and only felt the slow humbling of the Serahin, the night quiet in which their worldliness faded, and at last their new flashing eagerness to ride with us to whatever borne. Before dawn we called old Abd el Kader and taking him far aside among the sandy thickets, screamed into his dense ear that the Serahin would ride with us under his auspices to the Jaulan for Wadi Khalid after sunrise. He grunted that it was well: and we said to one another that never. If life was left to us would we take a deaf man for a conspirator again.

Chapter 82: Azrak and Anyadh

Afterwards we lay down a moment and were astir again very early in the morning to review the camel men of the Sirhan. They made a wild and ragged show dashing past us on their camels: but we thought them loose riders and they blustered too much about their prowess to be quite convincing. It was a pity they had no really good leader. Mteir was too old for service and ibn Bani was an indistinct man, ambitious rather as a politician than as a fighter. However they were the force we had, so there was an end to it, and at three in the afternoon we mounted for Azrak, since we agreed that another night in the tents would leave us picked to dry bones by the vermin. Today Abd el Kader and his servants mounted their mares, as sign that the fighting line was near. They rode just behind us.

It was to be Ali's first view of Azrak, and we hurried up the stony ridge in high excitement talking of the wars and songs and passions of the early shepherd kings with the names like music, who did so love this place, and of the Roman legionaries who had lingered here as garrison in yet earlier times. Then we drew rein and gazed as the blue fort on its rock above the rustling palms, with the fresh meadows and shining springs of water, broke suddenly on our sight. Of Azrak as of Rum one said, 'Numen mest' both were magically haunted by intangible presences but whereas Rum was vast and echoing and God-like, Azrak was steeped in an unfathomable pool of silence and past history instinct with strange knowledge of wandering poets and champions and lost kingdoms, all the crime and chivalry and dead magnificence of the legendary desert-courts of Hira and Ghassan, whose most sober story read like Arthur come again. Every stone and blade of it was radiant with poetry, thrilling with half-memory of the luminous misty Eden that had passed so long ago.

At last Ali shook his rein, and his camel picked her careful way down the lava flow, on to the rich turf behind the springs. There our puckered eyes opened wide with relief that the bitterness of many weeks was gone out of the reflected sunlight. Ali screamed, 'Grass', and flung himself off the saddle to the ground on hands and feet, with his face bowed down among the stems. Then he leaped up, tore off his head cloth, and raced boyishly along the field, bounding over the soft channels where the water stood brown between the reeds. His white feet flashed beneath the tossed folds of his cashmere robes. We in the West seldom learned that added beauty when the body was seen lightly poised on its bare feet. The rhythm and grace of movement then became visible. The play of muscle and sinew pointed the mechanism of each stride, and the balance of repose.

When we again paid attention to business, we missed Abd el Kader. We looked for him in the castle, in the palm-garden, over by the spring: he was nowhere to be found. Eventually we sent our men away to call him, and they came back with Arabs who told us that from just after Beidha he had ridden off northward through the flaky hillocks, and by now must be miles distant on his way towards Jebel Druse. The rank and file did not know our plans and hated him, and so had been glad to see him go: but it was bad news for us, and left us in a difficult position. Of our three alternative objects Hemme had been abandoned: without Abd el Kader, the Jaulan and Wadi Khalid were quite impossible.

This meant that we must necessarily attempt the bridge at Tell el Shehab. To reach it we had to cross the railway, and pass over the open land between the villages by Remthe and the Turks in Deraa. Abd el Kader was gone up to hostile country with full information of our plans and strength. The Turks would be forewarned and, if they took the most reasonable precautions on the night of November the seventh, would trap us at the bridge. We took council with Mifleh and Fahad, whom we had made leaders of our party, and finally decided to push on nonetheless, and trust to the usual incompetence of our enemy. It was not a confident decision, and our minds sank while we took it. In our new spirits the sunshine seemed less lambent than before, and Azrak not so aloof from fear.

We slept that night up the Mejaber valley, and next morning wound rather pensively along the flinty valley and over the ridge into Wadi el Harith, a broad tributary of Butmeh, whose green course had a sickening likeness to some lands at home. Ali rejoiced to see a rich pasture-valley bearing his family name, and was as glad as our camels when we found limpid pools of last week's rainwater in hollows among the bushes. We stopped and used the discovery for lunch, making a long halt to graze our camels who had been hungry since Ammari. Adhub went off with Ahmed and Awad to look for gazelle, and came back with three in splendid condition, as indeed gazelle usually were, even in the worst desert. So we stopped yet longer and made a second lunch, like a feast, of meat gobbets roasted on ramrods over the fire till the outside was charred black like coal while the heart remained juicy and sweet.

Unfortunately my time was spoiled for me by a bed of justice. The feud between Ahmed and Awad, which had been brewing, broke out during this gazelle chase (after the game had been killed) into a private duel, in which Awad shot off Ahmed's head rope, and Ahmed holed Awad's cloak. I disarmed them and gave loud order that the right thumb and forefinger of each should be cut off the terror of this drove them into an instant and violent and public kissing of peace, and a little later all my men went capital bail that the trouble had ended. I referred the case to Ali ibn el Hussein, who set them at liberty on probation, after sealing their promise with the ancient and curious nomad penance of striking the head sharply with the edge of a weighty Meccan dagger again and again till the issuing blood had run down to the waist-belt. It made a very painful but not dangerous scalp wound whose ache at first and whose scar later were supposed to remind the would-be defaulter of his bond.

We pushed on again over perfect going through rich country for the camels till we had passed the groups of ruins called Kseir el Hallabat, In front of them at Abu Sawana we found a flinty hollow in the valley bed which now, thanks to the rain of a few days before, was brimful of deliciously clear water in a narrow channel two feet deep, and perhaps ten feet wide, but nearly half a mile long. This would make a camping place, and serve as starting point for our bridge-raid. To be sure of its safety we rode a few yards further , to the top of a stony knoll, and there found ourselves looking quietly down upon a retreating party of Circassian horsemen, who had been sent out by the Turks from Mafrak to report if the water was occupied. They had missed us, to our mutual benefit, by about five minutes, and we watched them moving slowly away with great satisfaction.

Next morning we filled up all our water-skins, since we would find nothing to drink in front of us till we had done our bridge, and then marched very leisurely into Wadi el Butm. The last reach of this was a three-foot-deep depression, at the edge of a clean plain, which extended flatly to the metals of the railway line some miles away. We stopped here to wait till dusk should make it possible for us to move across this open to the railway unobserved. Our plan was to slip over secretly, raising no alarm and leaving no tracks, and then to hide in the hollows of Abyadh, a place known to our guides in the foothills beyond the line. These irregular hills, the Zumle, bordered the western side of the railway for its first thirty miles below Deraa. In the spring they were full of grazing sheep, for their hard valleys held abundant water, and the rain cloaked their low sides in new grass and flowers. With the coming of summer they dried up and became deserted, except when an occasional traveler crossed them westwards or eastwards. In this autumn season we might fairly calculate on lying in their folds for at least one day undisturbed.

We made our halt another opportunity of food, for we were using up our rations by recklessly eating all we could as often as we had a chance. It lightened our stores, and kept us from thinking too intolerably: but even with this help the day was very long. At last sunset came. The plain shivered, once, and the darkness, which for an hour had been gathering in the hollows of the hills in front, flowed slowly out and drowned us. We mounted. Two hours later after a quick march over smooth gravel, Fahad and I out scouting ahead, came to the railway and without difficulty found a stony place where our caravan would make no signs of passage. The Turkish rail-guards seemed very much at their ease, which relieved us, since it meant that Abd el Kader had not yet caused a panic by his news.

We rode along the other side of the line for half an hour, and then dipped down into a very slight rocky depression full of succulent plants. This was Ghadir el Abyadh, recommended by Mifleh as our ambush. We were in a rich confusion, for the descent though short had been abrupt, and our parties and loads were inextricably mingled. However, we took his surprising word for it that we were in cover, and lay down next our loaded beasts for a short sleep, before dawn would show us how far we were safe and hidden.

As day was breaking Fahad led me to the edge of our pit, some fifteen feet above where the camels sat, and from it we looked out directly across a slowly-dropping meadow to the railway, which seemed nearly within shot. It was most inconveniently close, but the Sakhr knew no better place, and anyhow it was probably safest to stay where we were. We had to stand-to all day, for we heard everything that passed up or down the line, and the situation demanded a constant watch and great care to keep our men under cover. Each time something was reported they ran to look at it, and then the low bank would grow a serried frieze of human heads. Also the camels had to be grazed, and required many guards to keep them from straying into view. Whenever a patrol passed we had to be very gentle in controlling the beasts, since if one of them had roared or truckled it would have drawn enemy attention to our hiding place. Yesterday had been long: today was longer, for we could not issue any food, as water was going to be scarce before we finished our effort. The knowledge made us thirsty.

Ali and I worked at the last arrangements for our ride tonight. It was clear we were penned up till sunset, and that we must reach Tell el Shehab forty miles away, blow up the bridge, and get back across the railway to its east side before dawn. This meant a ride of at least eighty miles in the thirteen hours of darkness, with an elaborate demolition thrown in. Such a performance was beyond the capacity of most of the Indians. They were not good riders, and had broken up their camels in the march from Akaba. An Arab would save his beast, and bring it home in fair condition after hard work. The Indians had done their best but had only tired out themselves, and their animals, in covering easy stages. So we picked out the six best riders, and put them on the six best camels, with Hassan Shah, their officer and greatest-hearted man, to lead them. He decided that this little party would be fittest armed with just one Vickers gun. It was a very serious reduction of our offensive power, and unhappily we had nothing Arab to supply in compensation. The more I looked at it, the less fortunate it seemed.

The Beni Sakhr was obviously fighting men, but we distrusted the Serahin. Finally Ali and I decided to make the Beni Sakhr under Fahad our attacking party. We would leave some of the Serahin to guard the camels, while we made our dismounted charge upon the bridge, and would bring along with us only so many of them as were needed to carry the blasting gelatin. To suit the new circumstances of hurried carriage down steep hillsides in the dark, we changed the shape of the explosive loads by stripping the single cartridges and kneading them into thirty-pound lumps which were put, each lump, into its own white cotton bag for visibility in the night. Visibility had a possible drawback in that the enemy might see it and shoot at it, and gelatin would detonate on impact: but so much the better if the charges were already in place, as I hoped would happen. Wood, who was of course coming with me, undertook to repack the gelatin and shared the rare headache we all got from handling it. However, even that helped pass the time.

My bodyguard had to be carefully distributed. One good rider, if possible a Sherari, was told off to each of the less-expert local men, whose indispensable virtue was that they knew the country we proposed to cross; the pairs so made were attached to one or other of my foreign liabilities, with instructions to keep close to him all night. Thus if the enemy or accident scattered us, we would all have equal chance of getting back to safety in the desert. Ali ibn el Hussein took six of his servants, and the party was completed by the twenty Beni Sakhr and forty Serahin. We left all the lame and weak camels behind at the Ghadir el Abyadh in charge of the balance of our men, who had instructions to get back over the line in the night and to wait by the Abu Sawana pool for news on the morrow. Two of my men developed sudden illnesses, which made them feel unable to ride with us. I excused them, for this night, and afterwards from all duties whatsoever.

Chapter 83: The Bridge Dash

At sunset we said goodbye to them, and went off up our valley, feeling very miserable and disinclined to go on at all. Darkness gathered slowly, as we rode over the first open ridge and turned to the westward, making for the abandoned pilgrim road, which would be our best guide for the Zumle portion of the journey. We were stumbling up and down the irregular hillsides, when suddenly the men in front of us dashed forward. We followed and found them surrounding a terrified pedal and his two wives, who had been coming our way, driving some donkeys laden with raisins and flour and native cloaks. We asked where they were going, and they said to Mafrak, the station just behind us. This was awkward, and we pondered what to do with them. In the end we told them to camp where they were, and left a Sirhani to see they did not stir till dawn when he was to let them go, and to escape himself over the line to Abu Sawana.

We went on plodding across country in the now absolute dark till we saw the gleam of the white furrows of the pilgrim road. It was the same road along which the Arabs had ridden with me on my first night in Arabia out by Rabegh, and since then for a year we had fought up it for more than a thousand kilometers of its length, past Medina and Hedia, Dizad, Mudowwara and Maan. There remained less than two hundred kilometers to the head in Damascus where our armed pilgrimage should end: but we were all apprehensive of the night. Our nerves had been shaken by the flight of Abd el Kader, the solitary traitor of our experience. Had we calculated fairly we would have known that we had a chance of doing what we needed in spite of him: but a dispassionate judgment lay not in our mood, and we thought half-despairingly how the Arab Revolt would never perform that last stage, but would remain one more example of the caravans that started out ardently for a cloud-goal, and died man by man in the wilderness before achievement.

Some shepherd or other scattered these thoughts by firing his rifle from just in front at our caravan, seen by him approaching silently and indistinctly in the dark. He missed widely, but began to cry out in his extremity of terror and poured shot after shot into the brown of us. Mifleh el Gomaan, who was guiding, swerved violently to the right, and in a blind trot carried our plunging line down a slope, over a break-neck bottom and round the far shoulder of a little hill. There we had peace and unbroken night once more, and swung forward in fair order under the stars. The next alarm was a barking dog on the left, and then a camel unexpectedly loomed up in our track. It was however a stray, and rider-less. We moved on again.

Mifleh chose me to ride with him in the van, and called me 'Arab' all this dash for the bridge, that he might not betray me to strangers by crying my known name aloud in the blackness. We were coming down into a very thick hollow when suddenly we smelt ashes, and next instant the dusky figure of a woman leaped from a bush beside the track and rushed shrieking out of our sight. She may have been a gypsy, for nothing followed. We came to a hill. At the top was a village which blazed at us while we were yet distant. Mifleh bore off to the right up a broad stretch of plough, which we climbed slowly, with creaking saddles. He led us to the very edge of the crest and halted. We were at the head of the Buweib, the northern end of the Zumle region of low downs.

Mifleh pointed away to the north, to some brilliant clusters of lights below our feet. They were the flares of Deraa station, lit up for a night spell of army traffic: and we felt something reassuring perhaps, but also a little blatant, in this Turk disregard for us. It was our revenge to make it their last illumination; Deraa was obscured from the morrow for the whole year till it fell. We collected together into a group, and rode to the left along the summit for a while. Then we went down a long valley into the beginning of the plain of Remthe, from which village an occasional red spark glowed out, far away in the darkness to the north-west. The going became flat, but it was land half-ploughed and very soft, so that our plunging camels sank fetlock-in and labored heavily. None the less, we had to put on speed, for the incidents and roughness of the way had made us late of our hoped time; Mifleh urged his camel into a trot.

I was better mounted than most, on the red camel of the Adham, that Sirhani who had led our procession into Beidha. She was a long raking beast, with a huge piston-stride very hard to suffer, pounding yet not fully mechanical, because there was courage and almost-human will in her persistent effort to out-march all the others, which carried her sailing to the head of the line. There, all competitors out-stripped, and opposition broken down, her ambition died into a solid step like any other animal's, but one which gave a confident feeling, as of all immense reserve of strength and endurance behind .

I rode back down the line and told them to press forward faster. The Indians, riding wooden like horsemen, did their best, with the others of our number, but the ground was so bad that the greatest efforts were not very fruitful and as the hours went on first one and then another of the party began to drop behind. Thereupon I chose the rear position with Ali ibn el Hussein, who was riding a rare old racing camel which he had got young from the Emir of Boreida

She must have been fourteen years old but never flagged or jogged the whole night. With her head low she shuffled along in the quick, broken-kneed Nejd pace which was so easy for the rider good enough to exact it from his mount. Our superior speed and our camel-sticks made life miserable for the last men and camels and forced the whole line forward.

Soon after nine o'clock we crossed the embankment for the new railway between Deraa and Irbid. There we left the plough, and the going should have improved: but it began to drizzle, and the rich surface of the land soon became slippery. A Sirhani camel fell. Its rider had it up in a moment and trotted forward. Then one of the Beni Sakhr came down. He also was unhurt, and remounted hastily. Then we found one of Ali's servants standing next his halted camel. Ali hissed him on, and when the fellow mumbled an excuse cut him savagely across the head with his cane. The terrified camel plunged forward, and the slave snatching frantically at the hinder girth was able to swing himself into the saddle. Ali pursued him with a rain of blows. Mustafa, my man, inexperienced with camels and a bad rider, but necessary to us on this night since he knew the country, fell off twice. He was splendidly looked after by Awad, his rank-man, who each time caught his halter, and helped him up again before we overtook them.

The rain stopped, and we went still faster. The road began to run downhill. Suddenly Mifleh rose in his saddle, and slashed with his stick at the air above his head. A sharp metallic contact from the night showed that we were passing under the telegraph line from Irbid to Mezerib. Then the grey horizon before us went more distant. We seemed to be riding down the camber of an arc of land, with a growing darkness at each side and in front. There came to our ears a faint sighing noise, like a wind among trees very far away, but continuous, and slowly increasing in strength and force. This must be from the great waterfall below Tell el Shehab, and we pressed forward confidently.

A few minutes later Mifleh pulled up his camel and beat her neck very gently till she sank silently on her knees. He threw himself off, while we reined up beside him on this grassy platform by a tumbled cairn. Before us was a lip of blackness from which came up very loudly the rushing of the river that had been so long sounding in our ears. It was the edge of the Yarmuk gorge and the bridge of our hunting must be just down the side valley to the right.

We all dismounted quietly helping down the Indians from their burdened camels that there might be nothing to betray us to listening watchmen. Then we mustered together in a whispering group on the clammy grass. The moon was not yet over Hermon but the night was only half-dark in the promise of its dawn with wild rags of tattered clouds driving across a livid sky. I served out the bags of explosive to the fifteen chosen porters and after a couple of minutes to prepare ourselves we walked forward down the steep grass slopes of the valley. The Beni Sakhr with Adhub at their head sank into the dark in front of us to scout out the way. The raindrops on the plants made the hill-slopes treacherous and only by driving our bare toes sharply into the soil could we keep a sure foothold. Two or three men slipped and fell heavily.

When we were in the steepest part where rocks seemed to crop out brokenly from the face a new noise was added to the roaring of the water as a train clanked slowly up from Galilee with the flanges of its wheels screaming on the curves and the steam of its engine panting up out of the hidden depth of the ravine towards us in white ghostly breaths. The Serahin hung back, and Wood drove them forward after us. Fahad and I leaped to the right and in the light of the boiler-flame believed we saw open trucks, in which were sitting and lying men in khaki clothes with perhaps Australian hats upon their heads. They may have been prisoners going up to Asia Minor.

A little further and there at last below our feet we saw a something blacker in the precipitous blackness of the valley and at its farther end a speck of flickering light. We halted to examine it with glasses. It was the bridge seen from this height in plan with a guard-tent pitched by the cutting at the other end under the shadowy wall of the opposite bank with the frowning houses of the village on its crest. It seemed to be about three hundred yards away and everything was quiet except the river and everything was motionless except the dancing flame on the hearth outside the tent.

So Wood was posted there for the moment (he was only to come down if I was hit) to get the Indians burdened with their gun, ready to spray the neighborhood of the guard-tent if affairs became general while Ali. Fahad, Mifleh and the rest of us with the Beni Sakhr and the explosive-porters crept on down the face of the ravine till we happened on the old graded construction path that had led down to the end of the near abutment. We stole down this in single file our brown cloaks and grey clothes blending perfectly with the limestone rocks above us and the depths below, till the first of us reached the metals just before they curved onto the bridge. There the crowd halted and I crawled on with Fahad to understand the place clearly.

We reached the naked abutment, and lying on it drew ourselves forward on our faces in the shadow of the rails and ballast till we could nearly touch the grey skeleton of under hung girders and see the single sentry leaning against the bank by the tent sixty yards away across the gulf. While we watched he began to move slowly up and down up and down before his fire without ever setting foot on the metal work of the dizzy bridge. I lay there staring at him fascinated feeling quite plain and helpless while Fahad shuffled back and dropped down by the abutment wall till he stood far below where it sprang clear of the hillside.

This was no good to me, for I wanted to attack the steel girders themselves, so I crept away to the path to bring on the Beni Sakhr and the gelatin. Before I reached them there was the loud clatter of a dropped rifle and a scrambling fall from up the bank. Someone had slipped. The sentry started and stared up at the noise, and saw, high up, in the zone of light with which the rising moon was slowly making beautiful the gorge, some Indian machine gunners climbing down the hillside from their old position, which was now illuminated to a new one in the receding shadow. He challenged loudly then lifted his rifle and fired wildly at them while yelling to the guard to turn out.

Instantly all was complete confusion. The invisible Beni Sakhr crouched along the narrow path above our heads blazed back at random at the bridge. The guard rushed out of the tent into the cutting and opened rapid fire at the Arab flashes. The Indians had been caught moving, so could not get their Vickers' in action to riddle the tent before it was empty. Firing became general, and the volleys of the Turkish rifles, echoing in the narrow place, were doubled by the impact of the crashing bullets against the rocks behind our storming party. The Serahin carrying the charges had been told by my bodyguard (who knew by bitter trial) that gelatin would go off if it was hit by bullets. So when the shots came splattering all about them on the hill face they dumped the sacks over the edge of the descent in a wild panic and fled. Ali leaped down to Fahad and me, where we stood on the obscure abutment beneath all the trouble, quite unperceived, but with empty hands, and told us that the explosives were lying scattered somewhere far below us in the deep bed of the ravine.

It was hopeless to think of recovering them now that hell was loose: so we scampered up the hill path with the Beni Sakhr through the Turkish fire without accident breathlessly to the top. There we met the disgusted Wood and the Indians, and told them it was all over. We hastened back to the cairn where the Serahin were scrambling on their camels. We copied them as soon as might be, and trotted off at speed, while the Turks went on blazing away in the bottom of the valley. The people of Turra, the nearest village, heard the clamor and joined in furiously. The other villages came awake, and lights began to sparkle out everywhere across the plain. They were often attacked by Bedouin, and had evolved an informal defense scheme, in which all co-operated to make life very difficult for a detected raider.

Our Serahin were sore at the part they had played, and possibly at something I had said in the heat of running away, and was looking for an outlet. In our wild rush we over-ran a party of peasants returning very late from Deraa market. They robbed them of everything. The victims, left there naked, dashed off with their women on foot through the moonlight, raising the whole district with the ear-piercing Arab calls for help. Remthe heard them, and its massed shrieks alarmed every sleeper in the neighborhood. Their mounted men turned out, and charged our flank, while all the settlements for miles about manned their house roofs and fired unsteady volleys in the air.

We left the Serahin offenders behind with their encumbering loot, and drove on over the plain in grim silence keeping together in what order we could while my trained men did marvelous service helping those who fell or mounting behind them those whose camels got up too hurt to canter on. The ground was still muddy and the ploughed strips more laborious than ever; but behind us was the riot spurring us and our camels to exertion like a peak hunting us into our refuge in the hills. At length we entered the Buweib and cut through there by a better road towards peace yet riding our jaded animals as hard as we could for dawn was getting very near. Gradually all the noise behind us died away and the last stragglers fell into place driven together as on the advance by the flail of Ali ibn el Hussein and myself in the rear.

The day broke just as we rode down by a dismantled construction house five miles north of If dein, to the railway: and Wood and Ali and the chiefs now in front with me to test the passage were amused by cutting the telegraph in many places while the tail of the procession marched over. We had crossed the line the night before to blow up the bridge at Tell el Shehab, and so to cut the only communications of the Turkish Army in Palestine with their base in Damascus... and we were actually cutting the telegraph between Damascus and Medin a, after all our pains and risks! Allenby's guns still shaking the air away there on our right was a bitter reminder to us of the failure we had been.

The grey dawn drew on with a gentleness in it foreboding the grey drizzle of rain which followed a drizzle so soft and hopeless that it seemed to mock our bitterness as we plodded broken footed out towards Abu Sawana. At sunset we reached the long water pool where we found the rejects of our party strong and well curious after the detail of our mistake. We were fools all of us equal fools and so our rage was fruitless. Ahmed and Awad had another fight young Mustafa refused to cook rice. Farraj and Daud knocked him about until he cried. Ali had two of his servants beaten: and none of us or of them cared a little bit. Our minds were sick with failure and our bodies tired after riding nearly a hundred strained miles over bad country in bad conditions between sunset and sunset without a halt or food.

Chapter 84: Waiting for Trains

The food was going to be our next preoccupation, and that evening we held a council in the cold driving rain, and considered what we might do. For lightness' sake we had each carried from Azrak three days' rations, which made us complete until tonight. If we rode there straight, tomorrow, we would get in with a just-convenient appetite: but we could not go back empty-handed. The Beni Sakhr wanted honor, and the Serahin were too conscious of their late disgrace not to clamor for more adventure. We had still in hand a reserve bag of thirty pounds of gelatin, and Ali ibn el Hussein, who had heard of the performances below Maan, and was as Arab as any Arab, said, 'Let's blow up a train: The word was hailed with universal joy, and they looked at me.

Blowing up trains was an exact science, when done deliberately by a sufficient party, with machine-guns in position. If scrambled at. it might become dangerous. The difficulty this time was that all the available gunners were Indian soldiers, who, though good men fed, were only half-men in cold and hunger. I did not propose to drag them off with us, without rations, on an adventure which might take a week. There was no cruelty to Arabs; they would not die of a few days' starving, and would fight as well as ever on empty stomachs, while, if things got too difficult, there were the riding camels to kill and eat: but the Indians had refused to touch camel-flesh.

I explained these delicacies of diet to the council, and Ali at once said that it would be enough for me to blow up the train. Leaving them to do their best without machine gun support, to complete the job. As in this unsuspecting district we might happen on a supply train with civilians or only a small guard aboard, I agreed to risk it: and we sat down in a cloaked circle, and finished our remaining food in a very late and cold supper (the rain made fire impossible), our hearts somewhat comforted by the chance of another effort.

At dawn, with the unfit of the Arabs, the Indians moved away for Azrak miserably. They had started up-country with me in high hope of a really military enterprise, and first they had seen the muddled bridge, and now would lose this prospective train. It was hard on them, and to soften the blow I asked Wood to go honorably with them. He agreed after a very decent argument, mainly for their sakes, since the race-prejudice between Arab and Indian never slept for long, and it was not safe to leave them together uncontrolled: but it proved a wise move for himself, as a little sickness which had been troubling him the last day or two began to show the early signs of pneumonia.

The balance of us, some sixty men, turned back towards the railway. Then it was discovered that none of them knew the country about the line: so I had to play the guide, and led them to Minifir, where with Zaal we had made such havoc in the spring. The re-curved hilltop was an excellent observation post, camp, grazing ground and way of retreat, and we sat there in our old place till sunset, shivering and looking out over the immense plain that stretched map-like from us to the clouded peaks of Jebel Druse, with Urn el Jemal and her sister-villages like ink-smudges on it through the rain.

In the first dusk we walked down to the railway, to choose where to lay the mine. The rebuilt culvert at Kilometer 172 seemed still the fittest place. While we stood looking at it there came a rumbling, and in the gathering darkness and the mist a train suddenly appeared, bearing down on us round the northern curve only a hundred yards away. We scurried quickly under the cover of the long arch, and heard it roll overhead. This was annoying but could not be helped, and when the course was clear again we all fell to, and began to bury the charge over the culvert. It was bitterly cold, with drifts of white rain blowing down our valley from the north against us.

The arch was of four meters span, of solid masonry and stood in an eighteen-foot bank, over a shingle water-bed that took its rise on the hilltop where we had left our camels. The winter rains had cut a channel about four feet deep, narrow and winding, in a course which served us as an admirable approach till within three hundred yards of the line. There it widened out, and ran straight towards the culvert, from whose head a great part of this later course lay open to the view. The hills swelled forward on each bank in low spurs, through which the railway passed in shallow cuttings: but the raised bank each side the culvert was longer than the ordinary train, and would leave all its carriages exposed to our fire from the hill.

We hid the explosive very carefully, on the crown of the arch, rather deeper than usual beneath a sleeper, so that the patrol walking on the metals would not feel its jelly softness underneath their feet. The wires were taken down the bank against the masonry revetment of the bridge, whose line covered the marks of their burying. At the bottom we led them into the shingle bed of the water-course, where concealment was quick, and up it as far as they would reach. Unfortunately this was only sixty yards, for there had been difficulty in Egypt over insulated cable and no more had been available when our expedition started. Sixty yards was plenty for the bridge, but little for a train: however, the ends happened to coincide with a little bush about ten inches high sticking out from the edge over the water course and we buried them beside this very convenient mark.

It was not possible to leave them out and connected to the exploder in the proper way since the spot was so close to the track that they would have been evident to the permanent way patrols as they passed their rounds. Further, we had no brush or bellows with us to remove the traces of our digging — not indeed that they would have been of much use in the mud: but consequently the job took longer than usual, and it was very nearly dawn before we finished, I waited under the draught arch till day broke, wet and dismal, and then went over the whole area of disturbance, spending another half-hour in effacing every sign of work, scattering leaves and dead grass over it, and watering down the broken mud from a shallow rain-pool near. Then they waved to me that the first patrol was coming, and I went uphill again to join the others.

Before I reached them they came tearing down into their prearranged places lining the water-course and behind the spurs while the look out signaled that a train was coming from the north. Hamud Feisal's long slave was carrying the exploder: but before he reached me a short train of closed box-wagons rushed by at top speed. The rain-storms on the plain and the thick morning had hidden it from the eyes of our watchmen, till it was almost upon us, and left no time to get ready. This second failure saddened us further, and Ali began to say that nothing would come right this trip. Such a statement was the next stage to the discovery of an evil eye present , so to divert attention I ordered new watching posts to be sent far out, one to the ruins on the north , another to the great cairn on the southern crest.

The others, having no breakfast, were to pretend not to be hungry. They all enjoyed doing this, and for a while we sat there quite cheerfully in the rain, huddling against one another behind a breastwork of our streaming camels for warmth. The moisture made the animals' hair curl up like a mat, so that they looked queerly disheveled. When the rain ceased, which it did frequently a cold moaning wind used to search out the unprotected parts of us, very thoroughly. After a time we found our wet cotton or silk shirts becoming clammy and comfortless things. We had nothing to eat and nothing to do, and nowhere to sit except on wet rock or wet grass or mud. However, this persistent weather kept on reminding me that it would delay Allenby's advance on Jerusalem, and rob him of his great possibility. So large a misfortune for another was a half encouragement. We would go on being partners into next year.

In the best circumstances waiting for action was trying. Today it was beastly. Even the enemy felt it, for their patrols stumbled along without care, working only perfunctorily against the rain. At last, near noon, in a snatch of fine weather, the watchmen on the south peak flagged their cloaks wildly in signal of a train. We reached our positions in an instant, for we had squatted the late hours on our heels in the streaming ditch near the line, so as not to miss another chance. The Arabs took cover properly, and I looked back from my advanced firing point at their ambush, and saw that nothing alarming was to be seen on the grey hillside.

I could not hear the train coming, but trusted, and knelt ready for perhaps half an hour when the suspense became intolerable, and I signaled to know what was up. They sent down to say it was coming very slowly, and was an enormously long train. Our appetites stiffened themselves, for the longer it was, the more loot. Then came the announcement that it had stopped. It moved again.

Finally, near one o'clock, I heard it panting. The locomotive was evidently defective (all these wood-fired trains were bad) and the heavy load on the up-gradient was proving too much for its capacity. I crouched behind my bush while it crawled slowly into view past the south cutting, and along the bank above my head towards the culvert. The first ten trucks were open trucks, crowded with troops. However, once again it was too late to choose, so when the engine was squarely over the mine I pushed down the handle of the exploder. Nothing happened. I pulled it up and pushed it down several times again.

Still nothing happened, and I realized that it had gone out of order, and that I was sitting on a naked bank in full view of a Turkish troop train, crawling past fifty yards away at walking pace. The bush which had seemed a foot high shrank till it was smaller than a fig-leaf, and I felt myself the most distinct object in the countryside. Behind me was an open valley for three hundred yards to the cover where my Arabs were waiting and wondering what I was at. It was impossible to make a bolt for it, or the Turks would step off the train and finish us. If I sat still there might be just a hope that they would ignore me as a casual Bedouin.

So there I sat, counting for sheer life, while eighteen open trucks, three box-wagons, and three officers' coaches dragged by. The engine panted slower and slower, and I thought every moment that it would break down, and end our last chance of escape. The troops took no great notice of me, but the officers were interested, and came out to the little platforms at the ends of their carriages pointing and staring. I waved back at them, grinning nervously, and feeling a most improbable shepherd in my Meccan dress, with its twisted golden circle about my head: but perhaps the mud-stains and the wet and their ignorance made me accepted. At any rate no one shot, and the end of the brake van slowly disappeared into the cutting on the north.

As it went I jumped up, buried my wires, snatched hold of the wretched exploder, and went like a rabbit uphill into safety. There I took breath and looked back to see that the train had finally stuck: and it waited about five hundred yards beyond the mine for nearly an hour to get up a head of steam, while an officers' patrol came back and searched all the ground where I had been seen sitting, very carefully. However, the wires were properly hidden: they found nothing: the engine plucked up heart again, and they went on.

Chapter 85: A Rout

The Arabs were now past tears, for they thought I had intentionally let the train through: and when they heard the real cause, said, 'Bad luck is with us'. Historically they were right: but they meant it for a prophecy, so to distract them I made sarcastic reference to their courage at the bridge the week before, hinting that it was Serahin preference to sit on camel-guard. At once there was uproar, the Serahin attacking me furiously, the Beni Sakhr defending. Ali heard the trouble, and came running down to part us.

When we had made it up, the original despondency was half forgotten. Ali backed me nobly, though the wretched boy was blue with cold and shivering in a bad attack of fever. He gasped that their ancestor the Prophet had given the Sherifs the faculty of sight', and by it he knew that our luck was turning. This was comfort, and the first installment of good fortune came when, in the wet, without other tool than my dagger, I got the exploder open and persuaded it to work again. The troublesome things were not made solid enough for our jolting life, and were often broke.

We returned to our vigil by the wires, but nothing further happened, and evening drew down with more squalls and beastliness, everybody full of grumbles. There were no trains, and it was too wet to light a cooking fire, and our only potential food was one of our camels. Raw meat did not tempt anyone that night, and we determined to hold out as we were, for one more watch, to see if perhaps something good would come to us.

Ali lay down on his belly, which position lessened the hunger ache, to try and sleep off his fever. Khazen, the servant, gave him his cloak for extra covering. For a spell I took Khazen under mine, but soon found it becoming crowded, and left it him, while I went downhill again and connected up the exploder in order not to miss any possible chance. I spent the night there by the singing telegraph wires, hardly wishing to sleep, so painful was the cold: nothing came all the long hours, and dawn, which broke wet, looked even uglier than usual. We were sick to death of Minifir by now.

I climbed up to the main body while the early patrol searched the railway, without seeing the hidden worms. Then the day cleared a little. Ali awoke, much refreshed, and his new spirit cheered everyone. Hamud the slave produced some sticks that he had kept under his clothes by his warm skin all night. They were nearly dry, and we shaved down some blasting gelatin, and with the hot flame got a fire going while some of the Sukhur hurriedly killed a mangy camel, the best-spared of our riding-beasts, and began with entrenching tools to hack it up for cooking.

Just at that moment the watchman on the north cried a train. We left the fire and did a breathless race of the six hundred yards downhill to the old position. The train came round the bend whistling its loudest, a splendid two engine thing of twelve passenger coaches, traveling at top speed on the favoring grade. I touched off under the first driving-wheel of the first locomotive, and the explosion was terrific. The air became full of whirling black things, and I was knocked over violently. I sat up with my shirt torn to my shoulder and the blood dripping down me from long ragged scratches on my left arm. Between my knees lay the exploder crushed flat under a twisted piece of sooty iron. When I peered through the dust and steam of the explosion, the whole boiler of the first engine seemed missing. Just in front of me was the scalded and smoking upper half of the body of a man.

I dully felt that it was time for me to get away to support, but there was a great pain in my right foot, because of which I could only limp slowly along, with my head swinging from the shock. However, it gradually cleared, and I hobbled towards the upper valley whence the Arabs were now shooting fast into the crowded coaches. I cheered myself on by talking repeatedly aloud but then the enemy began to return our fire, and I found myself much between the two. Ali saw me trip twice, and thinking that I was hard hit ran out with Turki and about twenty men of his servants and the Beni Sakhr to help me.

The Turks found their range, and got seven of them in a few seconds. The others, in a rush, were about me — fit models, in their activity, for a sculptor. Their full white cotton drawers drew in bell-like round their slender waists and ankles: and their hairless brown bodies and the lovelocks plaited tightly over each temple in long horns made them look like Russian dancers. We scrambled back into cover, together. By some wonderful fortune I had not once been really hurt, though besides the bruises and cuts of the boilerplate and a broken toe. I had about five bullet grazes on me (some of them uncomfortably deep) and my clothes ripped to pieces. From the water-course in comparative safety we could look about. The explosion had destroyed the whole arched head of the culvert and the frame of the first engine was lying beyond it at the near foot of the embankment having rolled down to the level ground. The second locomotive had toppled into the gap and was lying there across the ruins of the tender of the first. Its bed was all twisted and I judged them both beyond repair. The second tender had gone over the far side of the bank, and the first three coaches had telescoped and were smashed in pieces over the culvert.

The rest of the train was badly derailed with the listing coaches butted end to end at all angles zigzagged along the track. One of them was a saloon decorated with flags and in it had been Mehmed Jemal Pasha commanding the Eighth Army Corps, hurrying down to Jerusalem to defend it against Allenby. His chargers had been in the front wagon; his motor car was on the end of the train and we shot it up. Of his staff we noticed the Imam a fat priest whom we thought to be Assad Shukair, Imam to Ahmed Jemal Pasha and a notorious pro-Turk pimp. So we blazed at him till he dropped.

It was all long bowls and we could see that our chances of carrying the wreck were very slight. There had been some four hundred men on board and the survivors had now recovered from the shock, and were under shelter of the water-course or of the embankment and shooting hard at us. At the first moment our party on the north spur had closed and had nearly won the game. Mifleh on his mare had ridden across behind the train and had chased the officers from the saloon into the lower ditch. He was too excited to stop and shoot and so they had got away scar less. The Arabs following him had picked up some of the rifles and medals littering the ground and had then turned to grab bags and boxes from the train. If we had had a machine-gun on the flank covering the farther side according to my usual mining practice not a single Turk would have got away alive.

Mifleh and Adhub rejoined us on the hill and asked alter Fahad. We had not seen him but one of the Serahin told how he had led the first rush forward while I lay knocked out beside the exploder, and had been killed near it, and his body abandoned. They showed his belt and rifle as proofs that he was dead and that they had tried to save him. Adhub said not a word, but leaped out of the gully, and ran fast downhill. We caught our breaths till our chests hurt us, watching him: but the Turks seemed not to see. A minute later he was dragging a body behind the shelter of a bank on the left.

Milleh went back to his mare, mounted, and took her down behind the spur till he could reach him unobserved. Together they lifted the body on to the pommel of the saddle, and Mifleh sprang up behind and rode away to us. A bullet had passed through Fahad's face, knocking out four teeth, and gashing his tongue deeply. He had fallen unconscious: but had revived just before Adhub reached him, and was trying on hands and knees, blinded with blood, to crawl away. He now recovered enough to sit a saddle for a few minutes, and they led him off at once on his camel.

The Turks, seeing us so quiet, began to advance up the slope towards us. We let them come half-way across the open, and then poured in volleys which killed some twenty and put the rest to flight. The ground about the train was strewn with their dead, and the broken coaches had been crowded: but they were fighting under the eye of the General, and after the failure of the frontal attack (led by Hassan Bey, AD.C, who had been killed) they began to work round to the left and right behind the spurs to outflank us.

We were now only about forty in all, and obviously could do no more good against them. So we began to yield them the ground, and run in batches up the little stream-bed turning back at each sheltered angle to delay them with a few shots. Little Turki much distinguished himself by his quick coolness in these moments, though he was using a straight-stocked Turkish cavalry carbine, which made him expose his head too much, so that he got four bullets through his head cloth alone. Ali was angry with me for retiring so slowly. In reality my hurts were half crippling me, but to hide from him this real reason I pretended to be easy, interested in watching the Turks. My delays to recover courage for a new run kept him and Turki far behind the rest.

At last we reached the hilltop, and there each man jumped on the first camel to hand and we made off eastward at full speed into the desert after Fahad and his brother, for an hour. Then we sorted out our animals. I found that the excellent Rahail, in spite of all the excitement, had brought off with him, tied to his saddle girth, a huge haunch of the camel we had slaughtered just before the train arrived. This gave us a motive for a proper halt, and when just preparing for it, five miles further on, we suddenly saw a little party of four camels marching in the same direction away to the right. We swooped down to investigate, and found it was our old friend Matar, the Hesseni, coming back from Ajlun to rejoin us at Azrak with loads of raisins and village delicacies.

So we stopped at once, under a large rock in Wadi Dhuheil, where there was a barren fig tree, and cooked ourselves our first meal for three days. There also we bandaged up Fahad, who had a fair chance of recovery, though just now he was sleepy with the lassitude of his severe hurt. Adhub, seeing this, took one of Matar's carpets, and, doubling it across the camel saddle, stitched the ends into great pockets. In one they laid Fahad and Adhub crawled into the other as make-weight: and the camel bearing them in this tight litter was led off southward towards their tribal tents.

The other wounded men were seen to at the same time. Mifleh brought up to them the youngest boys of the party, and had them spurt into the wounds with their water, as a rude antiseptic. We whole ones meanwhile refreshed ourselves. I bought another mangy camel for meat for the rest, paid rewards to those who had done things special, compensated the relatives of the killed, and gave prize-money for the sixty or seventy rifles we had taken. It was small booty, but not to be despised. Some of the Serahin who had gone into the action without rifles were able only to throw unavailing stones, had now two guns apiece.

The Arabs were not sorry at the day's work, in spite of their losses: for they felt sure that it was jernal Pasha, since Mifleh swore he saw him running, and if so they would be famous. Also, the dead were not important men. I was most sorry for Hamud the long slave, a fine fighter who had ridden with me often, and was today shot through the heart running down, as he thought, to my rescue. Next day we moved into Azrak, boasting, God forgive us, that we were victorious , and receiving a great welcome therefore from the rest of the Sirhan, who had moved up from Beidha to be camped at the receipt of custom.

Chapter 86: Teaching

The min had now set in steadily, and the whole country was sodden wet. It confirmed us that Allenby had failed in his weather and that there could be no great advance to Haifa this year. However, unless the war ended (of which we saw no hope) he would need to do it next spring, and in the anticipation we determined to hold on to Azrak for the meanwhile. Partly it would be for us a preaching base, a point from which to spread our movement in the north country. Partly it would be a center of intelligence from which we would draw direct news of affairs in Damascus. Partly it would cut off Nuri Shaalan from the Turks. If we broke his relations with them he must fall into our hands, for he was a convinced nationalist, deeply committed to the Sherif, and hesitated to declare himself only because of his wealth in Syria, and the possible hurt to his tribesmen, if they were deprived of their natural market. We would make his mind up for him, and render him ashamed to go in to the enemy, by living in one of his main manors. Azrak lay in a very favorable place for us: and the old fort would be a convenient headquarters, if we made it strong and habitable enough to shelter us no matter how severe the winter. So we took steps at once to put it in order.

I decided to live myself in the upper room of the south gate tower, and therefore set Ahmed, Rahail, Abd el Aziz, Mustafa, Hassan and Mahmud, my Haumni boys (for whom manual labor was not disgraceful), to cover with brushwood, palm-branches and clay the split stone rafters which had for centuries stood open to the sky. Ali took up his quarters in the two rooms of the southeast comer tower, and we made his roof tight for him. The Indians weather-proofed their own north-west rooms themselves. We arranged the stores in the ground-floor of the western tower, by the little gate, for it was the soundest and driest place in the entire fort. The Biasha chose to live under me in the south gate. So we blocked that entry, and made a hall of it. Then we opened the great arch that gave from the court on to the palm-garden, and made a ramp, that our camels might be led up through it each evening into the yard.

Hassan Shah we made our seneschal. As a good muslim his first care was for the little mosque in the center of the square, with its baby mihrab. It had been half unroofed, and the Arabs had desecrated it by penning sheep within the walls. He set his twenty men to clear it, and in a few days they had dug out the filth, and swept the pavement clean. It then became a most attractive house of prayer. What had been a place shut off, dedicated to God alone, Time had broken open to the world and its ministering winds and rain and sunlight, which entered into the worship, and taught the worshipers what a part of life this was. Later the men felt imprisoned when they tried to pray within four walls, and grew to understand the Bedouin love of open spaces. The prudent jemadar's next labor was to make machine-gun positions in the upper towers, from whose tops all the approaches lay at his mercy. Then he placed a formal sentry (a portent and cause of wonder in Arabia) whose main duty was the shutting of the postern gate at sundown. The door was a huge poised slab of dressed basalt about a foot thick, turning on pivot hinges socked into threshold and lintel. It took a great effort to start it swinging, and at the end went shut with a metallic clang and crash which shook the west wall of the old castle.

Meanwhile we were studying to provision ourselves. Akaba was far off, and in winter the roads thither would be rigorous: so we prepared a caravan to go up to Jebel Druse, the neutral land, which lay only a day off. Matar went in charge of this for us, consigned to our good friend, Hussein Abu Naif, the Druse sheikh of Anz, by Salkhad. He took with him a long train of baggage camels, to carry back all the varieties of food that Hussein would buy on commission for our motley party. Besides my bodyguard, who were taught to live on what they got, we had the Indians, for whom pepper less food was no food at all. Ali ibn el Hussein wanted sheep and butter and parched wheat enough for his men and the Biasha. Then there were the guests and refugees whom we might expect to flock to us so soon as the news of our establishment was rumored in Damascus. Till then we would have a few days' repose: and we sat down to enjoy these dregs of autumn, the alternate days of rain and shine. We had sheep and flour and milk and fuel life, but for the mud and cold, went well enough. The peacefulness ended even sooner than we thought. Wood, who had been ailing for some time, went down with a sharp attack of dysentery. This was nothing, but the consequent weakness might have endangered his health in the more trying days when winter set in earnestly. Besides he was needed at Akaba, and except for my own comfort there was no justification for keeping him longer. So we made up a party for the coast. Ahmed, Abd el Rahman, Mahmud, and Abd el Aziz were to go down to Akaba with him, and to return forthwith with a new caravan of stores, particularly composed of the rations proper for the Indian gunners. The others of my people would stay here with me in chilly idleness till the situation developed far enough for us to see clearly which way it was tending. I took the opportunity of the enforced rest to liquidate on Farraj and Daud (not painfully) my promise to Sheikh Yusuf in the matter of his illuminated camel.

Then began our Hood of visitors all day and every day they came, now in the running column of shots, raucous shouting and the rush of camel-feet which meant a Bedouin parade, perhaps of the Rualla, or of the Sherarat, or the Serahin, the Serdiyeh, or the Beni Sakhr, chiefs of great name like ibn Zuh ail, ibn Kaeber, Rafa el Khoreisha; or some little father of a family demonstrating his goodwill or greedy expectation before the fair eyes of Ali ibn el Hussein ; or it would be a wild gallop of horse: friends from the Druses, or some of the ruffling warlike peasants of the rich Arab plain. Sometimes it was a cautious and slow-led caravan of ridden camels from which stiffly dismounted Syrian politicians or tradesmen not accustomed to the road. One day it would be a ragged trail of a hundred miserable Armenians, fleeing from starvation and the suspended terror of the Turk. Another time there would come a spick and span group of mounted officers, Arnb deserters from the Turkish armies followed as often as not by the compact marching company of their Arab rank and file. Always they came day after day till the desert to the north of us which had been trackless when we came, was all starred out with grey roads.

Ali appointed first one, then two, and at last three guest-masters, who received the rising tide of newcomers, sorted out the worshipful from the curious, and marshaled them at the due time before him or me. All wanted to know about the Sherif and the Arab army, and the English, and what each would do for them and for the Turks. Merchants from Damascus brought us presents: sweetmeats, caramel, apricot paste, nuts: silk clothes for ourselves, brocade cloaks and head cloths, sheepskins, felt rugs with colored strands beaten into them in arabesques, Persian carpets. We returned them coffee and sugar, rice, and rolls of white cotton sheeting, the necessities of which they had been deprived by war. Everybody learned that in Akaba there was plenty, coming across the open sea from all the markets of the outside world: and so the Arab cause, which was theirs by sentiment, and instinct and inclination, became theirs by interest also. Slowly our example and teaching converted them very slowly by our own choice that they might be ours more surely. We led their feeble spirits imperceptibly along sheltered by-roads, till they were abreast of the point where we needed them.

The greatest asset of Feisal's cause in this work up here in the north was Sherif Ali ibn el Hussein. The lunatic competitor of the wild tribesmen in their wildest feats was now turning all his force to greater ends. The mixed natures in him made of his face and body powerful arguments, carnal perhaps, except in so far as they were transfused by the wealth of his character. No one could see him without the desire to see him again, especially when he smiled, as he did rarely, with both mouth and eyes at once. His beauty was a conscious weep on with him. He dressed spotlessly, all in black or all in white, and he had studied gesture. To this, fortune had added unusual native grace, and physical perfection, but these qualities were only the just expression of his powers. They made obvious the pluck which never yielded, which would let him be cut to pieces holding on. His pride broke out ever and again in his war-cry, 'I am of the Harith', his two-thousand-year-old clan of freebooters: while the huge eyes, white with large black pupils slowly turning in them, emphasized the frozen dignity that was his ideal carriage, and to which he was always striving to still himself But as ever the bubbling laugh would shriek out of him unawares, and the youth, boyish or girlish, of him, the fire and devilry would break through his night like a sunrise.

Yet despite this richness there was a constant depression with him, the unknown longing which simpler restless people often feel, a need of abstract thought which their minds will not supply, and whose lack makes them unhappy. His bodily strength grew greater day by day, and he hated it, for it seemed to stifle, to flesh over, something humble that he wanted more. The wild mirth was only one sign of this vain wearing out of his desire. The swarm of strangers besetting him these days underlined his unwilling detachment from his fellows. In spite of his great instinct for confession and company he could find no intimates except Abd el Kher, his slave, and Khazen, his servant. Yet he could not be alone. If he had no guests Khazen had to serve the meals, while Ali and his slaves sat down and ate together.

In these slow nights we were secure from interruption by the world outside. For one thing, it was winter and, in the rain and the dark few men would venture either over the labyrinth of lava, or through the marshes, the two approaches to our fortress: and further we had ghostly guardians. Sometimes in the evening after dark when Hassan Shah had made the rounds, and the coffee was being pounded by the hearth, there came from outside a strange long wailing round the towers. The first night we were sitting with the Serahin, when suddenly ibn Bani seized me by the arm and held to me shuddering. I whispered to him, 'What is it?' and he gasped that the dogs of the Beni Hillal, the mythical builders of the fort, came each night, and quested the six towers for their dead masters. We strained to listen, and for a time heard nothing. Afterwards through Ali's black basalt window frame crept a rustling, which was the stirring of the night-wind in the withered palms below, an intermittent rustling, like the patter of autumn rain in England on yet-crisp fallen leaves. Then the cries came again and again and again, beginning very low, and rising slowly in power, till they sobbed round the walls in deep waves which died away choked and miserable. At such times our men used to pound the coffee harder and the Arabs to break into sudden song to occupy their ears against the misfortune. No Bedouin would lie outside in wait for the mystery and we saw nothing from our windows except the motes of water in the dank air, driving through the beam of our firelight. So they remained a legend, but wolves or jackals, hyenas, or hunting dogs, their ghost-watch kept our ward more closely than ever our own arms could have done.

In the evening when we had shut-to the gate, all the guests would assemble either in my room, or in Ali's, and coffee and stories would go round till the last meal, and after it till sleep came. On stormy nights we brought in brushwood and dry dung, and lit a great fire in the middle of the floor. About it were drawn the carpets and the saddle-sheepskins and in its light we would tell over our battles, or hear the traditions of our visitors. The leaping flames chased our smoke-muffled shadows strangely about the rough stone wall behind us, distorting them over the hollows and projections of its broken face. When the stories came to a period the circle would shift uneasily, turning over to the other knee or elbow, while the cups went clinking round, and one of the servants would rise and fan the blue reek towards the loophole with his cloak, making the glowing ash swirl and sparkle with his draught. Till the voice took up again we would hear the slow rain-spots hissing briefly as the damp from the stone-beamed roof dripped into the fire's heart.

At last the sky turned solidly to rain, and no man could approach us. In the loneliness we learned the full disadvantage of imprisonment in gloomy ancient palaces with walls without any mortar. The rain guttered down within their thickness, and spouted far into the rooms from chinks ten feet below the ceiling. We set rafts of palm branches to bear us clear of the streaming floor, covered them with felt mats, and huddled down on them under sheepskins, with another felt bent over us like a shield to throw off the water. It was icy cold, and we hid there without moving from murky daylight until dark, our minds seeming suspended within these massive walls, through whose shot-windows the piercing mist streamed like a white pennant before the wind. Past and future flowed over us like a river, leaving us hardly conscious of where we were. We dreamed ourselves into the spirit of the place, sieges and feastings, raids, murders, love-singing in the night time.

This escape of our wits from the fettered body was an indulgence, against whose enervation only change of scene could avail. Very painfully I drew myself again into the present, and forced my mind to say that it must profit by this wintry weather in which no man could fight, to explore the country lying about the junction at Deraa of the three railways. We had seen enough to be sure that if our lives lasted we would need further operations in this north: and next time we must know it well enough to plan with confidence the details of our fights and marches. So I decided to go off by myself secretly on this special errand, with two new men engaged for the new purpose. One was Daher, a lubberly dull good-tempered Sherari boy, and the other Mijbil, an old, bearded Haurani from the Jaulan district.

As I was thinking how I would ride, there came to us, unheralded, one morning in the rain, Taiai el Hareidhin, the famous sheikh of Tafas in the plain by Deraa. Taiai was an outlaw, with a price upon his head, but so great in his district that he rode about when and where he pleased, and lodged with whom he would. He had fallen out with the Turks over the military service of one of his villagers two years before, and in the first year and the second had killed, according to report, some twenty-three Turks with his own hand. He rode up to us with six followers, all splendidly mounted, himself the most dashing figure of a man in the height of Hauran fashion. His sheepskin coat was of the finest Angora obtainable, covered in green broadcloth, ornamented with silk patches, and designs in brown braid. His other clothes were silk, and his high boots, his silver saddle, his sword, his dagger, and his rifle, matched his reputation.

He swaggered in loudly to our coffee-hearth, a man sure of his welcome anywhere, and greeted Ali boisterously (all peasants sounded boisterous after long sojourn with the tribes), jesting and laughing at the weather and our old fort and the enemy. He looked about thirty-five, was short and strong, with a broad face, full lips, a trimmed beard and long pointed mustaches. His round eyes were made rounder and larger and darker by their thick rims of antimony, loaded on in villager-style. He was ardently for us, and since his name was one to conjure with in all the flat of Hauran, we rejoiced at his coming. When a day had made me sure of him I took him out quietly in the morning to the palm-garden, and there in secret asked him to help my ambition to see the Deraa neighborhood. The idea delighted him, and he companioned me for the few days' march as thoroughly and cheerfully as only a Syrian on a good horse can. His help was invaluable, and made an otherwise dangerous journey easy.

We rode by Urn el Jemal and Umtaiye to Taiyibe, where we tested the water-pits, and on to Ghazale, looking at the roads and wells, and lava-fields. Then we crossed the line by Miskin to Sheikh Saad, and turned south to Tafas where Taiai was at home. Next day we went on to Tell Khuman, or Arar as the peasants called it, a splendid position closing the Damascus railway, and commanding Deraa, which we were pleased to find now modestly dark of nights. Our raid had done it that much good. Afterwards we rode through very delicate and tricky rolling country to Mezerib, looking at the Palestine railway, till here also I could see the conduct of a profitable raid. I encouraged Taiai by sketching plans and operations for the next time when we would bring men and money and guns with us, and start the general rising which must end in inevitable victory. I hoped it would be not later than the spring, when Allenby made his great forward leap.

Chapter 87: Being Taught

To round off this spying of the Nugra, the hollow land of Hauran, it was necessary to visit Deraa, its chief town, and to examine its strength. It was clear that we could cut it off north and west and south, by destroying the three railways, but it would be quicker and more sure to rush the junction first, and then do these other things by working outwards. Taiai, however, could not venture in with me since he was too well known in the place. So we parted from him near Ataman with many thanks on both sides, and thence rode southward, alongside the line, till we were close to Deraa. There we dismounted, and gave the three ponies to Daher, with orders to take them round by the east to Nisib, the great village just south of Deraa, where he might expect us in the evening. My plan was to walk round the railway station and the town with Mijbil, and to reach Nisib after sunset. Mijbil was my best companion for the trip because he was an insignificant peasant, old enough to be my father, and respectable.

The respectability seemed only comparative as we tramped off in the watery sunlight, which was taking the place of the rain last night. The ground was muddy, and we were barefoot, and our cheap clothes showed the stains of the filthy weather to which we had been exposed all the week I was in ragged cotton things, with a torn Haurani jacket, and was yet limping from the broken toe gained when we blew up Jemal on the railway. The slippery track made walking difficult, unless we spread out our toes widely and took hold of the ground with them: and doing this for mile after mile was exquisitely painful for me. It would not do to be laying weight always on my troubles in our revolt: and yet it must be said that, looking back, I noted hardly one day in Arabia without its record of physical hurt to add to the corroding sense of my deceitfulness towards the Arabs, and the more lawful weariness of responsible command. Today we were a lame and draggled pair.

We stepped up on to the head of the curving bank of the Palestine railway, and from its vantage looked at Deraa station, but the ground on this side was too open to admit of our ever making a surprise attack across it. We decided to walk down the east face and examine the defenses closely: so we plodded on outside the fence, noting the German stores, the barbed wire here and there, and the rudiments of trenches. Turkish troops were passing between their tents and the latrines which were dug out on our side, and everything was unbuttoned and unsuspecting. However, all the east face was also too exposed for an advance in force. We reached the corner of the aerodrome at the south end of the station, and struck over it towards the town, as there was no wire there. We meant to cross the railway, and go up into the village to complete our survey.

There were two or three old Albatros machines in the sheds and a few men lounging about. One of these, a Syrian soldier, came up to us, and began to question us about our villages, and where they lay, and if there was much 'government' in our districts. He was probably an intending deserter, fishing for the offer of a refuge. We shook him off at last and turned away: when someone called out in Turkish. We walked on deafly, but an N.C.O. came after us, and took me roughly by the arm, saying, 'The Bey wants you.' There were too many witnesses for either fight or flight, so I went with him readily. He took no notice of Mijbil, who wisely slipped away at once.

I was marched through a tall fence into the compound which was set about with many low temporary huts and a few buildings. We passed some of these to a mud room, outside which was an earth platform, where, on a green tent-canvas, sat a fleshy Turkish officer. One leg was tucked under him, and he hardly looked at me when the sergeant brought me up and made a long report in Turkish. He asked my name: I told him Ahmed ibn Bagr 'An Arab?' I explained I was a Circassian from Kuneitra. 'A deserter?' 'But we Circassians have no military service.' He then turned round and stared at me curiously, and said very slowly, 'You are a liar. Keep him, Hassan Chowish, till the Bey sends for him.'

They led me into a guardroom, mostly taken up by large wooden cribs, on which lay or sat a dozen men in untidy uniforms. They took away my belt, and my knife, but let me sit on a spare place, made me wash myself carefully, and fed me with their own food: I passed the long day there unmolested. They would not let me go on any terms, but tried to reassure me. Tomorrow perhaps it would be permitted, if fulfilled all the Bey's pleasure this evening. The Bey seemed to be Hajim, the Governor though what he was to do with me I could not gather. If he was angry they said, I would be drafted to the depot in Baalbek. I tried to look as though there was nothing worse in the world than that for me.

Soon after dark they called me. I was waiting for the summons, to get away, but three men came with me, and one held me all the time. I cursed my littleness. They took me over the railway where were six tracks besides the sidings of the engine shop. We went through a side-gate north of the platform, and then turned to the left down a street past a square, and finally to a detached house standing back a little on the right. It was two-storied, with apparently a shop underneath and there was a sentry at the door and a glimpse of one or two others lolling in the dark entry. They took me upstairs to the Bey's room, which I was astonished to see was his bedroom.

He was another bulky man, a Circassian perhaps, sitting on his bed in a night-gown trembling and sweating as though with fever. When I was pushed in he kept his head down, and waved the guard out. Then in a breathless voice he told me to sit on the floor in front of him, and after that was dumb for several seconds, while I gazed at the top of his great shaved head, on which the bristling hair stood up stiffly no longer than the dark stubble on his cheeks and chin. At last he looked me over, and told me to stand up: then to turn round. I obeyed, and he flung himself back on the bed and dragged me down with him in his arms. When I saw what he wanted I twisted round and up again, glad to find myself equal to him in wrestling.

He then began to fawn on me, saying how white and clean I was, and how fine my hands and feet, and how he was all longing for me and would get me off drills and duties, make me his orderly, and pay me, if I would love him. Incidents like these made the thought of military service in the Turkish army a living death for wholesome Arab peasants, and the consequences pursued the miserable victims all their after-life, in revolting forms of sexual disease.

I was obdurate, so he changed his tone, and sharply ordered me to take off my drawers. When I hesitated he snatched at me, and I pushed him back. He clapped his hands for the sentry, who hurried in and seized me. The Bey then cursed me horribly, and threatened me, and made the man holding me tear my clothes away bit by bit till I stood there stark naked. His eyes rounded as he saw the half-healed places where the bullets of Jemal Pasha's guards had flicked through my skin a little while ago. Finally he lumbered to his feet, with a glitter in his eye, and began to paw me over. I bore it for a little, till he got too beastly, and then jerked up my knee, and caught him hard.

He staggered back to his bed, and sat there, squeezing himself together and groaning with pain, while the soldier shouted for the corporal and the other three men of the guard to come and hold my hand and foot. As soon as I was helpless the Governor recovered courage, and spat at me, saying he would make me ask pardon. He took off his soft slipper, and hit me repeatedly with it in the face. He leaned forward and fixed his teeth in the skin of my neck, and bit till the blood came. Then he kissed me. Afterwards he drew one of the men's bayonets. I thought he was going to kill me, and was sorry, but he only pulled up a fold of the flesh over my ribs, worked the bayonet point through, after considerable trouble, and gave it a half-turn. This hurt, and I winced a little, while the blood wavered down my side in a thin stream, and dripped on to the front of my thigh. He looked pleased and dabbled it over my stomach with his fingertips.

I got angry and said something to him. His face changed and he stood still; then controlled his voice with an effort and said significantly, 'You must understand that I know about you, and it will be much easier if you do as I wish.' I was dumbfounded by this, and we waited silently for another moment, staring at one another, while the men who had not seen an inner meaning shifted about uncomfortably: but it was evidently a chance shot by which he himself did not or would not mean what I feared. I could not again trust my twitching mouth which faltered always in emergencies but at last threw up my chin which is the sign for 'No' in the East and then he sat down and half-whispered to the corporal to take me out and teach me till I prayed to be brought back.

They kicked me to the landing at the head of the stairs and there threw me on the guard-bench and stretched me along it on my face pummelling me. Two of them knelt on my ankles bearing down with their arms on the back of my knees while two more twisted my wrists over my head till they cracked and then crushed them and my ribs against the wood. The corporal had run downstairs and now came back with a

Circassian riding whip of the sort which gendarmes carried. They were single thongs of supple black hide rounded and tapering from the thickness of a thumb at the grip (which was wrapped in silver, with a knob inlaid in black designs) down to a hard point much finer than a pencil.

He saw me shivering partly I think with cold and made it whistle through the air over my head taunting me that before the tenth cut I would howl for mercy and at the twentieth beg for the caresses of the Bey and then he began to lash me across and across with all his might while I locked my teeth to endure this thing which wrapped itself like flaming wire about my body. At the instant of each stroke a hard white mark like a railway darkening slowly into crimson leaped over my skin and a bead of blood welled up wherever two ridges crossed. As the punishment proceeded the whip fell more and more upon existing whales biting blacker or more wet till my flesh quivered with accumulated pain and with terror of the next blow coming. From the first they hurt more horribly than I had dreamed of and, as always before the agony of one had fully reached me another used to fall the torture of a series worked up to an intolerable height.

To keep my mind in control I numbered the blows but after twenty lost count and could feel only the shapeless weight of pain not tearing claws for which I was prepared but a gradual cracking apart of all my being by some too-great force whose waves rolled up my spine till they were pent within my brain and there clashed terribly together. Somewhere in the place was a cheap clock, ticking loudly, and it troubled me that their beating was not in its time.

I writhed and twisted involuntarily, but was held so tightly that my struggles were quite useless. The men were very deliberate, giving me so many, and then taking an interval, during which they would squabble for the next turn, ease themselves, play a little with me, and pull my head round to see their work. This was repeated time and again, for what may have been no more than ten minutes. They had soon conquered my determination not to cry, but so long as my will could rule my lips I used only Arabic, and before the end a merciful bodily sickness came over me, and choked my utterance.

At last when I was completely broken they seemed satisfied. Somehow I found myself off the bench lying on my back on the dirty floor, where I snuggled down, dazed, panting for breath but vaguely comfortable. I had strung myself to learn all pain until I died, and, no longer an actor but a spectator, cared not how much my body jerked and squealed in its sufferings. Yet I knew or imagined what passed about me. I remembered the corporal kicking me with his nailed boot to get me up: and this was true, for next day my left side was yellow and lacerated and a damaged rib made each breath stab me sharply.

I remembered smiling idly at him, for delicious warmth, probably sexual, was swelling through me: and then that he flung up his arm and hacked with the full length of his whip into my groin. This jerked me half-over, screaming, or rather trying impotently to scream, and only shuddering through my open mouth. Someone giggled with amusement, but another cried, 'Shame, you've killed him.' A second slash followed. A roaring was in my head, and my eyes went black, while within me the core of my life seemed to be heaving slowly up through the rending nerves, expelled from its body by this last and indescribable pang.

By the bruises, perhaps they beat me further: but I next knew that I was being dragged about by two men, each disputing over a leg as though to split me apart: while a third astride my back rode me like a horse. Then Hajim called. They splashed water in my face, lifted me to my feet, and bore me, retching and sobbing for mercy, between them to his bedside: but he now threw me off fastidiously, cursing them for their stupidity in thinking he needed a bedfellow streaming with blood and water, striped and fouled from face to heel. They had laid into me, no doubt much as usual: but my indoor skin had torn more than an Arab's.

So the crestfallen corporal, as the youngest and best-looking of the guard, had to stay behind, while the others carried me down the narrow stairs and out into the street. The coolness of the night on my burning flesh, and the unmoved shining of the stars after the horror of the past hour, made me cry again. The soldiers, now free to speak, tried to console me in their fashion, saying that men must suffer their officers' wishes or pay for it, as I had just done, with still greater suffering.

They took me over an open space, deserted and dark, and behind the Government house to an empty lean-to mud and wooden room, in which were many dusty quilts. They put me down on these, and brought an Armenian dresser who washed and bandaged me in sleepy haste. Then they all went away, the last of the soldiers whispering to me in a Druse accent that the door into the next room was not locked.

I lay there in a sick stupor, with my head aching very much, and growing slowly numb with cold, till the dawn light came shining through the cracks of the shed, and a locomotive began to whistle in the station. These and a draining thirst brought me to life, and I found I was in no pain. Yet the first movement brought anguish: but I struggled to my feet, and rocked unsteadily for a moment, wondering that it was not all a dream and I back five years ago in the hospital at Khalfati, where something of the sort had happened to me.

The next room was a dispensary, and on its door hung a suit of shoddy clothes. I put them on slowly and clumsily, because of my swollen wrists: and from the drugs chose some tablets of corrosive sublimate, as a safeguard against recapture. The window looked north on to a blank long wall. I opened it, and climbed out stiffly. No one saw me, which perhaps was the reason why I had been shut up in so weak a place.

I went timidly down the road towards the village, trying to walk naturally past the few people already astir. They took no notice, and indeed there was nothing peculiar in my dark broadcloth, red fez and slippers: but it was only by restraining myself with the full urge of my tongue silently to myself that I refrained from being foolish out of sheer terror. The atmosphere of Deraa seemed inhuman with vice and cruelty and it shocked me like cold water when I heard a soldier laugh behind me in the street.

By the bridge were the wells, with men and women already about them. A side-trough was free, and from its end I scooped up a little water in my hands, and rubbed it over my face: then drank, which was precious to me: and afterwards wandered aimlessly along the bottom of the valley for some minutes, towards the south, till out of sight of both town and station. So at last was found the hidden approach to Deraa for our future raiding party, the purpose for which Mijbil and I had come here it seemed so long ago.

Further on a Serdi, riding away on his camel overtook me hobbling up the road towards Nisib. To him I explained that I had business there, and was already footsore. He had pity, and mounted me behind him on his bony camel, to which I clung the rest of the way, learning the feelings of my name saint on his gridiron. The tribe's tents were just in front of the village, where I found Mijbil and Daher, very anxious about me, and curious to learn how I had fared. Daher had been up to Deraa in the night, and knew by the lack of rumor that the truth about me had not been discovered. I told them a merry tale of bribery and trickery, which they promised devoutly to keep to themselves, laughing aloud at the simplicity of the Turks.

We rested there the night, during which time I managed to get along towards the village, and to see the great stone bridge to the north of it, one of the most important in this neighborhood. Then we took horse, and rode very gently and carefully towards Azrak, without incident, except that on the Giaan el Khunna a raiding party of Wuld Ali let us and our horses go unplundered, when they heard who I was.

This was an unexpected generosity, for the Wuld Ali were not yet of our fellowship; and their action revived me a little. I was feeling very ill, as though some part of me had gone dead that night in Deraa, leaving me maimed, imperfect, only half myself It could not have been the defilement, for no one ever held the body in less honor than I did myself: probably it had been the breaking of the spirit by that frenzied nerve-shattering pain which had degraded me to beast-level when it made me grovel to it; and which had journeyed with me since, a fascination and terror and morbid desire, lascivious and vicious perhaps, but like the striving of a moth towards its flame.

Chapter 88: Jerusalem

In Azrak we found all well; our friend, Hussein el Atrash, the famous Druse chieftain of Anz, by Salkhad, was paying his first visit to Ali ibn el Hussein. He told us the rest of the history of Abd el Kader, the Algerian. After stealing away from us at Beidha he had ridden straight to Salkhad, and entered the village in triumph, the Arab flag displayed, and his seven horsemen cantering about him, firing joy-shots. The people were astonished, and the Turkish governor went across to Abu Naif, and protested that such doings were an insult to him. He was introduced to Abd el Kader, who, sitting in the divan, made a bombastic speech, that the Sherif now took over Jebel Druse through his agency, and that all existing officials were confirmed in their appointments.

Next morning he made a second progress through the district, and the long-suffering governor complained again. Abd el Kader drew his gold-mounted Meccan sword, and swore that with it he would cut off Jemal Pasha's head. Hussein reproved him, vowing that such things should not be said in his house before his Excellency the Governor. Abd el Kader called him whore-son, an ingle's accident, son of a dog, profiteering cuckold, pimp, and other incompatible terms, before the whole roomful of his villagers. Hussein got angry, and Abd el Kader flung raging out of the house, and mounted, shouting that when he stamped his foot all Jebel Druse would rise up on his side.

With his seven servants he spurred down the road to Deraa station, which he entered as he had entered Salkhad. The Turks knew his madness of old, and left him to play. They disbelieved even his yam that Ali and I would try the Yarmuk bridge that night. When, however, we did, they took a graver view, and sent him under custody to Damascus. Jemal's brutal humor was amused, and he enlarged him as a butt. Abd el Kader gradually softened down, and became amenable. After a little time the Turks began again to use him as *agent provocateur;* and go between for their purposes with the local peasantry.

The weather was now dreadful, with sleet and snow and rain continually: and it was obvious that at Azrak there would be nothing but the normal teaching and preaching in the next months. For this I was not eager. When necessary I had to convert new congregations, and did it as efficiently as I could, though conscious always of my strangeness, and of the fraudulence of an alien's preaching others' liberty. The war was a long, mental struggle with myself, to forget thought, to accept the idea of revolt as freely as the people and as trustingly. Especially was this difficult when tired and ill, for then the brain got impatient, and would not be deceived. The imitator might force himself to keep pace for a little, but then there was a reaction towards disgust, and these smooth townspeople provoked it in me. A Bedouin would thrust in, hailing me 'Ya Aurans', and put his need to me bluntly, without compliments. These others begged in false words for the favor of an audience, calling me 'Prince' and larding me with titles, which always seemed to me cowardice like body armor in a duel.

I had never been a lofty person, indeed I had tried to be accessible to everyone, and sometimes it felt as though most of them came and saw me every day. I had striven as eloquently as I could to keep plain the standard of existence by my own example in having no tents or cooks or body-servants: just my guards, who were fighting men, not servile: and here these Byzantine citizens were already setting out to corrupt our simplicity. So I flung away from them in a rage, determining to go south to the world again, and see if anything active was to be done in the cold weather about the bottom of the Dead Sea depression, which the enemy held as a trench dividing us from Palestine.

My remaining money was handed over to Sherif Ali, for his maintenance till the spring: and the Indians commended to his care. Particularly we bought them a fresh set of riding camels, in case the need to move came suddenly upon them in the winter, for news of a threat by the Turks against Azrak had been sent down by the Druses regularly for many days to Ali, who discounted it scornfully. Then we took an affectionate leave of one another. Ali gave me half his wardrobe, shirts, head cloths, belts, tunics. I gave him an equivalent half of mine, and we kissed like David and Jonathan, each wearing the other's clothes. Afterwards with Rahail only, on my two best camels, we struck away southward towards Kussair el Amruh, to avoid the mud-sloughs of the Ghadafon the direct road to Bair.

It was a toilsome starting out. We left Azrak near evening, riding into a glowing west, while over our heads schools of cranes flew into the sunset like the out-drawn barbs of arrows. Night was deep before we crossed Wadi Butm, where the conditions became very bad. All the plain was wet, and our poor camels slithered and fell time and again. We fell as often as the camels did, but at least our part of sitting still between falls was easier than the camels' part of movement. By midnight we had crossed the Ghadaf, and the quag felt too awful for further movement. The mishandling at Deraa had left me curiously faint; my muscles seemed at once pappy and inflamed, and all exertion frightened me: so we halted, as even Rahail was at last exhausted. We slept where we were in the mud, and rose up plated with it at dawn, and smiled crackly at one another.

This day the wind rose and the ground began to dry. It was important, for in the new circumstances at Azrak I wanted to reach Akaba before Wood's men started back with the return caravan, and this called for speed. My disinclination to ride hard was another perverse reason for forcing the march. Until noon we made poor traveling, for the camels still broke through the loose crust of flints, and foundered in the red under-clay. In the afternoon we did better, and closed rapidly on the Thlaithukhwat, gleaming today like white tents pitched in the sky above their lofty ridge, the southern boundary of our sight.

Suddenly, by the head of Muheiwir, shots rang out at close range, and four mouthing men dashed down the eastern slope towards us. I stopped my camel peaceably as they came. Seeing this they jumped off and ran up to us brandishing their arms. They asked who I was, and volunteered that they were Jazi Howeitat. This was an open lie, as their camel-brands were Faiz: when we said so they covered us with their rifles at about four yards, and told us to dismount. I laughed at them, which was good tactics with Bedouin at a crisis. They were puzzled. Then I asked the loudest if he knew his name. He stared at me, thinking I was mad. He came nearer with his finger on the trigger and I bent down to him and whispered that it must be Teras, since no one else could be so rude. As I spoke I covered him with my hidden pistol, from underneath my cloak.

It was a shooting insult but he was so astonished that anyone should provoke an armed man that he gave up for the moment his thought of murdering me took a step back, and looked round fearful that there was some reserve force somewhere, to give me confidence. At once I rode off, very slowly for about one hundred yards with a creeping feeling in my back, calling to Rahail to come along. They let him go too unhurt. When we were about two hundred yards away they repented themselves and began to shoot, but we dashed over the watershed into the next depression and across this galloped into safe ground. We learned afterwards that they were peasant clients of the Beni Sakhr, who had waited a week on a false rumor of our going down to Akaba with money. We complained to Mithgal, who sent them into Feisal, and there we reconciled ourselves with them.

From the level of the ridge at sunset we looked back for an instant upon the northern plain sinking greyly downward away from us except that here and there glowed specks or great splashes of crimson fire the reflections of the dying sun in the shallow pools of rainwater on the flats. These eyes of a dripping bloody redness were so much more visible than the plain on which they lay that they carried our sight miles beyond the limit of the haze and seemed to hang detached in the northern sky tilted up like mirage. We passed through Bair long after dark, when only its latest tent fires were still shining: and pushed straight on into the night over the Shomari for Jefer.

As we went we saw the stars mirrored in a valley-bottom and riding down were able to water our breathless camels in a new pool. This night-journeying was hard on both men and animals. By day the camels saw the irregularities of their path and undulated over them: and the rider too could swing his body to avoid the jerk of a long or short stride: but by night everything was blinded, and the march racked with shocks. I had a heavy bout of fever on me, which made me angry so that I paid no attention to Rahail's appeals for rest. That young man had maddened all of us for months by his abundant vigor, and his laughing at our weaknesses: so this time I was determined to ride him out without mercy. Before dawn he was blubbering with self-pity, but softly, lest I hear him.

Dawn in the Jefer plain was beautiful. It came imperceptibly through the mist, like a ghost of sunlight, which left the earth untouched, and demonstrated itself as a glittering blink against the eyes alone. Things stood out matt against the pearl-grey horizon, at their head clear, but at their foot melting softly into the ground. Our shadows had no edge: we scarce knew if that faint stain upon the soil below was cast by us or not. In the forenoon we reached Auda's camp and stopped half an hour for a greeting, and to eat a few Jauf dates in his tent. Then we mounted again, meaning to cross the railway in the early night, as soon as it was safe. Rahail was past protest now: he rode beside me white faced, bleak and silent, wrought up only to out-stay me, beginning to take a half pride in his pains.

He had the advantage anyhow over me in strength, even had we started fair: and this time I was nearly finished. Step by step I was yielding myself to a slow ache which conspired with my abating fever and the numb monotony of riding, to close up the gates of my senses. Perhaps I was at last approaching that insensibility which had always been for me beyond reach, but a delectable land for one born so sluggish that nothing this side of faintness would let the spirit free. Now that I was near it suddenly I found myself dividing into parts. There was one which went on riding wisely, sparing and helping every pace of the wearied camel. Another from above and to the right bent down curiously, and asked what the flesh was doing. The flesh gave no answer, for indeed it was conscious only of a ruling impulse to keep on and on: but a third garrulous one talked and wondered, critical of the body's self-inflicted labor, and contemptuous of the reasoned folly of the effort it maintained.

The night passed in these mutual conversations; now all of me could see the dawn-goal in front, the head of the pass below which that other world of Rum would lie out like a sunlit map: and they debated over me saying that the struggle might be worthy, but the end was just foolishness and a rebirth of trouble. The body toiled on doggedly and took no heed, quite rightly, for the divided selves said nothing which I was not capable of thinking in December Jerusalem cold blood; they were all my natives. When Telesius split up the soul he had perhaps been taught by some such experience. Had he gone on, and reached the furthest limit of exhaustion, he would have seen his conceived regiment of thoughts and acts and feelings ranking themselves around him as separate creatures, eyeing like vultures the passing in the midst of this common thing which gave them life.

Rahail collected me out of my death-sleep by jerking my rein and striking me, while he shouted that we had left the right way, and were wandering toward the Turkish lines below Aba el Lissan. He was right, and we had to make a long cast back to reach Batra safely. Afterwards we walked down the steeper portions of the pass, and then stumbled along Wadi Hafira. In its midst a gallant little Howeiti, aged perhaps fourteen, darted out against us, finger on trigger, and told us to stand and explain: which we did, laughing. The lad blushed deeply at himself, and pleaded that his father's camels kept him always in the field, so that he had not known us either by sight or by description. Then he begged that we should not do him shame by betraying his error. The incident broke the tension between Rahail and me, and chattering together we rode out upon the Gaa. There under the tamarisk we passed the middle hour of the day in sleep, since by our slowness in the night march over Batra we had lost the possibility of reaching Akaba within the three days from Azrak: and Rum's glory would not let a man waste himself in feverish regrets.

We rode up its valley in the early afternoon, easier now and exchanging jests with one another, as the long winter evening crept down on us. When we got past the Khazail in the ascent of Nejd, we found the sun veiled behind level banks of low clouds in the west, and enjoyed a rich twilight of the English sort, till later in Wadi Itm the mist steamed up gently from the ground, and collected imperceptibly into wool-white masses in the hollows. We reached Akaba at midnight, and slept outside the camp till breakfast, when I called on Joyce, and found the caravan not yet ready to start: indeed Wood was only a few days returned.

There were urgent orders for me to go up at once to Palestine by air. Croil came over in a machine, and flew me to Suez. Thence I went up to Allenby's headquarters beyond Gaza, and heard all the news of his great stroke at Beersheba, the fall of Gaza, the pursuit and battles in the Philistine plain, and the stern wrestle with the entrenched Turks in the fastnesses of the Judean hills. He was so full of victories that my short statement that I had failed to carry a Yarmuk bridge was accepted as sufficient, and the rest of my failure could remain concealed.

While I was still with him, word came from Chetwode that Jerusalem had fallen, and Allenby made ready to enter, in the official manner that the catholic imagination of Mark Sykes had devised. He was good enough, although I had done nothing to forward his success, to allow Clayton to take me with him as his Staff Officer for the day. The personal Staff tricked me out in their spare clothes till I looked like an ordinary major in the British Army, and Dalmeny lent me red tabs, and Evans gave me a brass hat, so that for once I had the gauds of my appointment; and then I shared in what for me was the most memorable event of the war, the one which, for historical reasons, made a stronger appeal than anything on earth.

It was strange to stand before the tower with the Chief, listening to his proclamation, and to think how few days ago I had stood before Hajim, listening to his words. Seldom did we pay so sharply and so soon for our fears. We would have been by now, not in Jerusalem, but in Haifa, or Damascus, or Aleppo, had I not shrunk in October from the danger of a general rising against the Turks. By my failure I had fettered the unknowing English, and dishonored the unknowing Arabs, in a way only to be repaired by our triumphal entry into a liberated Damascus. The ceremony of the Jaffa Gate gave me a new determination.

BOOK VII

The Dead Sea Campaign

Allenby however; had made fair progress and after the capture of Jerusalem he assigned us a limited objective to relieve his night. To this we added, on our own initiative, an operation against the Hejaz Railway, to make effective the siege of Medina.

We began well, and reached the Dead Sea without delay: but then bad weather and bad temper and division of purpose broke up our force.

I had a misunderstanding with Zeid, threw in my hand, and returned to Palestine to report that we had failed in the north and in the south and that my use with the Arabs was ended

Allen by was ill the hopeful midst of a great scheme for the coming spring lie sent me back at once to Feisal with new powers and duties.

Chapter 89: A Local Offensive

After the triumph: — which was not so much a triumph as homage by Allenby to the mastering spirit of the place — we drove back to Shea's headquarters. The A.D.C.s pushed about, and from great baskets drew a lunch varied and elaborate and succulent. On us fell a short space of quiet, to be suddenly shattered by Monsieur Picot, the French political officer (permitted by Allenby to march beside Clayton in the entry) who said in his fluting voice: And tomorrow, my dear General, I will take the necessary steps to set up civil government in this town.'

It was the bravest word on record, and a silence fell on us, as when they opened the seventh seal in heaven. Salad and chicken mayonnaise and *foie gras* sandwiches hung in our mouths unchewed, while we turned our round eyes on Allenby and waited. Even he seemed for the moment at a loss; we began to fear that the idol might betray a frailty.... But then he grew red and swallowed. His chin came forward in the way we loved, and he said firmly, 'In the military zone the only authority is that of the Commander-in-Chief, myself.' 'But Sir Edward Grey...' began M. Picot feebly. He was cut short. 'Sir Edward Grey referred to the civil government which will be established when I judge that the military situation permits': and then we got into our cars again, and, in the sunshine of a great thankfulness, sped down the mountainside into our saluting camp.

There Allenby and Dawnay told me what next to do. The British were marched and fought nearly to a standstill. Their line was drawn from Jaffa to Jerusalem. They could spare no men for the rocky western shore of the Dead Sea. The Arabs down there were not sure, and perhaps the Turks might slip round the south shore, from Kerak or Tafileh, and attempt something in the British rear.

So they would ask us to take opportunity of the present disorder of the Turks, and the pause in British operations, by coming north towards the Dead Sea until, if possible, we linked right up to its southern end in the shape of a fixed post. After such a move our line would be again continuous, as in the days of the Kuntilla post, and the Turks would be deprived of the alley of potential trouble between the fronts.

Fortunately before I left Akaba this had been provisionally discussed with Feisal: so I could reply that the Howeitat were at the moment being collected at points from which a converging movement on Tafileh and Shobek would be made: that Sherif Nasir and Sherif Mastur had been chosen to direct the several operations: and that Nuri Bey Said, with guns and regular mounted infantry from Maulud's unit, had been detailed to assist Nasir in the first stroke.

They found this pro per, a proof of Arab good sense. I tried to improve the moment by asking Allenby what he would do next. He thought he would be immobilized nearly in his present lines for two months, till supplies were again massed, and casualties made up by draft. Afterwards, perhaps in the middle of February, he would push down to Jericho, and get possession of the Jordan mouth. The Turks were there in considerable force, and the operation against them would be a large one. Much of the enemy food was being lightered to Jericho up the Dead Sea from the Kerak district, and he asked me to note that as a second objective if the effort to Tafileh and the Dead Sea coast prevailed.

I hoped to improve on this, and said that if the Turks were continually shaken we might join him at the Jordan mouth, pivoting ourselves on the region of Madeba, where we would have the undiminished help of the Beni Sakhr. From the sample of their help, given by Mifleh and Fahad on the bridge, it was clear that they were sound men, with the sense of rebellion firmly in them. Also they were very numerous, enough to keep safe their homeland if once they snatched it from the Turks. If Allenby could put the Arab base (requiring perhaps fifty tons a day, food and stores and ammunition) into Jericho, he would encourage us to abandon Akaba, and to transfer Feisal and his headquarters and the Arab regular army, now some three thousand strong, to the Jordan valley.

This idea commended itself to Allenby and Dawnay, and they said they could almost now promise to give us these facilities when the railway reached Jerusalem. For the moment there were great bridges missing, and it was with the utmost pains that our troops were being fed by motor-lorry. The engineers (General Wright, my explosives adviser, in charge) thought that the railway might be through on January the twenty-fifth. If Allenby's own stroke against Jericho succeeded before the end of February he might be able to offer us our base towards the end of March.

This talk left between us a clear understanding for the course of operations. The Arabs were to reach the Dead Sea as soon as possible: to stop the transport of food up the Dead Sea from Kerak to the Turks in Jericho before the middle of February: and to arrive opposite the British at the Jordan mouth before the end of March. Since the first movement would take a month to start, and since all possible preliminary steps towards it were in hand, I could take a holiday: and so I went down to Cairo, and stayed there a week in complete comfort, experimenting with methods of electric firing and new explosives.

After the week it seemed best to return to Akaba, to be sure that Nasir and the Howeitat were making proper haste: so I took ship from Suez in the little Arethusa, a four-hundred-ton coasting steamer affected to our service. We had three of these little vessels, and they were invaluable: though having been snugly built for the North Sea traffic they were hot as hell in the Red Sea for their unfortunate English officers.

We arrived on Christmas Day. The Humber was still our guard monitor, though her time was nearly up, and the military need of her had passed with Maulud's victory at Petra. Snagge, as senior officer in Akaba, was entertaining the British community to a great Christmas dinner. He had screened the after part of his deck and built tables, which took the hosts and the twenty-odd guests easily. For some of the shore-fellows it was the first decent meal for months. Snagge well understood how to act godfather to the land and by his unremitting hospitality by the loan of the ship's doctor, by her workshop, and most of all by his own cheery companionship, he kept up all our spirits, and materially increased the general efficiency.

In the early days of the revolt it had been the Hardinge which had been given leisure to play providence to us. Once, at Yenbo, Feisal had ridden to the port from the hills on a streaming day of winter, cold, wet, miserable and tired. Linberry had sent a launch ashore, and invited him to the ship, where he had found a warm cabin, a peaceful meal, and a bath made ready for him. Afterwards he lay far back in an armchair, smoking one of his constant cigarettes, and remarked dreamily to me that now he knew what the furnishing of heaven would be.

My own private account with Snagge was of this healthy sort many times repeated. Akaba gave me many rides which were either too hot or too cold, many disappointments and pains: but he was always at hand with water talk, and food. Looking for stories to make him laugh showed me the funny side of my accidents, and corrected for the time the almost insane tension of too constant striving after an ideal.

Joyce told me that things were well. In the hope of fine weather we had laid out an elaborate scheme for the winter movement on Tafileh, using all available irregular forces and our advantages of position. Tafileh a place of three thousand people the center of a group of hamlets was important as the market of an arable district. It lay in the first folds of a valley, just under the crest of the great scarp which sheered from the plateau of Western Arabia into the Dead Sea hollow. From these depths it was difficult to attack, as the slopes went up five thousand feet, nearly precipitously. Along the plateau it was easily reached by Shobek or from the railway.

Our problem was so to approach it by maneuver that reinforcements would not reach its garrison in time. To do this we had firstly to occupy Shobek and the Hisha Railway and secondly to immobilize the Turkish troops on the main Hejaz Railway between Amman and Maan until the operation was finished. Accordingly, we had determined to tackle it simultaneously from the east from the south, and from the west.

The attack from the east was to start from Jefer, where lay the Abu Tayi with Auda and Nasir the Fortunate in control. Their first objective would be not Tafileh but the railway at Jurf el Derawish: and that they might overwhelm this station whose loss would throw consternation into the command at Maan, we had sent them a mountain gun, four machine-guns, and a company of mounted infantry, under Nuri Bey Said the

Arab officer who had been active at Rabegh as chief of staff to Aziz el Masri, and was now acting similarly to Jaafar at Akaba. Nasir found the Abu Tayi slack and divided in council and called down five hundred of the Beni Sakhr from Bair under Mifleh and Adhub, in support. Their concentration and advance were hampered by the intense cold. Many of Nuri's regulars, who wore drill uniforms and had only the one blanket that Egypt would give us, were frozen to death as they slept out at night.

The attack from the south was planned from Wadi Musa, where the situation had sensibly changed since the date of Maulud's victory. After it the Turks had abandoned all attempts to invest Wadi Musa and Delagha, and had concentrated in Aba el Lissan to hold the top of the pass. We had distracted them by maintaining our series of raids against the line south of Maan; Abdulla and Ali did much the same between us and Medina, and the Turks, being pinched to guard the railway, had again and again to draw men from Aba el Lissan to strengthen weak sections.

With each such diminution the residue was confined more strictly to the passive role. Maulud boldly threw out posts to places like Sadaka and Basta, on the plateau within easy reach of Aba el Lissan, and began to harry the supply caravans that came out from Maan. He too felt the full severity of the rain and snow, and lost many men by exposure: but the Turks lost equally in men, and much more in transport, since their mangy camels died off rapidly in the storms and mud. The loss straitened them in food-carrying, and involved a further withdrawal from the Aba el Lissan garrison.

At last they were too weak to hold the wide position, and early in January, Maulud was able to force them out and back towards Mreigha. The Bedouin, who were the bulk of his forces as they were experienced and stood the hill winter better than the troops , caught the Turks moving, and almost without casualty to themselves cut to pieces the hindmost battalion. This loss made the Turks again modify their plan; they withdrew precipitately to Waheida, only six miles from Maan: and when we pressed after them menacingly, they saw that even Waheida was too exposed, and fell back into Semna, the outpost line of Maan, only three miles out. So by the seventh of January Maulud was containing Maan directly.

The forces in Wadi Musa were set entirely free by this clearing of the plateau. We withdrew the regulars and sent up two hundred Hudheil, half-nomad Hejaz camel riders, to strengthen the local men, with Sherif Abd el Mayin, a Harithi, in command. His orders were to move to Hisha, the forest of the branch railway, and thence to Shobek, when the west force was ready to co-operate.

The west force were the Jazi Howeitat, Auda's blood-enemies, under Hamd el Arar, their courtly and melancholy chief. They had just joined us, and we had sent old Mastur, the uncle of Abdulla el Feir, to collect them at Ifdein in Wadi Araba. Thence they would climb up the face of the plateau on to the flank of Shobek, in conjunction with the Wadi Musa men. The signal for this triple attack would be given by Nasir's capture of Jurf railway station, about the sixth or seventh of January. He would later join the others in Shobek, or near it, and the combined forces would proceed against Tafileh.

Chapter 90: Armoured Car Work

Such a date gave us ten days' leisure: and as it was very rare that Joyce and myself were at liberty together we decided to celebrate, by taking the armored cars towards the railway at Mudowwara down the avenue of mud-flats noted in September while we were blowing up the first train.

The cars were now at Guweira in permanent camp. Their officers, Gilman the veteran, and Dowsett, with their crews and fifty Egyptian soldiers as working party, had spent months in Wadi Itrn, building like engineers a motor-road through the rocky gorge. It had been a great work, but was now finished and in good order to Guweira. So we took the two Rolls tenders, filled them with spare tires, and petrol, and food and water for four days, and set off on our exploring trip.

The mud-flats were bone-hard, and afforded perfect going, as good as or better than any racing track could be; our ryes left only a faint white line across their velvet surface. It cheered up everybody, this twisting in and out among the flats, at top speed, skirting clumps of tamarisk, and roaring along under the great sandstone crags. The drivers rejoiced for the first time in nine months, and flung forward abreast in a mad race for miles. Their speed meters touched sixty-five miles an hour, not bad for loaded and unturned cars which had been so long plugging the sand and stones, with only such running repairs as their men had time and tools to give them.

Afterwards we had some difficulty in crossing the sandy neck from the first flat to the second but worked about till we found the narrowest place and built over it a corduroy road of brushwood which would bind the sand together under the wheel and bear their weight for months. When this was ready the old cars came steaming and hissing along it dangerously fast to avoid the risk of getting stuck, rocking from side to side over the hummocks in a manner which looked fatal for springs. However we knew that it was nearly impossible to break a Rolls-Royce and so were sorrier for the drivers. Thomas and Rolls and Sanderson from whose grip the jerks tore the steering wheel and left them breathless with bleeding hands after the crossing.

There we lunched and rested a little while Joyce and I the passengers walked back and looked at the four neat little parallel tracks pressed five or six inches into the sand and furred with tips of the broken tamarisk. They marked the way for our return journey and assured us that with each attempt the ground would become easier. We then had another burst of speed with a wild diversion in the middle when a gazelle was sighted over the flat and the two great cars lurched aside in chase.

At the end of this second flat, the Gao of Disi, we ground with laboring engines through the mouth of Heswa, the valley by which our second train-raid had returned from Shedia with Salem el Alayan. After it we entered the third flat of Abu Sawana, across which we had a final glorious blind of fifteen miles over the mud and over the equally firm flint plains beyond. We slept there that chilly night, happy with bully-beef and tea and biscuit with English talk and laughter round the fire golden with its shower of sparks from the fierce brushwood. When these things tired there was soft sand beneath our bodies and two blankets to wrap ourselves in. For me it was a holiday with not an Arab near before whom I must play out my tedious part.

In the morning we ran on to the watershed and down nearly to Mudowwara. This was all the information that we needed and at once we turned back, meaning to fetch down the armored cars to try their greater weight over the road made by our wheels till we reached the railway and could prove the actual ground conditions about its track. We decided further to undertake an immediate operation if this ground surface was good enough, and therefore ordered the mountain-gun section on Talbots to get ready with the Rolls-Royces.

This section was an odd unit which General Clayton had seen in Egypt, and had sent down to us in an inspired moment. Its six Talbot cars were specially geared for heavy work, and were good, but inferior to the Rolls in having artillery wheels (unstable in our changing climate) and only single wheels in front. This made them less nimble than the armored cars over treacherous surfaces, and in addition their torque-rod brackets were too weak and were continually breaking, until at last the railway workshop in Cairo made us a set in phosphor-bronze, and forever cured that difficulty.

They carried two ten pound guns, and were manned by British gunners who were technically excellent. It was wicked to have given good men such rotten tools: and yet the inferior weapons were hardly noticeable in the greatness of spirit of the men. Their Captain Brodie was a silent Scotsman, never very buoyant or very anxious, a man for whom difficulties were shameful to notice, and who stamped himself on his subaltern, Pascoe, and on his men. However hard the duty given to them, they attacked it with such untroubled determination that their will always prevailed. Brodie seemed able to pick up his unit, and carry it forward with him over every obstacle. On every occasion and in every crisis they were always in place at the right moment, perspiring but imperturbable, with never a word in explanation or complaint.

With this imposing array of eight cars we drove off from Guweira next day, and reached our old stopping place behind Mudowwara by sundown. It was most excellent going, and we camped, intending to find a road down to the line just north of the station in the morning. Accordingly we set off early in a Rolls tender and searched through the very nasty low hills till we found an easy pass: but it opened straight on Ramleh, the first station north of Mudowwara, and we had to go back and try other ways till evening, when we were at last in place behind the last ridge, a little above Tell Shahn, the second station.

We had talked vaguely of mining a train, but the country was too open , and the enemy blockhouses too numerous. Instead we determined to attack the little entrenched work across the valley opposite our hiding-place on the morrow. So late in the morning of January the first, 1918, a day as cool as a good summer's day in England, after a pleasant breakfast, we rolled gently over a stony plain to a little hill overlooking the Turkish post. There Joyce and I got out of our cars, and climbed to the summit, to look on at what would happen.

Joyce was in charge, and for the first time I was at a fight as a spectator. The novelty was most enjoyable; armored ear work seemed fighting de luxe, for all our own troops were steel covered and could come to no hurt. This relieved us of every anxiety and we made a field day of it like the best regular generals, sitting on our hilltop, and watching the battle intently through binoculars.

The Talbot battery opened the affair, coming into action in a spirited manner just below our point, while the three armored cars moved forward, and crawled about the flanks of the Turkish earthwork like great dogs nosing out a trail. The enemy soldiers popped up their heads to gaze at them, and everything was very friendly and curious, till the cars slewed round their Maxims and began to spray the trenches. Then the Turks realized that it was an attack, and got down behind their parapets, and fired raggedly. It was not very satisfactory, shooting at an armored car (about as deadly as trying to warm up a rhinoceros with bird-shot), so after a while they turned their attention to Brodie's guns and peppered the earth about them with bullets.

Obviously they did not mean to surrender, and obviously we had no means at disposal to compel them: and it would be silly to get a man hurt on so abortive an occasion: so we drew off, saying that we were contented with having prowled up and down the line, and proved the surface hard enough for car-operations at a deliberate speed. However, the men were not pleased, and looked for more: and to humor them we drove off gently southward till we were opposite Shahm. There Brodie chose a gun position at two thousand yards, and began to throw shell after shell neatly into the station yard.

The Turks hated this, and trickled off to a blockhouse on a knoll a few hundred yards beyond the line, while the cars approached the station, and put bullets through the doors and windows leisurely. It was probably deserted, and they might have entered it in safety, had there been point in doing so. As it was we called everybody off again and returned into our hiding-hills after an inconclusive day more jest than operation. Neither Joyce nor I had ever used an armored car before. Our anxiety and forethought had been all to reach the railway through the manifold difficulties of the plains and hills. When we did reach we were entirely unready for action with not a thought of tactics or method: and slight though our consequent proceedings were yet we learned much from them.

The certainty that in a day from Guweira we could be on the line operating along it meant that the traffic lay at our mercy to be held up at a day's notice for so long as we could keep the cars in petrol and water and food and ammunition. All the Turks in Arabia could not fight an armored car in open country. If they tried it would be a massacre: but I hoped not to have to prove it except in the event of their withdrawing the Medina garrison and that, though much talked of and frequently ordered was now almost beyond their power to do as our mining operations had reduced their rolling stock below the capacity to put in dumps for so great an operation.

To cut the line here prematurely was, as I have said to put the railhead at Maan, and great strength there just now would inconvenience us. We preferred to keep the bulk of our Turks in Medina five hundred miles from anywhere and the expense of maintaining these thirteen thousand men and one hundred guns was better on the enemy than on us. The Germans saw that and after Falkenhayn's visit to Maan, repeatedly urged the abandonment of everything south of it: but the Old Turk party valued Medina as the last remnant of Turkish sovereignty in the Holy Places this surviving claim upon the Caliphate: and sentiment swung the decision to their side.

The British authorities seemed curiously dense about Medina. They kept on saying that it must be taken and lavished money and explosive on the operations that Ali and Abdulla continually undertook from their Yenbo base. Once or twice I pleaded the contrary view but they treated it either as silly paradox or as sour grapes on my part.

Accordingly to excuse our seeming inactivity in the north we made a show of impotence and gave them to understand that the Arabs were too poltroon to cut the line near Maan and keep it cut. This reason satisfied their sense of fitness, and made them happy, for Englishmen were always ready to believe ill of native action, and took such inferiority as a national compliment. So we battened on our own reputation, an ungenerous stratagem perhaps, but the easiest way, for the Staff knew so much more of war than I did that they refused to learn from me anything unqualified of the strange conditions under which we had to act: and I could not be bothered to set up a kindergarten of the imagination for their benefit.

Chapter 91: My Bodyguard

On our return to Akaba that evening we found some domestic affairs, which engaged our remaining free days. My part mostly concerned the private bodyguard formed by me for my own protection, as rumor slowly collected about me a greater notion of importance. On our first going up country from Rabegh and Yenbo the Turks had been curious: and then annoyed, since they ascribed to us the direction and motive force of the Arab Revolt. This was a futile mistake on their part, but flattered their sense of superiority over the Arabs, much as we used to explain the Turkish efficiency by German influence, since instinctively we believed the Germans our worthier antagonists.

However, the Turks said it often enough to make it an article of faith, and by easy degrees began to offer a reward of one hundred pounds for a British officer's body, alive or dead. As time went on they grew to learn our names, and not only increased our general figure, but (perhaps because of my odd acquaintance with them or with Max von Oppenheim) made a special bid for me. After the capture of Akaba the price became respectable, and when Ali ibn el Hussein and I blew up Jemal Pasha they put us at the head of the list, worth twenty thousand pounds alive or ten thousand dead.

Of course the offer was equivocal, with no certainty that the money would be paid at all, or whether in gold or paper: and so the enterprise of taking us was less attractive than it should have been. Still there might be enough in it to justify my care, and for this and other reasons I began to increase my people into a troop, retaining those who were satisfactory, and adding to them such others as I found, lawless men, fellows whose dash and vigor had got them into trouble elsewhere. I needed hard riders and hard livers, men proud of themselves, without ties or families to drag upon them: and by good fortune three or four such joined me at the first, and set a tone and standard for all future applicants.

One afternoon I had been sitting quietly reading in Marshall's tent at Akaba (I lodged with Marshall as often as I was in camp) when there entered over the noiseless sand an Ageyli, thin, dark and short, most gorgeously dressed. He carried on his shoulder the richest Hasa saddlebag I had ever seen. It was a tapestry of green and red, white, orange and blue, with tassels woven over its sides in five rows, and from the middle and bottom hung five-foot streamers, of geometric pattern, tasseled and fringed, so long that when the camel was standing they would nearly reach the ground. The purpose of these trappings was mainly ornamental, but also they saved the camel's belly a very little from the flies.

The young man greeted me respectfully, threw the saddlebag on the floor of the tent, saying, 'For you', and disappeared as suddenly as he came, before I had said a word. Next day at the same hour he returned, carrying a camel-saddle of equal beauty, the long brass horns of its cantles adorned with exquisite old Yemen engraving. On the third day he reappeared, empty-handed, dressed in a single cotton shirt, and sank down in a heap before me, saying that he wished to enter my service. He looked odd, without his silk robes upon him: for his face, shriveled and torn with smallpox, and hairless, might have been of any age: and he had a lad's supple body.

His long black hair was carefully plaited into six shining plaits down his cheeks. His eyes were weak, and he kept them closed to narrow slits. His mouth was sensual, loose, wet, and gave him a good-humored, part cynical, expression. I asked him his name; he replied Abdulla, surnamed el Nahabi, or the Robber. I asked for the justification of it but he explained that he had not won it, merely inherited it from his respected father. His own adventures had been of an unprofitable sort. He was born in Boreida, amongst the Wahabis, and when young had suffered from the civil power, for his impiety. When half-grown, a misfortune in a married woman's house had made him leave his native town, and he had taken service with ibn Saud, Emir of Nejd.

In this service his hard swearing had brought him lashes and imprisonment, and consequently he had deserted to Kuweit, where again he had been amorous. On his release he had moved to Hail and had enrolled himself among the retainers of ibn Rashid, the Emir. Unfortunately, there he had disliked his officer to the point of striking him in public with his camel-stick. Return was made in kind and after a slow recovery in prison he had once more been thrust friendless on the world.

The Hejaz Railway was being built and in it he had sought fortune : but a contractor docked his wages for sleeping at noonday, and in his retort he had docked the contractor of his head. The Turkish Government interfered, and he found life very hard in the prison at Medina before trial. However, there was an open window, and he came to Mecca and for his proved integrity and camelmanship was made post carrier between Mecca and Jidda. To this employ he settled down, and laid aside his young extravagances bringing to Mecca his father and mother from Boreida, and setting them up in a shop to work for him.

After a year's prosperity he was waylaid, and lost his camel and his consignment. The merchants seized his shop in compensation and from the wreck he only saved enough to fit himself out as a man-at-arms for service in the Sherifian camel-police. Merit made him a petty officer but too much attention was drawn to his section by his habit of fighting with daggers and by his foul mouth which knew all human depravity, and had eaten filth in the stews of every capital in Arabia. His lips trembled with humor, sardonic, salacious, lying, once too often. He was reduced charged his downfall to a jealous Ateibi, and stabbed him in the Court of Justice before the eyes of the outraged Sharraf governor of Taif and later Feisal's second-in-command.

The Ateibi recovered, but Sharraf's stem sense of public decency punished Abdulla by the severest of all his chastisements, from which he very nearly died. Months later when he was well enough he entered Sharraf's service. On the outbreak of war he enlisted in the Camel Corps the very day of its formation, and became orderly to ibn

Dakhil, the captain of the Ageyl with Feisal. For a year his reputation grew: but then came the mutiny at Wejh, and ibn Dakhil became an ambassador and not a commander. Abdulla missed the comradeship of the ranks, and the common fighting, and ibn Dakhil had sent him to me with a written character to try to enter my service.

The letter said that for two years he had served faithfully but disrespectfully, being a son of shame. He was the most experienced Ageyli in the world having served every prince in Arabia, and having been without exception dismissed from each employment after stripes and prison for offenses of too great individuality Ibn Dakhil said that of all Arabs he knew, the Nahabi rode second only to himself: he was a master-judge of camels as brave as any son of Adam, easily, since he was too blind-eyed to see danger. In fact he was the perfect retainer and I engaged him at once as my head man, and never regretted it: nor had I ever to discipline him.

In my service only once did he taste confinement, and that was at Allenby's headquarters where a desperate provost-marshal rang me up to say that a wild man with weapons had been found sitting on the Commander-in-Chiefs doorstep, and had been led without riot to the guard room , where he had found a case of oranges and was eating them as though for a wager. He proclaimed himself my son, and one of Feisal's dogs and oranges were running short, and would I deliver them from him?

So Abdulla experienced his first telephone conversation told the A.P.M. that such a fitting would be a great comfort in all prison-cells and took a ceremonious leave. He scouted absolutely the notion that he might walk about Ramleh unarmed, and had to be given a special pass to make lawful his sword and dagger and pistol and rifle. His first use of the pass was to revisit the guardroom, to distribute cigarettes to his friends the military police on duty. Abdulla examined and proved all applicants for my service, and. thanks mainly to him and to the Zaagi. my other commander (a stiff man of the normal officer class) a wonderful gang of experts grew about me. The British at Akaba called them cutthroats, but they cut-throats only to my order. Perhaps in others' eyes it was a fault that they would recognize no authority in the world than mine... but when I was away they were kind to Marshall, our Scottish doctor and would hold him in incomprehensible talk about the points of camels and their breed and ailments, from dawn till night time. Marshall was very patient, and two or three of them would sit attentively by his bedside while he woke or slept

A good half of them (nearly fifty of the ninety) were Ageyl, the nervous limber Nejdi villagers who made the color and the parade in Feisal's army, and whose care for their riding camels was such a feature of their service. They would call them by name, from a hundred yards away: and would leave them in charge of their kit when they dismounted for any purpose. The Ageyl, being mercenaries, would not do well unless well-paid, and for lack of that condition had fallen into disrepute: yet the bravest single effort of the Arab war belonged to that one of them who twice swam down the water-conduit into Medina, and returned each time in safety, with a full report of the internal condition of the invested town.

I paid my men six pounds a month, the standard army wage for a man and camel, but mounted them on my own animals, so that the money was clear income, and this made the service enviable, and gave me the eager spirits of all the camp at my disposal. For my timetable's sake, since I was busier than most men in Arabia, my rides were customarily very long and hard and sudden. The ordinary Arab, whose single riding camel probably represented half his worldly wealth, could not afford causelessly to found it by traveling my speed: and such riding was painful for the man, and wore him as it wore the animal.

Consequently I had to have with me picked riders, mounted only on my own beasts, which we bought at long prices, and which were the fastest and strongest to be obtained anywhere. We chose them for speed and power, no matter how hard and exhausting they might be under the saddle: indeed often we chose the hard-paced, knowing that they would be equal to any journey which camels might do. They were changed or rested in our own camel-hospital when they became thin: and their riders likewise. The Zaagi held each man strictly responsible for his mounts good condition.

They were very proud of being in my bodyguard, and developed professionalism almost flamboyant. They dressed like a bed of tulips, in every imaginable color, leaving unused only white, since that was my constant wear, and they did not wish to seem to presume. In half an hour they would make ready for a ride of six weeks, that being the time for which food could be carried at the saddle-bow. Baggage camels they shrank from as a disgrace. They would travel day and night, at my whim and made it a point of honor never to mention fatigue. If one grumbled, the others would silence him or at least change the current of his complaint brutally.

They fought like devils when I wanted and sometimes when I did not, especially with Turks or with outsiders. For one guardsman to strike another was the last offense. When they did well they expected an extravagant reward and when they did ill an equal punishment. They made boast throughout the army of their pains and gains. By such unreason in each degree they were kept apt for any effort any risk.

Abdulla and the Zaagi ruled them by my authority, with an unalloyed savagery which could only be excused by the power of each man to quit the service if he wished. Yet we had only one resignation. The others, though adolescents full of carnal passion, tempted by their irregular life well-fed exercised, rich seemed to sanctify their fear, to be fascinated by their physical suffering. Servitude in the East was based like other conduct on their obsession with the antithesis between body and spirit, and these took pleasure in subordination in the utter degrading of the body to throw more into relief the freedom and equality of mind: almost they preferred servitude, as richer in experience than authority.

So the relation of master and man in Arabia was at once more free and more subject than elsewhere. Servants were afraid of the sword of justice and of the whip not because the one might put an arbitrary term to their existence and the other print red rivers of pain about their sides, but because these were the symbols and the means to which their obedience was vowed. They had a gladness of abasement, a freedom of consent to yield to their masters the last service and degree of their flesh and blood, because their spirits were equal and the contract voluntary.

In this pledging of their limit of endurance it disgraced men if from weakness of nerve or insufficiency of courage they fell anywhere short of the call. Pain was to them a solvent a cathartic almost a decoration to be fairly worn, so long as they survived it. Fear which might be the strongest motive in slothful man broke down and counted with us for nothing since love for a cause — or for a person — was aroused. For such an object penalties were discounted, and loyalty became open eyed, not obedient. To it men dedicated their being, and possessed by it had no room for virtue or vice. Cheerfully they fed it upon what they were, gave it their lives, and, greater than that, the lives of their fellowship; for it was many times harder to offer than to endure sacrifice.

It seemed almost as though an ideal, held in common by many, transcended that personal which had been the measure of the world for each of us. I sometimes wondered whether such an instinct might not point to our capacity someday for happily accepting a final absorption, in whose general pattern our discordant selves might find reasonable and inevitable purpose. Yet now this very transcending of our individual frailty made the ideal a transient thing. Its essence and principle became activity, unrest in mind and soul and body, extended beyond holding point to serve it with good and evil ability: and so always it vanished, leaving its worshipers saddened and exhausted, holding for false what they once pursued.

However, for the time the Arabs were possessed, and our cruelty of governance answered their need. Besides, these followers of mine were generally outlaws, men guilty of crimes of violence, which smooth measures would have repelled. They were the freelances of nearly thirty clans or tribes, from every district in Syria and North Arabia. Many were blood enemies and, only for my hand over them, would have murdered in the ranks each day. These internal feuds, and their unlikeness, prevented any number of them combining against me, and made for safety, while it gave me sponsors and guides wherever I went or sent, between Akaba and Damascus, between Beersheba and Bagdad.

They were personally loyal: many were used as spies, to go into their villages in the Hauran or the Ghuta, and bring me news of the Turks; and their trained intelligence made them good spies. They were wildly extravagant with my money and with their own: but I paid them out of the British funds of the Arab Movement, the half-million given us by Allenby for extraordinary work, and if they cost three times as much as any company in the army, on the other hand they did six times the work, and so their expense seemed just. Also they saved my life many times, and now I was almost a leader in the movement. In my service nearly sixty of them died.

Quaintly, but with justice, events forced me to live up to my bodyguard, to become as hard, as sudden, as heedless. The strain so put upon me was great, especially when the climate cogged the die. In winter I outdid them, with my allies of the frost and snow: but in the heat they could outdo me. In endurance there was less disparity. For years before the war, and during it, I had kept myself trim by constant training in carelessness. I had learned to eat much one time, and then to go two, three or even four days quite without food: and after to overeat, I made it a rule to avoid rules in food, not to regulate my life by hours or bells, never to have fixed meals, or a fixed number of meals. Such a course of exceptions accustomed me to no custom at all.

So physically I was every whit as efficient in the desert as my companions, felt neither hunger nor surfeit however great the feast or long the fast, and was never distracted by thought of food during my work. I had followed the same habit of avoiding habit in drink and sleep and rest, and on the march could go dry between wells (since to carry a water bottle was rightly thought Effeminate among the Arabs) and like the Arabs could drink greatly at wells both for the thirst of yesterday and against the thirst of tomorrow. No quality of water or food — and we met odd varieties of either — disturbed me.

In the like way, though sleep remained for me the richest pleasure in the world, I supplied its place by the uneasy swaying in the saddle of a night march, or missed it for night after laborious night without undue fatigue. Such liberties came from years of past control (contempt of use might well be the lesson of our manhood) and they fitted me peculiarly for my men and our conditions: but of course in me they were only the effect of training and trying, half from choice, half from poverty, and I was never able to assume them effortlessly, like the Arabs. Yet in compensation they had not my energy of motive, and their less-taut wills flagged before mine, and made me seem to them tough and active.

Together we often saw men push themselves, or be driven, to what some might have thought a cruel extreme of endurance: and yet never was there an intimation of physical break. The collapse of men from over strain always rose from a moral weakness eating into the body, which of itself, without traitors from within, had no power over the will. To men whose spirits were filled with desire there was no flesh. While we rode we were disembodied, all-unconscious of physical needs or feelings: and when at an interval this excitement faded and we did see our bodies it was with hostility, with a contemptuous sense that they reached their highest purpose, not as instruments of the spirit, but when, dissolved, their elements served to manure a field.

Chapter 92: Direct Action

Away from the fighting-line here in Akaba, during this pause, we saw the reverse of the shield: the reaction against, or the corruption of, our enthusiasms, which made the moral condition of life in the base unsatisfactory. The reckless habit which induced wild camel charges into Turkish posts, and daring raids by night and day through or behind the enemy lines, seemed to inspire in those who waited a disregard of decency and convention. The sacredness of women in nomad Arabia forbade prostitution, and there was no urban population to redeem the lack: while the extreme of temperature, the good food, abundance of money, uncertainty of life, and the consequent luxury of dress and behavior inflamed the never sedate instincts of the Arabs, and drove them into sexual perversities.

While these were voluntary and affectionate they were winked at: for they seemed amateurish when compared with the elaborate vices of oriental cities, or the bestialities of their peasantry with goats and asses. We left the regulation of such things to public opinion, and in hot climates where nature struck sharply and directly on the little-clothed body, public opinion was sometimes very slow and tolerant. The real danger, to my mind, was lest the contagion of example (and with it that still more dreaded physical contagion) spread to the British units. They were a handful of very nice fellows, and normally would have been proof: but in such strangeness nothing was granted, and we felt there might be reason for our fear.

It happened one evening of this week, as I sat with the Zaagi on his carpet under the palms, that there broke out a sudden hubbub beyond the men's fire. Abdulla slipped away to hear, and returned in a moment with Ali el Alayan, one of the youngest of the

Ageyl, a slight youth of seventeen. He had been caught in open enjoyment of a British soldier. However common in practice, such misconduct, when it came to light, was always sharply visited among the Ageyl, and Abdulla asked for Ali's immediate trial in company session. Five minutes later, he had been found deserving of the one hundred lashes appointed by the Prophet. By act of grace I reduced it to fifty with a cane. The modification passed willingly, as we were riding next day, and he was immediately trussed over a sand-heap and beaten lustily.

It was not a terrible ordeal, but certainly uncomfortable for little Ali whose writings were jeered at loudly by his fellows. Meanwhile I saw the English offender, Carson, a very decent A S.C. lad, and told him that I would have to turn him over to his officer, who returned to Akaba next day. He was miserable at his position.

A few minutes later the N.C.O. in charge of the car base appeared, and saluting (a rare thing with us) begged me very straightly to hush it up. This was the first crime in the British section. The shame of it was felt by them all. Carson was only a boy, not vicious or decadent. He could not explain how it had happened, except that Ali had excited him, and he had been carried away suddenly. He had been a year without opportunity of sexual indulgence, as my sentries had made the native women impossible. All this I could accept as true. The act was probably Ali's fault, for he was an ill-balanced youth, and our men's clothes struck the Arabs as a call to bawdiness. I had put my own guard over the three prostitutes in Akaba because they were so beastly that I could not stand the thought of their being touched by the British: even though deprivation drove the men into irregularities,

Driver replied that Carson had been too shy to tell any of the other fellows. I then pointed out that he was not being condemned by me morally, since neither my impulses nor my convictions were strong enough to make me a judge of conduct. It was because our position in the Revolt depended on our clean dealing. We shared good and ill fortune with the Arabs, who had already punished their offender in this case. So I could not in common equity let our man go free, and only regretted that we had no procedure summary and public to finish the matter out of hand.

The corporal reluctantly withdrew, to come back in half an hour rather breathlessly, and beg me to come across and see Carson at once. I jumped up asking if he were ill. Driver said he thought not, but that I must look at him. When I reached their camp, the half-dozen men were sitting in the open, round a bright fire of old petrol-cases. Carson was among them, lying covered up on a blanket. As I came he lifted his face up to me, and in the moonlight it looked drawn and ghastly, almost lead colored. I said, 'What on earth is the matter with you?' and he laid himself down again sullenly.

Driver bent over, and pulled off the blanket, and then I saw that the lad was stripped, and his back scored with heavy swollen lines. I turned to the corporal for explanation, and he related, rather hesitatingly, that they had talked over my words about fairness and an example to the Arabs, and had decided that it was up to them to give their fellow the like punishment which Ali had had. So they did it, all taking part, and as hard as they could, even giving him sixty instead of fifty because he was English! The Zaagi had been present as witness, and they hoped I would see they had done their best and call it enough.

I had not expected anything so drastic, and was taken aback, rather inclined to laugh. The Zaagi appeared noiselessly, and with his air of being able to say infinitely more than he did, muttered that by God they had beaten him: while Carson pleaded in great distress that this was much worse than a court-martial for him, and that he would rather anything than have had the other fellows shame him so.

The men, as a matter of fact, had done of their own accord the best thing possible for public opinion, and, so far as the Zaagi knew, by my orders. I was not sure if I could tell them so, quite directly, and compromised by saying to Driver that he had no right to take the law into his own hands, but it was done, and to prevent trouble spreading I would forget the whole affair, if nothing more was heard of it. They were relieved, for now that it was over they were afraid: and it was kept absolutely to them. Carson was unhappy for a time, but as soon as possible we took him up-country, where he showed himself one of our best men, always ready for any special job. The others learned from his misfortune, and we heard of no second case of British being mixed up with Arabs: which was a good thing for many reasons other than the sanitary.

Joyce and Snagge were also troubled mainly about the Egyptians under them as laborers and for mounting guards. It was all irksome, and we rejoiced when at last we were able to escape from this plague spot up-country again into the clean fresh hills about Guweira. The early winter gave us days hot and sunny or days overcast with clouds massed about the head of the plateau nine miles away, where Maulud was keeping his watch in the mist and rain. The evenings were just chill enough to add a delightful value to a thick cloak and a fire.

We waited in Guweira for a day or two till the post came in from Nasir, with the best of news. As usual he had directed his raid with great skill and deliberation. Jurf el Derawish, their objective was a strong station of three stone buildings with outer works and trenches in a broad valley up which the railway climbed from the basin of Hesa to the plains of Maan. Some hundreds of yards behind the station, to the south-east, was a low mound, trenched and walled, on which the Turks had set two machine-guns and a mountain gun. Beyond the mound lay a high sharp ridge. The north-western face of the last spur of the hills that divided Jefer from the watershed of Bair.

The weakness of the defense lay in this ridge, for the Turks were too few to hold both it and the knoll or station, and its crest overlooked the railway and the trenches at a range of little more than one thousand yards. Nasir knew it and moved by night from Jefer, and occupied the whole top of the hill without alarm. Then he began operations by cutting the line above and below the station in the dark. A few minutes later when it was light enough to see. Nuri Said brought up his mountain gun to the edge of the ridge and with a third lucky shot, a direct hit, silenced the Turkish gun.

The Arabs were greatly excited: and the Beni Sakhr brought up their camels and swore that they were going to charge in forthwith. Nuri thought it madness while the Turk machine-guns were still in action from their trenches: but his words had no effect upon the Bedu. In desperation he opened a rattling fire with all he had against the Turkish position and the Beni Sakhr swept round the foot of the main ridge and up over the knoll in a flash frightening rather than hitting the enemy in accordance with Guibert's maxim. When they saw this camel horde racing at them the Turks flung away their rifles and fled down into the station. Only two Arabs were hurt.

Nuri left his gunners on the hill to serve their piece against the station buildings their plunging fire tearing raggedly through the roofs while he ran down himself to the little knoll. The Turkish gun was undamaged and as it was heavier than his own he promptly slewed it round and discharged it point blank into the ticket office. The Beni Sakhr, in a mob behind the gun yelled with joy to see the wood and stones flying jumped again on their camels and loped into the station just as the enemy surrendered. The Turks had lost twenty killed and wounded but nearly two hundred including seven officers survived as prisoners.

The Bedu became rich: for besides the weapons there were twenty-five mules and in the siding two locomotives with seven trucks loaded full of delicacies for the officers' messes of the besieged garrison of Medina. There were things the tribesmen had only heard of, and things they had never heard of, and they were supremely happy. Even the unfortunate Arab regulars got a share and were able once more to enjoy the products of their native country as the Bedouin did not want olives and other Syrian food.

Nuri Said and the officers had artificial tastes and rescued tinned meats and liquors from the wilder men. They said all were forbidden things and had them thrown in disgust at their heads . There was one whole truck of tobacco and as the Howeitat did not smoke it was divided between the Beni Sakhr and the regulars. By its loss the Medina garrison became tobacco-less: and their sad plight later so worked on Feisal, a confirmed smoker, that he in compassion loaded some pack-camels with cheap cigarettes and drove them into Tebuk with his compliments.

After the looting the engineers got to work and fixed charges on the two engines in the water-tower and pump and between the points. They burned the trucks and damaged a bridge but all of it perfunctorily for as usual after victory everyone was too loaded and too hot to care for abstract labor. They camped behind the station and about midnight had an alarm when the noise and lights of a train came up from the south, and halted by the break of the evening before.

Auda sent scouts to report: but before they returned a solitary sergeant walked into Nasir's camp and reported himself as a volunteer for the Sherif's army. He had been sent out on the Turks' part to explore the station. His story was that there were only sixty men and a mountain gun on the relief train, and that if he went back with smooth news they would be surprised without a shot fired. Nasir called Auda, who called the Howeitat, and they went off silently to lay the trap: but, just before they got there, the men sent out scouting earlier decided to do their unaided best, and opened rapid independent fire against the coaches. In fear the engine reversed, and rolled the train back, unhurt, to Maan. It was the only sorrow of jurf.

Chapter 93: Tafileh

After this raid the weather once more broke. For three successive days came falls of snow. Nasir's force with difficulty regained the tents at jefer, and there, only on one night, ten of the Arabs were frozen stiff. This plateau about Maan lay between three and five thousand feet above sea level, open to every wind from the north and east.

They blew from the snow-covered mountains of Central Asia or from the Caucasus sweeping terribly over the great desert to these low hills of Edom, against which their first fury broke. The surplus bitterness lipped over the crest and made winter down below in Judea and Sinai.

Outside Beersheba and Jerusalem the British found it cold: but our Arabs fled there to get warmer, for unhappily the British Supply Staff realized too late that we were fighting in a little alp. They did not give us tents for one quarter of our troops, nor serge clothing, nor boots, nor blankets enough to issue two per head of the mountain-garrisons. Our soldiers accustomed to the heat of Arabia, and the comfort of the valleys of Syria, deserted in numbers, or died like butterflies of their exposure: or if they neither deserted nor died, existed in an aching misery which froze the hope out of them. Those leaders, who for the example went about in their fellowship tent less and barefoot and in cotton clothes, suffered enough to welcome any plausible excuse for inactivity.

According to our plan, the good news of Jurf was to send the Arabs of Petra under Abd el Mayin at once up their hills into the forest for Shobek. It was an uncanny march in the hoar mist, that of these frozen-footed Wadi Musa peasants in their winter sheepskins, up and down the sharp valleys and dangerous hillsides, out of whose snow-drifts the heavy trunks of the junipers, grudging in leaves, jutted like castings in grey iron. The ice and the frost broke down all the animals, and many of the men; but these hardy villagers of the hills had grown used to being cold throughout their winter: a state of body which we all now needed to learn, and learned well, but too late, just by when spring came.

The Turks heard of their coming and in a scared mob fled from the caves and shelters among the trees to railhead, littering the roads of their panic with cast baggage and equipment. Railhead, with its temporary sheds commanded from low ridges by the Arab gunfire, was no better than a trap. The Shobek tribes swarmed in a pack across the line further down the valley, and tore the enemy to pieces as they ran out from their burning and falling walls. One disciplined company of proper troops under an Albanian officer fought their way, with loss, to the main line at Aneyza; but the Arabs killed or took the others, with the stores at railhead, and the archives and officials in Shobek, the old Crusader fort of Monreale, poised high on a chalk cone, above its deep and winding valley. Abd el Mayin put his headquarters there, and sent word to Nasir and to Mastur. This capture of Shobek opened the way for the third part of the operation. Mastur drew his Motalga horse and foot from the comfort of their tents in the sunny depths of Araba by Ifdein, and with them climbed the hill-passes to Dana, Buseira and Rasheidiya, little villages nestling for shelter from the cold over the lip of the escarpment. The Jazi, now they were started, longed to be at Tafileh before their rivals of the Abu Tayi.

However, the advantage lay with Nasir, who leaped in one day from Jefer to Towana, and after a whirlwind night appeared at dawn on the rocky brink of the ravine in which Tafileh hid, and summoned it to surrender on pain of bombardment: an idle threat, for Nuri Said with the guns had gone back alter Jurf to Guweira. There were only one hundred and eighty Turks in the village but they had supporters in a clan of the peasantry the Muhaisin, not for love so much as because Dhiab el Auran, the vulgar head man of the chief faction of the place had declared for Feisal. So they shot up at Nasir a stream of ill-directed bullets and his rush was checked.

The Howeitat spread out along the cliffs climbing down them where it was convenient, and began to return the peasants' fire. This manner of going displeased Auda, the old lion, who raged that a mercenary village-folk should dare to resist their secular masters of the Abu Tayi. So he jerked his head-stall and cantered his mare down the path till he rode out plain to view on the little level beneath the easternmost houses of the village. There he reined in and shook his hand at them booming in his wonderful voice: 'Dogs, do you know Auda ?'... and when they realized that it was that implacable son of war their hearts failed them and an hour later Sherif Nasir in the town-house was sipping tea with his guest the Turkish governor consoling him upon the sudden changes of fortune in battle.

At dark Mastur rode in; with him were the Motalga, the main Jazi clan who looked blackly at their blood enemies the Abu Tayi lolling in the best houses as they passed. Nasir met him and the two Sherifs divided up the place hoping to keep their unruly followers apart. They had little authority to restrain them for by passage of time Nasir was nearly adopted into the Abu Tayi, and Mastur had been long with the Jazi.

When morning came the two factions were bickering and the day passed anxiously for besides these blood-enemies the Muhaisin were fighting the Auran for authority among the villager and further complications developed in two stranger elements one a colony of freebooting Senussi from North Africa, who had been intruded by the Turks into some rich but half-derelict lands of Rasheidiya to the bitter resentment of the owners and the other a plaintive but industrious suburb of nearly a thousand Armenians the few survivors of an inhuman deportation by the Young Turks in 1915. These clamored for food and protection: those for protection since the landowners had begun to close on them as soon as the Turks went

The people of Tafileh were in deadly fear of what the future would bring them. We were as usual short of food and short of transport, and they would remedy neither ill. They had com, wheat and barley, in their bins, but hid it till times were settled. They had pack animals, asses and mules, in abundance; but drove them away till times were settled. They could easily have driven us away too, but most of them were short of the sticking point. Incuriousness of the classes was the great foundation of our change, the most potentially four imposed order: for Eastern government rested not so much on consent or force, as on supine acquiescence, the lack of opposition, inertia, disinterestedness which gave a minority undue effect.

Feisal had delegated command of this push towards the Dead Sea to his half-brother Zeid, the youngest of the four sons of the Sherif of Mecca. It was Zeid's first office in the north, and he set out for it eager with hope. An adviser there came with him Jaafar Pasha, our general with a company of infantry and some gunners and machine gunners. Most of these were left, for lack of food in front, at Petra, where things were easier. But Zeid himself, with jaafar, and Rasim and Abdulla, the two experts of Wadi Yenbo, rode fast forward to Tafileh.

Things were almost at a break. Auda affected a magnanimity which was very galling to the Jazi boys, Metaab and Annad, sons of Abtan, whom Auda's son had killed. They, lithe, definite figures, very self-conscious, began to talk big about revenge torn tits threatening a hawk. Auda declared he would whip them in the marketplace, if they were rude. This was very well, but their followers were two to every one of his, and we were near having the village in a blaze. The young fellows, with Rahail my ruffler, went flaunting themselves in every street.

Zeid thanked and paid Auda, and sent him back to his desert beyond the railway to contain the garrisons of the Turkish stations. The enlightened heads of the Muhaisin had to go as forced guests to Feisal's tent. Dhiab their enemy was our friend, too fresh with services for us to flout direct: but we remembered regretfully the adage that the best allies of a violently successful new regime were not its old adherents, but its old opponents.

With Zeid's coming the economic situation improved by the plenty of gold with us. We appointed an officer-governor of the place instituted a market, and organized our villages for further attack. We began to think of Kerak, and Jaafar Pasha returned to Feisal, and arranged with him that Sherif Abdulla el Feir should advance from Ifdein with the semi nomad horsemen of the Beersheba Arabs, and occupy the thicket areas at the south end of the Dead Sea to fulfill the next stage of the program that Allenby had set us.

Chapter 94: The Turks Attack

However, these plans quickly went adrift. Before we were settled we were astonished by a sudden effort of the Turks to dislodge us by counter-attack. We had never dreamed of this for it seemed out of the question that they should hope to keep Tafileh or want to keep it. Allenby was just in Jerusalem, and for the Turks the whole issue of the war might depend on their successful defense of the Jordan valley against him. Unless Jericho fell or until it fell, Tafileh was for them an obscure village of no interest. For men so critically placed as the Turks to waste a casualty on it appeared the rankest folly.

Hamid Fakhri Pasha commanding the Forty-eighth Division and the Amman sector thought otherwise or had his orders. He collected about nine hundred infantry, made up of three battalions (in January 1918 a Turkish battalion was a poor thing) with an attached body of police one hundred cavalry two mountain howitzers, and twenty-seven machine-guns and sent them by rail and road to Kerak. There he impressed all local transport drew a fresh set of civil officials to staff his intended new administration in Tafileh, and marched southward to surprise us.

Surprise us he did. We first heard of him in the afternoon of January the twenty-fourth, when his cavalry advance-guard fell on our pickets in the Wadi Hesa, the gorge of great width and depth and difficulty that cut off the land of Kerak from the land of Tafileh, Moab from Edom. By early evening he had driven them back into Tafileh, and was upon us.

Jaafar Pasha had sketched out a defense position on the left bank of the great ravine of Tafileh, proposing if the Turks attacked from the north, to give them the village, and to defend only the steep heights to the south of it. This seemed to me unsound. The slopes were dead, and their defense as difficult as their attack. There was no reason to suppose the Turks would go for them, since their lines could be turned from the east: and by quitting the village we threw away the advantage of the local people, who would be for the occupiers of their houses.

However, it was the ruling idea, all Zeid had, and so about midnight he gave the order, and his servants and retainers saddled their animals and loaded up their stuff. The men proceeded to the south crest of the ravine, while the baggage train was sent off by the lower road to safety in Buseira. This move created a fearful panic in the town. The peasants thought we were running away (I think we were) and rushed to save their goods and their lives. It was freezing hard, and the ground crusted with noisy ice. In the blustering dark the crying and confusion through the narrow streets were terrible.

Dhiab the Sheikh had told us harrowing tales of the disaffection of the townspeople, to increase the splendor of his own loyalty: but my impression was that they were stout fellows, of great potential use. To prove it I made a point of sitting out on my roof, or of walking in the dark quietly up and down the steep alleys, cloaked against recognition, and my guards unobtrusively about me within call. So we heard what passed. The people were in a very passion of fear, nearly dangerous, abusing everybody and everything: but it was very clear that there was nothing pro-Turkish abroad. They were in horror of the Turks' returning, ready to do all in their physical capacity to support against them a leader with fighting intention. This was satisfactory.

Finally I met the young Jazi sheikhs, Metaab and Annad, beautiful in silks and gleaming silver arms, and sent them to find their uncle, Hamd el Arar. Him I asked to ride away north to the ravine, to discover what was happening, and to tell the peasantry who by the noise were still fighting the Turks up there, that we were on our way up to help them. Hamd, a gallant cavalier, galloped off at once with about twenty of his relations.

His passage at speed through the streets added the last touch required to perfect the terror. The housewives bundled their goods pell-mell out of doors and windows, though no men were waiting to receive them. Children were trampled on and yelled, while their mothers were yelling anyhow. The Motalga while they rode fired shot after shot into the air to encourage themselves, and as though to answer them the flashes of the enemy rifles became visible outlining the northern cliffs of the great gorge of Tafileh, in that last blackness of the sky before the dawn. I left the place and walked up the other bank to consult with Zeid.

He was sitting gravely on a rock sweeping the opposite country with his field-glasses for the enemy. As crises deepened Zeid always grew more detached nonchalant to a degree almost irritating. I was in a furious rage. The Turks should never by the rules of sane generalship have ventured back to Tafileh at all. It was pure greed a dog-in-the-manger attitude unworthy of a serious enemy, just the sort of hopeless thing a Turk would do. How could they expect a proper war when they gave us no chance to honor them? Our morale was continually being ruined by their follies, for neither could our men respect their courage nor do our officers respect their brains. We did not want Tafileh either. To us it was a leaping off place a stage towards Kerak and Madeba, not a line of defense. Also it was an icy morning and I had been up all night and was Teutonic enough to decide that they should pay for my changed mind and plan.

They must be few in number judging by their speed of advance. We had every advantage, and could checkmate them easily: but to my wrath that was not enough. We would play their kind of game deliver them a pitched battle such as they wanted on the pygmy scale of our Arab war and kill them all. I would wake up the old maxims and rules of the orthodox army text-book, and parody them in cold blood today.

This was villainous for both strength and ground were on our side and to make a conscious joke of victory was wanton. We could have won by refusing battle beaten them by maneuvering our center as on twenty such occasions before and since: but bad temper and conceit united to make me not content to know my power but determined to prove it to the enemy and to everyone. Zeid, now clearly convinced of the inconvenience of the defense line was very ready to listen to my tempting.

First I suggested that Abdulla go forward, with a few men on mules and two Hotchkiss guns to test the strength and disposition of the enemy. Then we talked of what might next be done, very usefully, for Zeid was a cool and gallant little fighter, with the temperament of a professional officer. We saw Abdulla climb the other bank. The shooting became intense for a time, and then more distant. His coming had stimulated the Motalga horsemen and the villagers, who had fallen on the enemy horse and driven them over a first ridge, across a little plain two miles wide, and over a ridge beyond it down the first step of the great Hesa depression. Some way behind this lay the Turkish main body, just getting on the road again after a severe night which had nearly frozen them in their places. They came properly into action, and Abdulla was checked at once. We heard the distant rolling of machine-gun fire, growing up in huge bursts, and laced by a desultory shelling. Our ears told us what was happening, as well as if we saw it, and the news was excellent. I wanted Zeid to come forward at once, on that authority: but his caution stepped in and he insisted that we wait for exact word from Abdulla.

This was not according to book, but they all knew I was a sham soldier, and took license to hesitate over my advice when it came suddenly. However, this time I held a hand worth twice of that, and went off myself for the front to prejudge their decision. On the way I saw my bodyguard, turning over the goods exposed for removal in the streets, finding much of interest to him. I told them to recover our camels from the pasture-land behind the village, and to bring them with their Hotchkiss automatic to the north bank of the gorge in a hurry.

The road dipped down into a grove of fig-trees, knots of blue twisting snaky boughs, bare as they would be long after the rest of nature was grown green. Then the road turned eastward, to wind lengthily up the valley to the crest. I left it, climbing straight up the cliffs to the plateau. An advantage of going barefoot was a new and incredible sureness upon rock when the soles had got hard by painful insistence, or were, like today, too chilled to feel jags and scrapes. The new way, while warming me, also shortened my time appreciably, and very soon at the top I found a level bit, and then a last ridge overlooking the plateau.

This last straight bank, with Byzantine foundations in it, seemed a very proper place for a reserve, or ultimate line of defense for Tafileh. To be sure we had no reserve as yet — no one had the least notion who or what we would have anywhere — but if we did have anybody, here was their place: and at that precise moment Zeid's personal Ageyl became visible, hiding coyly in a hollow. To move them they required words of encouragement of strength to unravel their plaited hair: but at last they were sitting along the skyline of this reserve ridge. They were about twenty, and from a distance looked beautiful, like the 'points' of a considerable army. I gave them my signet as a token, with orders to add all newcomers to their number, particularly my fellows with their gun.

Then I walked northward towards the fighting. On the way, there met me Abdulla, going back to Zeid with news. He had finished his ammunition, lost five men from shell-fire, and had one automatic gun destroyed. His idea was to get up Zeid with all his men, and fight: so there was nothing for me to add to his message, and no subtlety was required to let well alone, with my happy masters crossing and dotting their own right decisions. I knew Abdulla and trusted him, as an exquisite, but a fine officer whose advice would surely prevail with the already-willing Zeid.

It left me leisure to study the lie of the coming battlefield. The little plain was about two miles across, bounded by low green ridges, and roughly triangular, with my 'reserve ridge' as the base. The apex was to the north and through it ran the road to Kerak, dipping into the Hesa valley. The Turks were beyond the apex, fighting their way up this road. Abdulla's charge had taken the western or left-hand ridge, which was now our firing line, out by the apex near the Turks. The eastern, right-hand ridge was yet unoccupied.

Shells were falling freely in the plain, as I walked across it, with harsh stalks of the wormwood stabbing at my wounded feet. The enemy was firing at the ridge but the infusing was too long, so that the shells grazed the crest and burst away behind. One fell near me, and I learned its caliber from the hot fuse: as I went forward they began to shorten range, and by the time I got to the ridge it was being freely sprinkled by shrapnel. Obviously the Turks had got observation somehow, and looking round I saw them climbing along the eastern side beyond the gap of the Kerak road. From there they would soon outflank our end of the western ridge.

Chapter 95: The Arabs Reply

'We' proved to be about sixty men, some peasantry, and some Motalga horse. They were clustered behind the ridge in two bunches, one near the bottom, one by the top. The lower was made up of peasants, on foot, blown, miserable, and yet the only warm things I had seen that day. They said their ammunition was finished, and it was all over. I assured them it was just beginning and pointed to my populous reserve ridge, saying that all arms were there in support. A few of them then found cartridges, but I had these sent to the Jazi, and told the peasants to hurry back to the Ageyl, refill their belts and hold on there for good. Meanwhile we would cover their retreat by sticking here for the few minutes yet possible.

They ran off cheered, and I walked about among the upper group quoting how one should not quit firing from one position till ready to fire from the next. In command of them was young Metaab, stripped to his skimp riding-drawers for hard work, with his black love curls awry, his face stained and haggard. He was beating his hands together and crying hoarsely with vexation, for he had meant to do so well in this, his first fight for us.

My presence at the last moment, when the Turks were breaking through, was unwelcome: and he got angrier when I said that I only wanted to have a look at the landscape. He thought it flippancy, and screamed something about a Christian going into battle unarmed. I retorted with a word from Clausewitz, about a rearguard affecting its purpose more by being than by doing: but he was past laughter, and perhaps with justice, for the little flinty bank behind which we sheltered was crackling with fire. The Turks, knowing we were there, had turned some twenty machine guns against it. It was four feet high and fifty feet long, of bare flint ribs, off which the bullets slapped deafeningly: while the air above so hummed and whistled with them and their ricochets and chips that it felt like death to look over the top. Clearly we must leave very soon and as I had no horse I went off first, with Metaab's promise that he would wait, if possible, for another ten minutes.

The run warmed me, and as I went I counted the paces for convenience in ranging the Turks when they ousted us; since there was only that one position and it was poorly protected against the south. In losing this Motalga ridge we would probably win the battle by drawing into a death-trap the enemy ignorant of our game. So I too ran away in good spirits. The horsemen held on for almost their ten minutes and then galloped off without hurt. Metaab lent me his stirrup to hurry me along and at length we all found ourselves a little breathless among the Ageyl. It was just noon and we had leisure and quiet in which to think.

Our new ridge was about sixty feet high and a nice shape for defense. We had eighty men on it and more were constantly arriving. My guards were in place with their gun. Lutfi el Aseli, an engine destroyer rushed up hotly with his two and after him came another hundred Ageyl. The thing was becoming a picnic and by saying "excellent" and looking overjoyed, we puzzled the men and made them consider the position dispassionately. We had the automatics put on the skyline along the crest, with orders to fire occasional shots short to disturb the Turks a little but not too much; after the expedient of Massena in delaying enemy deployment. Otherwise a lull fell and I lay down in a sheltered place which caught a little sun and no wind and slept a blessed hour or two while the Turks occupied the old ridge and extended over it like a school of geese and about as wisely. Our men left them alone being contented with as free an exhibition of themselves as possible.

In the middle of the afternoon Zeid arrived with Mastur, and Rasim and Abdulla. They brought our main body comprising twenty mounted infantry on mules thirty more Motalga horsemen two hundred villagers' five more automatic rifles four machineguns and the old Egyptian Army Krupp which had fought about Medina and now had Petra and Jurf also to its credit. This was magnificent and I woke up to welcome them.

The Turks saw us becoming crowded and opened with shrapnel and machine-gun fire: but they had not the range and fumbled it. We reminded one another that movement was the law of strategy and started moving. Rasim became a cavalry officer and mounted with all the eighty owners of animals to make a circuit about the eastern ridge and envelop the enemy's left wing. Since the books advised attack not upon a line but upon a point and by going far enough along any finite wing it would be found eventually to end in a point of one single man. Rasim liked such a conception of his target, and promised to bring us that last man. Hamd el Arar took the occasion more fittingly. Before riding off he devoted himself to the death for the Arab cause, drew his sword ceremoniously, and made to it by name a heroic speech. Rasim took five automatic guns with him, which was good.

We in the center paraded about, so that Rasirn's departure might be unseen of the enemy, who were bringing up an apparently endless procession of machine-guns and dressing them by the left at intervals along the ridge, as though in a museum. It was lunatic tactics. The ridge was all of flint, without cover for a lizard, and we had seen how, when a bullet struck the ground, it and the ground spattered up in a shower of deadly chips. Also we knew the range, and elevated our Vickers' guns carefully, blessing their long, old-fashioned sights, and got our mountain-gun ready to let go a sudden burst of shrapnel over the enemy when the moment came that Rasim was in place.

As we waited, reinforcement was announced of one hundred men from Aima, a village on the northwest. They had fallen out with Zeid over war-wages the day before, but had grandly decided to sink old scores in the crisis. Their arrival convinced us to abandon Marshal Foch and to attack from, at any rate, three sides at once. So we sent the Aima men, with three automatic guns, to outflank the right or western wing. Then we opened against the Turks with all we had left in our central position, and bothered them terribly in their exposed lines with hits and ricochets.

The enemy felt the day no longer favorable. It was passing and sunset often gave victory to defenders yet in place. Old General Hamid Fakhri called to his Staff and headquarters, and told each man to take a rifle. 'I have been forty years a soldier, but never saw I rebels fight like this. Enter the ranks or we are lost...' but he was too late. Rasim pushed forward an attack of his five automatic guns, each with its two-man crew. They went in rapidly, unseen till they were in position, and crumpled the Turkish left.

The Aima men, who knew every blade of grass on these, their own village pastures, crept without loss till only three hundred yards from the Turkish machine-guns on the opposite flank. The enemy was held by our frontal threat, and first knew of the Aima men when they by a sudden burst of all their fire wiped out the gun-teams and flung the wing into disorder. We saw it and cried advance to the camel men and levies about us. Mohammed ibn Ghasib, comptroller of Zeid's household led them on his camel. In shining wind billowed robes, holding the crimson banner of the Ageyl high over his head. All who remained our servants and gunners and machine-gunners, rushed after him in a wide, vivid line.

The day had been too long for me, and I was now only shaking with desire to see the end: but Zeid beside me clapped his hands with joy at the beautiful order in which our plan unrolled itself in the frosty redness of the setting sun. On the one hand, Rasirn's cavalry were sweeping a broken left wing into the pit beyond the ridge; on the other, the men of Aima were bloodily cutting down fugitives. The enemy center was pouring back in a disordered mob over and through the gap, with our men after them on foot on horse, on camel. The Armenians crouching behind us all day anxiously now drew their knives and howled to one another in Turkish as they leaped forward.

I thought of the depths between the enemy and Kerak, the ravine of Hesa with its broken precipitous paths, the undergrowth, the narrows and defiles of the way. It was going to be a massacre and I should have been crying-sorry but after the angers and exertions of the battle my mind was too tired to care to go down into that awful place and spend the night saving them. I was frightened that, by my decision to fight, I had killed twenty or thirty of our six hundred men and the wounded would be perhaps three times as many. It was one-sixth of our force gone on a verbal triumph, for the destruction of the thousand poor Turks would not affect the issue of the war.

Had I maneuvered we would have worn them into ruin for a loss of perhaps five or six in all: and that power had lain neglected in the angry silence of my lips. Seldom did my misplaced humor let me pass a chance of speaking to the point: but a certain physical indolence and dreg of wisdom usually held me from action of a like untimely suddenness. With the odd difference in kind between word and deed it had grieved me always not saying a thing, but never not doing one: yet on this occasion, open-eyed, deeds and words had gone together, to my lasting shame.

In the end we had taken their two mountain howitzers (Skoda guns, very useful to us), their twenty-seven machine-guns, two hundred horses and mules, two hundred and fifty prisoners. Above six hundred were killed, and men said only fifty got back, exhausted fugitives, to the railway. The Arabs on their track rose against them and shot them ignobly as they ran. Our men gave up the pursuit quickly, for they were tired and sore and hungry and it was pitifully cold. A battle might be thrilling at a moment for the generals, though usually imagination played so vividly beforehand that the reality seemed sham, so quiet and unimportant that they ranged about, looking for its fancied core. This evening there was no glory left, but the terror of the broken flesh which had been our own men carried past us to their homes.

As we turned back it began to snow, and only very late and by a last effort did we get our wounded to the villages that night. The Turkish wounded layout, and were dead next day. It was indefensible, like the whole theory of war: but no special reproach lay on us for it. We risked our lives in the blizzard to save our own men: and if our rule in battle was not to lose Arabs to kill any number of Turks, still less might we lose them to save Turks.

Next day and the next it snowed yet harder, and we were weather-bound, and as the days passed in monotony we lost the hope of doing. We should have pushed to Kerak on the heels of victory, frightening the Turks to Amman with our rumor: as it was, nothing came of all the loss and effort, except a mean report which I sent over to the British headquarters in Palestine for the Staff's consumption. It was nicely written for effect, full of quaint similes and mock simplicities, and made them think me a modest amateur doing his best after the great models, not a leering clown frivolously whoring after them where they, with Foch bandmaster at their head, went drumming down the old road of effusion of blood into the house of Clausewitz. Like the battle, it was a nearly-proof parody of regulation use, and they loved it, and innocently to crown the jest offered me a decoration on the strength of it. We would have more bright breasts in the Army if each man wrote his own dispatch.

Chapter 96: The Weather Sums up

The sole profit of Hesa lay then in its lesson to myself never again were we combative, whether in jest, or betting on a certainty. Indeed only three days later our honor was partially redeemed by a good and serious thing we arranged through Sherif Abdulla ibn Hamza el Feir. He was camped beneath us in the Ghor el Safieh, that paradise of the Dead Sea's southern shore, a plain gushing with brooks of sweet water and rich in vegetation . We sent down the news of our victory to him, with details of a project to raid Mezraa, the lake-port of Kerak, and to destroy what of the Turks' inland flotilla lay there moored.

Abdulla chose out some seventy horsemen all well-mounted, and set over them Ibrahim Abu lrgeig the dashing chief of a main section of Beersheba Bedouin. They left camp at dusk, and rode in the night along the shelf of track between the hills of Moab and the lake's brim. Before dawn they had hidden themselves on the flat neck of the great promontory, the Lisan, which projected into the Dead Sea below Kerak: and in the first grayness when their eyes could reach far enough for a gallop they burst out of their undergrowth, and saw motor-launch and sailing lighters harbored in the northern bight, with their unsuspecting crews sleeping on the beach and in the reed huts nearby.

The officers and men were from the Turkish Navy, and not prepared for land fighting, still less for receiving cavalry: they were awakened only by the drumming of our horses' hooves as Ibrahim swept towards them in a headlong charge: and the engagement ended in a moment. The huts were burned, the stores all looted or thrown on the flames the shipping taken out to deep sea and scuttled. Then, without a casualty, and with their sixty prisoners, our men rode back to Abdulla praising themselves. It was January the twenty-eighth, and we had attained our second objective the stopping of the transport of enemy stores by water up the Dead Sea, a fortnight sooner than we had ventured to promise Allenby.

The third objective had been Kerak, Madeba and the Jordan mouth by Jericho, before the end of March, and it would have been a fair prospect, but for the paralysis that weather and the distaste for pain had brought upon us since the red day of Hesa. Conditions in Tafileh were mended. Feisal had sent us ammunition and food by caravan from Akaba to the foot of the Buseira Pass in Wadi Araba, whence we were ferrying the stuff up on the hired beasts of the peasantry. Prices were falling, as men grew to trust our strength. The tribes about Kerak, impressed by our victory, were in daily touch with Zeid, and proposed to join him in arms as soon as he moved forward.

This, however, was just what we would not do. The winter was too heavy for our energies, and its potency drove leaders and men into the houses of the village, and huddled them there together in a lackluster idleness against which the counsels of those few who wanted movement availed little. Indeed Reason also was within doors. Twice I ventured up to taste the snow laden plateau, upon who's even face the Turkish dead, poor brown loads of stiffened clothes, and was littered: but life there was not tolerable. In the day it thawed a little, and in the night it froze again. The wind cut open my skin: my fingers lost the power and sense of movement, and my toes also. My cheeks shivered like dead leaves till they could shiver no more, and then bound up their muscles in a witless ache.

Such conditions were unfit for our general advance. To launch out across the plains on camels, those beasts singularly inept on slippery ground, would be to put ourselves in the power of however few horsemen wished to oppose us: and as the days dragged on without essential change, even this last and dangerous possibility was withdrawn. Barley ran short in Tafileh, and our camels, already cut off by the snow from natural grazing, were now also cut off from artificial food. To save their lives we had to drive them down into the happier Ghar, to Abdulla ibn Harnza, a day's journey by road, round about through Buseira.

Though so far by the devious road, yet in direct distance the Ghor lay little more than six miles from us, and in full sight, five thousand feet below. Salt was rubbed into our miseries by the continual spectacle of that near winter-garden beneath us by the lake-side. We were penned in vermin houses of cold stone, lacking fuel, lacking food, storm-bound in streets like muddy sewers, with blizzards of sleet dashing over us every few hours, and an icy wind tearing us day and night: while down there in the valley was sunshine upon deep spring grass, full of Bowers, with the Bocks in milk, and the wind so warm that men went about always without their cloaks.

My private party were more fortunate than most of Zeid's men, as the Zaagi had found us an empty unfinished house, of two sound rooms and a courtyard. My money provided us with enough cooking fuel, and even some grain for the camels, which we kept sheltered in a comer of the yard, where Abdulla, the animal lover, could curry them and could teach every one by name to take a gift of bread gently with her loose lips like a kiss from his mouth when he called her. Still they were most unhappy days, since to have a fire was to be stained with the green smoke and in the windows were no panes of glass, only makeshift shutters of our own joinery. The mud roof dripped water all the day long, and the bees on the stone floor sang together for praise of the new meals given them.

While we waited here, my caravan of twenty laden camels for Azrak, where Ali ibn el Hussein and the Indians were still keeping their watch upon Deraa, started from Akaba, and marched comfortably along the warmth of Araba to the foot of the Buseira pass. As they climbed up through the trees towards the top, their faces grew paler with the increasing cold, and they reached Tafileh cloaked in mud and rain.

To have tried to cross the plateau to Bair in the face of such weather would have killed them: so we held them up, put their loads in our house upon the floor under us for warmth and because there was no other storage, and sent their camels in a drove back to the Araba to loaf and graze till the sky cleared. The eight extra men crushed into the house with us, so that we were twenty-eight in the two tiny rooms; which were no longer cold, but rather culture-boxes for vermin, and reeking with the sour smell of our crowd.

In my saddlebags was the *Morte D'Arthur*, which should have relieved my disgust: but the men had only physical resources, and in the confined misery their tempers roughened, and their oddness, which ordinary time packed with a saving-film of distance, now jostled angrily together directly beneath my notice; and irritated me the more that a grazed wound in my hip had refused to heal, and was throbbing painfully. Day by day the tension amongst us grew, as our state became more sordid, more animal. This fetid promiscuous life seemed to be forcing out in us what evil we possessed.

At last Awad, the wild Sherari boy, quarreled with little Mahmas, and in a moment their daggers clashed. The rest nipped the tragedy at its start, and there was only a slight wounding: but it broke the greatest law of the bodyguard, and as both guilt and example were blatant, the others went packing into the far room while their chiefs forthwith executed justice. However, the shrill cruelty of the whip strokes too nearly reminded me of that anguish in Deraa, and I stopped the protesting Abdulla before he was well warmed Awad, who had lain through his punishment without complaint, at this sudden release levered himself slowly to his knees and staggered away, with bent legs and swaying head, to his sleeping-place. It was then the turn of the waiting Mahmas, a tight-lipped youth with pointed chin and pointed forehead, whose beady eyes dropped at the inner corners with an indescribable air of impatience. He was not properly of my guard, but a camel-driver, for his capacity fell far below his own sense of it, and a constantly-hurt pride made him sudden and fatal in companionship. If worsted in argument, or laughed at, he would lean forward with his always-handy little dagger and rip up his friend. Now he was afraid and shrank back into a corner showing his teeth like an animal, vowing that he would be through the first who touched him. As I was perhaps the only one immune from his threat, I had myself to disarm him and drag him out. He was more sensitive, or less tolerant of pain than the Sherari, and, before Abdulla and the Zaagi had ended with him, was with good reason crying aloud. Arab habit called such weakness fear, since unlike us they did not dissect endurance, their crown of manhood, into material and moral parts, making allowance for nerves and spiritual courage. So when Mahmas was loosed he crept out disgraced into the night to hide himself and did not return to me for months.

I was sorry for Awad; and his hardness put me to shame, by stressing my inferiority even to the despised Sherari, one whose treatment from birth had broken the protest or rebellion out of him, and forced him to a dog-like unreasoning servility: and especially I was ashamed when next morning before dawn I heard a limping step in the yard, and looking out saw him fighting down his bruises in an attempt to do his proper duty by the camels. This was too much and I called him to me again excused him the day's work and gave him an embroidered head cloth as reward for faithful service. He had come in. pitiably sullen with a shrinking mobile readiness for more punishment: and my changed manner broke him down and brought the tears which he had held back the night before. By the afternoon he was singing and shouting happier than ever, as he had found a fool in Tafileh to pay him four pounds for my silken gift.

This nervous sharpening ourselves on each other's faults was so revolting that I decided to scatter the party and to go off myself in search of the extra money we would need when the fine weather came. Zeid had by now spent the first part of the sum we had set aside for Tafileh and the Dead Sea, partly on wages to the Beni Sakhr, the Howcitat, and the Tafileh peasants and party on supplies and in rewards to the victors of the battle of Seil el Hesa. At Kerak, at Madeba, wherever we put our next front line, we would have to enlist and pay fresh forces from the local people: for a cardinal principle in the rebellion was to use the district for its own operations: since only local men would know the qualities of their ground instinctively; and they laid the strongest stake in that they had to defend their homes and crops against the enemy.

By writing to Joyce the necessary funds would have been sent up: but not easily in such a season. It was surer to go down with my own explanation and carry back on my own camels the necessary fraction of our gold reserve: and anything seemed more moral than continued idleness in Tafileh. So five of us started off on February the fourth a day which before noon promised to be a little more open than usual. We made good time to Rasheidiya, and as we climbed the high saddle beyond it found ourselves momentarily above the clouds in a faint sunshine.

In the afternoon the weather drew down again, and the wind once more blew from the north and the east, and made us sorry to be out on the bare plain, exposed to all its bitterness. When we had forded the little river of Shobek a rain began to fall first in wild gusts but then more steadily reading down slantingly over our left shoulders, and seeming to cloak us from the main bleakness of wind. Where the rain-streaks hit the ground they furred out whitely like a spray. We pushed on without halting for a moment and tilt long after sunset urged our trembling camels with many slips and falls across the greasy valleys. We made nearly two miles an hour in spite of our difficulties, and the progress was become so exciting and unexpected that its mere exercise served to keep us warm. It had been my intention to ride all night, trusting to my knowledge of the country to reach the foot of the pass of Shtar, between Aba el Lissan and Guweira, at dawn: but near Odroh, night with mist came down about us in a low ring curtain over which the clouds, like tatters of a veil, spun and danced in the wind across the calmness of the moon. The perspective seemed to change so that high far hills looked small, and near hillocks looked distant and great. We bore too much to the right and lost the track.

This open country was rotten ground, though appearing hard to the eye. It broke beneath their weight and let our camels in four or five inches deep, at every stride. The poor beasts had been chilled all day and had bumped down so often that they were full of bruises, and had no more spirit. Consequently they made unwilling work of the new difficulties ran a few steps, stopped abruptly, looked round, tried to dart off sideways. We prevented their wishes, and drove them forward till our blind way took us into rocky valleys with a broken skyline dark to right and left and in front of us, apparent hills where on our road no hills should be.

Then it turned freezing once again, and the scabby stones of the valley slopes became sheets of ice. It was folly to push further on the wrong road through such a night. We looked for a larger outcrop of rock, and behind it where there should have been shelter but were certainly draughts, couched our camels in a compact group. We set them tails to wind, since if put facing it they would more quickly die of cold, and snuggled down beside them to hope for warmth and sleep ourselves.

The warmth I at least never got and hardly the sleep: for once I dozed off only to wake again with a start when slow fingers seemed to stroke my face and I stared out into a night livid with large soft snowflakes. They lasted only a minute, and then came rain and after it frost once more while I squatted in a tight ball. Aching every way but too miserable to move, till dawn. It was a hesitant dawn, but enough: for promptly I rolled over in the mud and stood up to see my men tightly knotted in their cloaks leaning against their beasts' flanks with on their faces the most dolorous expression of resigned despair.

They were four southerners whom fear of the winter had turned ill at Tafileh, and who were going to rest in Guweira till it was warm again: but now here in the mist they had made up their minds like he-camels that death was upon them: and though they were too proud to grumble at it yet they were sorry and not above showing me silently that this which they made for my sake was a sacrifice. They did not speak or move in reply to me. Under a flung camel it was best to light a slow fire to raise it: but I took one of these men by his head-curls and proved to him that he was still capable of feeling. At the same time the others got to their feet and we kicked up the stiff camels and led them out into the open. Our only loss in the night was the water-skin which had frozen to the ground and tore when we pulled at it: a good lightening of our load.

With the daylight the horizon had grown very close: and we saw that our proper road was just a quarter of a mile to our left. Along it we struggled afoot, past Basta and Aba el Adham for Aba el Lissan. The camels were too done any longer to carry our weight (all but my own died later of the overstrain of this march) and it was so muddy in the clay bottoms that as we led them we were hard put to it to keep our feet and slid and fell like them. However the Deraa trick helped of spreading wide the toes and hooking them down into the mud at each stride: and by this means in a group clutching and holding one another we maintained some sort of progress.

The air seemed cold enough to freeze everything but did not. The wind had changed during the night, and now swept into us from the west in mixed blizzards of hail and sleet, which were terrible obstacles to progress. Our cloaks were pulled out by the air like sails and against their drag we could scarcely move. At last we skinned them off, and went a little easier in our bare shirts wrapped tightly about our waists to deliver our skins from their slapping tails. The whirling direction of the squalls was shown to our eyes by the white mist which carried across the hills and dales. Our hands and feet were numbed into insensibility so that we knew the fresh cuts on them only by the red stains in the plastered mud with which they were hidden: but our bodies were not so chill and for hours quivered with the stinging drive of the hailstones before the storm. We used to twist ourselves to get the sharpness on an unhurt side, and tried to hold off our dripping shirts from the skin, to shield us momentarily. For all the good the clothes were, we might have been walking naked.

By late in the afternoon we had covered the ten miles to Aba el Lissan. Maulud's men were gone to ground in their earth shelters: and no one hailed us as we passed, which was as well, for we were filthy and miserable, stringy-looking like shaved cats. Afterwards the going was easier. The last two miles to the head of Shtar were frozen like iron, and we remounted our camels, whose breath escaped whitely through their protesting noses, and raced up to get the first wonderful view of the Guweira plain, warm and red and comfortable, as seen through the windows afforded us by the cloud gaps. The clouds had sealed the hollow strangely, cutting the Mid sky in a flat layer of curds at the level of the mighty hilltop on which we stood, and from which westward there was no hill its height before the Atlas: and we stood and gazed on them contentedly for whole minutes. Every little while a drift of this fleecy stuff would be torn away from the mass, and thrown against us at racing speed, like a wisp of sea-foam. We on the wall of bluffs would feel it slash across our faces, and turning would see it, almost within touch, draw like a white hem over the rough crest, be torn into shreds, and vanish in a powdering of white grains or a little trickle of water across the peat soil.

After having wondered at the sky, we slid and ran gaily down the pass, and a half-hour later were near Khabr el Abid on dry sand in a calm mild air. Yet the pleasure was not vivid as we had hoped. The pain of the blood fraying its passage once more about our frozen arms and legs and faces was as great and much faster than the slow pain of its driving out: and as we warmed we grew sensible that up there in the cold we had torn and bruised our unfeeling feet nearly to pulp among the stones. We had not felt them tender while each step was deep in icy mud: but this warm salty sand scoured out the cuts, and in desperation we had to climb up on our sad camels, and beat them Woodenly towards Guweira. However, the warmth had made them happier, and they brought us in sedately, but with success.

Chapter 97: Slow Progress

Three lazy nights in the armored car tents at Guweira were pleasant, with Alan Dawnay, Joyce and others talking, and the happenings of Tafileh to boast about. They were a little grieved at my luck, for the great expedition with Feisal in this fortnight to Mudowwara had been unprofitable. They had been ambitious, taking a great crowd of Beni Atiyeh, and guns, with a mind to do something desperate: but the rank and file had not been as ready as the leaders, and so the attack had miscarried after a first Turkish outpost had fallen to a bold rush.

Partly it was the old problem of the co-operation of regulars with irregulars, that rock on which so many elaborate and well-sounding plans had split. Partly it was the fault and the stupidity of old Sherif Mohammed Ali el Beidawi, who had been put over the Beni Atiyeh to organize them for fighting, and had come with them one day to water and cried, 'Noon-halt!' and then sat there for two months, pandering to Bedouin laziness, and to his own physical and mental weakness of good intention: but still more to that hedonistic streak among the Arabs which made them helpless slaves of carnal indulgences; and in Arabia, where life was so simple and life so hard, luxuries might be as plain as running water or a shady tree, whose rareness and misuse often turned them into lusts. Their story reminded me of Apollonius of Tyana: 'Come off it, you men of Tarsus, sitting on your river like geese, drunken with its white water!' Even where superfluities lacked, the temptation of necessary food lay always on men. Each morsel which passed their lips might, if they were not watchful, become pleasant to them.

To worry Feisal, Joyce, and Nuri Said, I suggested that their failure was their own doing, and we had a merry set-to about it, till we were all laughing at once. Then thirty thousand pounds in gold came up from Akaba in a car for me, and my cream camel, Wodheiha, the strongest and best of my remaining stud. She was Ateiba-bred, and had won many races for her old owner: also she was in splendid condition, fat but not too fat, her pads hardened by much practice over these northern flints, and her coat thick and matted. She was not a tall beast, and heavy looking, but docile and smooth to ride, turning if one tapped the saddle hum on the required side. So I rode her without a stick, comfortably reading a book during the march.

As my proper men were at Tafileh or Azrak, or out on missions, I asked Feisal for some temporary followers, and he lent me his two Ateiba horsemen, Seif and Ruweilim, and to help carry my gold, added to the party Sheikh Motlog ibn jemiaan, one of the heads of the northern Beni Atiyeh. Motlog was going up with thirty men to Zeid, to deal with the Maaza section of his tribe about Kerak, whose help was important to us. I was delighted at his company, for he was a lively good tempered clever fellow.

Motlog was the hero of a charming story when the armored cars explored the plain below Mudowwara, to find a road to Tebuk. He went as sponsor, pointing out the country from a perch high on the piled baggage of a box-Ford. They were dashing in and out of sand-hills at speed, to avoid getting stuck, with the Fords swaying like motor launches in a swell. At one bad bend they skidded half round, the car tilting on two wheels crazily. Motlog was tossed out of the back and landed fairly on his head in the dust. Marshall stopped the car and ran back contrite, making ready excuses for the driving: but Motlog standing up, ruefully rubbing his head, said gently, 'Don't be angry with me. I have not learned to ride these things.'

The gold was in thousand-pound bags, and I gave two each to fourteen men, and took the last two myself. Each weighed twenty-two pounds, and in such awful road-conditions two were weight enough for a camel, and swung fairly on either side in the saddlebags. We started off at noon, hoping to make a good first stage before getting into the trouble of the hills: but unfortunately it turned wet after half an hour and a steady line rain came down, soaked us through and through, and made our camels' hair curl like a wet dog's.

Motlog said this would never do and at that precise moment saw a tent, Sherif Fahad's, in a warm corner of a sandstone pike to the left. Despite my urgings, he voted to spend the night there, and see what it looked like on the hills tomorrow. I knew this would be a fatal course, wasting days in indecision: so I said farewell to him, and rode on with my two men, and with six Howeitat bound for Shobek who had joined themselves to our caravan.

The argument had delayed us, and consequently we only reached the foot of the pass at dark. With the sad soft rain we were made rather sorry for our virtue, inclined to envy Motlog his hospitality with Fahad — when suddenly we saw a red spark out to our left, and rode across to find Saleh ibn Shefia camped there in a tent and three caves, with a hundred of his freed-men fighters from Wadi Yenbo. Saleh, the son of poor old Mohammed, our jester on the way to Wejh, was the proper lad who had carried Wejh by assault on Vickery's field-day.

'Cheryf ent ; ('How are you?'), said I earnestly twice or thrice. His eyes sparkled at the Juheina greeting, and he came near me and with bowed head and an intense voice poured out a string of twenty 'Cheryf ents' before drawing breath. I disliked being outdone, so replied with a dozen as solemnly. He took me up with another of his long bursts, many more than twenty this time. So I gave up trying to learn how many possible salutations in Wadi Yenbo were. He welcomed me, in spite of my drenched condition, to his own carpet in his own tent, and gave me a new garment of his mother's sewing to put on while waiting for the hot stew of meat and rice. Then we lay down and slept a full night of great satisfaction, hearing the long patter of the rain on the double canvas of his Meccan tent.

In the morning we were off at dawn, munching a handful of Saleh's bread. As we first set foot on the ascent, Seif looked up and said, 'The mountain wears his skull-cap.' There was a white dome of snow on every crest, and as the Ateiba had not yet seen snow they pushed quickly and curiously up the pass to the crest, to feel the new wonder with their hands. The camels too were ignorant, and stretched their slow mouths down to it, and sniffed its whiteness twice or thrice in tired enquiry: but then drew their heads away and looked forward sadly without life-interest once more.

The inactivity lasted only another moment: for as we put our heads over the last ridge a wind from the north-east took us in the teeth, with a cold so swift and biting that we gasped for breath and turned hurriedly back into shelter. It seemed fatal to face it: but that we knew was silly, so we pulled ourselves together and rode hard through the first extreme to the half-shelter of the valley, where it did not hurt so much. Seif and Ruweilim were terrified of the new pains in their lungs, and thought they would strangle with them: and to spare them the mental struggle of passing a friendly camp, I led over by Fuweilah, behind Mauiud's hill, so that we saw nothing of his weather beaten force.

These men of Maulud's had been camped in this place, more than four thousand feet above the sea, for two months without relief they had no tents to live in, only shallow dug-outs in the hillside, lined with rough stone. They had no fuel except the sparse wet wormwood, over which they were just able to cook their necessary bread every other day. They had no clothes but the khaki drill uniform of the ordinary British summer sort. They slept in their vermin pits on empty or half-empty flour sacks, six or eight of them together in a knotted bunch, that enough of their worn out blankets might be pooled for warmth.

Rather more than half of them died or were mutilated by the cold and wet: and yet the others maintained their watch, wholly without available support, exchanging shots daily with the Turkish outposts, and protected only by the weather from crushing counterattack. We owed much to them, and more to Maulud, whose fortitude kept them to their duty. The old scarred warrior's history in the Turkish Army was a catalog of affairs provoked by his sturdy sense of Arab honor and nationality, a creed for which three or four times he had sacrificed his property and prospects. It must have been a strong creed that enabled him to endure cheerfully three winter months in front of Maan, and to share out enough spirit among five hundred men to keep them about him stout-heartedly. The nobility of the desert leaders was measurable by the greatness of these simple men serving in the ranks.

We, for our one day, had a fill of hardship. Just on the ridge of the range about Aba el Lissan the ground was crusted with frost, and only the smart of the wind in our eyes hindered us: but after Aba el Adham our real troubles began. The camels came to a standstill in the slush at the bottom of a twenty-foot bank of slippery mud, and lowed at it helplessly, to say that they could not carry us up that. We jumped off to help them, and slid back again ourselves just as badly. At last we took off our new and cherished boots, and hauled the camels up it barefoot, as on the journey down.

That was the end of our comfort, and we must have been off twenty times before sunset. Some of our dismounts were involuntary, when our camels side-slipped under us, and came down with the jingle of coin ringing through their hollow rumble like a cask. While they were strong this made them as angry as a she-camel could be: and afterwards plaintive, and finally afraid. We also grew short with one another, for the foul wind gave us no rest. Nothing in Arabia could be more cutting than a north wind at Maan, and today's was of the sharpest and strongest It blew through our clothes as though we had none, fixed our hands in claws not able to hold either halter or riding-stick, and cramped our legs so that we had no grip of the saddle-pin. Consequently, when thrown from our falling beasts, we pitched off helplessly, and crashed stiffly on the ground, still frozen brittle in the cross-legged attitude proper to riding.

However, there was no rain, and the wind felt like a drying one, so we held on steadily to the north. By morning we had almost made the rivulet of Basta. This meant that we were traveling more than a mile an hour, and for fear lest on the morrow we and our camels would both be too tired to do as well, I pushed on in the dark across the little stream. It was swollen, and the beasts jibbed at it, so that we had to lead the way on foot, splashing through three feet of very chilly water. Over the high ground beyond, the wind buffeted us like an enemy: at about nine o'clock the others flung themselves crying down on the ground and refused to go further.

I too was very near crying, sustained indeed only by my annoyance with their open lamentations; and therefore glad in my heart to yield to their example. So we built up the camels in a phalanx, tails to the wind, and lay between them in fair comfort listening to the driving wrack clashing about us as loud as the surges by night round a ship at sea. The visible stars were brilliant, seeming to change groups and places waywardly between the dark clouds which scudded low over our heads. We had each two army blankets, and a packet of cooked bread, so we were armed against all evil, and could sleep securely in spite of the mud and cold.

Chapter 98: Winter Sports

At dawn we went forward refreshed: but the weather had turned soft, with a grayness through which loomed the sad worm wood covered hills. Upon their slopes the limestone ribs of this very old earth stood wearily exposed. In their hollows our difficulties increased with the mud. The misty valleys were sluggish streams of melting snow: and at last new thick showers of wet flakes began to fall. We reached the desolate ruins of Odroh in at midday like at twilight: a wind was blowing and dying intermittently: and slowly moving banks of cloud and drizzle closed us in, all about.

I bore to the right to avoid the Naimat tents which lay between us and Shobek: but our Howeitat companions knew that mine was not the road and led us straight upon the camp. We had ridden six miles in seven hours and they were exhausted. The two Ateiba with me were not only exhausted but demoralized, and swore mutinously that nothing in the world should keep us from the shelter of the tribal tents. We wrangled by the roadside under the soft drift: but my wishes had no effect. They believed that they were already half-dead, and those hours more would be certain death. They wanted to compel me to rest with them to save their faces, as their disgrace of failing a comrade on the road would be indelible: and these were proud men who had marched and endured to the very limit of their courage.

For myself, I felt quite fresh and happy, averse from unnecessary tribal hospitality and its delay. Zeid was penniless, and would be hard put to it, if a new crisis arose at the moment, and such a chance was an excellent pretext for a trial of strength with the winter climate of Edom. Shobek was only ten miles further and daylight had yet five hours to run. So finally I decided to go on alone. It would be quite safe, for in this weather neither Turk nor Arab was abroad and the roads were mine. I took their four thousand pounds from Seif and Ruweilim, and cursed them off into the valley for cowards: which really they were not. Ruweilim was catching his breath in great sobs, and Seif in his nervous pain was marking each lurch of his camel with a running moan. They raved to God when I dismissed them and turned away.

The truth was that I had the best camel. The excellent Wodheiha struggled gamely forward under the weight of the extra gold. In flat places I rode on her: at ascents and descents we used to slide together side by side, with the most comic accidents, which she seemed rather to" enjoy. By sunset we were coming down to the river of Shobek, and could see a brown track straggling over the opposite bank to where the village lay. I tried a short cut across, but the frozen crust of the mud banks deceived me, and I crashed through the half-ice (which was sharp like knives) and got bogged so deeply in the quick-mire that I feared I was going to pass the night there, half in and half out of the water: or wholly in, which would be a tidy death.

Wodheiha, sensible beast, had refused to enter the morass: but she was now at a loss, and stood stupidly on the hard edge, and looked at me mud-larking. However, before I had sunk too deep I managed, with my still-held tow-rope, to persuade her a little nearer. Then I flung my body suddenly backward against the squelching quag, and grabbing wildly behind my head, laid hold of her fetlock. It frightened her, and she started back: and by the aid of this purchase I dragged myself clear. We crawled further down the bed to a safe place, and there crossed: while I sat in the stream and shivering washed the weight of stinking clay off me.

Afterwards I mounted her again, and we went over the ridge and down the chalk incline to the base of the impressive cone, whose mural crown was the ring-wall of the old castle of Monreale, very noble against the night-sky. The chalk was hard, and it was freezing, and the snow drifts lay a foot deep each side of the spiral path which wound about the hill to the crest. The white ice crackled desolately under my naked feet as we neared the gate, where, to make a stage entry, I climbed up Wodheiha's patient shoulder into the saddle: and repented it, since it was only by throwing myself agilely sideways along her neck that I avoided the voussoirs of the arch as she crashed underneath in half-terror of what this strange place was.

I knew that Sherif Abd el Mayin should be still at Shobek, so went in boldly, and rode up the steep silent street in the starlight which played with the black and white of moonbeams and their shadows among the bare walls and snowy roofs and ground. The camel stumbled doubtfully over the stairs hidden under a thick covering of snow: but I had no care of that, having reached my night's goal, and having, anyway, so powdery a blanket to fall on. At the cross-ways I called out the salutation of a fair night: and after a minute a husky voice protested to God through the thick sacking which stuffed a loophole of the mean house on my right. I asked for Abd el Mayin, and was told, 'in the old Government house', which lay at the other end of the castle.

Arrived there, I called again. A door was flung open, and a cloud of smoky light streamed across, recklessly whirling with motes, through which black faces peered to know whom I was. I hailed them friendly, by name, saying that I was come to eat a sheep with the master: and these slaves and Hudheil servants ran out, noisy with laughter and astonishment, and relieved me of Wodheiha, whom they led into the reeking stable where themselves lived. Then one lit me with a flaming log, recognizable splinter of a railway sleeper, up the stone outside-stairs to the house door, and between more servants down a winding passage, dripping with water from the broken roof, into a tiny room. There lay Abd el Mayin on a carpet on his face, breathing the least smoky level of air in the place.

My legs were shaky, so I dropped beside him, and gladly copied his position to avoid the choking fumes of a great brazier off laming wood which crackled in the embrasure of a shot-window in his outer wall. I showed him I was very wet, and hungry, and he searched out for me a waist-cloth and a sheepskin coat, while I stripped off my things and hung them to steam in front of the fire, which became less smarting to the eyes and throat as it burned down into red coals. Meanwhile Abd el Mayin clapped his hands for supper to be hastened, and served 'fauzan' (tea in the Harith slang, and so-named from his cousin, governor of their village north-east of Mecca, the same who led me to Aba el Naam), hot and spiced and often, till the mutton boiled with raisins in butter was carried in.

He explained with his blessings on the dish that next day they would starve or rob, since he had here two hundred men, and no food or money, and his messengers to Feisal were all held up in the snow. Whereat I too clapped my hands, and commanded my saddlebags, and then and there presented him with five hundred pounds on account, till his subsidy came. This was good payment for my food and we were merry with our tea and coffee, over my oddness of riding alone in winter with a hundredweight and more of gold for baggage. I repeated that Zeid, like himself, was straitened, and so I might not delay, and told of Seif and Ruweilim with the Naimat. The Sherif's eyes darkened, and he made passes in the air with his riding-stick. I explained that the cold did not trouble me, since the English climate was of this sort most of the year. 'God forbid it', said Abd el Mayin.

After an hour he excused himself, that he had just married a Shobek wife; we talked of their marriage, whose end was the bearing of children, and I withstood it, quoting Dionysus of Tarsus, who lived sixty years and never married: they were shocked, holding procreation and evacuation alike as inevitable movements of the body, and repeated their surviving half of the commandment to honor parents. I asked how they could look with pleasure on their children, walking about embodied proofs of consummated lust? And to picture the minds of the children, seeing crawl wormlike out of the mother that bloody blinded thing which were themselves. It sounded to him a most excellent joke, and after it we rolled ourselves up in the rugs and slept very warmly. The fleas were serried, but my nakedness, which was the Arab defense in a vermin bed, lessened their plague: and the lice and bruises did not prevail because I was too tired.

In the morning I rose with a splitting headache, and said I must go on. Abd el Mayin found two men who agreed to ride with me, though all said we would not reach Tafileh that night. No one had come or gone by the road since my party the week before, and the snow was now deeper in the Rasheidiya hills, However, I thought it could not be worse than yesterday, and so we skated timorously down the rapid path, and over the bottom to the plain across which still stretched the Roman road with its ruined blockhouses, and at the miles its groups of fallen milestones, inscribed by famous emperors.

On this plain, the mud was terrible, and the two faint-hearts with me slipped back to their fellows on the castle-hill. I proceeded, alternately on and off my camel, like the day before: though now the way was all too slippery, except where the pavement yet held together, as a last footprint of that Imperial Rome which had here, once, so much more preciously, played the Turk to the desert dwellers. On it I could ride: but I had to walk and wade the dips, where the floods of fourteen centuries had washed the very foundations out. It came on to rain, and soaked me, and then blew fine and freezing, till I crackled in white silk armor, like a theater knight: or perhaps more like a bridal cake, well iced.

We were over the plain in three hours, which was wonderful going: but I found the troubles not ended. The snow was indeed as my guides had said, and completely hid the path, which I knew wound with many turns uphill between the walls of fields, and ditches, and confused piles of stone. It cost me an infinity of pain to find it, and to turn the first two comers. Wodheiha was tired of wading to her bony knees in useless white stuff, and began perceptibly to flag. However, she got up one more steep bit, but there missed the edge of the path in a banked place, and we fell together eighteen feet down the hillside into a yard of drifted snow. This was too much, and she rose whimpering to her feet, and stood still, trembling.

When he-camels so baulked they would die on their spot, after days: and I feared that perhaps for the first time I had found this limit of effort in she-camels. I plunged in front of her, and tried to tow her out, vainly. Then I spent a long time hitting her behind, but she took no notice. I got on her back, and she sat down. I jumped off and heaved her up again and wondered if perhaps it was that the drift was too deep. So I went once more ahead and carved out for her a beautiful little road, a foot wide and three feet deep, and fifty feet long. It took a lot of trouble, for I had only my bare feet and hands as tools, and the snow was so frozen on the surface that it took all my weight first to break it down, and then to scoop it out. The crust was sharp, and cut my wrists and feet till they bled freely, and the roadside became lined with pink crystals, looking like pale, very pale, watermelon flesh.

Afterwards I went back to Wodheiha, patiently standing there, and climbed into the saddle, and started her easily. We went running at it, and such was her speed that the rush carried her right over the shallow stuff, back to the proper road. Up this we went cautiously, with me always sounding in front with my stick for the path, and digging new passes for her when the drifts were waist-deep. In three hours we were on the summit, and found it wind-swept on the western side. So we left the track which was buried far out of sight within the rim, and scrambled unsteadily along the very broken crest by Dana, looking down across its chessboard houses into sunny Araba, fresh and green, thousands of feet below.

When the ridge served no more we did further heavy work, and at last Wodheiha baulked again. It was getting serious and suddenly I realized how alone I was, for the evening was near, and if night found us yet beyond help on the hilltop, Wodheiha would die: and she was a very noble beast. There was also the solid weight of gold, and felt not sure how far, even in Arabia, could safely put six thousand sovereigns by the roadside, with my signet as mark of ownership, and leave them for a night. So I took her back a hundred yards along our beaten track, mounted, and again charged her at the bank she responded and we burst through and crashed over the lip, which looked down on Rasheidiya.

This face of the hill had been sheltered from the wind and open to the sun all afternoon, and had thawed. Underneath the coat of surface snow lay wet and muddy ground, and when Wodheiha ran upon this at speed her feet went from under her, and she sprawled, with her hind legs somehow locked. So on her tail, with me yet in the saddle, we went sliding round and down about two hundred feet. Perhaps it hurt the tail (there were stones under the snow) for on the level she sprang up unsteadily, grunting, and lashed it up and down like a scorpion's. Then she began to run at ten miles an hour down the greasy path towards Rasheidiya, sliding and plunging wildly, with me in terror of a fall and broken bones holding on, for what was worth, to the two horns of the saddle.

A crowd of Arabs, Zeid's men, weather-bound here on their way to Feisal, ran out of the houses when they heard her trumpeting approach, and shouted with joy at so distinguished an entry to the village. I asked them the news of Tafileh, and they told me all was well: and then remounted, and we did the last eight miles into Tafileh in four hours, with no more snow, and only the slippery ledges of the hill-path to guard against in the dark. I gave Zeid my letters and some money, and went very gladly to bed... flea-proof for another night.

Chapter 99: Resignation

In the morning I was nearly snow-blind, but otherwise vigorous, and cast about for something useful to fill the inactive days until the other gold arrived. The best thing seemed to make a personal examination of the approaches of Kerak, and of the ground over which we would later advance to Madeba and Jordan. I explained to Zeid, and asked him to take over from Motlog the coming twenty-four thousand pounds, and keep them (except for current expenses) till my return. This was the sort of arrangement tacit and customary between me and Feisal.

Zeid told me there was another Englishman in Tafileh. He astonished me, and I went off to learn. It was Kirk bride, a young Arabic-speaking lieutenant of Deedes' Intelligence Staff sent across here from Palestine to report on the information possibilities of the Arab Front. He had stayed long enough to see their importance, and now wished to go to Akaba to make arrangements for his permanent attachment to the Arab Army in the field. It was the beginning of a connection profitable to us and them, and creditable to Kirk bride, a taciturn, enduring fellow, only a boy in years, but ruthless in action. He lived and messed for months with the Arab Staff. Syrian and Mesopotamian officers with Eastern minds, but with habits molded after ours. My spirit, more sensitive to manner than to character, dared not mix with theirs for long. Kirk bride for eight months was their silent companion, either not noticing or not complaining.

His road to Akaba was mine to Dana: and we rode off together from Tafileh, till he turned south, and I north to Abdulla ibn Hamza's camp in the Ghor. Sherif Abdulla gave me a warm greeting in his happy camp, and we explored the ways up to the plateau of Kerak, deciding at last that the Turkish defence lines on the north crest of Wadi Hesa could be neatly and safely turned from this side. This was what we needed from the Dead Sea Zone, and I took leave and rode straight back to Tafileh, halted there for ten minutes, and went on northward across the highlands with one of the minor Majalli sheikhs of Kerak as my guide.

The cold had passed off now, and movement, even on the heights, was practicable. We crossed Wadi Hesa, where it was shallow and unguarded, out east by the railway, and then over the Katraneh-Kerak road which would be a danger-side of our advance. So we searched about till it was reasonably clear that a flanking force of ours in the broken valleys north of Lejun would hold up any attempted Turkish thrust from the line towards Kerak.

This was good, and freed us to go further. There we found the Mojeb, a parallel to Wadi Hesa, between Kerak and Madeba. Its obstacle-nature would be equally to our advantage as we reorganized ourselves after having captured Kerak. North of the Mojeb to Madeba the land was soft and open, and cried out for cavalry. We must have an understanding with the horsemen of the Faiz Beni Sakhr before we crossed the Mojeb. Madeba was not strategically interesting, but would make a good base for our regulars. Its communications with the Jordan were not good but would be made fit if the British held the town of Salt, and with it the motor road from Jericho to this eastern tableland.

We rode as far as the edge of the Jordan valley and looked down into its depths, noisy with Allenby's advance. They said the Turks yet held Jericho and its bridge. Then we turned back to Tafileh, after a complete and profitable reconnaissance very assuring for our future success. I felt that each step of our road to join the British to the north of the Dead Sea was possible for us: and most of them easy. The weather was so fine that we might reasonably begin at once: and we could hope to finish in a month.

Zeid heard me coldly. I saw Modog next him and greeted him sarcastically, and asked what his tally of the gold was: and then began to repeat my program of what we might fairly do. Zeid stopped me and said. 'But that will need a lot of money.' I said not at all: that our funds in hand would cover it and more. Zeid said that he had nothing: and when I gaped at him, muttered rather shamefacedly that he had spent what I had brought. I thought he was joking, but he went on to say that so much had been due to Dhiab el Auran, sheikh of Tafileh, and so much to the men of Senefhe, Aima, Buseira and the other villages: and so much to the jazi, and so much to the Zebn Beni Sakhr.

All such expenditure would be entirely profitless for an advance indeed was conceivable only if we were on the defensive. The peoples named were the sedentary and nomad elements centering in Tafileh, men whose blood-feuds made them impossible for any invasion of Kerak, or for use northward of Wadi Hesa. The Sherifs, as they advanced enrolled all the men of every district at a monthly wage: but it was understood on both sides that the wage was fictitious paid only if some special reason made that area critical. Feisal had more than forty thousand on his Akaba books: and his whole subsidy from England would not pay seventeen thousand. The wages of the rest were nominally due and often asked for: but not a proper debt. However Zeid said that he had paid them.

I was aghast for this meant the complete ruin of my plans and hopes: but remembered in time that the money had only arrived twenty-four hours earlier and that it was physically impossible to pay it out in so short a period. There were not enough clerks and secretaries available to count and enter it. But Zeid stuck to his word that it had all gone. We had an unpleasant scene and afterwards I went off to Nasir who was in bed with fever and asked him for the truth. He was very despondent and said that everything was wrong — those about Zeid stupid and cowardly and dishonest and Zeid too young and shy to counter them.

All night I thought over what could be done but found a blank wall staring me every way in the face: and when morning came could only send a last word to Zeid that if he would not return me the money. I must go away putting into words what had hitherto been better understood that I was in no way under his orders or responsible to him rather the contrary: that in all respects I expected to have my wishes considered and not acted against without due and previous explanation: and that where the British provided through me the whole resources for a particular operation it should follow as exactly as possible my instructions.

He sent back a supposed statement of account of the spent money and I had no choice but to leave at once. While we were packing our baggage Joyce and Marshall rode in without warning. They had ridden here from Guweira to give us a pleasant surprise and happened on this most inauspicious moment. I explained to them what Zeid had done and that I was going across to Allenby to explain and to put my further employment in his hands. There was no chance of my being sent back, since my explanation of the failure of our advance and of the loss of the money was the lame one that my faulty judgment had been still unable to distinguish between trusty and not trustworthy Arab agents: and I would be glad not to come back to the humiliation of being tricked in confidence after such and so long service with the Arabs. Joyce made a vain appeal to Zeid, and promised to explain to Feisal.

He would close down my affairs and disperse my bodyguard so with only four men I set off for Beersheba which was the quickest way to British headquarters late in the afternoon. The coming of spring made the first part of the ride along the so-known cliff path above Wadi Dhahal, surpassingly beautiful and I saw it with real regret for the last time. The ravines were clothed below with trees: but near to us by the top, they were a patchwork of close lawns, which tipped towards upright faces of bare rock of many colors. Some of the colors were minerals in the rock itself: but others were temporary and accidental due to the water from the melting snow and the springs now running out fully from the hollows of the hilltop and drifting over the cliff edge either in wisps of dusty looking spray or in glistening diamond-drops, showering down long tresses of green fern.

The people of Buseira, the little village on its hull of rock sheer over the abyss had seen us coming round the long path towards them and insisted that we halt to eat. I was willing since we could here feed our camels with a little barley and then ride all night to reach Beersheba on the morrow: but to avoid hours of delay I refused to enter their houses and instead sat down by the little cemetery, and fed there above a masonry tomb cemented into the joints of whose ashlar blocks were many severed plaits of hair, the cherished but sacrificed head-ornaments of the mourners.

Afterwards we went down the steep zigzags of the great pass into the hot depths of the bottom of the valley over which the cliffs and the hills so drew together that hardly could the stars shine into its pitch blackness. We halted a moment while our camels caught their breath and stilled the nervous trembling of their fore-legs after the strain of the terrible descent. Then we plashed fetlock-deep down the center of the running Dhahal stream under the long arch of rustling bamboos which met so nearly over our heads that if ever we left the center of the vaulted passage their fans brushed our faces. The strange noises in the tunnel frightened our camels, and made them trot faster.

Soon we were out of it, and then out of the horns of the valley, scouring across the open Araba. We reached the central water-bed, now dry and hard , and found that we were off the track: — not wonderful, for none of us knew the way and we were steering only on my three-year-old memories of the map I had helped oversee in the printing-shop of the War Office in London. The price we paid was a wasted half-hour, spent going up and down to find a ramp for the camels up the straight earth cliff of the western bank.

At last we found one, and threaded the windings of the marly labyrinth beyond — a strange place like a rough sea suddenly stilled and transformed itself with all its waves just as they had been tossing about, into hard, fibrous earth, sterile with salt, and very grey under tonight's pale half-moon. We wandered in this earth-maze for two miles, and then aimed westward till before us we saw the tall branched tree of Husb outlining itself against the sky, and heard the murmuring of the great spring which flowed out from the roots. We let our camels drink a little, before the next rush along the main Akaba-Beersheba road to the foot of the great pass of Safa. We had come down more than five thousand feet from the Tafileh hills, and had to climb nearly three thousand to the level of Palestine.

In the little foothills before Wadi Murra suddenly in a valley we saw a fire of large logs, freshly piled, and still at white heat. No one was visible, proof that the kindlers were a war party: and probably peasantry, for it was not kindled in the nomad fashion. The liveliness showed that they were still near it: the size that they were many: so prudence made us hurry on. Actually it was the campfire of a British section of armed Ford cars, under the two famous Macs, who were looking for a car-road from Sinai to Akaba. They were in the shadows watching us, and covering us with their Lewis guns.

We crossed Wadi Murra and climbed the steep and toilsome pass as day broke. There was a little rain, but it and the air felt balmy after the extreme of Tafileh. Rags of the thinnest white cloud stood unreasonably motionless all morning in hollows of the Kurnub hills, as we rode past them and over the comfortable plain into Beersheba about noon. I felt this was to be my last camel-ride, so had not hesitated to drive the animals, and we had done a good performance in consequence, getting here in twenty hours , down and up hills for nearly eighty miles.

They told us Jericho was just taken. I got a car, and went through in the dark, and on to Allenby's headquarters by the daylight train. To my astonishment, Hogarth was on the platform at Bir Salem to meet me. To him I said that I had made a mess of things: for me the play was over, and I had come to beg Allenby to find me some smaller part elsewhere. I had put all myself into the Arab business, and had come to wreck in it just as the tide turned towards success. The fault lay in my sick judgment, bitterest because the occasion was Zeid , own brother to Feisal, and a little man I really liked. I now had left no tricks worth a meal in the Arab marketplace, and wanted the security of custom, to be conveyed, to pillow myself on duty and obedience, irresponsibly.

Since landing in Arabia I had had options and requests, never an order: and I was surfeited, tired to death of free-will. My present yielding was of the spirit, for when we let our will shine out, the flesh melted like a mist. My flesh had been reasonably misused without complaint. For a year and a half I had been in motion, riding a thousand miles each month upon camels, with added nervous hours in crazy airplanes, or rushing across country in powerful cars. In my last five actions I had been hit, and my body so dreaded further pain that now I had to force myself under fire. Generally I had been hungry: and lately always cold: and that and the dirt had poisoned all my hurts, and made me a festering mass of sores.

However, these worries would have taken their due petty place had it not been for the rankling fraudulence which had to be my mind's habit: that pretense to lead the national uprising of another race, the daily posturing in alien dress, preaching in alien speech: with behind it a sense that the 'promises' on which the Arabs worked were worth what their armed strength would be when the moment of fulfillment came. The fraud — if fraud it was — was shared with Feisal in full knowledge: and we had comforted ourselves that perhaps peace would find the Arabs in a winning position (if such poor creatures not helped and untaught could defend themselves with paper tools), and meanwhile we conducted their necessary honorable war as purely and as cheaply as men could... but now by my sin this last gloss had been taken from me in Tafileh. To be charged against my conceit were the causeless and ineffectual deaths of those twenty Arabs and seven hundred Turks in Wadi Hesa, My will had gone, and I feared longer to be alone, lest the winds of circumstance or absolute power or lust blow my empty soul away.

Chapter 100: A New Engagement

Diplomatically, Hogarth replied nothing: but took me to breakfast with Clayton. There I gathered from the common talk how Smuts had come from the War Cabinet to Palestine, with news which had changed our relative situation. For days they had been telegraphing for me to come across to the conferences: and finally had sent out airplanes to find Tafileh, but the air had been so thick that the pilots did not see the place, and had dropped their messages near Shobek, among Arabs too weather-daunted to bring them to me.

I told Clayton a little how I felt, but he said that in the new conditions there could be no question of letting me off in his opinion the East was only now going to begin. Alier these few words he carried me off to Allenby, who told me that the War Cabinet were leaning heavily on his army, to repair the stalemate of the West. He was to go forward from his present line as soon as he could, and take at least Damascus, and if possible Aleppo. Turkey was to be put out of the war once and for all. He had plenty of men, plenty of guns, and the railways were nearly finished. Very soon he would be ready to flow forward over Palestine.

His difficulty lay with his eastern flank, the right, which today rested on Jordan. If he advanced up the coast, the Hejaz Railway became a threat to his security, and a burdensome threat, for it lay behind such difficult country, and so far away that he could operate against it only with his full store of transport. Therefore he called me to consider if the Arabs could play such a part there as to relieve him of care of it.

Things being in this case, I had to pocket my desires and prepare to take up again my mantle of fraud in the East: and, with a certain contempt which my nature always held for half-measures, I took it up quickly and wrapped myself in it completely. It might be fraud or it might be farce: no one should say that I could not act it. So in reply I did not even mention the reasons which had brought me across, since to have advanced them at that moment would have wasted my breath. Allenby's will and appetite and intention were marching fixedly together. Instead I pointed out that this was the Madeba scheme seen from the British angle. Allenby assented, and asked if we could still do it I said not at present, unless new factors were first checkmated.

The first was Maan. We would have to take the large force of Turks there before we could afford a second sphere. Allenby asked how we could take them, and I replied that if more transport gave a longer range to the units of the Arab Regular Army they would be sufficient for the purpose. By taking position some miles north of Maan and cutting the railway permanently they would force the Maan garrison to come out and fight them, and in the field the Arabs would easily defeat the Turks.

To transfer the Arab Regulars from Akaba to this point by Odroh or Aneyza, and to maintain them there, would require seven hundred baggage camels: and these could not be got in Arabia in the time. For long I had been buying all there were, and at a long price could only get about two a day, since the camel-trade had been thrown out by the war, and no animals came to market. Further we would require more guns and machine-guns, to make our victory over the Turks certain: and lastly, we would require assurance against flank attack from the Amman direction, while we were dealing with Maan.

On this basis a scheme was worked out. The battle of Seil el Hesa, or rather my story of it, had warmed the Staff towards us, and persuaded them that the Arabs could fight, and that therefore great good might come of them. So they were ready to invest in me, and the first subscription was the seven hundred camels. They ordered down to Akaba two units of the Camel Transport Corps, an organization of Egyptians under British officers, which had proved highly successful in the Beersheba campaign. It was a great gift, and meant that we could now keep our four thousand regulars eighty miles in advance of their base. The guns and machine-guns were also promised.

As for shielding us against attack from Amman, Allenby said that was easily arranged. He intended, for his own flank's security, shortly to take Salt, beyond Jordan, and to hold it with an Indian brigade.

If we wished it he could go on and destroy as much of the Hejaz Railway about Amman as we thought necessary. A Corps Conference dealing with the business was due next day, and I was to stay and take part in it.

At this conference it was determined that the Arab army move instantly to the Maan plateau, and take Maan, and rid itself of the southern section of the Hejaz Railway to Medina once and for all: that the British simultaneously, or earlier, cross the Jordan, occupy Salt, and proceed to destroy south of Amman as much of the railway as possible: especially the great tunnel. It was debated what share the Arabs should take in the more British operation. Bois thought we should join in the advance on Amman. I opposed this, since the later retirement to Salt would cause rumor and reaction, and it would be easier if we did not enter till this had spent itself.

Chetwode, who was to direct the advance asked how his men were to distinguish friendly from hostile Arabs, since their tendency was to be prejudiced against all wearing skirts. I was sitting among them in skirts myself, and replied naturally that skirt-wearers disliked men in uniform. The laugh clinched the question and it was agreed that we raise all the people between Madeba and Kerak, and support the British retention of Salt, only after they had come to rest there. As soon as Maan fell, the Arab Regulars would move to Madeba, and base themselves there, drawing supplies from Jericho. The seven hundred camels would come along, still giving them eighty miles' radius of action: enough to let them work above Amman in the second phase of the operation.

This second phase was to be Allenby's grand attack along the whole line from the Mediterranean to the Dead Sea. It was to lead to the capture of Damascus. The Arab role in this would be to cut the railway in the rear of the Turks in Palestine, probably near Deraa. Allenby suggested we ought to take Deraa, and be ready to fight the Turks in their retirement. This sounded like assault tactics, things of which I had no experience, and for which I thought the Arabs had no capacity. So I asked if he would consider lending me the Imperial Camel Brigade as shock troops.

This splendid unit, of picked Yeomen and Australians, mounted on Sudanese camels, had done good service in Sinai the year before, but was out of the picture in Palestine proper, and not now in much favor with the great, since the camels were expensive to keep up, and (as they complained) slower than cavalry and little more durable. I had kept some touch with them, and knew this heaviness was an accident, due to tactics and training, and that in fact any camel would out-march every horse.

These particular beasts, hand-fed and groomed, had grown too fat and so soft that one fast day would have foundered the lot. Partly for this reason they thought fifteen to twenty miles a fair march: partly because in movement they tried to keep march-discipline and formation. The camel was slow to turn and maneuver, and so they lost much time opening and closing: and their rigid lines deprived them of the advantage of the native tracks (woven as if by a shuttle across the flints) and drove their animals into rough places which tore their feet. Further they were too heavy. The massive men were inevitable, since England did not breed men little as the Bedouin, except in odd cases, like myself: but they added to their weight heavy food, too much ammunition, bulky kit; and worst of all, five gallons of water and fifty pounds of camel-meal. G.H.Q. did not in the least understand the tactical abilities of camels, and, deceived by their apparent immobility, had never given them a chance. They wished to save me from a bad bargain, and asked me therefore what I would do with the Brigade if I got it, how far a day it would have to march, how long the operation would take?

I said I would march it from the Jordan into the desert, to Azrak, and fall upon Deraa unawares. With fifteen hundreds of such men we could not fail to carry it first try: and the rest of the program would be easy. Their longest march would be only forty miles a day, and while the operation might take months, we could arrange to re-victual them after a fortnight.

At once Robertson, Dawnay's successor, cried out that it was impossible. The Camel Corps could not do it. However, I maintained they could. It was springtime, and the animals could now be taught to graze. Then we would get rid of the fifty-pound bag of grain. We would bring the men to water every other day, so that two water-bottles would be ample for each to carry. The camels so lightened of one hundred pounds of their load could comfortably bear the extra thirty pounds' weight of a soldier's ten days' food, and at the same time march further as the pasture-diet would make them hard and strong.

Smith the commander of the Camels was sent for to give his opinion. He was all for the effort, and swore that he would be fit on May the fifth, the appointed date. So this was agreed and he went off with permission to reshape his brigade for long-distance desert riding. My business was finished and I went down to Cairo for two days and then was flown to Akaba, in order to make my new terms with Feisal.

I told him I thought Zeid had behaved badly, in diverting to his own use money from the special account which, with Feisal's previous knowledge. I had drawn solely for the Dead Sea campaign. Consequently I had left Zeid: but Allenby had told me to return to him, and protest at the mismanagement of the advance on Kerak. A great opportunity had been missed, and now the Turks would retake Tafileh at once and without difficulty. It was a nearly impregnable place one on which a series of successes like Seil el Hesa could be arranged: but as things were, I proposed to let Zeid deal with them by his own methods.

Feisal was distressed fearing that the loss of Tafileh might do his reputation harm: and shocked by my apparent half-interest in its fate. To comfort him I pointed out that it now meant nothing to us. In March the two interests were going to be in the extremes of his area in Amman and Maan: and Kerak and Tafileh would be included in their fate. They were not worth losing a man over: indeed if the Turks moved there, and kept a main force there they would weaken either the garrison of Maan, or the garrison of Amman and make our real work easier.

He was a little reconciled with this but sent urgent letters to Zeid warning him of the coming danger: without avail, for six days later the Turks retook Tafileh. Meanwhile Feisal had rearranged the basis on which the funds of his army were to be administered and had begged me in future never to take offense till I had resorted to him, and had failed to get things put right I gave him the good news that Allenby, as thanks for Tafileh and Aba el Lissan, had put three hundred thousand pounds into the special credit, and given us seven hundred camels complete with personnel.

This raised great joy in all the Army, for one difficulty had been the lack of men for administrative work. Every enlisted man was a fighting man, served at the front, and refused to do non-combatant services. We had no base troops, but four thousand first-line men, and the baggage columns from Palestine would enable us to prove the value in the field of this regular army on which Joyce and so many Arab and English officers had worked for months. We arranged rough timetables and schemes, and then I shipped back to Egypt to rest a little, and to make minor arrangements.

BOOK VIII

The Ruin of High Hope

In conjunction with Allenby we laid a triple plan to join hands across the Jordan, to capture Maan, and to cut off Medina, in one operation. This was too proud and neither if us fulfilled his part. Allen by failed to establish himself in Salt, and failed before Maan.

So the spring offensive delivered the Arabs from the care if the Medina railway only to substitute the greater burden of investing, in Maan, a force as big as their available Regular Army.

To help us in this unwelcome duty Allenby increased our transport, that we might have longer range and more mobility. Maan was impregnable fir us, so we concentrated on cutting its northern rail way and diverting the Turkish attempts to relieve its garrison from Amman.

Clearly no decision lay in such tactics: but the German advance in Flanders at this moment withdrew from Allen by his British units, and consequently his advantage over the Turks. He noticed to us that he was unable to pass again to the attack

A stalemate, as we were, throughout 1918 was intolerable. We schemed to strengthen the Arab Army first autumn operations near Deraa and in the Beni Sam country. If this drew off one division from the enemy in Palestine it would make possible a British ancillary attach, one if whose ends would be our junction in the lower Jordan valley.

After a month's preparation this plan was dropped, partly because of us risk, partly because a better offered.

Chapter 101: A Big Scheme

In Cairo, where I spent four days, our affairs were now far from haphazard. Allenby's smile had given us Staff, and our own special little base, in the Savoy Hotel. We had a supply officer, a shipping expert, an ordnance expert, an Intelligence branch: and these were combined to work under Alan Dawnay, brother of the maker of the Beersheba plan. Dawnay was Allenby's greatest gift to us — greater than thousands of baggage camels. He was a professional officer, and so had the class-touch to get the best out of the proper staff at G.H.Q. He was a well-read practicing soldier, with all the necessary words natural to him: so that even his reddest hearer recognized his authentic redness. His was a brilliant mind, understanding to a degree, feeling instinctively the special qualities of rebellion, and developing them: at the same time his war training stood to him, and enriched his treatment of this antithetic subject.

He married war and rebellion in himself: in the way that of old in Yenbo it had been my dream every regular officer would do it. Yet in three years' practice only Dawnay succeeded, and he on his first visit, while I was up at Tafileh in the mists. He spent twenty days in Akaba and Guweira, and went back with dispatches to Allenby, showing all our needs (far more and other than we thought) in stores and funds and arms, and personnel and direction. His sense of fitness remodeled our standing.

He could not take complete direct command: because he did not know Arabic: and because his Flanders-broken health had already deprived him of one promising field-job. Yet he had the gift, rare among Englishmen, of making the best not merely of a bad thing, but of a good one also. He was exceptionally educated for an Army officer, and imaginative. His almost too-perfect manner made him friends wherever he went with all races and classes. From his advice and teaching we began to learn the technique of fighting, in subjects which we had hardly known to exist, and which we had been content to settle by rude and wasteful rules of thumb.

Also he kept account for us and maintained stocks and thought about them in advance so that we never ran short. If we needed any special appliance, he put his interest at our service till it came. Indeed his taking charge of us was a revolution in our history. Hitherto the Arab Movement had lived as a one-wild-man show, with its means as small as its duties and prospects. Henceforward Allenby counted it as an asset, a sensible part of his tactical scheme, and the responsibility upon us of doing better than he wished, knowing that forfeit for our failure would be paid in his soldiers' lives, removed it from the sphere of joyous adventure, and often frightened us with the forces we had called up. At such moments Dawnay gave us confidence, clear sight, and sympathy.

He and I went down to Akaba together, and there with Joyce we laid out our triple plan to support Allenby's first stroke. In our center would be the Arab Regulars, under Jaafar, with Maynard holding our brief They would occupy the line at a point a march north of Maan. While they held up the Turkish main force, Joyce with our armored cars would slip down southward to the Mudowwara section, and destroy the railway — permanently this time, for now we were ready and willing to cut off Medina finally. In the north, in the Madeba area, Mirzuk el Tikheimi would post himself with me attached. We were to join Allenby when he fell back, after destroying the Amman tunnel, to Salt. He would start his operation about March the twentieth: so we should start about the thirtieth.

Such a date gave me leisure for the moment: and I settled to go up to Shobek where Zeid and Nasir were still camped, watching the enemy in Tafileh. However, that phase was nearly over, as, with realization, at last wisdom had dawned upon the Turks. They had been a bare week in the place when their German units were withdrawn for the Jordan front, to face Allenby's now ominous concentration. The Turks felt lonely by themselves, and were happy to go under our pressure, so that our horse reentered the village the day after I arrived. The Wadi Hesa line was taken up by Jemal Pasha as his best front line in these parts: and since our design was to turn it, by a direct occupation of the Madeba district, I had little difficulty in persuading Zeid and Nasir not to put them about for it. In any case, our vacillation had made the Tafileh peasantry distrustful, and therefore useless for an offensive. So we lost nothing by idleness.

It was springtime, very pleasant after the biting winter, whose excesses seemed now dreamlike in the ease of our Shobek life. The green valley above the running brook (dammed up for our bathing) was so pleasant that it tempted us out of the cabined houses, and Nasir, the nomadic-amateur, pitched his great tents on a terrace by the mill, and I moved there with him to enjoy the new freshness and strength of nature...

for there was strength in this hilltop season, whose chill sharpness at sundown corrected the languid noon.

All life was alive with us: even the insects. In our first night by the mill I had slept out in the open, laying my cashmere head cloth on the ground under my head as a pad: and at dawn when I took it up again, there were twenty-eight lice tangled in its snowy texture. Afterwards we moved into the tent, and slept on its floor upon our sheepskin saddle-mats — the leather-lined fleece which in Arabia was hooked last of allover the saddle-load to make a sloppy and sweat-proof seat for the rider. Even so we were not left entirely alone. The camel-ticks which with blood from our tethered camels had drunk themselves into tight slat blue cushions, as thick as a bean, and as large as a thumbnail, used to creep under us for warmth, hugging the animal-like leather underside of the sheepskins: and if we rolled on them in the night (for men sleeping on the flat lay at first usually for softness on their faces) our weight would burst them into brown mats of dry blood and dust.

While we were living in this comfortable air, with fresh milk plentiful about us, news came in from Azrak, of Ali ibn el Hussein and the Indians, still on faithful watch, though their winter had been as severe as ours in Tafileh. One of the Indians had died of cold, and also Daud, my Ageyli boy, the friend of Farraj. It was Farraj himself who came and told us the story, returning with the empty caravan which Awad had taken up with food after the snow in Tafileh.

Farraj and Daud had been friends from childhood, going about during the day hand in hand, for the happiness of feeling one another, and diverting our march by their eternal gaiety. In camp they had worked together, and slept together, sharing the joy and misfortune of every scrape, with an openness and honesty in their love which proved its innocence; for with other couples we had seen how, when passion had thrust in, it had not been friendship anymore, but a half-marriage, a shamefaced union of the flesh.

So I was not astonished to see Farraj looking dark and hard of face, leaden-eyed and old when he came to tell me that his fellow was dead: and from that day till his service with me ended there was no more laughter made by him in camp. He took punctilious care, greater by far than before, of my camel, and of the coffee, and in the disposal of my clothes and saddles, and fell to praying his three regular praying every day, even when on the march. The others offered themselves to comfort him, but without effect, and as useless was their suggestion that he might go away to his home in Nejd. He wandered restlessly about, grey and silent, keeping very much alone.

When looked at from this torrid East our British conception of sex, or rather of woman, seemed Scandinavian, due to the cold climate which had in the same way rarefied our faith. In the Mediterranean, woman's influence and supposed purpose were circumscribed, and the posture of men before her sexual. In the West the growth of mind had set them free from that carnal conception: but bodies took longer to adjust, and so the physical power endured, and life became a struggle of reason and nature for the dominance of man.

European women were either volunteers or conscientious objectors in this war to govern men's bodies: whereas in the East it was ended long ago, by an understanding in which women were accorded all the physical: and this world they possessed in simplicity, unchallenged like the faith of the poor in spirit. They knew the necessity of their physical sphere, and had not to struggle for it, since there was no other open or imaginable for them.

Yet by this same agreement all the things men valued — love, companionship, friendliness became impossible heterosexually; for where there was no equality there could be no mutual affection. Woman became a machine for muscular exercise, satisfying the physical appetites of man: but his psychic side could be slaked only among his peers, and therefore carnal marriage was complemented by spiritual union, a fierce homosexual partnership which satisfied all that yearning of human nature for more than the attraction of flesh to flesh. Whence arose these bonds between man and man, at once so intense, so obvious, and so simple.

We Westerners of this complex century who, monks in our bodies' cells, searched and searched for something unknown which should fill our being full to speechlessness and senselessness, were by the mere effort of our search shut out from it forever. It came to children like these Ageyl, sitting still with their spirits' doors open: stronger than the actors of life, We racked ourselves with inherited remorse for others' flesh-indulgence in our gross birth, striving to pay for it by a lifetime of misery: but our frailty, instinct in, if not itself the very life-blood of purpose, drove us ever upon those momentary happiness by the wayside. So our minds, to let man meet life's overdraft, had invented him a compensating hell, and a ledger-balance of good or evil against a day of judgment.

When back at Aba el Lissan I found things not well with our scheme of attack in the center to destroy the Maan garrison. We had thought to collect stores at Aba el Lissan, with an advanced dump at Odroh, intending that the Arab Army should post itself strongly near Aneyza, over a break in the railway. Maan had only fourteen days' food, and since Allenby's attack by Amman would prevent help from the north, the besieged garrison would be forced to deliver themselves from starvation. If they did not surrender, they would have to turn us off the line. They were only three thousand strong. Jaafar had two thousand five hundred available for the actual battle, and had shown himself a good tactician in the Senussi war: so we would be in the happy position either of winning a battle or of having one refused, which was the same thing.

Feisal and Jaafar liked the scheme, and we began on it: but they had reckoned without their officers, old schoolfellows of the Turks, and heartily despising them. They clamored for a direct attack on Maan, which lay only a few miles before them in Waheida. Joyce said they could not take Maan — a remark which set them burning, since they thought it a slur upon their courage. Joyce vainly went on to point out their weakness in artillery and machine-guns, their untried men, the greater strategically wisdom of the Aneyza scheme: it was all of no effect. Maulud was hot for immediate assault, and wrote memoranda to Feisal upon the danger of English interference with their liberties.

At such a moment, Joyce fell ill of pneumonia. Dawnay came up to reason with the malcontents. He was our best card, with his proved military reputation, exquisite red tabs and field-boots — his air of well-dressed science: but he came too late, for the Arab officers now felt their honor engaged to make the first effort desperate, and a striking victory against odds. In the face of such a spirit there was nothing to be said:

only privately we implored Jaafar not to risk too great disaster. He replied that with officers and men both mad-keen there might be even a chance of success.

Joyce was sent to hospital in Suez. Dawnay, who decided himself to take his place on the Mudowwara operation, went back to Egypt for a short visit, to explain to Allenby that owing to this change of plan Maan would probably not be taken. We had agreed that we must give the Arab Army its head on such a point, since to force them to a detailed performance of our wishes would have been against the principle of our advisory position. The art of advising was to persuade to the best course by the better arguments, and in the long run — especially after the provision of a terrible example the good advice and the good adviser would win their way, since mankind decided reasonably in a fair field. Our fault this time had been in raising prejudice before our case was presented.

We were really all-powerful, at any rate to spoil the wishes of the Arabs, had we felt inclined. The money, the supplies, and now the transport, were in our hands: and we took credit to ourselves for our forbearance. If the people were slattern, why then should they have a slatternly government, after the spirit of Solon. Omnipotent advisers always had the temptation to go too fast, in order to see results in a lifetime, trying to raise their objects whole stages at a leap, forgetting that man climbed step by step: or when young, two steps at once. Particularly had the adviser to go slow with that self-governing democracy which was the Arab Army, where service was as voluntary as enlistment, for lack of a civil power to enforce the contract. Any dissatisfied soldier had his choice of escapes — either to the desert with the Bedouin, or unobtrusively back to Turkish Syria, or openly to British Palestine. Inevitably our life was hard, and the temptation to leave took many men: it would have been imprudent to have increased it by enforcing a strict curve of Army discipline on the usual model. So we had to discover and institute an alternative.

Between us we were familiar with the Turkish, the Egyptian and the British Armies: and mentally we compared and championed our respective taskmasters. Joyce alleged the magnificence on parade of the Egyptians — formal men who loved mechanical movement, and who surpassed the British Army in physique, in smart appearance, in perfection of drill. Before the war it had been forbidden to put Egyptian and British troops side by side for fear of invidious comparison. On the other hand, the Egyptian Army was a conscript army, a mere handful of the best men, picked annually from a huge population, and luxuriously appointed, with an artificial standard, and infinite control, since behind it stood a civil power so organized that a deserter had no escape.

I maintained the cause of the Turks that shambling ragged army of serfs, neither willing nor unwilling, neither daring to be disobedient nor anxious to be efficient. They were conscripts, under a sole rule of force, whose civil power had the ambition to be ruthless, but was so tattered that actually it was seldom disagreeable. The technical standard was the lowest of any civilized army's, reflecting the illiteracy of its non-commissioned officers and the ignorance of its officers. Barrack-life was mostly insecure off-time, sparely flavored with misuse. Formal duties were reduced to a minimum, like the expenses.

The British Army we all were acquainted with, in our fashion: and as we contrasted them, we perceived the basis of discipline and smartness in the degree of ordered force which served each as sanction. In Egypt, soldiers and convicts were excepted from civil rights and the men belonged to their officers without check of law or public opinion. Consequently they had a peace-incentive to perfection of formal conduct which produced astounding results under the intensive care of their expensive and qualified British and Egyptian officers. In Turkey the men were in theory equally the officers', body and soul, but their lot was mitigated by the possibility of escape: and their training vitiated by the incapacity and arbitrary impulses of their instructors.

In England public opinion had taken away from the Army the resource of inflicting physical pain: and had constrained it to indirect means of stimulating the nerves to which pain appealed directly: but in practice upon our less obtuse population the effects and severity of pack-drill and fatigues fell little short of the Egyptian and Turkish systems. Whereas in the Arab Army there was no power of punishment whatever; and no authority, either within or without the army, to enforce a refused order.

A difference showed itself very vital in all our constitution. We had little or no parade drill, no barrack square. The men disposed of their own time doing no more routine work than seemed to the common opinion just or necessary. There were no badges to clean no kits or tents to keep tidy no guards or parades. They had all passed through the Turkish Army and knew some drill: enough in their estimation. By mutual agreement they marched in rough lines. For convenience of pay and disposition they organized themselves in companies, battalions, divisions. Self-preservation persuaded them to keep their rifles clean and the technical (gunners, medicals, sappers) learned their private duties and rehearsed them sufficiently.

Otherwise there seemed no formality or discipline and certainly no subordination. All service was active; they were liable at any moment to be attacked by the Turks: and, like the army of Italy they recognized the duty of defeating the enemy. But for the rest they were not soldiers but pilgrims intent always to go a little farther.

I was not discontented with this state of things for it had seemed to me that discipline or at least formal discipline was a virtue of peace: a character or stamp by which to mark off soldiers from ordinary men and so to give them the professional spirit a capacity for pride in something or other which made esprit de corps. This pride of status was a thing necessary (my own bodyguard, with my help cultivated it to a mad degree) but I found it an unworthy limitation to confine or confound its spirit within the particular range of smartness in drill and parade. Pride in an unusual whiteness or blackness or swiftness or success among women might surely rank as high, and if equally a distinction have equal fighting value.

Not that I underestimated drill. It had a utilitarian side as had perfection of equipment in permitting a factor of carelessness to the officer commanding unintelligent troops since they would look after these trifles while he thought of important things: and drill might make it easier to pass a crowd through a gate or to turn them round without tangling their buckles and pouches. So far it had a cash value — for others. We had no crowds or gates and were fools if we wanted them. Our effort was to keep our men wide apart, each using his intelligence and there discipline would fail — or hinder.

For discipline seemed a training to obliterate the humanity of the individual. It resolved itself easiest into the restrictive the making men not do this or that and so could be fostered by a rule severe enough to make them despair of disobedience. It was a process of the mass, an element of the impersonal crowd, inapplicable to one man, since it involved obedience, a quality of will; and will itself seemed to become manifest only when a command had been obeyed, to exist only in the dual and plural, to be a mysterious double faculty, comprising a part which gave command and a part which executed it. In the Army an effort, more or less conscious, was made to persuade the recruit to surrender one half of his will. It was not to impress upon the man merely that his will must always actively second the officer's, for then there would have been, as in the Arab Army and among irregulars, that momentary pause for thought transmission or digestion, for the nerves to resolve the relaying private will into active consequence.

On the contrary, the Army sedulously rooted out this significant pause from its companies on parade. It tried to make obedience an instinct, a mental reflex, following as instantly on the command as though the motor power of the individual wills had been invested together in the system. It demanded surrender, for the term of service, of reason and initiative: the making of each soldier, or rather of each subordinate, an empty harp through which the will of the Commander-in-Chief could blow.

This was well so far as it increased quickness: but the giving to another a blank check of one faculty of mind led to danger, if or when that other disappeared. Necessary in the light of mortality was the weak assumption that each subordinate had his will-motor not atrophied, but reserved in perfect order, ready at the instant to take over his late superior's office and to direct those now subordinate, in turn, to himself In theory, as the officers from the general downwards were killed in action, the efficiency of direction passed smoothly down the hierarchy till it vested in the senior of the two surviving privates.

It had the further weakness, seeing men's jealousy, of putting unchecked power in the hands of arbitrary old age and its petulant activity: additionally corrupted by long habit of control, an indulgence which became an obsession and ruined its victim, by causing the death of his subjunctive mood. Also it was an idiosyncrasy with me to distrust instinct, which had its roots in our animalistic side. Sooner or later terror came to every fighting man, on the battle field generally because his instinct momentarily overcame his reason. If given time, very many men in a crisis would choose death rather than a failure of duty: but if the stress came suddenly, though there was no telling, yet the majority would fail. Reason seemed to give men something deliberately more precious than fear or pain: and this made me discount the value of peace smartness as a war education.

For with war a subtle change happened to the soldier. Discipline was modified, or supported, or even swallowed by a moral eagerness of the man to fight and win. This eagerness it was which brought victory in the moral sense, and often in the physical sense of the combat. War was made up of long inactions, of periods of mean activity, and then of a crisis of intense effort which turned the scale. For psychological reasons the generals wished for the least duration of this maximum effort: not because the men would not try to give it — usually they would go on till they dropped — but because each such effort weakened their remaining force. Eagerness of such a kind was nervous, and when present in high power, as with the Arabs or the British, it tore apart flesh from spirit, and overstrained the mind. During the war it obliterated, or much reduced, what had been cares of the individual before it possessed him. Slighting of family, slackening of physical attentions or of laws of conduct followed generally.

After the Armistice its aftermath was seen in the breaking down of States and persons: and thus it proved the sanity of the disciplinary training of our peace-army. To rouse the excitement of war for the creation of a military spirit in peacetime would be dangerous, like the too-early doping of an athlete. Consequently discipline, with its concomitant smartness (implying a measured sense of restraint and pain), took its place. If the soldier did not remain human, in spite of logic and his uniform, these peace-bonds would endure in war, and prevent the eagerness of victory by their automatism: but the British Army on such occasions rose superior to its habit: and the Arab Army, born in the fighting line, had never known a peace-habit, was never faced with problems of maintenance till Armistice-time: and then it failed signally.

The Egyptian Army, less fortunate, was over-disciplined, too anxiously routine to dare a fight. Some blamed this on the race of Egyptians, ignoring history, and the axiom that in the ranks the peaceful classes made the best soldiers, finding supine obedience easy. The unwarlike townsman had more of tractability, and of the courage of common sacrifice than the tribesman who had lived by his wits and rifle, through a lifetime of traceless feud. Always in the ranks: — since an irregular fighter needed to be self-reliant, and an officer, regular or irregular, was better for personality: but to understand his notion of what men should be, follow him as he looked with approval down the line of his new unit for the first occasion, and see his eye glisten as he muttered 'fine men!' to himself It was the supremacy of the physical in the basement of war, the instinct of battle expressing itself in the attitude and tone of a meat-merchant before a fresh drove of sheep.

Chapter 102: Amman Fails

After Joyce and Dawnay had gone I too rode off from Aba el Lissan, with Mirzuk. Our starting day seemed a crown of the spring freshness of this lofty tableland, as we marched through Waheida, and northward to the ruins which the Arabs called the flour-mill. A week before, there had been a furious blizzard which had wrecked a great raid upon the line, and some of the whiteness of the snow seemed to have passed into the light. The ground was washed, and vivid with new grass: and the sunlight, pale like straw color, mellowed the light west wind which fluttered among us. Over the open plain, seeming within a rifle-shot, but really distant, glanced the little station of Jerdun, half-way between Maan and Aneyza.

With us journeyed an immense caravan of two thousand Sirhan camels, carrying five thousand rifles, great quantities of ammunition, and food, for the adherents in the north, upon whom we might call for armed service in a month's time. For the convoy's sake we marched easily, setting to cross the railway after dark, on the flat which extended from Jerdun to Anazeh. To make sure of peace during the two hours which our scattered numbers would consume in crossing, a few of us rode forward, to scout up and down the line by daylight.

Most of my bodyguard was with me: and Mirzuk had his men, partly Ageyl, with his two famous racing-camels, the swiftest in all our army. So we were a troop, and the gaiety of the air and season caught us. Soon we were challenging to races, skirmishing or threatening one another. My imperfect camel-riding and my mood forbade me to thrust among the rest. They swung more to the north, while I worked on, ridding my mind of the lees of clamor and intrigue yet remaining from my days in camp. The abstraction of the desert landscape cleansed me: and then made rich my vacant mind with its superfluous greatness, a greatness not from the addition of thought to its emptiness, but by its subtraction. The weakness of the earth's life in it made the strength of heaven stronger.

It was near sunset when we reached the line. Mirzuk and the men halted on the last rise and looked to right and left along the deserted track which curved beautifully across the disclosed land among the low tufts of grass and bushes. I had steered straight, and was alone, far to their right; but seeing everything so peaceful, pushed on to cross the line, meaning to halt by it and watch the others over. There was always a little thrill in touching the rails which were the target of so many of our efforts.

As I rode up the bank my camel's feet scrambled in the loose ballast; and out of the long shadow of a culvert to my left, where no doubt he had slept all day, rose a single Turkish soldier. He glanced wildly at me and at the pistol in my hand, and then with sadness at his rifle leaning against the abutment yards beyond. He was a young man, stout but sulky looking. I stared at him for a little, and then said softly, 'God is merciful.' He knew the Arabic phrase, and raised his eyes like a flash to mine, while his heavy face began slowly to change into incredulous joy. I could see that here was a Turk who found life good enough to prize.

However, he said not a word, so I pressed my camel's hairy shoulder with my foot; she picked her delicate stride across the metals and down the further slope out over the desert towards the others: and the little Turk was man enough not to shoot me in the back, as I rode away feeling warm towards him, as ever towards a man to whom one had given life. When we were together again we sat down, and lit a coffee-fire as a beacon for the rest, and waited till their dark lines streamed out of the night, and passed by us northward into it again. Some foolish ones were afraid of our mark, and turned to the south. The moon came up late, splendidly riding the cloud masses in the sky. By its fitfulness the Turks in a blockhouse saw them, and in the panic the Serahin weaklings spilled some of the rifles and food from their rushing camels. However, we lost no one.

We crossed the low watershed next day, and marched beyond it into Wadi el Jinz, where were flood-pools, shallow eyes of water set in wrinkles of the clay, their rims lashed about with scrubby stems of brushwood. The water was grey with the hard merely soil of the valley bed, but sweet. By them we rested for the night. Mirzuk had stopped some miles back, at the first pools, but in the morning caught us up, and rejoiced with us since the Zaagi had shot a bustard, and their white meat was still as good as Xenophon had found it. While we feasted, the camels feasted. The bounty of spring was over all this country and the valleys knee deep in succulent green stuff.

The third night we settled near Wadi el Hafira, opposite Katraneh, in the desert. Some Sherarat tents were beside it, their Arabs watering from further rain-pools. The valley was broad, and its bed was filled with a hard mud-flat, very suitable, if need arose, for a temporary landing ground. Another easy march took us to the Atara, our goal, an area opposite the station of Khan Zebib, where the Zebn Beni Sakhr, under our old allies Mifleh, Fahad and Adhub, were now camped. Fahad was still stricken, but Mifleh with honeyed words came out to welcome us, his face eaten up by greed and his voice wheezy with it.

Our plan, thanks to Allenby's lion-share, promised simply for us. We would collect in the Atara, about its huge flood-ponds, and when ready cross the line to Themed, the main Beni Sakhr watering near Madeba. At Themed would join us Hatmal and Turki, the brother-chiefs of the southern Sukhur, bringing with them the garrisons of the four stations between Amman and Katrani. Turki had come down secretly to Feisal, offering this. His brother would remain friendly with the Turks till Allenby's occupation of Kissir had thrown them into confusion. Then he would give the cut-off posts asylum with himself and safe-conduct to the British prison camps to avoid bloodshed.

This Turk was an odd lad, more like one of the nervous types of the Syrian coast than an up lander. He was about eighteen, and excitably brave, but perverse. His fighting record was of acts of famous gallantry done at the spur of a moment's madness. He used to shave his face to a clean girlishness an unusual and unwholesome fashion in the desert, and was impressionable to a fault, with fits of self-abasement. When he first met Feisal his emotion flung him weeping at his feet, kissing them and swearing that his service would overpass the service of all other men. For the moment blind subordination to the Arab ideal filled him with content, and while this mood lasted we could trust him for extraordinary work: but as the novelty of Feisal dimmed he would go whoring after another. These flickering Syrian devotions were vivid like summer lightning with no real fire or destructiveness behind.

However, the taking of the four stations should be a picnic. We would then call to us Mithgal and Nawwaf heads of the main Faiz section of the Beni Sakhr, and under cover of a screen of their cavalry would move to Madeba, and collect there temporary supplies to fit it as our headquarters, while Allenby put the Jericho-Salt road in condition for our transport columns. We ought to complete this work and link up with the British comfortably without firing a shot.

Meanwhile we had only to wait in the Atatir, which to our joy were really green, with every hollow a standing pool, and the valley-beds tall with grass and painted with flowers. The bare chalky ridges, thick with salt framed the water channels rather delightfully. From the tallest point we could look north and south, and see how the rain, running down, had painted the valleys across the white in broad stripes of green, sharp and firm like brushstrokes. Everything was growing, and daily the picture was fuller and brighter, till the desert became like a water-meadow. The playful packs of winds came crossing and tumbling over one another their wide brief gusts surging through the grass, laying it momentarily in swathes of dark and light satin like young corn after the roller. On the hill we sat and shivered before these sweeping shadows expecting a cold heavy blast — and then there would come into our faces a warm and perfumed breath, very gentle, which passed away behind us as a silver-grey light down the plain of green. Our fastidious camels grazed an hour or so, and then lay down to digest, bringing up stomach full of butter-smelling green cud, and chewing it weightily.

At last a messenger came in, hot from Hatmal's tent, to say that the English had taken Amman, and that the garrisons of our four coveted stations had taken refuge with him, under his promise of their lives. He and the Faiz were sharing the booty. In half an hour we were making for Themed, across the deserted line. Turki met us there, with the first of their twelve hundred prisoners: but his latest messengers told him that the English were falling back, and though we had forewarned him of it, yet he was troubled.

A few minutes later another messenger rode up to say that the English had fled from Salt. This was plainly contrary to Allenby's intention, and I said straight out that it was not true. Then Adhub galloped in to say that the English had broken only a few rails south of Amman, after wasting their strength for two days in vain assaults against the town. I began to grow seriously disturbed in the conflict of rumor: and decided to send Adhub, who might be trusted not to lose his head, off to Salt with a letter for Chetwode or Shea, asking for a note on the real situation. For the intervening hours we tramped restlessly up and down the fields of young barley, our minds working out plan after plan for all events, with feverish activity.

Very late at night Adhub's racing horse-hoofs echoed across the valley and he came in to tell us that Jemal Pasha was now in Salt, victorious, hanging those local Arabs who had welcomed the English. The Turks were still chasing after Allenby's retreat, far down into the Jordan Valley. It was thought that Jerusalem would be recovered. My disappointment went hardly as far as this, but it was clear that something was very wrong.

We thought first of our own unenviable situation, here in Themed, with more than half the Beni Sakhr involved with us, and without resources to fight Jemal on our own. We held a council before dawn, and decided that Hatmal and Turki must carefully replace their captured Turks in the railway stations, and agree with them to say nothing about this well-meant effort to make safe their threatened lives. All the loot must be given back or made good, and confidence restored. Meanwhile we slipped off, bemused, to the Atatir again.

Chapter 103: Withdrawal

This reverse took us unawares, and so hurt the more. Allenby's plan had seemed to me not merely practicable, but modest: and that he should so fall down before the Arabs was deplorable.

It stained our reputation with the Beni Sakhr: or rather confirmed the haughty point from which the Arabs were wont to regard the outside world. They had never trusted us to do the great things which I foretold to them and now that we had failed, they returned to their independent thoughts and set out to enjoy their springtide here together. Their wish was abetted by some gypsy families which had appeared suddenly in the Atara, coming from the north, on donkeys, with the materials of their tinkering trade in panniers. They were old acquaintances of the Zebn, who greeted them with a humor I little understood — till I saw that, beside their legitimate profits of handicraft, the younger women were open to advances in other directions.

Particularly they were easy to the Ageyl, and for a while they prospered exceedingly, since our party was eager and very generous. Mirzuk had repeated junketing about the fire which the cool evenings made dear to us. His Ageyl were the main performers, and their sword-dances and chanting astonished the Beni Sakhr only less than the ventriloquial talent of one crack-voiced youngster who performed domestic tragedies of husband-beating or wife-murder each night behind a screen of a tent-wall. After a little the tinkers judged it wise to move on to more restful places.

First, however, I had made use of them to get us news of Amman, for, amongst other things, it would be good to know how much damage Allenby had done before he fell back. This they easily discovered. One rail was broken for two or three miles, and some culverts; a matter of three days for the enemy to repair. Then I wanted to know, from the Turkish side, why the English had fallen back so precipitately: and that was harder to learn: but at last our informant on the Army staff at Salt sent us his judgment on the operation. He thought the attack on Amman had been impromptu, carried out by disordered packets of mounted men, half-heartedly, not expecting resistance. When they first came, there were only staffs and depot troops in Amman, and the place undefended: but the British cavalry had gone away north, and missed that opportunity. Later there had been more serious attacks but by then the Turks had collected themselves, and received reinforcements by rail, and had made a stout stand. Our movements continued piecemeal, and we had exposed ourselves too much to the enemy machine-guns. Anyway the attacks had failed, and in the engrossment of them the British had failed to do real damage to the line.

The third purpose in which the gypsies could aid me was for a detailed examination of Amman itself Deraa I knew sufficiently. After it, Amman was the next-important Turkish point beyond Jordan, and so had a reflected importance for us. If the war lasted, one or other of these stations would fall to us — though neither was necessary. Our target was the line, anywhere. The Turks defended a myriad of points to cover it all, for every yard of it mattered to them. To us these points were alternatives. A few of them we wanted to take, many of them we could take: but there was no one of them we must take. The ease, the deliberation, the freedom were ours.

However, it seemed a pity to be at a loose end so near to Amman, and not bother to look at it. So Farraj and I hired three of the merry little women, and wrapped ourselves up like them, and together we strolled about the station and the village. The visit was successful, though my final determination was that the place should be left alone. We had one evil thrill, by the bridge when we were returning from the town. Some Turkish soldiers crossed our party, and taking us all for what we looked, wanted to be much too friendly. So we showed a very real coyness and a good turn of speed for gypsy women, and escaped intact. It was not a fair race, for we were feather-light, on our bare feet: and they, poor things, lumbered after us in their clumsy boots, as heavily as rutting camels. This was my second and last effort at disguise. For the future I kept to my first expedient — that of wearing ordinary British tommy-rig when exploring enemy camps. It was too obvious to be suspect, when carried off brazenly.

Mirzuk had his orders to stay up with the Zebn, but there was nothing for me to do with him, and I determined to return to Maan, to help Jaafar. At the same time I would withdraw the Indians from Azrak. There could be no immediate development up north demanding them. Nuri Shaalan was away east in his first pastures: the Turks had achieved nothing in their expedition against Azrak, and were little likely to come again. Ali ibn el Hussein would be safe sitting there by himself without machine-gun help. So I made up a drove of twenty-seven camels by purchase from the Sakhr, and sent them off under Mohammed and other men, to Hassan Shah, with orders to pack up and move to Akaba at once.

We started a little later, on a morning with one of those clean dawns which woke up the senses with the sun while the intellect, tired after the long thinking of the night, was yet abed. For an hour or two on such a morning the sounds, scents and colors of the world struck man individually and directly, not filtered through or made typical by thought; and seemed to exist for themselves, not for humanity, which became just one of them, self-contained and natural. When the mind was so asleep, the lack of design and of carefulness in creation no longer irritated.

We marched southward along the railway, expecting to cross the track of the slower-moving Indians from Azrak. Accordingly our ride was fast, and our little party on prize camels swooped from one point of advantage to another, on the look-out. The valleys were rich, though less wonderful than the Atara, and the still day encouraged us to speed to the heads of all the flint-strewn ridges, ignoring the multitude of desert paths which led only to the abandoned camps of last year, of the last thousand or ten thousand years ago: for once tread a road into such flint and limestone, and the face of the desert was marked for so long as the desert lasted.

While we marched down by Faraifra we saw a little patrol of Turks marching up the line. They were perhaps eight in all, and my men, fresh after the holiday in the Atatir, begged me to ride on them. I thought it too trifling, but when they chafed, agreed, and the younger ones instantly rushed forward at a gallop. We were on the north bank of a valley which opened very wide before turning in towards the railway, and the Turks were coming along the track near where it crossed our valley by a pair of culverts. When they saw us, about a thousand yards off, they ran into cover behind the embankment, and began a shaky fire.

I called out to my men to swing to their right, and cut across the line, in order to drive the enemy away from their shelter. The Zaagi saw what was wanted and swerved aside at once, Mohsin followed him a moment later, with his section, whilst Abdulla and I pushed forward steadily on our side, to take the enemy on both flanks together.

Farraj, who was riding in front of everyone, would not listen to our cries, or to the warning shots we fired past his head. He looked round, and no doubt saw our maneuver, but himself continued to canter madly towards the bridge, which he reached long before the Zaagi and his party had crossed the line. The Turks held their fire, and we supposed them gone down the further side of the embankment into safety: but as Farraj drew rein beneath the archway there was a shot, and he seemed to fall or leap out of the saddle, and disappeared. Immediately afterwards, the Zaagi got into position on the bank, and his party fired twenty or thirty ragged shots, forward, as though the enemy were still there.

I was very anxious about Farraj. His camel stood unharmed by the bridge, but he had not come back. He might be hit, or might be following the enemy. I could not believe that he had deliberately ridden up to them in the open and halted in front of them, and yet it looked like it. I sent Fahad to the Zaagi, and told him to rush along the far side as soon as possible, while we went at a fast trot straight in to the bridge.

We reached it together, and found there one dead Turk, and Farraj terribly wounded through the body, lying by the arch just as he had fallen from his camel. He looked unconscious, but when we dismounted, greeted us, and then fell silent, sunken in that loneliness which came to hurt men who believed death near. We tore his clothes away, and looked uselessly at the wound. The bullet had smashed right through him, and his spine seemed injured. The Arabs said at once that he had only a few hours to live.

We tried to move him, but he was helpless, though he seemed to feel no pain. We tried to stop the wide slow bleeding, which made poppy-splashes in the grass: but it seemed impossible, and after a while he told us to let him alone as he was dying, and that it was good to die as he had no more care of life: indeed, for long he had been so, and men very tired and sorry often fell in love with death, with that triumphal weakness coming home after strength has been vanquished in a last battle.

While we were fussing about him Abd el Latif shouted an alarm. Beyond the south ridge of the broad valley he could see about fifty Turks working up the line towards us, and soon after a motor trolley was heard coming from the north. We were only sixteen men, and had an impossible position. I said we must retire at once, carrying Farraj with us. They tried to lift him, first in his cloak, and afterwards in a blanket, but consciousness was now coming back to him, and he screamed so pitifully that we had not the heart to hurt him more.

We could not leave him where he was, to the Turks, because of their treatment of our wounded. When fighting Europeans the Turks were on their best behavior, and treated their prisoners, not indeed well, but with nothing worse than callous neglect, but against the Arabs they felt free to indulge all their desires, and we had seen them mutilate or burn alive our hapless men. For this reason we were all agreed, before action, to finish off one another, if too badly hurt to be moved away: but I had never realized that it might fall to me to kill Farraj.

I knelt down beside him, holding my pistol near the ground by his head, so that he should not see my purpose: but he must have guessed it, for he opened his eyes, and clutched at me with his harsh scaly hand, the tiny hand of these unripe Nejd fellows. I waited a moment and he said, 'Daud will be angry with you', the old smile coming back strangely to his grey face. I replied, 'Salute him from me', and he gave the formal answer, 'God give you peace', and shut his eyes to make my work easier.

The Turkish trolley was now very close, swaying down the line towards us like a dung beetle, and its machine-gun bullets stung the air about our heads as we fled back into the ridges, leaving Farraj lying there dead. Mohsin led his camel, on which were his sheepskin and trappings, still with the shape of his body in them, just as he had fallen by the bridge. Near dark we halted, and the Zaagi came whispering to me that everyone was wrangling who should ride the splendid animal next day. He wanted her himself, but I was bitter that these perfected dead had again robbed my poverty: and to make less the great loss with a little one I shot the poor beast with my second bullet.

Then the sun set on us. The day had been breathless, and in the flower-strewn valleys of Kerak the imprisoned air had brooded for hours without relief while the heat drew out the perfume from the flowers. With darkness the world moved once more, and a breath from the west crept out over the desert. We were miles from the grass and flowers, but suddenly we felt them all about us, as waves of this scented air, sticky from its stagnant dwelling over them all day, rolled past us with sweetness almost unbearable. However, quickly it faded, and the night wind, cool and damp and wholesome, followed. Abdulla brought me supper, rice and camel meat (Farraj's camel), and afterwards we slept.

Chapter 104: Maan Fails

In the morning, near Wadi el jinz, we met the Indians, halted by a solitary tree. We went to it, and rested a little, thankfully, in the shade: around on all sides the jealous desert pressed, as though wishful to root it out. Afterwards we set off together and it was like old times, like our gentle and memorable ride to the bridges the year before, to be going again across country with Hassan Shah, hearing the Vickers' guns still clinking in their carriers, and helping the troopers to re-tie their slipping loads, or to straighten an uneven saddle. They seemed just as unhandy on camels, and made it easy going for the rest of us, so that not till dusk did we cross the line, between Hesa and jurf without alarm.

Beyond the railway we happened upon a small party of Beni Sakhr, Trad ibn Nuweiris and his friends, going home from Aba el Lissan. Trad was not even shakily in his clan: but so forthright and doughty that his fame was growing greater than almost any man's in his tribe. In age and manner he a little resembled Auda, though without that magnificent assurance. We exchanged fierce greeting and Trad sent back by me to Feisal a cryptic but evidently impolite message, 'Upon my beard, without reward, in sixty years.'

There I left the Indians, because I felt restless, and movement fast in the night might cure my mind. The effort of hard riding on camels was great enough to inhibit thought, except of the goal, and if the goal was distant, even that became too difficult, and the mind dwelt on an intermediate point, since to our crawling spirits steps or stages were easier than an end. So we paced forward all the chill darkness, until hours before dawn we had crossed the rivulets of Shobek and were riding along the ridge above Jerba, with its memories of Crusades and early Islam.

We were riding for Odroh, where Mastur would give us news of Feisal, but when we topped the rise we noticed sudden gleams of fire away to our left, in the direction of the railway. Bright flashes went up constantly from a small area, very distant from us. It might be about Jerdun. We drew rein and heard the low boom of heavy explosions: and in half an hour a steady flare appeared, and grew greater, and divided into two. Perhaps it was the station burning, and we rode on quickly to ask Mastur.

However, his place at Odroh was dark and deserted, with only a jackal on the old camping-ground. I decided not to make for the line, but to push ahead to Waheida, to learn from Feisal what it was all about. We trotted our fastest, to be in before noon.

The road was bestial with locusts — though from a little distance they looked beautiful, for the air was silvered with the shimmer of their wings. The summer had come upon us unawares: my seventh consecutive summer in this East.

As we approached Waheida, we heard more firing in front and soon saw the bursting of our shells on Semna, the crescent mound which covered Maan villages, three miles to their west and south. On the mound lay the strong Turkish outposts and their first time of defense. While we looked through our glasses we saw parties of troops walk gently up our face of the hill and halt below the crest: and afterwards a gun was dragged up, and fire opened eastward towards the town, from the old Turkish trenches on the slope. Evidently we had taken the Semna, so we turned our camels to the left again and, leaving Waheida behind us, rode towards the new position.

We were on the flat before the valley this side of it when we met a camel with a pair of medical litters on its back. The man leading it knew me, and said, 'Maulud Pasha', pointing to his load. I jumped off and ran up to him and said, 'Is Maulud hit?' for he was one of the best officers in the army, a man I had found most honest and friendly towards us: not indeed, that admiration could anyhow have been refused to so sturdy and uncompromising a patriot. The old man replied out of his litter in a weak voice, saying, 'yes, indeed, Lurens Bey, I am hit in the thigh: but, thanks to God, it is not serious. We have taken Semna and prisoners and machine-guns.' I replied that I was going to look and Mauiud craned himself over the edge of the litter, hardly able to see or speak (his thigh bone was splintered into fragments above the knee), and pointed out to me point after point, begging me to see Nuri Said, and give him these ideas for organizing the hillside for defense.

When we reached the mound the Turks were just beginning to throw shells at it, but faintly, and with great inaccuracy. This astonished me, and made me fear a blind, for they had held this point for months, and must have records of its ranges. However, the fire grew no more dangerous and I went round to find Nuri Said, who it seemed was in command in jaafar's place. He was standing very coolly on the hilltop, staring at the enemy, giving detailed instructions to Jemil the gunner. Most men and all Arabs I had met except Zeid, talked faster under fire, and acted a betraying ease and joviality. Nuri grew calmer, and smiled unconcernedly at the others, who looked hot. The troops behind him were happy and confident in his supreme self-possession.

He told me they had fought for three hours, attacking the Semna on a wide front and had broken through in two places. Maulud from one had charged along the covered edge of the mound rolling up the Turkish defense cheaply; but many of the enemy had got back unscathed. Their escape angered Maulud, who had galloped after them alone and had been shot, with his horse, two hundred yards in front of our front. His men had brought him in but he was desperately hurt. Nuri had replaced him, and had brought up powerful groups of infantry and machine guns, expecting a Turkish counter attack: but nothing promised.

I asked where Jaafar was, and Nuri said that at midnight he was due to have attacked Jerdun with regulars and guns and Zeid's Howeitat. I told him of the night-flares, which must have marked his success, and while we were glad together his messengers arrived, reporting two hundred prisoners, and three machine-guns, while the station and three thousand rails had been destroyed. So splendid an effort would settle the line from the north for weeks, and then Nuri told me that at dawn on the twelfth, yesterday, he with French mountain guns and Arab Regulars, and Howeitat under Sherif Fahad, had rushed Ghadir el Haj station, wrecked it, and five bridges and one thousand rails, getting back only just to see Maulud take Semna.

This excellent operation had finished the threat of the line from the south, for the time being, as Jaafar had finished that from the north, and it was good news that the employed detachments were coming in hot-foot to reinforce the center, since Nuri had no reserve if Semna was overborne. However jaafar would be in at sunset, and Nuri's men an hour earlier, so that all looked well. It was late in the afternoon, and deadly quiet, after both sides had stopped their aimless shelling. I called my little party together and we rode back up the road towards Waheida.

They said that Feisal was moved there from Aba el Lissan. We crossed the little flooded stream with difficulty, because of its trampled muddy banks, and then passed a temporary hospital where Maulud lay. Mahmud, the red-bearded defiant doctor, thought that he would recover without amputation. Feisal was on the hilltop, and we rode up its central cleft to find him. The low sun threw a shadow down it, in which we climbed till near the top, where stood Feisal on the very edge, black against the sun, whose light threw a queer haze about his slender figure, and suffused his hair with gold through the floss-silk of his head cloth.

As we came up silently — for I forbade my men to shoot in the silly tribal way on entry, he pointed towards us and called Auda, next him, to see. I looked back wondering what it was which caught their eyes, and saw that the shaft of light now burned in my men's brown faces, and over their gay clothes, and about the fair heads of their camels, turning them all to the blazing red of its last brilliance, while their bodies remained obscure in the shadow of the ridge. I made my camel kneel before Feisal, who stretched out his hands crying, 'Please God, good?' I replied, 'The praise and the victory be to God', and he said, 'Cod be thanked', and swept me into his tent to hear the news.

Feisal had heard from Dawnay more than I knew of the British failure before Amman, of the bad weather and confusion of Shea's force, and how Allenby had stood at the telephone and talked with Shea, and had made one of his lightning decisions to cut the loss, and abandon all his holding on the plateau: — a wise decision, though it hurt us sorely. Joyce was still in hospital, and Dawnay was ready in Guweira to start for Mudowwara with all the cars and Peake's Egyptian Army Camel Corps, and Hornby to do demolitions. Nuri's break would cover him on the north, and he had a fair chance of doing decisively, if he did not run into a relief force from Medina for Maan. I asked Feisal if he had the Togatga, as we had suggested, and Feisal said yes, and also Sherif Hazaa, the Abdilli, who had been so long with the Arnran and had acquired such ascendancy over those feeble Arabs as to discipline them like troops.

He then asked me about Semna and Nuri and Jaafar, and I told him what I knew, and Nuri's opinion, and the prospects. Nuri had complained that the Bedouin, and especially the Abu Tayi, had done nothing for him all the day, and this opinion I repeated, adopting it, since Auda was present. He denied it, and I recalled the story of our first taking the plateau, and the gibe by which I had shamed the Abu Tayi into their charge at Aba el Lissan. The tale was new to Feisal, and hurt old Auda deeply.

He got up and swore vehemently that he had done his best today, only conditions were not favorable for tribal work: and when I withstood him further, he went out of the tent, very bitter.

Maynard and I spent the next four days watching jaafar's operations; the Abu Tayi helped now, and captured two outposts east of the station, while Saleh ibn Shefia advanced down the great valley between the Semnas and took a little work with a machine gun and twenty prisoners. These gains gave us liberty of movement round three sides of Maan, and on the third day Jaafar massed his artillery on the southern ridge, against the railway station, which the Turks covered from a rise between it and the villages.

The Arab guns sprayed this rise from the south-west, and the French guns from the south-east, while Nuri Said himself led a storming party into the sheds of the railway station. As he reached their cover, the French guns ceased fire. We were in a Ford car, and Nuri, perfectly dressed and gloved, and smoking his briar pipe, met us and sent us back to Pisani with an urgent appeal for support.

We found Pisani wringing his hands in despair, with every round expended. He said he had implored Nuri not to attack with him so nearly out of action. There was nothing to do, so we stood by and saw our men shelled and volleyed out of the railway station again. The road from it was littered with crumpled khaki figures, and the eyes of the wounded men, gone all rich with pain, stared accusingly at us as they were carried past. The human control had gone from their broken bodies, and their torn flesh took free play with its own nerves, and shook them helplessly. We could see everything and think dispassionately, but it was all soundless: hearing alone, of our five senses, was taken away by the knowledge that we had failed. It was hard when success — or half-success — had been almost in our grasp.

Afterwards when we thought back we understood that we had never expected such excellent spirit and work from our infantry, who fought steadily and cheerfully, under machine-gun fire, making clever use of their ground. The gunners worked well, and so little leading was required that we lost only three officers. The general conduct showed us that, given fair technical equipment, the Arabs were good enough for anything, with no need of British stiffening, however weighty the affair. This changed our course of mind for the future, and made us much freer to plan: so the failure was not wholly unredeemed.

The criticism lay against the direction, which was at fault in undertaking so large a problem with such slender resources, and which had persisted in face of the truth. I thanked my stars in the evening that always I had hindered bayonets coming down, for had we had them Nuri would have once more charged home, and all of us would have been spent. The tool in my estimation had its lawful occasion once in ten times — and the other nine it was a dear excuse for a dull soldier to neglect his intelligent rifle. Particularly did its passionate nature seem dangerous, for the infection would have carried everyone away. Nuri and I might have gone in with the folly of the mob, to shun the loss of respect in being the only ones sober of a crowd. As it was we had thrown away enough good men on an inferior object.

On the morning of the eighteenth of April, Jaafar wisely decided that he could not afford more loss, and drew back to the Semna positions which ringed round Maan at from two to five thousand yards. He was nearly as strong as the Turks and could hold there passively while he waited for ammunition and the long-range howitzers which Dawnay had promised him. With them he could enjoy himself cheaply, subjecting the Turks to an unanswerable bombardment

Meanwhile, the troops rested while Jaafar, an old college friend of the Turkish commandant, sent him in a white-flagged letter, inviting his surrender. The reply said that they would love to but had orders to hold out to the last cart ridge. Jaafar offered a respite, in which they could fire off their reserves: but the Turks hesitated till Jemal Pasha was able to collect troops at Aneyza from Amman, to re-occupy jerdun, and to pass a pack-convoy of food and ammunition, with reinforcements into the beleaguered town. The railway remained broken for weeks.

Chapter 105: D Awnay Succeeds

Meanwhile I took car from Waheida, and went down to Guweira, to join Dawnay in our old camp behind the toothed hill facing Tell Shahm station. I had been a little afraid of him by himself, for he was a regular fighting his first guerrilla battle, with that most involved and intricate weapon the armored car as his main asset. Also he was not an Arabist, and neither Peake the camel expert, nor Marshall, the Scotch doctor was fluent. His troops were mixed British, Egyptian and Beduin. The last two were antipathetic and trouble might easily arise. So I drove into his camp after midnight and offered myself, rather delicately, as his interpreter.

Fortunately he received me quite warmly, and took me round his lines in the dark. It was a wonderful show for the cars were parked geometrically here, and the armored cars placed there, and sentries and pickets were out in all the proper places with machineguns trained and ready. Everything was ready, even the Arabs, put in a tactical place behind a hill where they were in support but out of sight and hearing of the line: and by some magic Hazaa and himself had kept them where they were put. My tongue went far into my cheek with the wish to say that the only thing lacking was an enemy: but for all Dawnay knew the Turks might have been respectable foes, informed, capable of reconnaissance and of night attack they were not, of course, but if they had been, Dawnay was prepared.

His conversation, as he unfolded his plan, deepened my admiration to unknown depths. He unfolded a paper, and read me his operation orders, orthodox-sounding things with zero timings and a sequence of following movements. Each unit had its appointed duty. We would attack the 'Plain Post' at dawn (Armored Cars) from the vantage of the hillock on which Joyce and I had sat and laughed ruefully last abortive time. The cars, with closed cutouts, would take station before daylight, and carry the trenches by sunrise. Tenders Number One and Number Three would then demolish Bridges A and B on the operations plan (at zero 1.30) while the cars moved to Rock Post, and with the support of Hazaa and the Arabs rushed it (zero 2.15).

Hornby and the explosives in Talbots Number 4°5 31 and 41226 would move after them, and demolish Bridges D, E, and F, while the force lunched. After lunch when the low sun permitted sight through the mirage, at zero 8 hours, the united mass would attack 'South Post', the Egyptians from the East, the Arabs from the North, covered by long-range fire from the cars, and by Brodie's ten ponder guns, from Observation Hill.

The post would fall and the force would then transport itself to the station of Tell Shahm, which would be shelled by Brodie from the North-West, and bombed by Airplanes (at zero 10 hours) and approached by the Armored Cars from the West. The Arabs would follow the cars, while Peake with his Camel Corps descended from South Post on the North-East. 'The station will be taken at zero eleven-thirty', said the scheme, breaking into humor at the last: but there it failed, for the Turks, ignorantly and in a hurry, surrendered ten minutes too soon, and made the only blot on a bloodless day.

In a liquid voice I inquired if Hazaa understood, and was informed that as he had no watch to synchronies (by the way would I please put mine right now?) he would make his first move when the cars turned northward, and time his later actions by express order. I crept away and hid myself for an hour's sleep.

At dawn we were all afoot, and saw the cars roll silently on top of the still-sleeping sandy trenches , and the astonished Turks walk out to them with their hands up. It was like picking a ripe peach. Hornby dashed up in his two Rolls tenders put one hundred and twenty slabs of gun cotton under Bridge A (on the operation plan) and blew it up convincingly. The roar nearly lifted Dawnay and me out of our third tender in which we sat grandly overseeing all: and quickly we ran in. and I showed Hornby the cheaper way of the drainage holes as mine-chambers. The taught Turks had neatly blocked them with rubble and cement: but the car drivers who enjoyed destruction soon broke them out with lusty pick-work: and subsequent bridges came down for ten or fifteen slabs apiece.

While we were busy pecking at Bridge B. the cars concentrated their machine guns on the parapet of 'Rock Post' a circle of thick stone walls (very visible from their long early shadows) on a knoll too steep for wheels. However Hazaa was ready willing and excited and the Turks so frightened by the splashing and splattering of the four machine-guns that the Arabs took them almost in their stride so that was peach the second.

Then it was interval for the others but activity for Hornby and for myself, now become assistant engineer. With Dawnay we ran up and down the line in our Rolls-Royces, carrying some two tons of guncotton and bridges and rails roared up about us on all sides wherever fancy took us or there was a target. The officers and crews of the cars covered us and sometimes covered themselves under the turrets or wings of their cars when stones or iron fragments came over sailing musically through the smoky air. Only once was there a great hit, when a twenty-pound lump of flint dropped, with a sounding clang, plumb on a turret head and made a harmless dint. Other times everybody took photographs of the happy bursts. It was fighting de luxe and demolition de luxe and we enjoyed ourselves.

After the peripatetic lunch we went off to see the fall of 'South Post', at zero seven hours forty-five. It fell to its minute but not properly. Hazaa and his Arnran were too wound up to advance soberly in alternate rushes like Peake and his cautious Egyptians. Instead they thought it was a steeplechase and did a camel-charge up the mound and over into the breastworks and trenches. The Turks gave it up in disgust.

Then came the central act of the day the assault upon the station. Peake drew down towards it from the north moving his men with repeated efforts, hardly, for they were not fierce, or thirsty for honor. Brodie opened on it with his usual mathematical nicety, while the airplanes appeared overhead to the minute, circled round in their cold-blooded way, and dropped whistling bombs into its trenches. The armored cars went forward snuffing smoke, and a file of Turks waving white things rose slowly out of the ramp ending their main trench, and moved in a dejected group towards them.

We cranked up our Rolls tenders, the Arabs leaped onto their camels, Peake's now bold men broke into a run, and the force converged wildly, but ten minutes too soon, upon the station. Our car won the race, and I rushed into the office and came out with the station bell, a fine piece of dignified Damascus brass-work. The next man took the ticket punch and the third the office stamp, while the bewildered Turks, hungry for notice, stared at us, not understanding that their importance was secondary.

A minute later, with a howl, the Bedouin were upon us, and there was the maddest looting in their history. Two hundred rifles, eighty thousand rounds of ammunition, many bombs, much food, and clothes , were in the station, and everybody smashed and profited. An unlucky camel increased the confusion by firing one of the many Turkish trip-mines as it entered the yard. The explosion blew it parse over tip, and caused a panic, while the sheikhs besought me not to let the machines drop another bomb!

In the pause the Egyptian officer found an unbroken storehouse, and put a guard of his soldiers over it, since they were short of food. A dispute followed, as Hazaa's wolves were not yet sated, and did not recognize the Egyptians' right to share equally. Shootings began: but Hamaad el Tagtagi and Auda the Amrani kept their heads, and by their wise mediation we obtained that the Egyptians should pick first what rations they needed: and afterwards there followed a general scramble: in which the press nearly burst the storeroom walls.

The profit of Shahm was so great that in the morning only Hazaa and a handful of men, including the most excellent and dutiful Hamaad, were with us. Dawnay's program said Ramleh station, but the orders were inchoate, since the position had not been examined. So early in the morning we sent down Wade in his armored car, with a second in support, to go in gently and have a look at it He drove on, cautiously, stage by stage, in dead silence. At last he entered the station yard, carefully for fear of mines, without a shot fired.

The station was closed up, he put half a belt through the door and shutters, and, getting no reply, slipped out of his car, searched the building, and found it empty. The Turks had gone off, after burying their arms, in such haste that they had left their clothes, and had placed no booby-traps to engage us. We spent the day destroying miles more of the unoccupied line, till we judged that we had done more than a fortnight's damage, for the largest possible repair party.

The third day was to be Mudowwara, but we had no great hope or force left, after our surfeit of these two days. The Arabs were all gone, Peake's men were too little warlike, inclined to let him down when he had greatest need of them. The car soldiers were enough only as their crews; however, perhaps Mudowwara might panic like Ramleh, so we slept the night by our latest capture. As ever the unwearied Dawnay set out sentries, who did a Buckingham-Palace strut, up and down beside our would-be sleeping heads, till I got up and instructed them in the arts of desert watching.

In the morning we set off to look at Mudowwara, driving splendidly in our roaring cars over the smooth plains of sand and flint, with the low sun pale behind us in the east. The light hid us till we were close in and saw that a long train stood in the station. Reinforcement or evacuation? A moment afterwards they let fly at us with four guns, of which two were active and accurate little Austrian mountain howitzers. They reached to seven thousand yards, and did admirable shooting, while we made off in undignified haste, through the dropping shells, into some distant hollows to the south-east.

Brodie's guns were good only for three thousand yards, so the game was cogged against us, and anyway Mudowwara could only be carried, against resistance, by a co-operating force working in the western hills, along the line which Stokes and Lewis and I had found six months before. So we made a long circle in the cars, and came down again on the lower railway just north of Hallat Ammar, where with Zaal we had mined our first train. To annoy the new troops in Mudowwara we blew up there the long bridge under which the Turkish patrol had slept out that ten se midday.

Afterwards we returned to Ramleh, and went on destroying line and bridges, meaning to make our break a permanent one, a demolition too serious for Fakhri ever to restore: but that evening I left the force, and had I driven quickly over the mud-flats and through Guweira to Aba el Lissan. My mission was to tell Feisal of our Mudowwara work, that he might move against the wrecked section from the north.

However, the Togatga had already brought him news, news rather greater than the truth: and Zaal and Mohammed el Dheilan had started with all their men, and had taken Shedia, Fasoa, and Akebat el Hejazia, with their station-guards. Dawnay took Wadi Retem, below the escarpment, a day later, and so this eighty miles from Maan to Mudowwara, with its seven stations, fell wholly into our hands. Peake, Hornby, and others went down to it at their leisure, time after time in the next two months, and shattered till there was no more to shatter: and so it lay derelict till Feisal's government rebuilt it after the Armistice. The active defense of Medina ended with this operation.

Feisal made peace at this prosperous time between myself and Auda, turning our dispute over the inaction of the Howeitat before Maan into a jest. Auda soon forgave me, his 'world's imp' as he called me, for the laughter I used to bring to the so-serious councils of these grave people. It was part natural with me, part policy, for the more I laughed the more decorous and established grew their efforts: and after all it was not my doing, but theirs which would win this Arabian war: and just now they were doing so much, and such good things, that my spur even seemed superfluous.

So I determined to go up once more to Egypt, to discuss futures again with General Allenby. Jaafar was still investing Maan, and worrying the Turkish garrison of Jerdun by repeated attacks and feints.

Mirzuk was still in the north, keeping the Beni Sakhr as a menace to the flank of the Jordan Turks. A new officer, Young, had come from Mesopotamia to reinforce the advisory side of our staff. He was a regular of exceptional quality, with long and wide experience of war, and perfect fluency of Arabic. His intended role was to double mine, with the tribes, that our activity against the enemy might be broader, and better directed: and to let him play himself into our fresh condition I handed him over the possibility of combining Zeid, Nasir and Mirzuk into an eighty mile long interruption of the railway from Maan northward: while I went down to Akaba, and took ship for Suez.

Chapter 106: A Gift of Camels

Dawnay met me, and we talked over our brief before going up to Headquarters together to ask what would be the next thing they did. Bir Salem, their station, we reached as usual before breakfast. There stood General Bois, who smiled happily at us, and said, 'Well, we're in Salt all right.' To our amazed stares he went on explaining how the chiefs of the Beni Sakhr had come into Jerusalem, by Jericho, one morning, to offer the immediate co-operation of their twenty thousand tribesmen now camped in Themed: and how in his bath next day he had thought out a scheme, and had had it all fixed before the water chilled.

I asked who the 'chief of the Beni Sakhr was, and he said, 'Fahad el Zebn', obviously triumphing in his efficient inroad into what had been my province. It sounded to me madder and madder. I knew Fahad perfectly, and that he could in no circumstances raise more than four hundred men: since Mifleh was jealous of him, and Hatmal senior, while the Faiz branches followed Mithgal and Nawwaf and would have no part in anything the smaller Zebn did. At the moment there was not a single tent on Themed: and Young had just called the Beni Sakhr south towards Katraneh to help his sketched attack upon the line.

However, we did not begin to tell what we knew, but hurried to the office to hear the real story. Unfortunately there we learned that it was indeed as Bois had said. The British cavalry had gone impromptu up the hills of Moab on some airy promise of these Zebn sheikhs — greedy fellows who had ridden into Jerusalem only to taste Allenby's bounty by sweetening him with big words of their power. They were stealing a march on Mirzuk, and the British thought that they were stealing a march on us.

At this season there was no third partner at G.H.Q. Guy Dawnay, who had made the Jerusalem plan had gone to France, to Haig's Staff: and Bartholomew who was to work out the details for the autumn drive upon Damascus, was still with Chetwode. So the executive of Allenby's work in these months was much below the conception. There were miscarriages first of the Amman offensive, and then of this raid to Salt, faults of the gravest by which any less man than the conqueror of Jerusalem would have broken his neck. Only Palestine was now too little for Allenby to fall in.

For of course this raid miscarried even while I was in Palestine at Jerusalem, whither I had gone for two nights to solace myself against the inadequacy of Bois, in the company of Storrs, now the urbane and artful governor of the place. The Beni Sakhr were either supine in their tents or away with Young and Mirzuk in the desert east of Tafileh. General Chauvel, without the help of one of them, not even of Fahad the paid, saw the Turks reopen the Jordan fords behind his back and seize the road by which he had advanced to Salt, where his cavalry were almost cut off. We escaped a heavy disaster only because Allenby's instinct for a situation showed him his danger just in time, while his Staff was talking of sending me out by air to lead the detached expedition through the desert by the south end of the Dead Sea back to Palestine.

But for the lost men and guns, we on the Arab side would not have regretted the check, which had three good effects. It taught the British to be more patient with Feisal in his difficulties, showing them that local risings required as careful preparation as a regular advance. Afterwards they took us into their confidence before they planned schemes requiring Arab help. It convinced the Turks that the Amman sector was their danger point (and not their strongest point): so they strengthened it unduly at the expense of their Palestine front. It made the Beni Sakhr feel that the English were past understanding, not great fighting men perhaps, but ready on the spur of the moment to be odd. So in part it seemed to redeem the Amman failure by its deliberate repetition of what had looked accidental, and it kept the Arab mind in as unsteady a flux as the Turkish. At the same time it ruined our hopes of acting independently with the Beni Sakhr. This cautious and very wealthy tribe asked for dependable allies before they were to risk their own goods in action.

I feared a little its effect on Feisal. Our clean-cut movement had lost its way since we arrived at Akaba, in a bog of contingencies, no longer alone face to face with a simple enemy, but tied to a leading partner, ever and again playing a self-effacing or self sacrificing role for his advantage. Amman had hurt Feisal, and its grand repetition a month later might drive him to be foolish. Before him Jemal's traps of fair words were always open. It would be wise to get our version spread about Aba el Lissan before the Turkish songs of triumph sounded.

So in the morning G.H.Q. sent me to Sarona, where an R.E.S took me down to the hot valley of Akaba by noon, flying bumpily over Beersheba and Wadi Araba, past Petra, which looked very artificial from the air. At Akaba was an Air Force car just starting for Guweira, with rations for the detachment which Siddons, our incomparable flight commander, had put on Disi mud-flat by Rum, to bomb Maan and Mudowwara at ease. We were in Guweira at sunset, good going from Bit Salem, and thence another Crossley tender took me over the wire road across the soft Guweira plain, till it stuck in the sand hills below the Shtar pass at midnight: and in the airless damp heat of the covered ground our sweating efforts to push it out were of no avail.

I walked up in the dark to Feisal's tent at Waheida, arriving about four in the morning, and crouched down outside it, feeling the shiver of the mountain dawn strongly upon me, waiting for the first light when he would be stirring. It was not my part to make too heavy my news by rousing him specially. Actually I amused him, by spinning a good story of it. He promised so to admonish the Beni Sakhr that such double-dealing should not recur: but could not understand why Allenby had not warned him, or asked him to help, so that a real co-operation might have resulted Did the British mistrust him?

He was comforted a little by my suggesting that at such short notice, and after the Amman accident, perhaps we might have been unable to help very much: so that Bois' precipitancy had possibly saved us from confessing a failure. Then I walked back own the pass, and found my waiting car just dug out of its sand difficulties, and turned round ready for me. A little after noon we were in Akaba, before sunset in jaffa, and at Allenby's punctual table for dinner, with the last word from Feisal. This was important, for he was going to show me his new plans, and my suggestions for us depended wholly on them.

It was not good news. The German offensive in France made our line critical, and he had been called upon for all his white troops. They were already going. He would be left just enough to defend Jerusalem, but could not afford a casualty, much less an attack for months. The War Office promised him Indian divisions from Mesopotamia at once, and eventually Indian drafts to replace the men gone to France. When these came he would reorganize or rebuild his army on the Indian model, and perhaps after the summer, might be again in fighting trim: but for the moment, this was too far to fore see: we must, like him, just hold on and wait.

He told me this on May the fifth, the date chosen, under the Smuts arrangement, for the great heave northward of the whole army in prelude to the fall of Damascus and Aleppo. As first phase of this arrangement we had undertaken the liability of Maan: and Allenby's dropping his share stuck us with this siege of the superior force in a fortified position, with the advantage over us in guns. Now, in addition, their relief force was looking at them from Aneyza, and at Katraneh the Turks were making a base from which the Amman force would operate to sweep us off the plateau of Aba el Lissan, back into Akaba.

In so nasty a situation the common habit of joint operations cursing the other partner — weighed strongly upon me however, Allenby's wonderful staunchness to his subordinates was driving him out of his way to relieve us. He was threatening the enemy by a vast bridgehead across Jordan, and by continual deceptions to persuade them that he was about to cross a third time. So he would keep Amman tender. To strengthen us on our plateau he offered guns and what other technical equipment we needed.

We took the opportunity to ask for repeated air-raids on Amman and Katraneh. General Salmond was called in, and was as generous as the Commander-in-Chief Routine attacks upon the Hejaz Railway were arranged, and the Royal Air Force kept at this dull and troublesome business from now till the fall of Turkey. They served a very valuable strategic purpose, by causing heavy damage and uncertainty along the line, and so making any large concentration either of men or stores dangerous in the sector north of Maan. Much of the inactivity of the Turks, in this our lean season, was due to the disorganization of their railway traffic by air bombing. Then I asked for an air-taxi for myself next morning to fly over the desert beyond Katraneh, in case Young and Mirzuk had started, in order to turn them back towards Hesa, where it was now important that the railway should be extensively destroyed. Ross Smith, so Salmond said, was their keenest-eyed pilot, and at dawn in his machine, with another as escort, we flew over the Dead Sea, and over the noble castle of Kerak, and over Katraneh into Wadi Hafira. There my mud-flat of the month before winked up at us like a mirror in its polished smoothness.

Ross Smith swooped down to land, throwing out a smoke-ball to gauge the wind: and once more I noted the prior flatness of earth seen from a height, the absorbing crisis of landing on a virgin place, and when we were still, that sudden growth of hills and valleys and trees, all the vertical which from the air had been blotted out of view.

The water holes were dry and the Sherarat tents gone. Camels were pasturing in the plain, with their herdsmen: but when I ran out to them in my khaki uniform they were too afraid of my strangeness and of the new machines to let me near them. This meant that Mirzuk had not passed. So we refilled the Bristol Fighters, and going up again cruised southward over the valleys till Ross Smith saw a knot of Beni Sakhr marching in the scrub. We dived low at them to their evident horror, and dropped a message for Young, giving a veiled summary of the new tactical phase.

At tea-time, in Allenby's cool rooms. I complained of the desert mistrust of British uniform and its hindrance to the growth of our kind reputation. He laughed and reminded me of my hope to use the Camel Brigade out east, wondering how they would all have looked in skirts, and regretting that the chance for them was past, since he was just abolishing the Brigade to use its men as mounted reinforcements in the new stringency. I asked, 'What are you going to do with their camels' He laughed again, and said, 'Ask Q.'

Obediently, I went across the dusty garden and broke in upon the Quartermaster-General, Sir Walter Campbell, very Scotch, and repeated my question. He answered firmly that they were earmarked as divisional transport for the second of the new Indian divisions. I explained that I wanted two thousand of them. His first reply was irrelevant: his second that I might go on wanting. I argued but he seemed unable to see my side of the matter at all. Of course, it was of the nature of a 'Q' to be costive.

So I returned to Allenby, and said aloud before his party that there were for disposal two thousand two hundred riding-camels, and thirteen hundred baggage camels. They were all provisionally allotted to transport, but of course the riding camels were riding camels, and I would like them for Feisal's army. The Staff whistled pleasantly, and looked wise, as though they too doubted whether riding camels could carry baggage. Needless to say it made no difference, but a technicality in the path might be helpful, as every British officer had to understand animals or be silent in shame. So I was not astonished when Sir Walter Campbell was asked to dine with the Commander-in-Chief that night.

We sat on the right hand and on the left: and with the soup Allenby began to talk about camels. Sir Walter said that the providential dispersing of the Camel Brigade brought the transport of the 9th Division up to 10 strength — a godsend in the animal shortage, for all the Orient had been ransacked for camels. He over-acted, and Allenby, a great reader of good poetry and prose, had an acute sense of style; and the line was a weak one, for Allenby cared nothing for strengths, that fetish of the administrative branches.

He looked at me with a twinkle in his eye and said, 'And what do you want them for?' replied hotly, 'If I get them, I will put a thousand men of all arms into Deraa any day you please.' He smiled and shook his head at Sir Walter Campbell, saying sadly, 'Q, you lose.' The goat became giddy and the sheep sheepish for the evening. It was an immense, a regal gift, the gift of unlimited mobility. So far as the Arabs were concerned, they could now win their war when and where they liked.

Next morning I was off for Akaba, and on May the twenty second joined Feisal in his cold eye at Aba el Lissan. We discussed events, and tribes and their migration, and sentiments and pasturages at length. Finally I remarked incidentally that Allenby had given me two thousand camels. He gasped and caught my knee, saying, 'How?' I looked up and told him the entire story.

At its end he leaped up and kissed me: then clapped his hands loudly, and Hejris' black shape appeared at the tent door. 'Hurry: cried Feisal, 'and call them.' Hejris asked whom he meant. 'Oh, Fahad, Abdulla el Feir, Auda, Zaal, Motlog....' 'And not Mirzuk?' queried Hejris mildly. Feisal shouted at him for a mad fool, and the black ran off, while I said, 'It is nearly finished. In a little while you can let me go.' He protested strongly, saying that I must remain with them always, and not just till Damascus as I had promised him in Um Lejj.

In a few minutes feet came pattering to the tent door, and paused there a moment while the chiefs recovered their grave faces and set straight their head cloths for the entry. Then one by one they pushed in and sat down stilly on the rugs beside us, each saying unconcernedly, 'Please, God, good?' To each Feisal replied, 'Praise God', and they stared after his dancing eyes, wondering after the excitement.

When the last had rustled in, Feisal told them that God had sent them the means of victory, two thousand riding-camels, and that now our war was to march forward to its triumphant end, with freedom won. They murmured in astonishment, doing their best, as great men, to be calm, and looking at me to guess my share in the event. I said, 'The bounty of Allenby....' Zaal replied swiftly for them all, 'God keep his life, and yours.' I replied, 'We have been made victorious', stood up with a 'By your leave' to Feisal, and slipped away to tell Joyce, while they sat down again together and burst out into wild words of their coming wilder deeds — childish perhaps, but it would be a pretty war in which each man did not think that he was winning it.

Chapter 107: Covering Raids

Joyce also was glad and happy at the news of the two thousand camels. We let our minds for ten minutes run off the immediate needs, while we dreamed of the stroke to whose service they would be put: of their march overland from Beersheba to Akaba, where and with whom we could send out to graze for two months so vast a multitude of animals — for they must be broken of barley meals, and taught to live on the desert scrub, if they were going to be of use to us — and then the delirious prospect of the final dash.

These were not pressing thoughts. Joyce would turn them over and suggest a plan: but meanwhile we had to think how to maintain ourselves in position to attempt this final dash. It was May the twenty-third. To bring the camels over would take a month to prepare them for the expedition two months. Late in August we might be ready to move... which meant that all the summer we must cling on to the plateau at Waheida or Aba el Lissan, besieging Maan, keeping the railways cut, the Turks on the defensive. The task was difficult.

First of all about supply, the maintenance of the Arab Regulars in front of Maan. I had just thrown the existing arrangements out of gear. The Egyptian Camel Transport companies had been carrying steadily between Akaba and Aba el Lissan, but their efficiency was limited by corps rules of a fixed load for all their animals alike, weak or strong, and a fixed order and length of the march. Consequently we found them carrying less and marching less than our least sanguine estimate. They supplied us but barely, not putting in that margin for contingencies on which we had counted.

We urged them to increase weights and speeds, with some success: but found ourselves up against cast-iron regulations very wise and proper, no doubt, in the case of a millionaire government like the British, but too wasteful for a small fin like ourselves. Their framer was a British colonel who knew as much about camels as we had all forgotten. His idea was to keep down the figures of wastage: while we, by increasing them slightly could presently double the carrying capacity of the column, making it do the eight days' round in five or six: and it seemed so well worth it that at C.H.Q. I had offered to take over the animals from the Egyptian Transport people and send them back their officers and men.

The British were short of camel-men, for labor recruiting in Egypt had fallen off, as the stringency of service in Palestine during the winter capture of Jerusalem became known. So they jumped at my idea, almost too quickly for our resources. Coslett, single handed, had done supplies, transport, and ordnance paymaster, base commandant for everybody: and the work had become over great for him. Dawnay relieved him a little by getting us Scott, a perfect Irishman, for our base commandant. He had the good temper, the capacity, the spirit, and Akaba breathed quietly again.

Ordnance we gave to Bright, sergeant or sergeant-major (we never in Arabia quite knew our own or each other's ranks. Dawnay used to change them to keep pace with our growing duties, and we felt his happy results on our pay: but by ourselves we never had the titles or the badges, or the attitude of mind which seniority elsewhere involved): and now Young took over the transport, and general quartermaster work.

He had overstrained himself, riding furiously up and down the highlands between Maan and Katraneh, between the Howeitat, and Naimat, and Hejaia and Beni Sakhr, between Nasir and Mirzuk and Feisal, striving to combine them and move them in one piece. Incidentally he had furiously overstrained the Arabs, and we took the opportunity of his enforced rest to assign him to duties upon which his drive and ability would be better employed. Using his full power, he grappled with the thankless job of entire responsibility for the now-chaotic transport. He had no stores for his columns, no saddlers or clerks, or veterinaries or drugs, and few drivers, so that to run a harmonious and orderly train was impossible; but Young very nearly did it, in his curious ungrateful way, and thanks to him the supply question on the plateau eased itself, and a reserve up-country began to grow.

All this time, the face of our revolt was growing, and Feisal, veiled in his tent, continued day and night without surcease the teaching and preaching of his Arab Movement. His disciples up and down the desert and the fringe of the cultivated land transmitted his ideas, and gave wider currency to his nationality. Akaba boomed, even commercially, for we were making a point of trade, partly as propaganda, more to supply ourselves with the gold we needed to pay our troops and levies. Visitors arrived in daily droves from every part of Syria: and were sold Manchester cotton, and silks and luxuries and food, in return for their gold coin. Every Arab still under the Turkish hand, to Aleppo and Mosul, was now aware that the Sherif was close to him, and master in his own house, and rich.

Like our mind-work our field-work was going well. The Arab Regulars had just had their third success against Jerdun, the battered station, which they had almost made it a habit to take and lose, and upon which both officers and men had taught themselves the best way to fight the Turks. Our armored cars had happened once on a Turkish sortie from Maan by daylight up the line and had smashed it in such a manner that the opportunity never recurred.

Zeid had been put in command of half the army and with two thousand men had posted himself north of Waheida, between Fejeij and the ruined mill and was showing great force and vigor. His gaiety of spirit appealed more to the professional officer than did Feisal's poetry and lean earnestness, and this happy association of the two brothers gave every sort of man a sympathy with the leaders of the Arab Revolt. Each day something or other was being done to the line between Aneyza and Maan, and the Turks were no nearer controlling this sector than they had been a month before.

Yet there were clouds in the north. At Amman was a forcible Turkish concentration of troops, earmarked for the Maan district when supply conditions and the new harvest would let them move. At Katraneh was the beginning of this supply reserve being put in by rail from Damascus, as well as the air attacks from Palestine permitted. At Aneyza was a bridgehead and striking force, designed first to relieve Maan, and afterwards to act as a subsidiary base from which to conduct a double operation against Aba el Lissan, and thrust the Arab Army off the heights.

To make head against them Nasir had been appointed, in advance of Zeid, to take post in the Tafileh district, and do something great against the railway between Katraneh and Aneyza. He had camped in Wadi Hesa, near Tafileh, and with him had gone Hornby, full of explosives, and Peake with a trained section of his Egyptian Army Camel Corps, to guard Hornby and help him in his actual demolition. If they got to work promptly and well, the enemy's intentions against us would be greatly delayed.

At any rate, the Turks would have to drive off Nasir before thinking about Aba el Lissan: and as Nasir's men were irregulars, he should be able to confound them by evasive tactics, to keep his threat in being by refusing to fight. Nasir was our best guerrilla general our best man to wreck the ordinary army by playing the intangible ghost at it. Time till Allenby recovered was what we had to fight for, and if Nasir could secure our regulars a month's breathing space he would actualize our desire. We sent him word of the new importance of his mission, that he might surpass himself, in a make-believe of doing something great.

It was a difficult duty, and Nasir might fail. If he did we must expect the relief and reinforcement of Maan, and an onslaught upon Waheida and Aba el Lissan. We would be hardly able to meet this: certainly not at the same while to maintain our break between Maan and Mudowwara. We had done our best to destroy all that length of line, but it was simple desert railway, and we feared that in a month's leisure the Turks might bridge the gap. That would stultify our whole winter's work almost our coming to Akaba, and reduce us again to the weariness of desert raiding and a futile belligerent of Medina.

To prevent such a setback, our only means was to destroy the well at Mudowwara before Maan was free. I dreamed of a snap demolition, by running into the station after dark in an armored car, and dropping down the well a fused heavy mine. Siddons flew me over the place that I might work out my plan in full sight. It looked possible, by its sheer surprise, though dangerous, and we began to make reluctant preparations: but then came good news from Nasir, which postponed its urgency, and gladly I handed over to Marshall, our scholarly doctor, an alternative plan of attacking Hallat Ammar from Rum with the Beni Atiyeh, and went off myself to Aba el Lissan to get in touch with Nasir.

Chapter 108: Nasir Does Well

Nasir had attacked Hesa station at dawn on May the twenty-third in the old fashion, cutting the line to north and south the night before, and opening a sharp bombardment of the buildings when it was light enough to see. Rasim was the gunner, and the gun our Krupp antiquity of Wadi Yenbo, Jurf and Tafileh. A section of regulars served it, and Rasim had four Maxims under Subhi el Omari as covering troops. When the Turks weakened their reply, the Arabs had charged mounted into the station, Beni Sakhr and Howeitat trying for the lead.

We had, of course, no killed, and as soon as the capture was complete Hornby and Peake had got to work, and reduced the place to a heap of ruins. They blew in the well, the only all-the-year water on this part of the railway, and fired a small charge in the ground angle of the kidney-shaped water tower, which collapsed and crashed to the ground under the weight of its huge hundred-thousand gallon tanks, bursting open in a flood of water. They destroyed the engines, and the pumps, three buildings, three bridges, some rolling stock, and about four miles of rail.

Next day Nasir moved north, and attacked and destroyed Faraifra station, increasing his prisoners to nearly three hundred. Peake and Hornby continued their work on that day and the day following. Altogether it sounded like our biggest demolition, and came most opportunely. I determined to go up there for myself, and see how things would go.

A dozen of my men were ready to march with me (others being with Marshall, with Hornby, with Peake, with Young, or on independent mission). We set off from Waheida, by the now beaten and car-worn track to Zeid's, Thence past Odroh, and over the Shobek plain, now so leisurely ours. Below the Rasheidiya ridge we came to the lone tree, Shejerat el Tayar. My Haurani followers drew rein beside its tumbled cairn, under the thorny branches on which were impaled many tatters of wayfarers' offered clothes. Mohammed said, 'Upon you, O Mustafa'

Reluctantly Mustafa let himself down from his saddle, and piece by piece took off his clothes, till nearly naked, when he lay down on his back, arching himself over the pile of stones. The others dismounted, picked each a long thorn from the tree and in solemn file went up to Mustafa and drove their thorns (hard and sharp as brass) deep into his flesh and left them standing there.

My Ageyl stared open-mouthed at the ceremony, but before it ended swung themselves monkey-like down, grinning lewdly, and stabbed in their thorns where they would be most painful. Mustafa shivered quietly, and then Mohammed said, 'Get up', using the feminine inflexion. He got up, sadly pulled out the thorns, dressed and remounted, while we all rode forward. Abdulla had no not ion what was meant, and the Hauranis so clearly wished not to talk that I asked them nothing. Probably Mustafa was being punished for some private fault.

We reached Hesa to find Nasir with about six hundred men, concealed up and down the gorge under cliffs and bushes, afraid of the enemy aircraft which had been very active, and had killed many. For cover and grazing the Arabs were penned into the deep warm bed of this beautiful valley, and gave the Turkish machines an exceptional target, of which they had made too much use, so that now, with the frequency, their comparative harmlessness was becoming evident. Nevertheless they were troublesome. One bomb had fallen curiously into a pool at which a knot of eleven camels had been drinking, and had thrown them all, dead, in a symmetrical ring about the water-side among the torn flowers of the oleander bushes. We wrote to Air-Vice-Marshal Salmond for a great counterstrike to Katraneh, and sent the missive back to Joyce.

The railway was still in Nasir's hand, and whenever they had explosives Hornby and Peake went down to it, and destroyed bridges and rails. They had blown in a cutting, and were developing a new rail-demolition, turning over each section by main force, as it was cut. From Sultani in the north to Jurf in the south, the damage extended. They estimated it all at fourteen miles. Jurf had been tried, but was too active in artillery for their weakness. Nasir wanted it to be the target of a serious raid of Zeid's regulars.

He fully understood the importance of maintaining his activity, to give Waheida a breathing space, and there seemed a fair hope of his lasting as he had found a comfortable and bomb-proof cave between two limestone reefs which, articulated like teeth, broke forth from the green hillside. The heat and flies in the valley were not yet formidable. It was running with water, fertile with pasture. Behind in Tafileh, lay Sherif Abdulla el Feir, and if Nasir were short of food or hard pressed he had only to send off a message, and the mounted peasantry, on their rough ponies jangling with shrill bells, would come pouring over the range in his support.

The day of our arrival the Turks began to recover themselves, and sent a force of camel corps, cavalry, and infantry, down to the ruins of Faraifra to reoccupy them as a first counterstrike. Nasir at once was up and at them; while his machine-guns kept down the Turks' heads, the Abu Tayi charged in to within a hundred yards of the crumbling wall which was the main defense, and from the other end of the station cut out all the enemy camels, and some horses. To expose riding-animals to the sight of Bedouin was a sure way to lose them, and it was foolish but kind of the Turks to grant us this spur to victory.

Afterwards I was down with Auda, near the fork of the valley, when there came the throbbing and moaning overhead of Mercedes engines. Nature stilled itself, as even the birds and insects grew hushed in fear of what such greatness meant. We walked between the fallen boulders, screeds of the cliff-side, and heard the first bomb drop lower in the valley where Peake's camp lay hidden in a twelve-foot oleander thicket. The machines were flying up the bed towards us, for the next bombs were nearer, and the last just in front, with a shattering dusty roar out by our captured camels.

When the smoke cleared, two of them were kicking in agony on the ground and a man with his face torn away into strips of red flesh hanging about his bloody neck was stumbling frantically between the rocks, and screaming out. He crashed, blindly yelling, first into one and then into another, tripping and scrambling up again, to run off once more at a tangent, mad with pain and fear. He fell silent in a few minutes, and then we ventured out to him no longer afraid that he would rush at us: but already he was dead.

I went back to Nasir, safe in his cave, with Nawaf el Faiz, brother of Mithgai, the head of the Beni Sakhr, and chief of the Amman countryside. Nawaf was a shifty man, so full and careful of his pride that he would stoop to any mean crime to seem to preserve it: but mad like all the Faiz, uncertain like them, and voluble, with his eyes constantly flickering, as it were from round a corner.

We were old acquaintances (though we never showed it) not merely from before the war, but of a year ago also, when three of us had crept in after sunset to their rich family tents near Zizia, with letters to them from their fellow conspirators of the Fetah. Fawaz, their senior, was a notable Arab, a committee-man of the Damascus group, prominent in the party of progress and independence. True to profession he had received me with fair words and hospitality, fed us with a rich supper, and brought out for us, in the night after we had talked his richest quilts.

I had slept an hour or two when a charged voice, whispering through a smoke-smelling beard into my car, roused me. It was Nawaf the brother, to say that, under the friendly seeming, Fawaz had sent word by horsemen to Zizi, and soon the troops would be here to take me. I whispered back for his counsel, and he told me to follow, and crawled away through the tent-wall. I drew with me my few things in their light saddlebags, and found my camel knee haltered behind Nawaf's tent, which was the next.

With her were my two men, waiting, and Nawaf's mare, held ready. We mounted together, and Nawaf his rifle loaded across his thigh, led us to the railway, and beyond it into the desert, and there gave us the star-direction of our supposed goal in Bair. I asked him what return I could make, but in reply he asked only for silence, saying that the honor of his family was not yet repaired. A few days later Fawaz was dead, and though there was no evidence, yet my fears always bound it up with that clash between the brothers.

Peake and Hornby had done all the damage of which these near sections of the line were capable, and sighed for more bridges to root out. I meant to have another look at the Themed-Amman area, for a new plan was in my mind; and asked Hornby to ride the first part of the journey, with me and Trad, the old lion of the Mor, as far as Sultani, where my route would branch up to Kerak. We might blow up something there, and the loss of this last siding would make the Turkish revitalizing convoys walk from Katraneh to jurf eight more miles, with disproportionately more pains.

We reached the bridges north of Sultani early in the evening and, working together, had them out of the way in an hour without opposition. Afterwards I went off to the north, while Hornby lay down in the hills close to the line on the west, to gloat over his damage at sunrise. As a railway engineer he took pleasure in making work for a supposed colleague after the war. On this occasion no harm came to him: though he out slept the sight of the Sultani garrison running in terror towards Katraneh at dawn. They had thought the fate of Hesa and Faraifra upon them, when they heard the explosions between them and succor, in the night.

Chapter 109: A Changed Plan

Trad wanted to play a trick on Rufaifan, the pompous and futile headman of Kerak: so we raced across there after leaving Hornby, and made such speed that before midnight we were in its streets. We had our arms ready, while the Turks were caught unawares. They shut themselves into their barracks expecting the worst. Trad swore he was hungry, called for a sheep had it killed and cooked for us in public. Rufaifan was telephoning frantically to Katraneh for reinforcements, but we had had enough of our game, and slipped away, so that the tired soldiers an hour or two later arrived, only in an empty town.

We marched a little way, slept, marched again, and then slept till late afternoon, in some tents above the rift of the great valley of the Mojeb, the immense chasm which cut off Kerak from Therned, our goal. It was beautiful, this chasm of white limestone cliffs, as smooth as plaster, raising each side of a narrow stream, whose bed, half-choked by sallow, had something of the intimate friendliness of the birth of rivers. Such a pass would be impossible to force against even a few determined rifles, if they knew the ground. Trad wished not to cross it until dark.

The dark surprised us in it. Up above, the gold of sunset had been passing into twilight when we rode down the steep path: but in the narrow depths a pitched darkness swallowed us, and made our way a doubtful guess. However, Trad was a veteran of many crossings, and his white saddle-skin was a mark for me to follow: but the night, which so opened a little in front, closed in behind, and seemed to track us, with its companion silence, which filled the valley-deep about us, till our heart-strokes sounded crying discords in the vacancy.

At the foot, the path splashed into the stream: and the ripples of its star-shining water among the stones and roots with the chorus of croaking frogs was a glad break in the hot dizzy stillness of the descent. We waded for many yards till we passed to one side behind a thicket of trees which seemed standing in the water. There we paused. I thought I heard before us more than the noise of the rivulet: something long-drawn, like the dragging back of a lazy wave down the pebbles on a beach. Trad had heard it too, and from our hiding place he challenged firmly in a shout. A roar of shots followed, then stopped, in obedience to Turkish calls for silence, and the rough the failing echoes came the sounds of frightened cavalry on the cliff-path in front: their hooves kicking in the dust, or clinking on occasional stones, the snorting of horses, creak of leather and limbs moving.

My instinct acted while my mind was wandering, and I called out abuses in fluent Turkish, words which rose painlessly from my memory. Their last syllables mixed with the echoes of a new volley and fresh orders of silence, cannoning in repeated confusion off the cliffs. Afterwards we stood there, without moving, behind the swamp, while the enemy rode into the river and splashed across towards the way of our descent. The road they took left the yard thick screen of trees between us. The frogs fell silent. Birds disturbed by their passage whirled from their roosting places blindly over our heads. The boding precipices of this prison, their nearness, and the white knives of moonlight on their edges loomed over us uneasily, impenetrably, in the hush; while the brook chuckled past us with a horrid meaning in its tune. We waited till the clattering of the horses and their hoof-sparks had faded up into the hills again.

Next day we came to Urn el Rusas, a central place of the southern Beni Sakhr lands, with its ruined town and churches. Trad's Hegagish were camped there under their sick chief, Khallaf el Mor, and we had a vast talking until night, when I took my blanket out into the open, and slept there in peace, knowing Trad well enough so to reject his hospitality. After the peace and dignity of the empty lands, these half-peasant people were too human to be borne.

In the morning Trad and I wandered about the flat valleys north and east of the ruins, among the golden barley and the bearded wheat, till we had plotted a satisfactory aerodrome for the campaign I had come here to project. Later the Turks came over in the air and bombed the camps, wantonly no doubt practicing their aim. They mutilated some sheep, and scattered the herds. My haltered camel sprang up and tried to escape, when the aviators opened on the tents with machine-gun fire: and I stood still admiring the group of Salem, my Sherari squire wrestling with her. She was the tall Baha, the yapping camel, and tossed her head high in the air, straining him to his toes, with his arm extended, his back hollowed; while the thin clinging clothes for an instant revealed the exquisite grace and lithe proportions of his figure.

To avoid more interference, we moved in the evening with the tribe to Themed, the main summer watering of the pastoral Sukhur. There were now many of the Arabs about it, and we had great feastings every night, with preaching to follow, men's wills bowing before me like com in a wind. The day was only preparation for the night, the women gathering firewood, or brattling sheep, or swaying to one another over the running drone of the flour mill. Nidfaan took me about, and we went to Madeba and Amman, and to Hesban at the lip of the Jordan depression, above Allenby's bridgehead. Nidfaan was an old man, and a miser; the Arabs explained this disgrace as due to his having delayed seven years in the womb. His character was written in his narrow forehead, hairy eyebrows and deep, small, wrinkled eyes: and his horrible mouth, which opened to an oblong shape, gave a sense of crudity to all his speech.

My reconnaissance had been very satisfactory, and there was in my head a first draft of a plan of sudden occupation of this tempting district, for submission to Allenby on my return: and now it seemed time for this return, before my activity in the midst of their lines stung the Turks to reprisal. So we said farewell to Trad, and rode southward, keeping near the railway, so that we might cross the Mojeb tributaries in their shallow youth. Also I wanted to see Bisher, a wonderfully preserved Roman guardhouse near Katraneh.

Afterwards we rode over the level plain, expecting shortly to find the Kerak road, a thing to be crossed circumspectly, when through the calm morning sounded the song of airplanes, and we listened carefully into them, as into the deep note of a great bell, rolling out in close-following waves of tone. These had the intermittent swinging beat, the munch, munch, munch of Rolls Royce engines. I cheered my party with the news of friends, and a few minutes later we heard the booming of their bombs over Katraneh. Salmond had sent two more of his Australian machines upon our purpose.

Unfortunately they had seen us as they passed, and on their return, having dropped their loads, they dived down genially and kicked up the dust as with whips about us, emptying drum after drum of Lewis ammunition at our protesting heads. The Arabs could not understand it from friends, and unslung their rifles to shoot back: but I appealed to their strained sense of humor, and kept some of them laughing despite. It was bad shooting, and no one of us was hurt: but the fuss gave us away, and a squad of gendarmes on screws, patrolling the Kerak-Katraneh road, seeing us trespassing, took up the chase almost as soon as the Bristol Fighters left off.

Further on, we found Sultani station reoccupied by a small force of mounted men, who also sallied out to cut us off. It was gratifying to find that Nasir's sustained activity had so put life into the enemy. We found him still in his camp up Wadi Hesa, but happy now, for our airplanes were across so constantly as to make the air too dangerous for enemy machines. The Turkish aviators had the mean order to go down and land when they met Bristol Fighters, since they were not well enough equipped to fight them in the air.

I stayed only the afternoon with Nasir and Hornby and Peake, and then rode in the night along the level railway valley till opposite Jurf el Derawish. There we slept, to see it in the morning: for I had advised an expedition of Arab Regulars against it, to reduce it, and so deprive the enemy relief-force at Aneyza of their last waters supply. If we took it, we would compel the evacuation of the line from Sultani to Jerdun,

Unhappily the Turks saw us near them in the first light, and took pot-shots at us with their field-gun on the rise behind the station, and for eight thousand yards we had to run over the scaled rough basalt ground, in disagreeable heat. However, they sped up our going, so before noon we were near Aneyza. We were so light and fast a party that I kept close along the railway where the going was best: and consequently when explosions broke out ahead, and spouting columns of dust went up, we realized at once that heavy fighting was in progress too near us on the line just this side of Aneyza.

It was interesting, for some Rualla under Mijhem Shaalan had lately come to Bair, and perhaps Feisal had brought them raiding here. So we climbed the next ridge and then the next, to get a view: but the whole country seemed masked by these troublesome ridges, and I had turned towards the line to see quicker, when the two Nowasera with me called out in alarm. Behind us a small column of mixed horse and foot, in uniform, was moving fast up the valley from the railway to cut us off

A moment later more troops appeared in front. We were certainly caught. The Arabs jumped off their camels, and crouched in a covered place with their guns, meaning to fight to the last like cornered animals, and kill at least some of the enemy before they themselves died. Such tactics displeased me, for when combats came to the physical, bare hand against hand, I used to turn myself in. The disgust of being touched revolted me more than the thought of death and defeat: perhaps because one such terrible struggle in my youth had given me an enduring fear of contact: or because I so reverenced my wits and despised my body that I would not be beholden to the second for the life of the first.

Anyway I had not the instinct to sell my life dearly, and to avoid the indignity of trying not to be killed and failing, rode straight for the enemy to end the business, in all the exhilaration of that last and terrific and most glad pain of death; noting that the shock had paralyzed my intuition, and put reason on the throne. This was peculiar to me in company, when I felt fear, disgust boredom, but anger very seldom; and I was never passionate. Only once or twice, when I was alone and lost in the desert, and had no audience, did I break down.

When they saw me single, their horsemen galloped in advance, with their rifles out, but did not shoot when first I came up. Instead they reined back suddenly, stood still, and very slowly aimed at my body, calling to me a last warning in Arabic to testify, I said, 'There are no gods: — but God, and Jesus is His prophet' They gasped, stared, and then yelled, 'Urans' together, laughing. I was annoyed that they were mends after all, and asked whence their Turkish uniforms. They explained they were Hejaia, and had lately rushed two Turkish posts, and these clothes and guns and horses were spoils of the enemy cavalry. The infantry were sappers lent them by Jaafar, to blow up their sector of the line. They had never seen me before, and had supposed us some of Rufaifan's followers, with whom they had fought yesterday. The two Howeitat rejoined me, angry as men who had keyed themselves to a crisis and found it a fraud: and we went on together very fast to Aba el Lissan.

Chapter 110: King Hussein Refuses

I explained to Feisal that Nasir's cutting of the line would endure probably for another month: and after the Turks had got rid of him, it would be yet a third month before they were fit to attack us in Aba el Lissan. This nearly covered our dangerous period, for about then our new camels should be fit for use, and we enabled to forestall the enemy in an offensive.

This offensive would be really ours, in the sense that Allenby would now be the junior partner, and it was my opinion that we must strengthen the Arab Regulars numerically before we engaged ourselves in so great a hazard. I suggested that we ask his father to transfer to Akaba the regular units at present working with the Emirs Ali and Abdulla in front of Medina. Their reinforcement, and the yield of our normal recruiting from Palestine and elsewhere, would raise us to ten thousand strong in uniformed men.

Ten thousand men would scare the Turks from ever attacking Aba el Lissan. We would then divide them into three parts. The immobile would constitute a retaining force to hold quiet the Maan garrison. An expedition of a thousand, on our new camels, would attack the Deraa-Damascus sector, with the help of Nuri Shaalan and the Druses, reviving the plan of a Hauran rising rejected by me out of nervousness in October 1917. The remainder would form a second expedition, of two or three thousand infantry, prepared to move into the Beni Sakhr country, and from Madeba to connect up with Allenby at Jericho.

This third detachment would secure us a permanent advance. The long-distance mounted raid, by taking Deraa or Damascus, would compel the Turks to withdraw from Palestine one division, and perhaps a second, to restore their communications, and to blockade us securely in Jebel Druse or Azrak, whichever was our base. By so weakening the army of Liman von Sanders, we would give Allenby the power to advance his whole line from Jordan to the sea — not indeed to Haifa and Damascus, as in the abandoned Smuts' Plan — but at any rate to Nablus.

The fall of Nabius would cut the lateral communication through Salt, which made the Turks strong in Moab. It would make Salt a dangerous salient for the enemy: and they would be compelled, probably without fighting, to fall back on Amman, yielding us quiet possession of Madeba and the Jordan bottom.

Practically I was proposing that we use up the Hauran Arabs to let us reach Jericho, half-way to our Damascus goal. It was an expensive plan therefore: but the alternative was stagnation for English and Arabs in their present lines throughout next winter. We on the Arab front had been exciting eastern Syria, since 1916, for a revolt near Damascus, and our material was now ready and afoot. To hold it still in that excited readiness during another year risked our over passing the crisis ineffectually.

The danger of the scheme was that we would sacrifice the Hauran, hoping to gain Moab: and that after all the Belga and Beni Sakhr Arabs would remain idle (fearing a third exhibition of levity and raid tactics on the British part) till the Turks had recovered their shaken balance on the Amman front. To gauge this danger I had gone up with Trad to the Madeba district, and had convinced myself that it still held enough fighting material willing to strike for us, if we showed our solemn intention by investing in their revolt a sufficient stake of our own. It was for that purpose I had suggested a powerful infantry column, two or three thousand of Jaafar's men, to open the Madeba operation.

Feisal fell in with my proposal, and gave me letters to his father advising it, while at the same time he warned me that the old man was now little inclined to take his advice, out of green-eyed hatred for this son who was doing too well, and who was being disproportionately helped by, and cordial towards, the British. Also he was not sure what his brothers would say: but I knew that Abdulla would let go his regulars cheerfully, if he could keep his Ateiba, while Ali was full of public spirit. So this second point did not weigh heavily.

For dealing with the King I relied on a joint pressure by Wingate and Allenby, the paymasters. They would see that Medina was effectively besieged by Feisal's force covering the Mudowwara gap, and that the desire of Ali and Abdulla to possess it was pure politics. Its twelve or fourteen thousand Turks were shut up there harmlessly, indeed beneficially, self-supporting. They only bothered us because we blindly paid one hundred thousand pounds a month for the tepid efforts of the brothers to reduce them.

I decided to go up to Egypt personally to put my point, and press for letters and decisions of the necessary stiffness, while imparting the new plan to Allenby for his co-operation. If I carried my argument, afterwards I would go down to Jidda with it, and force it past the King: and in anticipation of success Feisal took the preliminary steps to get ready the Beni Sakhr and Nuri Shaalan for main events in September.

In Cairo, Dawnay agreed both to the transfer of the southern regulars, and to the independent offensive in the autumn, near enough to the rains for them to check a Turkish pursuit in time, if our attacks miscarried. We went to Wingate, and argued it with him, and convinced him that the ideas were good. He wrote me letters to King Hussein, strongly advising the reinforcement of Feisal, but would not go farther. I pressed him to make clear to the King that we regarded the move as vital, and that the continuance of our war-subsidy to him would depend on his giving effect to our advice: but he refused to be stringent, and couched the letter in terms of a vague politeness, which would be lost on the hard and suspicious old man in Mecca.

None the less the effort promised so much for us that, on June the eighteenth, we went up to Allenby, to beg his help in stopping the campaign in Hejaz — a delicate interference, for that sphere was Wingate's command, and the funds for it came direct from the Foreign Office. As soon, however, as we reached G.H.Q., we felt a remarkable difference in its air. The place was throbbing with energy and hope, but there were logic and co-ordination manifest in an uncommon degree.

Allenby had a curious blindness of judgment in choosing men, due largely to his positive greatness, which made good qualities in his subordinates look superfluous: and so usually his Staff was a very mixed one. Now however, Cherwode, who had brought forward Guy Dawnay to take Jerusalem, had interposed again, setting up Bartholomew, his own Chief of Staff, in the third place in the hierarchy. Bartholomew, not made broadly like Dawnay, nor with so many foreign sides, was yet more intricate, yet more polished as a soldier, more careful and conscientious; and seemed friendlier as a team-leader.

We laid out before him our scheme to start the ball rolling in the autumn, hoping by our pushes to make it possible for them to come in later vigorously in our support. He listened smiling, and at the end said that we were three days too late in our coming: for their new army was arriving to time from Mesopotamia and India: prodigious advances in grouping and training were being made: all records were being broken in their speedy rush towards becoming an efficient and coherent whole. On June the fifteenth, at a private conference, it had been the considered opinion that in September the army would be capable of a general and sustained offensive.

The sky was indeed opening over us, as we went in together to Allenby, who said outright that he would make a grand attack late in September, to fulfill the Smuts' Plan even to Damascus and Aleppo. Our role would be as already laid down then in the spring: only that as there was no longer a Camel Brigade to lend us, we must make the Deraa raid with our own men, mounted on the two thousand new camels which were just ready to start for us. Times and details would be fixed as the weeks went on, and as Bartholomew's calculations of possibility took shape.

Our hopes of final victory had been too often dashed, however, for me to take this any longer as assured. So for a second string I got Allenby's blessing of the transfer of Ali's and Abdulla's khaki clad contingents, and set off, fortified, to Jidda, where I met no more success than I expected. The King had got wind of my purpose, and took refuge in the pretext of Ramadan in Mecca: and once more I noted the truth of Storrs' commendation to European diplomacy of the advantages of a capital inviolable and inaccessible on religious grounds. We talked on the telephone, King Hussein sheltering himself behind the incompetence of the operators in the Mecca exchange, whenever the subject turned dangerous. My mind was not in the mood for farce, so I rang off, put Feisal's and Wingate's letters back unopened into my bag, and returned to Cairo in the next ship.

BOOK IX

Balancing for a Last Effort

A Denby had so surpassed all hopes in his rapid embodiment of the new relieves and drafts that he was able, after all, to plan an autumn offensive.

The near balance of the forces on each side meant that victory would depend on his subtly deceiving the Turks into the opinion that their entire danger lay beyond Jordan.

To assist in this the Arabs would have to lie quiet for six weeks, with an apparent feebleness which should tempt the Turks to mass on that flank.

The Arabs were then to lead off at the critical moment, by cutting the railway communications with Palestine, and by raising a revolt in Hauran.

Such bluff within bluff called fir most accurate timing since either a premature Turkish retreat in Palestine, or their premature attack across Jordan, would have wrecked us.

Every Arab element and resource was already engaged, so for the danger interval we borrowed from Allenby some Imperial Camel Corps to lend extra color to our feigned intention.

They did their work perfectly: while our final preparations went forward with no more check than an untimely show of pique on the part of King Hussein.

Chapter 111: Allenby Revives

On July the eleventh Dawnay and I were in the G.H.Q., again talking to Allenby and Bartholomew, and, of their generosity and confidence, seeing the working — in undress — of a general's mind. It was an experience, technical, reassuring, and very valuable to me, for I was mildly a general too in my odd show over there.

Bartholomew was now fine in the saddle, but as accessible and helpful as ever. Of the professional soldiers I met, only him, Alan Dawnay, and Allenby felt sure enough of their principles to break them, in advising on our difficulties of irregular war.

Allenby's confidence was like a wall: he went to see his troops a few days before the attack, when they were massed in dead secrecy waiting their signal, and told them in his exhorting speech that he was sure, with their good help, of thirty thousand prisoners: this when the whole game turned on a chance Bartholomew was more anxious. He said it would be desperate work to have the army re-formed and ready by the middle of September, but then everyone was working desperately, and so perhaps they might make it.

Yet even if they were ready (and so near did they cut it that actually some brigades met for the first time as brigades in the front line as they went over), we must not assume that the attack would follow as planned. It could be delivered only in the coastal sector, opposite Ramleh, where lay railhead, and where only could the necessary reserve of stores be gathered.

This fact seemed to him so obvious that he could not dream of the Turks staying blind: though it was true that for the moment their dispositions ignored it. The two unlucky raids to Amman and Salt had had the unexpected benefit of fixing the Turks' eyes exclusively beyond Jordan. Their reserves of men and guns all lay about the river, and every move there whether of British or Arabs, was accompanied by meticulous counter-precautions on the Turks' part, showing how fearful they were for it. In the coast sector, the point of real danger, the enemy had absurdly few men.

Allenby's plan was to move the bulk of his infantry and all his cavalry gradually into concealed camps under the orange and olive groves of Ramleh and Lod, just before the nineteenth of September, the day provisionally fixed for the great attack. Simultaneously he hoped to make, in the Jordan Valley, such demonstrations as should persuade the Turks of a concentration there in progress. After the Meinertzhagen successes of Beersheba, deceptions, which for the ordinary general had been just witty hors d'euvres before battle, were for Allenby a main point of strategy: and this time they were to be carried out with spirit.

Bartholomew would send to the Jericho valley, and erect there, all the condemned tents from the base stores in Egypt; would transfer veterinary hospitals and sick lines into the places of the former mounted camp, would put up dummy camps, dummy horses and dummy troops wherever there was plausible room, would throw more bridges across the river, would collect on our bank and open against enemy country all the captured guns that were serviceable, and, on the right days, would ensure along the dusty roads such movements of non-combatant bodies as would give the impression of eleventh-hour concentrations for the assault.

These means might lead the Turks aside from seeing our true dispositions, for at the same time our Air Force was going to fill the air with husbanded formations of the latest and best machines. These would obtain a mastery complete enough to deprive the enemy for days of the advantage of air reconnaissance. He wished us to supplement his efforts by similar false activities, carried out with all vigor and ingenuity, from our side of Amman.

Yet he warned us that even with this, the success of the operations would hang on a thread, since if the Turks by using their senses caught wind of the coming attack, or had an efficient spy, they could save themselves and their army, and give us our concentration to do over again, by the simple means of retiring their coast sector seven or eight miles towards Tul Keram, into the strong position which they had already outlined there in the hills.

The British Army would then be like a fish flapping on dry land, with its railways, its heavy artillery, its dumps, its stores, its camps all misplaced: and with no olive groves forward for them to hide in next time. We should be absolutely ruined, and it would be criminally or lunatic incompetent if the enemy did not see this in the next two months. So, while he guaranteed that the British were doing and would do their utmost, yet he implored us not to engage ourselves in a position from which we could not escape, relying on their sweeping success.

This success, if things did go well, and the British preparations were complete by the appointed date and the Turks remained bending, would be glorious. Allenby meant to break through by the coast, and to pour his mounted troops through in columns of divisions as fast as was possible, with objective Messudiyeh, and with the further hope that the defeat of the Turks would be so utter that Nablus would easily fall, and the British infantry have still energy in hand to go further. Bois had an obsession of Haifa: but Bartholomew laid more weight on Galilee, and would prevail, for Bois was to take leave while the plan was working out, Sir Walter Campbell was also to take leave, and Bartholomew and Evans, their deputies, would rearrange the army transport, independently of formations, with such elasticity that a pursuit could be sustained to any extent, and in the direction most in harmony with the conceptions of the General Staff.

The noble prospect sent Dawnay and myself back to Cairo in great fettle and cogitation. We were going to have a busy autumn, and since the two years' irregular work had used up some of my personal elasticity, I aimed at twelve days' rest in Cairo before setting out to Akaba for the final occasion: — and got the twelve days, but it was not all rest.

News from Akaba raised again the question of our liability for the siege of Maan, or rather our need to retain Aba el Lissan in face of the Turk intention to relieve Maan, and drive us down again into Guweira. In the last four days they had turned Nasir out of Hesa, and were contemplating a stroke against Mirzuk's subsidiary flying force which was active near Kerak. When they were rid of him they would move the decent forces they had now succeeded in collecting at Katraneh, Jurf and Aneyza, first to Tafileh , then to Shobek, and lastly to Odroh, for Waheida and Aba el Lissan.

They hoped for this about the end of August; but then our Deraa detachment should start off, so that unless we could further delay the Turks their threat might cripple us. We could not ask help of Allenby, who had his hands full till the nineteenth of September. The little ship of our war tacked about among these adverse winds, while we, the quartermasters, tried to keep clear in our minds our three duties, the first to hold tightly to our place on the plateau; the second, if we lost it, to keep the Medina railway yet cut; the third, not even for duty the first nor for duty the second to do anything to harm or hinder the expedition to Deraa which would end the war: an expedition planned and ready for months, which could be carried out as quickly as thought, so soon as the two thousand camels (arrived in Akaba on July the twelfth) were tempered to the skill of grazing.

We saw there was no harm in the Turks taking Tafileh, or even Aba el Lissan, after the Deraa expedition had well started, since it would be self-contained, and its success in the north would leave a more powerful enemy all the more bogged in the south. Yet the secrecy of Allenby's intention to attack on September the nineteenth forbade us to inform the Arab Army of the reasons for our confidence in marching off to Deraa at the end of August: and they might refuse to go, if a heavy Turkish threat was just then developing against their base. We must find some way to delay the Turks another fortnight.

At this juncture Dawnay was inspired to think of the surviving battalion of the Imperial Camel Corps which had been kept for patrol duties in Sinai. Perhaps G.H.Q. might lend us some of it, to confuse the Turks' reckoning by the sudden appearance of a new factor. We telephoned to Bartholomew, who instantly understood, and backed our request to Bois in Alexandria, and to

Allenby, with himself after an active telegraphing we got our way, and Colonel Buxton, with three hundred men, was lent to us for a month on two conditions: the first that we should forthwith furnish their scheme of operations, the second that they should have no casualties.

Bartholomew felt it necessary to apologies for the last condition, which he thought unsolder like but it confirmed my most honorable opinion of his brains and character, and I wished that all generals similarly distinguished the value in lives of essential and nonessential operations. As for the scheme, Dawnay went unlimited bail for the virtue and understanding of Buxton, so we sat down with a map, and measured that they should march from the Canal to Akaba, thence by Rum to carry Mudowwara by night attack, to Jefer, to Bair, to Kissir by Amman, to destroy the bridge and tunnel which Shea had left unhurt in March.

They must be back in Palestine as potential drafts for reinforcement on August the thirtieth, so we would bring them back from Kissir by Tafileh and Beersheba, after a busy and profitable month; for the fall of Mudowwara would seal the fate of Medina, and the destruction of the Amman bridge would put the Katraneh Turks out of action for three weeks. They would give us a peaceful August, in which our two thousand new camels would learn to graze, while putting out, if necessary, the extra dumps of forage and food which Buxton's force would expect at Rum, Jefer and Bair.

We had, unfortunately, to make these changes and additions ourselves, on the spur of the moment, without consulting Joyce and Young in Aba el Lissan, for our only touch with them was by wireless, and our cipher was a systematic one, which the Turks could puzzle out, and by which in consequence only false or routine news was passed: and just now Joyce and Young were far out of touch with developments.

As Dawnay and I were working out our new schemes there came to us by post from Akaba a most elaborate plan, worked out graphically by Young for Joyce, on our June understanding, for the independent Arab operations in Hauran and Belga. They had figured out the food and ammunition, supplies and forage, and transport for two thousand men of all ranks, to go from Aba el Lissan by Bair and Azrak to Deraa. They had taken into consideration all our pack animals, and worked out schedules, by which the dumps would be complete and the attack might begin in November.

Even had Allenby not pulled his army together this scheme would have broken down intrinsically. It depended on the immediate reinforcement of the Arab Army at Aba el Lissan, since we had lost many killed in action, and more had died, with cholera, typhus, typhoid, smallpox, recurrent fever and malignant malaria (which last, though in itself hardly a main disease, would break down one already enfeebled by privation or other illness), but our hopes of help had passed when King Hussein refused to meet me in Jidda: while November was too nearly winter in Hauran, when the first rains would make those muddy lands impossible for camels. To reach Azrak we must be on camels; to operate against Deraa in wet weather we must have horses, and we could not get so many in the time, or feed them if we got them.

Weather and strengths however, might be matters of opinion: while it was incontestable that the extrinsic factor of Allenby's wish put this November scheme out of the running. Allenby meant to attack on the nineteenth of September and wanted us to lead off not more than four nor less than two days before he did: so that our threat would be mature enough to unsettle the Turks, but not enough to have made them already fall back on the coast to Tul Keram. For the same reason preparation at Azrak on a great scale, weeks before we moved would not be wise.

The Chiefs words to us were that three men and a boy with pistols in front of Deraa on September the sixteenth would fill his conception: would be better than thousands a week before or a week after. A week too later — and we would have left the whole weight of the opening move on his burdened troops.

A week too soon and our cutting the line might compel that hand-to-mouth army which was the Turkish, to begin its retreat. The truth was he cared nothing for our fighting power, and did not reckon us as part of his tactical strength except in talk with me, and that to keep up my spirits. In his eyes our purpose was moral psychological, diathesis: to keep the enemy command intent on their trans-Jordan front: and any fighting we did beyond this, our business, was compound or unearned profit. In my English capacity I shared this view of Allenby's: but on my Arab side both agitation and battle seemed equally important, the one to serve the joint success, the other to establish Arab self-respect, without which victory would be unwholesome.

So, unhesitatingly, we laid the Young scheme aside and turned to build up our own. To reach Deraa by Azrak, our leaping-off place from Aba el Lissan, would take a fortnight: the cutting the three railways in Hauran and withdrawal to re-form in the desert, another week. Our raid must carry all its maintenance for three weeks. The picture of what this meant was in my head — we had been doing such raids for two years — and so at once I gave Dawnay my estimate that our two thousand camels, in a single convoy without advanced depots or supplementary supply columns, would suffice five hundred regular mounted infantry, the battery of French quick-firing .65 mountain guns, proportionate machine-guns, two armored cars sappers, camel-scouts and two airplanes until we had fulfilled our mission.

This was a liberal reading of Allenby's minimum three men and a boy: as a self-contained force it would be quick, intangible elastic and punctual and would leave no reasonable doubt of our keeping time and schedule. So we told Bartholomew our intentions and received G.H.Q. blessing on them. At the same time we drew from him twenty Hotchkiss automatic guns so that our mobile firepower might be in excess proportion to our number for our ambitions were to play a real part in this smashing-campaign coming. We could think of nothing else technical or general needed to improve our force.

Chapter 112: Resentment in Akaba

On July the twenty-eighth I was in Akaba, and at once went up to Aba el Lissan to tell Joyce and Young of the complete change which had just come over our situation. It was not a pleasing mission for to begin I had to say that their great scheme the fruit of such pains was torn up. Young had an orderly pragmatic mind logical in method mathematical in synthesis. His calculations had been worked out to an ounce providing food and water ammunition or forage or petrol for each man each animal each gun each car in the expedition. Forward dumps were to be put in and the operation would have gone as solemnly and as respectably as a British operation.

I did not say that it was top-heavy and too late: I threw the onus of change on Allenby's recovery. My new proposal — for which I had pledged their performance in advance — was an intricate dovetailing in the next crowded month and a half, of a British Camel Corps subsidiary raid and of a main raid in character rapid and self-contained to fall suddenly on the Turks by Deraa, and away again as suddenly.

Joyce felt that to introduce foreigners would unsettle and unman the Arabs (an untimely victory of my principles so preached from Yenbo) and that to let them go a month later would have an even worse impression. Young returned at once a stubborn combative July Resentment in Akaba 'impossible' to the scheme. The Camel Corps raid would engross the baggage camels, which might have enabled the Deraa force to reach its goal, and by trying to do two things I would end up in doing neither. I argued my case, and we had a battle.

In the first place I tackled Joyce concerning the Imperial Camel Corps and showed that I had no intention of letting these three hundred British act either with Bedouin or with Arab Regulars. On abundant experience I disapproved the using of mixed forces which laid the road open to many jealousies and a possible lowering of either British or Arab self-esteem. On their day and place the Arabs would fight splendidly, with more fire and speed than the British but with so much less persistence that the British would win on time. Each would look poor in the other's conditions and by avoiding too close comparison we avoided the risk of giving birth to either calumny.

Our promise, that there should be no casualties limited us to a night attack against an unsuspecting post, and the Mudowwara effort seemed to me the most profitable we could so undertake. For over a year we had been trying to destroy the Mudowwara well, to put beyond question or relief our stranglehold on the Medina army. The Camel Corps would arrive one morning at Akaba — no Arab suspecting them — and would vanish equally suddenly towards Rum. Their carrying the station was an easy certainty if their coming was secret, for Marshall's expedition against it during my absence at Jidda had proved that the Turks in the southern area were certainly less efficient than those in the north.

Marshall's had been the sad case of an excellent effort which ill-luck deprived of a double success. After consultation and reconnaissance he had begun against Hallat Ammar, the station which had beaten up Zaal and myself while we waited for the first mined train the year before: and so splendidly did he bring up his Beni Atiyeh, under the voluble Sheikh Motlog, that they had charged in and taken the station before the artillery preparation was complete. They captured seventy prisoners and much spoil.

The second stage of the plan had been to turn north against Mudowwara, now cut off from succor: but the too-pleased Arabs began instead to talk of going south towards Dhat el Haj, a larger operation but of no strategic value. Thinking round all sides of this new idea gave them time to realize their four killed and twenty wounded heavy losses in an irregular force. The reaction of victory set in and the booty was dragging man after man home to put it in safety. So they lost keenness and finally fell back on Rum, when, had they only known it, Mudowwara with its invaluable water supply lay empty to them. Its garrison, terrified at the firing and demolition just to their south, had buried their guns and fled up the ruined line, hoping forlornly to cross the dry eighty miles to Maan before the Arabs heard. The Howeitat cut up and captured most of them, but before news reached Rum, Fakhri had sent a relief train up from Tebuk and reoccupied Hallat Ammar and Mudowwara. It was an opportunity missed, except in so far as it showed us the deplorable morale of the isolated Turks in Hejaz.

Joyce was disarmed by these reasoning. I went on to show that from Mudowwara, Buxton's force would go through Jefer and Bair to Kissir. In other words their march would be in the desert, far from the sight of the Arab Army, and from the hearing of the villages. My object was to make the reports of them to the Turks so vague and contradictory that the enemy intelligence officers would conclude that the whole of the defunct Camel Brigade (which for two months they had been unable to place in Allenby's *ordre de hataile* was now on Feisal's front.

Such an accession of shock strength to Feisal would make them very tender of the safety of their railway and posts between Amman and Maan: while Buxton's appearance at Kissir, apparently on preliminary reconnaissance, would cause our wildest tales of our intention shortly to attack Amman to be believed. Joyce now understood my motives, and backed them with his favorable opinion. We concerted to send out, as soon as Mudowwara was taken, through my private means, such skilfully-colored reports of the Camel Corps ' strength and purpose, as should with good reason deceive the Turk.

For Young's transport troubles I had little sympathy to spare. It was a fixed mood of quartermasters to find difficult anything unusual: and Young was zealous for his office. He, a newcomer, said it was impossible to do all I wished — but I had done these things occasionally, without half his ability and concentration, and knew that they were not even difficult, unless the habit had been formed of thinking the daily rations an obligation, and not merely a desirable meal. In the British Army, too-regular transport had by sanction of time made food an expected routine. In the Arab Army it was not such a liability. The men expected to go hungry as often as not.

For the Camel Corps I left him alone to grapple with the weights and timetables, since the British Army was his profession: and though he would not promise anything (except that it would not be done), done of course it was, and two or three days before the necessary time. The Deraa raid was a different proposition, and there we took his figures, adjusted to our new numbers, and point by point I disputed his conception of the force and its necessary equipment.

I crossed out forage for the camels, after Bair. Young became ironic upon the patient endurance of camels: but the animals on July the twelfth had reached the Jazi pastures, and were learning by hunger to eat thorns and weeds. We were ruling them very moderate marches (twelve days to Azrak for the force), and such they could well do on what they picked up after Bair. To Bair the desert was barren, for the southern rains had failed: but in the Azrak-Deraa region this year the pasture was called grand by every one of the dozens of Bedouin I questioned, and by my own men whom I had sent up specially to report.

That saved the heaviest item of our load. From the men's food I cut off the provision for the duration of the second attack on the railway, and for the return journey. Young supposed aloud that the men would fight well hungry. I explained elaborately, as to a child, that we would live on the country. Young thought it poor country to live on. I called it very good.

He said that the ten days' march home after the attacks would be a long fast: but I had no intention of coming back to Akaba. Then he would be glad to know, just for his own account, whether it was certain defeat or certain victory which was in my mind? And when I said that we would win, he replied that of course he hoped so. I pointed out how, even if we retired, each man had a camel under him, and if we killed only six camels a day the whole force would feed abundantly on meat. Yet even this did not solace him.

I went on to cut down his ammunition, and the petrol, and the number of cars, and everything else, to the exact point which would meet the precise operations we planned , and reminded him of our motto for the Akaba base, 'No margins'. In riposte he became aggressively regular, and I further infuriated him by prosing forth on my old theorem that it was the irregularity that mirror of the real mind of the Arab Movement, which made it formidable. We lived by our raggedness, and beat the Turks by our uncertainty. If we became calculable we would gain in comfort, for ourselves and the British Staff, but would lose in weight and efficiency, since by subjecting ourselves to rule we would put in motion the numerical factor in our regard, and make our strength not more than a like strength of regulars.

The Turkish Staff not in the least afraid of enemy soldiers stood helpless before a rebellion: and by being familiar enough to confound ourselves with peasantry or tribes we made them think each such civilian a hypothetically to ourselves and a potential enemy for them. The Arab Regulars fought far better than the Bedouin and villagers: but it was these, and not the troops, who would win the war since our victory was expressed in territories occupied, not in battles gained or losses inflicted. Young's scheme was faulty because it showed a precise mind.

Instead we would march a camel column of one thousand men to Azrak, where their concentration must be complete on September the thirteenth. On the sixteenth we would envelop Deraa, and cut its railways, south , north and west, and isolate it, if we did not capture it. We would two days later fall back east of the Hejaz Railway and wait events ready to come forward at once if things went well with Allenby, or to establish ourselves in Jebel Druse or in the Arab villages, or at Azrak, if things dragged. As reserve against accident we would purchase barley in Jebel Druse, carry it to Azrak by hire and store it there for our use. To support and screen the expedition Nuri Shaalan would accompany us with a contingent of Rualla: also the Serdiyeh, Serahin, and Haurani peasants of the Hollow Land under Taiai el Hareidhin.

Young thought it a deplorable adventure and would not see the bearing it might have on Allenby's campaign, though I took both him and Joyce fully into the confidence of G.H.Q. Joyce who had loved our dog-fight in conference, was game to try, though doubting that it was ambitious, too difficult, and too elaborate for the short time available. However, I knew that both would do their best. July Resentment in Akaba now the thing was settled: and the organization would not be really difficult especially as Dawnay had procured from G.H.Q, for us Major Stirling a skilled Staff Officer, emollient and wise, to strengthen our local resources. Stirling spoke Arabic, and his passion for horses was a passport to intimacy with Feisal and the chiefs.

Among the Arab officers we distributed some British military decorations tokens of our having noticed their gallantry about Maan and in railway enterprises. Specially to Jaafar Pasha, the Arab Commander-in-Chief, fell a deserved C.M.G. Allenby called him to his headquarters in Palestine, and invested him personally, providing with rare humor a guard of honor from the same Yeomanry who had gained for themselves great credit in 1916 on the Senussi front, for galloping down the same Jaafar Pasha and taking him prisoner! Jaafar's great body shook with pleasure at the jest. These marks of Allenby's esteem heartened the Arab Army, with the conviction that they were truly playing a recognized and established part in the general war: and they put themselves with renewed vigor to ensure our plans as hotly as possible.

Nuri Pasha Said decided himself to command the Deraa expedition, for which his courage authority and coolness marked him as the ideal leader. He began to pick for it the best four hundred men in the Army, eliminating from Mauled's Hashimite Regiment which was the nucleus, those in whom their fellows had detected a failure to respond to the high sense of duty which the freedom of irregular service demanded for success. This was to us the profit of experience which made a bad man worse, and so rid us of him. Maulud was still in hospital in Egypt, slowly recovering. However, Tahsin was qualified to take his place, and with Nuri he overhauled the equipment and tested the officers and the technical units marked for the expedition.

Pisani, the French commandant, fortified by a Military Cross and urgent in pursuit of a hinted D.S.O., took bodily possession of the four Schneider mountain guns which Cousse had sent down to us after Bremond went, and spent agonized hours with Young, trying to put all his scheduled ammunition, and his mule-forage, and his men and his own private kitchen on to one-half the necessary camels. The camps buzzed with eagerness and preparation and all promised well.

Our own family rifts were distressing, but inevitable, and I discounted them. The Arab affair was now too considerable, and our rough and ready help organization which had grown up with it no longer met its needs. If the war lasted we would have to put straight ourselves by reorganizing on a different and larger basis, mechanical rather than personal. But the next was probably the last act, and by a little patience and ignoring of faults, we might make our present resources serve our turn.

The troubles were only between ourselves and there, thanks to the magnificent unselfishness and patience of Joyce, our commandant, lay enough of team-spirit to carry us to our goal. There was no earthly fear of a complete breakdown between us, however high-handed I might be... and I had a reserve of confidence to carry the whole thing, if need be, on my shoulders. They used to think me boastful when I said I could do such and such; but I never pretended to do it well — probably not so well as half those who heard me — it was only that I was willing to try.

My confidence was not so much ability to do perfectly, as a preference to botch it somehow rather than let it go by default of these brusher's of gentlemen's clothes. In case of need any man could do anything, except a work of art: and here I felt all-powerful since the Arab weapon had been tempering in my workshop for two years to this very effort. I trusted it to the limits of its nature, and knew it through and through: and the Arabs in return had a tradition of trust in me by which all went easily, without conscious strain or effort on my part.

Chapter 113: Buxton Begins Work

It was now the end of July, and by the end of August the Deraa expedition must be on the road. In the meantime Buxton's Camel Corps had to be guided through their program, Nuri Shaalan had to be warned and brought to agreement the armored cars must have their road broken to Azrak, and landing-grounds be found for our airplanes. Obviously it would be a busy month, and I must make a careful allotment of my time.

The Nuri Shaalan part, as the furthest, was tackled first. He was called to meet Feisal at Jefer about the seventh of August. We had long ago concluded our exact understanding with him, so merely we had to signify that now we were ready to pay the agreed price.

Buxton's force seemed the second need. They would arrive at Akaba on August the first. I went to Feisal, told him, under seal, of their coming, and of my plan to finish off Mudowwara with them as insurance against the very worst. He welcomed the idea, and suggested Hazaa as their best Sherifian second for the operation. As their arrival must strike Mudowwara with absolute surprise (to ensure their having no casualties), we decided that Hazaa should go to Rum with secret orders, to wait at the supply dump of five days' British rations which Young had put in there.

Hazaa's men were Arnran Arabs — but Mudowwara was Beni Atiyeh. So Feisal sent me Motlog ibn Jemiaan and Aid ibn Benaiyan, the two chiefs of the northern sections of the tribe as additional sponsors. They also would wait for me in Rum, for I had determined to guide Buxton so far myself. The first marches through the fag-ends of the Howeitat about Akaba were the most critical and I was nervous lest some unfortunate mischance occur.

Accordingly I went down to Akaba, where Buxton let me talk to the men of each company, and explain to them the hard conditions of their march, and the odd impatient nature of the allies whom they, unasked, had come to help, begging them to turn the other cheek if there was a row: partly because they were better educated than the Arabs, and therefore less prejudiced: partly because they were much fewer.

The program we had laid down for them, with the help of their officers, was one of which the British authorities thought them incapable. We wanted them to march nearly a thousand miles, in little more than a month, doing nearly twice the set daily march for the Camel Brigade, through desert country, on short rations for man and beast, with two intricate night attacks on Turkish posts thrown in. A breakdown of march-times would involve the unit in either thirst or starvation (or probably in both), while if they wore out their camels by too great effort or by careless riding, they would be stranded beyond succor in the desert.

After such solemnities came the ride up the oppressive gorge of Itm, and then by its right-hand branch through that slow preparation for the greatness of Rum — under the red cliffs of Nejd and over the breast-like curves of Imran — till they passed through the gap before the face of Khuzail, and into the inner shrine of the springs, with their worship-compelling coolness. There the landscape would not be accessory: but took the skies, and we chattering humans became dust at its feet.

The Howeitat there and on the road were too puzzled to know whence this white army had sprung, and whither it was going, actively to resent its unnecessary presence in their district.

I gave them all manner of vague replies, to keep rumor tossing back and forth among the tents, rather than running abroad to Tebuk, where the sons of Harb would have warned the enemy (for Mudowwara) of us.

In Rum the men had their first experience of watering in equality at an Arab watering place: and found it troublesome. The Beni Atiyeh were bringing some thousand camels to the four springs each day: and our four hundred in one drove made only a supplement on the blocked paths, which ran three hundred feet above the valley bottom, on their glorious shelf Some of the Egyptian camels were unused to mountain climbing, and delayed us, and all of them were clipped for mange, which frightened the Arabs, and made them feel us ill neighbors.

However, the men were wonderfully mild, and Buxton was an old Sudan official, speaking Arabic, and understanding Arab ways, very patient, good-humored, and sympathetic. Thanks to his diplomacy, and to the care of the rank and file, nothing untoward happened. Hazaa was helpful in admonishing the Arabs, and Stirling and Marshall, who both accompanied the column, were familiars of the Beni Atiyeh, and heard all their complaints. Aid ibn Benaiyan withdrew when he saw the alien nature of our force, but the energetic Motlog said he would ride with us, to Mudowwara or further.

I stayed at Rum with the Camel Corps for the first day, feeling the unreality there of these healthy-looking tummies, like stiff bodied schoolboys in their shirts and shorts, seeing them wander about the cliffs of Rum (which had been my private resort), anonymous and irresponsible, not knowing the privilege it was which their self-sacrifice had won them, of being able to visit and remember such a place.

Three years of Egypt and Sinai had burned all the color out of their faces to a deep brown — in which their blue eyes flickered weakly like sky-gaps, against the dark possessed gaze of my men. For the rest they were a broad-faced, low-browed people, blunt featured beside the decadent Arabs, whose fine-curved shapes had been sharpened by generations of breeding to a radiance ages older than these primitive blotched honest Englishmen. Continental soldiers looked lumpish beside our lean-bred fellows: but against my supple Nejdis the British in their turn looked lumpish.

Late the next day I left them, and rode for Akaba, passing again through the high-walled Itm, but now alone with my silent unquestioning fellows, who rode after me like shadows, harmonious and submerged in their natural sand and bush and hill; and a home-sickness came over me, reminding me vividly of my outcast life among these Arabs, exploiting their highest ideals, and making their love of freedom one more tool to help us win England the victory over her enemies.

It was evening, and the low sun was falling on the straight bar of Sinai ahead, its globe extravagantly brilliant in my eyes, because I was dead-tired of life, longing as seldom before for the peaceful moody sky in England. This sunset was fierce, stimulant, barbaric. Its intense glow revived the colors of the desert like a draught as indeed it did each evening, yet seeming ever a new miracle of strength and heat —

while my longings were for weakness and chill, and grey mistiness: that I might not be so crystalline clear, so sure of the wrong which I was doing.

We English, who lived years abroad among strangers, went always dressed in the pride of our remembered country, that strange entity impossible to rationalize or explain, but which had no part with the inhabitants, for those who loved England most, often liked Englishmen least. We idealized our country, so highly that when we returned, sometimes the reality fell too short of our dreams to be tolerable. When away, we were worth more than other men by our conviction that she was greatest, straightest and best of all the countries of the world, and we would die before knowing that a page of her history had been blotted by defeat. Here, in Arabia, in the war's need, I was selling my honesty for her sustenance, unquestioningly.

In Akaba my bodyguard was assembled, prepared for a long march, for I had promised my Hauran men that they should pass the great feast this year in their freed villages: and the date was near. So for the last time we mustered on the windy beach by the sea's edge, the sun on its brilliant waves glinting in rivalry with my flashing and changing men. They were sixty, and together we rode out of Akaba, and into the brown hills, for Guweira. Seldom had the Zaagi collected so many of his troops together, and he was busy sorting them in Ageyl fashion, center and wings, with a poet on the right and a poet on the left, among the best singers. So that our ride was musical. It hurt him that I would not have a banner, like a prince.

I was on my Ghazala, the old grandmother-camel, now again magnificently fit, though her baby had lately died and her milk was dried up. Abdulla, who rode next to me, had skinned the little carcass, and carried the dry pelt behind his saddle, like a crupper piece. We started well, thanks to the Zaagi's chanting, but after an hour or two, when we were again in Wadi Itm, the Ghazala lifted her head high, and began to pace slowly and uneasily, picking up her feet like a sword-dancer.

I tried to urge her: but Abdulla dashed up alongside me, swept his cloak about him, and sprang from his saddle, holding the calves skin in his hand. He lighted with a splash of gravel in front of my camel, which had come to a standstill, gently moaning. On the ground before her he spread the little hide, and drew her head down to it. She stopped crying, and snuffled with lips up and down its dryness, three or four times: then again lifted her head and, whimpering once, strode forward, as firmly as ever. Several times in the day this happened: but afterwards she seemed to forget.

At Guweira Siddons had an airplane waiting for me, as Nuri Shaalan and Feisal wanted me at once in Jefer. So I had my last flight in a B.E.2e, over the crest of Shtar. The air was thin and bumpy, so that we hardly scraped over the hilltop, and I sat in front wondering if we would crash, almost hoping it. I felt sure that Nuri wanted me for the dishonorable half-bargain understood between us, and the execution seemed more impure than the thought of it, and death in the air a short way out.

Yet I scarcely hoped it, not from fear, for only a deep man could grow deep fear, and I was too tired to be very much afraid: nor from scruple, for our lives had seemed to me the only things absolutely our own for us to keep or give away at will: but from habit, for lately I had risked myself only when it seemed profitable to the Arab cause, and this rule tore to pieces my instinct to end life now.

I was busied compartmenting-up my mind, finding instinct and reason as ever at strong war. Instinct said 'kill', but reason said that was only to cut the mind's tether, and loose it into freedom : better to seek some mental death, a slow wasting of the brain to sink it below these puzzlements, An accident would be more regretted than a deliberate fault: and if I did not hesitate to risk my life, why fuss to dirty it? yet life and honor seemed in different categories, not able to be sold for one another: and, for honor, had I not sold that a year ago, when for the best motive I assured the Arabs that England always kept her plighted world or was it like the Sibyl's Book, the more that was lost, the more precious the little that was left its part equal to the whole.

My self-secrecy had left me no arbiter of my responsibility. Mind-hunger could be allayed by drawing from others that converse and friction of ideas to light up our darkness: or by seeking within, where we could meet some needs by introspection, feeding upon ourselves, and even more, upon our bodies, drawing a perfect nourishment from all our pains, which became so many satisfactions to the mind looking inward. My trouble was a debauch of physical work, yet leaving a craving for it, while this everlasting doubt, and the questioning, bound my mind up in a giddy spiral, and left me never space for my own thinking.

Chapter 114: The Rualla

So we came at last, alive, to Jefer, where met us Feisal and Nuri in the smoothest spirits, with all arranged between them, and no mention of my price. The only need was to discuss last things, whether he should meet us in Azrak on the day of the new moon, or if I should meet him in the Blaidat and we go to Azrak together. It seemed incredible news that this old man had ungrudgingly joined himself to our youth: for he was very old, livid and worn, with a grey sorrow and remorse about him, and a bitter smile the only mobility of his face. Over his coarse eyelashes the eyelids wrinkled down, sagging in tired folds, through which, from the overhead sun, a red light glittered into his eyes and made them look like fiery pits in which the man was slowly burning. His hair and beard were dyed a vigorous black, and only the dead skin of the face, and the net of lines over it, betrayed his seventy years.

There was great talk about this dark little-spoken old leader, for with him were the head men of his tribe, famous sheikhs so bodied out with silks of their own wearing, or of Feisal's gift, that they rustled pettily while moving in state, like heifers. First of them was Faris, like Hamlet not forgiving Nuri his murdered father, Sotham: a lean man with drooping mustache, and white, unnatural face, who met the hidden censure of the world with a soft manner and luscious deprecating voice. 'Yifham', he squeaked of me in astonishment. 'He understands our Arabic' Trad was there, round-eyed, grave and direct-spoken, a chivalrous figure of a man, and their great leader of cavalry. Also Mijhem the rebellious had been brought in by Feisal, and reconciled with his unwilling uncle, who seemed only half to tolerate his small-featured bleak presence beside him, though Mijhem's manner was eagerly friendly: so eager that perhaps it disquieted his uncle's dourness, for Nuri was of all Arab chiefs the most masterful.

Mijhem was a great leader too, Trad's rival in the conduct of raids, but weak and cruel at heart. He sat next Khalid, Trad's brother, another healthy, cheerful rider, like

Trad in face, but not so full a man. Durzi ibn Dughmi swelled in and welcomed me, reminding me ungratefully of his greediness at Nebk: a one-eyed, sinister, hook nosed man, heavy built, menacing and mean, but brave. There was the Khaffaji, the spoilt child of Nuri's age; he looked for equality of friendliness from me, because of his father, and not for any promise in himself: but was young enough to be glad of the looming adventure of war.

Bender, the laughing boy, fellow in years and play with the Khaffaji, tripped me before them all by begging loudly for a place in my bodyguard. He had heard from my Rahail, his foster-brother, wild tales of their immoderate grieves and joys, and such servitude called to him with its unwholesome glamor. I fenced, and when he pleaded further, turned it by muttering that I was not a King to have Shaalan servants. Nuri's somber eye met mine for a moment, in tacit approval of my escape from the dilemma.

Behind me sat Rahail, very proud today, decked like a peacock, displaying his attractiveness by twisting his lusty self sinuously within his clothes. Under cover of the conversation he whispered to me the name of each chief, and thanks to him these and many more became known to me, less exhaustingly than usual. Of course I had learned their histories and families long ago, in readiness for a sudden campaign with them, and so was able, though an interloper, to thrust myself with dignity among such men of worship, without slighting any chance-met warrior by an ignorance of his standing in the scanty desert.

In return, they had not to ask who I was. My clothes and appearance saw to that for they were not disguise but not orient in the desert, and made me free of it. It was fame to be the only clean-shaven one, and I doubled it by wearing always the forbidden pure white silk, of the whitest (at least outside), with a gold and crimson Meccan head rope, and gold dagger. They were made in the fashion of the Sherifs, and by so dressing myself I marked my difference from the ordinary British officer in khaki, and staked a claim, which Feisal's public consideration of me confirmed, to my sweeping profit in quickly attaining weight and position among the tribes.

Many times in such councils had Feisal won over and set aflame new tribes, many times had the work fallen to me: but never until today had we been actively together in one company, reinforcing and relaying one another, from our opposite poles: and the work went like child's play: the Rualla melted in our double heat. We could move them with a touch, and a word. There was tenseness, a holding of breath, the glitter of belief in their thin eyes so fixed on us.

We brought nationality to their minds in a phrase, which set them thinking of Arab history and language: and then dropped into silence for a moment: for with these illiterate masters of the tongue, words were lively and they liked to savor each, unmingled, on the palate. Another phrase showed them the spirit of Feisal, their fellow and leader, sacrificing everything for the national freedom; and then silence again while they imagined him day and night in his tent, teaching, preaching, ordering, and making friends: and they felt something of the idea behind this pictured man, sitting there ironically, drained of desires, ambitions, weaknesses, faults; so rich a personality enslaved by an abstraction, made one-eyed, one-armed, with one sense and one purpose, only to live or die in its service.

Of course it was a picture-man, not of flesh and blood, but nevertheless true, for his individuality had proved weaker than the idea, weighed against which the wealth and artifices of the world had seemed less worthwhile. Feisal was hidden in his tent, veiled to remain a prophet, to keep alive the fiction of his leadership: while in reality he was nationality's best servant, our tool instead of our owner. None but a poor creature would have so yielded wholly to one notion, lost his third dimension, become a man, not an officer, a worker, not a master. Yet in the tented twilight nothing seemed nobler.

We went on to conjure up for them the enemy, dropping our tone between the heights, carrying their spirits from crest to crest, by hollow troughs of easy things, by commonplaces, by gentle laughs: since a continued height would be too smooth a plane for the quickening of these minds of clay. So the war became for our argument a half-jest, with the enemy girt round by ominous silence, on the eternal defensive, that hardest and most thankless war, whose best end was to have done no more than the necessary. While we were defended by this friendly silence, and swam calmly and coolly in it, till pleased to come ashore.

Our conversation was a shower of sparks, cunningly directed to set light to trains of their buried thoughts till the hidden charges set going their minds: that the excitement might be their own and the conclusions native, not inserted by us. Soon we felt them kindle, and leaned back, watching them move and speak, and vivify each other with mutual heat, till the air was vibrant, and in stammered phrases they expressed things greater than they could outline in form, experienced the first heave and thrust of notions which rose up beyond their sight. They turned to hurry us forward, felt themselves the begetters, and us laggard strangers in the gate, strove to make us comprehend the full intensity of their belief, forgot us, flashed out the means and end of our desire. A new tribe was added to our comity: though Nuri's plain, 'Yes', at the end carried more in it than all we had said.

In our preaching there was nothing merely nervous. Revolts had been begun so often out of plain vexation and we felt this undignified treatment of a great subject. We did our best to exclude the senses to appeal to mind to men's wit and instinct that their support might be slow, durable, unsentimental: and we were dealing with one of the shallowest and least patient races of mankind, a point which increased ten-fold our need of restraint.

We wanted no rice-converts and persistently refused to make our abundant and famous gold bring over those not spiritually convinced. The money was a confirmation: mortar not building stone. To have bought men would have been quick and cheap, and nasty; would have put our movement on the base of interest, a vulgar stump. Our followers must be ready to go all the way, without other mixture in their motives than human weakness. Even I the stranger the godless fraud inspiring an alien nationality felt a delivery from the hatred and eternal questioning of self in my imitation of their complete bondage to the idea: and for one to be comfortably surrendered others must surrender too.

A difficulty for me was the lack of instinct in my own performance. I could not for long deceive myself, and my eyes would open: but still my part was worked out so flippantly that none but Joyce and Nesib and Mohammed el Dheilan seemed to know

I was acting. To man-instinctive, anything believed by two or three had a miraculous sanction to which their individual ease and life might honestly be sacrificed. To man-rational, wars of nationality were as much a cheat as religious wars, and nothing was worth fighting for: while life was so deliberately private that no circumstances could justify one laying violent hands upon another's though a man's own death was his last free-will a saving grace and measure of intolerable pain; and earlier complaint was only a weakness for mother-comfort, like a child's whining.

We made our men strain on tiptoe to reach our creed, for it led to works a dangerous country where men might take the deed for the will. My fault, my blindness of leadership allowed them this finite image of our end which properly existed only in its unending effort towards unattainable imagined light. Our crowd seeking light in things was like the pathetic dogs snuffing round the shank of a lamppost: but shallow men could only identify a cause in the practice. Mankind hankered after the great in their worship; for some it was Feisal, for others the misty I in the darkness behind Feisal. It was only I who had nothing higher than the abstract.

The irony was in my loving objects before life or ideas, and in the infectious life of action, which laid weight on the diversity of things, and gave me no leisure to think through the forms, to their inner unity. We might have found free-will, if we had constantly not done what lay within our power to do: by choosing nothing, as often as we had a choice, we might have isolated ourselves, clear of circumstance, and so arrived at self-knowledge, which, unlike other human knowledge did not expire with its sister bad smell, the body. But our dutiful war forbade us such inactivity.

It was a hard task for me to straddle feeling and action. I had had one craving all my life — for the power of self-expression in some imaginative form — but had been too indolent and weak-willed ever to acquire technique. At last, accident with perverted humor had cast me as a man of action — and in the very height of doing I would momentarily forget my wished nature: yet always after such a crisis consciousness returned, asking how that had been done.

Then I would look back at my intention, trying to find a keyword for it in labored sentences like these which hid the reality, unless perhaps here and there it peeped out between the lines. Chance had given me place in the Arab Revolt, a theme epic to a direct eye and hand: and had given me taste for the subjective, for the words to mirror our motives or feelings of the time. Whence the indirection of my diary and of this book came built over it. I was excited only after mechanism, of how we adjusted ourselves to odd conditions. Memory Wave me no clue to the heroic, so that half the experience was lost to me. I could not feel Auda in myself he seemed as rugged and fantastic as the hills of Rum, as old and far from us as Malory.

Among the Arabs I was the disillusioned, the skeptic: and envied their cheap belief The unperceived sham looked so well-fitting and becoming a dress for shoddy man to wear. The ignorant, the superficial, the deceived, were the happy among us: and perhaps they had no real cause against us leaders. By our swindle they were made heroes. We paid, and they profited by the deepest feeling of their lives, in which therefore we too might take a distorted pride. The more we condemned and despised ourselves, the more we could admire them, our creatures. It was so easy to over-credit others: so impossible to write down their motives to the level of our own.

They were our dupes, wholeheartedly fighting the enemy with all their conviction. No one had deceived them but themselves and me, and they blew before our intentions like chaff, being not chaff, but the bravest, simplest, and merriest of men. *Credo quia sum?* But to be believed by many made for a sort of righteousness. The mounting-together of the devoted hopes of years or of nearsighted multitudes might endow even an unwilling idol with the attributes of a God, strengthened whenever men prayed silently to Him. Our search for the Unknown God, from the first day when He was born of our first thought, not cosmic nor incommensurate with us, but quite close and dear, might have been profitable more that He was unknown than that He was God.

Upon this text my mind went weaving across its space, towards whose dustiness the thoughts pierced like sunbeams, with motes of ideas dancing about them in intricate designs. Then I saw that this was a scapegoat idea, which lulled only to a false peace. To endure by order, or because it was a duty: that was straightforward and easy. The soldier suffered knocks harder than the general's, but involuntarily, which much lessened their hardship; whereas it was horrible to make one's own will play the ganger tin the workmen fainted. To stand in a safe place and thrust others into danger might be not merely painful but very brave. It would have been heroic to have offered up my own life for a cause in which I could not believe: but it was a theft of souls to make others die in sincerity for my graven image. They accepted our message as truth, and were ready to be killed for it, because it was true: but such a condition made their acts more proper than glorious, a logical bastard fortitude, suitable to a profit-and-loss balance of conduct. To invent a message, and then open-eyed to perish for its fraudulent self-made image — that was greater.

The whole business of the movement seemed to be expressible only in terms of death and pain, across which custom and excitement bore us. Whenever we were conscious of our flesh it was because it hurt us, and this we learned so thoroughly that sometimes we forgot it. Then the narcotic of pleasure would dull us for an instant to our proper element, with each such indulgence slackening the nerves of sense till it seemed as if by too much of this drugging our responsiveness might die. Better than such threatened flatness was it to be thrilled continually by fearlessly plucking hands, for so reaction was more felt. Joy came sharper from the long habitude of pain.

Our resources in suffering seemed greater than our capacity for gladness. Both emotions were in our gift, for our senses, like a philosopher's stone, changed pain into joy, happiness to shame, instantly. The rejoicing which passed to infinity transformed its nature and became painful, while infinite suffering brought death, our crowning mercy, in its train.

Our pain was full of eddies, confusing its purity. A reef on which many came to shipwreck was the use of flesh in the redemption of others, the fancy that our endurance might win joy, perhaps only for our tormentors, perhaps for all a race. Such false investiture bred a hot though transient satisfaction, in that we felt we had cheated ourselves of ourselves, assumed another's pain or experience, his personality. It was triumph, and a mood of enlargement; we had avoided ourselves, conquered our geometrical completeness and snatched a momentary 'change of mind'.

Yet in truth we had borne the vicarious for our own sakes, or at least pointed to our own benefit: and could escape from this knowledge only by a make believe in sense as well as in motive. The self-immolated victim profited first of all himself He took for his own the rare gift of sacrifice, and no pride and few pleasures in the world were so joyful, so rich, as this choosing voluntarily the evil that might have fallen to others. It was required to perfect a man, and there was a hidden selfishness in this, as in all perfections.

To each opportunity there could be only one vicar, and the snatching of it robbed the fellows of their due hurt. Their vicar rejoiced, while his brothers were wounded in their manhood. To accept humbly so rich a release was imperfection in them: to be glad at their saving of its cost was sinful in that it made them accessory, part-guilty of inflicting it upon their mediator. A purer part might have been to stand among the crowd, and let another by that suffering win the cleanness of a redeemer's name. By the one road lay self-perfection, by the other self immolation and the making perfect of a neighbor. Hauptmann told us to take as generously as we gave: but rather we seemed like the cells of a bee-comb, of which one might change only at the cost of all the rest.

To suffer in simplicity for another gave a sense of greatness, of super-humanity. There was no such loftiness as a Cross from which to contemplate the world The pride and exhilaration of it were beyond conceit. Yet each one occupied, robbed the latecomers of all but the poor part of copying: and the meanest of things were those done by example. The virtue of sacrifice lay within the victim's soul.

Honest redemption must have been free and child-minded. When the expiator was conscious of the under-motives and the after-glory of his act, both were wasted on him. So the introspective altruist appropriated a share worthless, indeed harmful, to himself, for had he remained passive his cross might have been filled by an innocent person. Today, natural man had grown so complicated that this was the general case: and so the truly heroic might be to let the ignorant assume the need of sacrifice in all sincerity, and by it gain the virtue of atonement played to the death, in the belief that it was for the general good.

To rescue simple ones from such evil by paying for them his complicated self would be futile or avaricious for the modem man. He, thought-riddled, could not share their belief in others' discharge through his hanging nailed in agony, and they, looking on him without understanding, might feel the shame which was the manly disciples' lot: or might fail to feel it, and incur the double punishment of ignorance.

Or was this shame a self-abnegation too, to be admitted and admired for its own sake? How was it right to let men die because they did not think or understand? Blindness and folly aping the way of right were punished more heavily than purposed evil, at least in the present consciousness and remorse of man-alive. Complex man, who knew how self-sacrifice uplifted the redeemer and cast down the bought, and who held back in this knowledge might so let a foolish brother take the place of false nobility and its later due of heavier sentence. There seemed no straight walking for us leaders in this crooked lane of conduct, ring within ring of unknown shame faced motives canceling or double charging their precedents.

Chapter 115: Peace Negotiations

The machine took me back to Guweira that evening, and after a telephone call took car in the night to Akaba and met Dawnay, just arrived. I told him that life was full but slipping smoothly, and that we would keep the promise to Allenby and Bartholomew of three men and a boy with pistols outside Deraa on the sixteenth.

Next morning we heard by airplane how at dawn Buxton's force had taken Mudowwara. They had left Rum on the fifth of August, and by the flat of Disi had been joined by Brodie with his ten-ponder guns on Talbots, and by Scott-Higgins to do demolitions. On the sixth, Buxton, with Marshall and Brodie had carefully examined Mudowwara station from a near hilltop to the west, and decided to assault it before dawn on the eighth mainly by means of bombers.

Accordingly, before midnight, white tapes were laid down, to guide the attacking parties from their starting point on the flat place south of the station, to their objectives. Buxton divided his force into three sections, of which a party of thirty men was to rush the station buildings; fifty were to carry the southern redoubt, while one hundred attacked the central redoubt. The isolated north post was left for later measures.

The attack had been timed for a quarter to four (the precision of modem armies!), but in the darkness the way proved difficult to find, and a delay of fifteen minutes ensued before the first blow was struck, so that daylight was almost upon them, and with it the attack would have been too costly to meet Bartholomew's condition. However, things began just in time against the southern redoubt, and after a number of bombs had burst in or about it the men rushed up and took it easily — to find that the station party had achieved their end a moment before. These alarms had prepared the middle redoubt, but only for defeat. Its men surrendered twenty minutes after the action began, before it was light enough to see plain.

The northern redoubt, which had a gun, seemed better-hearted and splashed its shot freely into the station yard and at the re-forming troops. Buxton put his headquarters in the cover of the southern redoubt, and from there directed the fire of Brodie's guns against the surviving point. Brodie and his crews, with their usual deliberate accuracy, sent shell after shell into the sangars. Siddons came over with his machines, and Buxton put out ground strip signals for them, to bomb the northern redoubt. This they did, while the Camel Corps closed in from north and east, and west, subjecting the breastworks to severe Lewis gun — fire from their six guns. At seven in the morning, the last of the enemy surrendered quietly. We had lost four killed and ten wounded. The Turks had lost twenty-one killed, and we took one hundred and fifty prisoners, with two field guns and three machine-guns.

Buxton at once set the Turks to work getting steam up on the pumping engine, so that he could water his now-thirsty camels; and while the cars captured a patrol which came up from the south to inquire into the noise, or carried the wounded of both sides down to Guweira, Scott-Higgins proceeded with the demolition. With his ton of guncotton he blew in the two wells, after choking them with railway rails, smashed the two engines and pumps, and the windmill, with two thousand yards of rails. At dusk he laid charges at the foot of the great water-tower, and spattered it in single stones across the plains: while Buxton, a moment later, called, 'Walk-march!' to his men, and the four hundred, rising like one and roaring like the Day of Judgment, started off for Jefer.

This fine performance settled the isolated fate of the Turkish corps in Medina beyond question, whatever might be our fortune away by Deraa, and whatever reverses our little containing army in front of Maan might suffer before or after: and Dawnay and I went up very brightly to Aba el Lissan, to greet Feisal. Allenby had sent him across with the latest news, and particularly to give Feisal a warning message. He was to beg him to do nothing rash, since the British push was a chance, and if it failed they would be massed on the wrong side of Jordan to afford the Arabs help. Particularly, Allenby begged Feisal not to rush too soon upon Damascus, but to hold his hand, till it was sure that events were favorable.

This very sound and proper caution had come on my account. Exasperated one night at GH.Q I had blurted out that to me 1918 seemed the last chance, and anyhow we would take Damascus, whatever happened at Deraa or Messudiyeh, since it was better to have taken it and lost it, than never to have taken it at all. This spirit alarmed them, and revived the faded opinion that I was sometimes rash. To my mind there was no more delightful story, and I tried hard to believe it on the principle that our character was what we were not aware of ourselves, and that any conscious quality presupposed the presence of its opposite: but my survival through two years of irregular fighting more truly marked my extreme caution. However, I greatly enjoyed Dawnay's homily.

Feisal smiled wisely as he listened and at the end replied, showing himself as heady as my reputation. He said he would go this autumn to Damascus though the heavens fell, and if the British were not able to carry their share of the attack he would not reproach them, or ask for help, but would save his own people by making his separate peace with Turkey. This was a new and strong idea, and afterwards when we were alone together I gave Dawnay a sketch of the grounds Feisal had for believing it possible.

The truth of the matter was that for months we had been in touch with elements in Turkey. Jemal Pasha had opened the correspondence by sending to Feisal in Wejh. He had known him intimately during those early months in Damascus, when Feisal had been half-guest, half-hostage, in his hands, and he believed that a reconciliation between them was yet possible, on grounds of community of faith. The idea was folly, because Feisal was an advanced thinker whose education had taught him the proper spheres of politics and religion, and in politics he had a creed of nationality. Indeed this was true not only of Feisal but of the whole Arab Movement, which was inspired by a true national sense, and was not to be warped by religious prejudice.

However, Jemal was simpler in mind. By instinct, when sober, he was Islamic, and his loyalty to Turkey was almost as much to the Sultan who was Caliph and held the Holy Places, as to the ideal of Ottoman over lordship in the Turanian family. In this old-fashioned outlook, Jemal stood alone among the Young Turks, and his surprising strength, which let him survive the envies of Enver and Talaat, was largely drawn from the clerical party. To him, as a sincere pan-Islamist, the revolt of Mecca was a judgment, and the defense of Medina Turkey's strongest duty. He was willing to say anything, or promise anything, or do anything, to compose this breach in Islam which was destroying his private justification of faith.

His letters betrayed his anxiety, and were, if only for this reason, illuminating. Feisal sent them to Mecca and Egypt, hoping that they would read into them what we did: but to our disappointment the points were taken literally, and we received return injunctions to reply shortly and worthily that the sword was now our judge. This was magnificent sounding, but we were at war, and so rich an opportunity of diathesis could not be missed.

It was true that peace with Jemal was not possible. He had lopped the tall heads of Syria and we would deny our friends' blood if we admitted him to our peace: but we could indicate this subtly to his Staff in our reply, and perhaps lead them to feel that Jemal's person was the main obstacle to an Arab accord. We knew the rifts in Turkey, and that Jemal's Islamism was old-fashioned in the eyes of seven in each ten of his nation. By suitably guarded phrases, we could throw the odium of the Revolt on the clerical party, and then perhaps the militarists might fall out with them.

They were constitutionally inclined to quarrel. The Nationalists, our particular target, were the old Turanian wing of the C.U.P. and a great and growing faction. Their heads were the anti-German sector of the General Staff, under Mustapha Kemal Pasha, a hero of Gallipoli. They were real nationalist, logical believers in their principles. By writing carefully to Jemal we could enlist their dispassionate judgment on our side, showing them the Arab and Turk nationalists were agreed to rid Turkey of her incubus of alien provinces, the dead weight which crippled her 'Turki ' mission. Self-government to the Arabic-speaking areas would set Anatolia free to cultivate the old cradle of its people's birth in Turkestan.

Accordingly Feisal with my full assistance sent back tendentious answers to Jemal, argumentative enough to cause to continue the exchange: and it continued brilliantly. The soldiers began to write to us, complaining of the pettiest, who put relics before strategy. The Nationalists wrote, saying that Feisal was only putting into premature and disastrous activity their cherished convictions, and how easily they could sit down together and work out the self determination of Turkey.

The knowledge of this ferment under him affected Jemal's determination. His offers became liberal as our preaching broadened. At first we were offered autonomy for Hejaz. Then Syria was admitted to the benefit: then Mesopotamia was added. Feisal seemed still not content, and Jemal's deputy (while his master was away in Constantinople) boldly added a Royal Crown to the offered share of Hussein of Mecca. We wondered smilingly what His Imperial Majesty Sultan Reshad knew! Lastly they told us that for their part, and their party's, they saw deep and reasonable logic in the claim of the Prophet's family to the spiritual leadership of Islam. Feisal saw himself, in cap and bells, playing Mutawakkil to Mohammed the Fifths Selim.

The comic side of the letters should not obscure their real help to us, at this critical stage, in dividing the Turkish General Staff on our count. The old-fashioned Muslims thought the Sherif an unpardonable sinner. The modernists thought him a sincere but impatient nationalist misled by British promises into espousing the wrong side. They had a real sympathy with him, and a desire to correct him by argument and not by military defeat.

Their strongest card was the Sykes-Picot agreement, an old-style division of Turkey between England, France and Russia. The Turks printed its text in all their papers, to show their Arab subjects the real duplicity of the Allies. Jemal read the more spiteful paragraphs at a public banquet in Beirut, and confused our friends. We received many copies by the hands of agents, and for a while the disclosure really hurt us, and justly, for we and the French had thought to plaster over a split in policy by a formula, vague enough for each to interpret in his divergent way.

Fortunately I had early divulged the existence of this thing to Feisal, and had convinced him that it was only to be set aside if the Arabs redoubled their efforts against the Turks, not with them in revenge; for we were sure to win the war, and would then have to enforce it. His only escape was to do so much to help the British that, after peace, they would not be able, for very shame, to shoot such allies down in fulfillment of a secret treaty.

Then at least there would be a modification, in which he would secure something; while if the Arabs did as well as I intended there would be no one-sided talk of shooting, for they would be in place to return shot for shot, and as armed men in their own houses to get their won freedom recognized by their victorious allies. I begged him not, like his father, to trust our promises — though one could not know if Hussein trusted us out of stupidity or out of craft — but to trust in his own performance and strength, a justification, by holding, of his right to hold.

Feisal, a reasonable and clear-eyed statesman, accepted my point of view as the normal between nations, and his conviction of the hollowness of promises and gratitude did not sap his energy. Yet I did not dare to take so frankly into confidence the other men in our movement, and they found the cheerfulness of Feisal and me under the blows of the Sykes-Picot agreement rather odd.

Fortunately, at this juncture the British Government in its joyous fashion gave with the left hand also. They promised to the Arabs, or rather to an unauthorized committee of seven Gothamites in Cairo, that the Arabs should keep for their own such territory as they conquered from Turkey in the war. Here was a new touch stone for the Sykes-Picot treaty, liable, if the war went as we hoped, to make parts of it look patchy. At least it made it all provisional, and the glad Arabs circulated the new word over Syria.

To help the downcast Turks, and to show us that its many hands as an ape's were ignorant of what one another did, and that it could give as many promises as there were parties, the British at once countered documents A to the Sherif, B to their allies, C to the Arab Committee, with document D to Lord Rothschild, a new power, who was promised something equivocal in Palestine. Old Nuri Shaalan, wrinkling his wise face, returned to me with his file of documents, asking in puzzlement which of them all he might believe. As before I glibly repeated, 'The last in date', and the Emir's sense of the honor of his word made him see the humor. Ever after he did his best for us, only warning me, whenever he failed in a promise, that he had superseded it by later intention.

However, Jemal went on hoping, he being an obstinate and ruffian man, and after Allenby's defeat at Salt, sent down to us Mohammed Said, the brother of the egregious Abd el Kader el Jezairi, whose services to Ali ibn el Hussein and myself in the ride to the bridge had been so embarrassing. Mohammed Said, a low browed degenerate with a bad mouth, was as devious as his brother, but less brave. He was very modest as he stood before Feisal and offered him Jemal's peace.

Feisal told him that he was come at an opportune moment, when he was disposed to come to terms. He would offer Jemal the loyal behavior of the Arab Army, if Jemal, on his part, would return the trust by evacuating north from Amman every Turk now south of it, and would hand over the province to Arab keeping. The silly Algerian thought that he had scored a resounding success, and rushed back to Damascus with his news: but the infuriate Jemal nearly hanged him for his pains.

Mustafa Kemal was alarmed, and begged Feisal not to play into Jemal's hands, promising that when the Arabs were installed in their capital, the disaffected in Turkey would rally to them, and ask to use their territory as a base from which to attack Enver and his German allies in Anatolia. Mustafa hoped that all the Turkish forces east of the Taurus would join him at the first blow struck and enable him from Aleppo to march direct on Constantinople.

Events at the end prevented our making positive use of these long, complicated negotiations: and their history will never be written, since they were not disclosed to Egypt or to Mecca, after the disappointing issue of our first confidence. We feared that the British might be shaken at Feisal's apparent mistrust of them, in entertaining separate negotiations, after their own model. Yet in fairness to the fighting Arabs we could not close all avenues of accommodation with Turkey. If the war failed it might be the cheapest way out: and there was always the lurking fear that Great Britain might forestall Feisal, and conclude its own separate peace, not with the nationalist, but with the conservative Turks.

The British Government had gone very far in this direction, without informing her allies, or at least her smallest ally. Our information of the precise steps, and of the proposals (which would have been fatal to so many of the Arabs in arms on our side), came not officially to me, but privately. It was only one of the twenty times on which my friends helped me more than did my Government: whose action and silence were at once an example and a spur and a license for me to do the like.

However this day I made to Dawnay a clean breast of so much of the secret situation as he needed to judge fairly of Feisal's strength to accord with Turkey, after he had taken Damascus, and before he had lost it again. He heard me out, and heard Feisal's appreciation of the internal state of the Turkish counsels, and gave us both reason in our hopes: but he thought he would not retail them too loudly in Palestine!

Chapter 116: By Car to Azrak

After the peace-talk we could set again to clean work. Buxton, now near Jefer, would wait there the night of the twelfth, and water his camels. We decided that we would all drive across and see him. Afterwards, Dawnay would spend a few days in Aba el Lissan, helping Young to do our necessary thinking. My next duty was to go with Buxton up to Kissir, for the bridge and back. However, as far as Bair anyone could guide him, and he would wait a day or two there, so that I had at least three days' leisure.

Joyce and myself decided to fill these by another of our joint car excursions, this time to Azrak, to break their trail so far, on the way to Deraa. For our final raid we purposed bringing up three armored cars and supplying them mainly by tender, and it was imperative that we should not calculate on this in blank ignorance of the running-time and surface. I was sure from my camel experience that cars would reach Azrak: but the only way to know how and when was by taking a car actually across.

So, on the afternoon of the eleventh of August, we ran out together to Jefer, to meet the victorious Buxton and consult with him as to the fitness of his men and animals to complete their arduous program. They came gliding in splendid trim and formal appearance, across the shining flat just before sunset, officers and men delighted at their Mudowwara success (though Lyall, commanding eleventh company, had been there wounded), and loving their freedom from orders and restraint out here on their own in the desert. Buxton said they were fit enough to go anywhere and do anything.

They would rest two nights, and draw four days' rations from their store, duly set out near Auda's tent by Young's care. Accordingly, on the morrow early, Joyce and I got into our tender, with the resourceful Rolls to drive us, and ran easily, over virgin country, through the Shomari, and up nearly to Jebel Erha before we turned east down the valleys into Wadi Bair.

At the wells lay camped Aiwain, Auda's young kinsman, a smooth-cheeked oppressed-looking silent man, hiding there with his section of the Abu Tayi in order to possess himself in peace, far from Auda. There were also Beni Sakhr and Rualla tents, but Aiwain was the greatest sheikh, and on behalf of everybody he promised us to give the Camel Corps the hospitality of his wells, and till they arrived he would guarantee the safety of their dump of rations (more of Young's pains-taking) and the proper conduct of the Bedouin they would meet on their road.

We stopped only the few minutes to arrange this with him, and then turned round our cars, and drove out as we had come, with the addition to our party of a young and very wild Sherari, to help us find our way. His camel-training would not make him very useful at first, road-picking for a five-ton armored car: but I did not like to rely only on myself as guide for so long a trip, and afterwards his knowing the track might serve other ears coming up by themselves.

The plateau of Erha was good going, since its flint opens were interspersed with beds of hard mud, permitting us speed. To avoid the tailings of valleys between Bair and the Thlaithukhwat on the direct road to Azrak I had determined to make a circuit round Erha to the west over the ground across which we had returned with Zaal from Minifir in 19IT and thence to swing round the outer slopes of Hadi and the Three Sisters, into Wadi Dhirwa on its eastern bank. We proceeded at a fast pace for miles, till we entered the shallow heads of Wadijinz, well grown with pasture.

There we saw large numbers of grazing camels, now being driven anxiously together by their ragged herdsmen of the Abu Tayi, who were riding bareheaded, with rifles in hand, and singing a war-chant. When they heard our roaring exhausts they rushed towards us with urgent shouts of mounted men just seen lurking in the low grounds ahead of us. We put the cars in the direction and after a little flushed five camel-riders who made off northwards at their best. However the going was firm so we ran them down in ten minutes. They couched their camels gracefully and came to meet us as friends — the only role left them since naked men could not quarrel with swifter men in armor.

They were Jazi Howeitat, undoubted robbers but now all kindness crying loudly at the pleasure of meeting me here suddenly. I was a little short with them and ordered them back to their tents at once on pain of instant complaint to Hamd el Arar, their courtly chief This was a real threat for Harnd was ruler of his tribe, and had come back from a political visit to Mecca a loyal and enthusiastic Arab nationalist with the loss of Tafileh (the occasion of his being sent away) quite made up. So they promised prompt obedience, and went off, crestfallen westwards.

We drove on over excellent surfaces till we were on the north face of the Thlaithukhwat ridge and crossed the springs of Wadi Dhirwa to enter Urn Kharag, its joint stream whose junction made the water-bed at Hazim in Sirhan. We followed its east bank finding the way firm but slow for there were the gutters of too many tributaries to cross and at each we had to stop and choose a smooth road or even lay down brushwood fascines, where the old bed of the flood-water was soft and full of sand. Towards the end of the day the valleys grew thick with tufted grass enough grazing for all our caravans. At dusk we halted for the night some thirty miles past Bair crow fly but many more by our indirect route.

In the morning the northern air and fresh wind of this desert were so cool to us that we made ourselves a hot breakfast before we cranked up the cars and purred onwards across the meeting of Urn Kharag and Dhirwa, and across the broad flat basin of Dhirwa itself, and over its imperceptible water-parting into the two Jesha water-carriers shallow systems in the elbow of the Ghadaf, running down into the Sirhan by Ammari, which I meant to visit; for supposing evil came to us at Azrak our next refuge should be Ammari, if it was accessible to cars. These battalions of 'ifs' skirmished about our plans continually. While we prospered they held back from attacking us: but when we met a check they were upon us with a thousand distractions: and it was a great part of my generalship to follow one plan, that which in advance seemed most profitable, to its furthest possibility: and at its end to have the courses of fifty others already mapped out in my slow mind, so that no sudden swerve could take me unawares. Our expedients proved fruitful in so far as they had been expected.

The night's rest had freshened Rolls and Sanderson, and they drove splendidly till near midday, over the saffron ridge of the little Jesha into the great valley which flowed by a straight bed ten feet below the plain-level, direct on Ammari wells. In the afternoon we saw the low chalk banks on north and south, and turned a little left down the pale ashy slopes into the Sirhan just by the water holes. This was most satisfactory and made our retreat always safe, for no enemy would be mobile enough to close both Azrak and Ammari at once to us and thrust us, very thirsty, into the flint desert.

So we refilled our radiators with the horrible water of the pool in which Farraj and Daud had played and drew out westward a little, over the open ridges, till we were far enough from the wells to acquit raiding parties from the need to stumble on us in the dark. There Joyce and I sat down and watched a sunset which grew from grey to pink, and to red, and then to a crimson so intolerably deep that we held our breath in trepidation for some stroke of flame or thunder to break its dizzy stillness: while the men cut open tinned meats, and boiled tea, and brought them with biscuits on a blanket for us to feast from. Afterwards we slept lusciously, having determined, since we were out for pleasure, to pluck all the comfort we could enjoy.

Next day we ran quickly across the delta of Ghadaf among the flint slopes trending northward along our road, till we came to the sand and scrub bed, where a branch cut sharply between Sirhan and the main depression south of the Azrak springs. Across this rotten ground we picked a careful way on foot through the sand blisters, with the great cars laboring after us. The wind had chased the sand into brushed curves by the tips of the lower branches of the drooping tamarisk.

Then we were out on the immense mud-flat which stretched southward and eastward for seven miles from the marshes by the old castle across all the hollow from the Ghadaf to Aiz el Beidha: but today the mirage blotted out its limits for us, lining them with blurs of steely blue, which were the tamarisk bounds, raised high in the air and smoothed into straight lines by the heat vapor. I wanted the Mejaber springs, down whose tree-bed we might creep unperceived into the fort: so Rolls made his car leap forward in a palpating rush across the great width. The earth blurred away in front of us, and a plume, like a greater dust-devil, rose into the air behind us along our track.

The brakes sang protesting as we slowed into the bed of the Ghadaf proper, a valley thick as a young plantation with tall stems of tamarisk, growing on heaps of wind-collected sand. We twisted through them on the hard intervening soil till the tamarisk ceased, and damp sand, speckled with close thorn-bushes, took its place. There we stopped the cars, behind the hummock of Ain el Assad, to fill their tanks under cover of this high-lipped cup of reeds, between whose vivid stems the water dripped like jewels.

We went forward gently across the valley and up the knoll of graves over the great Mejaber pools, and saw that the watering places were empty. The mirage hung over all the open spaces: but here, where the ground was bushed, no heat-waves could collect, and the strong sunlight showed us the valley as crystal clear as its running waters, and deserted except by herds of gazelles and flocks of wild birds who, alarmed by the people of our closed exhausts, were grouping together timidly in preparation for flight.

Rolls drew his tender past the graveyard above the Roman fish-pond; we got in again and skirted the high wall of the western lava-field, picking our way along the edge of the now-hard grass grown swamp, till we were under the blue walls of the silent fort, with its silken-sounding palms, behind whose intense stillness lay perhaps rather fear than peace. I felt guilty at introducing the great throbbing car and its trim crew of khaki-clad northerners into the remoteness of this most hidden medieval place: but my anticipations went astray, for it was the men who looked real, and the background which became scene-painting. The men's newness and certainty (nothing was more definite than British troops in uniform) made the old ruin more than ever my dream-palace of the days of legend: and did it greater honor than plain loneliness.

Chapter 117: Meeting at Bair

We stopped only a moment. Joyce and I climbed the western tower and agreed upon the manifold advantages of Azrak as a working base though to my sorrow there was no grazing here so that we could not linger in it with our army in the interval of our first and second raids. Then we ran back to the Mejaber mouth and crossed the isthmus between the fort and valley springs to the northern lobe of the mud-flat. It impressed us as a fit landing-ground for the machines which Siddons was adding to our flying column. Amongst other qualities was its visibility. Our airplanes flying two hundred miles to this their new base could not fail to see its electrum-shield, reflecting the sunlight for miles.

This completed the business. We went back to Ain el Assad where the armored car was turned round ready: and led it at a faster pace across the Ghadaf over the mud flat, and through the hummocks of the Sirhan branch out to the open flint desert once again. It was mid-afternoon, and very hot especially in the glowing metal of the steel-turreted car: but the sweating drivers kept at it and before sunset we had left our old Ammari road and were swinging right and left along the back of the dividing ridge between the Jesha valleys over fair going of flints to find a shorter and easier way than our coming.

I thought that by following up the watershed continually we might find a road without crosscutting valleys direct by Ras Muheiwir into the Hadi ridge near Bair, but night caught us not far south of Ammari, delayed by many punctures and we camped where we were on the top of the country with a cool northern breeze very precious after the blistering day coming down to us scent-laden from the flowering slopes of Jebel Druse. In the night it made us glad of the men's hot tea and afterwards of all the blankets with which we had softly padded the angles of the hard box-body.

The trip was one delight to me since I had no responsibility but to scout and guide and choose the road and the leisurely peace of rolling over the plains on which I was used painfully to ride was like a dream. Also there was the spice of the reflections of the Sherari boy about the others reflections naturally confided to me since I alone wore his sort of clothes and spoke his dialect. He, poor outcast, had never been treated as a considerate thing before and was astonished at the manners of the English, though of course they could not speak to him, but invited him always by gesture to move or act. Never once had he been struck or even threatened.

He said that each soldier carried himself apart like a family, and that he felt something of iron in their tight insufficient clothes and businesslike appearance. He was fluttering in skirts and head cloth and cloak. They had only shirts and shorts, puttees and boots, and the breeze could take no hold on them. Indeed they had worn these things so long, day and night, in heat and sweat, busied about the dusty oily cars that the khaki had set to the line of their bodies, like bark to a tree.

Then they were all dressed alike, and his eye, which most often distinguished man from man rather by clothes than by physical differences, here was baffled by their outward uniformity, and to know them apart had to discount their dress and learn their individual, as though naked, shapes. Their food took no cooking, their drink was hot, they spoke hardly at all to one another, and then just a word seemed what they needed to send them into fits of incomprehensible crackling laughter, unworthy and inhuman. His first belief was that they were my slaves, and he judged that there was little rest or satisfaction in their lives, though to a Sherari it would have been luxury so to travel like the wind, sitting down: and a privilege to eat meat, tinned meat daily.

In the morning we hurried along our ridge, meaning to reach Bair in the afternoon. Unfortunately there were more tire-troubles. The armored car's five tons were too heavy for the subsoil below the flints, and always it sank in a little, making heavy going on its third speed. This heated up the covers, and since we were a distant unit, far from inspection, unable to make prompt complaint, Egypt had palmed off on us a scrap consignment of Beldam tubes, whose felt-like rubber split and burst under the necessary air pressure, as soon as the temperature rose. The sharp flints had cut our few Dunlop tubes, and so after midday progress was a vexatious series of bursts, and stopping to jack up and change a wheel or tire. The day was hot, and we were hurried, so that the repeated exertion of levering and pumping wore thin all our tempers.

Just before noon we reached the Boseiri, the hills in the bend of the Ghadaf, and found that we were too far east to pass round them on the low valley level. We made resolutions for a new line in future, and put the cars at their steep four hundred feet of climb, and went over and down the other side along the great spinal ridge to Ras Muheiwir, the narrowest point of the Ghadaf-Dhirwa divide where Zaal and I had camped going to Ziza. From it I knew every foot to the Hadi, and promised the sulky drivers that it would be splendid going.

And it was. We all took new heart and even the tires were better while we rushed along the winding ridge, swinging in long curves from east to west and back again looking now to the left over the shallow valleys trending towards Um Kharag and the Sirhan, now to the right down a steep drop to the hollow plain of Ghadaf and Hafira, as far as the Hejaz Railway. The gleaming specks in the haze of distance were its white stations lit by the pouring sun.

However, it was late afternoon before we reached the end of the ridge and dipped into the hollow and roared at forty miles an hour up the breast of Hadi. Dark was near, so we decided not to follow our old road round the rim of Erha, but to cut across the furrows of Ausaji to Bair. This was short and quick, for it was less rough than we had expected bringing us in to Bair wells just after sunset in the first gloom. The valley was alive with fires, since Buxton and Marshall and the Camel Corps had arrived and were pitching camp after two easy marches from El Jefer.

There was heartburning among them for Bair had still only the two wells and both were beset. At one the Howeitat and Beni Sakhr were drawing for about six hundred of their camels. Just arrived thirsty from the pastures a day's journey to the south east, and at the other was a mob of one thousand camels, the mounts of a great disorderly caravan of Druses and Syrian refugees, Damascus merchants and Armenians on their way to Akaba. These were unhandy travelers with no notion how to water their mob of animals and cluttered up our access to the wells with their noisy straggles. However such difficulties had a natural end.

We sat down with Buxton and his officers in a council of war. Young had duly sent to Bair fourteen days' rations for man and beast, enough to take the two companies forward to Kissir for their attack on the bridge, to bring them back, and then to pass them by Tafileh to Beersheba. However, of the fourteen days' rations there remained only eight and a half days' for the men, and ten for the animals. The rest was deficient, due to gross pilfering on the road. The camel-drivers of the supply column had left Jefer half mutinous with fear of the desert, driven forward only by Young's strong will. They imagined themselves short of food, and had lost, stolen or sold the rest of Buxton's stores upon their way.

I suspected the complaining Armenians of part of the trouble, but nothing could be recovered from them, and we had to consider how to adjust the plan to its new circumstances. Buxton recast his column, leaving out any non-combatant elements and unfit animals: while I recast the march. We would do Kissir: but march then to Azrak, water, and return, by the abundant Um Kharag grazing, here to Bair, From Bair, instead of Tafileh they would go to Aba el Lissan, draw fresh supplies from Young's base reserve, and return to Beersheba by Wadi Araba. It would take three or four days longer, but would save some days of hunger: and there were yet spare days between their revised return date and Allenby's offensive.

We had meant to send with the column two armored cars, to cover its retreat from the destroyed bridge against the anticipated pursuit of Circassian horsemen from Amman; but now, to save petrol carriage, we would cut them down to one armored car. It was a risk, since single cars, like single machine-guns, were not advisable or trusty; but Buxton was willing to carry on, and this spirit made everything wise and possible.

Next day Joyce left Bair early, in the tender, for Aba el Lissan, to report that the road to Azrak was now found and marked by car tracks, and to help Feisal with the arrangements for the expedition of September, and Dawnay, Young and Stirling with the supply and transport preparation for it.

Chapter 118: A Birthday

Lazily and mildly I helped the Camel Corps in their long work of watering at the forty-foot wells, and enjoyed the kindness of Buxton and his three hundred fellows. The valley seemed alive with them, and the Howeitat, who had never imagined there were so many English in the world, could not have their fill of staring. I was very proud of my kind, for their dapper self-possession, and the orderly busyness of their self-appointed labor. British Tommies seemed to carry England about with them wherever they went, and were magnificently bound up always in their natural atmosphere. Beside them here the Arabs looked strangers in Arabia. Also Buxton's talk was a solid joy, for he was understanding and well read and bold: though mostly he was engaged in the difficulties of watering, and of weeding out his surplus and rearranging the rest into a single unit for the long forced march.

Accordingly I spent many of the daylight hours apart by myself, thinking of what was happening, and taking rough stock of where I stood, mentally, at this moment of my thirtieth birthday. It came to me, rather queerly, how as little as four years ago I had meant to be a general, and knighted, when I was thirty: and now, if I survived the next four weeks, both temporal dignities would be within my grasp: — only that my sense of the falsity of the Arab position, since McMahon went, had gradually put such crude ambitions beyond my acceptance, making me feel that nothing in this war was honorable for me, while it left my craving for good repute among men.

This craving made me profoundly suspicious of my truthfulness to myself Only too good an actor could so impress — or wish to impress — men, with his favorable opinion. Here were the Arabs believing me, Allenby and Clayton trusting me, my bodyguard dying for me: and I began to wonder how many established reputations were founded like mine, upon a fraud: how many people acted the dictator and felt like mean worms.

The praise-wages of such acting had now to be accepted. Any protestation of the truth from me was called modesty, self depreciation, and thought rather charming, for men were always fond to believe a romantic tale. It irritated me, this silly confusion of shyness, which was conduct, with modesty, which was a point of view. I was not modest but abnormally shy, ashamed of my awkwardness; and of my physical envelope; and of my solitary unlikeness, which made me no mend or companion, but an acquaintance; complete, angular, uncomfortable, as a crystal.

With men I had a sense always of being out of my depth. This led to elaboration, the vice of amateurs tentative in their arts. As my war was overwrought and over thought, because I was not a soldier, so my activity was overwrought, because I was not a man of action. In such outward spheres there was lacking to me the habit of mind to make them second nature. On the contrary, they were intensely conscious efforts, with my detached self always eyeing the performance from the wings in a spirit of criticism.

When there were added to this attitude the cross-strains of hunger, fatigue, heat, or cold, and the beastliness of living among the Arabs, the hysteria of my campaigns might be understood, and excuse made for the double-hysteria of my record of it. Instead of facts, details, and figures, my notebooks were full of states of mind, the reveries and self-questioning induced or reduced by our situations, expressed in abstract words to the dotted rhythm of the beat of camels' marching. The narrative hid in faint sentences, scattered through pages of opinion. Of course my diary had to be something not harmful to others if it fell into enemy hands: but even making this allowance it showed clearly that my interest lay in myself, not in my activities, and four-fifths of it were useless for this rewriting.

On this birthday in Bair, to satisfy my sense of sincerity, I began to dissect my own beliefs and motives, groping about in my pitch darkness, full of the wailing of the underworld. My self-distrusting shyness held a mask, often a mask of indifference or flippancy, before my face, and puzzled me. My thoughts clawed at this apparent peace, wondering what was underneath, knowing that it was only a mask because, despite my trying never to dwell on what interested me, there were moments too strong for control when my will burst out and frightened me.

I was very conscious of the bundle of powers and entities within me: it was their character which hid itself There was my craving for being liked: so strong and nervous was it that never could I open myself to another, to make him my friend. The terror of failure in an effort so important had frightened me from trying; and besides there was the standard, for intimacy seemed shameful unless the other could make the perfect reply, in the same language, after the same method, for the same reasons.

There was a craving for being known and famous, and a horror of being known to like being known. My contempt of my passion for distinction had made me refuse every offered honor. I cherished my independence almost as a Bedouin did, but found

I could realize it best by making another remark upon it, in my hearing. My impotence of vision showed me my shape best in painted pictures, and only the oblique overheard remarks of others taught me my created impression. So an eagerness to overhear and oversee myself was my assault upon my own inviolate citadel.

The lower creation I avoided, as an insult to our intellectual nature. If they forced themselves on me I hated them. To put my hand on a living thing was degradation to me: and it made me tremble if they touched me or took too quick an interest in me. This was an atomic repulsion, the power which guarded the intact course of a floating snowflake: but the opposite would have been my choice, if my head had not been tyrannous. I had a longing for women and animals and lamented myself most when I saw a soldier hugging a girl in silent ecstasy or a man fondling a dog: because my wish was to be as superficial and my galore held me back.

Always the feelings and the illusion were at war within me reason strong enough to win the victory but not strong enough to annihilate the vanquished or to refrain from liking them the better: and perhaps the truest knowledge of love was indeed to love what self despised. Yet I could only wish it: could see happiness in the supremacy of the material and could not surrender to it: could try to put my mind to sleep that suggestion might blow through me freely and could only remain bitterly awake.

I liked the things beneath me and took my pleasures and my adventures downward. There seemed a level of certainty in degradation, a final safety. Man could rise to any height but there was an animal point beneath which he could not fall. It was a solid satisfaction on which to rest the force of things years and an artificial dignity denied it me more and more, but there endured the aftertaste of a real liberty from one youthful submerged fortnight in Port Said coaling steamers by day with other outcasts of three continents, and curling up by night, to sleep on the breakwater by de Lesseps, with the sea surging past my head.

True there lurked always that will uneasily waiting to burst out. My brain was sudden and silent as a panther my senses like mud clogging its feet and myself (conscious always of itself and its shyness) telling the panther that it was bad form to spring and vulgar to feed upon the kill. So meshed in nerves and hesitation it could not be a beast to be afraid of: and yet it was a real panther and this book its mangy skin, dried stuffed with sawdust, set up squarely for men to look at.

I quickly outgrew ideas and devoured knowledge which gave me range beyond my real height, and capacity to take in the 'why' of things easily. Such lights were not odds and ends merely but illuminated my road in a new way showing me things from many angles, telling me how they might be added to. or improved. So I distrusted the judgment of experts who were often men confined within high walls, knowing indeed every paving-stone of their prison courts: — while I might know from what quarry the stones were hewn and what wages the mason earned. They thought me proud for gainsaying them: but it was carelessness only, for I had found materials always apt to serve man's purpose and many roads leading from purpose to achievement, with Will a sure guide through matter in the end. There was no flesh.

Many things I had picked up, dallied with, regarded, and lay down again, for the conviction of doing was not in me. Fiction seemed wiser than action or rather action only an introduction or material for fiction. Self-seeking ambitions visited me but not to stay since my critical self would make me fastidiously reject their fruits and take no good or evil of them. Always I grew to dominate these things into which I had drifted; but in none of them did I voluntarily engage. Indeed I saw myself a danger to ordinary men with my capacity for doing things veering about empty of conviction at the breath of their desires.

I followed, and did not institute; indeed had no desire even to follow. It was only weakness which delayed me from mind-suicide some slow task to choke at length this furnace in my brain. I had developed ideas of other men and helped them in their work, languidly: but had never created a thing of my own since I could not approve any creation. Nor did I ever work my fullest, except perhaps upon some pages of this book. When other men created and made me join them. I would serve and patch to make it as good as might be: for if it were sinful to create it was sin and shame added to create one-eyed or halt.

Always in working I had tried to serve for the scrutiny of leading was too prominent for me. Subjection to order achieved economy of thought, the painful and was a cold-storage for Character and Will, leading painlessly to the oblivion of doing. It was a part of my failure never to have found a chief to use me. All of them were weak and through incapacity or fear or liking allowed me to free a hand. I was always hoping for a master whom I could have fought till I dropped at his feet to worship: for with respect man could only worship the gods which had proved stronger than himself, and a tragedy of the world had been their fewness.

I used myself as I would have let no man use another; but needed over me one yet harder and more ruthless, who would have worn me to the last fiber of my strength. To him I could have given such service as few masters have had, and I would have given it zealously for voluntary slavery was a deep pride of a morbid spirit and vicarious pain its gladdest decoration . Instead of this they were all nice to me and valued me aloud and gave me license which I abused to raise their anger — but always reached insipid indulgence. An orchard fit to rob must have a guardian dogs a high wall barbed wire. I broke rules with joyless impunity.

My service of Feisal was mostly out of pity. He was such a brave, weak, ignorant spirit trying to do work for which only a genius a great prophet, or a great criminal was fitted. A much-loved man must always be a little weak on some side; but Feisal was less than weak, he was empty: only a great pipe waiting for a wind. A little breath rustled in him: while a full blast sounded a thundering organ note as from the finest instrument, one which called for a great man to play on it. I was not great for I could feel contempt a thin motive of effort: and yet chance made me his player.

The only great man who ever used me, Allenby, came nearest to my longings but I had to avoid him and keep out of the sight of the man whom I wanted to worship not daring to bow down for fear lest he show feet of clay with that friendly word which must shatter my allegiance. Yet what an idol the man was, prismatic with the sole quality of greatness instinct and compact with it! From such a height the world looked flat and at first I thought Allenby the only great man: but in time my senses, sharpened on him, began to distinguish elements of greatness, till then unseen, in others. However the Chief had no peer.

There were qualities like courage which could not stand alone but must be mixed with a medium, to appear good or bad. Greatness in Allenby showed itself other in category self-sufficient a facet of character, not of intellect. It made superfluous in him ordinary qualities; things like intelligence, imagination, acuteness, industry, looked silly beside it. He was not to be judged by our standards, any more than the sharpness of bow of a liner was to be judged by the sharpness of razors, they were our good points, and their contraries our bad points, but he dispensed with them by his inner power. We walked freely through the soft grass of normal life. He, like a tank, could smash through groves of guilty disaster. It reconciled to me the sanity of the vision of a super-man, or the mystical conception of God, including vice and virtue.

So extravagant an estimate of my Chief was partly as a refuge against the meanness of our enemy. The Turks were too-poor creatures for me to fight. Admiration of a beaten enemy had always in it something of the infect; admiration of the Turks would have been blatant self-praise, worthy of regard only if done consciously, to produce nausea in the hearers. Then it might have been that finest modesty which sought a bad impression, which denigrated itself by raising unwilling sympathy for the too-cheapened vanquished.

To hear other people praised made me despair jealously of myself, for I took it at its face value: whereas had they spoken ten times as well of me. I would have discounted it to nothing. I was a standing court-martial on myself; inevitably, because to me the inner springs of action were bare with the knowledge of how much was just exploited chance. The creditable must have been thought out beforehand, foreseen prepared, worked for. The self knew all detriment, and was forced into deprecating, by rebound off others' uncritical praise. It was a revenge of my trained historical faculty upon the evidence of public judgment, judgment which was always wrong, to those who knew, but from which there was no appeal, because the world was wider. Indeed having helped to produce history bred in me a contempt for our science, seeing that its materials were as faulty as our private characters, which supplied them.

When a thing was in my reach I no longer wanted it. My delight lay in the desire, and not in the desired. I believed that everything which my mind could wish for was attainable, and used to strive, until I had just to open my hand and take it. Then I would turn away. Other people used to pluck, and afterwards reject: I was content with the inner consciousness that it had been with in my strength. I sought only to assure myself, cared not a jot to make others know it and so preserved often for myself something of the secret illusion of the quest, for memory's sake.

There was a special attraction in a new beginning, an everlasting endeavor to free my personality from its accretions, and to project it encumbered on a fresh medium, that my curiosity to see its naked shadow might be fed. The hidden self was reflected clearest in the still water of another man's yet incurious mind. Considered judgments, which had in them of the past and the future, were worthless compared with the first sight, the instinctive opening or closing of a man as he looked at the stranger. Whence came our pleasure in disguise or anonymity. By getting alone or colorless we could fancy ourselves something.

Much of my doing was from intellectual curiosity, to see what I could. To exercise this conceit I would embark on little problems, observing the impact of this or that approach, treating fellow men as so many targets of my ingenuity. I would roughly annoy an individual, and then skill myself to smooth him, by some whimsical perversity, or intrigue him by some misplaced fiery earnestness: and run away, hoping that he wished to know who that odd creature was.

This futile pettiness made me uncomfortable with other men, lest my whim drive me suddenly to collect them as trophies of my marksmanship: also they were interested in so much of which my self-consciousness was ashamed. They talked of food and illness, games and pleasures: — with me, who felt that to recognize our possession of bodies was degradation enough, let alone to enlarge upon their needs and attributes. These others were outwardly so like me that I would feel shame for myself, seeing them wallow in what I judged shame: since the physical could be only a glorification of man's cross. Indeed the truth was always that I did not like myself.

Chapter 119: The Icc

I had reached this useful stage when there was a disturbance from the Toweiha tents, and shouting men ran towards me at a mad speed. I pulled myself together to appease a fight between the Arabs and the Camel Corps: but when they came up it was to appeal for help against a Shammar raid two hours since, away by the Snainirat. Eighty of their camels had been driven off, and they wanted Buxton's companies to leap out with them in pursuit.

I had the greatest regard for the Imperial Camel Corps, but this was hardly their work; their stated distance was twenty miles a day, and Alwain, by tomorrow, would have done a hundred. The essence of Arab tactics in their desert-raids was the whirlwind attack followed by an instant and headlong retreat, while the robbed party called up their fellows to pursue as fast and as far as camels would go. My bodyguard could do the distance, and were nimble enough to cope with the raiders when they caught them: but their camels were out by Erha, grazing. A fit armored car would have done the job before sunset; but the accident of our having been given Beldam tires was going to save those Shammar from their lives' surprise. However, not to seem wholly ungracious, I put the four or five of my men whose friends or relatives had suffered on our spare camels, and sent them off with Alwain's excited riders.

In the morning the watering was ended and we prepared to ride. As local sponsors with us were Sheikh Saleh, of the Faiz Beni Sakhr, and the heads of the two small sedentary or peasant clans which had settled nearest to the Kissir bridge, our goal. They went off in the mid-afternoon with Buxton and his men, while I delayed till evening, seeing my men load our six thousand pounds of guncotton on thirty Egyptian pack camels. My disgusted bodyguard was, for this ride, not merely to escort Buxton's men, but to lead or drive the explosives train — a duty which they found ignoble.

As usual other little points arose, and at sunset I was called in to settle some immediate difficulties between the Ben; Sakhr and the Howeitat, over the reception of these great caravans of merchants and refugees, which were continually passing between Syria and Akaba. It was Feisal's wish and wise policy that they ride through the desert toll-free: and as they exhausted the pasture, and fouled or drained the wells, the tribes grudged them passage. At sunset the Snainirat party returned, dejected having lost the Shammar trail in a dust-storm fifty miles out. Each un-plundered family would now have to subscribe a quota of their herd to maintain the others, till some successful raid should restore the balance. I added my returned men to my little party, and in the early dark we rode out from the tents, with the farewell good-wishes of Alwain sounding across the valley from the knoll into our ears.

We had judged that Buxton and his men, and mine, would sleep just short of the Hadi on the Muheiwir road that night , so we rode straight over the head valley of the Ausaji: but saw no camp-fire, and heard no noise of camp: nor was the track trodden. We went to the crest of the Hadi ridge, and looked over it, in the teeth of a bitter, strong north wind coming off Hermon into our flustered faces. The slopes beyond were black and silent: and to us town-dwellers, accustomed to winds reeking with smoke, or sweat, or the ferment of soil freshly-dug, there was something too searching, disquieting, almost dangerous, in the sword-sharp desert wind. So we turned back a few paces, and hid under the lip of the ridge, to sleep comfortably in its sheltered air.

In the morning we looked out across fifty miles of blank country, and wondered the more at this loss of our companions in the beginning of the adventure: but Daher shouted suddenly from the Hadi side, seeing their column winding up from the southeast. They had lost the track in the night, wandered a little, helplessly, and camped till dawn, and my men jested with humor against Sheikh Saleh, as one who could lose his road between the Thlaithukhwat and Bair — as one might say between the Marble Arch and Oxford Circus.

However, nothing mattered, for it was a perfect morning, with the sun hot on our backs, and the wind fresh in our faces. The Camel Corps strode splendidly between the stud of Hadi and the frosted tips of the three peaks, down the long slope into the green depths of Dhirwa. They looked a different set from the stiff respectful companies that had reached Akaba, for Buxton, a man of varied experience of life, with a supple brain and friendly observation, had taken in the points of irregular fighting, and had weighed their old training manual by their new needs.

He had changed their column formation, breaking its formal sub-divisions of two hard companies; he had changed the order of march, so that they came along clotted in groups which split up or drew together without delay upon each variation of road or ground surface, of old they had marched in immaculate lines which, with the roughness of the present track would have torn their camels' feet to shreds. He had lightened the loads, and re-hung them, thereby lengthening the camels' pace and the daily mileage. He had cut into their infantry system of clockwork halts every so often (to let the camels stale, as it was said!): and grooming was less thought of, whereas, in the old days, they had prinked their camels, cosseting them like Pekinese, and each halt had been lightened by a noisy flapping of the beasts' stripped humps with the saddle-blanket in massage, before the astonished, or rather ribald, Arabs. Now, any spare time was spent grazing.

Consequently, the Imperial Camel Corps had become rapid, elastic, enduring, silent: except when they mounted by numbers, and then the four hundred he-camels would roar in concert, giving out a wave of sound to be heard two or three miles across the night. Each day saw them more workmanlike, more at home on their animals, tougher, leaner, faster, so much more gracious and profitable was doctrine by example rather than by rule. They behaved like boys on holiday, and the easy mixing of officers and men made the general atmosphere delightful. They fitted without shock into the background of the country, and, when mounted, they conveyed no such feeling of strangeness or of being out of place, as did the running through the desert of our Rolls-Royce cars.

My camels were brought up to walk in Arab fashion, that bent kneed gait with much swinging of the fetlock. Always the rider's foot pressed on their right shoulder, urging them to make the stride a little longer and a little quicker than the normal. Buxton's camels strolled along at their native pace, unaffected by the men on their backs, who were kept from direct contact with them by their wood and steel Manchester-made saddles. The lighter Arab saddle, hugging the camel's shoulder, permitted her to be ridden: whereas the Englishmen were just carried neutrally from place to place.

Consequently, though I started each stage alongside Buxton in the van, I forged steadily in front with my five attendants, especially when I rode my Baha, the immensely tall, large-boned, upstanding beast, who got her name from the bleat-voice forced on her by a bullet through the chin. She was beautifully bred, but bad-tempered, half a wild camel, and had never patience for an ordinary walk. Instead, with high nose and wind-stirred hair, she would begin half-consciously to pace along in an uneasy dance, agony to my soft Ageyl, for it strained their backs and loins, but to me splendid in its suggestion of unlimited power in reserve. The roughest camel was not too rough for me (indeed, the rougher were generally the stronger), and I would let them jog-trot their joyful fill.

In this fashion we would gain perhaps three miles on the British in a couple of hours, and then would look about for a plot of grass, or some juicy thorns, and dismount to lie in the warm freshness of air, and let our beasts graze about while we waited to be overtaken: and a beautiful sight the Camel Corps would be, as it came up with us along this clean and narrow ridge between the haze-filled valleys of Dhirwa on the east and distant Hafira on the west.

Through the mirage of heat which flickered over the shining flint-stones of the ridge we would see, at first, only the knotted brown mass of the column, swaying in the haze. As it grew nearer, the masses used to divide and divide into little groups, which swung in and out, parting and breaking into one another, with each accident of track and ground. At last, when close to us, we would distinguish the individual riders, swimming like great water-birds breast-deep in the silver mirage, on a broad front, with Buxton's athletic splendidly-mounted figure leading his sun burnt khaki men, who laughed as they went at those allusive Scotch or English single-word quips which summed up their moments.

It was odd to see how diversely they rode. Some sat their camels naturally, despite the clumsy saddle: some pushed out their hinder-parts, and leaned forward like Arab villagers on the march: others lolled easily in the saddle, and seemed to think they were Australians riding horses in their loose fashion. I told my men how from that three hundred I would pick forty fellows who would have out-ridden and out-fought and out-suffered any forty Arabs in Feisal's armies.

At noon, by Ras Muheiwir, we halted an hour or two, for though the heat today was less than in Egypt in August, Buxton did not wish to drive his men through it without a break. The camels were loosed out, while we all lay and lunched and tried to sleep, defying the multitude of flies which had marched with us from Bair in colonies on our backs. Meanwhile my bodyguard passed through, grumbling and sweating at their new indignity of baggage-driving, making believe never to have been so shamed before, and praying profanely that the world would not hear of my tyranny to them.

Their sorrow was doubled since the baggage animals were Somali camels, whose greatest speed was about three miles an hour. Buxton's force marched nearly four, myself more than five: so that the marches were, for the Zaagi and his forty thieves, a torment of slowness, varied only by balking camels, or slipping loads, introduced only by the labor of roping up thirty packs of unhandy wooden boxes upon the noisy beasts. We abused their clumsiness, calling them drovers and coolies, offering, with a busman's humor, to buy their goods when they came to market, till they laughed at their plight. After the first day they kept up with us by lengthening the march into the night (only a little, for these ophthalmic-stricken brutes were blind in the dark), and by stealing from the breakfast and midday halts. They brought their caravan through without losing one of all their laden beasts a fine performance for such gilded gentlemen — only possible because under their gilt they were the best camel-masters for hire in Arabia.

That night we slept in Ghadaf by Tuba. The armored car overtook us as we halted, its delighted Sherari guide grinning in triumph on the turret lid. When they stopped, he came across and slept at our fire, confiding to me more of the pleasure of motoring, and of the gentleness of English soldiers. An hour or two later the Zaagi arrived, reporting all up and well. He wished that Buxton would not kill directly in the road such camels as broke down on the march, for his men could not leave such masses of meat to rot, but made each camel carcass a feast and a delay.

Abdulla was troubled to understand why the British shot their abandoned beasts. Was it sheer cruelty and love of killing, or that the unbelievers feared death so much that they would hurry even their animals past it? I pointed out how we Arabs shot one another if badly wounded in battle: but Abdulla replied that was to save us from being so tortured by the Turks that we might do ourselves shame. He believed there was not a man alive who would not choose a gradual death of weakness in the desert rather than a sudden cutting off: indeed in his opinion a slow death was the most merciful of all since the hopelessness would prevent the bitterness of a losing fight, and leave man's nature untrammeled to compose itself and him into the mercy of God. Our English argument, that it was kinder to kill quickly anything except a man, he would not take seriously.

Chapter 120: Self Denial

The morrow was like the day before a steady grind of some forty miles, till at dark we circled round the stiff whorls of the Umdeisisat and down the steepness of the northern hill into the narrow valley where we would sleep. The men had to walk their camels down the hillside along the innumerable paths, and from the bottom, looking up the smooth, tilted slope, the hundreds of grey men and camels moved pace by pace, silently and cautiously downwards across the face of the moon into our black shadow underneath.

Next day was the last before the bridge-effort and, for extra safety, I took half my men from the baggage-train and threw them forward on our line of march, to crown each hilltop, and secure us against the unexpected from the valley beyond. This was well done but did not profit us, for in midmorning, with Muagga, our ambush, in full sight, we were marching strongly and hopefully in the open plain, when a Turkish airplane came up from the south, flew the length of our column, and went down, before us, in Amman.

This gave us away and we plodded heavily into Muaggar by noon. We feared bombing, so hid our explosives and men in the substructures of the Roman temple-platform on the hill. Our watchers took post on the crest looking out over the harvested plains to the Hejaz Railway and northward to the stony ridge which hid Kissir and our bridge from sight Over these hill-slopes, grey stones seemed to line out like flocks of grazing sheep, when we stared through our glasses.

We sent Saleh and the local men, with some of my peasants, into the villages below us, to get news, and to warn the people to keep within doors, whatever noises they heard in the night. Saleh was away only a short time, and returned to say that chance was fighting against us. It was harvest time, and round the great heaps of winnowed com upon the threshing floors stood Turkish soldiers, sentries of the picket in each village, for the tax-gatherers were measuring the heaps for taxing, and these sections of mounted infantry went with them as guards. Three such troops, forty men, lay for this night in the three villages nearest the great bridge — villages through whose precincts we must go and come.

We held a hurried council. The Turkish airplane was our first difficulty. It had or had not seen us. In the first case, it would cause, at worst, the strengthening of the bridge-guard: but I had little fear of it. The Turks would believe that we were the prelude, or advance guard of a third British raid on Amman, and were more likely to concentrate there in the center, than detach more troops to the out-garrisons. Buxton's men were great fighters; he had laid admirable plans of attack in the dark against the bridge. We were certain to win.

The doubt was about the cost; about the value, in British life, of this bridge; about Bartholomew's prohibition of casualties; for the presence of these Turkish mule-riders in the villages meant that our retreat would not be unencumbered. The Camel Corps were to dismount nearly a mile from the bridge (their noisy camels!) and advance to take it on foot. The noise of their assault, not to speak of the firing of three tons of guncotton against its peers, would wake up the district. The Turkish patrols in the villages might stumble on our camel-park — a disaster for us — or at least would hamper us in the broken ground, as we carried back our wounded men, defending our retirement in the excited fashion inevitable at night.

Buxton's men could not scatter like a swarm of birds after the bridge explosion and find their own way back to Muaggar. In any night-fighting some would be cut off, and lost to us. We would have to wait for them, possibly losing more in the business. The whole cost might be fifty men, and I put the worth of the bridge at five. Its destruction was so to frightening and disturb the Turks, that they should leave us alone till August the thirtieth, when our long columns set out for Azrak. Today was the twentieth, and the Turkish preparations against Tafileh were yet incomplete.

The danger had seemed pressing in July, but had misused the intervening month, and now was no worse than then. Quite possibly it would linger till September, before it threatened actively our little army besieging Maan. Such a late date would suit admirably both Allenby and us, and the bridge, though desirable as a double insurance for it, was too dear at fifty men. Personally, I would have been loath to risk against it anyone except myself Buxton agreed with me, and we decided to cry off, and move back to Azrak for Bair at once. As we made our decision, more Turkish machines got up from Amman and quartered the rough hills northward from Muaggar, looking for us. We sat, well hidden in our unsuspected ruins, till they went down again.

The men groaned with disappointment when they heard the plan was changed. They set pride on this long raid, and were burning to tell incredulous Egypt that their ambitious program had been fulfilled to the letter. However, perhaps it was as fine to determine, in cold blood after such toils, that the far objective had become by ill-chance over-dear. Two days before, two days after, the villages would have been un-garrisoned, and our plan executed without trouble.

To gain what little we could, I sent Saleh and the other chiefs down to their people, to spread next day tall rumors of our numbers, and our coming as the first reconnaissance of a great wave of Feisal's army, to carry Amman by assault in the new moon. This was the story the Turks feared to learn: the operation they imagined, the stroke they dreaded. They pushed their cavalry cautiously into Muaggar, and found confirmation of the wild tales of the villagers, proof positive that there had been British there, for all the hilltop was littered with empty meat-tins, and the valley slopes were cut up by the deep tracks of enormous cars. Very many tracks there were! This alarm changed their plans, and at a bloodless price for us, kept them hovering a week, discussing a new disposition of covering troops. The destruction of the bridge would have gained us a fortnight.

We waited in Muaggar till the dusk was thick enough to mantle us against an airplane and then rode off down the shallow valley and out across the plain, for Azrak, fifty miles away. We pretended that the raid was become a tour and talked of Roman remains, and of Ghassanide hunting-palaces, while my thoughts were trying to walk steadily along the fine line between prudence and cowardice, and Buxton's thoughts were on the Turkish machines which might bomb us next day: he was urgent for us to make a long march, tonight, if the country suited, out of the danger zone.

The country suited very well, for it was that elastic plain of tough soil, a catch of Butmeh, which spilled into the Ghadafat Azrak. Across it camels, or cars or even airplanes might travel carelessly and we made a splendid marching. The Camel Corps had practice, almost a habit of night journeys so that their pace was as by day, and units never strayed or lost touch. There was a brilliant moon, at its full, and we marched till it was pale in the morning, passing the lone palace of Kharaneh about midnight, too pressed to turn aside and see its strangeness.

This was a pity, but part-blame lay on the moon, whose whiteness made our minds as frozen and shadow less as it did the earth, so that we sat still in our saddles, just sitting still, emptied of thought, and dead to all desire. At first I had had fear of a re-encounter with the Arab raiders who infested this plain, and might have attacked the Camel Corps in ignorance: so I put forward with my men, and rode some half-mile before the column: and as we slipped on with little heed, gradually we became aware of night-birds, flying up from under our feet in numbers, black and large. They increased, till it seemed as though the earth was carpeted in birds so thickly did they star up but in dead silence and dizzily wheeling about us in circles like feathers in a soundless whirl of wind. These weaving curves of their mad flight made us giddy, and their number and their quietness terrified my men who unsung their rifles, and lashed bullet after bullet into the flutter of them. After a mile or more the night became empty again and at last we lay down and slept a little in the fragrant wormwood till dawn roused us out.

In the afternoon tired, we came to Kussair el Amruh, the little hunting lodge of Harith the Shepherd King, patron of poets, which stood today so beautifully in the sweeping valley against the background of its rustling trees, Buxton put the headquarters in the cool duskiness of its great hall, and we lay there gazing at the vault, and puzzling out the worn fresco's of the wall, with more laughter than moral profit. Of the men, some sheltered themselves in other rooms, most, with the camels, stretched themselves beneath the trees, and there passed a slumberous afternoon and evening. The airplanes had not found us out — could not find us here — and we were quit of the fear of them: and tomorrow there was Azrak, and fresh water to replace this stuff of Bair which, with the passing days, was getting too tasty for our liking.

Also Azrak was a famous place, more beautiful than Amruh, queen of these oases, by virtue of its green rushes and its running springs. I had promised everyone a bathe, and the Englishmen, not washed since Akaba, were longing towards it. Meanwhile Amruh was wonder enough, and men asked me with astonishment what these Kings of Ghassan with their unfamiliar halls and pictures might have been. I could tell them of their poetry, and of the wars they made, but my memories were not sharp enough to draw themselves and their life. It was so distant and tinseled an age: and I was not sure whether all our knowledge, had I had it, would have helped me much.

Next day we walked gently towards Azrak. When we were over the last ridge of lava-pebbles, and saw the ring of the Mejaber graves — that most beautifully-put of all cemeteries — before us against the east, I trotted forward with my men, to be sure against accident in the place, and also to see it and to feel once more its remoteness before the others came. These soldiers seemed so secure in their England that I dreaded lest Azrak, which I liked so much, and which was to lead us to victory in three weeks' time, lose some of its rareness and be drawn back to the tide of life which had left it a thousand years ago.

However, both fears were silly. Azrak was empty of Arabs , as beautiful as ever, and even more beautiful a little later when its shining pools were brilliant with the white bodies of our men swimming, and the slow drifting of the wind through its reeds was drowned by their gay shouts echoed bell-like off the water, and by the slapping of the waves against the steep turf banks. We made a great pit, and buried in it our tons of guncotton, ready for the Deraa expedition in September, to save Young's sore-troubled transport camels so much of their load: and then roamed about collecting the scarlet sweet-water-berry of the sea bushes — Sherari grapes, my indulgent followers called them — for our gratification.

We rested there the twenty-second and the twenty-third, the refreshment of the place being so great. Buxton rode with me once to the fort, to see the Roman altar of Diocletian and Maximian, meaning to add a word in favor of King George the Fifth, from the Imperial Camels, after the fashion of our engraved record at Amruh: — but our stay was poisoned by the grey flies, and then ruined by a tragic accident. One of the Arabs, shooting fish in the fort pool, dropped his rifle, and the bullet passed through and killed instantly Lieutenant Rowan, of the Scottish Horse. So the little Mejaber graveyard, whose spotless quiet had long been my envy, received an English grave.

On the twenty-third we marched to Ammari, careful to graze the camels on the rich scrub which Joyce and I had marked a month before. Here we had to leave our armored car. It had marched with us day and night across unknown country, since we left Bair, a fine performance. We had brought with it petrol enough for the estimated journey, and all the tires we had: but today the last spare Beldam tube split along its rotten length. The accompanying tender still had air in its four wheels, and its crew thought that alone they had a sporting chance to get her back to Bair, where there should be a relief car, and fresh stores of tires and petrol.

So we lightened the tender of what we could, packing the stuff into the turret of the armored car, which then we drove heavily upon its rims five miles into the desert. There we screwed up her steel doors and shutters, and burred down the holding bolts of her engine covers: and abandoned her derelict, but still menacing upon the lofty ridge. Her crew climbed into the empty tender, and they set off by the short road to Bair, dreaming of return next day to rescue their armored toy.

We, on our camels, crossed the Jesha valleys and past Dhirwa into Urn Kharag, and up Urn Kharag to the Thlaithukhwat, all this old country whose nearly imperceptible variations I was come to know so well. By the Hadi we felt we were at home, and made a night march, the men joyful and strident through the darkness, with yells of, 'Are we well fed? No. Do we see life? YES.' thundering up the long slopes after me. Even when they tired of telling the truth I could hear them, from the rattle of their accoutrements hitched over the wooden saddles — eleven or fifteen hitching they had, each time they loaded up, in place of the Arabs' all-embracing saddlebag thrown on in one movement

I was so bound up watching their dark body and tail behind me, winding along after my head that, like Sheikh Saleh, I too lost my way between the Hadi and Bair. However, till dawn we went ahead steering by the stars (the men's next meal was in Bair, for yesterday their iron ration was exhausted) and day broke on us in a wooded valley which was certainly Wadi Bair, but for my life I could not tell if it was above or below the wells. I confessed my fault to Buxton and Marshall, and we teetered for a while till by chance Sagr ibn Shaalan, an old friend of the Wejh days, rode down the track, and put us on the road. An hour later the Camel Corps had new rations and their old tents, by the wells, and found to their joy that Salama the provident Egyptian doctor, calculating the need of their return today, had had his medical orderlies since midnight on the wells, and had filled the drinking cisterns with enough water to slake the half of their thirsty beasts.

To my astonishment, the armored car that we had left forlorn at Ammari was already here. The tender had arrived in four hours by a latter and better route skirting the west side of the Boseiri hills, and had filled up with petrol and tires, gone back for her at once, and found her safe. This was splendid. They needed now to take her in to Aba el Lissan for repairs, and I determined to go with them, for Buxton was now on proved ground among friends, and could do without my help.

So we drove fast down the scarp to the Jefer flat, and skipped across it at sixty miles an hour, ourselves the leading car. We threw up such a dust-cloud that we lost our sister, and when we reached the south edge of the flat she was nowhere visible. Probably tire trouble, so we sat down to wait for her, gazing back into the dappled waves of mirage which hurried over the streaming ground. Their dark vapor banks below the pale sky (which got more and more blue as it went higher) shifted a dozen times in the hour, giving US a false alarm of our coming friends, but at last a black spot came spinning through their grayness, waving a long plume of sun-shining dust.

This was Greenhill, tearing after us at top speed, through the shriveling wind, which eddied about his burning metal turret making it so hot that its naked steel seared the bare arms and knees of the crew hurled against it whenever the huge car lurched or plunged over soft ground: for the dust of the desert cut up by our running, was powdered by heat and lay in drifts, waiting for the low autumn wind to sweep it across the open places in one of those blinding storms which blotted out everything and left the land covered with a choking carpet.

Our car stood in the dust tire-deep, and. while we waited the men slopped a little petrol on the hillock of it, and boiled tea for us: Army tea, as full of leaves as flood water, and yellow with Ideal milk, but good for powdered throats. While we drank the others drew alongside, and reported two bursts of Beldam tubes in the heat of their mad swoop at a mile a minute across the scorching plain. We gave them of our boiled tea, and laughing they knocked the dust off their faces with their oily hands. They looked aged with its grayness in their eyebrows and eyelashes, and in the pores of their faces, except where the sweat had rolled down in dark-edged furrows bitten through to their red skin.

They drank hurriedly (for the sun was falling, and we had yet fifty miles to go) throwing out the last dregs from their mugs on the ground, where the drops ran apart like quicksilver over the dusty surface, till they were clotted and sank speckled like shot holes into its drifted grayness. Then we drove through the ruins of the station of Ghadir el Haj and through Waheida, to Aba el Lissan, where Joyce, Dawnay and Young reported all going marvelously. In fact, preparations were complete and they were breaking up, Joyce for Cairo to see a dentist Dawnay for G.H.Q. to tell Allenby we were prosperous and obedient.

Chapter 121: King Hussein Again

The ship which took on Joyce had come up from Jidda, with the Meccan mail for us. Feisal read his letters, and then opened his Kibla (King Hussein's gazette) to find staring at him a Royal Proclamation, saying that fools were calling Jaafar Pasha the General Officer Commanding the Northern Army, whereas there Was no such rank, indeed no rank higher than captain in the Arab Army wherein Sheikh Jaafar, like another, was doing his duty!

This gross insult to all of us had been published by King Hussein (after reading that Allenby had decorated Jaafar), without warning Feisal, out of pique at his son's too-great success, and to spite the northern town-Arabs, the Syrians and Mesopotamian officers, whom the King despised and feared. He knew that they were fighting, not to give him dominion, but to set free their own countries to govern themselves, and the lust for power had grown in the old man to a very disease, soon to make him not responsible for what he did under its prompting.

Now he had fairly torn apart our contentment at the most critical moment. Jaafar came in and proffered his resignation to Feisal, and there followed him our divisional officers and their staffs, and the regimental and battalion commanders. I begged them to pay no heed to the humors of an old man of seventy, out of the world in Mecca: and Feisal refused to accept their resignations, pointing out that the commissions were issued by himself and that he alone was discredited by the proclamation.

On this assumption he telegraphed to Mecca, and received a return telegram which called him traitor and outlaw. He replied laying down his command of the Akaba front. Hussein accepted the resignation, and appointed Zeid to succeed him. Zeid promptly resigned also; Hussein's cipher messages became corrupt with rage, and the military life of Aba el Lissan came to a sudden stop. Dawnay, from Akaba, just before the ship sailed, rang me up and asked dolefully if all our hopes were over. I answered that things hung on chance, but perhaps we would get through.

There were three courses before us. The first was to get pressure put on King Hussein to withdraw his statement, the second to carry on, ignoring it, the third to set up Feisal in formal independence of his father. There were advocates of each course, amongst the English as amongst the Arabs. We all knew that King Hussein's reliance was only upon the people of the Hejaz, an absurd attitude which at once excluded him from the real leadership of the Arab Movement. For two years his influence had been merely nominal: for a year he had been not even consulted about the conduct of the war.

In Hussein's place we had got Feisal chosen, and his breadth of mind, courage, and honesty had made him the ideal leader of a forlorn hope. From October 1916 till now his Army had moved from success to success. Because of this he had been helped more largely than his brothers, and the hopes and expectations of the Arabs were fixed on him. His prosperity was his fault in the jealous circle of Mecca, and in Abdulla's regard, and Abdulla had great influence with his father. Several trifling affairs had shown Hussein's displeasure, but Feisal, a quite dutiful son, had let them pass, even to the King's refusal to accept Jaafar's volunteered services.

However, this last was too hurtful to the fortunes of the nascent Regular Army for us English to endure, and we had pressed the old man till he gave Feisal sneering permission to do as he liked. The letter was ironic, meant to deceive us without empowering Feisal, written with the obscurity of sense and style which made all the King's letters unintelligible except to himself (and generally capable of changing their interpretation at his time and pleasure). However, to his surprise, Feisal read the letter literally, invited all the suspended officers to Wejh, and made Jaafar his Commander-in-Chief.

Jaafar worked hard, and had sufficient status from Turkish days to dominate the other volunteers. Gradually he drew them together, till with the help of Joyce and Feisal, the little trained force of the Northern Army was ready to make its creditable showing against Maan. It was bitter news to King Hussein, who took the opportunity of what seemed to him a lull in fighting to reassert his authority over Feisal: and his arbitrary manner of doing it was typical of the man. Alone, Feisal would have let it past, but his position forced him to stand champion of his officers, and they, who felt themselves higher in culture than the Koranic court in Mecca, seized on the pretext to snob King Hussein through the reputable instrumentality of Feisal and Jaafar. They demanded the withdrawal of Hussein's statement.

Legally their position was good, for Feisal had been handed over by his father, with full discretion in what concerned his Army, to Allenby's command. We wired to Allenby asking him either to smooth out the incident, or to procure the abdication of King Hussein. The second was possible, the first difficult, since Hussein was obstinate and crafty, and it might take weeks to force him out of his obstacles, to an apology. Normally we could have afforded these weeks: but at this unhappy season we were in the position that in three days if at all, our expedition to Deraa, and we hoped Damascus, must start. Hussein could not apologize in time, even if he acted to Allenby by return of telegraph, and we were compelled to some means of 'carrying on' despite him, to get us over our first difficulty.

My first duty was to send one of my men express to Nuri Shaalan to say that I could not meet him at the gathering of his tribes in Kaf but would be in Azrak from the first day of the new moon, expecting him. This was a sad expedient, for Nuri might take suspicion, and fail at the tryst, and without the Rualla half the efficiency and importance of our force before Deraa on the sixteenth would disappear. However, we had to risk this smaller loss since without Feisal and the regulars and Pisani's guns there would be no expedition, and with Joyce away my presence in Aba el Lissan was almost the only way to ensure their following our wishes.

My second duty was to start off the caravans for Azrak: — the baggage, the food, the petrol, the ammunition. Young prepared all these, rising as ever, to any occasion not of his own seeking. He was his own first obstacle, but would have no man hinder him. Never could I forget the radiant face of Nuri Said, after a joint conference, encountering a group of Arab officers with the cheerful words, 'Never mind, you fellows, he talks to the English just as he does to us!' Now he went down to the army camp, and saw that each echelon started — not indeed to time but only a day late — under its appointed officers according to program. It was our principle to issue orders to the Arabs only through their own chiefs, never directly, and we had followed this rule so exactly that they had no precedent for disobedience. Actually, off they went like lambs.

My third duty was to face a mutiny of the troops. They had heard false rumors of the real bearing of the crisis. Particularly, the gunners misunderstood, and one afternoon fell out with their officers, and rushed off to turn the guns on their tents. However, Rasim, the artillery commandant, had forestalled them by collecting all the breech-blocks into a pyramid inside his tent. I took advantage of this comic moment to go down to their Camp and meet the men. They were tense at first, but their curiosity eventually conquered, and they fell to talking with me. To them I was only an eccentric name, of one always with the Bedu, out on raid: and my aloofness, even mystery, made them interested to see me.

I told them the silly coffee-cup storm which was raging among the high heads, and they laughed merrily. Their faces were turned towards the north not the south towards Damascus not Mecca, and they cared for nothing outside their army. Their fear had been that Feisal had deserted the cause, since for days he had not been out. I promised to prove my case by asking Feisal and Zeid to come down and see them instantly: and when he, looking as usual drove through the lines in the green Vauxhall which Bois had made especially green for him, their eyes convinced them of their error, and he had to make no explanation.

My fourth duty was to start off the columns of troops for Azrak on the right day. For this, the solidity of the officers had to be in part restored. Stirling's tact affected this well enough to hold them together. Nuri Said, in command, was ambitious as any soldier would have been to make much of the great opportunity before him, and readily agreed to move as far as Azrak, pending the receipt of Hussein's apology. If it was unsatisfactory they could return, or throw off allegiance; and if it came, as I assured him it would, the unmerited services of the Northern Army meanwhile should bring a blush to the unfit old man's cheek.

The ranks responded to bluffer arguments. The enemy reminded them of the danger of too great a devotion to politics, by making gentle preliminary pushes towards Tafileh and Semna while they argued. We made plain that the gross questions of food and pay depended entirely on the maintenance of army organization. They yielded, and the separate columns, of mounted infantry, of machine-gunners, of Egyptian sappers, of Gurkhas, of Pisani's gunners, moved off in their courses, only two days late, according to the orders of Stirling and Young.

The last obligation was to restore Feisal's supremacy. To attempt anything serious between Deraa and Damascus without him would be a vain hope. We could put in the attack on Deraa, which was what Allenby expected from us: but the capture of Damascus which was what I expected from the Arabs, the reason why I had joined them in the field, and taken ten thousand pains, and spent all my wit and strength — that depended on Feisal's being present with us in the fighting line, ready to take over and exploit what our bodies conquered for him.

He would not desert his officers' cause: but offered to serve under me as a volunteer, in my Arab Movement. He said I had been the real leader for two years, so that it would only be to register a truth. I replied succinctly that I had not, and did not want, an Arab Movement: and if the Arabs could not at least pretend to lead one another, I was not going to help them.

There remained to get the apology from Mecca. Allenby and Wilson were doing their best, engrossing the cables. If they failed, my only course would be to force an open break between Feisal and his father: to promise to Feisal the direct support of the British Government, and to drive him into Damascus as sovereign prince. It was possible: indeed it was only to precipitate the inevitable, and in its reserve lay my confidence to Dawnay: but I wanted to avoid it except as a last necessity. It was my judgment that the Arabs hitherto in their Revolt had made clean history, and I did not wish our adventure to come to the pitiable case of scission before the common victory and its peace. Obviously Damascus could never form part of Hejaz — rather it was to be hoped that Hejaz would form part of Damascus — but these party politics should wait till the Turks gave in. For that reason I waited and waited for the reply from Mecca.

King Hussein behaved truly to type, protesting fluently, with endless circumlocution, showing no understanding of the grave effect of his invasion into Northern Army affairs. It was intolerable to be at the mercy of so crass a person. One would have wished such characters confined to Turkey, and indeed Hussein was 'palace Turk' in mind and manner, and in his habit of writing unintelligible nonsense and calling it official correspondence. To clear his mind we sent him some plain statements, which drew abusive returns. His wires came through Egypt to our operators in Akaba, and I had them sent up to me by car, for delivery to Feisal. The Arabic ciphers were simple, and I had each translated by Hilmi Bey, Joyce's capable and keen Egyptian Staff Officer, and used to mutilate undesirable passages by rearranging their figures into nonsense, before handing them in code to Feisal. By this easy expedient the temper of his entourage was not needlessly complicated.

This play went on for several days, Mecca never repeating a message notified corrupt, but telegraphing in its place a fresh version toned down a little from the original harshness at each re-editing. Finally there came a long odd message, whose first half comprised a withdrawal and lame apology of the mischievous proclamation, which the second half repeated in a new and glaring form. I suppressed this tail, and took the head marked 'very urgent' myself to Feisal's tent, where he sat in the full circle of his advisers and officers.

His secretary at once worked out the dispatch, and handed the dispatcher to Feisal. My hints had roused expectation and all eyes were on him as he read it. He was astonished, and gazed wonderingly at me, for the meek words were very unlike his father's querulous obstinacy. Then he pulled himself together, read the apology aloud, and at the end said thrillingly, 'The telegraph has saved all our honor.'

There came a chorus of delight in which he bent aside to whisper in my ear, 'I mean the honor of nearly all of us.' It was done so delightfully (we were really intimate) that I laughed aloud, and said demurely, 'I cannot understand what you mean.' He replied, 'I offered to serve under you: why was that not enough?' ... 'Because it would not go with your honor.' He murmured, 'You put mine before your own', and then sprang energetically to his feet, saying, 'Now, Sirs, praise God and work.' In three hours we had settled timetables, arranged for our successors here in Aba el Lissan, with their spheres and duties, and I took my leave. Joyce had just returned, and Feisal promised that he would come with him and Marshall to Azrak to join me on the twelfth at latest. All the camp was singing as I got into a Rolls tender and set off for Azrak, hoping to rally the Rualla in time for our attack on Deraa.

BOOK X

The House is Perfected

Our mobile column of airplanes, armored can, Arab Regulars and Bedouin *collected at Azrak. We determined to rot all through railways leading out of Deraa.*

The southern line we rot near Mafrak, then the northern at Arar, then the western by Mezeno. We circumnavigated Deraa and returned to Umtaiye, our advanced base in the desert.

Next day Allenby attacked, and in a few hours scattered the Turks beyond recovery.

Meanwhile, however; their airplanes established a supremacy over us. I flew to Palestine for help, and got it, together with my orders for the second phase of the thrust northward.

We moved behind Deraa to hasten its abandonment. General Barrow joined us and in his company we advanced to Ktszoe, where we found General Chauvel. The united forces entered Damascus unopposed.

There was some confusion in the city. While we strove to allay it, Allenby arrived and smoothed out all the difficulties afterward she let me go.

Chapter 122: Pleasure of Empty Azrak

It was an inexpressible pleasure to have left the mists behind and have no more friends, only a plain enemy to deal with. We caught at each other with thankfulness as we drove along. Winterton, Nasir and myself Lord Winterton was our latest recruit an experienced officer from Buxton's Camel Corps. Sherif Nasir was coming up to oversee the rally at Azrak, for he who had been the spear-point of the Arab Army since the first days of Medina, had been chosen by us for the field-work on this last occasion also. He deserved the honor of Damascus for his had been the honors of Medina, of Wejh, of Akaba, and of Tafileh.

In accord with my year-old principle Feisal would be kept in the background in reserve to be risked as a last card only if the situation was overtaxing our strengths, or if we were certainly victors. Until then to fill his place we needed an experienced and popular Sherif in command since we would have contingents of Rualla, of Serahin, of Druses, of Beni Sakhr, and of Howeitat tribesmen on this expedition to Deraa, besides masses of peasant horse and foot from the villages of the Hauran: — and everyone loved Nasir's gay simplicity.

A painstaking little Ford hung on in the dust behind our splendid car, as it drank up the now familiar miles through Jefer to Bair. While we moved, it was cool in the rush of air: but when we stopped the sun-blaze wilted us. Though strenuous the drive was two days of almost mournful comfort, compared with the past. Once I had been so proud of riding from Azrak to Akaba by Rum in three days: — and now we did the shorter road by routine nearly in two days, and slept well of nights after this kind exercise of driving in our Rolls-Royce's, like the great ones of war.

We noted again how easy their lives were, the soft body and the unexhausted sinews leaving the brain free to concentrate itself upon a work of which the fiercest might be done in an armchair. In those days, ours had been day-and-night effort for both brain and body only lying down for the stupor of an hour's sleep in the flush of dawn and the flush of sunset, the two seasons of the day through which the Arabs found it unwholesome to ride. For the rest it had been twenty-two out of the twenty-four hours in the saddle, each taking it in turn to lead the way through the dark hours to the chill before dawn, while the others let their heads nod forward over the pommel in nescience.

Not that it was more than a thin nescience: for even in the deepest of such sleep the foot went on pressing the camel's shoulder to keep it at the cross-country pace, and if the balance was lost ever so little when the beast lurched in a false stride or at a turn the rider awoke in a sickening clutch of recovery at the saddle-bow. Then we had had rain and snow and sun beating upon us without defense, little food, little water no safety on the way against either Turks or Arabs. Yet those forced months with the tribes had given me the freedom of the desert taught me the country and the people in a fashion to bring victory with a surety in planning affairs which seemed lunatic rashness to newcomers but which was no more than an exact knowledge of my materials.

This time the desert was not normal: indeed it was shamefully popular. From Ghadir el Haj up to Bair we were never out of sight of men; small groups or tenuous columns of troops and tribesmen and baggage on camels were strung out over the Jefer flat as long as the eye could see, all moving slowly and steadily northward. Past this activity of good omen for our punctual concentration at Azrak we roared at top speed, my excellent driver. Green achieving sixty-seven miles an hour for some minutes with his tender. The half-stifled Nasir in the box could only wave his hand across a furlong to each friend we overtook.

At Bair it was good to hear from the alarmed Beni Sakhr that the Turks, on the preceding day had launched suddenly westward from Jurf and Hesa, and had forced their way, with little fighting into Tafileh. Mifleh thought I was mad. or most untimely merry when I laughed outright at the news: but it was really rich, good as a bloodless victory so to have trapped the unsuspecting Turks.

Four days earlier their offensive would have held up the Azrak expedition: but now everyone was launched beyond recall into the desert and the enemy might take Aba el Lissan, Guweira, Akaba itself: — and welcome! We had pulled their leg nearly out of its socket with our formidable talk of advance by Kerak on Amman, and here the poor innocents were out to counter our feint! It was another splendid omen of success, for each man sent south was a man, or rather ten men, lost to them.

In Azrak on September the sixth we found just a few Blaidat men, servants of Nuri Shaalan, sent by him to occupy it till he came: and down on the mud-flat aerodrome was the Crossley car sent up from Akaba by Siddons, with a flying officer, a mechanic, some spares, and a canvas hangar for the Bristol Fighter and the B.E.I2, the two machines which he had settled to put here for aerial defense in advance of our concentration and while it was taking place. We did not want our force spotted and bombed at the outset of its adventure, and the Bristol was so superior in the air to the enemy machines that it should bring down any casual air patrol which the Turks might send over Azrak, before it could report us.

We spent our first night on the aerodrome and suffered for it. A reckless armor-plated camel — fly, biting like a hornet, occupied our exposed places until sunset. Then came a blessed relief, and we began to feel the itch becoming milder in the evening cool when the wind changed, and hot blinding showers of salty dust swept over us for three hours. We lay down behind such shelter as there was, and drew covers over our heads to shield them: but could not sleep. Each half-hour we had to throw out the new layer of sand which threatened to bury us. At midnight the wind ceased, and we issued out from our sweaty nests and restfully prepared to sleep when singing, a cloud of mosquitoes rolled over us, and then we fought till dawn.

Accordingly at dawn we changed camp to the height of the Mejaber ridge, a mile west of the water , and so free of the mosquitoes, a hundred feet above the marshes in enjoyment of all winds that blew: and there we rested a while, and then put up the hangar, and afterwards went off to bathe. In the silver pools, as we undressed beside them, the water was sparkling almost as though lit up from beneath, for the sides and floor were of pearl-white ground, reflecting the sky with a moony radiance. 'Delicious', I yelled as I splashed in and swam about. 'But why do we keep on bobbing under water?' asked Winterton a moment later, and then a horse-fly bit him behind, and he understood and leaped in after me. We swam about, desperately keeping our heads wet, to dissuade the swarm of grey flies: but they were too bold with hunger to be afraid of water: and after five minutes we struggled out, and frantically into our clothes: but were not covered before the blood was running down us from twenty of their dagger-bites.

Nasir stood and laughed at us: and later we journeyed together to the fort, to rest midday there. I went into Ali ibn el Hussein's old room in the corner tower above the garden where it was cool and peaceful, under this only roof in the desert. The wind gently stirred the palm-fronds outside to a frosty rustling. They were neglected palms, too northerly for their red date-crop to be good, so that the stems were thick with low branches, and threw a pleasant shade. Under them on his carpet sat Nasir smoking. I leaned through my square-framed basalt window and spoke with him in the quietness. The grey smoke of his thrown-away cigarette undulated out on the warm air, flickering and fading through the sun-spots which shone between the leaves. 'I am happy,' said he.

Indeed we were all happy here in this spot where Nature learning economy, had become a very careful artist. With one red flower at Azrak she gave us more pleasure than with a rose garden in Cyprus. In the afternoon an armored car came up, completing our necessary defense, though the risk of an enemy raid was minute. The Serahin covered the country between us and the railway, and both they and the Beni Hassan and Serdiyeh were our men, knew that we were here, and would report anything which moved: though indeed the enemy had little to move, for there were only forty horsemen in Deraa and none in Amman, and Azrak was a formidable march for infantry.

Also as yet they had no news of us. An airplane flew over on the morning of the ninth made a perfunctory circle of the place, and went off, probably without seeing us.

Good for it that Murphy in his Bristol Fighter was not here! Our camp on its airy summit looked out north, south, east, and west, and gave us splendid observation and command of the Deraa and Amman roads, and in it we slept comfortably at nights: or rather I did, enjoying the precious interval between the conquered troubles of Aba el Lissan and the unknown efforts of the next month. By day we twelve English, with Nasir and his slave, lazed about peacefully: roaming, bathing at sunset, sight-seeing and thinking about the future.

The preciousness would Seem to have been partly in myself, for in this march on Damascus (and such it already was in my imagination) my normal balance became weighed down. I could feel the tautness and power of the Arab excitement behind me. The climax of the preaching of years had come, and the united country was straining towards its historic capital in my inner confidence that this weapon, tempered by myself, was exalted enough for the utmost of my purpose, I seemed to have forgotten my English companions who stood outside my idea in the shadow of ordinary war, and to have failed to make them partners of my certainty.

Long after, by chance, I heard that Winterton rose each day before dawn, and went out to examine all the views to the horizon, fearing lest my carelessness subject us to surprise: and later at Umtaiye and Sheikh Saad the British for days thought we were a forlorn hope. Actually I knew (and surely said) that we were as safe as anyone in the world at war; and they were so proud that I never saw their doubt. I was walking by my inner light of experience and foresight: but my sureness seemed to them luck, and my clearness heady. So, unconsciously, I put an unnecessary strain upon their loyalty, and in amends must bear witness that hardly one ever failed me for an instant.

My plans, for what they mattered, were a parody of Allenby's, Their ends were a feint against Amman and a real cutting of the Deraa railways: further than this they hardly went, for it was ever my habit to keep the stages in solution. I knew to the last suspicion our present, and could see our goal in the sharpest outline: but the intermediate steps — on those my mind was yet open, ready to snatch any good or bad chance we met, to make them all guests at our feast, stepping-stones to our purpose.

The public often gave credit to the generals because it saw only the orders and the result: but the generals knew, for theirs was the idea, and they had seen it marred in execution, even when the executive, as here, was also myself usually the executives was other than the strategist, and tinged the plan, as it developed. Foch said (before he commanded troops) that generals won battles: but no general ever truly thought so. The Syrian campaign of September 1918 was perhaps the most scientifically perfect in English history, one in which force did least and brain most. The entire world, and especially those who served them, gave the credit of the victory to Allenby and Bartholomew: but those two would never see it in our light.

They knew how their inchoate ideas were discovered by application, and how it was their men who wrought them. The abstract envied the physical, as much as the physical despised and coveted thought. We subtracted our commanders from the fighting line, for the reason that it was impossible from a place of safety, in hot blood, to order another into danger. If they had the choice generals, for their self-respect, would assume the points of hardship or adventure, preferring to risk their own lives, which were in their discretion: except when they served a mastering ideal, and then to it they would offer a general sacrifice, willingly fitting others as teasers into the common design which comprehended all their consciousness.

Chapter 123: Our Slow Collection

However, with our establishment at Azrak the first part of our plan the feint — was accomplished: if indeed it did not happen that the powerful infection of general praise swept away the defenses of our dissatisfaction, so that we thought we had ordered all that fortuitously passed, and no more than passed! Anyhow, we had feinted, both of us, against Amman.

Allenby, while withdrawing every man of value, had filled up the Jordan with sham troops, to look massed for attack. We had sent our 'horsemen of St George', as the Italians called them, gold sovereigns, to the Beni Sakhr , purchasing all the heaps of barley on their threshing floors: begging them not to mention it, but we would require it for our animals and for the animals of our British allies in a fortnight. Dhiab of Tafileh — that jerky, incomplete hobbled boy — whose loyalty was now spotted, had also been sworn into our confidence and had gossiped the news through to Kerak: besides, the thousands we spent were enough to convince the most skeptical.

In addition, Feisal had warned the Zebn to Bair, for service: and Hornby, now perhaps a little prematurely wearing Arab clothes, and trying to obey their customs, was out making active preparations for a great assault on Madeba and Urn el Rusas, as I had planned with Trad in May this year. Hornby had grown fond of the Bedouin, seeing in them the key of operations, those who gave us access and domination — everything but defense. Also, very usefully, he was making himself a companion rather than an officer. The Arabs had men and to spare who would go in front. We were of the rank and file, a greater part than leadership, for our presence in the ranks raised the standard to our keenness: but unhappily no higher. Like most revolts, Feisal's was a combination of the poor and the illuminated and depended for its virtue on the excellence of the poor.

Hornby's plan was to let us get off to Azrak (where we supported his threat, being best suited to drive at Amman from the east), and then to move again into Wadi Hesa, for Madeba, about the nineteenth, when he heard that Allenby was started and ourselves engaged. His hope was to tie on to Jericho: so that if we failed by Deraa we could return to his area, and reinforce his movement. It then would be, not merely a feint, but a sane and proper scheme, the old second string to our bow. However, the Turks knocked it rather crooked by their advance to Tafileh, and Scott had to send up Hornby to defend Shobek against them.

Now at Azrak we were embarked on the Deraa business, and had to plan our attack proper. As a preliminary move we determined to cut the line between Deraa and Amman, nearer Amman. This would prevent the reinforcement of Deraa from the south two days later when we threatened it: and for those two days would maintain the conviction in Amman that our feint against it was real. It seemed to me that it could be done by our Gurkha party, with the Egyptian demolition-squad to do the actual destruction: their detachment for the purpose would not in any way distract our main body from the main purpose.

This main purpose was to cut the railways in the Hauran, and keep them cut for at least a week: and there seemed three ways of doing it. The first was to march north of Deraa, to the Damascus line, as on my ride with Taiai in the winter, cut it on a great scale, and then cross it to the Yarmuk line and blow up Tel Shehab bridge. The second was to march south of Deraa to the Yarmuk as with Ali ibn el Hussein in November 1911 and the third was to rush Deraa town.

The third scheme was the best, but it could only be undertaken if the Air Force would promise us so heavy a daylight bombing of Deraa station that we could risk an assault against it with our few men, in spite of our lack of fortress artillery. Salmond hoped to do this for us but it depended on how many D.H.9s and Handley Pages he had received or assembled in time. Alan Dawnay would fly over to us here with his last word on September the eleventh. Till then we would hold the schemes equal in our judgment. If the assault fell through, then the way round Deraa by the north seemed second in attraction.

In our supports, my bodyguard were the first to arrive prancing up Wadi Sirhan on the ninth , happy to see me, looking fatter than their camels, rested and amused after their month with the Rualla. They reported Nuri nearly ready to join us, and the contagion of the new tribe's first vigor had quickened in them life and spirit for the coming adventure. They made us jolly for they were good to look at most of them, and good to talk to some of them: and we were less constrained less swaddled in convention, together, than with any others of our movement. They spread through the bushes their little camps of groups of four or five, those fellows whom the hazards of war had attracted to one another.

On the tenth the two airplanes came through correctly from Akaba. Murphy, the Australian pilot of the Bristol Fighter, and junior, Siddons' choice for the B.E.I2 were both self-sufficing people and settled down without making too much of the horse flies who gamboled in the air about their juiciness. On the eleventh the other armored cars and Joyce drove in, with Stirling, but without Feisal. It frightened me for the moment with dreams of another mess, but Joyce said that Marshall remained to squire him up next day; and things were always safe to go well where Marshall the capable soul directed them with his cultivated humor, which was not so riotous as persistent. Young Peake, Scott-Higgins and the baggage arrived in due order. Azrak became peopled and its lakes were again resonant all day with voices and the plunge of brown and lean brown and strong copper-colored or white bodies into their transparent water.

I was interested to see how Azrak behaved itself before a crowd, and noting how differently we treated it Pisani, the Frenchman, liked it so much that he swore in peace time to build here a chalet and live in it: whereas the sentimental English wanted to creep away from it before either it or we lost the sense of freshness. We had to hold our breath to feel its strength — that Roman silence so much more durable than shouting — as it lay there remembering Diocletian, Harith and ibn Shedad. It would be odd to return to see if we merely ruffled the surface of its pools, or if it now had memories of Feisal, Nasir, and the armored cars.

On the eleventh the airplane from Palestine arrived. Unfortunately Dawnay was again ill, and the staff-officer who took his place had never been up flying before, had suffered severely from the roughness of the air on the way across, and had left behind the notes he was to bring us. His rather concrete assurance, that regard upon his world of the finished Englishmen, gave way before these shocks, and that final shock of our naked carelessness out there in the desert, without pickets or watching posts, signalers, sentries or telephones, or any apparent reserve, refuge or base anywhere.

So he forgot to give us his most important news, how on September the sixth Allenby had had a new inspiration and had said to Bartholomew, 'Why bother about Messudieh? Let the cavalry go straight to Afuleh, and afterwards to Nazareth': and so the whole plan had been changed and an enormous indefinite advance arranged, instead of a fixed objective. We got no notion of this, but by cross-questioning the pilot, whom Salmond had informed, we got a clear statement of his resources in bombing machines. They fell short of our minimum required to let us rush Deraa cheaply, so we asked just for a hamper-bombing of it, and decided to go north past Deraa, to Tell Arar, and make sure of destroying the Damascus line.

The next day Feisal arrived with Marshall, fit and glad to be out in the unfurnished world again, quit of telegraphs and politics, on an adventure. Behind him came the army of troops, with Nuri Said the spick and span, and Jemil the gunner, with Pisani's coster-like Algerians, and all the other items of our 'three men and a boy' effort. The grey flies had now two thousand camels to fatten upon, and in their weariness gave up Junor and his half-drained mechanics.

In the afternoon, Nuri Shaalan appeared, with Trad and Khalid, Faris. Durzi, and the Khaffaji. Auda Abu Tayi arrived, with Mohammed el Dhcilan, and Fahad and Adhub the Zebn leaders, with ibn Bani, the chief of the Serahin, and ibn Genj of the Serdiyeh Majid ibn Sultan of the Adwan near Salt, came across to learn the truth of our attack on Amman. Later in the evening there was a rattle of rifle fire in the north and Taiai el Hareidhin my old companion, came ruffling at the gallop with forty or fifty mounted peasants behind him, His sanguine face beamed with joy at our having at length arrived. Druses and Syrians, Isawiyeh and Hawarneh swelled our company. Even the barley for our return if the venture failed (a possibility we did not think on), began to arrive in a steady file of loads. Everyone was stout and in good health.

Except myself The crowd had destroyed my pleasure in Azrak, and I went off down the valley to our remote Ain el Essad, and lay there all day in my old lair among the tamarisk, where the wind was playing in the dusty green branches with such sounds as it made in English trees: and hearing it I wished very much to be safely there, out of it all. On the ground there was scratched again and again in English, 'He wrote his name in sand' — my epitaph which I had written unconsciously, was it last time, or the time before, or when I first came? Anyway this trip had fixed in my mind that the only honorable state was to be alone and that I was tired to death of these Arabs, and of my unlikeness to them. We English had an instinct so strong for compromise that it would be called a passion if its object were not the mean: whereas the Arabs. The petty incarnate Semite, reached heights and depths beyond our reach, though not beyond our sight. They realized our absolute, in their unrestrained capacity for good and evil; and for two years I had shammed to be their companion....

On September the thirteenth Peake with his Egyptian Camel Corps, now become a sapper party to blow up the line; Scott Higgins with a fighting escort of Gurkhas, and two armored cars as their insurance, went off to cut the railway by If dein, the place where Ali ibn el Hussein had crossed the line with me above Mafrak station, on our way to hide in Ghadir el Abyadh. There lay a stretch of five miles of line, which our airplanes had examined, and proved to hold only one little central redoubt in all its length.

Our scheme was for Scott-Higgins to rush this after dark with his nimble Indians — nimble on foot that was to say, for they were like sacks on camels. Peake was then to occupy the line and demolish till dawn, under cover of a car on each flank. The cars would cover his retreat eastwards in the morning, over the plain towards Urn el Jemal, where he would find us, the main body, marching north from Azrak for Umtaiye, the great pit of rainwater fifteen miles south-east of Deraa, which was to be our advanced base. We gave them Rualla guides, and saw them go off hopefully for this most important preliminary operation.

Chapter 124: The First Railway

At dawn on the fourteenth the column marched. Of them one thousand were the Aba el Lissan contingent: and three hundred were Nun Shaalan's nomad horse. He had in hand also some two thousand Rualla camel corps: but these we asked him to keep still in Wadi Sirhan. It seemed not wise, before the supreme moment, to launch so many disturbing Beduin among the villages of Hauran. The horsemen were either sheikhs or sheikhs' servants, all men of substance, under control.

Affairs to be discussed with Nun and Feisal held me some hours yet in Azrak, while the others marched away: but Joyce left me a tender, the Blue Mist, by which, on the morning of the fifteenth, I overtook the army in mid-morning. They were breakfasting among the grass-filled roughness of the Giaan el Khunna: and the camels, happy to be out of the barren circle of Azrak, were packing their stomachs hastily with this best of food.

Joyce had bad news. Peake's demolition-party had rejoined, reporting a failure to reach the line, because of trouble with the Arabs on their line of march. It perturbed me, for we had chosen them an area quite free of tribal encampments: but the guides explained that by a misunderstanding they had been made to go fifteen miles too far south, into the midst of the main sept of Serahin, whose fighting men were with us on the understanding that this area be kept outside the operations, and consequently of feared air reprisals against their families.

Their flocks were watering from Wadi Zerka, west of the railway, and would be lost if the Turks forbade their passage across. So when Peake turned up among them it seemed a breach of faith on my part, and the remaining men hotly refused to let him through to damage their part of the line. Accordingly, Peake with his camels and cars had to turn back: and instead of trying further north, thought it best to tell us quickly of this unfavorable local attitude.

We had set store on a breaking of the Amman railway, and the check was an offense to our wishes. To cast about for a means to set us right I left the car, took a load of guncotton, and mounted my camel, to push in advance of the force across the harsh tongues of lava which ran down from Safa westwards toward the railway. The others made a detour to avoid the worst of these, since they were bad for camels, but we, well-mounted, cut straight across by a thieves' path and came out, an hour ahead of everyone, on the open plain about the ruined Urn el jernal.

I was thinking hard what expedient would be quickest and best, puzzled to pick on one: and the puzzle of these ruins was added to my care. There seemed evidence of a certain bluntness of mind in these Roman frontier-cities, Urn el Jemal, Urn el Surab, Umtaiye. Such incongruous buildings in what was then and now a desert cockpit accused their builders of insensitiveness, almost of a vulgar assertion of man's right (Romans' right) to live unchanged in all his estate as if the standard of well-being were fixed. Italianate buildings — only to be paid for by taxing more docile provinces on these fringes of the world disclosed a prosaic blindness to the transience of their builders' politics. A house which survived the purpose of its master was a pride, a snatching at material authority, too trivial to honor the mind which conceived it.

Urn el jernal seemed so aggressive and impudent, and the railway beyond it so tiresomely intact that they blinded me to an air-battle between Murphy in our Bristol, and an enemy two-seater. It was a hard fight, and the Bristol was badly shot about before the Turk went down in flames between Urn el jernal and Ifdein. Our army were spectators, and delighted: but Murphy had to return at once to Azrak for repair, and finding the damage too great for his few materials, went over to Palestine in the morning. It was unfortunate, as Akaba had no other modern machine, and Palestine sent no successor: so that when our crisis came we found ourselves reduced to the B.E.12, a type so out of date that it was impossible for fighting, and little use for reconnaissance. This we discovered on the day: meanwhile we were as glad as the army at our man's win.

We reached our goal, Umtaiye, just before sunset. The troops were five or six miles behind, so, as soon as the Rualla scouts, sent here in advance to guard against enemy mischief, had announced all well, we watered our camels, and struck off to the railway, only four miles downhill to the westward, thinking to do a snatch demolition. The dusk let us get close without alarm, and to our joy we found that the whole going, though up and down, of valleys interspersed with fields of rock, was yet possible for armored cars: while just before us were two good bridges, and the line seemed very much at ease, insufficiently guarded.

These points decided me to do nothing now, but to return in the morning, with the cars and more guncotton, to abolish the larger, four-arched bridge. Its destruction would give the Turks some days' hard mending, and so set us free of Amman all the time of our first Deraa raid; thus the purpose of Peake's failed demolition would be fully supplied. It was a happy discovery, and we rode back, quartering the ground as well as we could in the gathering darkness, to pick the best car road.

As we climbed the last ridge, a high unbroken watershed which hid Umtaiye completely from the railway and its possible watchmen, the fresh north-east wind blew into our faces the warm smell and dust often thousand feet: and from the crest the view of the ruins was so startlingly unlike three hours before that we pulled up to take it in. The hollow ground was spangled with hundreds of little evening fires, freshly lighted, still twinkling with the flame reflections in their smoke. About them the force was making bread or coffee, while others drove their noisy camels to and from the water. After a year's stern limitation to mark-time raids, it was uplifting to be engaged in a thing of scale.

I rode to the dark camp, the British one, and sat there with Joyce and Winterton and Young, telling them of what we might do first thing in the morning. Beside us lay and smoked the British soldiers, very quiet, willing to risk their lives and bodies on this expedition of whose cause and purpose they knew nothing, simply because we wished it. It was a thing typical, as steeped and instinct with our national character as that babbling laughing turmoil over there was Arab. In their crisis the one race drew deep in, the other spread wide out.

In the morning Nasir sat in council with Joyce, Nuri Said, and me, while the army breakfasted, and thawed the dawn-chill from their muscles in the sun. We explained the fitness of the line here for a car-raid: and it was determined that two armored cars should run down to the bridge marked last night, and attack it, while the main body continued their march north, across Wadi Taiyibe, past Deraa, to Tell Arar on the Damascus railway, four miles north of Deraa station. They would take place there, possessing the line, at dawn tomorrow the seventeenth of September: and we with the cars would have finished this bridge and rejoined them before that.

We started about two in the afternoon, after Nuri Said and Nasir were clear, and as we drove down towards the railway had the great sight of a swarm of our bombing planes droning steadily up towards Deraa on their first raid. The place had hitherto been carefully reserved from air attack, so that the damage and disorder among the unaccustomed, unprotected, unarmed garrison were very heavy. The morale of the men suffered by it as much as the railway traffic: and till our onslaught from the north forced them to see us, all their efforts went in digging bomb-proof shelters for themselves. It helped our forthcoming attack on the bridge, and ensured Nuri Said's long and vulnerable column a safe march past Deraa to their far-fetched attacking point.

We lurched across plots of grass, with bars and fields of stones between them, roughly, in our two tenders of guncotton and two armored cars, but arrived all well behind the last ridge before the railway in the bed of a tributary valley which joined its main stream just this side of our target bridge. A stone blockhouse stood on the rise south of the bridge, held by Turks.

We settled to leave the tenders here, under cover. I transferred myself with one hundred and fifty pounds of guncotton on, ready prepared, to one armored car, deciding to drive down the bed of the valley towards the bridge till, if possible, its arches sheltered us from the lire of the post, and enabled us to get out and lay and light the demolition charges. Meanwhile the other, the lighting car, would go straight over to the blockhouse and engage it at short rang to cover my activities.

So the two cars set out simultaneously, mine crawling carefully downstream towards our bridge, which had a florid Turkish inscription on a white marble plaque inviting us, while the other finding the bed between it and the post too deep to cross directly, had to make a circuit to the left to compass it. The astonished garrison of seven or eight Turks, when they saw and heard us, got out of their trenches, and, rifles in hand, advanced in open order upon us, moved either by panic, by misunderstanding or by unmixed courage.

In a few minutes we heard the second car come into action against them: when four other Turks appeared beside the bridge and shot at us. Grisenthwaite halted the car, while our machine gunners ranged on them, and fired a short burst. One man fell another was hit: the rest ran a little way, thought better of it and returned making friendly signs. We drove close, took their rifles, and sent them up valley to the tenders, whose drivers, with Joyce and Winterton, watched us keenly from their ridge. Then we saw the second car appear on the railway bank above us by the blockhouse which they occupied. Thence they could enfilade the line and the other enemy wisely made off to the south with our goodwill, for we had no facility for prisoners and were very content to have taken the bridge, and the linesmen's hut, and this section of track in five minutes without loss.

Joyce rushed down in a tender with more guncotton, while the armored-ear crews kept watch upon the Turkish posts of some strength which stood some two miles north and south of us. Hastily we set about the bridge hoping for half an hour of quiet in which to finish. It was a pleasant little work, about eighty feet long and fifteen feet high. First we brought down, hoping to take away, the laudatory slab of Abd el Hamid: and then we stood on the pier-buttresses, which were conveniently flat-headed, to clear the drainage holes in the arch-spandrels. In these, six small charges were inserted zigzag, and with their explosion all the arches were scientifically shattered, the demolition being a fine example of that finest sort, which left the skeleton of the bridge intact indeed, but tottering, so that the enemy had a first labor to destroy the wreck, before they could begin to rebuild.

Meanwhile Joyce and Winterton tried their new hands with some 'tulips' (our latest track-demolition) on the line each side of the bridge. When we had finished the enemy were near enough to give us fair excuse for quitting. So we put the prisoners on the back of an armored car, and bumped off. Unfortunately we bumped too carelessly in our joy and at the first water-course there was a crash beneath my tender, and one side of its box body tipped downward till the weight came on the tire of the back wheel and we stuck.

We jumped out to look, and found that the front bracket of the near back spring had crystallized through by the chassis in a sheer break which nothing but a workshop could mend. We were in despair for we were only three hundred yards from the railway and stood to lose all our kit and the car when the enemy came along in ten minutes. A Rolls in the desert was above rubies and we had never lost one yet, though we had been driving in them for eighteen months without one inch of made road, across country of the vilest, at speed day or night doing perhaps twenty thousand mile carrying a ton of goods and four or five men up. This was our first structural accident in our team of nine.

Rolls the driver our strongest and most resourceful man, the ready mechanic largely by whose skill and advice it was that our cars kept in running order, was nearly in tears over his mishap. At last he said there was just one chance. If we lightened the car we might jack up the fallen end of the spring, and by scantling on the running-board wedge it in nearly its old position. The thin angle-irons of the running boards might carry the weight, with the help of ropes.

We had a piece of four-inch scantling tied to the car the beam which was placed between the double tires for the car to climb along if ever it got stuck in sand or mud. Three blocks of this would make the height. We had no saw, but quickly drove bullets through it cross-wise till we could snap it nearly off. The Turks heard us firing and halted cautiously. Joyce heard us and ran back to help. Into his car we piled our load jacked up the spring and the chassis, lashed in the wooden baulks, let her down on them (she bore splendidly) cranked up and drove off. Rolls eased her to walking speed at every stone and ditch on the way back, while we ran beside with cries of encouragement clearing her track for her.

In camp, by more rifle-shots, we made holes to stitch the blocks of scantling to one another with captured telegraph wire, and bound them together and to the chassis, and the spring to the chassis, till it looked as strong as possible: — and so enduring was the running board that we put back the load, and did all ordinary work with the car for the next three weeks, and took her so into Damascus at the end. Great was Rolls, and great was Royce! They were worth hundreds of men to us in these deserts.

Our darning the car delayed us for hours, and at the end we slept in Umtaiye, confident that, by starting before dawn, we would not be much late in meeting Nuri Said on the Damascus line tomorrow: and we could tell him that the Amman line was sealed, by the loss of a main bridge, for best part of a week. This was the line of quickest reinforcement for Deraa, and its death made our rear safe against enveloping attack while we demonstrated against Deraa and the Yarmuk. Even we had helped somewhat poor Zeid, behind there in Aba el Lissan: for the Tafileh and Amman Turks would stand still, waiting for their communications to be again open.

Our last campaign was beginning auspiciously.

Chapter 125: The Second Railway

Duly before dawn we woke, and drove upon the tracks of Stirling's cars, eager to be with them before their fight. Unfortunately the going was not helpful. At first we had a bad descent to the plain, and then difficult flats of jagged dolerite, across which we crawled painfully. At Taiyibe, the first village in its great valley, we crossed the derelict earthwork of the former branch-line to Bosra. Half the village helped us with excited directions. Their horsemen were in front, with Nasir: but those remaining, especially the lads, were vividly impressed with their privileges as rebels, and fought boisterously to climb aboard, or snatched what was portable, as souvenirs. We had to take sharp measures against being plundered.

Later we ran faster over ploughed slopes, winding about to miss the villages of Saida and Nueime, and their too-warm greetings. The soil was heavy for the cars, for with the summer drought this red earth of the Nugra cracked a yard deep and two or three inches wide, and in these cracks the wheels dropped, and between them they ploughed furrows four inches deep. The five-ton armored cars sank often to first speed, and nearly stuck: hard for their crews, for then the racing engine made inside the turrets intolerably hot, and today there was a powerful sun, not enough modified by the breeze.

Fortunately we had not to think of water, for the Rolls' generous radiator sufficed the amount for a day at least: and the tenders for many days: indeed they only twice or thrice in our year's running boiled. On the Fords, nothing but an added condenser made it possible to keep their hissing radiators full enough for a long journey in the desert: and even the Crossley, that enduring and capacious car, used to boil as a habit all the while it ran along, and was a serious drain upon the carried water of an expedition.

We overtook the Arab army about eight in the morning, on the crest of the slope to the railway, just while it was deploying to right and left to attack the little bridge-guarding redoubt which stood between us and Tell Arar, or Tell Khuman, as the peasants and tribes respectively called the commanding mound whose head overlooked all this northern countryside, from the far edge of Hauran by Mount Hermon, to Deraa, the junction, tucked under its southern face at short range.

The Rualla horsemen, led by Trad, dashed in front of us down the long slope and over the liquorice grown bed of the water-course up to the line. Young bounced after them in his Ford. From the ridge we thought the railway was taken without a shot fired, but while we gazed, suddenly from the neglected Turkish post came a vicious spitting fire, and our braves, who had been standing in splendid attitudes on the coveted line (wondering privately what on earth to do next), disappeared suddenly as everyone dived for cover in the ditch. Simultaneously a little party of twenty enemy horse disclosed themselves to the left down the valley: or rather they galloped violently out of it, making across the flat for Deraa.

We let them go: while Nuri Said moved down Pisani's guns into place and fired a few shots against the Turkish trenches. Then the Rualla and the troops rushed it easily, losing only one killed: so that the southern ten miles of the Deraa-Damascus line was freely ours before nine in the morning. It was the only railway, not merely of Palestine, but of Hejaz also, and I could hardly believe that our fortune was real, and our word to Allenby fulfilled so simply and so soon.

The Arabs streamed down from the ridge in rivers of men, horses, and camels, crossed the track, and swarmed upon the round head of Tell Arar, to look upon their plain, whose rimmed flatness the early sun made speciously relieved, by throwing as yet still more shadow than light. They could see Deraa and Mezerib and Chazale, the three key-stations, with their naked eyes. I was seeing further than them: northward to Damascus, the Turkish base. Their only communication with Constantinople and Germany now cut off: southward to Amman and Maan and Medina, all cut off: westward to Liman von Sanders in Nazareth and to Nablus, and the Jordan Valley all cut off: and today was September the seventeenth the promised day to G.H.Q., forty-eight hours before Allenby would throw forward his full power. In these next two days the Turks would decide to change their dispositions to meet our new danger, but would not have changed them before Allenby struck. Bartholomew had said. 'Tell me if he will be in his Auja line the day before we start, and I will tell you if we will win or not' Well he was and so we would win. It was only a question of how much.

I wanted the whole line destroyed in a moment : but things seemed to have stopped. The army had done its share, and Nuri Said was posting machine-gunners in proper places about the Arar mound to keep back any sortie from Deraa: but why was there no demolition going on? I rushed down to see, and found Peake's Egyptians having breakfast it was like Drake's game of bowls, and I was dumb with admiration: but they did not know they were magnificent, and so gained no merit. The Egyptian Army, proud of its regularity indeed one of the most formally beautiful alive fed gigantically several times each day. To the men, food was a solemn duty, enjoined, an exigency of service. No doubt it did them good, but today they vexed me. We others in these scrambling days of action ate nothing, or ate something unseen as we went whenever the raiding halted for a moment, and gave leisure for fatigue or hunger.

However in an hour or so they were mustered again and marched down to the line with their explosives on their pack-camels beside them, ready to begin their rhythmic demolition by numbers: while I had got the French gunners, who also carried guncotton, to descend with intention upon the Wadi Arar bridge. They were not very good, but at the second try did it some hurt.

From the head of Tell Arar we examined Deraa carefully through my strong glass, before the mirage had begun to dance over the plain in the risen sun, wanting to see what the Turks had in store for us this day: and the first sight was disturbing. The aerodrome was alive with men, who were pulling machine after machine into the open. I could count eight or nine being made ready now. Otherwise things were as we expected: few troops, and no mounted men beyond those fugitives. Some infantry were doubling out into the defense-positions, and their guns were being fired towards us: but we were four miles off Locomotives were starting off northward and westward: but they were unarmored trains. Behind us towards Damascus, the country lay as still as a map. From Mezerib on our right there was no sign of movement. Apparently we might do all the demolition we wished that day, unhindered except by air attack.

Our hope was to fire six hundred charges, tulip fashion, putting out of commission six kilometers of rail. Tulips had been invented by Peake and me for this occasion. They were a charge of thirty ounces of guncotton, buried beneath the center of the central sleeper of each ten-meter section of the track. The sleepers were steel, and their box-shape left an air-chamber above the explosive. The gas expansion filled this and blew the middle of the sleeper upward. If the charge was properly laid, not touching the sleeper, the metal did not tear, but humped itself, bud-like, two feet in the air. The lift of it pulled the two rails three inches up: the drag of it pulled the rails six inches together, and was exerted by the chairs on the bottom flange of the rail, which were warped inward seriously. The triple distortion put them beyond repair. Three or five sleepers would be likewise ruined, and a trench two feet wide driven across the earthwork: all this with one charge, fired by a short fuse, so that the first, blowing off while the third was being lighted, would cast its debris safely over the head of the lighter.

Six hundred such charges, if Peake managed them, would take the Turks a fair week to mend, with our bridge, and another one or two thrown in. This would be a generous reading of Allenby's 'three men and a boy with pistols': and it seemed possible. I turned to go back to the troops, and at that moment two things happened. Peake fired his first charge, like a poplar-tree of black smoke and dust with a low following report: and the first Turkish machine got up and came for us.

Nuri Said and I looked about, and found on the hill's southern face an outcrop of rock. It had fissured into deep natural trenches, which fitted us admirably, and there we waited coolly for the bomb: but it was only a reconnaissance machine, a Pfalz scout, which flew over and studied us, and then returned to Deraa with its news.

Bad news it must have been to the enemy, for their three two-seater's, and four scouts, and an old yellow-bellied Albatross got up in quick succession, and circled over us, leisurely dropping bombs, or diving at us with machine-gun fire. Nuri had put his Hotchkiss gunners in the rock cracks, and rattled back at them. Pisani cocked up his four mountain guns, and let fly some optimistic shrapnel. However, it disturbed the enemy, who circled off, and came back much higher. Their aim became uncertain.

We scattered out the troops and camels, while the irregulars, Rualla, Hauranis, Druses and the rest scattered themselves without our directions. To open out into the thinnest target was our only hope of safety, as the plain had not overhead cover for a rabbit: and our hearts rather mislead us when we saw what thousands of men we had, dotted out below. It was strange to stand on the hilltop looking at these two square miles of rolling country, liberally spread with men and animals, and bursting out irregularly here and there with lazy silent bulbs of smoke where bombs dropped (seemingly quite apart from their thunder) or with little sprays of dust from machine-gun groups.

Things looked and sounded hot, but the Egyptians went on working as methodically as they had gone on eating. Four parties dug in the tulips, while Peake and one of his officers lit each series as it was laid. The two slabs of guncotton in a tulip-charge were not enough to make a large explosion, and the airplanes seemed not to see what was going on. At least they did not wash them particularly with bombs, and as the demolition proceeded, the party drew gradually out of the danger-area, and worked up by themselves into the quiet landscape to the north. We traced their progress by the degradation of the telegraph. In virgin parts its poles stood trimly drilled by the taut wire: but behind Peake they leaned and tottered anyhow or fell.

By book, the six hundred charges should be fired by sunset or a little earlier and our duty as covering force was to guard them as they worked. It might be read to mean sitting still, which would have been admirable on a fine day but not now while it rained bombs. We looked for distractions and saw an engine drawing a single coach pull out of Deraa towards Mezerib. I rushed down to the line, for the armored cars had come down, and a Talbot had crossed, and I wanted in one to head the train off. The country between us and Mezerib was fit for cars and not far so that we might well catch the train in which clearly someone of importance was going to Palestine. Unhappily the ditch on the west side of the bank had checked the Rolls-Royce's, so the plan failed. Taiai told me later that it was Jemal Pasha, our old enemy, whom we had missed in that unfortunate battle at the culvert below Minifir with Ali ibn el Hussein and Fahad a year ago.

Another active possibility was to carry on our plan and top off the breaking of the Damascus and Hejaz railways by cutting the Palestine line if possible at Tell el Shehab. For this Nuri Said Joyce and I met in council, and wondered how to get at this Yarmuk section. It meant taking over there nearly all our men, which seemed hardly wise under such constant air observation. For one thing they would hurt us badly on the march across the open plain: and for another, by dividing our already small force we would put either part of it at the mercy of Deraa if the Turks plucked up courage to make a sally. For the moment they were evidently fearful: but time might make them brave as it did most men while ours with this continued air molestation were beginning to suffer in spirit. In the flesh they were doing very well. The first fifty bombs and three hours of machine-gun fire had killed only two of us. In such irregular warfare, when the ground force had unlimited maneuver area and was skilled to use it sporadic air attack was not very deadly.

While we hesitated in this dilemma things were marvelously solved for us. Junor the pilot of the RE. I 2 now alone at Azrak, heard from the disabled Murphy of the enemy machines about Deraa, and decided in his own mind to take the Bristol's place and carry out the air program we had arranged. So when things were at their thickest with us he suddenly arrived, and sailed into the middle of the circus.

We watched with very mixed feelings, for his machine was hopelessly old-fashioned, and made him cold meat for anyone of the enemy scouts or two-seater's: but at first he astonished them, as he rattled in with his guns, and they scattered to right and left for a careful look at this unexpected opponent He flew off westward across the line, and they went after in pursuit, with that amiable weakness of aircraft who had to desert the most valuable mixed objective, if a pure issue, a hostile machine, however unimportant, appeared.

This time they flew west and north out of our sight, and left us in perfect peace. Nuri caught at the opportune lull to collect three hundred and fifty regulars, with two of Pisani's guns, and we hurried them at once behind Tell Arar and over the saddle, beyond view of Deraa, on the first stage of their march to Mezerib. This cultivated land had a quilt-work appearance from the air, hiding small objects. If the airplanes gave us half an hour they would probably notice neither our lessened number on the mound, nor the scattered groups making along every slope and hollow across the stubble westward. The ground was tall with maize-stalks, and thistles grew saddle high about it in great fields.

We sent the peasantry off after the soldiers, and half an hour later I was just calling up my bodyguard, that we might get to Mezerib before the others, when again we heard the drone of engines, and to our astonishment, Junor, still alive, reappeared, attended on three sides by enemy machines spitting bullets. He was twisting and slipping splendidly, firing back. Their very numbers hindered them, but of course the affair could have only one ending.

In the faint hope that he might get down alive we rushed towards the railway where was a narrow strip of ground, not too boulder strewn. Everyone helped to clear it at top speed, while Junor was being driven every moment lower. He threw us a message once to say that his petrol was nearly finished, and he must land. We worked feverishly for another five minutes, and then put out a landing signal. He dived straight at it, but as he did so the wind flawed, and blew across at a sharp angle. The cleared strip was thirty yards wide and one hundred and fifty yards long, too little in any case. He took ground beautifully, but the wind puffed across once more and the strain was too great. His under coinage went and the plane turned over on its back in the rough.

We rushed up to rescue, but Junor were unstrapped and out in a second with no more hurt than a cut on the chin. He took off his Lewis gun and his Vickers, and picked up his drums of tracer ammunition. We threw them into Young's Ford and fled wildly from the spot, as one of the two-seater's dived viciously at us and dropped a bomb on the wreck.

However, no one got hurt, and Junor five minutes later was asking for another job. Joyce gave him a Ford, and he ran boldly down the line till near Deraa, and there blew a gap in the rails before the Turks saw him. They found such zeal excessive and opened on him with their guns, but he rattled away again in his Ford unhurt for the third time.

Chapter 126: The Third Railway

My bodyguard waited in two long lines on the hillside. I said goodbye to Joyce, who was staying in charge of Tell Arar and going to pose as the covering force with only a hundred of Nuri Said's men the Rualla, the Gurkhas and the cars; while we slipped across to break the Palestine Railway. My party would look like Bedouin and so I determined to move openly to go across to Mezerib by a direct line across country: since that would be the quickest course and would take us in view of Deraa, very far from Nuri Said's column to which it would be fatal to draw enemy attention.

Unfortunately we drew it ourselves. An airplane crawled over us dropping bombs one, two, three, misses: the fourth in our midst. Two of my men down. Their camels struggled on the ground, bleeding masses. The men had not a scratch, and leaped up behind two of their mends. Another machine floated past us, engine cut off. Two more bombs: and a shock spun my camel round and knocked me half out of my saddle with a burning numbness in my right elbow. I felt I was hard hit, and began to cry for the pity of it, to be put out just when another day's control would have meant a vast success. The blood was running down my arm; perhaps if I did not look at it I might carry on as if there was no hurt.

My camel swung to a spatter of machine-gun bullets and again nearly unseated me. Instinctively I clutched at the pommel with my damaged hand, and felt that my hand was there and efficient. I had judged it blown off. My left hand threw the cloak aside and felt for the wound — no more than a very hot little splinter of metal scarcely sticking in my flesh. It had been too light to drive through the folds of my camel-hair cloak. The trifle showed me that my nerve was on edge, to make such a fuss. Curiously enough, it was the first time in the war that I had been wounded from the air.

We opened out and rode greatly, knowing the ground by heart, checking only to tell the young peasants whom we met that the work was now at Mezerib, not at Deraa. The field paths were full of these fellows, pouring out afoot in arms from every village to help us. They were sharp and very willing: but our eyes had rested so long on the brown leanness of the desert men that these gay village lads with their flushed faces clustering hair and plump white arms and legs seemed like girls. They had kilted up their gowns above the knee for fast work: and the more active of them raced beside us through the fields chaffing back my veterans.

As we reached Mezerib, Durzi ibn Dughmi met us, with news that Nuri Said, with the soldiers was only two miles back, coming along well. We went forward more carefully, to find the upper spring deserted. At once we watered our camels, and drank deeply of it ourselves, for it had been thus far a long and hot day and was not nearly ended. Then we passed the half-abandoned village, and from behind the old fort looked over the lake and saw movement in the French railway station.

Some of the white-legged fellows told us that the Turks held it in force. However, the approaches were too tempting for us to resist. Abdulla led our charge, for my days of adventure were ended, with the sluggard reason that my skin must be kept for a justifying emergency. Also I wanted to enter Damascus. This station was too easy, and as a fact Abdulla took it bloodlessly before the ten Turks knew we were there. In it was stored grain: and also flour and some little booty of weapons, horses, ornaments. These excited my men, and new adherents came running to us across the grass, like flies to honey. Taiai arrived at his constant speed. We passed the stream by its low bridge, and walked together up the far bank, knee-deep in weeds, till we saw the Turkish station three hundred yards in front. We must take this before attacking Tell el Shehab. Taiai advanced carelessly. The Turks showed themselves to right and left. 'It's all right,' said he: 'I know the station-master': but when we were two hundred yards away twenty rifles fired a shocking volley at us. We dropped unhurt into the weeds, finding nearly all of them thistles, and crawled painfully back, Taiai swearing.

My men heard him, or the shots, and came streaming up from the river: but we returned them, fearing a machine-gun in the station buildings. In only half an hour Nuri Said was due. He came with Nasir and we considered the business. Nuri pointed out that a delay over Mezerib risked the loss of Tell el Shehab, a greater objective. I agreed, but thought this bird in hand might suffice us, since Peake's great demolition would stand for a week, anyhow, and the week's end would bring a new situation.

So up marched Pisani, unfolded his willing guns, and smashed in the trucks and roofs with a few rounds of point-blank high explosive. Under their cover, with our twenty machine-guns making a roof over his head, Nuri, immaculately gloved, walked forward unhesitatingly in front of a hundred infantry, and received the surrender of the place and the forty soldiers left alive in it.

This station was most rich; and the hundreds of Haurani peasants hurled themselves into it in frenzy, plundering. Men, women and children came running, and fought like dogs over every object. Even the doors and windows, the door-frames and window-frames, and the steps of the stairs were carried off One hopeful blew-in the safe, and found postage stamps inside. Others smashed open the long range of wagons in the sidings, to find in them all manner of goods for the Turkish army in Palestine. Tons were carried off yet more was strewn in wreckage on the ground.

Young and I cut the telegraph, first thing, from the station roof it was pleasant to imagine Liman von Sanders fresh curse, as each severed wire tanged back from the clippers. We did it slowly, with ceremony, to draw out the indignation. The Turks' hopeless lack of initiative made their army entirely 'directed', and destroying their telegraphs went far towards making them a leaderless mob. Besides it meant that Deraa would wireless all our history everywhere and Allenby would intercept and have quick notice of our doing: useful for the loss of our two airplanes left us marooned here. After the telegraph we blew in the points and planted some tulips: not very many but enough to annoy. While we worked a light engine came down the line from Deraa on patrol, to find out what we were at: but when it saw the dust of our tulips rising up it withdrew gently. Then an airplane visited us.

We looked through the captured rolling stock. Among it on platform trucks were two German army lorries of their Yiiderirn, former Pasha Corps going down to Palestine in new condition crammed with delicacies for some German canteen. The Arabs, not caring for tins and bottles had spoiled nearly everything: but we got some soups and meat and later Nuri Said gave us bottled asparagus. He had found an Arab prizing open the case and had cried, "pigs' bones!" in horror when the contents came to light. The peasant spat and dropped it and Nuri quickly stuffed all he could into his holsters.

The lorries had huge petrol tanks quite full of spirit perhaps a hundred gallons in each. Beyond them were some trucks of firewood and we laid sopped straw about them, with trails of chips and rags and set the whole afire at sunset when the plundering was finished and the troops and tribesmen had fallen back to the soft grass by the outlet from the lake.

The splendid blaze spreading along the whole line of wagons illuminated our evening meal. The wood burned with a solid glare and the fiery tongues and bursts of the petrol went towering up into the sky higher than the water-tanks. We let the men make bread and sup and rest a little before a night attempt on the Shehab bridge which lay only three miles to the westward. We had meant to attack at dark but the wish for food stopped us. and then we had swarms of visitors for our beacon-light advertised us half over the Hauran.

Visitors were our eyes and had to be welcomed. My business was to see every one of them with news and let him talk himself out to me selecting from each bundle of rumor the one fact I wanted and arranging and combining the truth of these points into a completed picture in my mind. It was to be called completed because it gave me actual certainty of judgment in any case: but it was assuredly neither conscious nor logical, for my informants were so many that they informed me to distraction and my single mind bent under all its claims. Yet my head must be the intelligence office for we had no supports and our weakness could be buttressed only by flawless knowledge.

Men came pouring down from the north in a solid stream on horse, on camel and on foot hundreds and hundreds of them in a terrible grandeur of enthusiasm, thinking that this was not a raid but the final occupation of the country, and that Nasir would seal his victory by taking Deraa in the night. Even the magistrates of Deraa came, to open us their town. By acceding we would hold the water supply of the railway station which must inevitably yield: yet later, if the ruin of the Turkish army came but slowly, we might be forced out again and the one failure would lose us the plainsmen between Deraa and Damascus in whose hands our final victory lay. It was a nice calculation, but on the whole the arguments were against taking Deraa, and we had to put off our friends with excuses within their comprehension.

Chapter 127: Check

It took time, and when at last we were ready, a new visitor appeared the boy-chief of the village at Tell el Shehab. His views were important, since his village was the key to the bridge. He described the position, the large guard, and how it was placed.

Obviously the problem was harder than we had believed if his tale was true: but on this very point we doubted, for his just-dead father had been hostile and the son sounded too-suddenly devoted to our cause. However he finished by suggesting a new plan that he should return in an hour with the officer commanding the garrison who was a friend of his and would join us for a safe-conduct to Feisal. This seemed proof of his honesty, and we sent him off to bring his Turk, telling our waiting men to lie down again.

Soon the boy was back with a captain in Turkish uniform who explained that he was an Armenian, anxious to harm his government in any way he could. Also, he was very nervous, and we had hard work to reassure him of our enlightenment. Then he outlined to us what he thought we had best do. He commanded the Tell Shehab detachment, but his subalterns were loyal Turks and some of the noncommissioned officers also. He proposed we move close to the village secretly, and lie there, while three or four of our most lusty men entered and hid in his room. He would call his subordinates one by one to see him, on pretexts, and as each entered our ambush might surprise and pinion him. Without these leaders he thought he could answer for the men, who were sick of the war, and of the Young Turks. If not it would be easily in our power to overwhelm them by a sudden attack.

This sounded to me in the proper descent from books of adventure, and we agreed enthusiastically. It was now nine o'clock at night. We would march at ten, and at eleven precisely would line up round the outskirts of the village and wait for the sheikh to show our strong men to the Commandant's house. The two conspirators departed, content at the way things were shaping, while we turned to wake up our army, now sleeping the sleep of exhaustion beside their loaded camels. It was pitched dark.

My bodyguard prepared bridge-rotting charges of blasting gelatin. I filled my pockets with fuse, detonators, and fuses in readiness. Nasir sent men to each section of the camel corps in turn, to ensure their mounting quietly, without the disaster of a roaring camel. Everything went very well. We told them of the coming adventure, that they might work themselves up to the height of it. Then, in a long double line, our force crept down the winding path, beside the irrigation ditch, on the crest of the ridge dividing Wadi Baje from Wadi Meddan.

If there was treachery before us, this bare road would be a death trap, without issue to right or left, narrow, tortuous, and slippery with the ditch-water. So with our men Nasir and I went first, their trained ears attentive to every sound, their eyes keeping constant guard in every direction. In front of us was the rushing of the waterfall, the great burdening roar which had given its character to that unforgettable night when, with Ali ibn el Hussein, we had attempted this Shehab Bridge from the other wall of the ravine. Only tonight we were so much nearer that, till we grew used to it, the noise flooded up oppressively and filled our ears to the exclusion of all else.

We crept very slowly and carefully now, soundless on our bare feet, while behind us the heavier soldiery snaked along, holding their breath as they rode in awe of the coming shock. They also were soundless, for camels moved always still at night, and this time we had packed the equipment not to tap, the saddles not to creak. The quietness of it made the dark deeper, and increased the menace of those whispering valleys on either side. Waves of dank air from the river met us, chilly in our faces, and then Rahail came down swiftly from the left and caught my arm, and pointed to a slow column of white smoke rising from the valley on his side.

We ran to the edge of the descent, and peered over, but the depth was grey with mist risen from the water, and we saw only dimness and this pale spire standing up out of its level fog-bank. Somewhere down there was the railway, and we stopped the march afraid that this was the suspected trap a machine gun waiting to burst out thence at us, on a signal, and sweep our disordered column with pitiless bullets as we huddled on the naked ridge.

Three of us went foot by foot down the slippery hillside till we could hear voices. Then suddenly the smoke broke and shifted, there came the panting of an opened throttle, and afterwards the squealing of brakes as an engine came again to a standstill. There must be a long train waiting in the fog beneath us, and. reassured, we marched on again, till we came to the very neck of the spur below the village, whose roofs stood out in cubes of blackness against the sky. We extended in line across the width of the neck, and waited for five minutes, ten minutes. They passed very slowly. The murk night before the moonrise was hushing in its solidity, and compelled patience on our usually restless fellows without the added warnings of the dogs, and the intermittent ringing challenge of the sentries about the bridge. At length we let the men slip quietly from their camels to the ground, and sat wondering what this delay meant, and why that silent train stood there below us in the valley. Our woolen cloaks got stiff and heavy with the mist upon them, and we shivered.

After a long while a lighter speck came through the dark towards us, and we saw it was the boy sheikh, holding his brown cloak open before his body to show his white shirt like a flag to us. He whispered that his plan had failed. They had got back to find a train (this one in the ravine) just arrived with a German colonel aboard , and the German and Turk reserve troops from Afuleh, sent up here from Palestine by Liman von Sanders, to the rescue of Deraa.

They had put the little Armenian under arrest for being absent from his post when they had come, and now there were machineguns all over the position, and sentries patrolling the approaches with ceaseless energy. In fact, there was a strong picket of them on this path , not a hundred yards from where we sat: and the oddity of our joint state made me laugh, though quietly. However, the boy was disgusted, because he felt himself in a delicate position.

Nuri Said came up to hear the news, and offered nevertheless to lead the men in an immediate dismounted rush with hand-grenades, and take the place by main force. We had bombs enough, and many pistol flares, and numbers and preparedness would be on our side. The Germans had the better position, but we knew it better than they did. It was a fair chance, but I was at the old game of reckoning the value of the objective in terms of life, and as usual finding it too dear.

Of course, most things done in war were too dear, and we would have followed good examples by going in and going through with it: but somehow it was much against the grain. I was secretly and disclaimed proud of the planning of our campaigns, and of the small cost for which we got our way. There were alternatives to the bridge demolition and by one or other of them we could keep the Turkish army cut off in

Palestine till Allenby had caught them all, choosing a way which would cost only a tenth of the thirty lives which must at least be reckoned for a charge tonight.

So I told Nuri that I voted against it. We had today already twice cut the Damascus-Palestine railway. This bridge was a luxury, and even in leaving it alone we had scored an unknowing success, for this German crowd's move up here would simplify Allenby down there. When he attacked tomorrow night he would find Afuleh open, which might save many casualties, and some hours in the first critical strokes of his cavalry offensive. We had fulfilled our bond to him with honor and paid heavy interest too. It would be foolish of us so to slaughter valuable men in gilding it.

Nuri, though a tiger for a fight, had a cool well-balanced brain, and after a moment's thought agreed with me. We said a very quiet "good night" to the lad who had honestly tried to do so much for us: we passed down the lines, and whispered to each man to turn about and retire in dead silence till far enough away to mount in safety. Then we sat down in a group with our rifles (mine Enver's gold-inscribed British trophy from the Dardanelles, presented by him to Feisal years ago), waiting and chatting till our men should be beyond the danger zone.

Oddly enough, this was the hardest moment of the night. Now the work was over we could hardly hold ourselves back from the temptation to rouse the spoil-sport Germans out. It would have been so easy to have crept in, and cracked off a Very light into their bivouac, and the solemn men would have turned out in a wild hurry, and shot as wildly into the bare and misty hillside silent at their feet. The notion came at once to Nasir, Nuri Said, and Me We blurted it out together, and at once each felt ashamed that the others had been as childish. We heartened one another by mutual cautions, and so kept our respectability, and wended wisely back to camp.

Arrived at Mezerib after midnight, we felt that something must be done to avenge the forfeited destruction of the bridge. So I found two small parties of my demolition fellows, with guides of Taial's men, and they went beyond Shehab, and cut the line twice behind it on deserted gradients. Their explosives echoed up the narrow valley and gave the Germans a bad night of it, for each time they all turned out and lit flares and searched up and down their neighborhood for the felt attack.

We were glad to give them as tiresome a night as we passed, for then they would be languid in the morning, not active to rout us out, or to go down to face Allenby, if the enemy at last saw that he was really coming. Our sleeplessness was due to our mends that were still coming in every minute to kiss our hands and swear eternal fealty. They trampled on their wiry little ponies through our misted camp, picking their way between the hundreds of circles of sleeping men, beside the uneasy camels whose great jaws munched all night the windy grass they had swallowed down in the day hours.

Before dawn, Pisani's other two guns and the rest of Nuri Said's troops arrived from Tell Arar. After Mezerib we had written to Joyce of our success and our intentions against Shehab, and that on the morrow we would return not by Arar, but southward by Remthe and Nisib, to make a complete circle of Deraa. It would be shorter to Urntaiye, than our coming road: and would confuse the Turks more, by appearing to threaten them from every side. Also we might attack Nisib on our way across the Deraa — Amman line and add one more damage to the Turk's debit. The bridge there I had coveted since November last year.

I suggested to Joyce that he should move straight back at dawn from Tell Arar by our old road through Taiyibe with the armored cars and the Egyptians and Gurkhas and Rualla, as far as Umtaiye and there wait for us: for it with its abundant water and splendid camel pasture and equidistance from Deraa and jebel Druse and the Rualla desert, seemed an ideal place for us to rally in and rest, while we waited news of Allenby's fortune in his part of our see-saw game. So long as we sat at Umtaiye we cut off the Turkish Fourth Army of beyond-Jordan (our special bird) from Damascus: and were in place quickly to renew our Tell Arar cut so soon as we heard the enemy had nearly set it right.

Chapter 128: The Nisib Bridge

Accordingly at dawn we pulled ourselves together for another day of effort called up the army, and moved in a huge straggle through Mezerib station, southward along the pilgrim road. Our fires in the yard had burned out, and the place stood disheveled, as after a bad night of storm. While the army moved over the line Young and I set leisurely to work, being too tired to put much spirit into it, and laid more tulips, making a general noise up and down the track. The Germans in Shehab held themselves in. to see whether we were coming at them or at Deraa decidedly for the while, the initiative was with us.

So we went on pursuing the unexpected. Our troops melted quietly into the broken ground towards Remthe, and under cover of the ridges keeping out of sight of both Deraa and Shehab, we marched quickly south-eastward making for Nisib and Umtaiye. Turkish airplanes were humming overhead, looking for us: so we sent most of our Haurani horse back again through Mezerib for their villages. Consequently the airmen reported only that we were very numerous, possibly eight or nine thousand strong, and that they could make nothing of our movements, which seemed to be complex, almost universal in every direction.

To increase their wonderment, the French gunners blew up the water-tower at Mezerib in a huge burst of long-fused guncotton hours after we had passed. Pisani enjoyed a real impression on something showy, and pleaded very hard for this liberty, till he got it: but to tell the truth it was wanton, for the tower did neither good nor harm, and some day we might want it. However, it went: and made the enemy think us still in the station. The Germans were marching out of Shehab at the moment: and its shock sent these humorless ones back to their defense positions, to stand there on guard till late afternoon.

Meanwhile we were far away, plodding steadily towards Nisib, till we reached the hilltop over it about four in the afternoon. There we gave the men a short rest while we examined the place hoping to take it without using our rifles or our tired mounted-infantry who had been marching or fighting for forty hours on end and were still the wrong side of the railway, with a possible fight to get across it to Umtaiye, To spare their energy till the last, we moved our gunners and machine-guns forward, down the hill, to the crest of the first ridge from which the ground fell away in a flat curve to the railway station.

We posted the guns there in shelter, with perfect observation, and had them open deliberately upon the station buildings at about two thousand yards. Pisani's two sections worked in emulation effectively, so that before long, ragged holes appeared in the roofs and sheds below us. At the same time to keep the enemy more occupied, we pushed our machine-gunners forward on the left of the ridge till within eight hundred yards and made them fire long concentrated bursts from their Vickers and Hotchkiss against the trenches in which the Turks had taken cover. Our plunging barrage made them lie very low: yet they were able to return a hot and obstinate fire. However, our troops had natural shelter nearly as good as their trenches and the advantage of the afternoon sun going down behind their backs. So we suffered no hurt.

Of course all this was just a game on our part, and the capture of the station not in our plan. The real objective was the great bridge, north of the village, which was itself north-west of the station. The ridge below our feet (a spur of the Buweib hills) curved out in a long horn to this bridge, serving as one bank of the valley which it was built to span. The village stood on a low mound, on the other bank, with the station beyond it. The Turks held the station in force, and the bridge by means of a small redoubt this side of it, on the tip of our hill-horn, within twenty yards of the line: while the station maintained touch with the bridge-post by means of the village, whose houses they had lined with riflemen.

When we understood all this, we rearranged ourselves. We turned two of Pisani's guns and six machine-guns on to the small but deeply-dug bridge-post, hoping to force its defenders out and back to the station. I took charge here while Nuri ran out along the middle crescent of the ridge, in front of the other machine-guns, and directed their fire on the village. In fifteen minutes its elders were out with us, very much perturbed. Nuri put as a condition of the cease-fire their instant rejection of the Turks from the houses. They promised, and carried it out. So the fire from the center of the enemy position ceased, and the station and bridge were divided.

We redoubled against them, and the firing from the four wings became violent, all our twenty-five machine-guns working, and the Turks being also plentifully supplied. Our infantry lay on their backs, sleeping: but the Turks were shooting their very hardest. If there was no other way we would storm the bridge, for it was worth casualties to us: but I still hoped that our searching gunfire would win it free of charge. At last we put all four of Pisani's guns against the little redoubt, and after a few salvoes thought we saw its guard slipping from the trenches into the valley, between our fire, and thence through the bridge into the cover of the far side of the railway embankment.

This embankment was twenty feet high, and the ground behind it dead to our efforts. If the bridge-guard chose to defend their bridge through its arches and from behind its bank they would be in a costly position, one only to be cleared by infantry attack. However, we reckoned that the attraction of the other fellows in the station would draw them away, up there, and tried to encourage them to go by putting some shells through the bridge, and shrapnel over its head, while I told off the half of my bodyguard carrying the explosives to move along the machine-gun crest, till near the bridge behind the shelter of the tip, along which they could move in safety till within a stone's throw of the redoubt.

It was a noble evening, yellow and mild and indescribably peaceful, a clear foil to our incessant cannonade. The declining light shone down the angle of the ridge, upon whose face its rays rested softly, modeling them and their least contour in a delicate complexity of planes. While we looked, the sun sank another second, and the whole surface of the hill became shadow out of which for a moment there rose, starkly, the innumerable stones strewing it, the western reflecting facet of each tipped , like a black diamond, with flame.

A very unfit afternoon for dying in, seemed to think my men: since for the first time their nerves failed me, and they refused to budge from safety over the ridge across which our path lay among the enemy's clattering bullets. They were dead tired, and their camels so marched-out that they could move only at a walk: besides they had to lead the explosives caravan, knowing that one bullet in the blasting gelatin would detonate them all, and send them sky-high. They were deafened by the machine-gun duel, and by the roaring of Pisani's guns over their heads: anyway, they would not face the rush across the open into shelter.

I tried to stir them up by jest, but failed, and lost my temper (also for the first time and thereby abating a little of myself): at last I cast them off, to go wherever they wanted out of my sight, choosing only Hemeid, the youngest and most timid of them all, to come up with me on the hilltop. He shook like a man in a sick dream, but I caught his headstall, and then he followed quietly. We rode squarely up the hollow and down the ridge to its furthest edge, from Which to have a last close look at the approach to the bridge,

Nuri Said was standing there, sucking his pipe, and cheering up the gunners, who were keeping a steady barrage over all the darkening roads between the bridge, the village and the station, and hindering the Turkish machine-guns. It being a hot place, Nuri was happiest and most possessed, and chatted with me, amid the bullets, of theories of attack, and alternative assaults against this station, which we did not wish to assault. We argued for about ten minutes on the skyline with Hemeid, white-faced clinging to his saddle in a piddling fear of the bullets some of which were over, spitting past us, some ricochets, humming like slow angry bees besides our ears but most of them proper hits splashing loudly into the flints, kicking up white chalk-dust, which hung transparently for a moment in the reflected light, and then was gone.

I told Nuri what I was going to try down by the bridge and he agreed to cover my movements as well as he could. Then I turned to poor trembling Hemeid, explained how little terrible things were and sent him back with my camel, to tell the rest that I would hurt them worse than bullets if they did not follow him across the danger-zone down along the half-mile spur to meet with me: for I meant to walk round till I could see into the bridge-post, and be sure it was empty.

He went back and delivered my message, so boastful at having twice passed the danger that the others were ashamed. While they hesitated, Abdulla the Nahabi, the imperturbable improvident, adventurous who feared nothing and the Zaagi, came on the scene. They had been behind with the other thirty guards whipping in the stragglers of our unhandy mounted-infantry, and were mad with fury when they heard how I had been let down. They dashed at the shrinkers, and the whole mob their faces large in the evening light pounded past me over the shoulder with only six casualties: for Nuri Said had broken down half the Turks' fire and the rest was wild.

My men were now full of courage and called loudly to me to come off the crest and join them below in the hollow. I was in an odd depression of spirit almost as though I had changed wills with Hemeid, encouraging him. He was now sedate, and I haunted by a shameless unknown disease, were out of the line of the crowd, and the enemy were unlikely to waste bullets on a single Bedawi walking round the rim of the long spur which bounded their flat: so I went on till I saw that the redoubt was indeed abandoned.

Then I ran down feeling that I had been a brave man to my bodyguard to tell them what I thought of them; however, they disarmed my anger, by cheering me loudly as I came up. It was interested politic praise, but pleased me for there was nearly full knowledge between us. They saw what I did and heard what I said and stood for, all day and every day, and how I was with Feisal, and why this or that was done. There was no acting towards them, and in return I knew each of them very well, and his motives and pleasures and character, and liked them, as a body and individually, proud of myself for being their master, proud of them for serving my whims composedly. Self-love and pride and greediness entered into this affection for subordinates — since by liking them so much we made them in a way our flesh and blood, and cast reflections of their high-light upon ourselves.

Now we dismounted, and rushed into the little fort, and signaled to Nuri to cease lire. There came a dead silence, in which we peeped discreetly through the bridge-arches, and found that the twenty men who had been in the post were some three hundred yards away, moving in the shadow of the earthwork towards the station. I called live or six men to me, and told them to line the tamarisk in to rent bed, and prevent the Turks' return. They were more zealous, and hurried their retreat with volleys which laid out most of them.

My other guards were unloading the explosives camels, splitting open the guncotton and gelatin boxes, and carrying their contents down the steep path to the bridge. We had been too long, and the fear of enemy reinforcement coming down by train from Deraa upon us was present in my mind. So I took the fused and primed slabs always in my saddle-bags, and ran five hundred yards along the line northward, to cut the metals there, and so stop the relief at least that far off. Meanwhile Young had ridden down and, hearing my noise, covered me till he saw whom I was. Then he joined in the good work, going yet further up the line with more gun cotton, so as to give us safe law in any case.

Abdulla ran after me, reporting the explosives all ready at the bridge, with the maddeningly stout cases of the army guncotton battered open for use. Hurriedly we piled the slabs against the piers, which were about five feet thick, and about twenty-five feet high, with three arches seven meters in spans — a good bridge, my seventy-ninth, and strategically one of our most critical, since we were going to live nearly opposite it at Umtaiye. So I was determined to leave not a stone of it in place, no light resolve in such haste, as it was built of basalt and cement, extravagantly strong.

However, we piled super charges, untamed, against the foot of each pier, using all our guncotton and gelatin, since there was plenty more at Umtaiye. We primed and put in detonators and fuses, and then went off to look at Nuri. He was hurrying the infantry and gunners and machine-gunners down from the hills in the thickening night, towards the line, with orders to cross over the cut part just above the bridge, and to get a mile beyond into the desert and there wait.

It was vital they should all be in safety and collected before a diversion came from north or south, and yet the passing of so many camels over the track must take tediously long. We sat and chafed under the bridge, matches and fuses in hand, to light at once if there was an alarm, but otherwise to wait Nuri's report that the force was clear. Fortunately everything went well, and after an hour Nuri gave me my signal. My guards went off with our camels, and half a minute later (my preference for six-inch fuses nearly let me in this time),just as I tumbled into the Turkish redoubt, the eight hundred pounds of stuff exploded in one burst, and the black air became sibilant with lying stones. The explosion was numbing from my twenty yards, and must have been heard half-way to Damascus.

Five minutes later Nuri, in great distress, fell in with me. He had given the 'all clear' signal before learning that one company of mounted infantry was missing, and in the dark and the noise it was hard for him to guess which way it had wandered. Fortunately my men were present, aching for redeeming service, and with them Taiai el Hareidhin of Tafas, who lost no chance of helping us. We scattered them every way up the hills back of the line we had just wrecked, while Nuri and I stood by the yawning pit which had been the bridge, and lashed an electric torch, screened from north and south, to give them a fixed point for their return.

It was hardly necessary, for tribesmen had a quality of direction which prevented their ever completely losing their way. As they marched, instinctively they understood the trend of the country, so that later, by its lie, they knew their point of compass, even if there were no stars. Consequently they never wandered helplessly in irritating circles like townsmen, Syrians almost worse than British in this respect, since they had no compasses, or would not look at them. However, tonight the difficulty was brief, for Mahmud came back in half an hour, triumphantly leading the lost unit. We fired shots to call the other searchers, and then rode two or three miles into the open towards Umtaiye. The going became very broken, over great screeds of slipping dolerite: so we called a halt the whole force together, and lay down in our ranks for an earned sleep.

Chapter 129: An Aeroplane Adventure

However, it seemed that Nasir and I were to lose the habit of sleeping. Our riotous noise at Nisib had proclaimed us as widely as the flames of Mezerib the night before, and hardly were we still when visitors came streaming in to pay their respects and to discuss the latest events. They told us Joyce was safely back in Umtaiye, where there was a large concourse very anxious to learn our plans, and disturbed by the speed and irregularity of our movements. It was being rumored that we were raiding, not occupying, and that later we would run away, as had Shea from Salt, leaving our local friends to pay our bills.

The night, for hour after hour was thus broken by these newcomers challenging all about our bivouacs, crying their way to us like lost souls, and, peasant-fashion slobbering over our hands with protestations that we were their highest lords and they our deepest friends. Perhaps in some respects our reception of them fell short of our highest standard, but in revenge they were applying the torture of keeping us awake and uneasily awake. We had been at strain for three days and nights thinking, ordering and executing and now, on our road to rest, it was bitter to play away this fourth night also, at the old game of keeping friends or adding new ones.

And their shaken morale impressed us worse and worse, till Nasir drew me aside and whispered that the tone was moving so against us that clearly there existed an active focus of discontent in some center near. I lost out some of my peasant bodyguard to mix with the villagers on their way in, and find me the truth: and from their reports it seemed that the cause of distrust lay in the first village of Taiyibe, which had been shaken by the return of the armored cars yesterday by some chance incidents, and by a just fear that they were the spot most exposed in our retreat.

I saw that anyhow I would get no sleep where I was, so called to me Abd el Aziz, and we mounted and rode over the rough stretches of lava, apparently trackless, and piled across with high walls of broken stone, straight to Taiyibe. The village was astir, and in the head-man's hut sat the conclave which infected all our visitors passing through to us. They were debating whom to send next day to implore mercy from the Turks, when we walked in unannounced. Our single coming frightened them, as we had reckoned, by its assumption of our supreme security. They were abashed into silence. We talked irrelevantly a while about crops and farmyard prices, and then rose to go. Behind us their babble broke out again, but now their inconstant spirits had veered to what seemed our stronger wind, and they sent no word to the enemy: though next day they were bombed and shelled for their stubborn complicity with us.

We got back just before dawn, and stretched out to sleep an hour: when there came a loud boom from the railway south of Nisib, and a shell shattered just beyond our sleeping host It seemed that, to the bridge broken on the sixteenth by our armored cars, the Turks had sent down a repair party, on an armored train, mounted with a field gun, and this had been cut off by our blowing up Nisib bridge, and in its vexation was making fair shooting from five thousand yards, at us. By myself I would have changed the gun, for my sleep had been just long enough to make me rage for more; but the army had slept six hours, and was moving.

So we hurried across horrible going feeling very tired and sore. An airplane came over, and circled round to help the gunners, who got better. Shells began to keep accurate pace with our line of march. We doubled our speed, and broke into a ragged procession of very open order. One such group which crossed my road proved to be Kirk bride and his Scotch soldier-servant, bearded, deepened and dirty as Hauran peasants. Till then I had hardly known they were up with us.

Fortune was favorable, for the directing airplane faltered suddenly, swerved aside towards the line, and seemed to land by it in Wadi Butm, Either it was damaged, or they had an aerodrome there. The gun went on doing its best alone, and put in one lucky shot, which killed two more of my Ageyl camels: but for the rest it lost accuracy, and after about fifty shots we began to draw out of range. They switched off from us, and began to punish Taiyibe for their agreement with me last night.

Joyce, at Umtaiye, had been roused by the shooting, and came out to welcome us. Behind his tall figure on the ridge showed up the ruins, crested by a motley band, seeming to be sample men from every village and tribe in the Hauran, come to do us homage and offer at least lip-service. To Nasir's tired disgust I left these to him, while I went off with Joyce and Winterton, telling them of the airplane which had come down over there, and suggesting that we start off at once in an armored car, and beat it up at home. At that moment, two more enemy machines appeared, and landed in the same place. A new aerodrome so near would be intolerable, whether directed against us, or against the British bombing squadrons, which had now three times laid waste Deraa with their attacks.

However, breakfast was being got ready, and it was some time since we had fed. So we sat down and first I told them what we had done at Mezerib and Nisib. Joyce related their difficult return from Tell Arar, and how the villagers of Taiyibe had fired at them as they came through. Some thought they fired to hit but we had had no casualties, and these gazelle hunters could hit hard enough if they wished: so probably their shooting was only to show their opinion of strangers who stirred up all a hornets' nest of Turks, and then hopped off Raiding parties were so seldom popular with established people, especially when going away!

A second story was how yesterday Joyce had seen the Turks busily mending our ruined bridge at Kilo. 149. Winterton, with Junor the irrepressible, had driven down to interrupt them. With cutouts closed they had reached the little bluff behind which we had concealed the tenders last time, and had climbed to its head to study their enemy Junor, hugging his beloved Lewis gun, had said to Winterton that the enemy looked so peaceful they made him quite ashamed to shoot.

Winterton had half-agreed, when there were explosions on the repair train standing by the work, and two shells curved screaming through the air and burst just beyond the car. He gasped out, 'It's an armored train', just as a rapid blaze of musketry was opened on them from further up the line. They chose the wiser part, and made off, the big car leaping like a scalded cat at forty miles an hour over the rough valleys, out of range, while Junor, with interest, watched the shells bursting this side and that, and coolly remarked that this was his first real shelling on the earth and how amusingly safe it felt since one could not possibly be hit! Once in the air over Amman had made the land counterpart of Junor's remark to my pilot, while he was slipping and diving to confuse the enemy gunners and had equally annoyed him with what he thought my pose: but with shell-fire it was familiarity which brought the fear.

However, breakfast ended and we called for a volunteer car to drive to the enemy aerodrome. Everybody came forward, with a silent goodwill and readiness which caught me by the throat. I was accustomed callous now to the Arabs' courage for they were fighting for their freedom, a very urgent end: but these English were men as good as ourselves yet moved only by duty or the mass instinct of industry. For the moment their desire to be exploited nearly put me off, and I turned to call up my tired bodyguard instead. It seemed mean to use people so innocently trustful of our half-trained direction.

Finally Joyce chose two armored cars one for Junor and one for me, and we drove for five rough miles to the valley in whose mouth I judged the planes had landed. We silenced the cars and crept slowly down its course. When about two thousand yards from the railway it turned a corner and opened out into a flat meadow, by whose further side stood the three machines drawn up in line. This was magnificent and we leaped forward with the accelerator jammed down — to meet a deep ditch with straight banks of cracking earth, quite impassable.

We ran frantically along it looking for a flat place, but there was none. However, by a diagonal route, it brought us nearer the enemy till we were twelve hundred yards from them. The pilots were pulling round their propellers: and as we stopped two of them started. We opened fire searching the right range by our dust-spurts on the ground: but before we could get on to them they had run their distance, and were off the ground, swaying round over our heads.

The third engine was sulky. Pilot and observer pulled the propeller round and round, while our shots drew nearer. Finally we got the range and they leaped into the railway ditch, as we put bullet after bullet into the fuselage till it danced under their rain. The enemy shot back and there were many of them, apparently with a machine-gun. At least they struck us several times, one bullet cutting Junor's flying helmet, and gently parting his hair, as he stood out in the open to get a better view. We fired fifteen hundred bullets at our target till we judged it shot to bits (they burned it in the afternoon), and then turned home.

Unfortunately the two escaped machines had had time to go to Deraa; and they came back, feeling spiteful. We were in the bad ground, crawling among the stones at a foot's pace. One was not clever, and dropped his four bombs from a height, missing us widely. The other seemed to know that our machine-gun would not elevate to his angle, and swooped down low at us; dropping one bomb each time with the utmost care. We crept on defenselessly slowly, feeling like sardines in a chosen tin, as the bombs fell closer. Two nearly got us; one sent a shower of small stuff through the driving-slit of the car, to whiz round inside the turret between our heads; but the only hurts were cut knuckles. One tore off a front tire, and nearly lurched the car over.

It was unmixed horror to be shut up in this steel pillbox with five other fellows, and be so knocked about. Normally, armored car fighting was a gay luxury, against unarmored enemies: but on such bad ground they were helpless against air attack, and being bombed in the open air on camel-back was pleasure in comparison. Fortunately they had only four bombs each, and the rest were further off So we reached Umtaiye well, and reported our third-success to Joyce. At least we had proved to the Turks that that aerodrome was not fit for use: and Deraa lay so equally open to car attack that we must have set them a nearly infinite problem to think over.

Chapter 130: Over to Allenby

Afterwards I lay down in the shadow of a car and slept: all the Arabs in the desert, and the Turkish airplanes which came and bombed us, having no effect upon my peace. It was not an exhausted peace, for a man both tired and busy, like myself, would feel strangely tireless, with a feverish energy: but today we had finished our first round, fortunately, and it was necessary that I lie down a little, to clear my mind upon what we should next do. As usual when I lay down I dropped asleep, and slept till the afternoon.

Our present business was to hold on to Umtaiye. Strategically it was a wonderful place, which gave us command, at will, of Deraa's three railways. If we held it another week we would have strangled the Turkish armies by our own efforts,

T.E. Lawrence

whatever fate Allenby was having in the west. Yet tactically Umtaiye was a dangerous place, only four miles from the railway, and an easy march from Deraa. A force made up exclusively of regulars, without guerrilla screen, could not safely hold it: and yet to that we would shortly be reduced, if our air-helplessness continued.

The damage to the Bristol and the loss of the RE.12 had wiped out our air force. The Turks now had at least nine machines, probably more. We were camped twelve miles from their aerodrome, in the open desert about the only possible water supply, with great herds of camels and many horses necessarily grazing round us. The Turks had found us out, and had made a beginning of bombing, enough to disquiet the irregulars who were our eyes and ears. Unless they could be delivered from overhead risk, they would break up and go home, and our usefulness would be ended: and Taiyibe too, that first village which covered us from Deraa: — it lay defenseless and quivering under repeated attack. If we were to remain in Umtaiye, Taiyibe must be content with us.

Accordingly, to fulfill our duty of remaining here, we must, in the first place, get air-strength from Allenby. He had arranged if he did not hear from us before, to send a machine to Azrak on September the twenty-first (the day after tomorrow) to exchange news of our respective attacks. We had meant to send in letters only: but in the present disquieting and pregnant case I judged that it would be more profitable for me to go across myself, and talk with the Commander-in-Chief I could start tomorrow and be back on the twenty-second. Umtaiye could hold out so long for we could always fox the airplanes a while by moving camp away to Urn el Surab, the next ruined Roman village, near enough to send up here for water.

Whether it was Umtaiye or Urn el Surab, to be safe we must keep the initiative. The Deraa side was temporarily closed by the suspicion of the peasants: there remained to us a field of activity on the Hejaz line. The Nisib bridge was a week's repair: this one at Kilo. 149 were nearly mended. We should smash it again and smash another more to the south, to deny the repair-trains access to it. Winterton's effort showed that the first was a matter for troops and guns: the second was an objective for a raid. I went across to my bodyguard to test their spirit and see if they could do it with me on our way to Azrak.

Among them I felt that something had happened. They were red-eyed, hesitant, trembling: and at last I understood that while I was away in the cars this morning, the Zaagi and Abdulla and their other chiefs had taken them to one of the ruined houses, and there gone mercilessly through the tale of those who had flinched at Nisib, battering them till the pain overmastered their endurance quicker perhaps than usual, for they were born with the strain of fighting and the present uncertainty, sore from their days in the saddle, hungry, sleepless, and tired.

It was their right for since the incident of Tafileh I had left its discipline to the company, seeing that to each was his standard of pain and danger, and the longing for it; and knowing that these vigorous fellows needed, more than ordinary weaklings, to satisfy their health and strength: but today I was a Benthamite, shrinking from anything that hurt, and accordingly I saw something bestial in their deliberate search after abnormality, their breeding for it. After wrong-doing they would expect almost claim, their punishment, as an honor due welcoming it as a means of self-knowledge by which to explore themselves, to learn how far beyond the bounds of daily fortitude their bodies could endure.

Afterwards since memory of pain was so short they made a fantasy of it toying with it running its risk: that in passionate excitement they might ride the neck of this unknown force so much stronger than themselves thrilling with the joy of surf-bathers who snatched life like a cork between elemental powers. Pain became an allurement, like danger, of which the best that was, and the worst that was, remained secret, brooded upon and coloring them inwardly. What was this hoarding of extremes, this laying up of the highest and lowest, as the prime mental food?

The effect for the moment was to disgust me with them, and to make them useless for my purpose. Such cruel punishment was preceded by fear: but the memory of its infliction provoked only wilder lawlessness among the stronger victims, and a greater likelihood of as violent offenses among the witnesses. Accordingly, after so general a stimulus as that of today, the wisest thing was to leave them alone a while to calm down. They would have been dangerous to me, to themselves, or to the enemy as the whim and opportunity provided, had we gone into action together tonight.

So instead I went to Joyce and suggested that the Gurkhas and Egyptians had now served our purpose and might return to Akaba, to spare us the present difficulty of feeding them: proposing that he further lend me an armored car, in which I should go down with them on their first stage before midnight to the railway, just north of Ifdein, and do what could be done. Afterwards I could drive on to Azrak for Palestine, to ask Allenby for airplanes Joyce agreed, and we went up to Nasir and Nuri Said, and told them about it, and that I would be back on the twenty-second with two fighting-machines to deliver us forever from Turkish air-bombing and observation. Meanwhile we would salve Taiyibe with money for the Turkish damage, and Joyce would lay out landing-grounds, both here and at Urn el Surab, against my return. Nasir entrusted me with his dispatches for Feisal at Azrak.

The demolition of the night was a fantastic muddle. We moved off at sunset, and proceeded cautiously to an open valley, from which we had an easy run of three miles to an apparently undefended section of the railway. Trouble would threaten from the south, where lay the large garrison of Mafrak station. So I arranged to drive down to that lank in my armored car, with Junor attendant in a Ford, to stop any hostile advance. The Egyptians with whom was Marshall the fighting doctor, would move on their own, direct to the line, and lay and fire their charges as quickly as possible.

It seemed a lawlessly simple scheme, but my guiding fell through, and on the car we wandered for three hours, lost in a maze of valleys, not able to find the railway, or the Egyptians or our starting-point. At last we saw a speck and drove for it, to find ourselves in front of Mafrak station on the line certainly, but six miles too far to the south. We turned about to get into place, and at that moment heard the clank of a train running northward out of the station. We chased its intermittent fan of light, hoping to catch it between us and the broken bridge, but before we overtook it there came flashes and explosions fur up the line, as Peake fired twenty or thirty quick charges.

Some mounted men, probably Ifdein Circassians, galloped headlong past us towards the station. We fired at them, and then saw the glare of the patrolling train, backing at its best speed away from the danger north of it in the dark. We should have derailed it with a charge: but I had forgotten my detonators, and so our guncotton was useless. Instead we ran alongside, about eighty yards off, and opened on the dense moving trucks with our Vickers, while Junor ranged up in his Ford and sent a green shower of tracer bullets from his Lewis across the dark.

Above our shooting and the noise of the engine we heard the Turks howling with terror of this new luminous attack. They began to fire back raggedly and, as they did so, the big car suddenly choked and stood still. We jumped out, and found that an unlucky bullet had pierced the unarmored end of our petrol tank, and so destroyed our pressure. It was the only unarmored tank in all our team of cars, and had been spared me, therefore, and now it lost us the certainty of smashing up a train. Junor pursued a little way alone in his Ford, and then came back to see what was wrong with us, fearing that we had run into some rock or hole in the dark. It took us an hour to plug the villain leak.

Later we drove along the silent line to where we had heard the demolition going on, and found the twisted rails and gaping culverts, but no trace of our friends. Obviously it was useless to look for them till daylight; so we drew a mile back from the line, and there at last I had my sleep out, three perfect hours of it before the dawn. When I awoke I was fresh and recognized our place. Probably it was only my fifth sleepless night which had made my wits woolly the evening before.

We pushed forward on the Azrak road, overtaking the Egyptians and Gurkhas, who were puzzling over our non-appearance. They were on the highway, with the car-tracks to follow across Wadi Dhuleil and the Giaan: so we pushed ahead of them, and reached Azrak in the early afternoon. There were Feisal and Nuri Shaalan, eager to hear all our news. We explained particularly, and then I went over to Marshall, in his temporary hospital which Young had got carried up for him from Akaba on Brodie's Talbot cars. He had our badly wounded here in his quiet care: but they were fewer than he had expected so that he spared me a bed and on it I slept a long night.

At dawn Joyce unexpectedly arrived. He had made up his mind that in this lull it was his duty to go down to Aba el Lissan to help Zeid and Jaafar before Maan, and to press forward Hornby among the Beni Sakhr, that the south might profit by the success of the north. Then the plane from Palestine arrived and we went across to the aerodrome together and heard the amazing first chronicle of Allenby's victory. He had smashed and burst through and driven the Turks inconceivably. The face of our war was changed and we gave hurried word of it to Feisal, with counsels of the general rising that we must swiftly undertake to profit by the coming situation.

We explained to the pilot that I was coming back to Palestine with him so that his observer must stay meanwhile at Azrak till relieved. They took it calmly and we flew off by way of Zerka, for I had a notion that cars and camel-men might go for its big bridge together and pin the Fourth Army with all its rolling stock into Amman station. So we came down low and studied the ground till I saw the best means, while the Turks fired hopeless shots at us.

From Ramleh the Air Force gave me a car up to Headquarters and there I found the great man sitting at work in his office unmoved except for the light in his eye each time Bois bustled in. on an average once in fifteen minutes, with a fresh telegram of some wider success. Allenby had boasted to his Australians before they went over that he was going to have thirty thousand prisoners, so that the result was to him almost boredom: but no scientific general ever built could see his intricate plan carried out over an enormous extent in every particular with complete success and not face inward gladness: especially when he knew it to be intellectually so deserved, the result of his breadth and independence of judgment which had let him conceive such unorthodox movements had made him break up the proper book of his administrative services to suit them, and had supported them by every moral and material asset regular and irregular military or political within his grasp.

He sketched to me his next intentions. Historic Palestine was as good as his, and the broken Turks were in the hills expecting a slackening of the pursuit: not at all! Bartholomew and Evans controlled his transport together, and accordingly the British range was not nearly spent They were ready to provision three more thrusts, one across Jordan to Amman, to be done by Chaytor and his New Zealanders; one across Jordan to Deraa, to be done by Barrow and his Indians; one across Jordan to Kuneitra , to be done by Chauvel and his Australians. Chaytor would rest at Amman: Barrow and Chauvel, on attaining their first objectives would turn slightly and converge on Damascus. We were to assist them: but I was not to carry out my saucy threat to take Damascus, till we did it all together.

I then explained our private prospects, and how everything was being wrecked by air-impotence and our lack of petrol for the cars. He pressed a bell and asked for Air Force 'Generals', and in a few minutes Salmond and Borton were conferring with us. Their machines had taken a definite and indispensable part in Allenby's scheme (the perfection of this man who could use infantry and cavalry, artillery and air force, navy and armored cars, deceptions and irregulars, each in its best fashion!) and had fulfilled it. There were no more Turks in the sky — except on our side, as I hurriedly explained. So much the better said Salmond; they would send two Bristol Fighters over to Umtaiye to sit with us so long as we needed them. Had we spares? Petrol? Not a drop? How was it to be got there? Only by air? An air self-contained fighting unit? Unheard of!

However, Salmond and Borton were two men avid of novelty and the unheard-of sounded to them most attractive. They sat down and worked out loads for a D.H.9 and Handley-Page, how to create this new force: while Allenby sat by, listening and smiling, very sure that it would be done. The cooperation of the Air with his ever-unfolding scheme had been so ready and elastic the liaison so complete and informed and quick, that he had perfect confidence in any future test. It was the Air Force which had turned the Turkish retreat into a rout, which had destroyed their telephone and telegraph connections, had blocked their lorry-columns had scattered their infantry units.

The Air Chiefs turned on me and asked if our aerodromes were good enough far landing a Handley-Page with full load. I had seen the big machine once in a shed, but unhesitatingly said, —Yes—... though they could best send an expert over with me in the Bristols tomorrow and make sure. He could be back by noon and the Handley come at three o'clock, Salmond got up and said to Allenby, 'That's all right, Sir we'll do all that is necessary'... and I went out and breakfasted.

Allenby's headquarters was a perfect place a cool airy whitewashed house proof against flies with its screened doors and windows and made musical by the moving of the wind in the trees outside I felt immoral enjoying these white table-cloths, and coffee and soldier-servants while our people up at Umtaiye were lying like lizards among the stones eating unleavened bread and waiting for the next plane to bomb them; and I felt as restless as the dusty sunlight which splashed the paths in a diaper through the chinks between the leaves because after a long spell of the restrained desert, flowers and grass seemed to fidget and the everywhere-burgeoning green of nature was boisterous almost vulgar in its fecundity.

However Clayton and Deedes and Dawnay were friendliness itself, and also the Air Force Staff; while the spirit of good cheer and conscious strength which flowed from the presence of the Commander-in-Chief was a bath of comfort to a weary person after long strained days. Bartholomew gave me new draughts of military science and moved maps about showing what they had done and would do. I added to his knowledge of the enemy for thanks to the Arabs. I was probably the best-served intelligence officer on the whole front: and in return he made me sure and safe against all happenings. It corrected my knowledge of the Arab feebleness and added perspective to my survey of events to hear again that we were part of a great plan directed by a master of strength who was allied to a master of wit and that our tiny effort maintained so near breaking-point might help to give this slow mass in reserve time and opportunity to acquire its momentum.

Chapter 131: Back to the Desert

At dawn it was Ramleh again to the Australian aerodrome on which stood two Bristols and a D.H.9 waiting to start. In one Bristol was Ross Smith the Australian my old pilot who had been picked out of all the pilots in the Middle East to fly the new Handley-Page, the single machine of its class in Egypt. It had been flown across Europe and the Mediterranean to be here in time for the offensive, and was the apple of Salmond's eye. The sacrifice of lending it to us, to fly over the enemy line on so Iowan errand as baggage-carrying, was a measure of his goodwill towards us.

We reached Umtaiye in an hour, and saw by the look of it that the army had gone: so I waved ourselves back to Urn el Surab, and there they all were, the defensive group of cars, the Arabs hiding from our suspect noise here and there and everywhere, the camels dispersed singly over the plain, filling themselves with the wonderful grazing which made our unsupplied maintenance in this key position possible. Young had out a landing signal and smoke bombs as soon as he saw our friendly markings, and we came down one by one, and made excellent landings on the great turf aerodrome which his care and Nuri Said's had swept clear of stones.

Ross Smith anxiously began to pace out the length and breadth of the prepared space, and to study its chance imperfections: but when he rejoined us where the drivers were making breakfast by the cars his face had cleared. The ground was O.K. for the Handley. Young told us stories of the repeated bombings of Umtaiye yesterday and the day before; how they had killed some of the regulars, and some of Pisani's gunners, and had tired the life out of everyone, so that they had moved in the night to

Urn el Surab: and how the idiot Turks were still bombing Umtaiye, though our men went to it only in the neutral noon and nights to draw water.

Also he told of Winterton's last blowing-up the railway, an amusing night of it, in which, while laying his charges, he had met an unknown soldier, explained to him in his broken Arabic how well they were getting on, and how the soldier had thanked God for His mercies and disappeared in the dark, whence a moment later machine-gun fire opened from left and right! Nevertheless, Winterton had got all his charges fired, and had withdrawn in good order without loss. Nasir came to us, and told how this man had been hurt, and that killed, how this clan were getting ready, and those had joined us, but those others gone home again — all the news and gossip of the countryside.

The three shining airplanes with me had restored the Arabs. They lauded the worth of the British, and their own bravery and endurance, while I told them the scarce-credible tale of Allenby's success — Nablus taken and Afuleh taken, and Beisan, and Semakh, and Haifa, with still more new terrors getting ready for the Turk. It was a wonderful epic of victories, and as I told it I could feel my hearers' minds drawn after me like flames. Taiai took fire, and boasted, while the Rualla shouted for an instant march upon Damascus. Even my bodyguard, still bearing witness to the Zaagi's severity in their muddy eyes and constrained faces, cheered up, and began to flaunt themselves a little among the crowd, with a dawn of happiness.

A shiver of self-assertion and self-confidence ran across the camp. I had made myself the magnet of their hidden longings, and knew that they were ready to do any service we asked of them. The whole country lay willing to our grasp, and I determined to bring up Feisal and Nuri Shaalan to the front, and go through with it completely: though my lethargy also made me happy there, lying on the ground, reluctant to rise or do the routine work, while quite prepared to do the unreal myself, and to drag the changed hopes and loves of half a nation madly after my whim.

Meanwhile it was breakfast time, with a smell of sausage in the air. We sat round, very ready for it, but the watcher on the broken tower yelled, Airplane up! seeing one coming over from the Deraa aerodrome. Our Australians scrambled to their feet, rushed wildly across to their yet-hot machines, and had them started in a moment. Ross Smith, with his observer, leaped into one, for he had been a famous fighting pilot, put later to the onerous but unwarlike Handley-Page, and this was his morning out, and he meant to taste the old joys of Bristol-work. He climbed like a cat up the sky. After him went Peters and his pal, while the third pilot, Traill, stood beside the D.H.9 and looked hard at me.

I seemed not to understand him. Lewis guns, Scarfe mountings, sights, rings which turned, vanes, knobs which rose and fell on swinging parallel bars; to shoot, one aimed with this side of the ring or with that according to the varied speed and direction of oneself and the enemy. Yes, I had been told the theory, could even repeat some of it: but it was in my head, and rules of action were only snares of action till they had run out of the empty head into the hands, by use. No, I was not going up to air-fight, no matter what caste I lost with the pilot. He was not an Arab, but an Australian, one of a race delighting in additional risks. I need not play to his gallery.

He was too respectful to speak: only he looked his reproach at me while we watched the battle in the air. There were one enemy two-seater and three scouts. Ross Smith fastened on the big one, and after live minutes of sharp rattle of machine-gun fire, the German dived suddenly towards the railway line. As it flashed behind the crest of the low ridge there broke out a long plume of black smoke and from its falling place came up a soft, dark cloud. An 'Oh' came from the Arabs about us. The scouts went low and sneaked home undamaged, but their two-seater was finished, and live minutes later Ross Smith was back, with Peters, and jumped gaily out of his machine, saying that the Arab front was the place.

The sausages were still hot, and we ate them, and drank the tea, (our last English stores, broached for our visitors) but were hardly at the grapes which Jebel Druse had sent us, when again the watchman tossed up his cloak and screamed, 'An airplane'. This time Peters won the race, Ross Smith second, and Traill disconsolate in reserve: but the shy enemy turned back too soon. Our people were out an hour, for Peters did not catch his quarry till near Tell Arar: there he drove them down fighting but still to his mind alive though damaged. A few days later when the wave of war rolled back thither, we found their hopeless crash and two charred German bodies.

Ross Smith wished he might stay forever on this Arab front, with an enemy every half-hour and deeply envied Peters his coming days at Urn el Surab. However, he must go back to Palestine, to bring across the Handley-Page that afternoon with petrol, food and spares. These two fighting trips had used up so much that there was only just enough for the return journey. The third machine was for Azrak, to rescue the observer I had marooned there yesterday: and I went down so far with him to see Feisal and Nuri Shaalan, and get the last move afoot.

Time was long to those who flew: we were in Azrak before noon, having filled a busy thirty hours. Stirling was there preparing with the cars and Gurkhas and Egyptians to attack Zerga bridge, when they got my news of it. Instead, I told them we would leave it to Chaytor, whom Allenby was starting instantly: and they might get back to Urn el Surab for our new urgent demolitions in the north. Then, with Feisal and Nuri Shaalan, I packed into the green Vauxhall, which its British soldier, proud of his prince to drive, kept always spick and shining; a heart-breaking contrast to our dingy war-cars: and off we went in the midday, wishing to reach Urn el Surab in the afternoon, to see the great Handley-Page alight there with its supplies.

Accordingly we ran at speed over the smooth flint or mud-flat, letting the strong car throb itself fully: but luck was hostile. A dispute was reported to us by one group of travelers, and so we had to turn aside and stop in the main Serah in camp, near the head of the Giaan el Khunna. However, we turned our loss to profit by calling up all their fighting men to Umtaiye: and had them send word of the complete victory across the railway to the Beni Hassan and the Chaabneh, that the roads through the Ajlun hills might be closed to the broken pieces of the Turkish armies, as they tried to escape through into safety.

Then Feisal took leave of the Serahin, and we flashed northward again. Twenty miles short of Urn el Surab we perceived a single Bedawi running southward at his best pace, all in a flutter, with his long grey hair and grey beard flying in the wind, and his shirt (tucked up in his belly-cord) puffing out behind him. He altered course to pass near us, and raising his bony arms, yelled aloud, 'The biggest airplane in the world', before he flapped on into the south, to spread his great news among the tents. Word of mouth would so carry rumor a hundred miles a day, till it overtook our more ingenious telegraphs.

At Urn el Surab there stood the Handley, majestic on the grass with the Bristols and 9A like chickens beneath its spread of wings. Round it admired the Arabs, saying, Indeed and at last they have sent us the airplane, of which these little things were the asses': and before night rumor of Feisal's immense resource went over Jebel Druse and across the hollow of Hauran, telling people that the balance of success was weighted on our side.

Borton himself had come over in the machine, as a passenger with Ross Smith, to greet us, and concert further help: also to see the strange conditions of the Arab front. Which by now had a body of its own legend among the Staff in Palestine. We talked with him while our men drew, from her bomb-racks and fuselage, forty-seven four-gallon tins of petrol, and oil and spare parts for Bristol fighters with tea and sugar and rations for our men and letters. Reuter telegrams and medicines for ourselves I found myself wondering what would be the added value to our force, if a daily Handley came to us: but that would be too much to ask the gods.

Nevertheless Borton offered it saying that this was the first occasion to his knowledge on which a Handley-Page had crossed an enemy front in broad day and how glad he would be to repeat it when we needed him again. While I thanked him and Young offered tea we passed the word to our car-drivers and they subtracted from the pile of cans before it was counted one can for each car to give them a radius of a last hundred miles, up to Damascus. Then the great machine rose into the early dusk, on her flight back to Rarnleh, with an agreed program of night-bombing against Deraa and Mafrak, to complete that ruin of the railway traffic which our guncotton had begun.

We for our share would keep up this guncotton pressure. Allenby had assigned to us the Turkish Fourth Army to harass and contain till Chaytor forced them out of Amman; and afterwards to cut up on their retreat. We were not to think about Damascus till we had settled them for at Deraa were stores and reserve troops, with whose help if we gave them an unmolested passage they might re-form themselves enough to dispute Barrow's rough passage of the Irbid hills, and so throw out of gear Allenby's double drive against Damascus and his hope to sweep their ruins far beyond it without pause.

At the same time this retirement of the Fourth Army was only an affair of days and it was as certain as things could be in war that we would raise all the plains between us and Damascus next week. So Feisal decided that Nuri Shaalan should add himself to our column, with the Rualla camel-men whom he would send up from Azrak to join us here. It would increase us to about four thousand strong, more than three-fourths irregular but reliably so for the Hauran peasants obeyed Taiai implicitly, and Nuri, the hard, silent rather cynical old man, held his tribe between his lingers like a tool.

He was that rarity in the desert, a man without the sense of argument. He either would or would not and there was no more to it. He listened to others, often with a quiet humor in his eye, and when they finished would announce his will in a few flat phrases and wait calmly for obedience, which came, for he was feared by those below him, for his harshness. He was old and wise, which meant tired and disappointed: so old that it was my abiding wonder that he should understand our enthusiasm and be so determined on our side. Youth had before him, a candid sense that its admission into the already working and established world was an intrusion, deservedly grudged, but tolerated, by his wisdom.

Personally I found him delightful to work with for his intelligence and wisdom and quick sight. It intoxicated me to have another, unprompted announce my secret beliefs: confirmed me in them, and exasperated my mind to rush them forward to an unwarrantable extreme of credulity. In a little while, one fool would make his company all of them follies: and with Nuri Shaalan the contagion of wisdom seemed as quick.

On the next day the twenty-third of September, I rested, sitting with Nasir in his tent among the visitors from every village in Hauran, sorting out the too abundant news furnished us by their quick wit and good will. Every change in enemy disposition, almost every variation of mood so came to our camp sooner or later often without the consciousness of the teller. Our duty was to listen so closely that we might walk with a firm step through the storm of strange circumstances which beat about us; and with the help of these trained Sherifs, bred to sift true from false, we did it well. Some thought our course was luck, or a guessing after the probable: but in reality it was the patient result of infinite care the fruits of our two years' work with these people, grafted in Nasir's case on a lifetime of habit, in my case on seven years' study of their land and language.

During my rest-day, Nuri Said, with Pisani and two guns, with Stirling, Winterton, Young, their cars, and a considerable force, went down openly to the railway, cleared some of it by approved military means, and destroyed nearly a kilometer of rail, and much of the tentative wooden structure with which the Turks had tried to mend the bridge blown up by the armored cars. Nuri Shaalan, the old man of seventy, personally led his Rualla horsemen, galloping in his black broadcloth cloak with the best of them. Under his eye the tribe showed a valor which drew praise from Nuri Said: and Arab Regulars, whether Syrian or Mesopotamian, were less sympathetic to Bedouin, and less likely to give them praise even than British officers.

Chapter 132: A Surprise Move

We did not know it, but the operation of today was the Turks' final blow, after which they gave up effort to restore the line between Amman and Deraa. We still had the threat of it as a bogy over us, and were still urgent to put out of action a yet longer stretch. I conceived a plan of attacking it by armored car below Mafrak, since even a temporary railhead must be at a siding, and if we deprived the Fourth Army of the Mafrak access they would have to march from Sumra to Deraa, a distance of thirty miles, instead of the fifteen which was now their penance.

Accordingly, next day, while the soldiers rested, Winterton and Jemil the gunner and I went out on two armored cars to examine the line between Minifir and Ifdein. The going was admirable, and we ran in confidently just south of Mafrak station: however, the Turks had a gun there, a little thing, but even so it seemed a pity to give it a chance. So we drew out and ran further south and again turned in towards a bridge.

This time we were received with machine-gun fire of a vigor and direction and intensity beyond any of our experience on the Turkish side. Later we captured the experts and found they were a German machine-gun unit of the Yiiderirn army. For the moment we drew out, puzzled, and went further to turn in once more to a tempting bridge. My plan was to run right under it in the car, till beneath the vault, and lay the charge against its pier in its own shelter. So I transferred myself to an armored car, put the necessary sixty pounds of guncotton on the back-board, and told the driver to push in under the arch.

Winterton and Jemil came behind in the supporting car. 'It's very hot,' said Jemil. 'It's going to be still hotter where we're going,' replied Winterton, as we drew in slowly over indifferent ground, with a few aimless shells falling harmlessly about. We were puzzling our way forwards about fifty yards from the bank, with, rattling off our armor, enough machine-gun bullets for a week's fighting, when someone from behind the line flung a hand-grenade at us.

It burst short, but was a new condition, which made impossible my plan of getting under the bridge in the car to fix the charge. For one thing, a hit on the back of the car would have set off our guncotton and blown us to blazes: for another, the car was helpless against a grenade bowled at it under-arm. So we drew off again, very puzzled to understand this new strength of defense lavished on a bit of railway: and very interested, indeed amused, at meeting worthy opposition after such long ease. In our imaginations, Check was a short, compact, furious man, darting glances every way from beneath his tangled eyebrows for an end to his troubles: beside him Victory seemed a lanky, white-skinned, rather languid woman.

If we tried again it must be after dark, when we might reasonably hope to get in and out before the bombers reached our spot. So we drove back to Urn el Surab, and found that Nasir wished to fix the camp once more at Umtaiye. The grazing was as good, the water was to hand, and we were nearer both to our enemies the Turks and to our friends the Hauranis. Also it was a first stage of our journey to Damascus. So his wish delighted me, and we moved, winning thereby good excuse for doing nothing this night to the line. Instead we sat and told stories about the Young Turks, and waited for midnight when the Handley-Page was heard in the distance. It had come to bomb Mafrak station and one hundred-pound bomb after another crashed down into the packed sidings, till they caught fire and the Turks' shooting stopped.

When the machine had gone we went off to sleep, having given the prize of the night to a tale of Enver Pasha, in the Balkan War, after the Turks had just retaken Sharkeui. He went out to see it, in an old penny steamer, with Prince Jemil and a gorgeous staff. The Bulgars, when they came, had massacred all the Turks, and when they retired the Bulgar peasants went with them. So the town was empty, and the Turks found hardly any women there to kill. However, they caught an old man, who was led on board for the Commander-in-Chief to bait. At last Enver, tired of this, signed to two of his brave A.D.C.s, and throwing open the furnace door, said, 'Push him in: The old man struggled and screamed but the officers were stronger and the door was slammed to on his jerking body. 'We turned feeling sick, to go away, but

Enver, his head on one side, listening, held up his hand. So we listened, too, and there came a crash from within the furnace. He smiled and nodded, saying. "Their heads always pop like that":

All night the fire among the trucks burned, and next day, growing greater and greater. It was proof, if any were needed, of the breakdown of the Turks, which the Arabs had been rumoring since yesterday. They said the Fourth Army was streaming up from Amman in a loose mob of carts and guns and lorries, of horses, mules, donkeys and men. The Beni Hassan, who were cutting off their stragglers and weak detachments, said they were like gypsies on the march.

We held a council, where I brought forward a fresh set of thoughts. The Beni Hassan news showed that our work against the Fourth Army in Amman was finished. Those remnants which avoided out of the hands of the Arabs would reach Deraa after their forced march only as unarmed stragglers. Our new endeavor should be to force the quick evacuation of Deraa, that the Turks there, giving up the hope of re-forming the fugitives into a rearguard, might join the common flight towards Damascus. This evacuation, I thought, would be best brought about by our sudden thrust upon the rear of Deraa So I proposed that we march at once across Wadi Taiyibe, and further north, past Tell Arar and Ghazale, over the railway at dawn tomorrow, and into Sheikh Saad village, west of the line. It lay in a Rualla district, in familiar country with abundant water, perfect observation, and a secure retreat west, or north, or even south-west, if we were directly attacked. Its advantages had been shown me by Taiai a year ago. It cut off Deraa from Damascus, and Mezerib also. The Turkish flight would have to pass below our eyes, often below our guns from Sheikh Saad, and we could take our desired action against them, circumspectly.

Taiai agreed with fervor Nuri Shaalan gave his nod Nasir was all for the move. Nuri Said accepted it. So we decided to go off at noon, and prepared at once to strike camp. The armored cars could not come with us, for beyond Sheikh Saad lay lava country, into which we might be driven. They could not stay here: so they had better go back to Azrak, where Marshall was, till Deraa fell and we sent for them to help us into Damascus. The Bristol Fighters likewise had done their work. Turkish airplanes seemed to have ceased to exist. They might go to Palestine, with news of our sudden move to Sheikh Saad, where we promised to layout an aerodrome for them to rejoin us if there was need later.

They circled off We, watching their line of light, noticed a great cloud of apparent dust added to the slow smoke rising from the ruined yard at Mafrak station. It puzzled us, unless it was the broken van of the Fourth Army in its light: but one of our machines turned back and dropped a scribbled message to say that a large body of hostile cavalry was heading out from the railway towards us.

This was most unwelcome news, for we were not in trim for a fight. The cars had gone, the airplanes had gone one company of the mounted infantry had marched. Pisani's mules were packed and drawn up in open columns. I went off to Nuri Said, standing with Nasir on a dust-heap at the head of the hill, and we wavered whether to run or to stay and stand. At last it seemed wiser to run, since Sheikh Saad was a more profitable stop-block. So we hurried the rest of our regulars away.

Yet things could hardly be left like that; accordingly, I went to Nuri Shaalan and to Taiai and got them to lead the Rualla horse and the Hauran horse back down the lava slopes we knew so well, to delay the pursuit. They had an unexpectedly, for our cars on their way to Azrak had seen the enemy, and of their own accord had gone down to look at them. With such support, our mounted irregulars had no difficulty, for after all the Turks were not cavalry coming to attack us, but deluded elements seeking a shorter way home. We took some hundreds of thirsty prisoners and much transport, causing such a panic that the main rout in the plain cut the traces of their limbers and guns, and rode off on the bare horses, leaving everything slow abandoned in the open. The infection of terror spread up and down the line, and the troops, who had been marching heavy-laden and in some order, threw away all they had even to their rifles, and made a mad rush towards the supposed safety in Deraa.

However, this interruption delayed us, for we could hardly march a khaki-clad body of regular camel corps across the Hauran plain at night without enough screen of local cavalry to go bail for us to the suspicious villagers that we were not Turks. So we crossed Wadi Taiyibe late in the afternoon and halted for Taiai and Nasir and Nuri Shaalan to catch up.

This halt gave us time to review the wisdom of our proceeding, and some began to question the need of our crossing the railway a second time to put ourselves in the dangerous position of Sheikh Saad, astride the retreat of the main Turkish forces. Finally about midnight Young appeared where I lay, in the midst of the army, on my carpet, awake and thinking what various possibilities might come to us. He suggested that we had done enough. Allenby had appointed us watchmen of the Fourth Army. We had just seen it in disordered flight. Our duty was complete, and we might honorably fall back eastward to Basra Eski Sham, the town twenty miles out of the way, where the Druses were collecting under Nesib el Bekri to help us. We might wait with them for the British to take Deraa and for our reward, in the victorious dose of the campaign.

This attitude passed me by, since if we withdrew to Jebel Druse, we ended our active service before the game was won, leaving the last brunt on Allenby. To be sure he had given us the Fourth Army, and our formal 'duty' was completed: but I had always been shy of this word 'duty', which seemed to imply a bargain with a third party for a certain performance, a half-price with life, as though there was a bound where our strength might rest: — while I had found its limit only in the will which failed us, seduced by the longing for a moment's forgetfulness of life. It seemed meanness, in cold blood, to formulate a set limit and call it 'duty': and it would be an added meanness to rest while we were capable of doing more.

To my mind we owed no duty to anyone; though we served Allenby to our best ability, because there lay our interest to win the war. Yet I was very jealous for the Arab honor, and for them would go forward at all costs. They had joined the war to win their freedom, and while winning it was easy, the abiding resolve to keep it could be sealed only by their blood and effort. Scientifically speaking we had perhaps done enough for this: at least we had earned the right to it: but we were dealing with masses in their ignorance, and the recovery of their old capital by the force of their own arms was the sign they would most fully understand.

However, let us suppose we were serving Allenby out of sense of duty, not by conviction. By thrusting behind Deraa into Sheikh Saad we put unrivaled pressure on the Turks and did them more harm than any British unit was in place to do. It would forbid the Turks fighting again this side of Damascus, for which end, even if we all lost our lives in the business (an improbability which I would do all in my power to avert), such a cost would be cheap payment. By it we as good as took Damascus, which meant the end of this war in the East, and I believed the end of the general war.

In the general war the unknit Allies had survived the end of Serbia, and the end of Russia, without enfeeblement in France; and they could have survived the loss of Mesopotamia, of Palestine, and of Salonika as easily; but the Central Powers were a single body with one front, a use of force economical and yet most dangerous, since it made them interdependent, and the breaking of the weakest link, Turkey, would swing loose them all. Therefore for every reason, strategically, tactical, political, even moral, we were going on.

Young's stubborn resistant mind was not convinced. He returned with Pisani and Winterton, as though for a conference to debate our movements, and began to put the question to me again, speaking slowly and distinctly because Nuri Said was lying on the rug beside me, only half asleep, and he wanted to impress him also with the madness of my plan.

Accordingly, he put things only on the military basis, of our fulfilled purpose, and of the danger of trying to cross the Hejaz Railway. I had planned to be over it at dawn. This delay made us too late to cross tonight. In the daytime it would be madness to attempt such an operation: while tomorrow night it would be guarded from end to end by the tens of thousands of Turks pouring into Deraa, and we would certainly be cut off and captured; even if they let us over we would only be in the greater danger with it held behind us.

Joyce, he said, had appointed him military adviser to the expedition (his splendid work with the transport had earned him a share in our operations, and we had asked him to come along and help, in the informal way we did things among ourselves), and it was his duty to point out, reluctantly, that he was a regular officer, and knew his business.

I was in no mood for a debate at this time of night, or at this stage of our journey, when no new circumstance had arisen to change our plan. Also in a debate I might have lost my temper and told Young that had I been a regular officer I would have found his upsetting my subordinates irregular. So I endured his complaints silently and patiently, sighing upon occasion, for I thought that was perhaps the most irritating answer to the protestant. At the end I said wonderingly that I wanted to go to sleep, since we would have to be up early, to go forward across the line and yet reach Sheikh Saad by daylight: and it was my intention to go in front with my bodyguard, among the Bedouin, wherever they were, for it was odd that Nuri Shaalan and Taiai had not overtaken us. Anyway, I was going to sleep now.

Pisani, whose long military life had been all as a subaltern, said with correctness that he took his orders, and would follow after. I liked him for that, and tried to soothe what evidently were his honest doubts by reminding him that we had worked for eighteen months together without his ever finding cause to call me rash. He replied with a French laugh that he thought it all very rash; but that in war it was proper to take risks open-eyed: and that he was very much a soldier.

Winterton was silent, but I knew that his instinct would join him to the weaker and more sporting side of my choice. I reproached myself for not having understood that the other British perhaps did not see the rights of our proceedings as clearly as me. My knowledge that the Arabs were the main partners, the workers whom we watched, and that they were very ignorant, had led me to devote myself to them, cultivating them day and night so fully and so repeatedly that my plans became commonplaces to me, and with the British for relief I would talk of indifferent subjects, forgetting that they too should be kept informed.

Nuri Said had lain silently through our talk, pretending to be asleep, but when Young went away grumbling, he rolled over to me and whispered, 'Is it true?' I replied that I saw no unusual risk in going on tomorrow and crossing the line in mid-afternoon; and that with care we should be able to avoid traps at Sheikh Saad. He lay back satisfied.

Chapter 133: In Hiding

It was a glorious, fresh morning. We had not passed the crest before we met Nasir and Nuri Shaalan and Taiai. They had overshot us in the dark, and had slept there to find us in the morning. Our joined forces marched with a heady breeze in the teeth northward across these rich plough-lands, between Saida and Gharija: fat happy villages. Over the harvested fields whose straw had been rather plucked than reaped grew thistles tall as a child but now yellow and dried and dead. The wind snapped the more hollow ones off, short at the root, and they fell pitch-polling on their branchy tops along the level ground thistle blowing against thistle and interlocking their spines till a huge matted ball of them careered merrily across the fallows.

Arab women, out with their donkeys to carry water ran to us in alarm, saying that an airplane had landed a little while since in a near hollow. Taiai sent a galloper to see and he came back with word that it bore the round rings of the Sherifian camel-brand upon its body. Peake was nearest, and rode across — to find an Australian pilot and observer who Bristol had been hit by a bullet in the radiator over Deraa, and brought down here over-hot. They were glad and even astonished to find themselves among friends. The leak they had plugged with asbestos and wire and we levied water from the women to fill them up again. After which they took off and flew home safely.

Our force marched forward keeping together for security in this uncertain country. Men rode up every minute from both sides and joined us, while by each village the adventurous young ran out on foot, and entered our ranks. As we moved on, so closely knit in the golden sunlight, we were able, for one of our rare chances, to see ourselves in a body: and quickly we seemed to grow a character to become an organism, in whose pride each of us was uplifted. We knew that we were Mohammed or Awad, Auda or Nuri, Rahail or Nasir whose manhood it was that made the force: but also it was something exterior which we had created, a work of art, in honoring which we glorified ourselves: and we cracked bawdy jokes at one another to set off its beauty.

At noon we entered the sweltering basaltic bed of Wadi Ghar, near Horeik, in its water-melon fields. The army ran upon them, while we went up a little and spied out the line, which lay quivering in the sunlight, but deserted, across our front. As we watched there, resting an hour to ease the regulars a train suddenly passed down towards the south. This was our first news that Peake's break at Tell Arar had been amended, and I sent for some of the local people. They reassured our vanity by protesting that only last night had the rails got through, and only three trains had yet passed.

This was better and after our halt we moved over the plain in a horde two miles across, upon the line, and reached it without opposition. There we tore down the telegraph, and began to blow up things, hastily, anyone who had explosive using it upon his fancy in any fashion which seemed to him good. There were hundreds of novices with us, full of zeal, and the demolitions to them were great joy. So many hands albeit uninstructed, did a wide damage in fifteen minutes.

Clearly our return had taken the distracted enemy quite by surprise; and we felt that we must extend and improve this happy chance. So we went to Nuri Shaalan, to Auda Abu Tayi, and to Taiai, and asked each what local effort he would undertake. Taiai the energetic answered first that he would attack Ezraa, the big station and grain depot just north of us: Auda was for Khirbet el Ghazale, the corresponding station to the south: Nuri said he would sweep his men down the main Damascus road, towards Deraa, on the chance that Turkish parties were struggling up it northward.

These were three good ideas, and the three chiefs went to put them into being, while we pulled our column to its shape again and pursued our road, past the ruined colony of Sheikh Miskin, very gaunt in the moonlight. The obstacle of its water-ditches muddled together all our thousands, so that we halted in confusion on the stubble plain beyond, near dawn. Some made fires against the penetrating mist of this clay Hauran land: others lay down as they were on the dew-slimy ground, for a short rest: but there was no rest, for lost men went about the army calling their friends in that sharp full-throated wail of the Arab villager. The moon had gone down, and the world was black and very cold.

Later I roused my bodyguard, and we rode on in front so briskly that we entered Sheikh Saad with the dawn. As we passed between the rocks into the field behind the trees, the earth sprang to life again with the new sun. The morning airs flashed the olive yards to silver, and men ran out from a great goat-hair tent on the right, and called us in to guest with them. We asked whose camp it was... they said, 'Ibn Srneir's.' This was a sorry complication. He was an enemy of Nuri Shaalan's, unreconciled chance-met.

At once we sent warning to Nasir, and then crossed to the tent, to find that, fortunately, ibn Smeir was absent. So all would be easy They would be our temporary guests, and Nuri as a host would observe the rules, It was a relief, for already we had hundreds of deadly enemies in our ranks (their feuds only suspended by Feisal's peace), and the strain of keeping them in play when they met before our faces, and of employing their respective hot-heads in separated spheres, balancing opportunity and service that our direction might be esteemed as above jealousy: all that was evil enough. The conduct of the war in France would have been harder if each division, almost each brigade, of our army had hated each other with a deadly hatred, and fought when they met suddenly. However, we had kept them quiet in such conditions for two years, and it would be only a few days now.

The parties of the night returned, enriched Tala had taken Ezraa, which was feebly defended by Abd el Kader, the Algerian who had tried to betray us in 1917. He had his personal followers, some volunteers, and troops with two guns and some machine-guns. When Taiai came, the volunteers went over to him; the troops fled, and the retainers were so few that Abd el Kader had to abandon the place without fighting. He rode off angrily towards Damascus, and our men were too heavy with the great booty of Ezraa to catch him.

Auda came in, boasting that he had taken Ghazale by storm, capturing a derelict train, with guns and two hundred men, of whom some were Germans. Nuri Shaalan reported four hundred prisoners, with mules and machine-guns. The rank and file had been farmed out to remote villages to work for their keep till called for.

An English airplane appeared and flew round and round us, wondering if we were the Arab force or not. Young spread out his ground signals, and then on him they dropped a message to say that Bulgaria had surrendered to the Allies. We did not even know there was an offensive in the Balkans, so the news was too much by itself: however there it was, circumstantially, one more proof that the end, not only of our war, but of the great war was very near. We thought that after another sharp effort our trial would be over and everyone able to go back to his affairs forgetting the madness: because to most of us it was our first war, and we looked forward to its end as rest and peace.

The army arrived, and the groves became thronged with men and camels as each detachment picked out the best vacant place and unsaddled there, whether under fig trees, or under palms, or olives. The birds, hearing our noise, burst out from them in frightened clouds with multitudinous crying. The animals were taken to water at the stream, while we wandered through the gardens seeing green bushes and flowers, and cultivated fruits, which had been strange for the years of our wandering in the flinty desert.

The people of Sheikh Saad came shyly to look at us. Feisal's army had been a whispered legendary thing for so long to them and here we were in their village in our diversity, led by people renowned or formidable, Taiai, Nasir, Nuri, Auda, names to hush even boastful men. We stared back envying their peasant life, sheltered from the current of war and engaged in normal husbandry, knowing that for us there would not be peace till the major armies were disbanded; but determined meanwhile to enjoy Sheikh Saad, this interval of no more than comfortable danger.

We let the men stretch the saddle stiffness from their legs after the days of riding, while we went up some five or six of us to the height above the ruin whence we could look across the southern plain and see the measure of security in store for us. To our astonishment we saw in the valley just over the walls a thin company of men in uniform, Turks, Austrians, Germans, with eight machine-guns on pack-animals. They were toiling up from Galilee towards Damascus after their defeat by Allenby, hopeless but careless marching at case thinking themselves fifty miles from any war.

We did not give an alarm, to spare our tired troops further pains: just Durzi ibn Dughmi, with the Khaffaji and others of the family, and a few tenants, mounted quietly and fell on them from a narrow lane. The officers showed fight, and were killed instantly. The men threw down their arms and in five minutes had been searched through and robbed and were being shepherded in file along the water-paths between the gardens to an open pound which seemed fit for our prison. Sheikh Saad was paying soon and well.

Next away to the west appeared three or four black knots of people moving northward. We loosed the Howeitat on them and after an hour they returned in laughter each man leading a new mule or pack-horse: poor tired galled brutes showing all too clearly the straits of the beaten army. Their riders had been unarmed. Were just ragged Turkish soldiers fleeing from the British. The Howeitat had disdained to make such prisoners. 'We gave them to the boys and girls of the villages for servants: said Zaal, with his thin-lipped smile: but indeed it was the merciful course for they would be fed and let sit about and help on the threshing floors till there was a government to make inquisition for them. Had we collected these thousands about us they would have died of hunger and disease.

A boy came running from the west to say that small companies of Turks some still commanded by their officers, were retiring into their villages from jisr Benat Yakub, broken by Chauvel's attacks. We sent to find them armed parties of Nairn a great peasant tribe of the northern and western Hauran, who had joined us as appointed last night at Sheikh Miskin. All the villagers from the Kuneitra road to the railways on the east and south were muttering among themselves by night , wondering what they could do against any weak bodies of Turks within their districts. The mass rising so long prepared by us was now in flood rising higher as each fresh success armed more of the rebels. In two days' time we might have sixty thousand armed men in movement beyond Jordan at our disposal under orders of the sheikhs who had been long in correspondence with us. The teaching and preaching of Ali ibn el Hussein. Nesib el Bekri, and Faiz el Ghusein, in Jebel Druse and elsewhere, was at last bearing fruit.

We snapped up some further trifles on the Damascus road and then of a sudden smoke rose heavily above the hill beyond which lay Deraa: and a horseman cantered into Taiai with news that the Germans had set fire to their five airplanes and to their storehouses and the Turks were getting ready to evacuate the town. We sent scouts to give us long warning of such a movement and then a British airplane visited us and dropped a message that Barrow's troops were nearing Remthe, and that two Turkish columns, one of four thousand, one of two thousand, were nearing us from Deraa and Mezerib respectively.

It seemed to me that these six thousand men were all that remained of the Fourth Army, from Deraa, and of the Seventh Army, which had been disputing Barrow's advance from Beisan: and that with their destruction would end our purpose here. Yet for the moment we must still defend Sheikh Saad, with both regulars and irregulars, and we could not as well send out two offensive detachments. So the larger column, the four thousand, we would let pass for the moment, only fastening to them Khalid and his Rualla, with some northern peasantry, to harry their flanks and rear, hurting and hindering them at every favorable accident of ground.

The nearer two thousand seemed more our size. We would meet them with five hundred men, and scatter them. Therefore we called up half our mounted infantry, with most of the Hotchkiss automatics, and two of Pisani's guns, to go down south against them. Taiai was anxious, for their indicated route would bring them through Tafas, his own village. So we determined to make speed there, and seize the ridge south of it, to attack them in the flank as they came unsuspectingly along the track.

Chapter 134: A Night of Storm

Unfortunately speed was only a relative term with men so tired. Nuri Said undertook to start them off, while I rode away at once with my troop to Tafas, hoping to occupy a shadow-position beyond it, and fight a retiring action till the rest came up. Half-way on the road there met us mounted Arabs herding a drove of stripped prisoners towards Sheikh Saad. They were driving them mercilessly, and the bruises of their urging were blue across the ivory backs: but I left them to it, for these were Turks of the police battalion of Deraa, beneath whose iniquities the Arabs of the neighborhood had run with tears and blood innumerable times: and I thought that a taste of such bitterness as their customary own would not kill them, but might make them thoughtful for the future, less-docile instruments of tyranny. With some of them I had my own account.

The Arabs told us that the Turkish column was mostly of mounted men, Jemal Pasha's lancer regiment, who were already entering Tafas. When we got within sight, we found their news true. They had taken the village (from which sounded an occasional shot), and were halted about it. Small pyres of smoke were going up between the houses. On the rising ground to this side, knee deep in dried thistles, stood a distressed remnant of the inhabitants, old men, women and children, telling terrible stories of what had happened when the Turks rushed in an hour before.

It was too late to do anything but hope for the others, so we lay there on watch, crawling down through the thistles till we were quite near and saw the enemy re-form close column to march out in an orderly body towards Miskin, cavalry in front and in the rear, infantry and machine-guns as a flank-guard, guns and transport in the center. We opened fire on the head of their line when it showed itself beyond the houses. They made an active return from two field guns, unlimbered behind the village. Their shrapnel was over-fused, and passed above us into the rough.

At last Nuri came with Pisani. Before their ranks rode Auda Abu Tayi, expectant, and Taiai nearly frantic with the tales his people poured out of the sufferings of the village. The Turks were now nearly quit of it, and we slipped down behind them to end Taial's suspense, while our infantry took position and fired strongly with the Hotchkiss, and the French high-explosive threw their rearguard into confusion.

The village lay there still before us, under the slow wreaths of white smoke, as we rode to it guardedly. Some grey heaps seemed to hide in the long grass, embracing the ground in that close way which corpses had. These we knew were dead Arab men and women: but from one a little figure tottered off, as though to escape from us. It was a child, three or four years old, whose dirty smock was stained red all over one shoulder and side. When near we saw that it was blood from a large half-fibrous wound, perhaps a lance thrust, just where neck and body joined.

The child ran a few steps, then stood still and cried to us in a tone of astonishing strength (all else being very silent), 'Don't hit me, Baba.' Abd el Aziz, choking out something — this was his village, and she might be of his family — flung himself off his camel, and stumbled, kneeling in the grass beside the child. His suddenness frightened her, for she threw up her arms and tried to scream: but instead dropped in a little heap, while the blood rushed out again over the clothes: and then, I think, she died.

We left Abd el Aziz there, and rode on past the other bodies, of men and women, and four more dead babies, looking very soiled in the clear daylight, towards the village whose loneliness we now knew meant that it was full of death and horror. On the outskirts were some low mud walls, of sheepfolds, and on one lay something red and white. I looked close and saw the body of a woman folded across it, bottom upwards, nailed there by a saw bayonet whose haft stuck hideously into the air from between her naked legs. She had been pregnant, and about her lay others, perhaps twenty in all, variously killed, but set out in accord with an obscene taste.

The Zaagi burst out in wild peals of laughter, and those who were not sick joined him hysterically. It was a sight near madness, the more desolate for the warm sunshine and the clear air of this upland afternoon. I said, 'The best of you brings me the most Turkish dead', and we turned and rode after the fading enemy, on our way shooting down those who had fallen out by the road-side and came imploring our pity. One wounded Turk, half-naked, not able to stand, sat and cried to us. Abdulla turned away his camel's head: but the Zaagi crossed him, and whipped three bullets from his revolver through the man's bare chest. The blood came out with his heart beats, throb, throb, throb, slower and slower.

Taiai had seen what we had seen, He gave one moan like a hurt animal, and then rode heavily to the upper ground and sat there a long while on his mare, shivering and looking fixedly after the Turks. I moved near to speak to him, and lead his mind away: but Auda caught my rein and stayed me. After some minutes Taiai very slowly drew his head cloth about his face, and then seemed to take hold of himself, for he dashed his stirrups into his horse's flanks, and galloped headlong, bending low and swaying in the saddle, right at the main body of the enemy.

It was a long ride, down the gentle slope, and across the hollow, and we sat there like stone while he rushed forward, the drumming of the hoofs sounding unnaturally loud in our ears, for we had stopped shooting and the Turks had stopped shooting. Both armies waited for him, and he flew on in the hushed evening till only a few lengths from the enemy. Then he sat up in the saddle and cried his war cry, 'Taiai, Talal', twice in a tremendous shout. Instantly their rifles and machine-guns crashed out together, and he and his mare, riddled through and through with bullets, fell dead among their lance points.

Auda looked very cold and grim. 'God give him mercy: we will take his price.' He shook his rein, and moved slowly forward after the enemy. We called up the peasants, now drunk with fear and blood, and sent them from this side and that against the retreating columns. Auda led them like the old lion of battle that he was. By a skillful turn he drove the Turks into bad ground, and split their formation into three parts.

The third part — the smallest — was mostly made up of German and Austrian machine-gunners grouped round three motor-cars, which presumably carried high officers. They fought magnificently and repulsed our attacks time and again despite our hardiness. The Arabs were fighting like devils, the sweat blurring their eyes, dust parching their throats: while the flame of cruelty and revenge which was burning in their bodies so twisted them about that their hands could hardly shoot. By my orders we took no prisoners, for the only time in the war.

At last we left this stern section behind us, though they said it held Sherif Bey, commanding the lancers: and pursued the faster two. They were in panic, and by sunset we had destroyed the smallest pieces of them, gaming as and by what they lost. Parties of peasants flowed in on our advance, each man picking up his arms from the enemy. At first there were five or six to every rifle: then one would put forth a bayonet; another a sword; a third a pistol. An hour later, those who had been on foot would be on donkeys. Afterwards every man would have a rifle, and the most other arms as well. At last all were on captured horses. Before nightfall the horses were heavy-laden, and the rich plain behind us was scattered over with the dead bodies of men and animals. There lay on us a madness, born of the horror of Tafas or of its story, so that we killed and killed, even blowing in the heads of the fallen and of the animals, as though their death and running blood could slake the agony in our brains.

Just one group of Arabs, who had been to the side all day, and had not heard our news, took prisoners, the last two hundred men of the central section. That was all to survive, and even their respite was short. I had gone up to learn why it was, not unwilling that this remnant be let live as witnesses of Taial's price: but while I came, a man on the ground behind them screamed something to the Arabs who with pale faces led me down to see. It was one of us, his thigh shattered. The blood had rushed out over the red soil, and left him dying, but even so he had not been spared. In the fashion of today's battle he had been further tormented, bayonets having been hammered through his shoulder and other pinning him out like a collected insect.

He was fully conscious, and we said, 'Hassan, who did it?' He dropped his eyes towards the prisoners, standing there so hopelessly broken. We ranged our Hotchkiss on them, and pointed to him silently. They said nothing in the moment before we opened fire: and at last their heap ceased moving, and Hassan was dead , and we mounted again and rode home slowly (home was just my carpet at Sheikh Saad) in the gloom which felt so chill now that the sun had gone down.

However, I found that I could not rest or speak or eat for thinking of Taiai, the splendid leader, the fine horseman, the courteous and strong companion of the road: and after a while had my other camel brought, and, with one of my bodyguard, rode out in the night towards Sheikh Miskin, to join our men who were hunting the great Deraa column, and learn how they had fared.

It was very dark with a wind beating in great gusts from the south and east, and only by the noise of shots it tossed across to us, and by occasional gun-flashes did we at length come to the fighting. Every field and valley had its Turks, stumbling blindly northward. Our men were clinging on tenaciously. The fall of night had made them bolder, and they were closing with the enemy, firing into them at short range. Each village as its turn came took up the work, and the black icy wind was wild with rifle shots and shootings, volleys from the Turks and gallops as small parties of one or other side crashed frantically together.

The enemy had tried to halt and camp at sunset, but Khalid had shaken them into movement again. Some had marched some had stayed. As they went many dropped asleep in their tracks with fatigue. They had lost all order and coherence and were drifting through the storm in lost packets ready to shoot and run at every contact with us or with each other and the Arabs were as scattered and nearly as uncertain.

Exceptions were the German detachments and here for the first time I grew proud of the enemy who had killed my brothers. They were marching for their homes two thousand miles away, without hope and without guides in conditions mad enough to break the bravest nerves. Yet each section of them held together marching in firm rank, sheering through the wrack of Turk and Arab like an armored ship dark, high-set and silent. When attacked they halted faced about took position, fired to order. There was no haste no crying no hesitation. They were glorious.

After many encounters at last I found Khalid, and asked him to call off all possible Rualla, and leave this routed enemy to time and the peasantry. Heavier work, perhaps lay to the southward. There had been a rumor at dusk that Deraa was empty and Trad with the rest of the Anazeh had ridden off to make sure. I feared a reverse for him since there must still be men in the place and more struggling towards it up the railway and through the Irbid hills in hope of safety there. Indeed unless Barrow had lost contact with his enemy there must be that fighting rearguard yet to follow. Disaster in this eleventh hour was possible: almost likely for the Arabs in their distracted situation, and I wanted Khalid to go help his brother with what fellows he could collect from the night battle.

He agreed at once and after an hour or two of shouting his message down the wind hundreds of horsemen and camel-men had rallied to him. On his way to Deraa he charged through and over several formed detachments of Turks, in the star-blink, and arrived to find Trad in secure possession. He had won it at dusk, taking the station at a whirlwind gallop jumping the trenches and blotting out the scanty elements that still tried to resist.

Then with the help of the local people they had plundered all the camp especially finding booty in the fiercely burning storehouses which the German troops had fired when they left. They entered them and snatched goods from beneath their flaming roofs at peril of their lives: but this was one of the nights in which mankind went crazy, when death seemed impossible however many died to the right and left, and when others' lives seemed just toys to break and throwaway.

Meanwhile Sheikh Saad passed a troubled evening, all alarms and shots and shouts, threatening to murder the prisoners of the day as added price of Taiai and his village. The active Sheikhs were out with me or hunting the Turks, and their absence and the absence of their retainers deprived the Arab camp of its chiefs and of its eyes and ears. The sleeping clan-jealousies had come to life in the blood thirst of the afternoon of killing, and Nasir and Nuri Said, Young and Winterton, were up nearly all the time, keeping the peace.

I got in long after midnight, and found Trad's messengers just arrived with news of Deraa. Nasir left at once to join him. I had wished to sleep, for this was my fourth night of riding: but my mind would not be still enough to feel how tired my body was; so about two in the morning I mounted a third camel, and splashed out towards Deraa, down the Tafas track again, passing to windward of the dark village and its plangent, miserable women.

Nuri Said and his Staff were riding the same road, and our parties hurried along together till the half-light came. Then my impatience and the cold would not let me travel horse-pace any longer. I gave liberty to my camel, the grand but rebellious Baha, and she stretched herself out against the entire field, racing the other camels for mile upon mile with great piston-strides like an engine, so I entered Deraa quite alone in the full dawn.

The men about the smoking ruins of the military stores told me where Nasir was, and I rode past my old hospital (now gutted by fire) and over the bridge up into the town, to find him at the Mayor's house. There we worked together for a while, arranging a military governor, and police, and for an inquisition of the place, and putting guards over the pumps and engine sheds, and over what remained of the tool shops and stores.

Chapter 135: With Tile British

My bodyguard arrived, and after them a man from the west, who told us that he had been fired on by the English, now in position to attack the town. To prevent such accident, I took the Zaagi with me, and we two rode up the first slopes of the Buweib, on whose crest was visible a strong post of Indian machine gunners. They trained their weapons very fiercely on us, and looked proud of the splendidly-dressed prizes they had taken. However, an officer soon showed himself with some British troopers, and to them I explained myself.

It was true that they were in the midst of a great enveloping movement against Deraa, and while we watched from the hill their airplanes bombed the luckless Nuri Said as he rode into the railway station. It was his penalty for losing the race from Sheikh Saad: but to stop its getting worse I hurried down to Barrow who had just driven up to this his outpost in a car.

I told him that we had spent the night in the town, and that the shooting which he heard was not at him, but our joy-firing, or the Arabs testing their captured rifles at the butts. He was short with me, but I had little pity for him, since he had delayed a day and night watering at the poor wells of Remthe, when his maps showed him the lake and river of Mezerib in front of him, on the road by which his enemy were escaping his pursuit, and when his airplanes told him that the country thither was empty, and we ourselves active just beyond.

However, his orders were Deraa, and to Deraa he would go: and if he could not make a conqueror's entry, he would make a second best entry. He told me to ride beside him into the town: but had not reckoned on my camel. His horse hated her, so that the General and his Staff plunged and bucked along the ditch, while the Zaagi and I soberly paced the crown of the road. I showed him the village. He said he must post sentries in the street to keep the populace in order. I explained gently that the Arabs had installed their own military governor and dual control might be confusing. At the wells he said he must send his sappers to inspect the pumps. I replied that I would welcome them, for we had lit the furnaces at dawn and hoped to begin watering his horses in an hour. He snorted that we seemed to be at home and that he would garrison and picket only the railway station. I pointed to the engine moving out towards Mezerib (where our little sheikh had just prevented the Turks from blowing up the Tell el Shehab bridge) and asked that his sentries be instructed not to interfere with our proper working of the line.

He had had no orders of what was to be the status of the Arabs after he joined them. Clayton did us this service thinking that we would deserve what we could assert: so Barrow who had come in thinking of us as a conquered people, was dazed at my calm assumption that he was my guest and had no option but to follow the lead of such assurance. My head was working full speed in these minutes since now or never was the moment to put the Arabs in control to prevent those fatal first steps by which the unimaginative British with the best will in the world usually deprived the acquiescent native of responsibility and created a situation which called for years of agitation and successive reform bills and rioting to mend.

I had studied Barrow and was ready for him from the day of his being ordered to cross Jordan. Years before he had published his confession of faith in Fear as the main motive of moral activity in war and peace. Now I found Fear a mean and over-rated motive no deterrent and an unsatisfactory poisonous stimulant whose every application consumed more of the system. In my view war and government could only be maintained by people whose fear had been conquered — or rather transmuted. Instead of making them afraid I tried to make them eager for some remote unintelligible unearthly ideal (in this Arab instance Freedom was what we called it) that their lifted eyes might ignore or see in their true smallness the obstacles which would hurt their flesh upon its way. No end which could be circumscribed would carry far the men who so saw it.

Therefore Barrow and I could never have worked together as I could have no alliance with this pedant belief of scaring men into heaven: and it was better that we part at once. My instinct with a thing inevitable was to rush upon it, or to provoke it in the quickest and fullest measure. Therefore I was very spiny and high towards him, and staved him off easily. My exotic dress and Arab companions helped to confuse him, for he could not treat one so unlike a decent colonel as a mere subordinate in the military hierarchy: besides I took my orders and sent my reports to Allenby, who alone cemented the British and Arabs into a concrete front.

He surrendered himself by asking me to find him the forage and food-stuff needed for his force. I persuaded him into sending two of his brigades to Mezerib, after all, and borrowed his telegraph to send my messages. Indeed as soon as we understood one another we got on quite well, for he had an intelligent and popular side. In the station square I showed him Nasir's little silk pennon, propped on the balcony of the Governor's office, with a yawning sentry lolling underneath. Barrow drew himself up and saluted sharply, while a thrill of pleasure at the General's compliment ran round our officers and men.

We also did not let our self-assertion pass the strict bounds of political necessity. On all Arabs, civil and military, we impressed that these Indian troops were their guests, and must be permitted, nay helped, to do whatever they wished. In some ways the doctrine took us into unexpected places: thus every chicken disappeared from the village: and three privates carried off Nasir's pennon, having coveted the silver knobs and spike of its dainty staff. This pointed a contrast between the English General who saluted it and the Indian trooper who stole it: a contrast welcome to the Arab race hesitation towards the Indians, who liberally returned their feeling.

Meanwhile everywhere we were taking men and guns. Our prisoners could be counted in thousands. Some we handed over to the British, who counted them again: most, as before, we boarded out in the villages to help till the soil. Our reports of the end reached Feisal, and a day later he drove in along the Bosra road, with most of our armored cars following his Vauxhall. He installed himself in Deraa station, and at once was full of work. I called on him when he arrived to give the record of my stewardship: and as my tale was finished our first-floor room in which we sat shook in an earthquake. The windows broke, and his table-furniture rolled on the boards.

Barrow was now watered and fed. Then he warned me that Chauvel was nearing Damascus, and it was his day to leave, that they might enter the city together. I replied that Allenby had told me to go up with him: he asked us to take the right flank, which suited me, for there our men were still fighting, along the Hejaz line beyond Miskin, near Mesmiyeh, hanging on to the Turkish retreat, reducing their numbers by continuous attack day and night, at the smallest cost to themselves. Also our best villages lay along the desert edge, by the railway line. So I said we would guarantee that part, and our regular troops marched off with his on the morning. I had still very much to say and do, and therefore waited in Deraa till the thirtieth, enjoying its quiet now the troops had gone; for the station stood at the limit of the open country , and the Indians round it had angered me by their out of placeless, The essence of the desert was the lonely individual, the son of the road, moving always, as much apart from the world as in a grave. These troopers went about in flocks like slow sheep, and looked not worthy of the privilege of space.

Perhaps the unspoken Arab disdain — founded on that not reasonable race-prejudice — worked in me. At least my mind seemed to feel in the Indian troops something puny and confined, an air of thinking themselves mean, almost a careful, esteemed subservience, so unlike the abrupt, wholesome Bedouin of our joyous Army. The superior manner of the British officers towards their Indian men struck my bodyguard with horror. It was the expression of a relation three or four generations older than our occupation of Egypt and, by so much, more assured and dominant. They had never seen or imagined personal inequality before, and this novel Indian opinion of themselves bruised their self-respect.

I was not certain. It was safest to be one's own maker of emotion, apart from the irresistible current of the crowd, which carried away my slower solitary feeling like a cork on its strong wave. So to know the truth I would withdraw somewhat from their assemblies: yet not so far nor for so long as to forget all standard of comparison. A man by himself found himself the devil of a fellow. For this time I withdrew to the aerodrome, and lay for my last night in the open, out on its emptiness.

By the charred hangars had pitched my vivid guards, as fickle surfaced as the sea, and for the last time Abdulla brought me cooked rice in the little silver bowl, and after supping I lay there in the blankness, and tried to think forward: but my mind was as blank. My dreams had been puffed out like candles by this strong wind of success. In front was only the shadow of our too-tangible goal: but behind was all the effort of two years, its misery now forgotten or glorified. Names ran through my head, memories of our best places, each in imagination a superlative of some sort. Rum the magnificent brilliant Petra Azrak the remote. Batra the very clean.

Sleep did not come to me: so very early, before the light, I woke Stirling and my drivers and we four climbed into the Blue Mist our light Rolls tender which I had made my own, and set out for Damascus along the dirt road which was at first deeply rutted and then nearly blocked by the slow transport columns and rearguard of Barrow's division. They held up our car, so after a little while we cut across country westward to the earthwork of the French railway, whose metals had been taken up to make the Palestine extension in the first year of the war.

The old flat ballast gave us a clear, if rugged, road for our wheels and we put on speed, for such going was heaven to the ill-used driver, At noon we caught up Headquarters and saw Barrow's pennon by a stream, where he was watering his horses. My bodyguard was nearby, so I took my camel and rode over to him. Like some confirmed horsemen, he had been a little contemptuous of the camel and had suggested rather too grandly in Deraa, that we might hardly keep up with his cavalry division, which was going to Damascus in not more than three forced marches.

So when he saw me freshly riding up he was astonished and asked when we had left Deraa; I said, 'This morning' and his face fell. 'Where will you stop tonight?' was his next question. 'Damascus: said I gaily and rode on, having made another enemy. It a little smote me to play him these tricks for he was generous towards my wishes: but my play was for high stakes, high beyond his sight and I cared nothing what he thought of me so that I won. By being personally objectionable to the great men I transferred their anger from my cause to my manner and gained from them all I wanted so long as it was not for me this was a useful discovery and later in Paris and London. Where events made me a big brother of Arab independence, I was able to divert much of the odium to myself: though new nations were necessarily disliked, thrusting as they did, parvenus, into the most exclusive society in the world.

I returned to Stirling and the car, and we drove ahead, now in front of the army. At each village we stopped and got news from the people, and left with them notes for the British advance-guards, telling them how far on we were, and how far beyond us the enemy. The Arabs knew us and told us freely what they knew which was that there were no Turks in front of us for miles. So it irked Stirling and myself to see the caution of Barrow's advance the scouts scouting the empty valleys, sections crowning every deserted hill, the screen drawn forward so carefully over friendly country. It marked the difference between our certain movements based on sure knowledge, and the tentative processes of normal war.

There could be no crisis till Kiswe, this side of Jebel Mania. Beyond it Damascus was visible but at Kiswe we were to meet Chauvel, and there too the Hejaz Railway met our road. Up the railway were riding Nasir and Nuri Shaalan and Auda with the horsemen and camel-men of the tribes still harrying that column of four thousand (but in truth nearer seven) marked by our airplane near Sheikh Saad three busy days ago.

We let the car slide forward to the watershed, from which we could look down and across to the empty line.

As we drove up we heard firing and saw the bursts of shrapnel behind a ridge to our right, where the railway was. Soon appeared the heads of a Turkish column of about two thousand men, marching in ragged groups, halting now and then to fire their mountain guns. We ran ahead to see their pursuers, our great blue Rolls very plain to the eye on its white open road.

Some Arab horsemen galloped out from behind the Turks and across the fields towards us, bucketing unhandled across the irrigation ditches. When they were near we recognized Nasir and old Nuri Shaalan and about thirty of their servants, on exhausted mares. They told us that these few were all that remained of the seven thousand Turks. The Rualla were hanging on to both flanks while Auda Abu Tayi had ridden behind Jebel Mania to gather the Wuld Ali his friends and lie in wait there for this column, which the Rualia hoped to drive over the hill into his ambush.

I told them that the British in force were just behind. If they could delay the enemy only an hour we might take them overwhelmingly in flank. Nasir looked ahead and saw the walled and wooded farmstead of Khaira barring the level making with the hill a defile through which lay the road both of the railway and of the Turks. He called to Nuri Shaalan and they went thither at their best pace, to check the Turks before it with their rifle-fire.

We drove back three miles to the leading Indian regiment and told their ancient surly colonel what a gift the Arabs brought him. He seemed not too pleased to upset the beautiful order of his march but at last, grumbling opened out one squadron and sent them slowly across the plain towards the Turks who turned the little guns their way and tried to range on them as they came forward.

One or two shells burst nearly among the files and then to our horror (for the Arabs had put themselves in jeopardy expecting our courageous help) the colonel at once ordered a retirement and fell back quickly to the road. Stirling and I were hopping mad. We dashed down to him and begged him not to be afraid of mountain guns whose missiles were no worse than Very pistols': but neither to kindness nor to wrath did the old man budge an inch. We turned the car round and raced a third time back along the road in search of higher authority.

A red-tipped aide told us that over there was General Gregory asking what all the firing was about. We blessed him. Stirling's professional pride nearly in tears at the mismanagement: but myself less astonished for my irregularity had warned me to expect little good from so crusted a vintage as that colonel. So we thrust our friend aboard and found his General to whom we showed the exhibition and lent our car that he might send his brigade major with hot orders to the cavalry. A galloper hurtled back for the horse artillery which came up in ten minutes was run forward into place and opened fire just as the last of the light fled up the hill to its summit and took refuge in the clouds. Middlesex Yeomanry appeared, and were pushed in among the Arabs to charge the Turkish rear in the dark: and as the night fell we saw the break-up of the enemy who abandoned their guns and their transport and all their stuff, and went streaming up the col towards the two peaks of Mania, into what they thought was empty land beyond.

However, in that empty land was Auda waiting for them, and in that night of his last battle against the Turks the deadly old man killed and killed, plundered and plundered, captured and captured, till dawn came and showed him his work finished. There ended the Fourth Army, our stumbling-block for two years.

Gregory's happy vigor heartened us again to face Nasir, and we drove on to Kiswe, where we had agreed that we would meet before midnight. After us came the press of Indian troops: but I had never liked them much, and today's work had destroyed my last conceit in them, so we moved away seeking a retired spot. But there were men everywhere, and at last we felt we must bed down as we were, resigned to a crowd. Nonetheless, the movement and cross-currents of so many minds working in so confined a place disturbed me, and drove me about restlessly like themselves.

In the night my color was unseen, and I could walk as I pleased, not noticed nor saluted, an unconsidered Arab: and this finding me among but cut off from my own kin made them doubly strange. Our armored-car men were persons to me, from their fewness and our long company, and also in themselves, for the flaming sun, and their months unshielded from the bullying wind, had worn and refined them into individuals. In this mob of unaccustomed soldiers, British and Australian and Indian, they went about nearly as strange and timid as myself, distinguished also by their dress for, with the weeks of wearing, their clothes had become rather integuments than wrappings, molded to them by their sweat, and by use, and by the accidents of living in and caring for their cars.

But these others were really soldiers, a novelty to me, the first met in two years, and it came upon me freshly how the secret of uniform was to make solid, dignified, impersonal, a crowd: to give it something of the singleness and tautness of one upstanding man. This death's livery veiled its bearers from ordinary life, was sign that they had sold themselves to the State for wages; and that in the great game which States ever played with death, some few of these their servants would at times be lost. Such were the hazards of their hire.

They had contracted themselves into a service none the less abject for that its beginning was voluntary, some of them obeying the instinct of lawlessness, some because they were hungry: others thirsting for glamor, for the supposed color of a military life: and of them all those only received satisfaction who had sought to degrade themselves, for to the peace-eye they were fallen below humanity. Only women with a leech were called by those witnessing clothes: their pay, beneath the dignity of any laborer, was enough only to let them drink sometimes, and forget.

Convicts had violence put upon their bodies: but the soldier assigned his owner the twenty-four hours' use of his flesh, and the conduct of his mind and passions. A convict had license to hate the rule which confined him (and all humanity outside himself, if he were greedy in hate); but the sulking soldier was a bad soldier, indeed not a soldier. His very affections became hired pieces on the chess-board of living. He might love only the friends of the King his paymaster fight only His enemies. Some even of the instincts remaining free to slaves he must renounce to be a true soldier — his opinions.

The strange power of war which had made us all as a duty so demean ourselves! These Australians shouldering me in unceremonious horse play had put off half civilization with their civil clothes. They were dominant tonight, too sure of themselves to be careful: and yet did not impress me with their own conviction of themselves. I felt them thin tempered, hollow: they seemed so merely instinctive always going to do great things, with a disquieting suppleness as of blades recklessly half-drawn from the scabbard, lazily swaggering those quick bodies, all curves with never a straight line: yet with such old and disillusioned eyes.

The British tommies were not instinctive except so far as their matter-of-fact instinct was to be more on guard, neater, self conscious. They were not negligent like the Australians but held themselves with a slow-eyed, almost sheepish care. They were prim in their dress, quiet and fresh, going shyly about in pairs. The Australians stood in groups and walked singly. The British clung two and two for company, not out of simple strangeness feeling a need of material support in this far country: but out of an active friendliness of spirit, which expressed the level of the ranks the commonness of their Army clothes. 'Holding together' they called it: a war-time yearning to keep suppressed such emotions as were deep enough to hurt.

About the soldiers hung the Arabs, gravely gazing men from another sphere. My crooked duty had banished me among them for two years. Tonight I was nearer to them than to the tommies, and I resented it, felt it shameful. With a new longing for home I began to cut myself away from the Arabs in spirit, however allied I might be in appearance. The direct contrast sharpened my faculties, and made fertile my distaste, till not merely did I see their unlikeness of race, and hear their unlikeness of language, but I learned to pick between their smells — the heavy, standing, curdled sourness of dried sweat in cotton which hung over the Arab crowds, and the feral smell of the English soldiers, that hot pissy aura of thronged men in woolen clothes, a tart pungency, breath catching, ammoniac, a fervent fermenting naphtha-smell.

Chapter 136: Damascus

We were forced to sleep that night in Kiswe, for the Arabs told us that the roads were dangerous, and we had no wish to die stupidly in the dark at the gate of Damascus. In our minds was the sense that our war was ended, and we shrank from hurrying forward to confirm it. These sporting Australians saw the campaign as a point-to-point, with Damascus the post which the best horse would pass first. We saw it as a serious military operation, in which any unordered priority would be a meaningless or discreditable distinction. We were all under Allenby, and Damascus was the fruit of his genius, and Bartholomew's.

What we, their instruments could claim would be not to have spoiled their conception by our poor work: just as subordinate virtue was rewarded by having avoided punishment. Allenby's tactical scheme properly put the Australians north and west of Damascus across its railways before the southern columns might enter it: and his word to General Chauvel had been, 'You will let the Arabs go in first, if possible:

The 'if possible' had pleased me, for the great man knew that for weeks it had been physically possible for us to enter, and that we had waited only by his command, for his troops to march with us: but the word meant that he never questioned our fulfilling what he ordered . His power lay somewhat in the calm assumption that he would receive as perfect obedience as he gave trust.

He hoped we would go in first, partly because he was generous, and knew how much more than a mere trophy of victory Damascus would be to the Arabs: and partly for prudential reasons. Feisal's movement it was which made this enemy country friendly to the Allies as they advanced, which enabled convoys to go up and down without escort, towns to be administered without garrison: and Allenby valued and used the Arabs not for their fighting, but for their preaching.

For this reason Nuri Said had ridden in Barrow's ranks up from Deraa, and Stirling and Nasir and Nuri Shaalan and I had kept in front of him. It was our burden to make each new yard of country ours in sentiment before we took it. Allenby had appointed to the Australians an envelopment of Damascus by the west and north: but perhaps they might be forced to enter the town at dawn tomorrow, and if anyone resisted them there it would spoil the future. In the one night we must convince the Damascenes to receive the British as their allies.

This was a revolution in behavior, if not in opinion, but we had good hopes of success in it, since Feisal had in Damascus a powerful committee, who for months had been prepared to take over the reins of administration when the Turks crashed. We had now only to get in touch with the to tell them the movements of the Allies, and what was required of them. So, as the dusk deepened into night, Nasir and I consulted with Nuri Shaalan and decided to send the Rualla horse galloping into the town, to Ali Riza Pasha, the chairman of our committee, and to Shukri el Ayubi, his assistant, with orders to reconstruct a government at once.

As a matter of fact it had been done at four o'clock in the afternoon, before we took action. Ali Riza was absent, put in command at the last moment by the Turks of the retreat of their army from Galilee before Chauvel: so they hoist him with the defense of the Aswad-Mania line of his own fortification; works intentionally laid out to be useless against attack. He joined us later, but Shukri el Ayubi, in charge of our work while he was away, had found unexpected support from the Jezairi brothers, Mohammed Said and Abd el Kader. With the help of their retainers the Arab flag was hung out on the Town Hall before sunset. The last echelons of Germans and Turks defiled past it on their way to the station of the Beirut line. They say the hindmost general saluted it, ironically.

I dissuaded Nasir from going by himself, saying that this would be a night of confusion and terror, and it would better serve his dignity if he entered serenely at dawn. He and Nuri Shaalan lined out their personal retainers between Jebel Mania and Kiswe, to intercept the second body of Rualla camel-men, who had started out with me from Deraa this morning before dawn. They came along, and with them the first contingent of Druses. We sent them all forward into Damascus, to support the Rualla sheikhs, in case they and our committee had opposition to encounter: so at midnight, when at length we went away to rest, we knew that we had four thousand of our armed men in the town.

I wanted to rest, for my work was coming on the morrow: but could not. This was the climax of our two years' uncertainty, and my mind was distracted by tags of all the ideas which had been used or rejected in that time. Also, Kiswe was stifling, the air warm and breathless with the exhalations of too many trees, too man y plants, too many human beings. I felt I was going back into the crowded world and hated it.

As the Germans left Damascus they set fire to the dumps and ammunition stores, so that miles away though we were, yet every few minutes we were jangled by explosions, whose first shock would set the sky white with flame. At each such roar the earth seemed to shake under us, and we would lift up our eyes to the north, and see the pale sky prick out suddenly in sheaves of yellow points as the shells, thrown to terrific heights by each bursting charge in their turn, burst in irregular clusters like rockets. I turned to Stirling and muttered, 'Damascus is burning', sick at heart to think of the great town laid in ashes as the price of the freedom we were bringing her.

When dawn came we drove to the head of the ridge, which stood over the oasis of the city, almost afraid to look out north for the ruins we would sec: but instead of ruins were the silent gardens, blurred green with the early mist, in whose circuit nestled the glowing city, beautiful as ever, like a pearl in the morning sun. The uproar of the night had shrunk to a thin column of black smoke which rose up sullenly from the store-yard two miles below the town by the Kadem station.

We drove down the hill towards the road which lay straight banked through the watered fields in which the peasants were just beginning their day's work. A horseman galloping towards us checked at the sight of our head cloths in the car and rode to us with a merry salutation holding out a bunch of yellow grapes saying: 'Good news: Damascus salutes you.' He came from Shukri, to tell us that our friends held the city.

Nasir was beyond us and to him we carried the tidings that he might have the honorable entry, a fair privilege of his fifty battles of the war. With Nuri Shaalan beside him he forced a last gallop from his weary mare and vanished down the long road in a cloud of dust which hung reluctantly in the air between the water splashes. To give him a fair start, Stirling and I set out to tell another general (General Clarke I think he was) from Chauvel's column. On the way we found a little stream, clean in the depths of a steep channel. By it we stopped and cleaned ourselves and shaved.

Some Indian troopers peered at us and our car and its ragged driver in Army shorts and tunic, topped with Arab headgear. I was pure Arab in dress; Stirling but for his head-covering, was pure British staff-officer. They called in their language to their N.C.O., an obtuse and bad-tempered person who thought he had taken us prisoner. It took us so long to deliver ourselves from his arrest that we judged we might go forward after Nasir. It was the early morning of October the first just two years since I had landed at Rabegh and gone up alone into Jebel Subh, on the forlorn hope of finding in Feisal the leader whom the Arab Movement lacked.

Quite quietly we drove in. up the long street to the government buildings on the bank of the Barada. All the way was packed with people, lined solid on the side-walks in the road itself at the windows of the houses and on their balconies and roof-tops. Many of them were crying a few of them cheered faintly, some of the bolder ones cried my name aloud: but mostly they just looked and looked, joy in this deliverance almost too great to be credible, shining in their eyes. Movements like a breath in a long sigh from gate to heart of the city, marked our course.

However, at the Town Hall things were different. Its steps and stairs were packed with a swaying mob, yelling against one another, embracing, dancing and singing. They crushed a way through the midst for us, to the antechamber, where were the gleaming Nasir, and Nuri Shaalan, seated. On either side of them stood Abd el Kader, my old enemy, and Mohammed Said his brother. I was dumb with amazement, and, seeing this, Mohammed Said leaped forward and shouted that they, grandsons of Abd el Kader the Emir, with Shukri el Ayubi, of Saladin's house, had formed the emergency government and proclaimed Hussein King of the Arabs from the Town Hall steps yesterday into the ears of the humbled Turks and Germans.

While he ranted I turned to Shukri, who was no statesman, but a beloved man, almost a martyr in the people's eyes, because of what he had suffered from Jemal. He told me how the Algerians alone of all Damascus had stood by the Turks, till they saw them actually running. Then they had come with their Algerian retinue, and burst in upon Feisal's committee where it sat in secret, and brutally assumed control, naming themselves governors of a provisional state.

They were fanatics of the bad Islamic type, whose ideas were theological, not logical, and I turned to Nasir, meaning through him to check their impudence now from the start: when there came a diversion. The screaming press about us parted as though a ship drove through, men going down to right and left among the ruins of the chairs and tables, while a terrific roaring in a voice I knew triumphed over all the rest and stilled them dead .

In the cleared space were Auda Abu Tayi and Sultan el Atrash, chief of the Druses, tearing one another; their followers bounded forward, while I jumped in to drive them apart, crashing upon Mohammed el Dheilan with the same good purpose. Together we broke them, and forced Auda back a pace, while Hussein el Atrash hustled the lighter Sultan into the crowd and away to a side room.

Auda was too blind with rage to be fairly conscious, and we got him into the great state-hall of the building, an immense pompous gilded room, quiet as the grave, since all doors but ours were locked. We pushed him into a chair and held him there while in his fits he foamed and shouted at us till his voice was cracked, his body twitching and jerking with rage, his arms lunging wildly at any weapon within reach , his face swollen with blood, bareheaded, with his long hair scattered over his eyes.

The old man had been hit in the face by Sultan with a stick, and his ungovernable spirit, drunk with the wine of self-will all his life, was raving to wash out the insult with Druse blood. Zaal came in, with the Hubsi, and the four or five of us united to restrain him: but it was half an hour before he calmed enough to hear us speaking, and another half hour before we ventured to stand back from him, with his promise to leave his satisfaction for three days in the hands of Mohammed and myself I went out and had Sultan el Atrash taken secretly out of the town with all speed; and then could look round for Nasir and Abd el Kader, to set in order their Government.

However, they were gone. It was mid-morning, and the Algerians had persuaded Nasir to their house for refreshment. It was a good hap, for there were more pressing public things. We must prove the old days over, and a native Government at last in power. For this Shukri Pasha would be my best instrument, as a local notable, known to every man in the town. He had better be temporary Governor. Ali Riza Pasha Rikabi had been Feisal's Governor-Designate, but was missing. Shukri could fill his place for a day or two: so together we got into the Blue Mist, and set off to show ourselves about the town, his enlargement in authority a banner of revolution for the citizens.

When we came in, there had been some miles of people greeting us: now there were thousands for every hundred then. Every man, woman, and child in this city of a quarter-million souls was out on the streets: and as the miracle of victory was at last confirmed, they waited only the spark of our appearance to unchain their spirits. Damascus went mad with joy. The men tossed up their tarbushes to cheer, the women tore off their veils. Householders threw their flowers, their hangings, their carpets into the road before us. Their wives leaned through the lattices and splashed cups and vases, even bath-dippers of scent at us.

The poor dervishes came together, and made themselves our running footmen in front and behind, howling and cutting themselves with frenzy: and over all the local cries and the shrilling of the women, there came the measured roar of men's voices chanting, 'Feisal, Nasir, Shukri, Urens', in waves which began here, and rolled along the squares, and through the market, down the long street to the East Gate, round the wall, back up the Maidan, and grew to a solid wall of shouts around us by the citadel. We English had been too long free to keep even a memory of its first delirious taste: so that this named gratitude and thanks from a hundred thousand voices broke us with the humiliation of over-great honor.

They told me Chauvel was coming, so with great difficulty I drove alone into the southern outskirts, where our cars met in the road. I described the excitement in the city, and how our new Government was getting into order but would not be prepared to guarantee administrative services before the following day: but then I would wait on him, to discuss his needs and mine together: and meanwhile I made myself responsible for the town, only begging him for the moment to keep his men outside it, since tonight would be a carnival such as the town had not seen for six hundred years, and its hospitable abandon might mislead strangers and pervert their discipline.

Chauvel unwillingly followed my lead, his vain ignorance ruled by my certainty. Like Barrow, he had no instructions from Allenby what to do with the captured city, and since we had confidently taken possession, knowing our road, with clear purpose, prepared processes, and assets in hand, he had no choice but to let us carry on. He was as weak a corps commander as he was a conqueror, and his Chief of Staff, Godwin, who did his technical work, like a good soldier was conscious of his enemy in being behind the hills, and delighted to shelve the responsibility of civil government. His advocacy confirmed my assumption.

Indeed it was confirmed and recognized in Chauvel's next words, which asked liberty for himself to drive round the town and look. I gave this so gladly that he asked if it would be convenient for him to make his formal entry with his troops on the morrow. I said certainly, and we thought a little of the route. There flashed into my head the pleasure of our men at Deraa when Barrow saluted their flag — and I quoted it as an example good to follow before the Town Hall when he marched past.

It was a casual thought of mine, but he saw significance in it: and grave difficulty for him to salute any flag but his own. I wanted to make faces at his folly: but instead to be kind I kept him company, seeing like difficulty in his passing our flag deliberately not noticed. We stumbled round this grave problem, while the joyful unknowing crowd cheered us. As a compromise I suggested we leave the Town Hall out, and invent another route, passing, say, by the Post Office. I meant this as screaming farce, for my patience with him had broken down: but he took it seriously, thought it a helpful idea; and would concede in return, for my sake and the Arabs, a great point.

Instead of an 'entry' he would make a 'march through': it meant that instead of going in the middle he would go at the head, or instead of at the head, in the middle. I forgot, or rather did not well hear, which: for I would not have cared if he had crawled under or flown over his troops, or split himself to march both sides of them: I had no skills in flunkey-work or ceremonial antics: but he must have risen fresh from the study of a book of it.

While we discussed manners there was a world of work inside and outside for each of us to do. It was a little bitter for me to waste my powers playing down to such a part: I grudged lavishing my brain on men who had not earned my respect, and hardly my courtesy: also the won game of grab left a bad taste in my mouth, spoiling my entry much as I spoiled Chauvel's. However, it was part payment for the equivoque which had launched the body of Arabs so deep into the war: and therefore my due. Another twelve hours and we would be safe, with the Arabs put in so strong a place that their hand would hold through the long wrangle and appetite of politics which we foresaw must break out about this luscious spoil.

Chapter 137: Making a State

We sneaked back through the stunning welcome of the people to get to grips at the Town Hall with Abd el Kader: but he had not returned. I sent for him, and for his brother, and for Nasir: and got a curt reply that they were sleeping. So should I have been, but instead was eating a snatch-meal, in the gaudy salon, sitting on gold chairs which writhed about a gold table whose legs also writhed, obscenely.

I explained pointedly to the messenger what I meant. He disappeared, and in a few minutes, Taher, one of the family, came up very agitated, and said they were already on their way. This was an open lie, but I replied that it was very well, since in half an hour I would have called the British and looked carefully for them. The Emir ran off very quickly to report that I was really in earnest, and Nuri Shaalan, who had heard me speak, asked quietly what I meant to do.

I said I would depose Abd el Kader and Mohammed Said, and appoint Shukri in their place till Feisal came: but did it in this gentle fashion because I was loath to hurt Nasir's feelings, and had no strength of my own if men resisted. He asked if the English would not come. I said certainly, but the sorrow was that afterwards they might not go. He thought a moment, and said, 'you shall have the Rualla if only you do all your will, and quickly.' Then he went out on the great steps of the hall, and sent his family to muster the tribe in the square, ready to take my orders as his own.

The Algerians came to the tryst with their bodyguards and with murder in their eyes: but on the way saw the massed lowering tribesmen of Nuri's preparation, and then how Nuri Said with his regulars held the end of the square, and within how my reckless guardsmen were lounging in the ante-chamber. From that moment they knew the game was up: and yet it was a stormy meeting.

In my capacity as regent for Feisal, I pronounced their civil government of Damascus abolished, and named Shukri Pasha Ayubi as acting Military Governor of Syria. Nuri Said was Commandant of Troops. Azmi Adjutant-General. Jemil Chief of Public Security Mohammed Said replied in a bitter speech denouncing me as a Christian and an Englishman, and calling on Nasir to assert himself

Poor Nasir was far out of his depth and could only sit and look miserable at this falling out of friends. Abd el Kader, disappointed in him leaped up and cursed me virulently, puffing himself up to a white heat of passion. His motives seemed to me dogmatic irrational: so I took no heed: which maddened him yet more: till suddenly he leaped forward and drew his dagger.

Like a flash Auda was on him, the old man bristling with the chained-up fury of the morning, and longing for a fight. It would have been heaven for him to have shredded someone there and then with his great fingers. Abd el Kader was daunted and Nuri Shaalan closed the debate by saying to the carpet (so enormous and violent a carpet it was) that the Rualla were now mine, and no questions asked. The Algerians rose and swept in high dudgeon from the room. I was sure they should be seized and shot; but could not make myself fear their power of mischief, nor set the Arabs an example of precautionary murder as part of politics.

I excused myself to Nasir for the urgency which had lain on me, and explained the fantastic unfitness of these Algerian degenerates to represent Feisal for a moment: then we passed to work. Our aim was to make an Arab Government, to lay foundations of a State large enough and native enough to employ the enthusiasm and self-sacrifice of the rebellion, translated into terms of peace. We had to save some of the prophetic personality of the Arab Movement, and add a superstructure to please the conservative classes, that ninety per cent of the population who had been too solid to rebel, and on whose solidity the new State must rest. Rebels, especially successful rebels, were of necessity bad subjects and worse governors. Feisal's new duty would be to rid himself of his war-friends, and to take up with those elements that had been most useful to the Turkish Government. His administrative performance would depend on his understanding of this, and on the degree to which he achieved it. Nasir was too little a political philosopher to feel it, much less to say it. Nuri Said knew, and Nuri Shaalan knew: but neither could take the first steps towards it. Those fell on me.

My reading of history told me that the steps were humdrum: appointments, organization, and departmental routine. We began with the police: chose a commandant, and assistants: allotted districts, provisional wages, indents, uniforms, responsibilities. It began to function. Then came a complaint of water supply. The conduit was foul with dead men and animals. We formed an inspectorate, and gave them labor: drafted an emergency regulation.

The day was drawing in the world was in the streets, riotous. So we passed to lighting, and chose a man to superintend the electric power-house, charging him at all pains to illuminate the town that night. No more signal proof of peace and restoration could be given the public than to resume that street lighting which the war scare had put out. It was done, and to its shining quietness some of the order of the people in this first evening of victory belonged: though our new police were zealous, and we made the grave sheikhs of the many quarters patrol with them, reinforcing fresh activity by old knowledge.

Then sanitation the streets were full of the debris of the broken army, derelict carts and cars, baggage, material, corpses. Typhus, dysentery and pellagra were rife among the Turks, and sufferers had fallen out and died in any shadow there was, along the line of march. We prepared scavenger-gangs to make a first clearing of the roads, and rationed out our doctors among the hospitals, promising them drugs and food next day, if we could find any.

Next a fire-brigade. The local engines had been smashed by the Germans as they left, and the army store-houses still burned unchecked, making the town dangerous. So mechanics were cried for, and trained men, pressed into service, sent down to circumscribe the flames. Then the prisons there were no warders left, and few inmates. We made a virtue of it by a general amnesty civil, political, military. Also the citizens must be disarmed — or at least the war habit of carrying a rifle everywhere must cease. A proclamation was the treatment, followed up by good-humored banter merging into police activity. It would affect our end without malice in three or four days.

Relief work the poor were destitute and had been half-starved for days. We arranged a free distribution of the damaged food from the army store-houses. It would have rotted before we could have received tenders and sold it. After that we must think of food for the general. Damascus would be starving in two days for there were no stocks in the city. To get temporary supplies from the near villages was easy if we restored confidence, safeguarded the roads, replaced the transport animals which the Turks had carried off by others from the pool of captures. Chauvel would not hear of it. We shared out our own animals, and our army transport.

For the routine feeding of the place we needed the railway points men, drivers, and firemen, shop-men traffic staff had to be found and re-engaged immediately. Then the telegraphs: the junior staff were available: we had to find directors, and send out the linesmen to put the system in repair. The post could wait a day or two: but quarters for ourselves and the British were urgent, and so was the resumption of trade, the opening of shops, and their corollary needs of markets and currency.

The currency was horrible. The Australians had looted millions in Turkish notes, the only stuff in use, and had reduced it to no value by throwing it about. One trooper gave a five-hundred pound note to a lad who held his horse three minutes . We tried our Prentice-hands at bolstering it up with the last remnant of our Akaba gold: but new prices had to be fixed everywhere, and for that we needed a printing-press, and hardly was that settled when we had to start a newspaper. Also, as heirs of the Turkish Government, we must maintain its records of fiscal, property, register: and all the old staffs were taking jubilant holiday.

Requisitions plagued us while we were half-hungry. Chauvel had no forage and forty thousand horses. If forage was not brought him he would go seek it, and our new-lit freedom puff out like a match. Our status hung on his satisfaction, and he grudged our being, so that we would find little mercy in his judgments.

Taken all in all, it was a busy evening: but we reached an apparent end by sweeping delegation of office (too often, in our haste, to hands unworthy), by a summary cutting down of efficiency, and by the willing help of Stirling the suave, Young the capable, and Kirk bride the summary. They were backed by the open-minded power of the Arab officers, who saw that their continued independence depended on these two days: and so all did their best that night.

Only time could tell if our best was enough: but at least the Government then instituted endured for two years without foreign advice, in a country wasted by war, in alien occupation, and in the teeth of the opposition of important elements among the Allies. When I left Damascus on October the fourth, it was with the knowledge that the Syrians had a defect to government, a de facto constitution, the nucleus of an Army, and a rifle for every able bodied man. If with these they could not keep the freedom they had won, then either fortune would have treated them hard, or they would have shown themselves unfitted for its gift.

Later, I was sitting alone in my room, working and thinking out as firm a way as the turbulent memories of the day allowed, when it came to the hour of last prayer, and the muedhdhins began to send their call through the warm moist night over the feasting and the illuminations of the city. From a little mosque, quite near, there was one who cried into my open window, a man with a ringing voice of special sweetness, and I found myself involuntarily distinguishing his words : 'God alone is great: I testify there are no gods: but God: and Mohammed the Prophet of God. Come to prayer: come to security. God atone is great: there are no gods: but God:'

At the close he dropped his voice two tones, almost to speaking level, and very softly added: 'And He is very good to us this day, O people of Damascus: The clamor beneath him hushed suddenly, as everyone seemed to obey the call to prayer for this first night in their lives of perfect freedom: while my fancy showed me, in the overwhelming pause, my loneliness and lack of reason in their movement: since only for me, of the tens of thousands in the city, was that phrase meaningless.

I had been born free, and a stranger to those whom I had led for the two years, and tonight it seemed that I had given them all my gift, this false liberty drawn down to them by spells and wickedness and nothing was left me but to go away. The dead army of my hopes, now turned to fact confronted me, and my will, the worn instrument which had so long frayed our path, broke suddenly in my hand and fell useless. It told me that this Eastern chapter in my life was ended. There was the morrow and the next day of unrelenting care, that Feisal might surely gain the fruits of battle: and that was all my work. Or was it just a dream from which I would awake again in the saddle, with before me other months of effort, preaching, risk?

Chapter 138: Sanitary Men

After midnight they woke me with word that Abd el Kader was making rebellion. I sent across to Nuri Said, glad that the fool was digging his own pit. He had called to him his men, told them these Sherifs were only English creatures, and conjured them to strike with him a blow for the religion and the Turkish Caliph, while there was yet time. They took his word for it, and set out to make war on us.

He asked the Druses to help him: and the Druses, who had not joined Feisal's revolt till the war was won and for whose tardy services I had this night sharply refused reward listened to him. They were sectaries caring nothing for Islam or Caliph or

Turk or Abd el Kader; but an anti-Christian rising meant at least plunder, and perhaps Maronites to kill. So they ran to arms and began to burst open shops.

I counseled that we hold our hands till day, for our numbers were not so great that we could throwaway our advantage in weapons, and go out in the strange city to fight in the darkness which made a fool and a wise man equal: but when dawn hinted itself we moved men to the upper suburb and drove the rioters towards the river districts of the center where all the roads crossed bridges and were easy to control.

Then at once we saw how small the trouble was. Nuri Said had covered the river parades with machine-gun sections who with a continuous rattle barraged them across to blank walls. Into these our sweeping parties urged the dissident. The appalling noise made the Druses drop their booty and flee like hares down side-alleys. Mohammed Said not so brave as his brother was taken in his house, and led to goal in the Town Hall. Again I itched to shoot him but waited till we had the other.

However Abd el Kader seeing his cause failed broke back, and fled into the country. We killed three of his servants and the others yielded. At noon it was all over by our own effort, not using the British. When things began I had called up Chauvel and told him their bad aspect. At once he offered his troops. I thanked him and asked for a second company of horse to be drafted to the Turkish barracks (the nearest Australian post) to stand by against call: but the fighting was too petty for that call.

Its best consequence was among the press-men living in the Hotel Victoria whose river-wall was the stop-block of one barrage. They had not dipped their pens in much blood during this campaign which had run faster than their cars: but here was a godsend at their bedroom windows and they wrote and telegraphed till Allenby, away in Ramleh, was frightened and asked me for a report, sending me a copy of a press dispatch which recalled two Balkan wars, and five Armenian massacres but never carnage like today's: the streets paved with corpses, the gutters running blood, and the swollen Barada spouting crimson through all the fountains in the city! My reply was a death-roll, showing the five victims, and the hurts of the ten wounded. Of the casualties three fell to Kirk bride's ruthless revolver!

The Druses were expelled from the city to Jaraman, and lost horses and rifles in the act, at the hands of the citizens of Damascus whom we had formed for the emergency into a civic guard under their quarter sheikhs, and issued with captured arms. They gave the town a very warlike look, patrolling till the afternoon when things were quiet again, and street-traffic normal, with sweetmeats, and iced-drinks, and flowers, and little Hejaz flags being hawked round by their pedals as before.

We returned to the organization of the public services, begun yesterday, and dealt with each new call as it arose, to the best of our slender endeavor. An amusing event for me personally was an official call from the Spanish Consul, a polished English-speaking individual, who introduced himself as the chargi daifizires of seventeen nationalities (including all the combatants of any side except the Turks), in search of the constituted legal authority of the town. I could not help him further than the defect to head : but he was as gratified at our expressed readiness to serve him, as he was disappointed when he found our lack of resources. However, we gave him a military guard for his Consulate, which was something: indeed, it amounted to a soldier per nationality interested.

At lunch an Australian doctor begged me, for the sake of humanity, to take notice of the military hospital. I ran over in my mind our three hospitals, the military, the civil, the missionary, and told him they were all three cared for as well as we had means. We could not invent drugs, nor would Chauvel give them us. He complained further, describing an enormous range of buildings in a filthy state, packed with a thousand dead and dying, mainly dysentery cases, but at least some typhoid, and, it was only to be hoped, no typhus or cholera. There was not a single medical officer or orderly to attend them.

I questioned him further, and in his descriptions recognized the Turkish barracks, which had never been a hospital, and which were occupied by the Australian two companies of town-reserve; they had sentries at the gates. Yes, he said, that was the place, but it was full of Turkish sick, and he implored me to go and see its horror for myself.

I walked up at once and parleyed with the guard who had orders to keep all natives out lest they massacre the patients — a misapprehension of the Arab fashion of making war common among the British. As a fact, within my experience, only on that red afternoon of Tafas, and then by my direct order, and reluctantly, did the Arabs ever kill an unarmed Turk or refuse a prisoner. At last my English speech got me through the gate of the little lodge, whose dry garden was filled with two hundred wretched prisoners in the last stages of exhaustion and despair.

I went in through the great door of the barrack building, and called up the dusty echoing corridors, but no one answered or moved. The place seemed deserted: however, out in the courtyard were signs of recent occupation. The huge sun-trapping area was squalid with rags and rubbish. The guard told me that when they first entered they had driven thousands of prisoners in here, but had yesterday sent them out to a camp beyond the town. Since then no one had come in or out.

I walked across to the far side, and there entered the thoroughfare to the back yard. On my left was a smaller doorway, to a lobby whose shuttered window made it black after the blazing sunlight of the plastered court. I stepped in to see what was there, and met a sickening stench and, as my eyes grew open, a sickening sight. The stone floor was covered with dead bodies laid out side by side, like sacks, some in full uniform, some in underclothing, some stark naked.

There might be thirty there, and they crept with rats who had gnawed wet red galleries into them. A few were corpses nearly fresh, perhaps only a day or two old: others must have been there for long: but there were all stages. Of some the flesh, just going putrid, was yellow and blue and black. Others were already swollen twice or thrice life-width, their round inflated heads laughing with black mouths in jaws harsh with stubble. Of others the softer parts were fallen in, while the worst had burst open, and were liquescent with decay.

Beyond was the vista of a great room, from which I thought there came a groan. So I trod over to it, across the soft mat of bodies, whose clothing, yellow with dung, crackled dryly under me. Inside the ward the air was raw and still, and the dressed battalions of filled beds so quiet that I thought these too were dead, each man rigid on his stinking pallet, from which the liquid muck had dripped and stiffened on the floor. However, I picked forward a little between their lines, holding my white skirts about me, and careful not to dip my bare feet in the softness of their puddle running, and suddenly heard a sighing breath and turned abruptly to meet the open eyes of these outstretched men fixed on me like beads, while 'Aman, Aman', (,pity, pity, pardon'), rustled from their twisted lips. There was a brown wavering as they tried to lift their hands, and a thin fluttering like withered leaves, as they vainly fell back again upon the beds.

No one of them had strength to speak aloud, but there was something which made me laugh at their whispering their appeal in unison, as if by command. No doubt occasion had been given them to rehearse it all the last two days, each time a curious trooper had peered into their halls, and gone away, adding despair to their deadly sickness, and their thirst and hunger: and as I realized the multitude crushed into this moldering barrack, their despair came over me also. Outside the walls we could hear Damascus and its hundreds of thousands merry-making, drunken on liberty after five subject centuries, too happy to see misery or to relieve it: and within the walls lay these hundreds enduring, in our neglect, not Death the strong spirit, with quiet hands and wings, but slow physical corruption, a piecemeal rotting of the envelope of flesh about the hopeless spirit longing to escape.

I tip-toed out, and ran through the arch into the garden across which the Australians were picketed in lines. I asked for a working party. They refused. Tools: they had none. Doctors: busy. Kirk bride came and we walked back into the court. Under its kiosk lay a Turk able to move. He told us how the three hundred Red Crescent orderlies of the hospital had confounded themselves yesterday with the prisoners in the court, and had gone out with them to the idleness of the prison-camp.

The doctors, he thought, were upstairs, shut into their quarters. He guided us up and we broke open a door to find seven men in night-gowns, collected in a great room, sitting on their unmade beds, boiling toffee over a spirit-stove. One was the Commandant, and we convinced them quickly of the wisdom of dressing and running down to sort out the living and the dead and have ready for me in half an hour a tally of their numbers. Kirk bride wore heavy army boots which fitted him to oversee their work: while I went to the Town Hall and got hold of Ali Riza Pasha, now returned and made Governor. He detailed me one of our four Arab Army doctors.

When he came we went to the lodge and pressed the fifty fittest of the miserable prisoners there as a labor party. We bought some biscuits off a barrow and fed them as earnest: then led them out of the dusty bushes into the white sunshine to a corner where there were some Turkish tools. With these we armed them and set them in the back yard to dig a pit for a common grave. The Australian officer protested it was an unfit place whose smell might drive them from their garden. In fury I told him I hoped to God it would.

It was cruelty to work men so tired and ill: but we had no choice in our haste. By the kicks and blows of their non-commissioned officers they were at last got obedient. There was an old hole in one place the foundation of a building. We tried to deepen it, but beneath was a cement floor: I said that it would do if they could enlarge the edges. It was six feet deep, but nearby was much quicklime which mixed with earth, would help to cover it effectually.

Kirk Bride took charge of the digging while I went to see the doctors, who told me of fifty-six dead two hundred dying seven hundred more not yet dangerously ill. There was not one wounded man in the entire place. We formed a stretcher-party to carry down the corpses, of which some were lifted easily: others with shovels were scraped up piece-meal and piled together for the trip. The bearers were hardly strong enough to stand: indeed before we finished we had added two of our workmen to the pit.

We shot the bodies in by tipping the stretcher as it was held across the middle. The trench was too small and they had to pile up one upon the other but so fluid was the mass that each newcomer fell softly and the others just jellied out the edges of the heap a little under the weight. I was ill before the work finished: it was after midnight and I had not slept three hours since we left Deraa four days ago: so I left Kirk Bride (a boy in years, doing two men's work these days) to finish the burying and scatter the earth and lime over the grave.

At the hotel was waiting for me a bunch of urgent matters: some death sentences, a new justifier, a famine in barley for the morrow if the train did not work. Also a messenger from General Chauvel, with a complaint, 'to wait reply', that some of the Arab troops were slack about saluting Australian officers. For a moment the wish to answer him worthily quivered in me: but he seemed too poor a thing to teach, and Godwin, our friend, already suffered from him all that he could bear. So I sent a soft note that Arab regulations prescribed a salute only when wishing to address an officer: but I would attend to it: and on the morrow send him for action the names of some Australian troops who had failed to salute Arab officers. He never replied.

Chapter 139: Allenby Triumph

In the morning, after the sudden fashion troubles had, they were ended and our ship sailing under a clear sky. Our armored cars came in, and the pleasure of seeing the men's sedate faces heartened me. Pisani had arrived, and made me laugh, so bewildered was the good soldier by the political hubbub around him. He gripped his military duty as if it was a rudder to steer him through. Damascus was normal, the shops open, street merchants trading, the electric tram cars restored, grain and vegetables and fruits coming in well from outside.

The streets were being watered to lay the terrible dust: though no surface treatment would much allay the damage of three war-years' lorry-traffic. The crowds were slow and happy, and a goodly sight to me were numbers of British troops wandering about to see the town, unarmed. The telegraph was now restored and open with Palestine, with Sidon and Beirut. It grieved me that the Arabs had sent across and occupied Beirut last night. As long ago as Wejh I had warned them when they took Damascus to leave the Lebanon as a sop to the French, but to take Tripoli instead, since as a port it outweighed Beirut, and England would have played the honest broker for it on their behalf in the Peace Settlement. So I was sorry they had made this open mistake, and yet glad to see that they now felt themselves grown-up enough to disobey me.

Even the hospital was better. I had urged Chauvel to take it over, but he said he could not. At the time I thought he meant to overstrain me, and then point at our confusion to justify his taking away our government of the town. However, since, I have understood that the trouble between us was largely made by my ragged nerves, and that I was unjust in ascribing to him designs against us. Certainly he won the last act, and made me feel mean, for when he heard that I was leaving, he drove round with Godwin and thanked me very kindly for what he called my help in his difficulties.

Still, the hospital was improving of itself the fifty prisoners, now called orderlies, had cleaned up the courtyard, collecting the lousy clothes and boots and dung into heaps, and burning them. Others had gone through the wards, lifting and washing each patient, putting them into clean shirts, and reversing their mattresses, to have a tolerably clean side up. We had found a little suitable food, even for the most critical cases, and now nobody was thirsty: while in each ward there was always someone in hearing if a sick man called. One room we had cleared of beds, brushed out and sprinkled with disinfectant: and were just about to transfer into it the less ill cases, to clean their room in turn.

At this rate three days would have seen things very fit, and I was proudly arranging other benefits when an Army medical major strode up and asked me shortly if I spoke English. I said, 'Yes', and with a glance of disgust at my skirts and sandals he said, 'You're in charge?' I replied that in a way I was, and then he burst out, ...scandalous, disgraceful, outrageous, ought to be shot.... At this sudden onslaught I cackled out like a duck, with the wild laughter which often took me at moments of strain : and it was extraordinarily funny to be so cursed just as I was pluming myself on having bettered the apparently hopeless.

He had not entered the Charnel-house of yesterday, or smelt it, or seen us burying those bodies of ultimate degradation, whose memory had woken me up again and again, sweating and trembling in my bed this early morning. So he misunderstood, and glared at me, muttering about a bloody brute. I laughed out again, and angered him so much that he smacked me over the face and stalked off, leaving me more ashamed than angry, for in my heart I felt that he was right, and that anyone who had, like me, pushed through to success a rebellion of the weak against their masters, must come out of it so stained that nothing in the world would make him clean again.

It was a poor performance, but the last two months had been times of strenuous responsibility, when by my own force I had salved the pains of an over-growing movement, and patched an inadequate staff and direction so that they fulfilled the last necessary duty. This extreme period had come only after two years of exposure to trying physical and mental conditions in the desert, with enough of unavoidable hardship to wear down a man strong and active, much more a book-reader like myself.

Also now in Damascus I knew things were nearly over, and no longer bothered to waste time on sleeping and eating carefully.

Things were indeed very nearly over, for when I got back to the hotel crowds were besetting it, and at the door stood a grey Rolls-Royce, which I knew for Allenby's. I ran in and found him there with Clayton and Cornwallis and other noble people. He gave me his approval of my steps in imposing Arab government, here and at Deraa, upon the chaos of the entry. He confirmed the appointment of Ali Riza Rikabi as his Military Governor, under the orders of Feisal, his Army Commander, and regulated their sphere and Chauvel's. He agreed to take over my hospital, and the working of the railway. In ten minutes all difficulties had slipped away, before a confidence and decision and kindness which were dreamlike.

Then we were told that Feisal's train had just arrived from Deraa. A message was hurriedly sent him by Young's mouth, and we waited, tilt the tide of cheering beat up against our windows, and then Feisal came in. It was fitting the two chiefs should meet for the first time in the heart of their greatest victory; with myself still the interpreter between them.

Allenby gave me a telegram from the Foreign Office, recognizing to the Arabs the status of belligerents, telling me to translate it to the Emir: but none of us knew what it meant in English, let alone in Arabic, and Feisal, smiling through the tears which the welcome of his people had forced from him, put it aside to satisfy the ambition of a year, and thank the Commander-in-Chief for the trust which had made him and his movement. They were a strange contrast, Feisal, large-eyed, colorless and worn, like a fine dagger: Allenby gigantic and red and merry, fit representative of the Power which had thrown a girdle of humor and strong dealing round the world.

The interview lasted only a few minutes and when Feisal had gone I made to Allenby the last (and also I think the first) request I ever made for myself — leave to go away. For a while he would not have it, but I reasoned pointing out how much easier the New Law would be if my spur were absent from the people. In the end he agreed, and then at once I knew how much I was sorry.

Epilogue

Needless to say when the Arab thrust northward from Hejaz began. Damascus was not my ultimate end: but by the time it was taken most of my springs of action were exhausted and so I withdrew myself. Throughout my strongest motive had been a personal one omitted from the body of the book, but not absent. I think, from my mind waking or sleeping for an hour in all those years. Active pains and joys flung themselves up among my days like towers: but always fluent as air this persisting hidden urge reformed and became a very element of life: till near the end. It was dead before we reached the town.

Next in order had been the superficial but powerful motive of a wish to win the war with the conviction that we must have Arab help if we were to win the Eastern war at a price we could afford. Throughout I tried to make the hurt of so exploiting the blood and hope of another people as small in degree as it seemed necessary in kind. When Damascus fell the Turkish war and probably the German was decided: and so this motive also died.

Then I was moved by intellectual curiosity by the desire to feel myself the inspiration of a national movement thrilling with the ideals and efforts of all a race. From this cup I drank as deeply as any man should do when we took Damascus: and was sated with it. More would have set in me the vice of authority and smirched my hope clean as I felt it to create some lively thing of black marks on white paper. For three days I was arbitrary: and by use that motive died.

There was left to me ambition the wish to quicken history in the East as the great adventurers of old had done. I fancied to run up in my own life that new Asia which inexorable time was slowly bringing upon us. The Arabs made a chivalrous appeal to my young instinct and when still at the High School in Oxford already I thought to remake them into a nation client and fellow of the British Empire.

I had conceived that our possessions in Asia were behind the spirit of our day that devolution of our brown provinces imposed itself and that our race at home was now sensitive and weary enough to make the allowances also for the other side in linking our developed institutions with the first thoughts of their student minds. I had intended to inaugurate this new Imperialism in the Arab World thinking to be the only person with a clear intention when Damascus fell and had planned even on paper the successive stages of that Arab advance by which without my leading they yet took Antioch before the Allies expelled them from Beirut.

The necessary Turkish elements to reshape Anatolia were ready to my hand could be grasped before the Allies saw the hollowness of their victory, while they were still made generous by the German army in Flanders. A strong Syria might dominate Mecca. Yemen was not difficult, and then the center of gravity would have shifted eastward and Bagdad have been ceded to me gracefully.

However this remained a dream because of the insubstantiality of abstract ambition by itself as sole motive: and is here written only for men to call fantastic. It was a fantasy: to believe that an illiterate spirit of nationality without authority, without a city or a ship or a factory or a shop or a rifle or a leader of its own could meet Turkey in arms and wrest away its old capital. They gave me the arts and objects of our fighting materials for my share. I studied them to the best of my ability and used them as far as I could make them go in a fashion neither dull nor negligent. After such training with material resources to reinforce the spiritual, the rest of my intention might have been not difficult.

'Not the light that was quenched for us nor the deeds that were,
Nor the ancient days.
Nor the sorrows not sorrowful nor the face most fair
of perfect praise.'